AMERICA

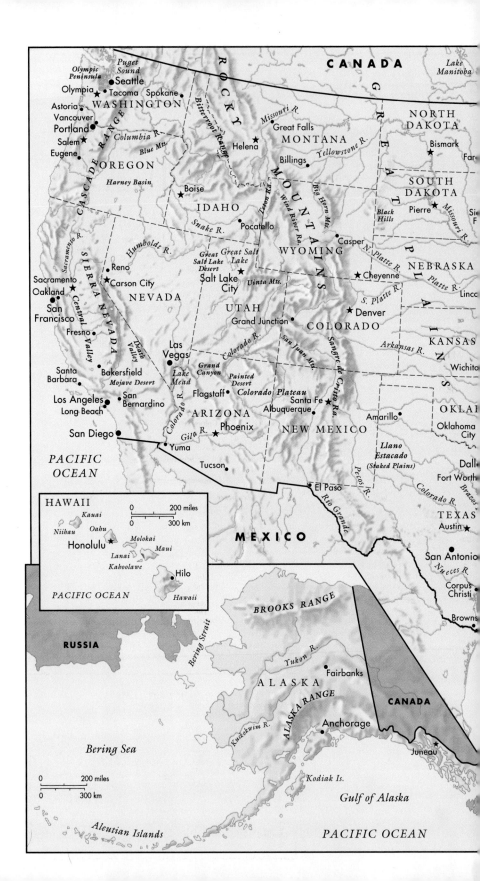

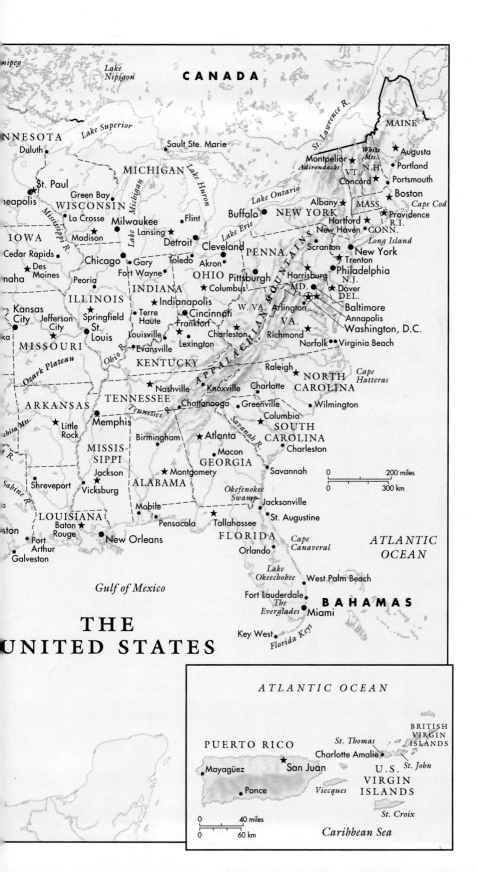

THE
UNITED STATES

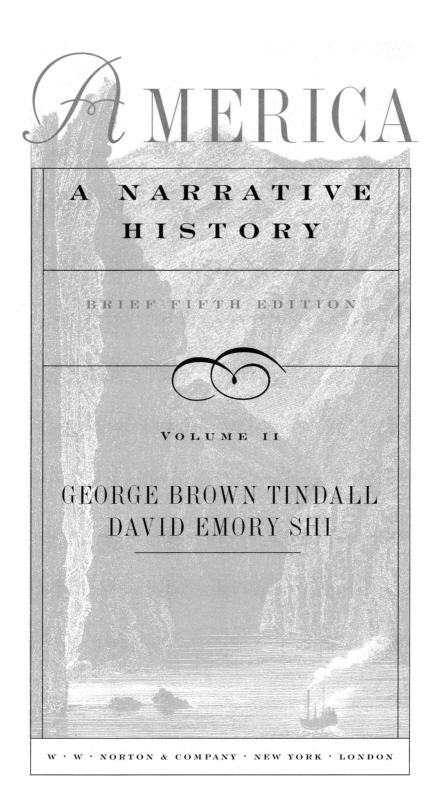

AMERICA

A NARRATIVE HISTORY

BRIEF FIFTH EDITION

VOLUME II

GEORGE BROWN TINDALL
DAVID EMORY SHI

W · W · NORTON & COMPANY · NEW YORK · LONDON

Copyright © 2000, 1999, 1997, 1996, 1993, 1992, 1989, 1988, 1984
by W. W. Norton & Company, Inc.

The text of this book is composed in Fairfield Light,
with the display set in Torino.
Composition by The PRD Group.
Manufacturing by Courier Corp.
Book design by Antonina Krass.
Cover art by Diego Rivera, *Detroit Industry* (detail of North Wall), 1932–1933.
Fresco. The Detroit Institute of Arts. Gift of Edsel B. Ford.
Reproduced with the approval of Instituto Nacional de Bellas Artes and Banco de Mexico.
Photograph © The Detroit Institute of Arts.

Cartographer: CARTO-GRAPHICS/Alice Thiede and William Thiede,
with relief maps from Mountain High Maps®, Digital Wisdom, Inc.

Acknowledgments and copyrights appear on p. A61,
which serves as a continuation of the copyright page.

The Library of Congress has catalogued the one-volume edition as follows:

Tindall, George Brown.
   America : a narrative history / George Brown Tindall, David Emory
Shi. — Brief 5th ed.
      p.   cm.
   Includes bibliographical references and index.
   1. United States—History.   I. Shi, David E.   II. Title.
E178.1.T55 2000
973—dc21   99-43626
                                                 CIP

ISBN 0-393-97444-8 (pbk.)

W. W. Norton & Company, Inc., 500 Fifth Avenue, New York, N.Y. 10110
http://www.wwnorton.com

W. W. Norton & Company Ltd., 10 Coptic Street, London WC1A 1PU

1 2 3 4 5 6 7 8 9 0

FOR BRUCE AND SUSAN
AND FOR BLAIR

FOR
JASON AND JESSICA

CONTENTS

PART SIX / MODERN AMERICA

36 | CULTURAL POLITICS   1268

APPENDIX   A1

CREDITS   A61

INDEX   A63

MAPS

PREFACE

Just as history is never complete, neither is a historical textbook. We have learned much from the responses of readers and instructors to the first four editions of *America: A Narrative History*. Perhaps the most important and reassuring lesson is that our original intention has proved valid: to provide a compelling narrative history of the American experience, a narrative animated by human characters, informed by analysis and social texture, and guided by the unfolding of events.

To help students better grasp the major themes and developments throughout the text, we have integrated key pedagogical features into *America*. Part openers introduce the major ideas emphasized in upcoming chapters. Chapter openers present important thematic threads that serve as a guide through the narrative. "Making Connections" boxes appear on the final page of each chapter to link significant events to issues in surrounding chapters. Seven new narrative timelines, one for each major section of the book, also make connections by drawing out the central themes within each time period through political, global, social, and economic entries.

We have also introduced a new map program. All the maps in the book have been reconsidered and redrawn to make them clearer and more helpful to students. The new maps and the larger format and two-color design produce a more attractive, easier-to-read text that instructors and students should find even more inviting.

In this edition of *America* we have highlighted aspects of popular culture, beginning with the culture of everyday life: how Americans spent their leisure time, what forms of recreation and entertainment captured their interest, and how the performing arts helped people to understand and deal with traumatic events such as wars and economic depressions.

For example, we have incorporated new material dealing with the architecture of colonial homes, the role of taverns in eighteenth-century social life, the evolution of national holidays such as Independence Day, dueling as a manifestation of the cult of honor in the antebellum South, political parties as a source of entertainment and social life during the Gilded Age, the evolution of professional sports and the performing arts, the popularity of minstrel shows and jazz, the development of the radio, television, and film industries, and the rise of rock 'n' roll music.

Taken together, these activities, as well as others like them, document the importance of popular culture in unifying a disparate nation. Colonial taverns served as gathering places for discussions that led to revolution; revival meetings provided a meeting ground for people living isolated lives on the frontier; popular magazines, mail-order catalogues, and later radio and films gave people in both isolated rural areas and crowded cities a common ideal of what life should be like. Such collective forms of social activity have made American life more inclusive and accessible to the masses. In turn, such developments in popular culture inform our understanding of major trends in social and political life. Understanding the role of these aspects of popular culture and others like them helps expand and enrich our understanding of what "history" includes.

In the previous edition, we emphasized the role of the frontier and immigration on the American experience. We have continued and expanded on this emphasis. For example, we have included a new section on the Wilderness Trail and the settling of Kentucky. We also have described how immigrants and native-born Americans began to participate in outdoor recreation and formed social clubs and attended vaudeville and Wild West shows in the cities, later going to football and baseball games and boxing matches.

Moreover, we have expanded our discussion of political culture. For example, we describe the rise of a new political atmosphere during the Jacksonian era and the expansion of the suffrage. We include new material on the political rallies and campaigns that gave working men (women could not vote until 1920) a break from the tedium of their everyday lives. We have added more on the activities of political parties during the Gilded Age and more on state and local efforts at reform during the Progressive Era. We also have added more on technology. We now have a new section on the second industrial revolution and the scientific research and innovations that permitted the expansion of transportation and communication, the construction of high-rise buildings, and the tremendous growth of cities.

The Fifth Brief Edition includes new sections on women and minorities: the difficulties faced by white women in the South during the Civil War, black migration to the West after the Civil War, the treatment of minorities during the New Deal, developments in civil rights after World War II, and how major league baseball was racially integrated. Other new sections include new interpretations of the presidencies of Dwight Eisenhower and Ronald Reagan, a new section on the computer revolution, a section on the rightward shift of the Supreme Court and the backlash against affirmative action programs, the role of America in dealing with the ethnic clashes that have marked the end of the cold war, and a new discussion of *fin-de-siècle* America.

To help students and instructors, we have an outstanding ancillary package that supplements the text. *For the Record: A Documentary History of America,* by David E. Shi and Holly A. Mayer (Duquesne University), is a rich resource with over 300 primary source readings from diaries, journals, newspaper articles, speeches, government documents, and novels. It also has four special chapters on interpreting illustrations and photographs as historical documents. The *Study Guide,* by Charles Eagles (University of Mississippi), is another valuable resource. It contains chapter outlines, learning objectives, timelines, vocabulary exercises, short-answer questions, essay questions, as well as source readings for each chapter. *America: A Narrative History WebBook,* prepared by Tom Pearcy (Slippery Rock University), is an on-line collection of tools for review and research. It includes chapter summaries, review questions, interactive map exercises, timelines, and research modules. *Norton Presentation Maker* is a CD-ROM slide and text resource that includes all images from the text, four-color maps, 1,000 additional images from the Library of Congress archives, and thirty audio files of significant historical speeches. Finally, the *Instructor's Manual and Test Bank,* by David Parker (Kennesaw State University), includes a test bank of short-answer and essay questions, as well as detailed chapter outlines, lecture suggestions, and bibliographies.

In preparing the Brief Fifth Edition, we have benefited from the insights and suggestions of many people. The following scholars have provided close readings of the manuscript at various stages: Lucy Barber (University of California at Davis), Michael Barnhart (State University at New York at Stony Brook), Saul Cornell (Ohio State University), Charles Eagles (University of Mississippi), Timothy Gilfoyle (Loyola University), Tera Hunter (Carnegie-Mellon University), Walter Johnson (New York University), Peter Kolchin (University of Delaware), Christopher Morris (University of Texas at Arlington), Arwen Mohun (University of Delaware), David Parker (Kennesaw State University), Thomas Sugrue (University of Pennsylvania), and Marilyn Westerkamp (University of California at Vera Cruz). Our special thanks go to Tom Pearcy (Slippery Rock University) for all of his work on the timelines. Once again, we thank our friends at W. W. Norton, especially Steve Forman, Jon Durbin, Sandy Lifland, Steve Hoge, Kate Nash, Candace Kooyoomjian, and Robert Stillings, for their care and attention along the way.

—George B. Tindall
—David E. Shi

AMERICA

17   RECONSTRUCTION: NORTH AND SOUTH

CHAPTER ORGANIZER

This chapter focuses on:

- the different approaches to Reconstruction.

- congressional efforts to reshape southern society.

- the role of African Americans in the early postwar years.

- national politics in the 1870s.

In the spring of 1865 the wearying war was over. At the frightful cost of 630,000 lives and the destruction of the southern economy and much of its landscape, American nationalism emerged triumphant, and some 4 million slaves emerged free. But peace had come only on the battlefields. "Cannon conquer," recognized a northern editor, "but they do not necessarily convert." Now the North faced the imposing task of "reconstructing" a ravaged and resentful South.

THE WAR'S AFTERMATH

In the war's aftermath, important questions faced the victors in the North: Should the Confederate leaders be tried for treason? How should new governments be formed? How and at whose expense was the South's economy to be rebuilt? What was to be done with the freed slaves? Were they to be given land? social equality? education? voting rights? Such complex questions required sober reflection and careful planning, but policy makers did not have the luxury of time or the benefits of consensus.

ECONOMIC DEVELOPMENT IN THE NORTH To some Americans the Civil War had been more truly a social revolution than the War of Independence, for it reduced the once-dominant power of the planter elite in the national councils and elevated that of the northern "captains of industry." It is easy to exaggerate the profundity of this change, but government did become subtly more friendly to businessmen and unfriendly to those who would probe into their activities. The wartime Republican Congress had delivered on the major platform

The Grand Review of Union Troops in Victory, *Washington, D.C., May 1865.*

promises of 1860, which had cemented the allegiance of northeastern businessmen and western farmers to the party of free labor.

In the absence of southern members, Congress during the war had seized the opportunity to centralize national power. In this regard, it passed the Morrill Tariff, which doubled the average level of import duties. The National Banking Act created a uniform system of banking and bank-note currency, and helped to finance the war. Congress also passed legislation confirming that the first transcontinental railroad would run along a north-central route from Omaha to Sacramento, and donated public lands and public bonds to ensure its financing. In the Homestead Act of 1862, moreover, Congress voted free homesteads of 160 acres to settlers. They had to occupy the land for five years before gaining title. The Morrill Land Grant Act of the same year conveyed to each state 30,000 acres of public land per member of Congress from the state, the proceeds from the sale of which went to create colleges of "agriculture and mechanic arts." Such measures helped stimulate the North's economy in the years after the Civil War.

DEVASTATION IN THE SOUTH   The postwar South, where most of the fighting had occurred, offered a sharp contrast to the victorious North. Along the path of General William T. Sherman's army, one observer reported in 1866, the countryside "looked for many miles like a broad black streak of ruin and desolation." Columbia, South Carolina, said another witness, was "a wilderness of ruins," Charleston a place of "vacant houses, of widowed women, of rotting wharves, of deserted warehouses, of weed-wild gardens, of miles of grass-grown streets, of acres of pitiful and voiceless barrenness." The border states of Missouri and Kentucky had experienced a guerrilla war that lapsed into postwar anarchy perpetrated by marauding bands of bushwhackers turned outlaws, such as the notorious James boys, Frank and Jesse.

Throughout the South, property values had collapsed. Confederate bonds and money were worthless; railroads were damaged or destroyed. Cotton that had escaped destruction was seized as Confederate property or in forfeit of federal taxes. Emancipation of the slaves wiped out perhaps $4 billion invested in human flesh and left the labor system in disarray. The great age of expansion in the cotton market was over. Not until 1879 would the cotton crop again equal the record harvest of 1860; tobacco production did not regain its prewar level until

1880; the sugar crop of Louisiana not until 1893; and the old rice industry of the Tidewater and the hemp industry of the Kentucky Bluegrass never regained their prewar status.

A TRANSFORMED SOUTH   The defeat of the Confederacy transformed much of southern society. The freeing of slaves, the destruction of property, and the free-fall in land values left many among the former planter elite destitute and homeless. Amanda Worthington, a plantation mistress from Mississippi, saw her whole world destroyed. In the fall of 1865, she assessed the damage: "None of us can realize that we are no longer wealthy—yet thanks to the yankees, the cause of all unhappiness, such is the case."

Genteel southerners such as Worthington were now forced to rebuild lives and families without the help of slaves. Women accustomed to relying on slaves for their every need were unprepared for the tasks at hand. Those who still had some money often recruited former slaves to work as domestic servants. Now, however, they had to pay for the services. "It seems humiliating to be compelled to bargain and haggle with our servants about wages," wrote one exasperated woman. After the Civil War, many former Confederates were so embittered by defeat and so resistant to the idea of living under northern rule that they abandoned their native region rather than submit to "Yankee rule." Some migrated to Canada, Europe, Mexico, South America, and Asia. Others preferred the western territories and states. Still others moved north, settling in northern and midwestern cities on the assumption that their educational and economic opportunities would be better among the victors.

Most of those who remained in the South returned to find their farms and homes and communities transformed. One Confederate army captain reported that on his father's plantation "Our negroes are living in great comfort. They were delighted to see me with overflowing affection. They waited on me as before, gave me breakfast, splendid dinners, etc. But they firmly and respectfully informed me: 'We own this land now. Put it out of your head that it will ever be yours again.'"

Unreconstructed Confederates, both men and women, planted in their children a hatred of Yankees and a defiance of northern rule. One mother said that she trained her children to "fear God, love the South, and live to avenge her."

LEGALLY FREE, SOCIALLY BOUND In the former Confederate states, the newly freed slaves suffered as well. According to Frederick Douglass, the black abolitionist, the former slave remained dependent: "He had neither money, property, nor friends. He was free from the old plantation, but he had nothing but the dusty road under his feet. . . . He was turned loose, naked, hungry, and destitute to the open sky."

A few northerners argued that what the ex-slaves needed most was their own land. But even dedicated abolitionists shrank from endorsing measures of land reform that might have given the freed slaves more self-support and independence. Citizenship and legal rights were one thing, wholesale confiscation of property and land redistribution quite another. Instead of land or material help, the freed slaves more often got advice and moral platitudes.

In 1865 Representative George Julian of Indiana and Senator Charles Sumner of Massachusetts proposed to give freed slaves forty-acre homesteads carved out of Rebel lands taken under the Confiscation Act of 1862. But their plan for outright grants was replaced by a program of rentals since, under the law, confiscation was effective only for the lifetime of the offender. Discussions of land distribution, how-

According to a former Confederate general, recently freed blacks had "nothing but freedom."

ever, fueled rumors that freed slaves would get "forty acres and a mule," a slogan that swept the South at the end of the war. As a black man in Mississippi put it: "Gib us our own land and we take care ourselves; but widout land, de ole massas can hire us or starve us, as dey please." More lands were seized as "abandoned lands" under an act of 1864, and for default on the direct taxes that Congress had levied early in the war, than under the Confiscation Act.

The most conspicuous example of confiscation was the estate of Robert E. Lee and the Custis family, which became Arlington National Cemetery, but larger amounts were taken in the South Carolina Sea Islands and elsewhere. Some of these lands were sold to freed blacks, some to Yankee speculators.

THE FREEDMEN'S BUREAU On March 3, 1865, Congress set up within the War Department the Bureau of Refugees, Freedmen, and Abandoned Lands, to provide "such issues of provisions, clothing, and fuel" as might be needed to relieve "destitute and suffering refugees and freedmen and their wives and children." The Freedmen's Bureau would also take over abandoned or confiscated land, but the amount of such land was limited. Agents of the Freedmen's Bureau were entrusted with negotiating labor contracts (something new for both blacks and planters), providing medical care, and setting up schools, often in cooperation with northern agencies such as the American Missionary Association and the Freedmen's Aid Society. The bureau had its own courts to deal with labor disputes and land titles, and its agents were further authorized to supervise trials involving blacks in other courts.

White intransigence and the failure to grasp the intensity of racial prejudice, however, thwarted the efforts of Freedmen's Bureau agents to protect and assist the former slaves. Congress was not willing to strengthen the powers of the Freedmen's Bureau to deal with such problems. Beyond temporary relief measures, no program of Reconstruction ever incorporated much more than constitutional and legal rights for freedmen. These were important in themselves, of course, but the extent to which even these should go was very uncertain, to be settled more by the course of events than by any clear-cut commitment to equality.

THE BATTLE OVER RECONSTRUCTION

The problem of reconstructing the South involved deciding what governments would constitute authority in the defeated states. This problem arose first in the state of Virginia at the very beginning of the Civil War, when the thirty-five western counties of Virginia refused to go along with secession. In 1861 a loyal state government of Virginia was proclaimed at Wheeling, and this government in turn formed a new state called West Virginia, admitted to the Union in 1863. The loyal government of Virginia then carried on from Alexandria, its reach limited to that part of the state that the Union controlled. As Federal forces advanced into the South, Lincoln in 1862 named military governors for Tennessee, Arkansas, and Louisiana. By the end of the following year, he had formulated a plan for regular civilian governments in those states and any others that might be liberated from Confederate rule.

LINCOLN'S PLAN AND CONGRESS'S RESPONSE   Acting under his pardon power, President Lincoln issued late in 1863 a Proclamation of Amnesty and Reconstruction, under which any Rebel state could form a Union government whenever a number equal to 10 percent of those who had voted in 1860 took an oath of allegiance to the Constitution and Union and received a presidential pardon. Participants also had to swear support for laws and proclamations dealing with emancipation. Excluded from the pardon, however, were certain groups: civil, diplomatic, and high military officers of the Confederacy; judges, congressmen, and military officers of the United States who had left their federal posts to aid the rebellion; and those accused of failure to treat captured black soldiers and their officers as prisoners of war.

Under this plan, loyal governments appeared in Tennessee, Arkansas, and Louisiana, but Congress refused to recognize them. In the absence of any specific provisions for Reconstruction in the Constitution, politicians disagreed as to where authority properly rested. Lincoln claimed the right to direct Reconstruction under the presidential pardon power, and also under the Constitutional obligation to guarantee each state a republican form of government.

A few conservative and most moderate Republicans supported Lincoln's program of immediate restoration. A small but influential group known as Radical Republicans, however, demanded a sweeping transformation of southern society that would include making the freed slaves full-fledged citizens. The Radicals hoped to reconstruct southern society so as to mirror the North's emphasis on small-scale capitalism. This meant thwarting the efforts of the old planter class to reestablish a caste system and keep the freed blacks in a state of peonage.

The Radicals were talented, earnest men who maintained that Congress, not the president, should supervise the Reconstruction program. To this end, they helped pass in 1864 the Wade-Davis Bill, sponsored by Senator Benjamin Wade of Ohio and Representative Winter Davis of Maryland. In contrast to Lincoln's 10 percent plan, the Wade-Davis Bill required that a *majority* of white male citizens declare their allegiance and that only those who swore an "ironclad" oath that they had always remained loyal to the Union could vote or serve in the state constitutional conventions. The conventions, moreover, would have to abolish slavery, deny political rights to high-ranking civil and military officers of the Confederacy, and repudiate Confederate war debts. Passed during the closing days of the 1864 session, the bill went unsigned by Lincoln, and this "pocket veto" provoked the bill's sponsors to issue the Wade-Davis Manifesto, a blistering statement that accused the president of usurping power and attempting to use readmitted states to ensure his reelection.

Lincoln issued his final statement on Reconstruction in his last public address, on April 11, 1865. Speaking from the White House balcony, he dismissed the theoretical question of whether the Confederate states had technically remained in the Union as "good for nothing at all—a mere pernicious abstraction." These states were simply "out of their proper practical relation with the Union," and the object was to get them "into their proper practical relation" as quickly as possible. Lincoln hoped to get former Confederate state governments in operation before Congress met in December. He worried that Congress might push through a harsher Reconstruction program. Lincoln wanted "no persecution, no bloody work," no dramatic restructuring of southern social and economic life.

That evening Lincoln went to Ford's Theater and his rendezvous with death. Shot in the head by John Wilkes Booth, a crazed actor and Confederate zealot, the president died the next morning. Pursued into Virginia, Booth was trapped and shot in a burning barn. His last words were: "Tell mother I die for my country. I thought I did for the best." Three collaborators were tried and hanged, along with Mrs. Mary Surratt, at whose boardinghouse they had plotted. Three other conspirators received life sentences, including a Maryland doctor who set the leg Booth had broken when he jumped from Lincoln's box onto the stage. The doctor achieved lasting fame by making common a once obscure expression. His name was Mudd.

JOHNSON'S PLAN Lincoln's death suddenly elevated to the White House Vice-President Andrew Johnson of Tennessee, a man whose state remained in legal limbo and whose party affiliation was unclear. He was a War Democrat who had been put on the Union ticket in 1864 as a gesture of unity. Of humble origins like Lincoln, Johnson had moved as a youth from his birthplace in Raleigh, North Carolina, to Greenville, Tennessee, where he became proprietor of a tailor shop. Self-educated with the help of his wife, Johnson learned to write, and over the years he grew quite prosperous, acquiring several slaves in the process.

Beginning in the 1830s, Johnson emerged as one of the leading Jacksonian Democrats. A bitter critic of the "swaggering" planter aristocracy "who are too lazy and proud to work," he was a fervent populist who promoted free land for the poor, defended slavery, and promoted white supremacy. A notoriously stubborn man, he became a self-righteous, hot-tempered orator who enjoyed strong drink and employed abusive

Andrew Johnson.

language to belittle his opponents. His fiery speeches and firm principles helped him win election as mayor, congressman, governor, and senator.

Like many other whites living in mountainous eastern Tennessee, Johnson ardently believed in the Union. In 1861 he was the only southern senator from a Confederate state to vote against secession, leading critics to denounce him as a "traitor" to the region. Yet his devotion to the Union did not include opposition to slavery. He hated the Confederacy because he hated the planter elite. "Damn the Negroes," Johnson bellowed to a friend during the war, "I am fighting those traitorous aristocrats, their masters."

Abraham Lincoln selected Johnson, who had been military governor of Tennessee, as his running mate in 1864 solely for political reasons. He and his advisers thought that the addition of a southern Democrat and Unionist would strengthen the Republican ticket in the face of northern impatience with the war effort. The strategy worked, and Lincoln was reelected, but Johnson did not get off to a good start as the nation's new vice-president. On the morning of Lincoln's inauguration, Johnson was not feeling well, so he drank some whiskey—too much, as it turned out. As he delivered his inaugural speech in the Senate chamber, it quickly became evident that he was drunk. A New York newspaper reported the next day that Johnson was "a drunken boor."

Some of the Radicals at first thought Johnson, unlike Lincoln, was one of them. Johnson had, for example, asserted that treason "must be made infamous and traitors must be impoverished." Ben Wade loved such harsh talk. "Johnson, we have faith in you," he pledged. "By the gods, there will be no trouble now in running this government." But Wade would soon find him as untrustworthy as Lincoln, if for different reasons.

Johnson's very loyalty to the Union sprang from a strict adherence to the Constitution. Given to dogmatic abstractions that were alien to Lincoln's temperament, Johnson nevertheless arrived by a different route at similar objectives. The states should be brought back into their proper relation to the Union because the states and the Union were indestructible. In 1865 Johnson declared that "there is no such thing as Reconstruction. Those states have not gone out of the Union. Therefore Reconstruction is unnecessary."

Johnson's plan to restore the Union thus closely resembled Lincoln's.

A new Proclamation of Amnesty (May 29, 1865) added to the list of those Lincoln had excluded from pardon everybody with taxable property worth more than $20,000. These wealthy planters and merchants were the people Johnson believed had led the South into secession. But those in the excluded groups might make special applications for presidential pardon, and before the year was out Johnson had issued some 13,000 such pardons.

In each of the Rebel states not already organized by Lincoln, Johnson named a native Unionist provisional governor with authority to call a convention of men elected by loyal voters. Lincoln's 10 percent requirement was omitted. Johnson called upon the conventions to invalidate the secession ordinances, abolish slavery, and repudiate all debts incurred to aid the Confederacy. Each state, moreover, was to ratify the Thirteenth Amendment, which ended slavery. Like Lincoln, Johnson endorsed limited voting rights for blacks. He reminded the provisional governor of Mississippi, for example, that the state conventions might "with perfect safety" extend suffrage to those blacks with education or with military service so as to "disarm the adversary"—the adversary being "radicals who are wild upon Negro franchise."

The state conventions for the most part met Johnson's requirements. But a northern visitor found in the South "an *utter absence of national feeling* . . . and a desire to preserve slavery . . . as much and as long as possible." Southern whites accepted the situation because they thought so little had changed after all. Emboldened by Johnson's indulgence, they ignored his advice to move cautiously in restoring their political and social traditions. Suggestions of black suffrage were scarcely raised in the conventions, and promptly squelched when they were.

SOUTHERN INTRANSIGENCE When Congress met in December 1865, for the first time since the end of the war, it faced the fact that new state governments were functioning in the South, and they were remarkably like the old. Among the new members presenting themselves to Congress were Georgia's Alexander H. Stephens, late vice-president of the Confederacy, four Confederate generals, eight colonels, six cabinet members, and a host of lesser Rebels. The Congress forthwith denied seats to all members from the eleven former Confederate states. It was too much to expect, after four bloody years, that Unionists would welcome ex-Confederates back like prodigal sons.

Furthermore, the new southern legislatures, in passing repressive "Black Codes" restricting the freedom of blacks, baldly revealed that they intended to preserve the trappings of slavery as nearly as possible. As one southerner stressed, the "ex-slave was not a free man; he was a free Negro," and the Black Codes were intended to highlight the distinction. They extended to blacks certain new rights, but they also insisted that the freed slaves be set aside as a separate caste subject to special restraints.

The details of the Black Codes varied from state to state, but some provisions were common. Existing black marriages, including common-law marriages, were recognized (although interracial marriages were prohibited), and testimony by blacks was accepted in legal cases involving them—in six states in all cases. Blacks could own property. They could sue and be sued in the courts. On the other hand, blacks in Mississippi could not own farm lands, and in South Carolina they could not own city lots. Blacks were required to enter into annual labor contracts, with provision for punishment in case of violation. Dependent children were subject to compulsory apprenticeship and corporal punishment by masters. Vagrant blacks were punished with severe fines, and, if unable to pay, they were forced to work in the fields for whites who paid the courts for such cheap labor. To many people it seemed that slavery was being revived in another guise.

THE RADICALS   Faced with such evidence of southern intransigence, moderate Republicans drifted more and more toward the Radical camp. Having excluded southern members, the new Congress set up a Joint Committee on Reconstruction, with nine members from the House and six from the Senate, to gather evidence and submit proposals. As a parade of witnesses testified to the Rebels' impenitence, initiative on the committee fell to determined Radicals: Benjamin Wade of Ohio, George W. Julian of Indiana, Henry Wilson of Massachusetts—and most conspicuously of all, Thaddeus Stevens of Pennsylvania and Charles Sumner of Massachusetts.

Stevens, a crusty old bachelor with a chiseled face, thin, stern lips, and brooding eyes, was the domineering floor leader in the House. Driven by a genuine, if at times fanatical, idealism, he angrily insisted that the "whole fabric of southern society *must* be changed." Sumner, Stevens's counterpart in the Senate, agreed. Now recovered from

"Bully" Brooks's 1856 assault, Sumner strove to see the South *recon-structed* rather than simply restored. This put him at odds with Johnson. After visiting the White House, Sumner found the president "harsh, petulant, and unreasonable." He was especially disheartened by Johnson's "prejudice, ignorance, and perversity" regarding the treatment of blacks. Sumner and other Radicals now grew determined to take matters into their own hands. He argued that "Massachusetts could govern Georgia better than Georgia could govern herself." The southern plantations, seedbeds of aristocratic pretension and secession, he later added, "must be broken up, and the freedmen must have the pieces."

Most of these Radical Republicans had long been connected with the antislavery cause, and they approached the question of black rights with a sincere humanitarian impulse. Few, however, could escape the bitterness bred by the long and bloody war or remain unaware of the partisan advantage that would come to the Republican party from "Negro suffrage." But they reasoned that their party, after all, could best guarantee the fruits of victory and that granting suffrage could best secure black rights. Stevens reflected the mixed motives of the Radicals when he proclaimed: "I am for negro suffrage in every rebel state. If it be just, it should not be denied; if it be necessary, it should be adopted; if it be a punishment to traitors, they deserve it."

The growing conflict of opinion over Reconstruction policy brought about an inversion in constitutional reasoning. Secessionists—and Johnson—were now arguing that their states had in fact remained in the Union, and some Radicals were contriving arguments that they had left the Union after all. Stevens argued that the Confederate states had indeed seceded and were now conquered provinces, subject to the absolute will of the victors. Sumner maintained that the southern states, by their acts of secession, had in effect committed suicide and reverted to the status of unorganized territories subject to the will of Congress. But most congressmen embraced the "forfeited rights theory," which held that the states continued to exist, but by the acts of secession and war had forfeited "all civil and political rights under the Constitution." And Congress was the proper authority to determine conditions under which such rights might be restored.

JOHNSON'S BATTLE WITH CONGRESS   A long year of political battling remained, however, before this idea triumphed. By the end of

1865, Radical views had gained only a slight majority in Congress, insufficient to override presidential vetoes. But the critical year 1866 saw the gradual waning of Johnson's power and influence, much of this self-induced. Johnson first challenged Congress in February, when he vetoed a bill to extend the life of the Freedmen's Bureau. The measure, he said, assumed that wartime conditions still existed, whereas the country had returned "to a state of peace and industry." Since it was no longer valid as a war measure, Johnson believed it violated the Constitution. For the moment, Johnson's prestige remained sufficiently intact that the Senate upheld his veto.

Three days after the veto, however, Johnson undermined his already weakening prestige by launching an intemperate assault on Radical leaders during an impromptu speech on George Washington's Birthday. From that point forward, moderate Republicans backed away from the president, and Radical Republicans went on the offensive. Johnson was now "an alien enemy of a foreign state," Stevens declared.

In mid-March 1866, Congress passed the Civil Rights Act. A direct response to the Black Codes, this bill declared that "all persons born in the United States . . . excluding Indians not taxed," were citizens entitled to "full and equal benefit of all laws." The grant of citizenship to native-born blacks, Johnson claimed, went beyond anything formerly held to be within the scope of federal power. It would, moreover, "foment discord among the races." He vetoed the measure, but this time, in April 1866, Congress overrode the presidential veto. Then in July it enacted a revised Freedmen's Bureau Bill, again overturning a veto. From that point on, Johnson's public and political support steadily eroded.

THE FOURTEENTH AMENDMENT   To remove all doubt about the validity of the new Civil Rights Act, the Joint Committee recommended a new constitutional amendment, which passed Congress in 1866 and was ratified by the states in 1868. The Fourteenth Amendment, however, went far beyond the Civil Rights Act, and it would have significant and unforeseen effects long thereafter. The first section asserted four principles: it reaffirmed state and federal citizenship for all persons—regardless of race—born or naturalized in the United States, and it forbade any *state* (the word "state" was important in later litigation) to abridge the "privileges and immunities" of citizens; to deprive any *person* (again an important term) of life, liberty, or property without "due process of law"; or to deny any person "the equal protection of the laws."

The last three of these clauses have been the subject of lawsuits resulting in applications not foreseen at the time. The "due-process clause" has come to mean that state as well as federal power is subject to the Bill of Rights, and it has been used to protect corporations, as legal "persons," from "unreasonable" regulation by the states. Other provisions of the amendment had less far-reaching effects. One section specified that the debt of the United States "shall not be questioned," but declared "illegal and void" all debts contracted in aid of the rebellion. Another section specified the power of Congress to pass laws enforcing the amendment.

Johnson's home state was among the first to ratify the Fourteenth Amendment. In Tennessee, which had harbored probably more Unionists than any other Confederate state, the government had fallen under Radical control. But the rest of the South steadfastly resisted the Radical challenge to Johnson's program. In 1866 bloody race riots in Memphis and New Orleans added fuel to the flames. Both incidents sparked indiscriminate massacres of blacks by local police and white mobs. The rioting, Radicals argued, was the natural fruit of Johnson's foolish policy.

RECONSTRUCTING THE SOUTH

THE TRIUMPH OF CONGRESSIONAL RECONSTRUCTION As 1866 drew to an end, the upcoming congressional elections promised to be a referendum on the growing split between Johnson and the Radicals. Johnson embarked on a speaking tour of the Midwest, a "swing around the circle," which provoked undignified shouting contests between the president and his audiences. In Cleveland he described the Radicals as "factious, domineering, tyrannical" men. Once, while Johnson was speaking from an observation car, the engineer mistakenly pulled the train out of the station, making the president appear quite the fool. Such incidents tended to confirm his image as a "ludicrous boor," which Radical papers eagerly projected. When the election returns came in, the Republicans had well over a two-thirds majority in each house, a comfortable margin with which to override any presidential vetoes.

The Congress actually enacted a new program even before new members took office. On March 2, 1867, two days before the old Congress expired, it passed three basic laws of congressional Reconstruction over Johnson's vetoes: the Military Reconstruction Act, the Command of the Army Act, and the Tenure of Office Act.

The first of the three acts prescribed conditions under which new southern state governments should be formed. The other two sought to block obstruction by the president. The Command of the Army Act required that all orders from the president, as commander-in-chief, go through the headquarters of the general of the army, then Ulysses S. Grant. The Radicals trusted Grant, who was already leaning their way. The Tenure of Office Act required the consent of the Senate for the president to remove any officeholder whose appointment the Senate had to confirm in the first place. In large measure, it was intended to retain Secretary of War Edwin M. Stanton, the one Radical sympathizer in Johnson's cabinet. But an ambiguity crept into the wording of the act. Cabinet officers, it said, should serve during the term of the president who appointed them—and Lincoln had appointed Stanton, although, to be sure, Johnson was serving out Lincoln's term.

The Military Reconstruction Act, often hailed or denounced as the triumphant victory of "Radical" Reconstruction, actually fell short of a

This cartoon appeared at the time of the 1866 congressional elections. It shows "King Andy I" approving the execution of Radical leaders in Congress.

thoroughgoing transformation. Originally intended by the Radical Republicans to give military commanders in the South ultimate control over law enforcement and to leave open indefinitely the terms of future restoration, it was diluted by moderate Republicans, until it boiled down to little more than a requirement that southern states accept black suffrage and ratify the Fourteenth Amendment.

Tennessee, which had already ratified the Fourteenth Amendment, was exempted from the application of the act. The other ten southern states were divided into five military districts, and the commanding officer of each was authorized to keep order and protect the "rights of persons and property." The Johnson governments remained intact for the time being, but new constitutions were to be framed "in conformity with the Constitution of the United States," in conventions elected by male citizens twenty-one and older "of whatever race, color, or previous condition." Each state constitution had to provide the same universal male suffrage. Then, once the constitution was ratified by a majority of voters and accepted by Congress, and once the state legislature had ratified the Fourteenth Amendment, and once the amendment became part of the Constitution, any given state would be entitled to representation in Congress. Persons excluded from officeholding by the proposed amendment were also excluded from participation in the process. Before the end of 1867, new elections had been held in all the states but Texas.

Having clipped the president's wings, the Republican Congress moved a year later to safeguard its program from possible interference by the Supreme Court. On March 27, 1868, Congress simply removed the power of the Supreme Court to review cases arising under the Military Reconstruction Act, which Congress clearly had the constitutional right to do under its power to define the Court's appellate jurisdiction. The Court accepted this curtailment of its authority on the same day it affirmed the notion of an "indestructible Union" in *Texas* v. *White* (1868). In that case, it also acknowledged the right of Congress to reframe state governments, thus endorsing the Radical point of view.

THE IMPEACHMENT AND TRIAL OF JOHNSON (1868) By 1868, Radical Republicans were convinced that not only did the power of the Supreme Court and the president need to be curtailed, but Johnson had to be removed from office. Horace Greeley, the prominent editor of the *New York Tribune,* called Johnson "an aching tooth in the national jaw, a screeching infant in a crowded lecture room. There can be no peace or comfort till he is out."

Johnson, though hostile to the congressional Reconstruction program, had gone through the motions required of him. He continued, however, to pardon former Confederates and transferred several of the district military commanders who had displayed Radical sympathies. Johnson was revealing himself to be a man of limited ability and narrow vision. He lacked Lincoln's resilience and pragmatism. In the process of promoting his lenient southern strategy, Johnson allowed his temper to get the better of his judgment. He castigated the Radicals as "a gang of cormorants and bloodsuckers who have been fattening upon the country." During 1867, newspapers reported that the differences between Johnson and the Republicans were irreconcilable.

The Republicans unsuccessfully tried to impeach Johnson early in 1867, alleging a variety of flimsy charges, none of which represented an indictable crime. The head of the Secret Service, for example, shared rumors about an alleged presidential affair with a woman seeking pardons for former Confederates. Johnson was also accused of public drunkenness, and one congressman even tried to implicate him in the assassination of Lincoln. After listening to the hodgepodge of charges, a House member from Iowa concluded: "While the President has been guilty of many great follies and wickedness," it is better to "submit to two years of misrule . . . than subject the country, its institutions and its credits to the shock of an impeachment." But the impasse between the congressional leadership and the president continued.

At last, Johnson himself provided the occasion for impeachment when he deliberately violated the Tenure of Office Act in order to test its constitutionality. Secretary of War Edwin Stanton had become a thorn in the president's side, refusing to resign despite his disagreements with Johnson's Reconstruction policy. On August 12, 1867, during a congressional recess, Johnson suspended Stanton and named General Grant in his place. When the Senate refused to confirm Johnson's action, however, Grant returned the office to Stanton.

The Radicals now saw their chance to remove the president, and they were quite explicit about their political purposes. As Charles Sumner declared, "Impeachment is a political proceeding before a political body with a political purpose." The debate in the House was clamorous and vicious. One congressman said Johnson had dragged the robes of his office through the "filth of treason." Another denounced the president as "an ungrateful, despicable, besotted traitorous man—an incubus." Still another called Johnson's advisers "the worst men that ever crawled like filthy reptiles at the footstool of power." On February 24, 1868, the House passed eleven articles of impeachment by a party-line vote of 126 to 47.

Of the eleven articles of impeachment, eight focused on the charge that Johnson had unlawfully removed Stanton and had failed to give the Senate the name of a successor. Article 9 accused the president of issuing orders in violation of the Command of the Army Act. The last two articles in effect charged him with criticizing Congress by "inflammatory and scandalous harangues." Article 11 also accused Johnson of "unlawfully devising and contriving" to violate the Reconstruction Acts, contrary to his obligation to execute the laws. At the very least, it stated, Johnson had tried to obstruct Congress's will while observing the letter of the law.

The Senate trial began on March 5, 1868, and continued until May 26, with Chief Justice Salmon P. Chase presiding. It was a great spectacle before a packed gallery. Witnesses were called, speeches made, and rules of order debated. Johnson wanted to plead his case in person, but his attorneys refused, fearing that his short temper might erupt and hurt his cause. The president thereupon worked behind the scenes to win over undecided Republican senators, offering them a variety of political incentives.

As the weeks passed, the trial grew tedious. Senators slept during the proceedings, spectators passed out in the unventilated room, and poor acoustics prompted repeated cries of "We can't hear." Debate eventually focused on Stanton's removal, the most substantive impeachment charge. Johnson's lawyers argued that Lincoln, not Johnson, had appointed Stanton, so the Tenure of Office Act did not apply to him. At the same time, they claimed (correctly, as it turned out) that the law was unconstitutional.

As the five-week trial ended and the voting began in May 1868, the Senate Republicans could afford only six defections from their ranks to ensure the two-thirds majority needed to convict. In the end, seven moderate Republicans and all twelve Democrats voted to acquit. The final tally was 35–19 for conviction, one vote short of the two-thirds needed for removal from office. The renegade Republicans offered two primary reasons for their controversial votes: they feared damage to the separation of powers among the branches of government if Johnson were removed, and they were assured by Johnson's attorneys that he would stop obstructing congressional policy in the South.

In a moment of high drama, the deciding vote was cast by Edmund Ross, a first-term Kansas Republican who in the days leading up to the verdict was "hunted like a fox" by both sides. He insisted that his decision was an act of courage based on principled constitutional scruples: "If the president must step down upon insufficient proofs and from partisan considerations, the office of president would be degraded" and "ever after subordinated to the legislative will."

Historians have since discovered that Ross was not so principled: he demanded several political favors from Johnson in exchange for his vote. Whatever his motives, Ross's defection infuriated those promoting impeachment. One of his constituents fired off a bitter telegram: "Kansas repudiates you as she does all perjurers and skunks."

Although the Senate failed to remove Johnson, the trial crippled his already weak presidency. During the remaining ten months of his term, he initiated no other clashes with Congress. In 1868 Johnson sought the Democratic presidential nomination but lost to New York governor Horatio Seymour, who then lost to Republican Ulysses Grant in the general election. A bitter Johnson refused to attend Grant's inauguration. His final act as president was to issue a pardon to former Confederate president Jefferson Davis. In 1874, after failed bids for the Senate and the House, Johnson won a measure of vindication with election to the Senate, the only former president ever to do so, but he died a few months later. He was buried with a copy of the Constitution tucked under his head.

As for the impeachment trial, only two weeks after it ended, a Boston newspaper reported that people were amazed at how quickly "the whole subject of impeachment seems to have been thrown into he background and dwarfed in importance" by other events. Moreover, impeachment of Johnson was in the end a great political mistake, for the failure to remove the president damaged Radical morale and support. Nevertheless, the Radical cause did gain something. To blunt the opposition, Johnson agreed not to obstruct the process of Reconstruction, and thereafter Radical Reconstruction began in earnest.

RADICAL REPUBLICAN RULE IN THE SOUTH   In June 1868 Congress agreed that seven states had met the conditions for readmission, all but Virginia, Mississippi, and Texas. Congress rescinded Georgia's admission, however, when the state legislature expelled twenty-eight black members and seated some former Confederate leaders. The military commander of Georgia then forced the legislature to reseat the black members and remove the Confederates, and the state was compelled to ratify the Fifteenth Amendment before being readmitted in July 1870. Mississippi, Texas, and Virginia had returned earlier in 1870, under the added requirement that they too ratify the Fifteenth Amendment. This amendment, ratified in 1870, forbade the states to deny any citizen the right to vote on grounds of race, color, or previous condition of servitude.

Long before the new governments were established, partisan Republican groups began to spring up in the South, promoted by the Union League, an organization founded in 1862 to rally support for the federal government. Its representatives enrolled blacks and loyal whites as members, initiated them into the secrets and rituals of the order, and instructed them "in their rights and duties." These Union Leagues became a powerful source of Republican political strength in the South and as a result drew the ire of unreconstructed whites.

THE RECONSTRUCTED SOUTH

THE FREED SLAVES   To focus solely on what white Republicans did to reconstruct the defeated South creates the false impression that the freed slaves were simply pawns in the hands of others. In fact, however, southern blacks were active agents in affecting the course of Reconstruction activities. Although many of them found themselves liberated but destitute after the fighting ended, and often widely separated from family members, the mere promise of freedom raised their hopes about achieving a biracial democracy, equal justice, and economic opportunity. "Most anyone ought to know that a man is better off free than as a slave, even if he did not have anything," said the Reverend E. P. Holmes, a black Georgia preacher and former domestic servant. "I would rather be free and have my liberty."

Participation in the Union army or navy gave many freedmen a training ground in leadership. Black military veterans would form the core of the first generation of African-American political leaders in the postwar South. Military service provided many former slaves with the first opportunities to learn to read and write. Army life also alerted them to alternative social choices and to new opportunities for advancement and respectability. "No negro who has ever been a soldier," reported a northern official after visiting a black unit, "can again be imposed upon; they have learnt what it is to be free and they will infuse their feelings into others." Fighting for the Union cause also instilled a fervent sense of nationalism. A Virginia freedman explained that the United States was "now *our* country—made emphatically so by the blood of our brethren."

Former slaves established independent black churches after the war, churches that would serve as the foundation of African-American community life. In war-ravaged Charleston, South Carolina, the first new building to appear after the war was a black church on Calhoun Street; by 1866, ten more had been built. Blacks preferred Baptist churches over other denominations, in part because of their decentralized structure that allowed each congregation to worship in its own way. By 1890, there were over 1.3 million black Baptists in the South, nearly three times as many as any other black denomination. For many former slaves, churches were the first institutions they owned and controlled. In addition to forming viable new congregations, freed blacks organized thousands of fraternal, benevolent, and mutual-aid societies, clubs, lodges, and associations. Memphis, for example, had over two hundred such organizations; Richmond boasted twice that number.

The freed slaves, both men and women, also hastened to reestablish and reaffirm families. Marriages that had been prohibited were now legitimized through the assistance of the Freedmen's Bureau. By 1870, most former slaves lived in two-parent households. One white editor in Georgia, lamenting the difficulty of finding black women to serve as house servants, reported that "every negro woman wants to set up house keeping for herself and her family." The freed slaves would not live in the old slave quarters and wanted their own cabins, far from the old master's house.

The freed slaves had little money or technical training and were thus faced with the prospect of becoming wage laborers to support themselves. To avoid this and to retain as much autonomy as possible over their productive energies and those of their children on both a daily and seasonal basis, many former slaves chose to become sharecroppers. This meant that they were tenant farmers who gained access to separate plots of land owned by whites in exchange for a share of their crop. In payment for the use of the land and cabin, and sometimes even for use of the tools, seed, and fertilizer needed to farm the land, they gave between one-half and two-thirds of the harvested crops to the white landowner. This gave them higher status than they would have had as wage laborers; it gave them the freedom to set their own hours and work as much or as little as they pleased; and it enabled mothers and wives to devote more of their time to domestic needs while still contributing to family income.

Black communities in the postwar South also sought to establish schools. The antebellum planter elite had denied education to blacks because they feared that literate slaves would organize uprisings. After the war, the white elite worried that education programs would encourage both poor whites and blacks to leave the South in search of better social and economic opportunities. Economic leaders wanted to protect the competitive advantage afforded by the region's low-wage labor market.

The general resistance among the former slaveholding class to new education initiatives forced the freed slaves to rely on northern assistance or to take their own initiative. A Mississippi Freedmen's Bureau agent noted in 1865 that when he told a gathering of some 3,000 former slaves that they "were to have the advantages of schools and education, their joy knew no bounds. They fairly jumped and shouted in gladness." Black churches and individuals helped raise the money and often built the schools and paid the teachers. Soldiers who had acquired some reading and writing skills often served as the first teachers, and the classes included adults. A Florida teacher reported that a sixty-year-old former slave woman in her class was so excited by literacy that she "spells her lesson all the evening, then she dreams about it, and wakes up thinking about it."

BLACKS IN SOUTHERN POLITICS The new role of blacks in politics caused the most controversy, then and afterward. If largely illiterate and inexperienced in the rudiments of politics, they were little different from millions of whites enfranchised in the age of Jackson or immigrants herded to the polls by political bosses in New York and

Black Suffrage. *The Fifteenth Amendment was passed in 1870 and guaranteed the right of citizens, including the right to vote, regardless of race, color or previous condition of servitude, on the federal level. But former slaves had been registering to vote and voting in large numbers in state elections since 1867, as shown here.*

other cities after the war. Some freedmen frankly confessed their disadvantages. Beverly Nash, a black delegate in the South Carolina convention of 1868, told his colleagues: "I believe, my friends and fellow-citizens, we are not prepared for this suffrage. But we can learn. Give a man tools and let him commence to use them, and in time he will learn a trade. So it is with voting."

Several hundred black delegates participated in the statewide political conventions. Most had been selected by local political meetings or by churches, fraternal societies, Union Leagues, and black federal army units, although a few simply appointed themselves. "Some bring credentials," explained a North Carolina black leader, "others had as much as they could to bring themselves, having to escape from their homes stealthily at night" to avoid white assaults. The black delegates "ranged all colors and apparently all conditions," but free mulattoes from the cities played the most prominent roles. At Louisiana's Republican state convention, for instance, nineteen of the twenty black delegates had been born free.

By 1867, former slaves began to gain political influence and to vote in large numbers, and this revealed emerging tensions within the black community. Some southern blacks resented the presence of northern brethren who moved South after the war, while others complained that few ex-slaves were represented in leadership positions. Northern blacks and the southern free black elite, most of whom were urban dwellers, tended to oppose efforts to confiscate and redistribute land to the rural freedmen, and many insisted that political equality did not mean social equality. As an Alabama black leader stressed, "We do not ask that the ignorant and degraded shall be put on a social equality with the refined and intelligent." In general, however, unity rather than dissension prevailed, and blacks focused on common concerns such as full equality under the law.

Brought suddenly into politics in times that tried the most skilled of statesmen, many blacks served with distinction. Nonetheless, the derisive label "black Reconstruction" used by later critics exaggerates black political influence, which was limited mainly to voting, and overlooks the large numbers of white Republicans, especially in the mountain areas of the upper South. Only one of the new conventions, South Carolina's, had a black majority, 76 to 41. Louisiana's was evenly divided racially, and in only two other conventions were more than 20 percent of the members black: Florida's, with 40 percent, and Virginia's, with 24 percent. The Texas convention was only 10 percent black, and North Carolina's 11 percent—but that did not stop a white newspaper from calling it a body consisting of "baboons, monkeys, mules . . . and other jackasses."

In the new state governments, any black participation was a novelty. Although some 600 blacks—most of them former slaves—served as state legislators, no black man was ever elected governor and few served as judges. In Louisiana, however, Pinckney B. S. Pinchback, a northern black and former Union soldier, won the office of lieutenant-governor and served as acting governor when the white governor was indicted for corruption. Several blacks were elected lieutenant-governors, state treasurers, or secretaries of state. There were two black senators in Congress, Hiram Revels and Blanche K. Bruce, both from Mississippi, and fourteen black members of the House during Reconstruction. Among these were some of the ablest congressmen of the time.

CARPETBAGGERS AND SCALAWAGS   The top positions in southern state governments went for the most part to white Republicans, whom the opposition soon labeled "carpetbaggers" and "scalawags," depending on their place of birth. Northern opportunists who allegedly came South with all their belongings in carpetbags to reap political spoils were more often than not Union veterans who had arrived as early as 1865 or 1866, drawn South by the hope of economic opportunity. Others were lawyers, businessmen, editors, teachers, social workers, or preachers who came on missionary endeavors.

The "scalawags," or southern white Republicans, were even more reviled and misrepresented. A Nashville editor called them the "merest trash that could be collected in a civilized community, of no personal credit or social responsibility." Most "scalawags" had opposed secession, forming a Unionist majority in many mountain counties as far south as Georgia and Alabama, and especially in the hills of eastern Tennessee. Though many were indeed crass opportunists who indulged in corruption at the public's expense, several were quite distinguished figures. They included former Confederate general James A. Longstreet, who decided after Appomattox that the Old South must change its ways. To that end, he became a successful cotton broker in New Orleans, joined the Republican party, and supported the Radical Reconstruction program. Others were former Whigs who found the Republican party's expansive industrial and commercial program in keeping with Henry Clay's earlier American System.

THE RADICAL REPUBLICAN RECORD   Former Confederates not only resented "carpetbaggers" and "scalawags," they also objected to the new state constitutions, primarily because of their provisions for black suffrage and civil rights. Nonetheless, most of the state constitutions remained in effect for some years after the end of Radical control, and later constitutions incorporated many of their features. Conspicuous among Radical innovations were steps toward greater democracy such as requiring universal manhood suffrage, reapportioning legislatures more nearly according to population, and making more state offices elective.

Given the hostile circumstances in which the Radical governments arose and operated, their achievements were remarkable. In most of the South, they established the first state school systems, however inadequate and ill supported at first. Some 600,000 black pupils were in schools by 1877. State governments under the Radicals also gave more attention than ever before to poor relief and to orphanages, asylums, and institutions for the disabled of both races. Public roads, bridges, and buildings were repaired or rebuilt. Blacks achieved new rights and opportunities that would never again be taken away, at least in principle: equality before the law, and the right to own property, carry on business, enter professions, attend schools, and learn to read and write.

Yet several of these Republican regimes also practiced systematic corruption. In Louisiana, the carpetbag governor acknowledged the situation: "Why," he said, "down here everybody is demoralized. Corruption is the fashion." Public money and public credit were often voted to privately owned corporations, notably railroads, under conditions that invited influence peddling. Bids for contracts were accepted at absurd prices, and some public officials took their cut. Taxes and public debt rose in every state. Still, the figures of taxation and debt hardly constitute an unqualified indictment of Radical governments, since they then faced unusual and inflated costs for the physical reconstruction of public works in the South. Corruption was not invented by the Radical regimes, nor did it die with them. In Mississippi, the Republican governments of Reconstruction were quite honest compared to their Democratic successors.

WHITE TERROR The case of Mississippi suggests that whites were hostile to Republican regimes less because of their corruption than because of their inclusion of blacks. Most white southerners remained unreconstructed, so conditioned by slavery that they were unable to conceive of blacks as citizens or even free agents. In some places, hostility to the new regimes took the form of white terror. Efforts to oust Republican rule focused largely on violence. Said one unreconstructed Mississippian, "Carry the election peaceably if we can, forcibly if we must."

The prototype of terrorist groups was the Ku Klux Klan (KKK), first organized in 1866 by some young men of Pulaski, Tennessee, as a social club with the costumes, secret ritual, and mumbo-jumbo common to

This Thomas Nast cartoon chides the Ku Klux Klan and the White League for promoting conditions "worse than slavery" for southern blacks after the Civil War.

fraternal groups. At first a group of pranksters, they soon began to intimidate blacks and white Republicans, and the KKK spread rapidly across the South in answer to the Republican party's Union League. Klansmen rode about the countryside hiding under masks and robes, spreading horrendous rumors, harassing blacks, and wreaking violence and destruction.

In Mississippi, Klansmen mutilated a black Republican leader in front of his family. Three white "scalawag" Republicans were murdered in Georgia in 1870. That same year, an armed mob of whites disrupted a Republican political rally in Alabama, killing four blacks and wounding fifty-four. In South Carolina the Klan was especially active. Virtually the entire white male population of York County joined the Klan, and they were responsible for eleven murders and hundreds of whippings. In 1871 some 500 masked men laid siege to the Union County jail and eventually lynched eight black prisoners. Although most Klansmen were poor farmers and tradesmen, middle-class whites—planters, merchants, bankers, lawyers, doctors, even ministers—also joined the group and participated in its brutalities.

Congress struck back with three Enforcement Acts (1870–1871) to protect black voters. The first of these measures levied penalties on persons who interfered with any citizen's right to vote. A second placed the election of congressmen under surveillance by federal election supervisors and marshals. The third (the Ku Klux Klan Act) outlawed the characteristic activities of the Klan—forming conspiracies, wearing disguises, resisting officers, and intimidating officials. In 1871, the federal government singled out nine counties in upcountry South Carolina as an example, and pursued mass prosecutions that brought an abrupt halt to Klan terrorism. The program of federal enforcement broke the back of the Klan, whose activities declined steadily as recalcitrant southerners resorted to more subtle methods of racial intimidation.

CONSERVATIVE RESURGENCE   The Klan in fact could not take credit for the overthrow of Republican control in any state. Perhaps its most important effect was to weaken the morale of blacks and Republicans in the South and strengthen in the North a growing weariness with the whole "southern question." Republican control in the South gradually loosened as "Conservative" parties—Democrats used that name to mollify former Whigs—mobilized the white vote. Scalawags, and many carpetbaggers, drifted away from the Radical ranks under pressure from their white neighbors. Few of them had joined the Republicans out of concern for black rights in the first place. And where persuasion failed to work, Democrats were willing to use chicanery. As one enthusiastic Democrat boasted, "the white and black Republicans may outvote us, but we can outcount them."

Such factors led to the collapse of Republican control in Virginia and Tennessee as early as 1869, in Georgia and North Carolina in 1870. Reconstruction lasted longest in the Deep South states with the heaviest black population, where whites abandoned Klan hoods for barefaced intimidation in paramilitary groups like the Mississippi Rifle Club and the South Carolina Red Shirts. In overwhelmingly black Yazoo County, Mississippi, vengeful whites used violence to reverse the political balance of power. In the 1873 elections, the Republicans cast 2,449 votes and the Democrats 638; two years later, the Democrats polled 4,049 votes, the Republicans 7. By 1876, Radical regimes survived only in Louisiana, South Carolina, and Florida, and these all collapsed after the elections of that year.

The erosion of northern interest in promoting civil rights in the postwar South reflected both weariness as well as interest in other activities. Western expansion, Indian wars, economic development, and political debates over the tariff and currency distracted attention from

RECONSTRUCTION, 1865–1877

▨	States with Reconstruction governments
1868	Date of readmission to the Union
1870	Date of reestablishment of conservative rule
2	Military districts set by Reconstruction Act, 1867

Means by which slavery was abolished

▲	Emancipation Proclamation, 1863
■	State action
◆	Thirteenth Amendment, 1865

southern outrages. In addition, a business panic that occurred in 1873 led to a sharp depression and created both social problems and new racial tensions in the North and the South.

THE GRANT YEARS

THE ELECTION OF 1868 Ulysses S. Grant, who presided over the collapse of Republican rule in the South, brought to the presidency little political experience. But in 1868 the rank-and-file voter could be expected to support "the Lion of Vicksburg" because of his brilliant record as a war leader. Both parties wooed him, but his falling-out with President Johnson pushed him toward the Republicans and built trust in him among the Radicals. They were, as Thad Stevens said, ready to "let him into the church."

The Republican platform endorsed Radical Reconstruction, cautiously defending black suffrage as a necessity in the South, but a matter each northern state should settle for itself. It also urged payment of the nation's war debt in gold rather than in the new "greenback" paper currency printed during the war. More important than the platform were the great expectations of a soldier-president and his slogan: "Let us have peace."

The Democrats took an opposite position on both Reconstruction and the debt. The Republican Congress, the platform charged, had "subjected ten states, in the time of profound peace, to military despotism and Negro supremacy." As to the public debt, the party endorsed Representative George H. Pendleton's "Ohio idea" that, since most bonds had been bought with depreciated greenbacks, they should be paid off in greenbacks unless they specified payment in gold. With no conspicuously available candidate in sight, the convention turned to Horatio Seymour, war governor of New York and chairman of the convention. The Democrats made a closer race than expected, attesting to the strength of traditional party loyalties. While Grant swept the electoral college by 214 to 80, his popular majority was only 307,000 out of a total of over 5.7 million votes. More than 500,000 black voters accounted for Grant's margin of victory.

Grant had proven himself a great leader in the war, but in the White House he seemed blind to the political forces and influence peddlers around him. Shy and withdrawn, he was uncomfortable around intellectuals and impatient with idealists. Grant preferred watching horse races to reading about complex issues. Although personally honest, he was dazzled by men of wealth and unaccountably loyal to greedy subordinates who betrayed his trust. In the formulation of policy he passively followed the lead of Congress. This approach endeared him at first to party leaders, but it left him at last ineffective and caused others to grow disillusioned with his leadership. At the outset, Grant consulted nobody on his cabinet appointments. Some of his choices indulged personal whims; others simply reflected bad judgment. Secretary of State Hamilton Fish of New York turned out to be a fortunate exception; he masterfully guided foreign policy throughout the Grant presidency.

THE GOVERNMENT DEBT   Financial issues dominated the political agenda during Grant's presidency. After the war, the Treasury had assumed that the $432 million worth of greenbacks issued during the conflict would be retired from circulation and that the nation would revert to a "hard-money" currency—gold coins. Congress in 1866 granted the Treasury discretion to do so gradually. Many agrarian and debtor groups resisted this contraction of the money supply, believing that it would mean lower farm prices and harder-to-pay debts. They were joined by a large number of Radicals who thought a combination of high tariffs and inflation would generate more rapid economic growth. In 1868 "soft money" supporters in Congress halted the retirement of greenbacks, leaving $356 million outstanding. There matters stood when Grant took office.

The "sound" or "hard" money advocates, mostly bankers, merchants, and other creditors, claimed that Grant's election was a mandate to save the country from the Democrats' "Ohio idea" of using greenbacks to repay government bonds. Quite influential in Republican circles, the "sound-money" advocates also had the benefit of a deeply ingrained popular assumption that hard money was morally preferable to paper currency. Grant agreed, and in his inaugural address he endorsed payment of the national debt in gold as a point of national honor.

SCANDALS   Within less than a year of his election, Grant fell into a cesspool of scandal. In the summer of 1869 two brilliant, if crass, young railroad entrepreneurs, the crafty Jay Gould and the flamboyant Jim Fisk, connived with the president's brother-in-law to corner the gold market. Gould concocted an argument that the government should refrain from selling gold on the market because the resulting rise in gold prices would raise temporarily depressed farm prices. Grant apparently smelled a rat from the start, but he was seen in public with the speculators. As the rumor spread on Wall Street, gold rose from $132 to $163 an ounce. Finally, on "Black Friday," September 24, 1869, Grant ordered the Treasury to sell a large quantity of gold, and the bubble burst. Fisk got out by repudiating his agreements and hiring thugs to intimidate his creditors. "Nothing is lost save honor," he said.

The plot to corner the gold market was only the first of several scandals that rocked the Grant administration. In 1872 the public first learned about the financial buccaneering of the Crédit Mobilier, a construction company that had milked the Union Pacific Railroad for exorbitant fees to line the pockets of insiders who controlled both firms. Rank-and-file Union Pacific shareholders were left holding the bag. This chicanery had transpired before Grant's election in 1868, but it now touched a number of prominent Republicans who had been given shares of Crédit Mobilier stock in exchange for favorable votes. Of thirteen congressmen involved, only two were censured.

Even more odious disclosures soon followed, and some involved the

The People's Handwriting on the Wall. *An 1872 engraving comments on the corruption engulfing Grant.*

president's cabinet. Grant's secretary of war, it turned out, had accepted bribes from merchants who traded with Indians at army posts in the West. He was impeached, but he resigned in time to elude trial. Post-office contracts, it was revealed, went to carriers who offered the highest kickbacks. In St. Louis a "Whiskey Ring" bribed tax collectors to bilk the government of millions in revenue. Grant's private secretary was enmeshed in that scheme, taking large sums of money and other valuables in return for inside information. There is no evidence that Grant himself participated in any of the fraud, but his poor choice of associates earned him widespread censure.

REFORM AND THE ELECTION OF 1872   Long before Grant's first term ended, Republicans broke ranks. Their alienation was a reaction against the Radical Reconstruction measures and the incompetence and corruption in the administration. The Liberal Republicans favored free trade, gold to redeem greenbacks, a stable currency, restoring the rights of former Confederates, and civil service reform. Open revolt broke out first in Missouri, where Carl Schurz, a German immigrant and war hero, led a group of Liberal Republicans that, with Democratic help, elected a governor in 1870 and sent Schurz to the Senate.

In 1872 the Liberal Republicans held a clamorous national convention that produced a compromise platform condemning the Republican party's "vindictive" southern policy and favoring civil service reform, but which remained silent on the protective tariff. The delegates stampeded toward an anomalous presidential candidate: Horace Greeley, editor of the *New York Tribune,* a strong protectionist and enthusiastic reformer. During his long journalistic career, Greeley had promoted vegetarianism, brown bread, free-thinking, socialism, and spiritualism. His image as a visionary eccentric was complemented by his open hostility to Democrats, whose support the Liberals needed. One reporter suggested that there had been "too much brains and not enough whiskey" at the convention. The Democrats gave their nomination to Greeley as the only hope of beating Grant and the Radical Republicans. Greeley's promise to end Radical Reconstruction and restore "self government" to the South won over Democrats who otherwise despised the man and his beliefs.

The 1872 election result surprised no one. Republican regulars duly endorsed Radical Reconstruction and the protective tariff. Grant still had seven carpetbag states in his pocket, generous support from business and banking interests, and the stalwart support of the Radicals. Above all he still evoked the glory of Vicksburg and Appomattox. Greeley, despite an exhausting tour of the country—still unusual for a presidential candidate—carried only six southern and border states and none in the North. Devastated by his crushing defeat and the simultaneous death of his wife, Greeley entered a mental sanitarium and died three weeks later.

PANIC AND REDEMPTION A paralyzing economic panic followed closely upon the public scandals besetting the Grant administration. Contraction of the money supply brought about by the Treasury's postwar withdrawal of greenbacks and the reckless overexpansion of the railroads into sparsely settled areas helped precipitate a financial crisis. During 1873 some twenty-five strapped railroads defaulted on their interest payments. Caught short, the prominent investment firm of Jay Cooke and Company went bankrupt on September 18, 1873. A financial panic in Vienna forced many financiers to unload American stocks and bonds. The ensuing stampede of selling forced the stock market to close for ten days. The Panic of 1873 set off a depression that lasted for six years. It was the longest and most severe that Americans had yet suffered, marked by widespread bankruptcies, chronic unemployment, and a drastic slowdown in railroad building.

Hard times and corruption hurt Republicans in the midterm elections of 1874, allowing the Democrats to win control of the House of Representatives and gain seats in the Senate. The new Democratic House immediately launched inquiries into the Grant scandals and unearthed further evidence of corruption in high places. The panic meanwhile focused attention once more on greenback currency. Since greenbacks were valued less than gold, they had become the chief circulating medium. Most people spent greenbacks first and held their gold or used it to settle foreign accounts, which drained much gold out of the country. To relieve this deflationary spiral and stimulate business, therefore, the Treasury reissued $26 million in greenbacks previously withdrawn.

For a time, the advocates of paper money were riding high. But Grant vetoed an attempt to issue more greenbacks in 1874, and in his annual message he called for their gradual withdrawal and the resumption of payments of gold for greenbacks. Congress obliged the president by passing the Resumption Act of 1875. The resumption of paying gold to customers who turned in their greenbacks began on January 1, 1879, after the Treasury had built a gold reserve for the purpose and reduced the value of greenbacks in circulation. This act infuriated those promoting an inflationary monetary policy and provoked the formation of the National Greenback party. The much debated "money question" would remain one of the most divisive issues in American politics until the end of the century.

THE COMPROMISE OF 1877   Grant yearned to run for president again in 1876, but the recent scandals precluded any challenge to the two-term tradition. James G. Blaine of Maine, former Speaker of the House, emerged as the Republican front-runner, but he too bore the taint of scandal. Letters in the possession of James Mulligan of Boston linked Blaine to some dubious railroad dealings. Newspapers soon published these "Mulligan Letters," and Blaine's candidacy was dealt a body blow.

The Republican convention therefore eliminated Blaine and several other hopefuls in favor of Ohio's favorite son, Rutherford B. Hayes.

Three times governor of Ohio and an advocate of hard money, Hayes had a sterling character and had been a civil service reformer. But his chief virtue, as Henry Adams put it, was "that he is obnoxious to no one."

The Democratic convention was abnormally harmonious from the start. The nomination went on the second ballot to Samuel J. Tilden, millionaire corporation lawyer and reform governor of New York, who had directed a campaign to overthrow first the corrupt Tweed Ring that controlled New York City politics and then the Canal Ring in Albany that had bilked New York State of millions.

The campaign generated no burning issues. Both candidates favored the trend toward restoring conservative rule in the South. During one of the most corrupt elections ever, both candidates favored civil service reform. In the absence of strong differences, Democrats waved the Republicans' dirty linen. In response, Republicans "waved the bloody shirt," which is to say that they engaged in verbal assaults on former Confederates and the spirit of rebellion, linking the Democratic party with secession and with the outrages committed against both black and white Republicans in the South. As one Republican speaker insisted, "Every man that tried to destroy this nation was a Democrat. . . . The man that assassinated Abraham Lincoln was a Democrat. . . . Soldiers, every scar you have on your heroic bodies was given you by a Democrat!"

Early election returns pointed to a Tilden victory. Tilden had a 300,000 edge in the popular vote and had 184 electoral votes, just one short of a majority. Hayes had 165 electoral votes, but Republicans also claimed 19 doubtful votes from Florida, Louisiana, and South Carolina. The Democrats laid a counterclaim to 1 of Oregon's 3 votes. The Republicans had clearly carried Oregon, but the outcome in the South was less certain, and given the fraud and intimidation perpetrated on both sides, nobody will ever know the truth of the matter. In all three of the disputed southern states, rival canvassing boards sent in different returns. The Constitution offered no guidance in this unprecedented situation. Even if Congress were empowered to sort things out, the Democratic House and the Republican Senate proved unable to reach an agreement.

The impasse dragged on for months, and there was even talk of public violence. Finally, on January 29, 1877, the two houses decided to set up a special Electoral Commission that would investigate and report its findings. It had fifteen members, five each from the House, the Senate, and the Supreme Court. Members were so chosen as to have seven from each major party, with Justice David Davis of Illinois as the swing man. Davis, though appointed to the Court by Lincoln, was no party regular and was in fact thought to be leaning toward the Democrats. Thus, the panel appeared to be stacked in favor of Tilden.

But as it turned out, the panel got restacked the other way. Short-sighted Democrats in the Illinois legislature teamed up with minority Greenbackers to name Davis their senator. Davis accepted, no doubt with a sense of relief. From the remaining justices, all Republicans, the panel chose Joseph P. Bradley to fill the vacancy. The decision on each state went by a vote of 8 to 7 along party lines, in favor of Hayes. After much bluster and threat of filibuster by Democrats, the House voted on March 2 to accept the report and declare Hayes elected by an electoral vote of 185 to 184.

Critical to this outcome was the defection of southern Democrats who had made several informal agreements with the Republicans. On February 26, 1877, a bargain was struck at the Wormley House, a Washington hotel, between prominent Ohio Republicans (including James A. Garfield) and powerful southern Democrats. The Republicans promised that, if elected, Hayes would withdraw federal troops from Louisiana and South Carolina, letting the Republican governments there collapse. In return, the Democrats pledged to withdraw their op-position to Hayes, to accept in good faith the Reconstruction amend-ments, and to refrain from partisan reprisals against Republicans in the South.

Southern Democrats could now justify deserting Tilden. This so-called Compromise of 1877 brought a final "redemption" from the "Radicals" and a return to "home rule," which actually meant rule by native white Democrats. Other, more informal promises bolstered the secret agreement. Hayes's friends pledged more support for Mississippi River levees and other internal improvements, including a federal sub-sidy for a transcontinental railroad along a southern route. Southerners extracted a further promise that Hayes would name a white southerner as postmaster-general, the cabinet position with the most patronage jobs at hand. In return, southerners would let Republicans make Garfield Speaker of the new House. Such a deal illustrates the relative weakness of the presidency compared to Congress during the period.

THE END OF RECONSTRUCTION   In 1877 Hayes withdrew federal troops from the state houses in Louisiana and South Carolina, and the Republican governments there soon collapsed—along with much of Hayes's claim to legitimacy. Hayes chose a Tennessean as postmaster-general. But after southern Democrats failed to permit the choice of Garfield as Speaker, Hayes expressed doubt about any further subsidy for railroad building, and none was voted. Most of the other Wormley House promises were either renounced or forgotten.

As to southern promises regarding the civil rights of blacks, only a few Democratic leaders remembered them for long. Over the next three decades, those rights crumbled under the pressure of white rule in the South and the force of Supreme Court decisions narrowing the application of the Fourteenth and Fifteenth Amendments. Radical Reconstruction never offered more than an uncertain commitment to racial equality before the law. Yet it left an enduring legacy, the Thirteenth, Fourteenth, and Fifteenth Amendments—not dead but dormant, waiting to be revived. If Reconstruction did not provide social equality or substantial economic opportunities for blacks, it did create the opportunity for future transformation. It was a revolution, sighed North Carolina governor Jonathan Worth, and "nobody can anticipate the action of revolutions."

MAKING CONNECTIONS

- The political, economic, and racial policies of the conservatives who overthrew the Republican governments in the southern states are described in Chapter 18.

- Several of the political scandals mentioned in this chapter were related to the railroads, a topic discussed in greater detail in Chapter 19.

- This chapter ends with the election of Rutherford B. Hayes: for a discussion of Hayes's administration, see Chapter 21.

FURTHER READING

Reconstruction has long been "a dark and bloody ground" of conflicting interpretations. The most comprehensive treatment is Eric Foner's *Reconstruction: America's Unfinished Revolution, 1863–1877* (1988). More specialized works give closer scrutiny to the aims of the principal political figures. For a study of Andrew Johnson, see Hans L. Trefousse's *Andrew Johnson: A Biography* (1989).

Scholars have been fairly sympathetic to the aims and motives of the Radical Republicans. See, for instance, Herman Belz's *Reconstructing the Union* (1969) and Richard Nelson Current's *Those Terrible Carpetbaggers: A Reinterpretation* (1988). The ideology of these Radicals is explored in Michael Les Benedict's *A Compromise of Principle: Congressional Republicans and Reconstruction, 1863–1869* (1974).

The intransigence of southern white attitudes is examined in Michael Perman's *Reunion without Compromise* (1973), Dan T. Carter's *When the War Was Over: The Failure of Self-Reconstruction in the South, 1865–1867* (1985), and Richard Zuczek's *State of Rebellion: Reconstruction in South Carolina* (1996). Allen W. Trelease's *White Terror* (1971) covers the various organizations that practiced vigilante tactics, chiefly the Ku Klux Klan. The difficulties former laborers had in adjusting to the new labor system are documented in James L. Roark's *Masters without Slaves* (1977). Books on southern politics during Reconstruction include Michael Perman's *The Road to Redemption* (1984), Terry L. Seip's *The South Returns to Congress* (1983), and Mark W. Summer's *Railroads, Reconstruction, and the Gospel of Prosperity* (1984).

Numerous works have appeared on the freed blacks' experience in the South. Start with Leon F. Litwack's *Been in the Storm So Long* (1979),which covers the transition from slavery to freedom. Willie Lee Rose's *Rehearsal for Reconstruction* (1964) examines Union efforts to define the social role of former slaves during wartime emancipation. Joel Williamson's *After Slavery* (1965) argues that South Carolina blacks took an active role in pursuing their political and economic rights. For works concerning the political activity of freed slaves in other areas of the South, see Howard N. Rabinowitz's *Southern Black Leaders of the Reconstruction Era* (1982) and Edmund L. Drago's *Black Politicians and Reconstruction in Georgia: A Splendid Failure* (1982). Peter Kolchin's *First Freedom* (1972), a study of freed slaves in Alabama, is also useful. The role of the Freedmen's Bureau is explored in William S. McFeely's *Yankee Stepfather: General O.O. Howard and the Freedmen* (1968). The situation of freed slave women, which was often quite different from that of freed slave men, is discussed in Jacqueline Jones's *Labor of Love, Labor of Sorrow: Black Women, Work, and the Family from Slavery to Present* (1985).

The land confiscation issue is discussed in Eric Foner's *Politics and Ideology in the Age of the Civil War* (1980); Beth Bethel's *Promiseland* (1981), on a South Carolina black community; and Janet S. Hermann's *The Pursuit of a Dream* (1981), on the Davis Bend experiment in Mississippi.

The politics of corruption outside the South is depicted in William S. McFeely's *Grant: A Biography* (1981). The political maneuvers of the election of 1876 and the resultant crisis and compromise are explained in C. Vann Woodward's *Reunion and Reaction* (1951) and William Gillette's *Retreat from Reconstruction, 1869–1879* (1979).

For an examination of the lives of southern men and women who moved North between 1865 and 1880, see Daniel E. Sutherland's *The Confederate Carpetbaggers* (1992).

PART FIVE

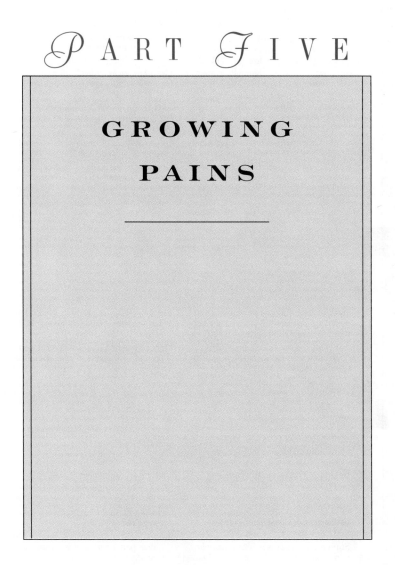

GROWING
PAINS

	POLITICAL	GLOBAL
1876	No president wins a majority of the popular vote (1876–1896) Rutherford B. Hayes becomes president after disputed election (1877–1881) Granger movement brings about passage of Granger laws to help farmers (1870s) Bourbons (planter-merchant elite) dominate southern politics and use poll taxes, literacy tests, and grandfather clause to disenfranchise blacks (1877–1890s) Socialist Labor party is organized in America (1877) Greenback party, which favors expansion of currency through issue of additional paper money, elects 15 congressmen (1878)	Large numbers of Irish, British, and Germans emigrate to U.S., including many European anarchists (1870s–1880s) Japan industrializes and rises to world power status (1870s–1890s) Great famine in China leads to migration of many Chinese men to America (1877–1878) First shipments of frozen meats arrive in Europe from Argentina and Australia (1870s) Queen Victoria of England proclaimed Empress of India (1877) Congress of Berlin gives Austria the right to "occupy and administer" the Ottoman provinces of Bosnia and Herzegovina (1878)
1880	Growth of governmental services such as water, sewers, street lighting, and fire and police protection (1880s–1900) Urban party machines help provide food, coal, money, and food for the poor (1880s–1910s) James A. Garfield becomes president (1881) Chester A. Arthur becomes president when Garfield is assassinated (1881–1885) Civil Rights Act of 1875 is declared unconstitutional (1883) Congress passes Pendleton Civil Service Reform Act to insure distribution of government jobs based on merit (1883) Grover Cleveland becomes president (1885–1889) Greenback party disintegrates (1885) In *Wabash Railroad* v. *Illinois,* U.S. Supreme Court denies states the right to regulate interstate commerce (1886) Cleveland administration creates the Interstate Commerce Commission (1887) Dawes Severalty Act disrupts Indian culture by privatizing their lands (1887) Farmer's Alliances turn to politics but fail to achieve significant gains for rural America (1880s–1890) Benjamin Harrison becomes president (1889–1893)	European drive for raw materials and markets leads to scramble for colonies in Africa (1880s–1890s) French Panama Canal Company begins to dig canal through Panama (1881–1887) Pro-imperialist Colonial League established; British occupy Egypt (1882) Austria, Germany, and Italy form the Triple Alliance (1882) England's Third Reform Bill gives vote to nearly all adult males (1884) Berlin Conference on imperialism (1884–1885) Canadian Pacific transcontinental railroad completed (1885) Indian National Congress formed to foster Indian participation in government (1885) Three Emperors' League of Germany, Russia, and Austria collapses (1887) Germany enacts social security reform laws (1884–1889) Second Socialist International begins (1884–1914)

"Flood tide" of migrants go west; harsh life leads to more equality between men and women (1870s–1890s)	Additional mining, dry farming, and irrigation further open the West for settlement (1870s–1890s)	1876
Black Exodusters move from South to Kansas (1870s–1880s)	Southern coal production increases from 5 million tons to 49 million tons (1875–1900)	
Vaudeville houses established in cities across U.S. (1870s–1890s)	John D. Rockefeller consolidates oil refining industry into Standard Oil Company of Ohio, which comes to control 90%–95% of nation's oil (1870s)	
Colleges and high schools start football teams (1870s–1900s)		
Andrew Carnegie invests $120 million on public libraries and education (1870s–1910s)	Second Industrial Revolution connects national transportation and communications networks leading to international market for American goods (1870s)	
Indians defeat Custer and his men in Battle of Little Bighorn (1876)	Building of transcontinental railways and trunk lines extends miles of railways from 35,000 to 200,000 (1870s–1890s)	
Alexander Graham Bell patents the telephone, making possible unprecedented rapid communication over long distances (1876)	Grangers promote farmer-owned cooperatives for buying and selling farm products (1870s)	
	Rise of bonanza farms for mass production of crops and livestock in West (1870s–1890s)	
	Great Railroad Strike of 1877 erupts when workers oppose wage cuts (1877)	
Thomas Edison invents the phonograph (1877) and the first successful incandescent light bulb, as technology impacts leisure and work (1879)	Knights of Labor becomes national movement (1878)	
Construction of taller buildings made possible by iron and steel frame construction and electric elevators leads to larger numbers of people who live and work in cities (1880s–1890s)	Andrew Carnegie consolidates steel industry in Pittsburgh (1880s)	1880
	Expansion of textile production in the South, where number of mills increases from 161 to 400 (1880s–1900)	
Immigrants from Europe and Asia gather in large numbers in America's largest cities providing much-needed labor while sometimes provoking ethnic and racial tensions (1880s–1890s)	Sagging crop prices make it increasingly difficult to own land (1880s–1890s)	
	Rise of sheep herding and barbed wire fencing disrupts cattle grazing, causing "range wars" between small farmers and cattle barons (1880s)	
The Atlanta Constitution heralds the advent of a "New South" (1880s)		
Proponents of "New South" espouse idea of "separate but equal" (1880s)	Edison establishes the Edison Electric Illuminating Company, the world's first public utilities company, in New York City (1882)	
State referenda on prohibition of alcoholic beverages (1880s–1890s)		
Chinese Exclusion Act prohibits immigration of Chinese for ten years (1882)	Foran Act passed, penalizing employers who import contract labor from abroad (1885)	
Mark Twain publishes The Adventures of Huckleberry Finn (1884)	Workers at Chicago's International Harvester Plant strike, culminating in Haymarket bombing (1886)	
Baseball becomes national pastime (1880s)		
Depletion of buffalo and capture of Geronimo (1886) leads to collapse of Indian resistance movement (1880s)	Founding of American Federation of Labor (1886)	
Amusement parks appear in many major cities (1880s–1900s)	George Westinghouse's invention of the 1st alternating current system enables factories to locate wherever they wish (1886)	
Increase in number of employed women (1880s–1890s)		
Black players banned from minor league baseball teams (1887)	Texas Farmer's Alliance unsuccessfully promotes Alliance Exchange to free farmers from dependence on processors and banks (1887)	
Andrew Carnegie's Gospel of Wealth published (1889)		

POLITICAL	GLOBAL

1890

Mississippi constitutional convention effectively disenfranchises blacks (1890)

National American Woman Suffrage Association established with Elizabeth Cady Stanton as its 1st president (1890)

People's party established, otherwise known as the Populist party (1892)

Grover Cleveland becomes president for 2nd time (1893–1897)

Populists poll 1.5 million votes for congressional candidates (1894)

Supreme Court rules in case of *In re Debs* that force may be used to enforce federal law (1895)

Plessy v. *Ferguson* sanctions "separate but equal" segregation (1896)

William Jennings Bryan runs for president as Democratic-Populist-Silverite candidate on a free silver platform (1896)

Struggle between urban and rural America culminates with 1896 election, and the collapse of the Populist party signals the failure of agrarian activism (1896)

First southern states adopt Democratic primary, which effectively excludes black voters (1896)

Eugene Debs organizes Social Democratic party (1897)

William McKinley becomes president (1897–1901)

GLOBAL

Bismarck is dismissed as prime minister of Germany (1890)

Japan adopts a constitution (1890)

Large numbers of people from eastern and southern Europe emigrate to U.S. (1890s–1900s)

Doctrine of Social Darwinism fuels imperialism (1890s)

French acquire Indochina (1893)

France and Russia form the Dual Alliance (1894)

Sino-Japanese War furthers Japan's imperialism (1894–1895)

Spanish-American War (1898)

Hawaii is annexed by U.S.; Puerto Rico, Guam, and the Philippines become U.S. territories (1898)

Fashoda crisis in the Sudan brings British and French to brink of war (1898)

U.S. appoints military governor of Cuba (1899)

Boer War in South Africa (1899–1902)

Beginning of Open Door trade policy in China (1899)

1900

Boxer Rebellion in reaction to Western presence in China (1900)

Britain agrees to establishment of Commonwealth of Australia (1900)

Foraker Act establishes a civil government in Puerto Rico (1900)

William Howard Taft is sent by McKinley to the Philippines to set up a civil government (1900)

"Streetcar suburbs" spring up as a result of transportation revolution, leading to exodus of middle and upper classes from city centers (1890s)

12% of whites and 50% of blacks are illiterate (1890)

College enrollment increases from 52,000 (1870) to 157,000 (1890); professors increasingly have Ph.D.s (1890s)

Ongoing nativism leads to further immigration restrictions (1890s–1950s)

Ghost Dance movement leads to bloodbath at Wounded Knee (1890)

Annual lynchings average 187; 82% occur in the South (1890–1899)

Severe winters decimate open range (1886, 1887); 10 years of drought in West follow (1890s)

U.S. surpasses Britain in iron and steel production (1890s)

Sears and Roebuck come to dominate mail-order industry (1890s)

Congress defeats Farmer's Alliance subtreasury plan for storage of crops and loans to farmers (1890)

Dependent Pension Bill provides funds to veterans who cannot work (1890)

5 vertically integrated companies produce 90% of all meat shipped in interstate commerce (1890)

Tenant farmers and sharecroppers constitute a majority of farm workers in the Deep South (1890)

Sherman Silver Purchase Act (1890)

McKinley Tariff raises duties on manufactured goods 49.5% (1890)

Sherman Anti-Trust Act prohibits businesses from monopolizing trade (1890)

Dr. James Naismith invents basketball (1891)

Chinese Exclusion Act of 1882 renewed for another 10 years (1892)

Opening of Ellis Island as reception area for new immigrants (1892)

Frederick Jackson Turner presents his "The Significance of the Frontier in American History" in Chicago (1893)

Homestead Strike among steel workers at Pittsburgh's Homestead Works (1892)

Supreme Court of Ohio orders dissolution of Standard Oil Company (1892)

Depression of 1893 destroys many small businesses (1893)

President Cleveland rescinds Sherman Silver Purchase Act, worsening the debate that divides the nation regarding silver coinage (1893)

American Railway Union is founded by Eugene Debs (1893)

Pullman Strike among employees of Pullman Palace Car Co. in Illinois (1894)

J.P. Morgan and other financiers supply gold to buy up government bonds and to stop demands on Treasury (1895)

Stephen Crane publishes *The Red Badge of Courage* (1895)

Booker T. Washington's "Atlanta Compromise" urges blacks to accommodate white racism and domination (1895)

W.E.B. DuBois calls for "ceaseless agitation" among blacks (1897)

Nearly 100 settlement houses dot urban America (1900)

Number of public schools in America increase from 800 (1880) to 6,000 (1900)

30% of residents of major cities are foreign born (1900)

Dingley Tariff raises tariff to 57% of the value of imported goods, the highest tariff in U.S. history (1897)

Gold Standard Act ends silver movement (1900)

The northern victory in 1865 restored the Union and in the process helped to accelerate America's transformation into a modern nation-state. A distinctly national consciousness began to displace the sectional emphases of the antebellum era. During and after the Civil War, the Republican-led Congress pushed through legislation to foster industrial and commercial development and western expansion. In the process, the United States abandoned the Jeffersonian dream of a decentralized agrarian republic and began to forge a dynamic new industrial outlook generated by an increasingly national market.

After 1865, many Americans turned their attention to the unfinished business of settling a continent and completing an urban-industrial revolution begun before the war. Huge new national corporations based upon mass production and mass marketing began to dominate the economic order. As the prominent sociologist William Graham Sumner remarked, the process of industrial development "controls us all because we are all in it. It creates the conditions of our own existence, sets the limits of our social activity, and regulates the bonds of our social relations."

The industrial revolution was not only an urban phenomenon; it transformed rural life as well. Those who got in the way of the new emphasis on large-scale, highly mechanized commercial agriculture and ranching were brusquely pushed aside. Farm folk, as one New Englander stressed, "must understand farming as a business; if they do not it will go hard with them." The friction between new market forces and traditional folkways generated political revolts and social unrest during the last quarter of the nineteenth century. Fault lines appeared throughout the social order, and they unleashed tremors that exerted what one writer called "a seismic shock, a cyclonic violence" upon the body politic.

The clash between tradition and modernity came to a climax during the decade of the 1890s, one of the most strife-ridden in American history. A deep depression, agrarian unrest, and labor violence provoked fears of a class war. This turbulent situation transformed the presidential election campaign of 1896 into a clash between two rival visions of America's future. The Republican candidate, William McKinley, campaigned on behalf of modern urban-industrial values. By contrast, William Jennings Bryan, the nominee of both the Democratic and Populist parties, was an eloquent defender of America's rural past. McKinley's victory proved to *be a watershed in American political and social history. By 1900, the United States would emerge as one of the world's greatest industrial powers, and it would thereafter assume a new leadership role in world affairs.*

18 ❧ NEW FRONTIERS:
SOUTH AND WEST

CHAPTER ORGANIZER

This chapter focuses on:

• the economic and political policies of the states in the post-Reconstruction South.

• race relations in the New South.

• the farmers', miners', and cowboys' frontiers.

• late-nineteenth-century Indian policy.

*A*fter the Civil War, the West and the South provided enticing opportunities for pioneers and entrepreneurs alike. Before 1860, most people had viewed the region between the Mississippi River and California as a barren landscape unfit for human habitation or cultivation, an uninviting land suitable only for Indians and animals. Half of the state of Texas, for instance, was still not settled at the end of the Civil War. After 1865, however, the federal government encouraged western settlement and economic development. The construction of transcontinental railroads, the military conquest of the Indians, and a liberal land distribution policy combined to help lure thousands of pioneers and expectant capitalists westward.

As a result of the mass migration to the West, fourteen new states were created out of America's western territories during the century after the Civil War.

Although the first great wave of railroad building occurred in the 1850s, the most spectacular growth took place during the quarter century after the Civil War. From about 35,000 miles of track in 1865, the network grew to nearly 200,000 miles by 1897. The transcontinental rail lines led the way, and they helped populate the plains and the Far West. Of course, the expense of such massive railroad development was enormous, and the long-term debt required to finance construction would become a major cause of the Panic of 1893 and the ensuing depression.

Meanwhile, southern rail lines were rebuilt and supplemented with new branch lines. The defeated South, although not a frontier in the literal sense of the term, offered capitalists a fertile new ground for investment and industrial development. Proponents of a "New South" after 1865 argued that the region must abandon its single-minded preoccupation with agriculture and pursue industrial and commercial development. As a result, the South as well as the West experienced dramatic social and economic changes during the last third of the nineteenth century. By 1900, these new "frontiers" had been transformed in ways that few could have predicted.

THE NEW SOUTH

A FRESH VISION   After the Civil War, many southerners looked back wistfully to the plantation life that had characterized their region before the firing on Fort Sumter. A few prominent leaders, however, insisted that the postwar South must liberate itself from such nostalgia and create a new society of small farms, thriving industries, and bustling cities. The major prophet of this "New South" was Henry W. Grady, the thirty-six-year-old editor of the *Atlanta Constitution*. During the 1880s, Grady set forth the vision that inspired a generation of southerners: "The Old South rested everything on slavery and agriculture, unconscious that these could neither give nor maintain healthy growth. The New South presents a perfect democracy . . . a social system compact and closely knitted, less splendid on the surface, but stronger at the core—a hundred farms for every plantation, fifty homes for every palace—and a diversified industry that meets the complex need of this complex age."

It was a compelling vision, and other advocates of this New South Creed soon emerged. In the aftermath of the Civil War, these men, and their Yankee patrons, preached the gospel of industry with evangelical fervor. The Confederacy, they reasoned, had lost because it relied too much on King Cotton. In the future, the South must follow the North's example and industrialize. From that central belief flowed certain implications: that a more diversified and efficient agriculture would be a foundation for economic growth, that more widespread education, especially vocational training, would promote material success. By the late 1870s, with Reconstruction over and the Panic of 1873 forgotten, a mood of progress permeated the editorials and the speeches of the day.

ECONOMIC GROWTH   The chief accomplishment of the New South movement was an expansion of the area's textile production, which began in the 1880s and overtook its older New England competitors by the 1920s. From 1880 to 1900, the number of cotton mills in the South grew from 161 to 400, and the number of mill workers (among whom women and children outnumbered the men) increased fivefold.

Tobacco growth also increased significantly, entering a new era with the development of two new varieties of the weed: burley, which first appeared in southern Ohio, and bright leaf, which was grown on otherwise infertile soils and cured by a charcoal process discovered by a slave in 1839. Knowledge of the bright-leaf type remained chiefly local until, in what seemed a misfortune, Union soldiers swarmed over central North Carolina in 1865.

One victim of their looting was John Ruffin Green, whose bright-leaf tobacco factory was ransacked by soldiers loitering around Durham Station. Within a few weeks, orders began to pour into Green's factory for the Best Flavored Spanish Smoking Tobacco "that did not bite." With this revival, Green adopted as his trademark a bull's head similar to that on Colman's mustard, made in Durham, England. It did not take long for Green and his successors to make the image of Bull Durham ubiquitous, so much so that years later Mark Twain, who was notorious for embellishing a good story, claimed that when he visited Egypt he never saw the pyramids because they were obscured by Bull Durham signs.

Even more important in the rise of tobacco and the city of Durham was the Duke family, who inhabited a nearby farm. At the end of the Civil War, the story goes, old Washington Duke had only fifty cents obtained from a Yankee soldier in exchange for a souvenir Confederate five-dollar bill. He took a load of tobacco, and with the help of his three sons, beat it out with hickory sticks, stuffed it in bags, hitched two mules to his wagon, and set out across the state, selling bright-leaf tobacco as he went. By 1872 the Dukes had a factory producing 125,000 pounds of tobacco annually, and Washington Duke prepared to settle down and enjoy success.

His son Buck (James Buchanan Duke), however, had the same entrepreneurial drive that animated the Carnegies and Rockefellers of that day. Buck Duke recognized early that the tobacco industry was "half smoke and half ballyhoo," so he poured large sums into advertising schemes. Duke also undersold competitors in their own markets, and cornered the supply of ingredients. Eventually his competitors were ready to take the hint that they join forces, and in 1890 Duke brought most of them into the American Tobacco Company, which controlled nine-tenths of the nation's cigarette production. In 1911 the Supreme Court ruled that the company was in violation of the antitrust laws and ordered it broken up, but by then Duke had found new worlds to conquer in hydroelectric power and aluminum.

Systematic use of other natural resources helped revitalize the area along the Appalachian Mountain chain from West Virginia to Alabama. Coal production in the South (including West Virginia) grew from 5 million tons in 1875 to 49 million tons by 1900. At the southern end of the mountains, Birmingham, Alabama, sprang up during the 1870s as a major steel-producing center and soon tagged itself the "Pittsburgh of the South."

Industrial growth created a need for wood-framed housing, and after 1870 lumbering became a thriving industry in the South. By the turn of the century, it had surpassed textiles in value. Tree cutting seemed to know no bounds, despite the resulting ecological devastation. In time the industry would be saved only by the warm climate, which fostered quick renewal, and the rise of scientific forestry.

Two forces that would impel an even greater industrial revolution were already on the southern horizon at the turn of the century: petroleum in the Southwest and hydroelectric power in the Southeast. In

1901 the Spindletop oil gusher in Texas brought a huge bonanza. Electrical power proved equally profitable, and local power plants dotted the South by the 1890s. Richmond, Virginia, boasted the nation's first electric streetcar system in 1888, and Columbia, South Carolina, boasted the first electrically powered cotton mill in 1894. The greatest advance would begin in 1905 when Buck Duke's Southern Power Company set out to electrify entire river valleys in the Carolinas.

AGRICULTURE, OLD AND NEW   Although there was some industrial growth, at the turn of the century, most of the South remained undeveloped, at least by northeastern standards. Despite the optimistic rhetoric of New South spokesmen, the typical southerner was less apt to be tending a loom or forging than, as the saying went, facing the eastern end of a westbound mule. King Cotton survived the Civil War and expanded over new acreage even as its export markets leveled off. Louisiana cane sugar, probably the most war-devastated of all crops, also flourished again by the 1890s.

The majority of southern farmers were not flourishing, however. A prolonged deflation in crop prices affected the entire western world

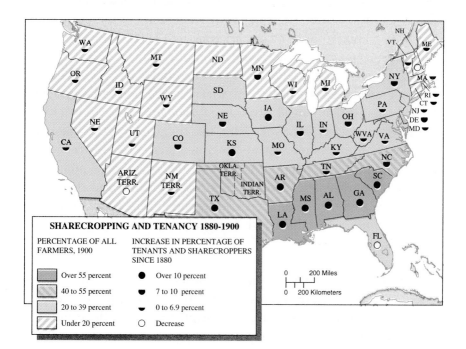

SHARECROPPING AND TENANCY 1880-1900

PERCENTAGE OF ALL FARMERS, 1900	INCREASE IN PERCENTAGE OF TENANTS AND SHARECROPPERS SINCE 1880
Over 55 percent	● Over 10 percent
40 to 55 percent	◗ 7 to 10 percent
20 to 39 percent	◞ 0 to 6.9 percent
Under 20 percent	○ Decrease

0   200 Miles
0   200 Kilometers

during the last third of the nineteenth century. Sagging prices made it more difficult than ever to own land. Sharecropping and tenancy grew increasingly prevalent. By 1890, most southern farms were worked by people who did not own the land. High tenancy rates in the Deep South belied the rosy rhetoric of New South prophets: South Carolina, 61 percent; Georgia, 60 percent; Alabama, 58 percent; Mississippi, 62 percent; and Louisiana, 58 percent.

How did the system work? Sharecroppers, who had nothing to offer the landowner but their labor, tilled the land in return for supplies and a share of the crop, generally about half. Tenant farmers, hardly better off, might have their own mule, a plow, and credit with the country store. They were entitled to claim a larger share, commonly three-fourths of the cash crop and two-thirds of the subsistence crop, which was mainly corn. The system was horribly inefficient, for the tenant lacked incentive to care for the land, and the owner had little chance to supervise the work. In addition, the system bred a morbid suspicion on both sides. The folklore of the rural South was replete with tales of tenants who remained stubbornly shiftless and scheming landlords who kept books with crooked pencils.

The crop lien system was equally flawed. At best, it supplied credit where cash was scarce. It worked this way: country merchants furnished supplies in return for liens (or mortgages) on farmers' crops. To a few tenants and small farmers who seized the chance, such credit offered a way out of dependency, but to most it offered only a hopeless cycle of perennial debt. The merchant, who assumed great risks, generally charged interest that ranged, according to one journalist, "from 24 percent to grand larceny." The merchant, like the planter (often the same man), required his farmer clients to grow a cash crop that could be readily sold at harvest time. Thus, for all the New South promoters' ballyhoo about diversification, the routines of tenancy and sharecropping were geared to a staple crop, usually cotton. The resulting stagnation of rural life held millions, white and black, in bondage to privation and ignorance.

THE BOURBON REDEEMERS   In post–Civil War politics, habits of deference and elitism still prevailed. After Reconstruction ended in 1877, a planter-merchant elite, collectively known as Redeemers or Bourbons, dominated southern politics. The supporters of these postwar leaders referred to them as "Redeemers" because they supposedly "redeemed," or saved, the South from Yankee domination as well as from the limitations of a purely rural economy. The Redeemers included a rising class of entrepreneurs who were eager to promote a more diversified economy based on industrial development and railroad expansion.

The opponents of the "Redeemers" labeled them "Bourbons" in an effort to depict them not as progressives but as reactionaries. Like the French royal family which, Napoleon said, forgot nothing and learned nothing in the ordeal of revolution, Bourbons of the postwar South were said to have forgotten nothing and learned nothing in the ordeal of the Civil War.

The term "Bourbon" came to signify the leaders of the Democratic party, whether they were real reactionaries or, more commonly, champions of an industrial New South who, if they had forgotten nothing, had at least learned something. They may have worshipped at the shrine of the old social order, but they embraced a new order of economic development.

The Effects of Radical and Bourbon Rule in the South. *This 1880 cartoon shows the South staggering under the oppressive weight of military Reconstruction* (left) *and flourishing under the "Let 'Em Alone Policy" of Hayes and the Bourbons* (right).

These Bourbons of the New South perfected a political alliance with northeastern conservatives and an economic alliance with northeastern capitalists. They generally pursued a government policy of laissez-faire, except for the tax exemptions and other favors they offered to business. They avoided political initiatives, making the transition from Republican rule to Bourbon rule less abrupt than is often assumed. The Bourbons' favorable disposition toward the railroads was not unlike that of the Radicals. And despite their reputation for honesty, Bourbon office-holders were occasionally caught with their fingers in the till.

The Bourbons focused on cutting back the size and cost of government. This spelled austerity for public services, including the school systems started during Reconstruction. In 1871 the southern Atlantic states were spending $10.27 per pupil; by 1880 the figure was down to $6.00, and in 1890 it stood at only $7.63. Illiteracy rates at the time ran at about 12 percent of the white population and 50 percent of the black population.

The Bourbons' urge to economize led them to adopt the degrading system of convict leasing. The destruction of prisons during the Civil War and the poverty of state treasuries afterward combined with the demand for cheap labor on the railroads, in the mines, and in lumber camps, to make the leasing of convict labor a way for southern states to avoid expenses and generate revenue. The burden of detaining criminals grew after the war because freed slaves, who had been subject to the discipline of masters, were now subject to the criminal law. Convict leasing, in the absence of state supervision, allowed inefficiency, neglect, and disregard for human life to proliferate.

The Bourbons scaled down not only state expenditures but also the public debt, and by a simple means—they repudiated a vast amount of debt that had been issued by the Radical state regimes. The corruption and extravagance of Radical rule were commonly advanced as justification for the process, but repudiation did not stop with Reconstruction debts. Altogether nine states repudiated more than half of what they owed to bondholders and various other creditors.

These scrimping Bourbon regimes did respond to the demand for commissions to regulate the rates charged by railroads for commercial transport. They also established boards of agriculture and public health, agricultural experiment stations, agricultural and mechanical colleges, teacher-training schools and women's colleges, even state colleges for

African Americans. Nor can any simplistic interpretation encompass the variety of Bourbon leaders. The Democratic party was then a mongrel coalition that threw Old Whigs, Unionists, secessionists, businessmen, small farmers, hillbillies, planters, and even some Republicans together in alliance against the Reconstruction Radicals. Democrats therefore, even those who bore the Bourbon label, often marched to different drummers, and the Bourbon regimes never achieved complete unity in philosophy or government.

Perhaps the ultimate paradox of the Bourbons' rule was that these paragons of white supremacy tolerated a lingering black voice in politics and showed no haste about raising legal barriers of racial separation. Blacks sat in the state legislature of South Carolina until 1900, of Georgia until 1908, and of Virginia until 1890; some of these black representatives were Democrats. The South sent black congressmen to Washington in every election until 1900 except one, though they always represented gerrymandered districts into which most of the black voters had been thrown. Under the Bourbons, the disenfranchisement of black voters remained inconsistent, a local matter brought about mainly by fraud and intimidation, although it occurred often enough to ensure white control of the southern states.

A like flexibility applied in other areas of race relations. The color line was drawn less strictly than it would be in the twentieth-century South. In some places, to be sure, racial segregation appeared before the end of Reconstruction, especially in schools, churches, hotels and rooming houses, and in private social relations. In other public places such as trains, depots, theaters, and soda fountains, however, segregation was more sporadic.

DISENFRANCHISING BLACKS   During the 1890s, the attitudes of patrician benevolence that permitted such moderation eroded swiftly. One reason for this was that, despite signs of progress, many whites claimed that blacks, freed from the restraints of slavery, were "retrogressing" toward bestiality, especially the younger blacks born after emancipation.

Another reason was political. The rise of populism, a farm-based protest movement that culminated in the creation of a third political party in the 1890s, divided the white vote to such an extent that in some places the black vote became the balance of power. Some populists courted black votes. In response, the Bourbons revived the race issue, which they exploited with seasoned finesse, all the while controlling for their ticket a good part of the black vote in plantation areas. Nevertheless, the Bourbons soon insisted that the black vote be eliminated completely from southern elections. It was imperative, the Louisiana governor told the state legislature in 1894, that "the mass of ignorance, vice and venality without any proprietary interest in the State" be denied the vote. Some farm leaders hoped that disenfranchisement of blacks would make it possible for whites to divide politically without raising the specter of "Negro domination."

But since the Fifteenth Amendment made it illegal to disenfranchise blacks as such, racists accomplished their purpose indirectly with devices such as poll taxes (or head taxes) and literacy tests. Some opposed such devices because they also ensnared poor whites, and this led to the creation of loopholes through which illiterate whites could slip.

Mississippi led the way to near-total disenfranchisement of blacks. The state called a constitutional convention in 1890 to change the suffrage provisions of the old Radical constitution of 1868. The resulting Mississippi plan set the pattern that seven more states would follow over the next twenty years. First, a residence requirement—two years in the state, one year in the election district—struck at those black tenant farmers who were in the habit of moving yearly in search of a better chance. Second, voters were disqualified if convicted of certain crimes, many of them petty. Third, all taxes, including a poll tax, had to be paid by February 1 of election year, which left plenty of time for white officials to lose the receipt before the fall vote. This proviso fell most heavily on the poor, most of whom were black. Fourth and finally, all voters had to be literate. The alternative, designed as a loophole for whites otherwise disqualified, was an "understanding" clause. The voter, if unable to read the Constitution, could qualify by "understanding" it—to the satisfaction of the registrar. Fraud was thus institutionalized by "legal" disenfranchisement.

In other states, variations on the Mississippi plan added a few flourishes. In 1898 Louisiana invented the "grandfather clause," which allowed illiterates to qualify if their fathers or grandfathers had been eligible to vote on January 1, 1867, when blacks were still excluded. By 1910 Georgia, North Carolina, Virginia, Alabama, and Oklahoma had adopted the grandfather clause. Every southern state, moreover, adopted a statewide Democratic primary which became the only meaningful election outside isolated areas of Republican strength. With minor exceptions, the Democratic primaries excluded black voters altogether. The effectiveness of these measures can be seen in a few sample figures: Louisiana in 1896 had 130,000 black voters registered, and in 1900, 5,320. Alabama in 1900 had 121,159 literate black males over twenty-one, according to the census; only 3,742 were registered to vote.

SEGREGATION SPREADS   What came to be called "Jim Crow" segregation followed disenfranchisement and in some states came first. From 1875 to 1883, any racial segregation violated a federal Civil Rights Act, which forbade discrimination in places of public accommodation. But in 1883 the Supreme Court ruled on seven *Civil Rights Cases* involving discrimination against blacks by corporations or individuals. The Court held, with only one dissent, that the force of federal law could not extend to individual action because the Fourteenth Amendment, which provided that "no State" could deny citizens the equal protection of the laws, stood as a prohibition only against state, not individual, action.

This left as an open question the validity of state laws *requiring* separate public facilities under the rubric of "separate but equal," a slogan popular with the New South prophets. In 1888 Mississippi required railway passengers, under penalty of law, to occupy the car set aside for their race. When Louisiana followed suit in 1890, the law was challenged in the case of *Plessy* v. *Ferguson,* which the Supreme Court decided in 1896.

The test case originated in New Orleans when Homer Plessy, an octoroon (a person of one-eighth black ancestry), refused to leave a white railroad car when asked to do so. He was convicted, and the case rose on appeal to the Supreme Court. The Court ruled that segregation laws "have been generally, if not universally recognized as within the competency of state legislatures in the exercise of their police power."

Very soon the principle of statutory racial segregation extended into every area of southern life, including street railways, hotels, restaurants, hospitals, recreations, sports, and employment. If an activity was overlooked by the laws, it was not overlooked in custom and practice. The editor of the *Richmond Times* expressed the prevailing view in 1900:

"God Almighty drew the color line and it cannot be obliterated. The negro must stay on his side of the line and the white man must stay on his side, and the sooner both races recognize this fact and accept it, the better it will be for both."

Violence accompanied the so-called Jim Crow laws that mandated segregated facilities. From 1890 to 1899, lynchings in the United States averaged 187 per year, 82 percent of which occurred in the South; from 1900 to 1909, they averaged 93 per year, of which 92 percent occurred in the South. Whites constituted 32 percent of the victims during the first period, only 11 percent in the latter. A young Episcopal priest in Montgomery remarked that extremists had proceeded "from an undiscriminating attack upon the Negro's ballot to a like attack upon his schools, his labor, his life."

WASHINGTON AND DU BOIS A few brave souls, black and white, spoke out against such attitudes, but by and large blacks had to accommodate as best they could. Some blacks even began to make a virtue of necessity, and the chief spokesman for this accommodationist philosophy was Booker T. Washington, the black prophet of the New South Creed. Born in Virginia of a slave mother and a white father, Washington had fought extreme adversity to get an education at Hamp-

Booker T. Washington.

ton Institute, one of the postwar missionary schools, and then, in 1881, to build at Tuskegee, Alabama, a leading college for blacks.

Washington argued that blacks should not antagonize whites by demanding social or political equality; instead they should concentrate on establishing an economic base for their advancement. In his speech at the Atlanta Cotton States and International Exposition in 1895, which propelled him to fame and was later labeled the "Atlanta Compromise," Washington advised fellow blacks to begin "at the bottom of life" and stress their opportunities rather than their grievances: "Cast down your bucket where you are—cast it down in making friends . . . of the people of all races by whom we are surrounded. Cast it down in agriculture, mechanics, in commerce, in domestic service, and in the professions." He conspicuously omitted politics and implied an endorsement of segregation: "In all things that are purely social we can be as separate as the five fingers, yet one as the hand in all things essential to mutual progress."

Some people bitterly criticized Washington, in his lifetime and after, for making a bad bargain: the sacrifice of broad education and of civil rights for the dubious acceptance of white conservatives and the creation of economic opportunities for blacks. W. E. B. Du Bois led blacks in this criticism of Washington. A native of Great Barrington, Massachusetts, the son of free blacks, Du Bois once said defiantly that he was born "with a flood of Negro blood, a strain of French, a bit of Dutch,

W. E. B. Du Bois.

but thank God! no 'Anglo-Saxon.'" Du Bois first experienced southern racial practices as an undergraduate at Fisk University in Nashville. Later he earned a Ph.D. in history from Harvard and afterward attended the University of Berlin. In addition to an active career in racial protest, he left a distinguished record as a teacher and scholar. Trim and dapper in appearance, sporting a goatee, cane, and gloves, he possessed a combative, fiery spirit. Not long after he began his teaching career at Atlanta University in 1897, he began to assault Washington's accommodationist philosophy of black progress and put forward his own program of "ceaseless agitation."

Washington, Du Bois argued, preached "a gospel of Work and Money to such an extent" that it overshadowed "the higher aims of life." The education of blacks, he maintained, should not be merely vocational but should nurture leaders willing to challenge segregation and discrimination through social protest and political action. He believed in work, "but work is not necessarily education. Education is the development of power and ideal." He demanded that disenfranchisement and legalized segregation cease and that the laws of the land be enforced. And he provided the formula for attaining such goals: "By voting where we may vote, by persistent, unceasing agitation, by hammering at the truth, by sacrifice and work." Du Bois minced no words in criticizing Washington's "Atlanta Compromise" philosophy: "We refuse to surrender the leadership of this race to cowards and trucklers."

THE NEW WEST

For vast reaches of western America the great epics of the Civil War and Reconstruction were remote events hardly touching the lives of Indians, Mexicans, Asians, and white trappers, miners, cowboys, traders, and Mormons scattered through the plains and mountains. There the march of Manifest Destiny continued its inexorable course, propelled by a lust for land and a passion for profits. On one level, the settlement of the West beyond the Mississippi constitutes a colorful drama of determined pioneers overcoming all obstacles to secure their visions of freedom and opportunity amid the region's awesome vastness. On another level, however, the colonization of the Far West involved short-sighted greed and irresponsible behavior, a story of reckless exploitation that nearly exterminated the culture of Native Americans, scarred the land, and decimated its wildlife. Both images of the process of western settlement are accurate in some respects.

In the second tier of trans-Mississippi states—Iowa, Kansas, Nebraska—and in western Minnesota, the last frontier of farmers began spreading out onto the Great Plains after the Civil War. From California the miners' frontier stretched east through the mountains as scattered mining enclaves sprang up at one new strike after another. From Texas the nomadic cowboys migrated northward into the plains and across the Rockies into the Great Basin. Now there were two frontiers of settlement, east and west, and even a third in the south; in another generation there would be none.

As settlement moved west, the environment gradually altered. The scarcity of water and timber in the Great Plains rendered obsolete the axe, the log cabin, the rail fence, and the usual methods of tilling the soil. For a long time, the region had been called the Great American Desert, a barrier to cross on the way to the Pacific, unfit for human habitation and therefore, to white Americans, the perfect refuge for Indians. But that pattern changed in the last half of the nineteenth century as a result of new finds of gold, silver, and other minerals, completion of transcontinental railroads, destruction of the buffalo, the rise of the range-cattle industry, and the dawning realization that the arid region need not be a sterile desert. With the use of what water was available, techniques of dry farming and irrigation could make the land fruitful after all.

THE MIGRATORY STREAM During the second half of the nineteenth century, an unrelenting stream of migrants flowed into the largely Indian and Hispanic West. Millions of Anglo Americans, African Americans, Mexicans, and European and Chinese immigrants transformed the patterns of western society and culture. Most of the settlers were relatively prosperous white, native-born farming families. Because of the expense of transportation, land, and supplies, the very poor could not afford to relocate. Three-quarters of the western migrants were men.

The largest number of foreign immigrants came from northern Europe and Canada. In the northern plains, Germans, Scandinavians, and Irish were especially numerous. Not surprisingly, these foreign settlers tended to cluster together according to ethnic and kinship ties.

An American family on their way west.

In the aftermath of the collapse of Radical Republican rule in the South, thousands of blacks began migrating west from Kentucky, Tennessee, Louisiana, Arkansas, Mississippi, and Texas. Some 6,000 southern blacks arrived in Kansas in 1879 alone, and as many as 20,000 may have come the following year. They came to be known as Exodusters, making their exodus out of the South in search of a haven from racism and poverty.

The foremost promoter of black migration to the West was Benjamin "Pap" Singleton. Born a slave in Tennessee in 1809, he escaped and settled in Detroit, where he operated a boardinghouse that became a refuge for other runaway slaves. After the Civil War, he returned to Tennessee, convinced that God was calling him to rescue his black brethren. He decided that the brightest future for African Americans lay not in sharecropping or tenant farming but in farm ownership. When Singleton learned that land in Kansas could be had for $1.25 an acre, he began distributing a recruiting pamphlet entitled "The Advantage of Living in a Free State" to former slaves. In 1878 Singleton led the first party of 200 colonists to Kansas, bought 7,500 acres that was formerly an Indian reservation, and established the Dunlop community.

Over the next several years, thousands of African Americans followed Singleton into Kansas, leading many southern leaders to worry about the loss of laborers from the Old South. In 1879 white Mississippians closed access to the river and threatened to sink all boats carrying black colonists to the West. An army officer reported to President Rutherford B. Hayes that "every river landing is blockaded by white enemies of the colored exodus; some of whom are mounted and armed, as if we are at war." One black migrant to Kansas who returned to Mississippi to retrieve his family was seized by whites who cut off his hands and threw them onto his wife's lap, yelling, "Now go to Kansas to work!"

The exodus to Kansas and Oklahoma Territory died out by the early 1880s. Many of the settlers were unprepared for the quite different living and working conditions on the plains. Their homesteads were not large enough to be self-sufficient, and most of the black farmers were forced to supplement their income by hiring themselves out to white ranchers in the area. Drought, grasshoppers, prairie fires, and dust storms led to crop failures. The sudden influx of so many people taxed resources and patience. Although sympathizers formed the Kansas Freedmen's Relief Association and collected thousands of dollars for food and clothing, they could not keep up with the needs of the swelling tide of migrants. Many of the black pioneers soon abandoned their land and moved to the few cities in the state. Life on the frontier was not always the "promised land" that people had been led to expect. Nonetheless, by 1890, some 520,000 blacks lived west of the Mississippi River. As many as 25 percent of the cowboys who participated in the Texas cattle drives were African Americans.

In 1866 Congress passed legislation establishing two "colored" cavalry units and dispatched them to the western frontier. Nicknamed "Buffalo Soldiers" by the Indians, the soldiers were mostly Civil War veterans from Louisiana and Kentucky. They built and maintained forts, mapped vast areas of the Southwest, strung hundreds of miles of telegraph lines, protected railroad construction crews, subdued hostile Indians, and captured outlaws and rustlers. For this they were paid $13 a month. Eighteen of the "Buffalo Soldiers" won Congressional Medals of Honor for their service in the West.

MINING THE WEST   Miners were also ethnically diverse. Every race and nationality was represented in the mining communities. The California miners of 1849 (the "Forty-niners") set the typical pattern in which the disorderly rush of prospectors was quickly followed by the arrival of the camp followers, a motley array of saloonkeepers, prostitutes, card sharps, hustlers, and assorted desperadoes, out to mine the miners. An era of lawlessness eventually gave way to vigilante rule and, finally, to a stable community and more subtle forms of exploitation.

The drama of the 1849 gold rush was reenacted time and again in the following three decades. Though the California fever had passed by 1851, and no big strikes were made for seven years, new finds in Colorado and Nevada revived hopes for riches. While nearly 100,000 early rushers were crowding around Pike's Peak in Colorado in 1859, miners discovered the Comstock Lode at Gold Hill, Nevada. The lode produced gold and silver, and within twenty years had yielded more than $300 million from shafts that reached hundreds of feet into the mountainside. Yet in both Arizona and Montana, the most important mineral proved to be neither gold nor silver, but copper.

The growing demand for orderly government in the West led to the hasty creation of new territories, and eventually the admission of a host of new states. In 1861 Nevada became a territory, and in 1864 the state of Nevada was admitted in time to give its three electoral votes to Lincoln. After Colorado was admitted in 1876, however, no new states entered for over a decade because of the party divisions in Congress. Democrats were reluctant to create states out of territories that were heavily Republican. After the sweeping Republican victory of 1888, however, Congress admitted the Dakotas, Montana, and Washington in 1889, and Idaho and Wyoming in 1890, completing a tier of states from coast to coast. Utah entered in 1896 (after the Mormons abandoned the practice of polygamy), Oklahoma in 1907, and in 1912 Arizona and New Mexico finally rounded out the forty-eight continental states.

THE INDIAN WARS   As the frontier pressed in from east and west, the Indians were forced into what was supposed to be their last refuge. Perhaps 250,000 Indians in the Great Plains and mountain regions lived mainly off the buffalo herds that provided food and, from their hides, clothing and shelter. In 1851 the chiefs of the principal Plains tribes had gathered at Fort Laramie in Wyoming Territory, where they had agreed to accept more or less definite tribal borders and to leave the emigrants unmolested on their trails. The treaty worked for a while, with wagon trains passing safely through Indian lands and the army building roads and forts without resistance from the Indians. Fighting resumed, however, as the emigrants began to encroach upon Indian

INDIAN WARS, 1864–1890

lands rather than merely passing through them. From 1850 to 1860, for example, 150,000 whites moved into Sioux territory in violation of treaty agreements.

From the early 1860s until the late 1870s, the frontier raged with Indian wars, and intermittent outbreaks continued through the 1880s. In Colorado, where Cheyenne and Arapaho chiefs were forced to accept a treaty reducing their lands, Indians began sporadic raids on trains and mining camps. In 1864 Colonel J. M. Chivington's poorly trained "90-day" volunteers fell upon an Indian camp along Sand Creek that was flying a white flag of truce, and slaughtered 150 to 200 Indians—men, women, and children. One general called the "Sand Creek Massacre" the "foulest and most unjustifiable crime in the annals of America."

With other scattered battles erupting, a congressional committee began to gather evidence in 1865 on the grisly Indian wars and massacres. Its 1867 *Report on the Condition of the Indian Tribes* led to an act to establish an Indian Peace Commission charged with removing the causes of Indian wars in general. Congress decided this was best accomplished at the expense of the Indians, by persuading them to take up life on out-of-the-way reservations. This solution continued the persistent encroachment on Indian hunting grounds.

In 1867 a conference at Medicine Creek Lodge, Kansas, ended with the Kiowa, Comanche, Arapaho, and Cheyenne reluctantly accepting lands in western Oklahoma. The following spring, the Sioux agreed to settle within the Black Hills reservation in Dakota Territory. But Indian resistance in the southern plains continued until the Red River War of 1874–1875. Soldiers led by General Philip Sheridan, the hard-charging Civil War cavalryman, scattered the Indians and finally forced them to terms in the spring of 1875.

By then trouble was brewing once again in the north. In 1874, Lieutenant-Colonel George A. Custer, a reckless, glory-seeking officer who graduated last in his class at West Point but who distinguished himself as a cavalry officer during the Civil War, led an exploring expedition into the Black Hills, accompanied by gold seekers. Miners were soon filtering into the Sioux hunting grounds despite promises that the army would keep them out. The army had done little to protect the Indian lands, but when ordered to move against wandering bands of Sioux hunting on the range according to their treaty rights, the army moved vigorously.

What became the Great Sioux War was the largest military event since the end of the Civil War. It lasted fifteen months, and entailed some fifteen battles in a vast area of present-day Wyoming, Montana, South Dakota, and Nebraska. After several indecisive encounters, Custer found the main encampment of Sioux and their northern Cheyenne allies on the Little Bighorn River. Separated from the main body of his men, Custer and 210 soldiers were surrounded by 2,500 warriors and annihilated.

Instead of following up their victory, the Indians threw away their advantage in celebration and renewed hunting. The army regained the offensive, and the Sioux were forced to give up their hunting grounds and the gold fields in return for payments. Forced onto reservations situated on the least valuable lands in the region, the Indians soon found themselves struggling to subsist under harsh conditions. Many of them died of starvation or disease. In response to the peace commission that imposed a settlement, Chief Spotted Tail said: "Tell your people that since

The Battle of Little Bighorn in a pictograph by an Oglala Sioux, Amos Bad Heart Bull, 1876.

the Great Father promised that we should never be removed, we have been moved five times. . . . I think you had better put the Indians on wheels and you can run them about wherever you wish."

In the Rockies and westward the same story of hopeless resistance was repeated. In Idaho the peaceful Nez Percés finally refused to surrender lands along the Salmon River. Chief Joseph tried to avoid war, but when some unruly braves started a fight, he directed a masterful campaign against overwhelming odds, one of the most spectacular feats in the history of Indian warfare. After a 1,500-mile retreat through mountains and plains, he was finally caught thirty miles short of the Canadian border, and exiled to Oklahoma. A generation of Indian wars virtually ended in 1886 with the capture of Geronimo, a chief of the Chiricahua Apaches, who had fought encroachments in the Southwest for fifteen years.

There would be one tragic epilogue, however. Late in 1888 Wovoka (or "Jack Wilson"), a Paiute in western Nevada, fell ill and in a delirium imagined he had visited the spirit world where he learned of a deliverer coming to rescue the Indians and restore their lands. To hasten the day, he said, they had to take up a ceremonial dance at each new moon. The Ghost Dance craze fed upon old legends of a coming Messiah and spread rapidly. In 1890 the Sioux took it up with such fervor that it

Issue Day. *Native Americans confined to Pine Ridge Reservation in South Dakota could no longer hunt for themselves and had to wait for government-issued food rations.*

alarmed white authorities. An effort to arrest Sioux Chief Sitting Bull led to his death. Shortly afterward, on December 29, 1908, a bloodbath occurred at Wounded Knee, South Dakota. An accidental rifle discharge led nervous soldiers to fire into a group of Indians who had come to surrender. Nearly 200 Indians and 25 soldiers died in the "Battle of Wounded Knee." The Indian wars had ended with characteristic brutality.

Over the long run, the collapse of Indian resistance resulted as much from the killing off of the buffalo herds on which they subsisted as from warfare. White hunters felled buffaloes for sport, sometimes firing from train windows merely for the pleasure of seeing the large animals die. In the 1870s, a systematic slaughter of the buffalo served the demand of fashionable easterners for buffalo robes and overcoats. By the mid-1880s, the herds were near extinction.

INDIAN POLICY   Most frontier folk had little tolerance for moralizing on the Indian question, but many easterners who were far removed from frontier dangers decried the slaughter and mistreatment of Indians. Well-intentioned reformers sought to "Americanize" the Indians by dealing with them as individuals rather than as tribes. The Dawes Severalty Act of 1887 proposed to introduce the Indians to individual land ownership and agriculture. The Dawes Act permitted the president to divide the lands of any tribe and grant 160 acres to each head of family and lesser amounts to others. To protect an Indian's property, the government held it in trust for twenty-five years, after which the owner won full title and became a citizen. In 1901 citizenship was extended to the Five Civilized Tribes of Oklahoma, and in 1924 to all Indians.

But the more it changed, the more Indian policy remained the same. Although well-intended, the Dawes Act created new chances for more plundering of Indian lands, and it disrupted what remained of the traditional cultures. The Dawes Act broke up reservations and often led to the loss of Indian lands to whites. Those lands not distributed to Indian families were sold, while others were lost to land sharks because of the Indians' inexperience with private ownership, or simply because of their powerlessness in the face of fraud. Between 1887 and 1934, Indians lost an estimated 86 million of their 130 million acres. Most of what remained was unsuited for agriculture.

CATTLE AND COWBOYS   While the West was being taken from the Indians, cattle entered the grasslands where the buffalo had roamed. The cowboy enjoyed his brief heyday, then faded into the folklore of the Wild West. From colonial times, especially in the South, cattle raising had been a common enterprise just beyond the fringe of settlement. In many cases, the early slaves took care of the livestock. Later, in the West, black cowboys were still a common sight, although they were lost from view in the novels and "horse operas" that pictured a lily-white frontier.

Much of the romance of the open-range cattle industry derived from its Mexican roots. The Texas longhorns and the cowboys' horses had in large part descended from stock brought over by the Spaniards, and many of the industry's trappings had been worked out in Mexico first: the cowboy's saddle, chaps (*chaparejos*) to protect the legs, spurs, and lariat.

For many years, wild cattle competed with the buffalo in the Spanish borderlands. Natural selection and contact with "Anglo" scrub cattle produced the Texas longhorns: lean and rangy, they were noted more for speed and endurance than for providing a choice steak. They had little value, moreover, because the largest markets for beef were too far away. At the end of the Civil War, perhaps as many as 5 million longhorns roamed the grasslands of Texas, still neglected—but not for long. In the upper Mississippi Valley, where herds had been depleted by the war, cattle were in great demand, and the Texas cattle could be had just for the effort of rounding them up.

So the cattle drives after the Civil War took on a scale far greater than before. In 1866 a large Texas herd set out for Sedalia, Missouri, the western terminus of the Missouri-Pacific Railroad. But that route proved unsuitable because it was subject to raids by postwar bushwhackers (bandits), obstructed by woodlands, and opposed by Arkansas and Missouri farmers. New opportunities arose as railroads pushed farther west, where cattle could be driven through relatively vacant lands.

Joseph G. McCoy, an Illinois livestock dealer, realized the possibilities and encouraged railroad executives to run a line from the prairies to Chicago, the meat-packing center. The Kansas-Pacific Railroad liked McCoy's vision, and with its help he made Abilene, Kansas, the western terminus of a new line. In 1867, the first shipment of Texas cattle went to Chicago. As the railroads moved west, so did the cowtowns. These included Ellsworth, Wichita, Caldwell, and Dodge City, all in Kansas; and farther north Ogallala, Nebraska; Cheyenne, Wyoming; and Miles City, Montana.

During the twenty years after the Civil War, some 40,000 cowboys roamed the Great Plains. They were young—the average age was twenty-four—and from diverse backgrounds. Thirty percent were either Mexican or African American, and hundreds were Indians. Many others were Civil War veterans from North and South who now rode side by side, and a number had come from Europe. The life of a cowboy, for the most part, was rarely as exciting as motion pictures and television shows have depicted. Being a ranchhand involved grueling, dirty, wage labor interspersed with drudgery and boredom.

The cattle industry spurred rapid growth. The population of Kansas rose from 107,000 in 1860 to 365,000 ten years later and reached almost a million by 1880. Nebraska witnessed similar increases. During the 1860s, the cattle would be delivered to rail depots, loaded onto freight cars, and shipped east. By the time they arrived in New York or Massachusetts, some would be dead or dying and all would have lost significant weight. The secret to higher profits for the cattle industry was to devise a way to slaughter the cattle in the Midwest and ship the dressed carcasses east and west. That required refrigeration to keep the meat from spoiling. In 1869 G. H. Hammond, a Chicago meat packer, shipped the first refrigerated beef in an air-cooled car from Chicago to Boston. Eight years later, Gustavus Swift developed a more efficient system of mechanical refrigeration, an innovation that earned him a fortune and provided a major stimulus to the growth of the cattle industry.

But it was one thing to develop the processes to produce refrigerated meat; it was another to convince people to eat it. This required a major marketing campaign. Consumers balked at eating beef that had been butchered a thousand miles away. "The idea of eating meat a week or more after it had been killed," Swift's son noted, "met with a nasty-nice horror." What gradually changed public taste was the fact that dressed meat was significantly cheaper than fresh beef. In addition, Swift introduced the practice of displaying various cuts of dressed beef in butcher shops. He urged his agents in eastern cities to cut up the meat "and scatter the pieces," for "the more you cut, the more you sell." The combination of shrewd marketing and low prices soon convinced customers to prefer dressed meat.

The flush times of the cowtowns soon passed. The long cattle drives played out because they were economically unsound. The dangers of the trail, the wear and tear on men and cattle, the charges levied on drives that crossed Indian territory, and the advance of farms across the trails combined to persuade cattlemen that they could best function near the railroads. As railroads spread out into Texas and the plains, the cattle business spread with them as far as Montana and on into Canada.

In the absence of laws governing the open range, cattlemen at first worked out their own arrangements when rights and uses conflicted. As cattle wandered onto others' property, cowboys would "ride the line" to keep them off the adjoining ranch. In the spring, they would "round up" the mixed herds and sort out ownership by identifying the distinctive mark "branded" into the cattle.

All this changed in 1873, when Joseph Glidden, an Illinois farmer, invented the first effective barbed wire, which ranchers used to fence off their claims at relatively low cost. Five years later an eastern promoter, John W. "Bet-a-Million" Gates, one of the early agents for Glidden, gave a persuasive demonstration of the barbed wire in San Antonio. Skeptical cattlemen discovered that their meanest longhorns shied away from the fence which, as Gates put it, was light as air, stronger than whiskey, and cheaper than dirt. Orders poured in, and Gates eventually put together a virtual monopoly in the American Steel and Wire Company.

END OF THE OPEN RANGE A combination of factors conspired to end the open range. Farmers kept crowding in and laying out homesteads. The boundless range was beginning to be overstocked by 1883, and expenses mounted as stock breeders formed associations to keep intruders out of overstocked ranges, to establish and protect land titles, to deal with railroads and buyers, to fight prairie fires, and to cope with rustlers and predatory beasts. The rise of sheep herding by 1880 caused still another conflict with the cattlemen. A final blow to the open-range industry came with two unusually severe winters in 1886 and 1887, followed by ten long years of drought.

Those who survived the hazards of the range, established legal title and fenced in the lands, restricted the herds to a reasonable size, and provided shelter and hay against the rigors of winter. Moreover, as the long cattle drives ended with the advent of more rail lines and refrigerated cars, the cowboy settled into a more sedentary existence. Within merely two decades, 1866–1886, the era of the cowboy had come and gone.

RANGE WARS The growth of the cattle industry placed a premium upon land. Conflicting claims over land and water rights ignited violent disputes between ranchers and farmers. Ranchers often tried to drive off neighboring farmers, and farmers in turn tried to sabotage the cattle barons, cutting their fences and spooking their herds. The cattle ranchers also clashed with sheepherders over access to grasslands. A strain of ethnic and religious prejudice heightened the tension between ranchers and herders. In the Southwest, shepherds were usually Mexican Americans; in Idaho and Nevada, they were Basques or Mormons. Many Anglo-American cattlemen and cowboys viewed these ethnic and religious groups as un-American and inferior. This helped them rationalize the use of violence against the sheepherders. Conflict faded, however, as the sheep for the most part found refuge in the high pastures of the mountains, leaving the grasslands of the Plains to the cattlemen.

There also developed a perennial tension over grassland use between large and small cattle ranchers. The large ranchers fenced in huge tracts of public lands, leaving the smaller ranchers with too little pasture. To survive, the smaller ranchers cut the fences. In central Texas this practice sparked the Fence-Cutters' War of 1883–1884. Several ranchers were killed and dozens wounded before the state ended the conflict by passing legislation outlawing fence cutting.

An even more violent confrontation between large and small ranchers occurred in Wyoming when members of the Wyoming Stock Association organized an assault against small ranchers, who they charged were rustling their stock. In Johnson County, Wyoming, in 1889, the cattle barons lynched James Averell, a small rancher, and Ella Watson, a prostitute embroiled in the dispute. The vigilantes were brought to trial, but the case was dismissed when the four witnesses to the hanging refused to testify.

Two years later, in 1891, the large ranchers grew bolder. They organized a "lynching bee" to eliminate rustlers in Johnson County and hired gunmen from Texas to do their bidding. On Tuesday, April 5, 1892, two dozen Texan mercenaries and an equal number of ranchers who dubbed themselves "regulators" set out to wipe out the rustlers. After killing two men, the vigilante group headed north, only to find itself surrounded by a band of small ranchers who had been alerted to their arrival. The timely arrival of federal cavalry prevented a massacre. The cattle kings thereupon turned to a bounty hunter, Tom Horn, who murdered "rustlers" until he himself was caught, convicted, and hanged.

FARMERS AND THE LAND   Among the legendary figures of the West, the sodbusters projected an unromantic image in contrast to the cowboys, cavalry, and Indians. After 1860, on paper at least, the federal land laws offered favorable terms to the farmer. Under the Homestead Act of 1862, a farmer could either realize the old dream of free land simply by staking out a claim and living on it for five years, or by buying the land at $1.25 an acre after six months.

The unchangeable fact of aridity, rather than land laws, however, shaped institutions in the New West. Where farming was impossible, the ranchers simply established dominance by control of the water, regardless of the laws. Belated legislative efforts to develop irrigable lands finally achieved a major success when the Newlands Reclamation Act (aptly named after Senator Francis G. Newlands of Nevada) of 1901 set up the Bureau of Reclamation. The proceeds of public land sales in sixteen states created a fund for irrigation works, and the Reclamation Bureau set about building such major projects as Boulder (later Hoover) Dam on the Nevada-Arizona line, Roosevelt Dam in Arizona, and Elephant Butte Dam and Arrowrock Dam in New Mexico.

The lands of the New West, as on previous frontiers, passed to their ultimate owners more often from private hands than directly from the government. Many of the 274 million acres claimed under the Homestead Act passed quickly to cattle ranchers or speculators, and thence to settlers. The land-grant railroads got some 200 million acres of the public domain in the twenty years from 1851 to 1871, and sold much of this land to build population centers and traffic along the lines. The New West of ranchers and farmers was in fact largely the product of the railroads.

The first arrivals on the sodhouse frontier faced a grim struggle against danger, adversity, and monotony. Though land was relatively cheap, horses, livestock, wagons, wells, fencing, seed, and fertilizer were not. Freight rates and interest rates on loans seemed criminally high. As in the South, declining crop prices produced indebtedness that soon became a chronic condition that led strapped western farmers to embrace virtually any plan to inflate the money supply. The virgin land

Woman and her family in front of their sodhouse. The difficult life on the prairie led to more egalitarian marriages.

itself, although fertile, resisted planting; the heavy sod broke many a plow. Since wood was almost nonexistent on the prairies, pioneer families used buffalo chips (dried dung) for fuel.

Farmers and their families also fought a constant battle with the elements: tornadoes, hailstorms, droughts, prairie fires, blizzards, and pests. Swarms of locusts would cloud the horizon, occasionally covering the ground six inches deep and consuming everything in their path. A Wichita newspaper reported in 1878 that the grasshoppers devoured "everything green, stripping the foliage off the bark and from the tender twigs of the fruit trees, destroying every plant that is good for food or pleasant to the eyes, that man has planted."

As time passed and farmers were able to lay aside some money from their labor, farm families could leave their dugouts or sod houses and build frame houses with lumber carried by the railroads arriving from Chicago. New machinery also helped open fresh opportunities for farmers. In 1868 James Oliver of Indiana made a successful chilled-iron plow. With further improvements his "sodbuster" was ready for mass production by 1878, easing the task of breaking the shallow but tough grass roots of the Plains. Improvements and new inventions lightened the burden of labor but added to the capital outlay of the farmer.

To get a start on a family homestead required a minimum investment of $1,000. And while the overall value of farm lands and farm products increased in the late nineteenth century, the small farmers did not keep up with the march of progress. Their numbers grew but decreased in proportion to the population at large. The wheat produced in the eastern Plains from Minnesota and North Dakota down to Texas, like cotton in the antebellum period, provided the great export crop that evened America's balance of payments and spurred economic growth. For a variety of reasons, however, few small farmers prospered. And by the decade of the 1890s, many were in open revolt against the "system" that thwarted their efforts and denied their dreams.

PIONEER WOMEN The West remained a largely male society throughout the nineteenth century. In Texas, for example, the ratio of men to women in 1890 was 110 to 1. Women continued to face traditional legal barriers and social prejudice. A wife could not sell property without her husband's approval. In Texas women could not sue except for divorce, nor could they serve on juries, act as lawyers, or witness a will.

But the fight for survival in the trans-Mississippi West often made husbands and wives more equal partners than their eastern counterparts. Prairie life also allowed women more independence than could be had by those living domestic lives back East. One woman declared that she insisted on leaving out of their marriage vows the phrasing about "obeying" her husband. "I had served my time of tutelage to my parents as all children are supposed to. I was a woman now and capable of being the other half of the head of the family." Similar examples of strong-willed femininity abound. Explained one Kansas woman: "The outstanding fact is that the environment was such as to bring out and develop the dominant qualities of individual character. Kansas women of that day learned at an early age to depend on themselves—to do whatever work there was to be done, and to face danger when it must be faced, as calmly as they were able."

A VIOLENT CULTURE   Although often exaggerated in films and television shows, the western frontier during the second half of the nineteenth century was indeed a violent place. Guns, rifles, and knives were prevalent, and people readily used them to resolve their disputes. The brutal requirements for self-preservation on the frontier or in the mining communities led to a change in the long-standing premise of English common law that required a person to flee or retreat in the face of a violent threat. In 1876 a court ruled that a "true man" was no longer obligated "to fly" from an assailant.

The need to protect one's family or homestead in the face of threats and the frontiersman's obsessive preoccupation with masculine honor helped nourish what came to be called the Code of the West. It stressed the need for a man to stand and fight when threatened or wronged, and this spawned a reckless preoccupation with individual courage. As the famous frontier marshal James Butler ("Wild Bill") Hickok explained, "Meet anyone face to face with whom you disagree," and "if you meet him face to face and took the same risk as he did, you could get away with almost anything [including killing], as long as the bullet was in the front."

Most of the individual violence associated with the "Wild West" occurred in the cattle towns and mining communities, where young single men abounded and liquor was the most popular refreshment. Bodie,

California, in the heart of the mining region, developed a reputation as a "shooter's town." Between 1877 and 1883, there were forty-four shootings, leaving twenty-nine dead. The courts convicted only one man of murder. A few roughnecks in Bodie preferred weapons other than guns. For several months, Man Eater McGowan terrorized the town. He gained his nickname from his tendency to chew on his opponent's appendages. Before being run out of town, he bit the sheriff's leg, broke a pitcher over a waiter's head, and bit or chewed off the noses or ears of a dozen others.

"THE FRONTIER HAS GONE" American life reached an important juncture in the last decade of the nineteenth century. After the 1890 population count, the superintendent of the census noted that he could no longer locate a continuous frontier line beyond which population thinned out to fewer than two persons per square mile. This fact inspired the historian Frederick Jackson Turner to develop the influential frontier thesis, first outlined in his paper "The Significance of the Frontier in American History," delivered to the American Historical Association in 1893. "The existence of an area of free land," Turner wrote, "its continuous recession, and the advance of American settlement westward, explain American development." The frontier had shaped the national character in striking ways. It was

> to the frontier [that] the American intellect owes its striking characteristics. That coarseness and strength combined with acuteness and acquisitiveness; that practical, inventive turn of mind, quick to find expedients; that masterful grasp of material things, lacking in the artistic but powerful to effect great ends; that restless, nervous energy; that dominant individualism, working for good and for evil, and with all that buoyancy and exuberance which comes with freedom—these are traits of the frontier, or traits called out elsewhere because of the existence of the frontier.

But, Turner ominously concluded in 1893, "the frontier has gone and with its going has closed the first period of American history."

Turner's "frontier thesis" guided several generations of scholars and students in their understanding of the distinctive characteristics of American history. His view of the frontier as the westward-moving source of America's democratic politics, open society, unfettered economy, and rugged individualism, far removed from the corruptions of urban life, gripped the popular imagination as well. But it left much out of the story. Turner's description of the frontier experience exaggerated the homogenizing effect of the physical environment and virtually ignored the roles of women, blacks, Indians, Mormons, Hispanics, and Asians in shaping the diverse human geography of the western United States. Turner also implied that the West would be fundamentally different after 1890 because the frontier experience was essentially over. But in many respects that region has retained the qualities associated with the rush for land, gold, timber, and water rights during the post–Civil War decades. The mining frontier, as one historian has recently written, "set a mood that has never disappeared from the West: the attitude of extractive industry—get in, get rich, get out."

MAKING CONNECTIONS

- The problems of southern and western farmers described in this chapter will set the stage for the rise of the populists as discussed in Chapter 21.

- This is a crucial period in the evolution of race relations in the South, bridging the antebellum period and the twentieth century.

- This chapter closes with the observation that, as of 1890, according to the superintendent of the census and the historian Frederick Jackson Turner, "the frontier has gone." Where would Americans now look to fulfill their expansionist urgings?

FURTHER READING

The classic study of the emergence of the New South remains C. Vann Woodward's *Origins of the New South, 1877–1913* (1951). A more recent treatment of southern society after the end of Reconstruction is

Edward L. Ayers's *Southern Crossing: A History of the American South, 1877–1906* (1995).

For Bourbon politics, see Jack P. Maddex's *The Virginia Conservatives, 1867–1879* (1970) and William J. Cooper's *The Conservative Regime: South Carolina, 1877–1890* (1968). On the development of southern politics since Reconstruction, see Dewey W. Grantham's *The Life and Death of the Solid South: A Political History* (1988).

A good survey of industrialization in the South is James C. Cobb's *Industrialization and Southern Society, 1877–1984* (1984). Scholarship on the textile industry, which formed the heart of the New South's aspirations, includes Patrick J. Hearden's *Independence and Empire: The New South's Cotton Mill Campaigns, 1865–1901* (1982), David L. Carlton's *Mill and Town in South Carolina, 1880–1920* (1982), and Jacqueline D. Hall et al.'s *Like a Family: The Making of a Southern Cotton Mill World* (1987). For developments in the tobacco industry, consult Robert F. Durden's *The Dukes of Durham, 1865–1929* (1975). A fine study of convict leasing is Alex Lichtenstein's *Twice the Work of Free Labor: The Political Economy of Convict Labor in the New South* (1996).

C. Vann Woodward's *The Strange Career of Jim Crow* (3rd ed., 1974) remains the standard on southern race relations. Some of Woodward's points are challenged in Howard N. Rabinowitz's *Race Relations in the Urban South, 1865–1890* (1978), Joel Williamson's *The Crucible of Race* (1984), and John W. Cell's *The Highest Stage of White Supremacy* (1982).

Leon Litwack's *Trouble in Mind: Black Southerners in the Age of Jim Crow* (1998) treats the rise of legal segregation. David M. Oshinsky focuses on race relations and convict leasing in Mississippi in *"Worse Than Slavery": Parchman Farm and the Ordeal of Jim Crow Justice* (1996). J. Morgan Kousser's *The Shaping of Southern Politics: Suffrage Restriction and Establishment of the One-Party South, 1880–1910* (1974) handles disenfranchisement. An award-winning study of white women and the race issue is Glenda Gilmore's *Gender and Jim Crow: Women and the Politics of White Supremacy in North Carolina, 1896–1920* (1996).

Several good books discuss developments in southern agriculture. Roger L. Ransom and Richard Sutch's *One Kind of Freedom: The Economic Consequences of Emancipation* (1977) examines the origins of sharecropping. A more recent sociological analysis is Edward Royce's *The Origins of Southern Sharecropping* (1993).

Good overviews of the transformation of the West are Rodman W. Paul's *The Far West and the Great Plains in Transition, 1859–1908* (rev. ed., 1998) and Geoffrey Ward, David Duncan, and Ken Burns's *The West: An Illustrated History* (1996). The Turner thesis is best presented by Frederick Jackson Turner himself in *The Frontier in American History* (1920).

For powerful and provocative reinterpretations of the frontier and the development of the West, see William Cronon's *Nature's Metropolis: Chicago and the Great West* (1991), Patricia Nelson Limerick's *The Legacy of Conquest: The Unbroken Past of the American West* (1987), Richard White's *"It's Your Misfortune and None of My Own": A New History of the American West* (1991), Donald Worster's *Under Western Skies: Nature and History in the American West* (1992), and *Under an Open Sky: Rethinking America's Western Past* (1992), edited by William Cronon, George Miles, and Jay Gitlin.

The role of blacks in western settlement is the focus of William L. Katz's *The Black West* (1996) and Nell Painter's *Exodusters: Black Migration to Kansas after Reconstruction* (1992). The best account of the conflicts between Indians and whites is Robert Utley's *The Indian Frontier of the American West, 1846–1890* (1984). For a presentation of the Native American side of the story, see Peter Nabokov and Vine Deloria's *Native American Testimony: A Chronicle of Indian-White Relations from Prophecy to the Present, 1492–1992* (1992).

Federal government efforts to facilitate western agriculture are detailed in William D. Rowley's *Reclaiming the Arid West: The Career of Francis G. Newlands* (1996).

19 BIG BUSINESS AND ORGANIZED LABOR

CHAPTER ORGANIZER

This chapter focuses on:

- factors that fueled the growth of the post–Civil War economy.

- the methods and achievements of major entrepreneurs.

- the rise of large labor unions.

America's rise as an industrial and agricultural giant in the late nineteenth century is a fact of towering visibility. Between 1869 and 1899, the nation's population nearly trebled, farm production more than doubled, and the value of manufactures grew sixfold (in constant dollars). Within three generations after the Civil War, the nation that had long been a predominantly rural society became a highly structured, increasingly centralized, urban-industrial society buffeted by the imperatives of mass production, mass consumption, and time-clock efficiency. Bigness became the prevailing standard of corporate life, and social tensions worsened with the rising scale of business enterprise.

The Rise of Big Business

The industrial revolution created huge corporations that came to dominate the economy—as well as political and social life—during the late nineteenth century. Businesses became so large and concentrated after the Civil War because an older economy dependent upon small business and craftspeople could not satisfy the rapidly growing national market. Entrepreneurs who recognized this development focused their attention on developing systems of mass production and distribution. To do so, they took advantage of many technological innovations and generous government support. As the volume of these businesses grew, the owners sought to integrate all the processes of production and distribution into single companies, thus producing even larger firms. Others joined forces with their competitors through "pools" or "trusts" in an effort to dominate entire industries. This process of industrial combination and concentration transformed the nation's social order. It also provoked widespread dissent and the emergence of an organized labor movement.

THE SECOND INDUSTRIAL REVOLUTION   The industrial revolution "controls us all," said Yale sociologist William Graham Sumner, "because we are all in it." Sumner and other Americans living during the

The Hand of Man, *photogravure by Alfred Stieglitz, 1902.*

second half of the nineteenth century experienced what economic historians have termed the second industrial revolution. The first industrial revolution began in Britain during the late eighteenth century. It was propelled by the convergence of three new technologies—the coal-powered steam engine; textile machines for spinning thread and weaving cloth; and blast furnaces to produce iron.

The second industrial revolution began in the mid–nineteenth century and was centered in the United States and Germany. It was sparked by an array of innovations and inventions in the production of metals, machinery, chemicals, and foodstuffs. While the first industrial revolution helped accelerate the growth of the early American economy, the second transformed the economy and society into its modern urban-industrial form.

The second industrial revolution involved three major interrelated developments. The first of these was the creation of an interconnected *national* transportation and communication network that in turn facilitated the emergence of a national and even international market for American goods and services. Contributing to this development were the completion of the national telegraph and railroad system, the emergence of steamships, and the laying of the undersea telegraph cable spanning the Atlantic Ocean and connecting the United States with Europe.

During the 1880s, a second major breakthrough—the use of electric power—accelerated the pace of change. Electricity created dramatic advances in the capacity and efficiency of industrial machinery. It also spurred urban growth through the addition of electric trolleys and subways, and it greatly enhanced the production of steel and chemicals.

The third major aspect of the second industrial revolution was the systematic application of scientific research to industrial processes. Laboratories sprouted across the country, and scientists and engineers worked at finding dramatic new ways to improve industrial processes. Researchers, for example, discovered how to refine kerosene and gasoline from crude oil. They also developed improved techniques for refining steel from iron. Such innovations and inventions accelerated production, created new products—telephones, typewriters, adding machines, sewing machines, cameras, elevators, and farm machinery—and lowered consumer prices. These advances in turn expanded the scope and scale of industrial organizations. Capital-intensive industries such as steel and oil, and processed food and tobacco, took advantage of new technologies to gain economies of scale that emphasized maximum production and national as well as international marketing and distribution.

BUILDING THE TRANSCONTINENTAL RAILROADS Railroads were the first big business, the first magnet for the great financial markets, and the first industry to develop a large-scale management bureaucracy. The railroads opened the West, connected raw materials to factories and markets, and in so doing created a national market for the nation's goods and produce. At the same time, they were themselves gigantic markets for iron, steel, lumber, and other capital goods.

The renewal of railroad building after the Civil War filled out the railway network east of the Mississippi, but the most spectacular exploits were the transcontinental lines built across the Plains and mountains. Running through sparsely settled lands, they served the national purpose of binding the country together.

Before the Civil War, sectional differences over routes delayed the start of a transcontinental line. Secession finally permitted passage of the Pacific Railway Bill, which Lincoln signed into law in 1862. The act authorized a line along a north-central route, to be built jointly by the Union Pacific Railroad westward from Omaha and the Central Pacific Railroad eastward from Sacramento.

Both railroads began construction during the war, but most of the work was done after 1865. The Union Pacific pushed across the Plains at a rapid pace, avoiding the Rockies by going through Evans Pass in Wyoming. The work crews, with large numbers of ex-soldiers and Irish immigrants as laborers, had to cope with bad roads, water shortages, rugged weather, and Indian attacks. Construction of the rail line and bridges was hasty and much of it was so flimsy that it had to be redone later. Moreover, the movable encampments of rail workers, with their retinue of peddlers, gamblers, and prostitutes, were aptly dubbed "Hell-on-wheels."

The Central Pacific construction crews were mainly Chinese workers lured first by the California gold rush and then by railroad jobs. Thousands of Chinese men migrated to America, raising their numbers in the United States from 7,500 in 1850 to 105,000 in 1880. Most of these "coolie" laborers were single males intent upon accumulating money and then returning to their homeland, where they could then afford to marry and buy a parcel of land. Their temporary status and dream of a good life back in China apparently made them more willing than American laborers to endure the dangerous working conditions and low pay of railroad work. By 1867, the Central Pacific Railroad's 12,000 Chinese laborers represented 90 percent of its workforce.

Clearing trees, handling explosives, operating power drills, and working in snowdrifts was dangerous work, and many Chinese died on the job. Fifty-seven miles east of Sacramento the construction crews encountered the towering Sierras, but they were eventually able to cut through to the more level country in Nevada. The Union Pacific had built 1,086 miles to the Central Pacific's 689 when the race ended on the salt plains of Utah near Ogden, at Promontory. There, on May 10, 1869, Leland Stanford, governor of California and one of the organizers of the Central Pacific Railroad, drove a gold spike that symbolized the railroad's completion.

The next transcontinental railroad linked the Atchison, Topeka and Santa Fe Railroad with the Southern Pacific Railroad in southern California. The transcontinentals soon sprouted numerous trunk lines that in turn encouraged the building of other transcontinentals. The result

The celebration after the last spike was driven at Promontory, Utah, on May 10, 1869, completing the first transcontinental railroad.

was a massive railroad building boom that lasted into the 1890s and in turn stimulated the rest of the economy.

FINANCING THE RAILROADS   The railroads were built by private companies that raised money for construction primarily by selling railroad bonds to American and foreign investors. While constitutional scruples over state sovereignty initially constrained federal aid for internal improvements, many states subsidized the building of railroads within their own borders. Finally, in 1850, Stephen Douglas managed to secure from Congress a federal grant of public lands to subsidize two north-south railroads connecting Chicago and Mobile. Over the next twenty years, transcontinentals received generous government aid in the form of federal land grants, as well as loans and tax breaks from federal, state, and local governments. For example, the Pacific Railway Act authorizing the construction of the first transcontinental railroad was

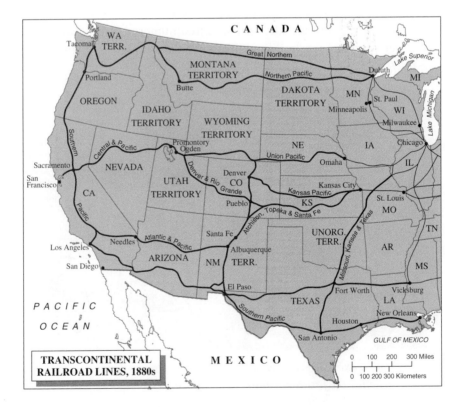

TRANSCONTINENTAL
RAILROAD LINES, 1880s

amended in 1864, at which time the federal government donated to the Union Pacific Railroad and the Central Pacific Railroad twenty sections of land per mile of track, in alternating blocs of railroad and government property, and granted loans from $16,000 to $48,000 per mile, depending on the difficulty of the terrain.

In the long run, the federal government recovered much if not all of its investment in transcontinentals. As farms, ranches, and towns sprouted around the rail lines, the value of the alternate sections of government land on both sides of the tracks skyrocketed. The railroads also benefited the public by hauling government freight, military personnel and equipment, and the mails at half fare at no charge. Moreover, by helping to accelerate the creation of a national market, the railroads spurred economic growth and thereby increased government revenues.

The vast sums of money used to finance the building of the transcontinental lines, however, also generated shameless profiteering through construction companies controlled by insiders who overcharged the railroad companies. One scandal involved the Crédit Mobilier Company, a construction company that had charged the Union Pacific exorbitant fees in order to line the pockets of insiders who controlled both firms. Crédit Mobilier, according to a congressional investigation, bought congressmen like sacks of potatoes and charged the Union Pacific $94 million for construction that actually cost at most $44 million.

Eastern rail lines engaged in similar acts of financial buccaneering, which centered first on the Erie Railroad, the favorite prey of manipulators. Prince of the railroad "robber barons" was Jay Gould, a secretive trickster who mastered the art of buying rundown railroads, making cosmetic improvements, and selling out at a profit, meanwhile using corporate funds for personal speculation and bribes. Nearly every enterprise he touched was either compromised or ruined, while Gould built a fortune that amounted to $100 million upon his death.

Few railroad fortunes were built in those freewheeling times by purely ethical methods, but compared to opportunists such as Gould, most railroad entrepreneurs were giants of honesty. They at least took some interest in the welfare of their companies, if not always in that of the public. Cornelius Vanderbilt, called "Commodore" by virtue of his early exploits in steamboating, stands out among the railroad barons. Already rich before the Civil War, he decided to give up the hazards of wartime shipping and move his money into land transport. His great achievement was consolidating separate trunk lines into a single power-ful rail network led by the New York Central. After the Commodore's death in 1877, his son William Henry extended the Vanderbilt lines to include more than 13,000 miles in the Northeast. This consolidation trend was nationwide. About two-thirds of the nation's railroad mileage fell under the control of only seven major groups by 1900.

MANUFACTURING AND INVENTIONS   The story of manufac-turing after the Civil War shows much the same pattern of expansion and merger in both old and new industries. The Patent Office, which had recorded only 276 inventions during its first decade of existence, the 1790s, registered 234,956 in the decade of the 1890s. And whether or not necessity was the mother of invention, invention was the mother of new industries—and new departures in old ones. The list of innova-tions after the Civil War can be extended indefinitely: barbed wire, farm implements, the air brake for trains, steam turbines, gas distribu-tion and electrical devices, the typewriter (1867), vacuum cleaner (1869), and countless others. Before the end of the century, the inter-nal combustion engine and the motion picture were laying foundations for new industries of the twentieth century.

These technological advances altered the lives of ordinary people far more than politics or intellectual developments. In no field was this truer than in the applications of electricity to communications and power. Few if any inventions of the times could rival the importance of the telephone, which Alexander Graham Bell patented in 1876 and demonstrated at the Philadelphia Centennial Exposition the same year.

To promote the new device, the inventor and his supporters formed the Bell Telephone Association, out of which grew in 1879 the National Bell Telephone Company. Its stiffest competition came from Western Union, which, after turning down a chance to buy Bell's "toy," employed Thomas Edison to develop an improved version. Edison's telephone, with its separate transmitter and receiver, became the prototype of the modern instrument. But Bell had a prior claim on the basic principle, and Western Union, rather than risk a legal defeat, sold its rights and properties for a tidy sum, clearing the way for the creation of a monop-oly. In 1885 the Bell interests organized the American Telephone and Telegraph Company. By 1899, it was a huge holding company in control of forty-nine licensed subsidiaries and itself an operating company for long-distance lines.

In the rise of electrical industries, the name of Thomas Alva Edison stands above those of other inventors. He started his career at an early age selling papers and candies on trains, soon learned telegraphy, and began making improvements in that and other areas. In 1876 Edison went full-time into the "invention business." He invented the phonograph in 1877, and the first successful incandescent light bulb in 1879. At his laboratories in Menlo Park, New Jersey, he created or perfected hundreds of new devices and processes, including the storage battery, dictaphone, mimeograph, dynamo, electric transmission, and the motion picture. In the process, Edison and his assistants demonstrated the significance of "research and development" activities to American business.

In 1882, with the backing of financier J. P. Morgan, the Edison Electric Illuminating Company began to supply current to eighty-five customers in New York City, beginning the great electric utility industry. A number of companies making light bulbs merged into the Edison General Electric Company in 1888. Financially secure, Edison retired from business to devote full time once again to invention.

The use of direct current limited Edison's lighting system to a radius of about two miles. To get more distance required an alternating current, which could be transmitted at high voltage and then stepped down by transformers. George Westinghouse, inventor of the air brake, developed the first alternating-current system in 1886 and manufactured the equipment through the Westinghouse Electric Company. Edison considered the new method too dangerous, but just as Edison's instrument supplanted Bell's first telephone, the Westinghouse system won the "Battle of the Currents," and the Edison companies had to switch over. After the invention of the alternating-current motor in 1888, Westinghouse acquired and improved the motor, which started a revolution by enabling factories to locate wherever they wished. Capable now of using electricity as a power source, they no longer had to cluster around waterfalls and coal supplies.

ENTREPRENEURS

Edison and Westinghouse were rare examples of inventors with the luck and foresight to get rich from the industries they created. Most of the architects of industrial growth—the great captains of industry—

were not inventors but pure entrepreneurs, men skilled mainly in organizing and promoting industry. Three post–Civil War business titans stand out for their achievements and for their greed, guile, and enterprise: John D. Rockefeller, Andrew Carnegie, and J. Pierpont Morgan. Each of them in different ways replaced the small-scale economy of the early republic with vast new industries that forever altered the size and scope of the nation's business. Two other entrepreneurs, Richard Sears and Alvah Roebuck, perfected a new way of retailing and distributing the goods produced by the large-scale manufacturers in the new economy.

ROCKEFELLER AND THE OIL TRUST   Born in New York State, the son of a flamboyant, adulterous con man and a frugal, devout Baptist mother, Rockefeller moved as a youth to Cleveland. Soon thereafter, his father abandoned his family and started a new life under an assumed name with a second wife. Raised by his mother, John Rockefeller developed a passion for systematic organization and self-discipline. He was obsessed with precision, order, and tidiness. And early on, he decided to bring order and rationality to the chaotic oil industry.

Cleveland's railroad and ship connections made it a strategic location for servicing the oil fields of western Pennsylvania. In economic importance the Pennsylvania oil rush of the 1860s far outweighed the California gold rush of just ten years earlier. Well before the end of the Civil War, derricks checkered the area around Titusville, Pennsylvania,

John D. Rockefeller, whose Standard Oil Company dominated the oil business.

where the first oil well was struck, and refineries sprang up in Pittsburgh and Cleveland.

Of the two cities, Cleveland had the edge in transportation, and John D. Rockefeller made the most of the fast-growing commercial city's advantages. His desire for personal advancement and material gain was obsessive. While other young men were going off to fight the Civil War, young Rockefeller, blessed with icy efficiency and tenacious daring, moved aggressively into the oil business. In 1862 he backed a refinery started by his friend, Samuel Andrews, with whom Rockefeller then formed a partnership. The firm expanded, and in 1870 Rockefeller incorporated his various interests as the Standard Oil Company of Ohio.

Rockefeller's refinery was already the nation's largest and most efficient, but as he put it, "the butcher, the baker, and the candlestick maker began to refine oil." As a result, "the price went down and down until the trade was ruined." Rockefeller resolved to bring order out of chaos by stamping out the competition, and he soon hatched an ingenious scheme.

In 1872 the inscrutable Rockefeller created the South Improvement Company, which he made the marketing agent for a large percentage of his oil shipments. By controlling this traffic, he gained clout with the railroads, which gave him large rebates (or secret refunds) on the standard freight rates in order to keep his high-volume business. In some cases, they even gave him information on competitors' shipments. Rockefeller then approached his Cleveland competitors and pressured them to sell out at his own price. Most of them complied. Those who resisted were forced out. As one competitor recalled, we were told that "if we did not sell out, we should be crushed out." In less than six weeks, Rockefeller took over twenty-two of his twenty-six competitors. By 1879, Standard Oil had come to control 90 to 95 percent of the oil refined throughout the country.

Much of Rockefeller's success reflected his determination to "pay nobody a profit." Instead of depending on the products or services of other firms, known as "middlemen," Standard undertook to make its own barrels, cans, and whatever else it needed. Economists label this "vertical integration." The company kept large amounts of cash reserves to make it independent of banks in case of a crisis. Rockefeller also set out to control his transportation needs. With Standard owning most of the pipelines leading to railroads, as well as the tank cars and the oil-storage facilities, it was able to dissuade the railroads from servicing eastern competitors. Those rivals who insisted on holding out then faced a giant marketing organization capable of driving them to the wall with price wars.

Eventually, in order to consolidate scattered business interests under more efficient control, Rockefeller and his advisers resorted to the legal device of the "trust." Long established in law to enable one or more people to manage property belonging to others, such as children or the mentally incompetent, the trust now was used for another purpose—centralized control of business across state lines. In 1882 all of the thirty-seven stockholders in various Standard Oil enterprises conveyed their stock to nine trustees, getting "trust certificates" in return. The nine trustees were thus empowered to give central direction to all the Standard companies.

The original plan, never fully carried out, was to organize a Standard Oil Company in each state in which the trust did business. But the trust device, widely copied in the 1880s, proved legally vulnerable to prosecution under state laws against monopoly or restraint of trade.

In 1892 the Supreme Court of Ohio ordered the Standard Oil Trust dissolved. For a while the company managed to unify control by the simple device of interlocking directorates, through which the board of directors of one company was made identical or nearly so to the boards of the others. Gradually, however, Rockefeller took to the idea of the holding company, a company that controlled other companies by holding all or at least a majority of their stock. He was convinced that big business was a natural result of capitalism at work. "It is too late," he declared in 1899, "to argue about the advantages of industrial combinations. They are a necessity." That same year Rockefeller brought his empire under the direction of the Standard Oil Company of New Jersey, a holding company. Though less vulnerable to prosecution under state law, some holding companies, as we will see, proved vulnerable to the Sherman Anti-Trust Act of 1890. Meanwhile the term "trust" had become so fixed in the public mind that it was used to describe large combinations under holding companies as well.

Rockefeller not only made a fortune, he also gave much of it away, mainly to education and medicine. A man of simple tastes, who opposed the use of tobacco and alcohol and believed his fortune was a public trust awarded by God, Rockefeller became the world's leading philanthropist. He donated more than $500 million during his ninety-eight-year life. "I have always regarded it as a religious duty," Rockefeller said late in life, "to get all I could honorably and to give all I could."

CARNEGIE AND THE STEEL INDUSTRY Andrew Carnegie, like Rockefeller, experienced the untypical rise from poverty to riches that came to be known in those days as "the typical American success story." Born in Scotland, he migrated with his family to Allegheny, Pennsylvania, in 1848. Then thirteen, he started out as a bobbin boy and engine tender in a textile mill at wages of $1.20 per week. At fourteen he was getting $2.50 per week as a telegraph messenger. Quick-witted, shrewd, and brilliant, he worked hard, and in 1853 he became personal secretary and telegrapher to the district superintendent of the Pennsylvania Railroad. When the superintendent became the president of the line, Carnegie took his place, and the pace of his career accelerated. During the Civil War, Carnegie went to Washington, where he developed a military telegraph system and personally helped evacuate the wounded from Bull Run.

Carnegie kept on moving—from telegraphy to railroading to bridge building, then to iron and steel-making, and investments. In 1865 he quit the railroad to devote full time to his own interests. These were mainly in iron and bridge building, but the versatile entrepreneur also

Andrew Carnegie, apostle of "The Gospel of Wealth."

made money in oil and sold railroad bonds in Europe. In his *Autobiography* Carnegie recalled his growing determination to allow "nothing to interfere for a moment with my business career." He kept his pledge. In 1872 he netted $150,000 on a trip during which he also met Sir Henry Bessemer, inventor of a new process of steel-making. The process dazzled Carnegie, and he returned to America a converted prophet of steel, exclaiming to a friend: "The day of iron has passed!" The next year Carnegie resolved to concentrate on steel, or as he put it, to put all his eggs in one basket and then watch the basket. As competitors arose, Carnegie picked them off one by one.

Steel was the miracle material of the post–Civil War era not because it was new but because it suddenly was cheap. Until the mid–nineteenth century, the only way to make steel was from wrought iron—itself expensive—and in small quantities. Then in 1856 Bessemer invented what became known as the Bessemer converter, a process by which steel could be produced directly and quickly from pig iron by using forced air to heat the metal. As the volume of steel rose, its price dropped and its uses increased. In 1860 the United States produced only 13,000 tons of steel. By 1880 production had reached 1,400,000 tons.

Carnegie was never a technical expert on steel. He was a promoter, salesman, and organizer with a gift for finding and using men of expert ability. Fiercely competitive and obsessed with efficiency and innovation, he always insisted on up-to-date machinery and equipment, and he used times of recession to expand more cheaply. Carnegie retained a large part of his annual profits during good times to tide the business over during lean years. During business depressions, when construction costs were low and competitors were forced to the wall, Carnegie used his surplus capital to buy them out and expand. He also preached to his employees a philosophy of constant innovation in order to reduce operating costs.

In much of this, Carnegie was a typical businessman of the time, if abler and luckier than most. But he stands out from the lot as a thinker who publicized a philosophy for big business, a conservative rationale that became deeply implanted in the conventional wisdom of some Americans. Carnegie argued that the captains of industry were on the whole public benefactors. In "The Gospel of Wealth," published in 1889, he argued that the contrast between the millionaire and the laborer measures the distance society has come. "Not evil, but good, has come to the race from the accumulation of wealth by those who have the ability and energy that produces it." The process had been costly in many ways, but the law of competition was "best for the race, because it insures the survival of the fittest in every department." He believed that the best way to dispense a fortune was to administer it during one's lifetime for the public good: "The man who dies rich dies disgraced." Carnegie insisted that the wealthy should provide means for people to help themselves by supporting universities, libraries, hospitals, parks, halls for meetings and concerts, swimming baths, and church buildings—in that order. To his credit, Carnegie devoted his wealth to many such benefactions and to the cause of world peace. He spent some $60 million on public libraries and another $60 million on higher education.

J. P. MORGAN, THE FINANCIER   J. Pierpont Morgan was born to wealth in Hartford, Connecticut, and increased it enormously. Morgan's father was a partner in a London banking house, and his wealth enabled him to send young Pierpont to boarding school in Switzerland and Germany. After a brief apprenticeship, Morgan in 1857 began work in a New York firm that represented his father's London bank, and in 1860 he set himself up as its New York agent under the name of J. Pier-

J. Pierpont Morgan. *This is the famous portrait by the photographer Edward Steichen, done in 1903.*

pont Morgan and Company. This firm, under various names, channeled European capital into the country and grew into a financial power in its own right.

As an investment banker, Morgan bought corporate stocks and bonds wholesale and then sold them at a profit. The growth of large corporations put Morgan's and other investment firms in an increasingly strategic position in the economy. Since the investment business depended on the general good health of client companies, investment bankers became involved in the operation of their clients' firms, demanding places on boards of directors and helping to shape their fiscal dealings. By these means, bankers could influence company policies, often emphasizing fiscal matters to the detriment of technical innovation.

Morgan realized that railroads were the key to the times, and he picked up and reorganized one rail line after another. After the Panic of 1893, when hard times gutted the net worth of many railroads, Morgan took over the Erie, Philadelphia and Reading, the Northern Pacific, and organized the Southern Railway; he already had a hand in the Vanderbilt and Pennsylvania lines. By the 1890s, he alone controlled one-sixth of America's railway system.

Morgan's crowning triumph was the consolidation of the steel industry. In 1901 he bought out Carnegie's huge steel and iron holdings. Carnegie set his own price, which came to nearly $500 million, of which Carnegie's personal share was nearly $300 million. After closing the deal, Morgan told the steel king, "Mr. Carnegie, I want to congratulate you on being the richest man in the world." Like Rockefeller, Morgan scorned competition as wasteful, and, in rapid succession, he added other steel mills. Altogether the new United States Steel Corporation, a holding company for these varied interests, was capitalized at $1.4 billion, a total that was heavily "watered" (valued well above the company's actual assets) but was soon made solid by large profits. The new giant was a marvel of the new century, the first billion-dollar corporation, the climactic event in that age of corporate consolidation. By 1904 there were some 318 industrial trusts in the United States, capitalized at over $7 billion, with nearly 5,300 distinct plants.

SEARS AND ROEBUCK American inventors helped manufacturers after the Civil War produce a vast number of new products, but problems of distribution remained acute. The most important challenge was how to extend the reach of modern commerce to the millions of people who lived on isolated farms and in small towns. In the aftermath of the Civil War, a traveling salesman from Chicago named Aaron Montgomery Ward decided that he could reach more people by mail than on foot and in the process could eliminate the "middlemen" whose services increased the retail price of goods. Beginning in the early 1870s, the Montgomery Ward Company began selling goods at a 40 percent discount through mail-order catalogs.

By the end of the century, a new retailer came to dominate the mail-order industry: Sears, Roebuck and Company, founded by two young midwestern entrepreneurs, Richard Sears and Alvah Roebuck, who began offering a cornucopia of goods by mail in the early 1890s. The Sears, Roebuck and Company catalog in 1897 was 786 pages long and was published in German and Swedish as well as in English. It included groceries, drugs, tools, bells, furniture, ice boxes, stoves and household utensils, musical instruments, farm implements, boots and shoes, clothes, books, and sporting goods.

The Sears catalog helped create a truly national market and in the process transformed the lives of millions of people. With the advent of free rural mail delivery in 1898 and the widespread distribution of Sears catalogs, families on farms and in small towns and villages could pur-

Sears, Roebuck, and Company, catalog cover, *1897. Sears' extensive mail-order service and discounted prices allowed its many products to reach people in both cities and backcountry.*

chase by mail the products that heretofore were either prohibitively expensive or available only to city dwellers. By the turn of the century, 6 million catalogs were distributed each year, and the catalog had become the single most widely read book in the nation except for the Bible.

LABOR CONDITIONS AND ORGANIZATION

SOCIAL TRENDS   Accompanying the spread of these giant industrial combinations was a rising standard of living for most people. If the rich were still getting richer, a lot of other people were at least becoming better off. The continuing demand for workers meanwhile was filled by new groups entering the workforce at the bottom: immigrants above all, but also growing numbers of women and children. Because of a long-term decline in prices and the cost of living, real wages and earnings in manufacturing went up about 50 percent between 1860 and 1890, and another 37 percent from 1890 to 1914. By latter-day standards, however, working conditions then were dreary indeed. At the turn of the century, the average hourly wage in manufacturing was 21.6 cents, and average annual earnings were $490. The average workweek was fifty-nine hours, which amounted to nearly six ten-hour workdays, but that was only an average. Most steelworkers put in a twelve-hour workday, and as late as the 1920s, a great many worked a seven-day, or eighty-four-hour, workweek.

Moreover, although wages were steadily rising, working and living conditions remained precarious. In the crowded tenements of immigrant neighborhoods in the major cities, the death rates ran substantially higher than in the countryside. Factories often maintained poor health and safety conditions. In 1913, for instance, there were some 25,000 factory fatalities and some 700,000 injuries that required at least four weeks' disability—more than half the number of American casualties in World War I. In this new industrial world, ever-larger numbers of people were dependent on the machinery and factories of owners whom they seldom if ever saw. In the simpler world of small shops, workers and employers could enter into close personal relationships; the larger corporation, on the other hand, was likely run by a bureaucracy in which ownership was separate from management. Much of the social history of the modern world in fact turns on the transition from a world of personal relationships to one of impersonal and contractual relationships.

DISORGANIZED PROTEST   In these circumstances it was far more difficult for workers to organize for mutual benefit than for a few captains of industry to organize for personal profit. Civic officials and business leaders respected property rights more than the rights of labor. Among workers recently removed from an agrarian world, the idea of permanent unions was slow to take hold. Immigrant workers represented diverse and frequently antagonistic cultures and spoke different languages. Many, if not most, saw their jobs as transient, the first rung on the ladder to success. They hoped to move on to a homestead, or to return with their earnings to the old farms of their European homelands. With or without unions, though, workers often staged impromptu strikes protesting long working hours and wage cuts. Such action often led to violence, and three incidents of the 1870s colored much of the public's view of labor unions thereafter.

The decade's early years saw a reign of terror in the eastern Pennsylvania coal fields, attributed to an Irish group called the Molly Maguires. Taking their name from an Irish patriot who had directed violent resistance against the British, the group was incited by the miserable, dangerous working conditions in the mines and the owners' brutal efforts to suppress union activity. Convinced of the justness of their cause, the Molly Maguires aimed to right perceived wrongs against Irish workers by such methods as intimidation, beatings, and killings. Their terrorism reached its peak in 1874–1875. At trials in 1876, twenty-four of the Molly Maguires were convicted, and the next year twenty of them were hanged. The trials also resulted in a wage reduction in the mines.

THE RAILROAD STRIKE OF 1877   Far more significant, because more widespread, was the Great Railroad Strike of 1877, the first major interstate strike. Wage cuts caused the Great Strike. After the Panic of 1873 and the ensuing depression, the major rail lines in the East had cut wages. In 1877 they made another 10 percent cut, which provoked most of the railroad workers at Martinsburg, West Virginia, to walk off the job and block the tracks. Without organized direction, however, their picketing groups degenerated into a mob that burned and plundered railroad property.

Walkouts and sympathy demonstrations spread spontaneously from Maryland to San Francisco. The strike engulfed hundreds of cities and towns, leaving in its wake over a hundred people killed and millions of dollars in property destroyed. Federal troops finally quelled the violence. The greatest outbreak began at Pittsburgh, when the Pennsylvania Railroad put on "double-headers" (long trains pulled by two locomotives) in order to reduce crews. Public sympathy for the strikers was so great at first that local militiamen, called out to suppress them, instead joined the workers. Militiamen from Philadelphia managed to disperse one crowd at the cost of twenty-six lives, but then found themselves besieged in the railroad's roundhouse, where they disbanded and shot their way out.

Looting, rioting, and burning went on for another day until the frenzy wore itself out. A reporter described the scene as "the most horrible ever witnessed, except in the carnage of war. There were fifty miles of hot rails, ten tracks side by side, with as many miles of ties turned into glowing coals and tons on tons of iron car skeletons and wheels almost at white heat." Public opinion, sympathetic at first, shifted until it tended to blame the workers for the looting and violence. Eventually the strikers, lacking organized bargaining power, had no choice but to drift back to work. Everywhere the strikes failed.

For many people, the strike raised the specter of a worker-based social revolution like the Paris Commune of 1871, in which disgruntled mobs chanted "Bread or Blood." As a Pittsburgh newspaper warned, "This may be the beginning of a great civil war in this country between labor and capital." Equally disturbing to those in positions of corporate and political power was the presence of many women among the protesters. A Baltimore journalist noted that the "singular part of the disturbances is the very active part taken by the women, who are the wives and mothers of the [railroad] firemen." From the point of view of organized labor, however, the Great Railroad Strike demonstrated potential strength and the need for tighter organization. As the labor leader Samuel Gompers later recalled, "The railroad strike of 1877, was the tocsin that sounded a ringing message of hope for us all."

THE "SAND LOT" INCIDENT In California the railroad strike indirectly gave rise to a political movement. At San Francisco's "Sand Lot," a meeting to express sympathy for the strikers ended with attacks on some passing Chinese. Within a few days, sporadic anti-Chinese riots led to a mob attack on Chinatown. Depression had hit the West Coast especially hard, and the Chinese were handy scapegoats for frustrations.

Soon an Irish immigrant, Dennis Kearney, organized the "Workingmen's Party of California." Its platform called for the end of further Chinese immigration. A gifted agitator, himself only recently naturalized, Kearney harangued the "sand lotters" about the "foreign peril" and assaulted the rich for exploiting the poor—sometimes at gatherings beside their mansions on Nob Hill. In 1878 his new party won a hefty number of seats in a state constitutional convention, but managed to incorporate in the state's basic law little more than ineffective attempts to regulate the railroads. The workingmen's movement peaked in 1879 when it elected many members of the new legislature and the mayor of San Francisco. Kearney lacked the gift for building a durable movement, but as his party went to pieces, his anti-Chinese theme became a national issue. In 1882 Congress voted to prohibit Chinese immigration for ten years.

TOWARD PERMANENT UNIONS   Meanwhile, efforts to build a permanent union movement had begun to bear fruit. Earlier efforts, in the 1830s and 1840s, had largely been dominated by reformers with schemes that ranged from free homesteads to utopian socialism. But the 1850s witnessed the beginning of "job-conscious" unions in certain skilled trades. By 1860 there were about twenty such unions, and during the Civil War, because of the demand for labor, these craft unions grew in strength and numbers.

There was no overall federation of these groups until August 1866, when the first National Labor Union (NLU) convened in Baltimore. The NLU was composed of delegates from labor and reform groups more interested in political and social change than in bargaining with employers. The groups espoused ideas such as the eight-hour workday, workers' cooperatives, paper money, and equal rights for women and blacks. But the organization lost momentum after the death of its president in 1869, and by 1872 it had entirely collapsed. The National Labor Union, however, was not a total failure. It was influential in persuading Congress to enact an eight-hour workday for federal employees and to repeal the 1864 Contract Labor Law, which allowed employers to bind immigrant laborers (contract laborers) by paying for their passage from Europe. That such immigrants were willing to work for low wages made them unpopular with American workers.

THE KNIGHTS OF LABOR   Before the National Labor Union collapsed, another labor group of national standing had emerged, the Noble and Holy Order of the Knights of Labor. The name evoked the aura of medieval guilds. The founder of the Knights of Labor, Uriah S. Stephens, a Philadelphia tailor, was a habitual "joiner" involved with several secret orders, including the Masons. Secrecy, he felt, along with a semireligious ritual, would protect members against retaliation and at the same time create a sense of solidarity.

The Knights of Labor, started in 1869, grew slowly, but during the years of depression after 1873, as other unions collapsed, it spread more rapidly. In 1878 its first General Assembly established a national organization. Its preamble and platform endorsed producers' and consumers' cooperatives, hoping to replace the wage-labor system with worker-owned factories. The Knights also called for free homesteads, bureaus of labor statistics, elimination of convict-labor competition, the eight-hour workday, and the acceptance of greenbacks as currency in order to enlarge the money supply and ease credit. One plank in the platform, far ahead of the times, called for equal pay for equal work by both men and women.

Throughout their existence the Knights emphasized reform measures and preferred boycotts to strikes as a way to put pressure on employers. They also had a liberal membership policy, welcoming all who had ever worked for wages, except lawyers, doctors, bankers, and those who sold liquor. Theoretically it was one big union of all workers, skilled and unskilled, regardless of race, color, creed, or sex.

Stephens was elected as the first Grand Master Workman to head the organization. In 1879 he gave way to Terence V. Powderly, the thirty-year-old mayor of Scranton, Pennsylvania. In many ways Powderly was unsuited to the new job. At once mayor, head of the Knights, county health officer, and part owner and manager of a grocery store, he had too many irons in the fire. He was physically frail, sensitive to criticism, and indecisive at critical moments. Powderly was temperamentally opposed to strikes, and when they did occur, he did not always back up the locals. Yet the Knights ironically owed their greatest growth to strikes that occurred under his leadership.

In the mid-1880s membership in the Knights grew rapidly. In 1884 a successful strike against wage cuts in the Union Pacific shops at Denver led many railroad workers to form new local chapters. Then, in 1885, the Knights scored a startling victory over Jay Gould. Late the previous year and early in 1885 Gould had cut wages on several of his railroads. A spontaneous strike on these lines in 1885 spread to Gould's Missouri-Pacific, and as organizers from the Knights of Labor moved in, Gould restored the wage cuts. Such successes allowed the Knights to grow rapidly from about 100,000 members to more than 700,000 in 1886.

But the Knights peaked in 1886 and then went into rapid decline. Jay Gould in 1886 provoked another strike by firing a foreman in the Texas-Pacific shops. When the Knights struck, Gould refused arbitration and hired Pinkerton agents to harass strikers and keep the trains running. The Knights had to call off the strike. The organization was further damaged by an incident in Chicago's Haymarket Square that very night, with which the Knights had little to do but which provoked widespread revulsion against labor groups in general.

ANARCHISM   The tensions between labor and management during the late nineteenth century in both the United States and Europe helped generate interest in the doctrine of anarchism. The anarchists believed that government, any government, was in itself an abusive device used by the rich and powerful to oppress and exploit the working poor. Anarchists dreamed of the eventual disappearance of government altogether, and many of them believed that the transition to this stateless society could be hurried along by promoting revolutionary action among the masses. One favored tactic was the use of dramatic acts of violence against representatives of the government. Many European anarchists emigrated to the United States during the last quarter of the nineteenth century, and they brought with them this belief in the impact of "propaganda of the deed."

THE HAYMARKET AFFAIR   On May 3, 1886, Chicago's International Harvester plant was the site of an unfortunate clash between strikers and policemen in which one striker was killed. Leaders of a minuscule anarchist movement in Chicago scheduled an open meeting the following night at Haymarket Square to protest the killing. Under a light drizzle the crowd listened to long speeches promoting socialism and anarchism, and was beginning to break up when a group of policemen arrived and called upon the activists to disperse. At that point someone threw a bomb at the police, killing one and wounding others. The police responded by firing into the crowd, killing four demonstrators. Six policemen were also killed. In a trial marked by prejudice and hysteria, seven anarchist leaders were sentenced to death, despite the lack of any evidence linking them to the bomb-thrower, whose identity was never established. Of the seven, two were reprieved and some years later pardoned, one committed suicide in prison, and four were hanged. The episode helped stamp in anxious American minds the stereotype of bearded and swarthy alien anarchists and labor radicals. All but one of the group were German-speaking, but that one held a membership card in the Knights of Labor.

Despite his best efforts, Powderly could never dissociate in the public mind the Knights from the anarchists. He clung to leadership until 1893, but after that the union evaporated. By the turn of the century, it was but a memory. A number of problems accounted for the Knights' decline: a leadership devoted more to reform than to pragmatic organization, the failure of the Knights' cooperative enterprises, and a preoccupation with politics rather than negotiations with management.

The Knights nevertheless attained some lasting achievements, among them the creation of the Federal Bureau of Labor Statistics and the Foran Act of 1885, which penalized employers who imported contract laborers from abroad. The Knights also spread the idea of unionism and initiated a new type of union organization: the industrial union, an industry-wide union of both the skilled and unskilled.

GOMPERS AND THE AFL   The craft unions opposed the industrial unionism of the Knights. They organized workers who shared special skills, such as typographers or cigarmakers. Leaders of the crafts feared that joining with the unskilled would mean a loss of their separate craft identities and a loss of the bargaining power held by skilled workers. In the summer of 1886, delegates from craft unions met at Columbus, Ohio, and organized the American Federation of Labor (AFL). In structure it differed from the Knights in that it was a federation of national craft organizations, each of which retained a large degree of autonomy and exercised greater leverage against management.

Samuel Gompers served as president of the AFL from its start until his death in 1924. Born in London of Dutch-Jewish ancestry, Gompers came to the United States as a teenager, joined the Cigarmakers Union in 1864, and became president of his New York local in 1877. This background was significant. The Cigarmakers tended to be the intellectuals of the labor movement; to relieve the tedium of their task, they hired young men to read aloud as they worked, and debated such weighty topics as socialism and Darwinism. But Gompers and other leaders of the union focused on concrete economic gains, avoiding involvement with utopian ideas or politics. "At no time in my life," Gompers once admitted, "have I ever worked out a definitely articulated economic theory." Adolph Strasser, head of the Cigarmakers, put it more strongly: "We have no ultimate ends," he told a Senate hearing. "We are going on from day to day. We are fighting only for immediate objects—objects that can be realized in a few years."

Such job consciousness became the policy of the AFL under Gompers, whose lifetime concern was the effectiveness of the federation. Gompers hired organizers to spread unionism and worked as a diplomat to prevent overlapping unions and to settle jurisdictional disputes. The federation represented workers in matters of national legislation and acted as a sounding board for their cause. On occasion it exercised its power to request dues from members for the support of strikes. Gompers, it turned out, was temperamentally more fitted than Powderly for the rough-and-tumble world of unionism. He had a thick hide, liked to talk and drink with workers in the back room, and advocated using the strike to achieve labor's objectives. His preference, though, was to achieve these objectives through agreements with management that included provisos for union recognition in the form of closed shops (which could hire only union members) or union-preference shops (which could hire others only if no union members were available).

The AFL at first grew slowly, but by 1890 it had already surpassed the Knights of Labor in membership. By the turn of the century, it claimed 500,000 members in affiliated unions; in 1914, on the eve of World War I, it had 2 million; and in 1920, it reached a peak of 4 million. But even then the AFL embraced less than 15 percent of the nonagricultural workers. All unions, including the unaffiliated railroad brotherhoods, accounted for little more than 18 percent of these workers. Organized labor's strongholds were in transportation and the building trades. Most of the larger manufacturing industries, including textiles, tobacco, and packinghouses, remained almost untouched.

THE HOMESTEAD STRIKE   Two violent labor incidents in the 1890s scarred the emerging industrial union movement and set it back for forty years to come—the Homestead Steel Strike of 1892 and the Pullman Strike of 1894. The Amalgamated Association of Iron and Steel Workers, founded in 1876, had by 1891 a membership of more than 24,000 and was probably the largest craft union at that time. But it excluded the unskilled and had failed to organize the larger steel plants. The Homestead Works at Pittsburgh was an important exception. There the union had enjoyed friendly relations with the Carnegie company until H. C. Frick became its president in 1889. A showdown was delayed, however, until 1892, when the union contract came up for renewal. Andrew Carnegie, who had expressed sympathy for unions in the past, had gone to Scotland and left matters in the hands of Frick. Carnegie, however, knew what was afoot: a cost-cutting reduction in the number of workers through the use of labor-saving devices, and a deliberate attempt to smash the union.

As negotiations dragged on, the company announced it would deal with workers as individuals unless an agreement was reached by June 29. A strike, or more properly a lockout of unionists, began on that date. Even before the negotiations ended, Frick had begun barricading the plant and hired as plant guards 300 Pinkerton detectives whose specialty was union-busting. But on the morning of July 6, 1892, when the Pinkertons floated up the Monongahela River on barges, discharged union workers were waiting behind iron breastworks on shore. Who fired the first shot remains unknown, but a battle erupted in which nine workers and seven Pinkertons died. In the end, the Pinkertons surrendered and marched away, to the taunts of crowds in the street. Six days later 8,000 state militiamen appeared at the plant to protect the strikebreakers hired to restore production. The strike dragged on until November, but by then the union was dead at Homestead. Its cause was not helped when an anarchist shot and wounded Frick. Much of the local sympathy for the strikers evaporated.

THE PULLMAN STRIKE   The Pullman Strike of 1894 was perhaps the most notable walkout in American history. It paralyzed the economies of twenty-seven states and territories making up the western half of the nation. It grew out of a dispute at the "model" town of Pullman, Illinois, just outside Chicago, which housed workers of the Pullman Palace Car Company in neat brick homes nestled on grassy lots along shaded streets. The town's idyllic appearance, however, was deceptive. Employees were required to live there, pay rents and utility costs higher than in nearby towns, and buy their goods from company stores. With the onset of the depression in 1893, George Pullman laid off 3,000 of 5,800 employees, and cut wages 25 to 40 percent, but not his rents and other charges. When Pullman fired three members of a grievance committee, a strike began on May 11, 1894.

During this tense period, the Pullman workers had been joining the American Railway Union, founded the previous year by Eugene V. Debs. The tall, gangly Debs was a charismatic man who led by example and by the electric force of his convictions. A child of working-class immigrants, he quit school in 1869 at age fourteen in order to go to work for an Indiana railroad. There he soon "learned of the hardships of the rail in snow, sleet, and hail, of the ceaseless danger that lurks along the iron highway, the uncertainty of employment, scant wages and alto-

Eugene V. Debs, founder of the American Railway Union and later candidate for president as head of the Socialist Party of America.

gether trying lot of the workingman, so that from my very boyhood I was made to feel the wrongs of labor." He felt them so deeply that he eagerly accepted an invitation to start a local of the railroad brotherhood, a craft union of skilled workers.

Still, it was not until the Haymarket bombing that Debs came to see an inevitable conflict between labor and management. By the early 1890s, he had become a tireless spokesman for labor radicalism, and he launched a crusade to organize *all* railway workers—skilled and un-skilled—into the American Railway Union. His earnest appeal generated a tremendous response, and soon he was in charge of a powerful new labor organization. He quickly turned his attention to the Pullman controversy.

After Pullman refused Debs's plea for arbitration, the union workers in June 1894 stopped handling Pullman cars and by the end of July had tied up most of the railroads in the Midwest. The rail owners then brought strikebreakers from Canada and elsewhere, instructing them to connect mail cars to Pullman cars so that interference with Pullman cars also meant interference with the federal mail. Attorney-General Richard Olney, a former railroad attorney, swore in 3,400 special deputies to keep the trains running. When clashes occurred between these and some of the strikers, lawless elements ignored Debs's plea for an orderly boycott and repeated some of the violent scenes of the 1877 strike.

Finally, on July 3, 1894, President Grover Cleveland answered an appeal from the railroads to send federal troops into the Chicago area, where the strike was centered. Illinois governor John Peter Altgeld issued a vigorous protest, insisting that the state could keep order, but Cleveland claimed authority and a duty to ensure delivery of the mails. "If it takes every dollar in the Treasury and every soldier in the United States to deliver a postal card in Chicago," he vowed, "that postal card should be delivered."

As strikers clashed with troops and burned hundreds of cars, the federal district court granted an injunction forbidding any interference with the mails or any combination to restrain interstate commerce. On July 13 the union called off the strike, and on the same day the district court cited Debs for violating the injunction and sentenced him to six months in jail. The Supreme Court upheld the decree in the case of *In re Debs* (1895) on broad grounds of national sovereignty: "The strong arm of the national government may be put forth to brush away all obstructions to the freedom of interstate commerce or the transportation of the mails." Debs served his term, during which time he read deeply in socialist literature, and he emerged to devote the rest of his life to that cause.

SOCIALISM AND THE UNIONS   The major American unions, for the most part, never allied themselves with the socialists, as many European labor movements did. But socialist ideas had been abroad in the country at least since the time Robert Owen visited America in the 1820s. The movement gained little notice before the rise of Daniel DeLeon in the 1890s as the dominant figure in the Socialist Labor party. A native of the Dutch West Indies, DeLeon had studied law and lectured for some years at Columbia University. He proposed to organize industrial unions with a socialist purpose, and to build a political party that would abolish the state once it gained power. His ideas seem to have influenced Lenin, leader of Russia's Bolshevik revolution of 1917, but DeLeon preached revolution at the ballot box, not by violence.

Yet Debs was more successful at building a socialist movement in America. To many, DeLeon seemed doctrinaire and inflexible. Debs, however, built his new party by following a method now traditional in the United States: he formed a coalition, one that embraced viewpoints ranging from moderate reform to doctrinaire Marxism. In 1897 Debs announced that he was a socialist and organized the Social Democratic party from the remnants of the American Railway Union. He received over 4,000 votes as its candidate for president in 1900. In 1901 his followers joined a number of secessionists from DeLeon's party, led by Morris Hillquit of New York, to set up the Socialist Party of America. In 1904 Debs polled over 400,000 votes as the party's candidate for president and more than doubled that to almost 900,000 votes in 1912, or 6 percent of the popular vote.

By 1912 the Socialist party seemed well on the way to becoming a permanent fixture in American politics. Thirty-three cities had socialist mayors. The Socialist party sponsored five English daily newspapers, eight foreign-language dailies, and a number of weeklies and monthlies. Its support was not confined to urban workers and intellectuals. In the Southwest the party built a sizable grassroots following among farmers and tenants. But the party reached its peak in 1912. During World War I, it was wracked by disagreements over America's participation in the war, and it was split thereafter. The Great Depression of the 1930s served only to interrupt, not halt, its decline.

THE WOBBLIES   During the years of Socialist party growth, there emerged a parallel effort to revive industrial unionism, led by the Industrial Workers of the World (IWW), dubbed the Wobblies. The chief base for this group was the Western Federation of Miners, organized at Butte, Montana, in 1893. Over the next decade, the Western Federation was the storm center of violent confrontation with unyielding bosses who mobilized private armies against it in Colorado, Idaho, and elsewhere. A radical manifesto issued from the founding convention of the IWW in 1905, arguing that the IWW "must be founded on the class struggle, and its general administration must be conducted in harmony with the recognition of the irrepressible conflict between the capitalist class and the working class."

But the IWW waged class war better than it articulated class ideology. Like the Knights of Labor, it was designed to be "One Big Union," including all workers, skilled or unskilled. Its roots were in the mining and lumber camps of the West, where unstable conditions of employment created a large number of nomadic workers, to whom neither the AFL's pragmatic approach nor the socialists' political appeal held much attraction. The revolutionary goal of the Wobblies was an idea labeled syndicalism by its French supporters: the ultimate destruction of the state and its replacement by one big union. How it would govern remained vague.

Like other radical groups, the IWW witnessed internal disputes. William D. "Big Bill" Haywood of the Western Federation emerged as the leader of those who remained in the IWW and managed to hold the group together. Although since embellished in myth, Haywood was indeed an imposing figure. Well over six feet tall, handsome, broad-shouldered, one-eyed, and rippling with muscles, he commanded the attention and respect of his listeners. This thirty-six-year-old hardrock miner, union organizer, and socialist from Salt Lake City had nothing but disdain for the AFL and its conservative labor philosophy. Haywood promoted the concept of one all-inclusive union whose credo would be the promotion of a socialism "with its working clothes on."

Haywood and the Wobblies reached out to the fringe elements that had the least power and influence, chiefly the migratory workers of the West and the ethnic groups of the East. Always ambivalent about diluting their revolutionary principles, they heaped scorn on the usual labor agreements, even when they participated in them. They engaged in spectacular battles with corporate America but scored few victories. The largest was a textile strike at Lawrence, Massachusetts, in 1912; the strikers won wage raises, overtime pay, and other benefits. But the next year a strike of silk workers at Paterson, New Jersey, ended in disaster, and the IWW entered a rapid decline.

The fading of the movement was accelerated by the hysterical opposition it engendered. Branded as anarchists, bums, and criminals, the IWW was effectively destroyed during World War I, when most of its leaders were jailed for their militant opposition to the war. Nonetheless, the Wobblies left behind a rich folklore of nomadic working folk and a gallery of heroic agitators such as Elizabeth Gurley Flynn, a dark-haired Irish girl who at age eighteen, ardent and pregnant, chained herself to a lamppost to impede her arrest during a strike. The movement also bequeathed martyrs such as the Swedish singer and labor organizer Joe

Textile workers strike, Lawrence, Massachusetts, *1912. The IWW of this Lawrence mill engaged in a violent strike for increased wages, overtime pay, and other benefits.*

Hill, framed (so the faithful assumed) for murder and executed by a Utah firing squad. His last words were written to Haywood: "Goodbye, Bill. I die like a true blue rebel. Don't waste any time mourning. Organize." Such intensity of conviction and devotion to a cause ensured that the IWW's ideal of a classless society did not die.

A Nation Transformed

By the end of the nineteenth century, the ever-accelerating industrial revolution had transformed the nature of work and social life, generated a new urban consciousness and culture, and provoked rising class tensions. With each passing year, more and more people jettisoned traditional rural folkways in favor of new urban environs, a more secular outlook, and enticing new economic and social opportunities.

The modern city's frenetic pace, its sprawl, disorder, beauty, and energy, all combined to give it a commanding presence and almost sensual allure. As centers of production and consumption, the new industrial cities controlled the pace of national life. Instead of solitary farmers tending fields, the city brought together workers crowded into congested apartments. People living amid the marvels and miseries of metropolitan America saw their habits of mind profoundly altered.

The industrial revolution occurred at different rates and produced different effects across the expanding nation. Despite the energetic efforts of "New South" boosters, the states of the former Confederacy, burdened by a chronic shortage of capital and a poorly educated populace, lagged well behind the rest of the nation in industrial development, urban expansion, and per capita income. Most southerners also clung to a romanticized past rather than confront a sobering present.

The recurring theme of American life after the Civil War was an acute sense of accelerated social and intellectual change. Of course, the pressure of history, the pneumatic push of extraordinary new social developments and ideas, never rests. Yet the velocity and scope of change at mid-century and after seemed especially bewildering. "When I reflect what changes I, a man of fifty, have seen, how old-fashioned my ways of thinking have become," poet James Russell Lowell confessed to a friend in 1869, "the signs of the times cease to alarm me."

To Lowell and others, the United States seemed to have lost much of its stability and cohesion as a result of urban-industrial development and western expansion. It had become a loose aggregate of competing individuals, divided from one another by economic differences and ethnic, racial, and class prejudices. How to restore a sense of community and cohesion would become the collective challenge of all Americans.

MAKING CONNECTIONS

- The Darwinian ideas implicit in the attitudes of many leading entrepreneurs, especially Andrew Carnegie, are described in greater detail in the next chapter.

- In response to the growth of the railroads, reformers in the 1880s and 1890s began to push for regulation, a trend explored in Chapter 21.

- The economic and industrial growth described in this chapter was an important factor in America's "new imperialism" in the late nineteenth century, as shown in Chapter 22.

- The socialist approach to reform was a significant influence on the progressive movement, covered in Chapter 23.

FURTHER READING

For a masterly synthesis of post–Civil War industrial development, see Walter Licht's *Industrializing America: The Nineteenth Century* (1995). Of more specialized interest are Alfred D. Chandler's *The Visible Hand: The Managerial Revolution in American Business* (1977), and Maury Klein's *The Flowering of the Third America: The Making of an Organizational Society, 1850–1920* (1992).

On the growth of railroads see Albro Martin's *Railroads Triumphant: The Growth, Rejection, and Rebirth of a Vital American Force* (1992) and Sarah Gordon's *Passage to Union: How the Railroads Transformed America, 1829–1929* (1997). Walter Licht's *Working for the Railroad: The Organization of Work in the Nineteenth Century* (1983) treats the life of the railroad workers. Gabriel Kolko's *Railroads and Regulation, 1877–1916* (1965) argues that the entrepreneurs themselves sought government regulation.

On entrepreneurship in the iron and steel sector, see Thomas J. Misa's *A Nation of Steel: The Making of Modern America, 1865–1925* (1995). The best biography of the leading business tycoon is Ron Chernow's *Titan: The Life of John D. Rockefeller, Sr.* (1998). A new book on J. Pierpont Morgan is Jean Strouse's *J. P. Morgan: American Financier* (1999).

Nathan Rosenberg's *Technology and American Economic Growth* (1972) documents the growth of invention during the period. For an absorbing biography of the foremost inventor of the era, see Neil Baldwin's *Edison: Inventing the Century* (1995).

Much of the recent scholarship on labor stresses the traditional values and the culture of work that people brought to the factory. Herbert G. Gutman's *Work, Culture, and Society in Industrializing America* (1976) best introduces these themes. The best survey remains David Montgomery's *The Fall of the House of Labor: The Workplace, the State and American Labor Activism, 1865–1925* (1987).

For the role of women in the changing workplace, see Alice Kessler-Harris's *Out to Work* (1983), Susan E. Kennedy's *If All We Did Was to Weep at Home: A History of White Working-Class Women in America* (1979), and S. J. Kleinberg's *The Shadow of the Mills: Working-Class Families in Pittsburgh, 1870–1907* (1989).

As for the labor groups, Gerald N. Grob's *Workers and Utopias* (1961) examines the difference in outlook between the Knights of Labor and the American Federation of Labor. For the Knights, see Leon Fink's *Workingmen's Democracy* (1983). Also useful is Susan Levine's *Labor's True Woman* (1984), on the role of women in the Knights. To trace the rise of socialism among organized workers, see Nick Salvatore's *Eugene V. Debs: Citizen and Socialist* (1982) and Robert J. Constantine's *Letters of Eugene V. Debs* (1990). Strikes are discussed in Kevin Kenny's *Making Sense of the Molly Maguires* (1998), Paul Avrich's *The Haymarket Tragedy* (1984), and Paul Krause's *The Battle for Homestead, 1880–1892: Politics, Culture, and Steel* (1992).

20 ❧ THE EMERGENCE OF URBAN AMERICA

*D*uring the second half of the nineteenth century, the United States experienced an urban revolution unparalleled in world history up to that time. As factories, mines, and mills sprouted across the landscape, cities grew up around them. The late nineteenth century, declared an economist in 1899, was "not only the age of cities, but the age of great cities." Between 1860 and 1910, the urban population grew from 6 million to 44 million. The United States was rapidly losing its rural flavor. Indeed, by 1920, more than half of the population would be living in urban areas.

The rise of big cities during the nineteenth century created a distinctive urban culture. People from different ethnic and religious back-

The elevator at Lord & Taylor store, 1873.

grounds and representing every walk of life poured into the high-rise apartment buildings and ramshackle tenements springing up in every major city. They came in search of jobs, wealth, and new opportunities. Rising wages and the availability of inexpensive consumer goods in the dazzling new downtown department stores improved the material standard of living for millions—while widening the gap between the poor and affluent.

The rise of metropolitan America also created an array of social problems. Rapid urban development produced widespread poverty and political corruption. It also produced dirt and disease, crowded substandard housing, and unsafe working conditions in factories, mines, mills, and slaughterhouses. People needed basic services like access to education, transportation, sewers, fresh water, inoculations against disease, and factory inspections to prevent unsafe working conditions. Eventually broadened access to public education and to public health services would improve literacy and lower infant mortality rates (although the death rate for adult black males would remain quite high). Breakthroughs in medical science would bring cures for tuberculosis, typhoid, and diphtheria—although these infectious diseases would remain the century's leading killers. But in the meantime, the problems of how to feed, clothe, shelter, and educate the new arrivals taxed the imagination—and patience of many Americans.

AMERICA'S MOVE TO TOWN

The urban-industrial revolution greatly increased the national wealth and transformed the pace and tenor of American life. City people and folks who worked in factories rather than on farms, while differing significantly among themselves, also became distinctively and recognizably urban in demeanor and outlook.

EXPLOSIVE URBAN GROWTH   The frontier was a safety valve, the historian Frederick Jackson Turner said in his influential thesis on American development. Its cheap lands afforded a release for the population pressures mounting in the cities. If there were such a thing as a safety valve in his own time, however, he had it exactly backward. The flow of population toward the city was greater than toward the West, and "country come to town" epitomized the American people better than the occasional city "dude" who turned up in cow country.

Much of the westward migration in fact was itself an urban movement, spawning new towns near the mining digs or at the railheads. The Pacific coast boasted a greater urban proportion of the population in the West than anywhere else; its major concentrations were first around San Francisco Bay and then in Los Angeles, which became a boom town after the arrival of the Southern Pacific and Santa Fe Railroads in the 1880s. Seattle also grew quickly, first as the terminus of three transcontinental railroad lines, and by the end of the century as the staging area for the Yukon gold rush. Minneapolis, St. Paul, Omaha, Kansas City, and Denver were no longer the mere villages they had been in 1860. The South, too, produced new cities: Durham, North Carolina, and Birmingham, Alabama, which were centers of tobacco and iron manufactures, and Houston, Texas, which handled cotton and cattle, and later, oil. The industrial explosion powered the growth of new cities during this period.

The cities expanded both vertically and horizontally to absorb their huge populations. In either case, technological innovations played an important role: steam heating and radiators, elevators, streetcars, and, before the end of the century, the first automobiles. In the 1870s heating innovations, such as steam circulating through pipes and radiators, contributed to the building of multiple-apartment dwellings, since landlords no longer had the expense of providing fireplaces and fuel to

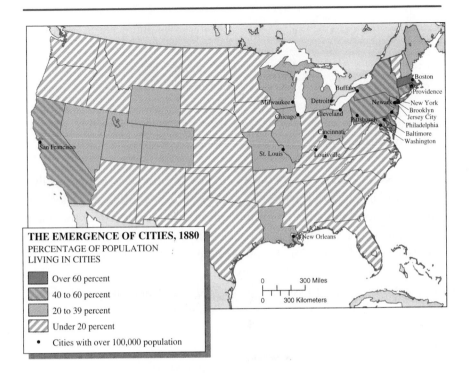

THE EMERGENCE OF CITIES, 1880
PERCENTAGE OF POPULATION
LIVING IN CITIES

Over 60 percent

40 to 60 percent

20 to 39 percent

Under 20 percent

• Cities with over 100,000 population

heat every room. In 1889 the Otis Elevator Company installed the first electric elevator, which made possible the erection of taller buildings. Before the Civil War, few structures had gone higher than three or four stories. During the 1880s, engineers developed cast-iron and steel-frame construction, which was stronger than brick, and therefore facilitated the development of higher stories in apartment and office buildings. Many architects designed "skyscrapers" with steel frames and girders in the new style of design promoted by Chicago architects. Because Chicago had to be rebuilt after the great fire of 1871, it provided a laboratory for new architectural ideas.

Before the 1890s, the chief power sources of urban transport were either animals or steam. Horse- and mule-drawn streetcars had appeared in antebellum cities, but they were slow and cumbersome, and cleaning up horse manure from the streets added to their cost. In 1873 San Francisco became the first city to use cars pulled by steam-driven cables. Some cities used steam-powered commuter trains or elevated tracks, but by the 1890s electric trolleys were preferred. Mass transportation received an added boost when around the turn of the century

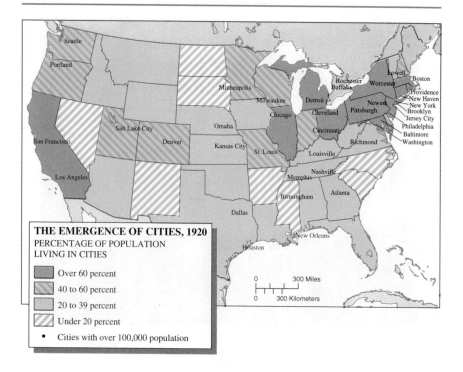

THE EMERGENCE OF CITIES, 1920
PERCENTAGE OF POPULATION
LIVING IN CITIES

- Over 60 percent
- 40 to 60 percent
- 20 to 39 percent
- Under 20 percent
- • Cities with over 100,000 population

subway systems began to function in Boston, New York, and Philadelphia. Moreover, advances in bridge building through the use of steel
and the perfection of the steel-cable suspension bridge also extended
the reach of mass transportation.

The spread of mass transit made it possible for large numbers of people to become commuters, and a growing middle class (laborers often
could not afford even the nickel fare) retreated to quieter, tree-lined
"streetcar suburbs" whence they could travel into the central city for
business or entertainment. The pattern of urban growth often became a
sprawl, since it took place usually without plan in the interest of a fast
buck, and without thought to the need for parks and public services.

The use of horse-drawn railways, cable cars, and electric trolleys
helped transform the social character of cities. Until the implementation of such new transportation systems, people of all classes lived and
worked together in the central city. After the Civil War, however, the
emergence of suburbs began to segregate people according to their economic standing. The more affluent moved outside the city, leaving the
working folk, many of whom were immigrants, behind. The poorer dis-

Central Park Tunnel, 1903. *The subway system helped abate the street-level congestion that plagued cities at the turn-of-the-century.*

tricts in the city became more congested and crime-ridden as the population grew, fueled by waves of newcomers from abroad.

ALLURE AND PROBLEMS OF THE CITY   The wonder of the cities—their glittering new arc and electric lights, their streetcars, telephones, vaudeville shows and other amusements, newspapers and magazines, and a thousand other attractions—cast a magnetic lure on the youth of the farms. The new cities threw into stark contrast the frustration of unending toil and the isolation and loneliness of country life. In times of rural depression, thousands left for the cities in search of opportunity and personal freedom. The exodus from the countryside was especially evident in the East, where the census documented the shift in population from country to city, and stories began to appear of entire regions where buildings were abandoned and going to ruin, and where the wilderness was reclaiming farms that had been wrested from it during the previous 250 years.

Yet, those who moved to the city often traded one set of problems for another. Workers in the b g cities often had no choice other than to live in crowded apartments, most of which were poorly designed. In 1900 Manhattan's 42,700 tenements housed almost 1.6 million people, an average of 37 residents per building. Before the day of high-rise apartments, this represented an extremely high density, and such unregulated urban growth created immense problems of health and morale.

As the number of new arrivals mushroomed during the last quarter of the nineteenth century, cities became so cramped and land so scarce that designers were forced to build upward. In New York City this resulted in the "dumbbell" tenement house. These structures, usually six to eight stories tall and jammed tightly against one another, derived their name from the fact that housing codes required a two-foot wide air shaft between buildings, giving the structure the appearance of a dumbbell when viewed from overhead. Twenty-four to thirty-two families would cram into each building. Some city blocks housed almost 4,000 people. The tiny air shaft provided little ventilation; instead, it proved to be a fire hazard, fueling and conveying flames from building to building.

The early tenements were poorly heated and had toilets outside in the yard or alley for communal use. By the end of the century, they would feature two toilets on each floor, available to all comers. Shoe-horned into such quarters, families had no privacy, free space, or sunshine; children had few places to play except in the city streets; infectious diseases and noxious odors were rampant. Not surprisingly, the mortality rate for the urban poor was much higher than that of the general population. In one poor Chicago district at the end of the century, three babies of every five died before their first birthday.

CITY POLITICS   The sheer size of the cities helped create a new form of politics. Since individuals could hardly provide for themselves necessary services such as transit, paving, water, sewers, street lighting and cleaning, and fire and police protection, they came increasingly to rely on city government support. Because local government was often fragmented and beset by parochial rivalries, a need grew for a central organization to coordinate city-wide issues such as public transportation, sanitation, and utilities. Urban political machines developed, consisting of local committeemen, district captains and leaders, and culminating in a political boss. While these political bosses engaged in patronage favors and graft, buying and selling votes, taking kickbacks and payoff money, they also provided needed services. They distributed food, coal, and money to the poor; found jobs for those who were out of work; sponsored English-language classes for immigrants; organized sports teams, social clubs, and neighborhood gatherings; fixed problems at city hall; and generally helped newcomers adjust to their new life. As one ward boss in Boston said: "There's got to be in every ward somebody that any bloke can come to—no matter what he's done—and get help. Help, you understand, none of your law and justice, but help." In return, the political professionals felt entitled to some reward for having done the grubby work of the local organization.

THE NEW IMMIGRATION

The industrial revolution brought to American shores waves of new immigrants from every part of the globe. By the end of the century, nearly 30 percent of the residents of major cities were foreign-born. These newcomers provided much-needed labor, but their arrival also provoked ugly racial and ethnic tensions.

AMERICA'S PULL   European immigrants increasingly moved from the great agricultural areas of eastern and southern Europe directly to the foremost cities of America. They wanted to live with others of like language, customs, and religion, and they lacked the means to go west and settle on farms. Though cities of the South and West (excepting the Far West) drew their populations mainly from the native-born of their regions, American cities as a whole drew more residents from abroad. During the peak decade of immigration, 1900–1910, 41 percent of the urban newcomers arrived from abroad.

This nation of immigrants continued to draw new inhabitants for much the same reasons as always, and from much the same strata of society. Immigrants took flight from famine, cholera, or the lack of economic opportunity in their native lands. They fled racial, religious, and political persecution and compulsory military service.

Yet more immigrants probably were pulled by America's opportunities than were pushed out by conditions at home. American industries, seeking cheap labor, sent recruiters abroad. Railroads, eager to sell land and build up the traffic on their lines, distributed tempting propaganda

Steerage Deck of the S.S. *Pennland,* 1893. *These immigrants are about to arrive at New York's Ellis Island.*

in a medley of languages. Many of the western and southern states set up official bureaus and agents to attract immigrants. Under the Contract Labor Law of 1864, the federal government itself encouraged immigration by allowing companies to recruit foreign workers by paying for their passage and then recouping the money from the immigrants' wages. The law was repealed in 1868, but not until 1885 did the government forbid companies to import contract labor, which put immigrants under the control of their employers.

After the Civil War, the tide of immigration rose from just under 3 million in the 1870s to more than 5 million in the 1880s, then fell to a little over 3.5 million in the depression decade of the 1890s, and rose to its high-water mark of 8.8 million in the first decade of the new century.

A NEW WAVE   During the 1880s, the continuing search for cheap labor combined with renewed persecutions in eastern Europe to bring a noticeable change in the source of immigration. Before 1880 immigrants were mainly of Germanic and Celtic origin, hailing from northern and western Europe. But by the 1870s, there were signs of change.

The proportion of Latin, Slavic, and Jewish people from southern and eastern Europe rose sharply. After 1890, these groups made up a majority of the newcomers, and by the first decade of the new century they formed 70 percent of the immigrants to this country. Among these new immigrants were Italians, Hungarians, Czechs, Slovaks, Poles, Serbs, Croats, Russians, Romanians, and Greeks—all people of markedly different cultural and language stocks and of different religions, including Judaism and Catholicism.

ELLIS ISLAND   As the number of immigrants passing through the Port of New York soared during the late nineteenth century, the state-run Castle Garden receiving center overflowed with corruption. Money-changers cheated new arrivals, railroad agents overcharged them for tickets, and baggage handlers engaged in blackmail. With reports of these abuses filling the newspapers, Congress ordered an investigation of Castle Garden, which resulted in the closure of the facility in 1890. Thereafter the federal government's new Bureau of Immigration took over the business of admitting newcomers to New York City.

To launch this effort, Congress funded the construction of a new reception center on a tiny island off the New Jersey coast, a mile south of Manhattan and some 1,300 feet from the Statue of Liberty. The statue, unveiled in 1886, was a centennial gift from the French government commemorating the Franco-American alliance during the Revolutionary War. It soon came to be viewed as a symbol of hope for immigrants passing under "Lady Liberty." In the base of the statue, workers had chiseled the poet Emma Lazarus's tribute to the promise of new life in America:

> Give me your tired, your poor,
> Your huddled masses yearning to breathe free,
> The wretched refuse of your teeming shore.
> Send these, the homeless, tempest-tossed to me,
> I lift my lamp beside the golden door!

In 1892 Ellis Island opened its doors to the "huddled masses" of the world. In 1907, the reception center's busiest year, more than a million new arrivals filtered through the cavernous Great Hall, an average of about 5,000 per day; in one day alone, immigration officials processed some 11,750 arrivals. These were the immigrants who traveled crammed into the steerage compartments of ship hulls. Those immigrants who could afford first- and second-class cabins did not have to visit Ellis Island; they were examined on board ship, and most of them simply walked down the gangway onto the docks in lower Manhattan.

Ellis Island was not a comforting place. Its bureaucratic purpose was to process immigrants, not welcome them. An army of inspectors, doctors, nurses, and public officials questioned, examined, and documented the newcomers. Inspectors asked probing questions: Have you money, relatives, or a job in the United States? Are you a polygamist? An anarchist? Doctors and nurses poked and prodded, searching for any sign of debilitating handicap or infectious disease. All the while, the immigrant worried: "Will they let me in?" Although some who were sick or lame were detained for days or weeks, the vast majority of immigrants received stamps of approval and were on their way after three or four hours. Only 2 percent of the newcomers were denied entry altogether, usually because they were criminals, strikebreakers, anarchists, or carriers of some "loathsome or dangerous contagious disease," such as tuberculosis or trachoma, a contagious eye disease resulting in blindness.

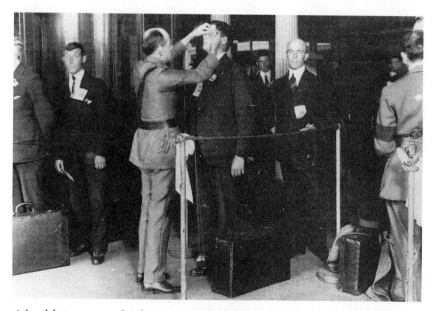

A health inspector checks immigrants on Ellis Island, *1909. Before being granted entry, each immigrant was examined for contagious diseases, including trachoma, an eye disease that could lead to blindness.*

These luckless folk were then returned to their places of origin, with the steamship companies picking up the tab.

Between 1892 and 1954, 70 percent of all European immigrants circulated through Ellis Island. (Others landed at Boston, Philadelphia, Baltimore, New Orleans, and Galveston.) Among the arrivals at Ellis Island were many youngsters who would distinguish themselves in their new country: songwriter Irving Berlin (Russia), football legend Knute Rockne (Norway), Supreme Court justice Felix Frankfurter (Austria), singer Al Jolson (Lithuania), and comedian Bob Hope (England). But many others found America's opportunities harder to grasp.

MAKING THEIR WAY   Once on American soil, the immigrants felt exhilaration, exhaustion, and usually a desperate need for work. Many were greeted by family and friends who had come over before, others by representatives of the many immigrant aid societies or by agents offering the men jobs in mines, mills, and sweatshops. Since most knew little if any English and nothing about American employment practices, the immigrants were easy subjects for exploitation.

In exchange for providing men with a bit of whiskey and a job, obliging recruiters claimed a healthy percentage of their wages. Among Italians and Greeks these agents were known as *padrones,* and they came to dominate the labor market in New York. Other contractors provided train tickets for immigrants to travel inland to jobs in cities such as Buffalo, Pittsburgh, Cleveland, Chicago, Milwaukee, Cincinnati, and St. Louis.

Eager to retain a sense of community and to use the skills they brought with them, the members of ethnic groups tended to cluster in particular vocations. Poles, Hungarians, Slovaks, Bohemians, and Italians used to the pick and shovel flocked to coal mines, just as the Irish, Cornish, and Welsh had done at mid-century; Slavs and Poles comfortable with muscle work gravitated to the steel mills; Greeks preferred working in textile mills; Russian and Polish Jews peopled the sewing trades and pushcart markets of New York. The vast majority of female immigrants found work as domestic servants. Others worked in textile mills or urban "sweatshops." A few determined peasants uprooted from their agricultural heritage made their way west and were able to find work on farms or even a parcel of land for themselves.

Most of the immigrants, however, settled in the teeming cities. Strangers in a new land, they naturally gravitated to neighborhoods populated by their own kind. These immigrant enclaves—nicknamed Little Italy, Little Hungary, Chinatown, and so on—served as crucial transitional communities between the newcomers' Old World past and their New World future. In such kinship communities the immigrants could practice their religions and native customs, converse in their native tongue, and fill an aching loneliness. But they paid a price for such community solidarity. When the "new immigrants" moved into an area, older residents typically moved out, taking with them whatever social prestige and political influence they had achieved. The quality of living quickly deteriorated as housing and sanitation codes then went unenforced.

THE NATIVIST RESPONSE   Many Americans of longer standing saw the new immigration as a threat, and the undercurrent of nativism so often present in American culture surfaced during the late nineteenth century, mainly in anti-Catholic and anti-Semitic sentiments. But more than religious prejudice underlay hostility toward the latest newcomers. Cultural differences confirmed in the minds of nativists the assumption that the Nordic peoples of the old immigration were superior to the Slavic and Latin peoples of the new immigration. Many of the new immigrants were illiterate, and more appeared so because they could not speak English. Some resorted to crime in order to survive in the new land, and political and social radicals turned up among these immigrant groups in sufficient numbers to encourage nativists to blame labor disputes on alien elements.

Nativism led to a movement to restrict immigration, but it had mixed success beyond the exclusion of certain individuals deemed undesirable. In 1891 Representative Henry Cabot Lodge of Massachusetts took up the cause of excluding illiterates—a measure that would have affected much of the new immigration, even though the language of literacy did not have to be English. Several times during the next twenty-five years Congress passed bills embodying the restriction, but they were vetoed by Presidents Cleveland, Taft, and Wilson. In 1917, however, Congress overrode Wilson's veto.

Advocates of immigration restriction during the late nineteenth century did succeed in excluding the Chinese, who were victims of everything the new European immigrants suffered and color prejudice as well. By 1880 there were some 75,000 Chinese in California, about one-ninth of the state's population. Railroad owners found them hardworking and submissive. "They prove nearly equal to white men in the amount of labor they perform," one owner wrote, "and are much more reliable. No danger of strikes among them." Many white workers resented the Chinese for accepting lower wages, but their greater sin, a New York editor stressed, was perpetuating "those disgusting habits of thrift, industry, and self-denial."

Exclusion of the Chinese began in 1880, when the urgent need for railway labor had ebbed. A new treaty with China permitted the United States to "regulate, limit, and suspend" Chinese immigration, and in 1882 President Chester Arthur signed a bill authorizing a ten-year suspension of Chinese immigration. The legislation closing the doors to Chinese immigrants received overwhelming support. One congressman explained that because the "industrial army of Asiatic laborers" was increasing the tension between workers and management in the American economy, "the gate must be closed." The Chinese Exclusion Act was periodically renewed before being extended indefinitely in 1902. Not until 1943 were such barriers to Chinese immigration finally removed.

The West Coast counterpart to Ellis Island was the Immigration Station on rugged Angel Island, six miles offshore from San Francisco. Opened in 1910, it served as a processing center for tens of thousands of Asian immigrants, most of them Chinese. Although the Chinese Exclusion Act had sharply reduced the flow of Chinese immigrants, it did not stop the influx completely. Those arrivals who could claim a Chinese-American parent were allowed to enter, as were certain officials, teachers, merchants, and students. The powerful prejudice the Chinese immigrants encountered helps explain why over 30 percent of the arrivals at Angel Island were denied entry. Those who appealed such denials were housed in prisonlike barracks for weeks or months. One of the detainees scratched a moving poem on the wall:

> This place is called an island of immortals,
> When, in fact, this mountainous wilderness is a prison.
> Once you see the open net, why throw yourself in?
> It is only because of empty pockets. I can do nothing else.

Popular Culture

As more people moved to large towns and cities, the urban environment created new patterns of recreation and leisure. Whereas people in rural areas were tied into the rituals of the harvest season and intimately connected to their neighbors and extended families, most middle-class urban whites were mobile and lived in nuclear families (made up of only parents and children), and their affluence enabled them to enjoy greater leisure time and rising discretionary income.

Middle- and upper-class urban families spent much of their leisure time together at home, usually in the parlor, singing around the piano, reading novels, or playing cards, dominoes, backgammon, chess, and checkers. A new invention called the "stereopticon" was all the rage. It was a hand-held device that placed several photographs or paintings at facing angles to one another. When looked at through binocular glasses, it gave the appearance of three-dimensional views.

Where social and economic conditions remained the same as in earlier periods, popular culture remained much the same. For example, most blacks continued to live in rural areas and operated within extended family networks that included cousins, aunts, uncles, and other relatives who provided assistance and emotional support. Popular culture in rural areas included many traditional forms of entertainment, centered on the family and the planting and harvesting of crops, or the arrival of an itinerant evangelist intent upon conducting a revival or camp meeting.

In the towns and cities, however, people were not as dependent upon mobile ministers or harvest rituals and festivities, and popular culture took on new or greatly expanded dimensions that endowed life with a more cosmopolitan quality. For example, traveling circuses brought entertainment to large cities and small towns. Creative promoters such as Phineas T. Barnum and James A. Bailey made the circus the most eclectic form of entertainment. The midwestern writer Hamlin Garland recalled how the circus came to rural hamlets "trailing clouds of glorified dust and filling our minds with the color of romance. . . . It brought to our ears the latest band pieces and taught us the popular songs. It furnished us with jokes. It relieved our dullness. It gave us something to talk about."

In the congested metropolitan areas, politics became as much a form of public entertainment as it was a process of providing civic representation and public services. People flocked to hear visiting candidates give speeches in cavernous halls, outdoor plazas, or from railway cars. Huge crowds regularly attended political rallies, and membership in a political party in cities such as New York, Philadelphia, Boston, and Chicago was akin to belonging to a social club. In addition, labor unions also included activities that were more social than economic in nature, and members often visited the union hall as much to socialize as to discuss working conditions. The sheer numbers of people congregated in cities also helped generate a market for new forms of mass entertainment such as traveling Wild West shows, vaudeville shows, and spectator sports.

WILD WEST SHOWS   One of the touring extravaganzas that enjoyed incredible popularity during the last quarter of the nineteenth century was "Buffalo Bill's Wild West" traveling show. William "Buffalo Bill" Cody was a rugged frontiersman and sharpshooter. Born in Iowa and raised in Kansas, he became a rider for the Pony Express in 1860 and later served as a Union scout during the Civil War. After the war, he

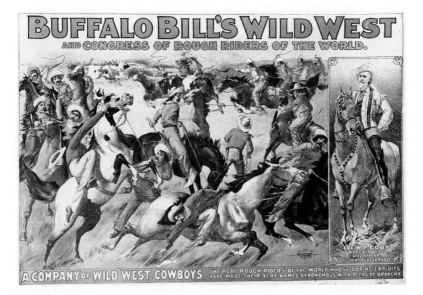

Buffalo Bill's Wild West Show. *Although the shows included geniune cowboys and authentic Indians, they romanticized the American West.*

operated a hotel and a freight business, but Indians captured his wagons and horses. He thereafter became a renowned buffalo hunter, providing meat for the crews building railroads. His hunting ability earned him the nickname Buffalo Bill. From 1868 to 1872, Cody served as a scout for army troops and was awarded the Congressional Medal of Honor after a ferocious battle with Indians on the Platte River. Four years later, he participated in a skirmish with Cheyennes during which he killed and scalped a young chief, Yellow Hand.

Cody's exploits attracted the attention of writer Ned Buntline, who wrote a series of popular novels that brought international celebrity to Buffalo Bill. Always alert to financial opportunity and ever eager to exaggerate his own accomplishments, Cody took advantage of his popularity to organize a stage show. By 1883 he had broadened its scope into a traveling spectacle that included live elk and buffalo, hundreds of horses, genuine cowboys, authentic Indians, rope tricks, shooting exhibitions, cowgirl Annie Oakley, and Cody himself as the star attraction.

Indians were prominently featured in the show. In 1885 Cody hired Sitting Bull, the most famous Indian chief, to ride around the arena and sign autographs. One advertisement promised "a horde of warpainted Arapahoes, Cheyenne, and Sioux Indians." Their role in the show was to stage attacks on wagon trains and stagecoaches, as well as to reenact the battle between Indians and soldiers in George Custer's last stand at the Little Bighorn. The Indians were always portrayed as the aggressors, and the whites as the victims. These images of murderous Indians attacking helpless whites set in motion the mythic depiction of the West that later became the staple of television and movie Westerns.

For three decades, this outdoor spectacle crisscrossed the United States and the world. The Wild West shows visited metropolises such as Chicago and New York as well as smaller cities—Oakland, Memphis, and Raleigh. The shows could accommodate up to twenty thousand people for each performance and promised to present "actual scenes and genuine characters" from the West. When Buffalo Bill died in 1917, his shows died with him, but he bequeathed to Americans a new form of entertainment that has since taken deep root: the rodeo.

VAUDEVILLE Growing family incomes and innovations in urban transportation—cable cars, subways, electric streetcars and streetlights—

enabled more people to take advantage of urban cultural life. Attendance at theaters, operas, and dance halls soared. Those who were interested in serious music could attend symphony concerts by orchestras that were appearing in every major city by the end of the nineteenth century.

But by far the most popular—and diverse—form of theatrical entertainment in the late nineteenth century was known as vaudeville. The term derives from a French word meaning a play accompanied by music. It emerged in the United States in saloons whose owners wanted to attract more customers by offering free shows.

Vaudeville "variety" shows featured comedians, singers, musicians, blackface minstrels, farcical plays, animal acts, jugglers, gymnasts, dancers, mimes, and magicians. Because variety shows were held in seedy beer halls populated by drunks and prostitutes and because the entertainers often included vulgar material, they quickly developed a bad reputation. To combat such an image so as to encourage families to attend, promoters of variety shows built elegant new theaters, banned alcoholic beverages, upgraded the performers, hired policemen and bouncers to handle "rowdies," and began to use the more elegant French word "vaudeville" to describe the genre.

Vaudeville houses sprouted like mushrooms in cities across the United States in the 1870s and 1880s. They quickly became popular gathering places for all social classes and types—men, women, and children—all of whom were expected to behave according to middle-class standards of gentility and decorum. Ushers walked the aisles and handed out cards to unruly patrons. One of them read: "Gentlemen will kindly avoid the stamping of feet and pounding of canes on the floor, and greatly oblige the Management. All applause is best shown by clapping of hands." Raucous cheering, booing, and tobacco spitting were expressly prohibited. The diverse vaudeville shows would run all day and well into the night. They included something to please every taste and, as such, reflected the heterogeneity of city life. To commemorate the opening of a palatial new Boston theater in 1894, an actress read a dedicatory poem in which she announced that "All are equals here." The vaudeville house was the people's theater; it knew "no favorites, no class." She promised the spectators that the producers would "ever seek the new" in providing entertainers who epitomized "the spice of life, Variety," with its motto, "ever to please—and never to offend."

OUTDOOR RECREATION   The congestion and diseases associated with metropolitan life led many people to participate in forms of outdoor recreation intended to restore their vitality and improve their health. People sought places within the city to escape the tenements and factories and offices, and New York City in the 1850s set up a park commission, which hired Frederick Law Olmsted to design and plan Central Park. Olmsted viewed city parks as much more than recreational centers; he sought to create oases of culture that would promote social stability and cohesion. He was convinced that Central Park would exercise "a distinctly harmonizing and refining influence upon the most unfortunate and lawless classes of the city—an influence favorable to courtesy, self-control, and temperance." Olmsted went on to design parks for Boston, Brooklyn, Chicago, Philadelphia, and San Francisco.

Although originally intended as places where people could walk and commune with nature, the parks soon offered more vigorous forms of exercise and recreation—for men and women. During most of the nineteenth century, prevailing social attitudes scoffed at the notion of proper young women participating in even the lightest athletic endeavors. Women were deemed too delicate for such behavior. Before the Civil War, women essentially had only one exercise option: pedestrianism, the formal title for outdoor walking. After the war, however, the growing number of women enrolled in colleges began to participate in physical education, and they in turn demanded access to more vigorous sports.

Croquet and tennis courts were among the first additions to city parks because they took up little space and required little maintenance. Croquet was born in the British Isles in the mid–nineteenth century and soon migrated to most other English-speaking countries. Because croquet could be played by both sexes, it combined the virtues of sport with the opportunities of courtship. Croquet as a public sport suffered a setback in the 1890s, however, when Boston clergymen lambasted the drinking, gambling, and licentious behavior associated with it on the Boston Common, where croquet matches were held.

Lawn tennis was invented by an Englishman in 1873 and arrived in the United States a year later. By 1885 Central Park had thirty courts. Lawn tennis was originally viewed as a leisurely sport best suited for women. The Harvard student newspaper declared in 1878 that the sport was "well enough for a lazy or *weak* man, but men who have rowed or taken part in a nobler sport should blush to be seen playing Lawn Tennis."

Even more popular than croquet or tennis was cycling or "wheeling." In the 1870s, bicycles began to be manufactured in the United States, and by the end of the century, a "bicycle craze" had swept the country. The first bicycles were called "high-wheelers" or "boneshakers" because the front wheel was huge, as much as five feet high, while the rear wheel was tiny, no more than a foot in diameter. The high-wheelers were hard to ride, uncomfortable, and dangerous, as they had no brakes. During the 1880s, an Englishman named J. K. Starley produced the first "safety bicycle." These bicycles had wheels of equal size and axles with ball bearings, which made them easier and safer to ride than high-wheelers. By 1890, bicycles had air-filled rubber tires and brakes. Millions of middle-class Americans (who could afford the new invention) discovered a new mobility and freedom through the bicycle, which

Tandem Tricycle. *In spite of the danger and discomfort of early bicycles, wheeling became a popular form of recreation and mode of transportation.*

had few of the drawbacks of horses. Bicycles went where pointed, did not need to be fed, and did not leave droppings in the road.

Bicycles were especially popular with women who chafed at the restricting conventions of Victorianism. The new vehicles offered exercise, freedom, and access to the countryside. Female cyclists were able to discard their cumbersome corsets and full dresses in favor of bloomers and split skirts. Critics feared that the bicycle mania was encouraging young women to grow independent and shun conventional domestic responsibilities. Some guardians of morality believed that cycling was also sexually provocative. In 1899 the Reverend W. W. Reynolds expressed outrage because a "large number of female bicyclists wear shorter dresses than the laws of morality and decency permit, thereby inviting the improper conversations and remarks of the depraved and immoral." He found cycling "detrimental to the advancement of morality."

The working poor in the cities could not afford to acquire a bicycle or join a croquet club. Nor did they have as much free time as the affluent. They toiled long hours, six days a week, and at the end of their long days they eagerly sought recreation and fellowship on street corners or on the front stoops of their apartment buildings. Organ grinders and musicians would perform on the sidewalks among the food vendors. Those with a few extra dollars to spend frequented the saloons and dance halls available in each city. In 1900 New York City alone had 10,000 saloons featuring five-cent beer and free lunch. In the late nineteenth century, saloons often doubled as gymnasiums. Back rooms housed handball courts, pool tables, bowling alleys, and dart boards.

Many ethnic groups, especially the Germans and the Irish, formed male singing, drinking, or gymnastic clubs. Working folk also attended bare-knuckle boxing matches or baseball games, and on Sundays they would gather for picnics. By the end of the century, large-scale amusement parks such as New York's Luna Park on Coney Island provided entertainment for the entire family. Yet many inner-city youth could not afford the trolley fare to visit a suburban amusement park, so the crowded streets and dangerous alleys became their playgrounds.

SPECTATOR SPORTS   In the last quarter of the nineteenth century, horse racing and prizefighting remained popular, but team sports also began to attract legions of fans. New spectator sports such as college football and basketball and professional baseball gained mass popularity, reflecting the growing urbanization of American life. People could gather easily for sporting events in the large cities. And news of the games could be conveyed quickly by newspapers and specialized sporting magazines relying upon telegraph reports. Saloons also posted the scores. Athletic rivalries between distant cities were made possible by the network of railroads spanning the continent and facilitating team travel. Spectator sports became urban extravaganzas, unifying the diverse ethnic groups in the large cities and attracting people with the leisure time and ready cash to spend (or bet) on watching others perform.

Football emerged as a modified form of soccer and rugby. The College of New Jersey (Princeton) and Rutgers played the first college football game in 1869. Soon 200 students and spectators saw Rutgers win 6–4. The teams at first used twenty-five players at a time, and players literally kicked the ball along the ground. By 1880, the number of players had been reduced to eleven, and they carried the ball rather than kicking it. The players wore no protective padding or headgear, and the games often resembled organized fights. In fact, advocates of football portrayed it as a "blood sport" that provided a modern substitute for the frontier experience.

By the end of the century, scores of colleges and high schools had started football teams, and some college games attracted more than 50,000 spectators. Early games featured unregulated mayhem, with slugging and kicking commonplace. Scores of players died from injuries. In 1905 alone, 18 players were killed and 150 seriously injured. Gambling on college football games was also widespread, and many college coaches provided cash incentives to lure players to enroll. The president of Cornell University grew so digusted with the evils infecting the sport that he prohibited the football team from playing the University of Michigan squad, refusing to "permit 30 men to travel 4,000 miles to agitate a bag of wind."

Football became so controversial that President Theodore Roosevelt intervened in 1905. He had long promoted strenuous exercise and "rough, manly sports" as antidotes needed by young Americans leading sedentary lives in cities. With the closing of the frontier, he feared that young boys growing up in urban centers would become effeminate and anemic. Roosevelt championed football as a means of instilling in young men the virtues of "pluck, endurance, and physical address," yet he appealed to coaches, professors, and alumni to "come to a gentlemen's agreement not to have mucker play." His appeal did little good, and the roughness and foul play continued. As a result, Columbia University and the Massachusetts Institute of Technology abolished football. Stanford and the University of California replaced it with rugby. In a further effort to curb injuries and abuses, the National Collegiate Athletics Association (NCAA) was founded in 1910.

Basketball was invented in 1891 when Dr. James Naismith, a physical education instructor, nailed two peach baskets to the walls of the YMCA training school in Springfield, Massachusetts. Naismith wanted to create an indoor winter game that could be played between the fall football and spring baseball seasons. The baskets were ten feet high because that was the height of the balcony at each end of the gym to which the baskets were attached. The first game had nine men on a side, and they used a soccer ball. Basketball quickly grew in popularity among both boys and girls. Vassar and Smith Colleges added the sport in 1892. In 1893, Vanderbilt became the first college to field a men's team.

Baseball laid claim to being America's national pastime at mid-century. Contrary to popular opinion, Abner Doubleday did not invent the game. Instead, Alexander Cartwright, a New York bank clerk and sportsman, is recognized as the father of organized baseball. In 1845 he gathered a group of merchants, stockbrokers, and physicians to form the Knickerbocker Base Ball Club of New York. They began playing a bat-and-ball game on a field at the corner of Twenty-seventh Street and Fourth Avenue in Manhattan. Soon they moved to a field in Hoboken, New Jersey. After their games, they would gather at a nearby hotel bar. There they drafted a list of rules that included setting the bases 90 feet apart and allocating nine players to a side. Initially the pitcher stood 45 feet from home plate and threw the ball underhanded. Three strikes resulted in an out, but the batter had to take three swings. There were no called strikes.

The first professional baseball team was the Cincinnati Red Stockings, which made its appearance in 1869. Seven years later, seven other teams joined the Red Stockings in creating the National League. Reporters began to cover the games, and sports sections appeared in every newspaper. Professionalization brought changes in the sport. Umpires

Professional Baseball Game, 1887. *The excitement of rooting for the home team united all classes as they watched the athletes who graced the playing field.*

were added to call balls, strikes, and outs; pitchers threw overhand rather than underhand; fielders began to use gloves; catchers donned protective equipment. Other changes in the late nineteenth century included the addition of a "walk" after four balls and fixing the distance from the pitcher to home plate at 60 feet 6 inches. In 1901 the American League was organized, and two years later the first World Series was held.

Baseball became the "national pastime" and the most democratic sport in America. People from all social classes (mostly men) attended the games, and ethnic immigrants were among the most faithful fans. The *St. Louis Post-Dispatch* reported in 1883 that "a glance at the audience on any fine day at the ball park will reveal . . . telegraph operators, printers who work at night, travelling men [salesmen] . . . men of leisure . . . men of capital, bank clerks who get away [from work] at 3 P.M., real estate men . . . barkeepers . . . hotel clerks, actors and employees of the theater, policemen and firemen on their day off . . . butchers and bakers." Cheering for a city baseball team gave rootless people a common loyalty and a sense of belonging.

Only white players were allowed in the major leagues. African Americans played on "minor league" teams or in all-black "Negro leagues." In 1867 the National Association of Base Ball Players excluded black clubs from membership. And the National League followed suit when it was organized nine years later. In 1887 black players were banned from minor league teams as well. That same year, the Cuban Giants, a barnstorming team made up of black players, traveled the country. A few major league white teams agreed to play them. An African-American-owned newspaper announced in early 1888 that the Cuban Giants "have defeated the New Yorks, 4 games out of 5, and are now virtually champions of the world." But it added, "the St. Louis Browns, Detroits and Chicagos, afflicted by Negrophobia and unable to bear the odium of being beaten by colored men, refused to accept their challenge."

By the end of the nineteenth century, sports of all kinds had become a major cultural phenomenon in the United States. A writer in *Harper's Weekly* announced in 1895 that "ball matches, football games, tennis tournaments, bicycle races, [and] regattas, have become part of our national life." They "are watched with eagerness and discussed with enthusiasm and understanding by all manner of people, from the day-laborer to the millionaire." One reporter in the 1890s referred to the "athletic craze" that was sweeping the American imagination. Moreover, it was in 1892 that a Frenchman, Pierre de Coubertin, called for the revival of the ancient Olympic games; the first modern olympiad was held four years later.

EDUCATION AND THE PROFESSIONS

THE SPREAD OF PUBLIC EDUCATION   The growth of public education, spurred partly by the determination to "Americanize" immigrant children, helped quicken the emergence of a new America after the Civil War. By the 1870s, America's commitment to public education was nearly universal. In 1870 there were 7 million pupils in public schools; by 1920 the number had tripled. Despite such progress, educational leaders had to struggle against a pattern of political appointments, corruption, and incompetence in the public schools.

The spread of secondary schools accounted for much of the increased enrollment in public schools. In antebellum America, private academies had prepared those who intended to enter college. At the beginning of the Civil War, there were only about 100 public high schools in the whole country, but their number grew rapidly to about 800 in 1880 and to 6,000 at the turn of the century.

HIGHER EDUCATION American colleges at this time sought to instill discipline, morality, and a curriculum heavy on mathematics and the classics (and in church schools, theology), along with ethics and rhetoric. History, modern languages and literature, and some science courses were tolerated, although laboratory work was usually limited to a professor's demonstration in class. The college teacher was apt to be a young man seeking temporary refuge, or a broken-down preacher seeking safe harbor. In 1871 one writer called the typical professor "nondescript, a jack of all trades, equally ready to teach surveying and Latin eloquence, and thankful if his quarter's salary is not docked to whitewash the college fence."

Nevertheless, the demand for higher learning drove the college student population up from 52,000 in 1870 to 157,000 in 1890 and to 600,000 in 1920. During the same years, the number of institutions rose from 563 to about 1,000. To accommodate the diverse needs of these growing numbers, colleges moved away from rigidly prescribed courses toward an elective system. The new approach allowed students to favor their strong points and colleges to expand their scope. But as Henry Cabot Lodge complained, it also allowed students to "escape without learning anything at all by a judicious selection of unrelated subjects taken up only because they were easy or because the burden imposed by those who taught them was light."

Women's access to higher education improved markedly in this period. Before the Civil War, a few colleges had already gone coeducational, and state universities in the West were commonly open to women from the start. But colleges in the South and East fell in line very slowly. Vassar (1865) was the first women's college to teach by the same standards as the best of the men's colleges. In 1875 two more excellent women's schools appeared in Massachusetts: Wellesley and Smith, the latter being the first to set the same admission requirements as men's colleges. Thereafter the older women's colleges rushed to upgrade their standards in the same way.

The dominant new trend in American higher education after the

Civil War was the rise of the graduate school. Heretofore, most professors had a knowledge more broad than deep. With some notable exceptions they engaged in little research, nor were they expected to advance the frontiers of knowledge. Gradually, however, more and more American scholars studied at German universities, where training was more systematic and focused. After the Civil War, the German system became the basis for the modern American graduate university. By the 1890s, the Ph.D. was fast becoming the ticket of admission to the guild of professors.

THE RISE OF PROFESSIONALISM   The Ph.D. revolution was but one aspect of a growing emphasis on professionalism, with its imposition of uniform standards, licensing of practitioners, and accreditation of professional schools. The number of professional schools grew rapidly in fields such as theology, law, medicine, dentistry, pharmacy, and veterinary medicine.

Along with advanced schooling went a movement for licensing practitioners in certain fields. During the second half of the nineteenth century, the first state licensing laws were enacted for dentistry, pharmacy, veterinary medicine, accounting, and architecture. Such licensing benefited the public by certifying competence in a given field, but it also benefited members of the profession by controlling the number of practitioners and thereby limiting competition.

REALISM IN THOUGHT, CULTURE, AND LITERATURE

Just as popular culture was transformed as a result of the urban-industrial revolution, so, too, did intellectual life adapt to its incessant demands. Before the Civil War, various forms of idealism dominated American thought. Although quite diverse in motive and method, idealists shared a basic conviction that fundamental truths rested in the unseen world of ideas and spirit or in the distant past rather than in the tangible world of fact and contemporary experience. The most prominent writers, artists, and philosophers were more concerned with romantic or biblical themes than with common aspects of "real" life.

At mid-century and after, however, a more realistic sensibility began to challenge this idealistic tradition. A writer in *Putnam's Monthly* noted in 1854 a growing emphasis in American life on "the real and the practical." This realistic movement matured into a full-fledged cultural force during the second half of the nineteenth century. More and more thinkers and artists focused their attention on the emerging realities of scientific research and technology, factories and railroads, cities and immigrants, wage labor and social tensions.

The rise of realism resulted from a transformed social, intellectual, and moral landscape. The horrors of the Civil War led many people to adopt a more realistic outlook. An editor attending an art exhibition in 1865 sensed "the greater reality of feeling developed by the war. We have grown more sober, perhaps, and less patient of romantic idealism."

Another factor contributing to the rise of realism was the growing impact of a modern scientific outlook that empirical evidence constituted the only admissible basis for knowledge. By producing what one writer called a "mania for facts," a new generation of professional scientists served as the first shock troops for the realistic crusade in thought and the arts. "This is a world of reality," lamented a romantic writer, "and romance breaks against the many hard facts." The idealistic tradition, she claimed, had been displaced by a "scientific age" which valued only "facts that can be seen or heard or weighed or measured."

The prestige of empirical science increased enormously during the second half of the nineteenth century as researchers explored electromagnetic induction, the conservation of matter, the laws of thermodynamics, and the relationship between heat and energy. Breakthroughs in chemistry led to new understandings of the formation of compounds and the nature of reactions. Fossil discoveries opened up new horizons in geology and paleontology, and greatly improved microscopes enabled zoologists to decipher cell structures. The "stupendous power of Science," announced one editor, will rid American thought of "every old-time idea, every trace of old romance and art, poetry and romantic or sentimental feeling" and wash away the "ideal . . . and visionary.

DARWINISM AND SOCIAL DARWINISM   Every field of thought in the post–Civil War years felt the impact of Charles Darwin's *On the Origin of Species* (1859). It argued that existing species, including humanity itself, had evolved through a long process of "natural selection" from less complex forms of life. Those species that adapted to survival by reason of quickness, shrewdness, or other advantages reproduced their kind, while others died away. The idea of species evolution shocked people with conventional religious views by contradicting a literal interpretation of the creation stories in the biblical Book of Genesis. Heated arguments arose among scientists and clergymen. Some of the faithful rejected Darwin's doctrine, while others found their faith severely shaken. Most of the faithful, however, eventually came to reconcile science and religion, viewing evolution as a natural process designed by God.

The pervasive effect of Darwinism in late nineteenth-century American intellectual circles was comparable to the effect of romanticism in the first part of the century. Like the earlier reaction against the Enlightenment's praise of reason, the trend in social thought now was turned against abstract logic and toward concrete reality.

Though Darwin's theory actually applied only to biological phenomena, other thinkers applied its premises and metaphors to human society. In the milieu of Darwinism, for example, the study of history flourished. The historian, like the biologist, studied the process of development, but in the origins and the evolution of society. Under the influence of German scholarship and the new emphasis on science, history aspired to become "scientific." This meant examining documents and manuscripts critically, using external and internal evidence to determine validity and relevancy. The ideal of the scientific historian was to reproduce history with perfect objectivity, a noble if unreachable goal.

The temptation to apply evolutionary theory to the social world proved irresistible. Darwin's fellow Englishman Herbert Spencer became the first major prophet of what came to be called Social Darwinism, and he exerted an important influence on American thought. Spencer argued that human society and institutions, like species, passed throught the process of natural selection, which resulted in what he called the "survival of the fittest."

If, as Spencer believed, society naturally evolved for the better, then individual freedom was inviolable, and any governmental interference with the process of social evolution was a serious mistake. Social Darwinism thus endorsed a hands-off governmental policy, then known as laissez-faire; it decried the regulation of business, the proposals for a graduated income tax, sanitation and housing regulations, and even protection against medical quacks. Such initiatives, no matter how well intended, would only help the "unfit" survive and thereby impede progress. The only acceptable charity was voluntary, and even that was of dubious value. Spencer warned that "fostering the good-for-nothing at the expense of the good, is an extreme cruelty."

For Spencer and his many supporters, successful businessmen and corporations were the engines of social progress. If small businesses were crowded out by trusts and monopolies, that too was part of the evolutionary process. John D. Rockefeller told his Baptist Sunday school class that the "growth of a large business is merely a survival of the fittest."

The ideas of Darwin and Spencer were quickly popularized in America. Their most powerful advocate was William Graham Sumner, a professor at Yale who preached the gospel of natural selection to his classes and in writings such as *What Social Classes Owe to Each Other* and "The Absurd Effort to Make the World Over."

REFORM DARWINISM   The influence of Darwin and Spencer on American intellectuals did not go without challenge. Reform found its major philosopher in an obscure civil servant, Lester Frank Ward, who had fought his way up from poverty and never lost his empathy for the underdog. Ward's book *Dynamic Sociology* (1883) singled out one product of evolution that Spencer and others had neglected, the human brain. Humans, unlike animals, had a mind that could plan for and shape the future. Far from being the helpless pawn of powerful evolutionary forces, Ward argued, humanity could actively shape the process of evolution. The competition extolled by Sumner, Spencer, and other Social Darwinists was in fact highly wasteful, and so was the natural competitive process: plant or cattle breeding, for instance, could actually improve on the results of natural selection.

Ward's Reform Darwinism challenged Sumner's conservative Social Darwinism, holding that cooperation, not competition, would better promote progress. Government could become the agency of progress by striving to ameliorate poverty, which impeded the development of the mind, and to promote the education of the masses. "Intelligence, far more than necessity," Ward wrote, "is the mother of invention," and "the influence of knowledge as a social factor, like that of wealth, is proportional to the extent of its distribution." Intellect, rightly informed by science, could plan successfully. In the benevolent "sociocracy" of the future, Ward argued, legislatures would function mainly to sanction decisions worked out in the sociological laboratory.

PRAGMATISM Around the turn of the century, the evolutionary idea found expression in a philosophical principle set forth in mature form by William James in his book *Pragmatism: A New Name for Some Old Ways of Thinking.* James, a professor of philosophy and psychology at Harvard, shared Lester Frank Ward's concern with the role of ideas in the process of evolution. Truth, to James, arose from the testing of new ideas, the value of which lay in their practical consequences. Similarly, scientists could test the validity of their ideas in the laboratory and judge their import by their applications. Pragmatism thus reflected a quality often looked upon as genuinely American: the inventive, experimental spirit focusing on tangible results.

John Dewey, who would become the chief philosopher of pragmatism after James, preferred the term "instrumentalism," by which he meant that ideas were instruments of practical use, especially for promoting social reform. Dewey, unlike James, threw himself into movements for the rights of labor and women, the promotion of peace, and the reform of education. He believed that education was the process through which society would gradually progress toward greater social equality and harmony. Dewey became the prophet of what was later labeled "progressive education," which emphasized the teaching of history, geography, and science in order to enlarge the child's personal experience. Dewey also pointed out that social conditions had so changed that schools now had to find ways to inculcate values once derived from participation in family and community activities.

THE LOCAL COLORISTS Writers of American fiction in this period also sought new ways to capture concrete reality, present and past. What came to be called the local color movement expressed the nostalgia of a people for places where old values and folkways survived. Sarah Orne Jewett depicted the down-easters of her native Maine most enduring in the stories and sketches collected in *The Country of the Pointed Firs* (1896). Jewett's creative glance was always backward-looking and affectionate, as she identified more with her forebears than her peers.

This local color impulse was not limited to New England. Once the passions of war and Reconstruction were spent, the South became for many northern readers an inexhaustible gallery of quaint types and picturesque settings. George Washington Cable exploited the local color of the quaint Louisiana Creoles and Cajuns in *Old Creole Days* (1879), *The Grandissimes* (1880), and other books. Joel Chandler Harris, a white newsman and columnist, wove authentic African-American folk tales into the unforgettable stories of Uncle Remus.

CLEMENS, HOWELLS, AND JAMES   The best of the local colorists could find universal truths in local life, and Samuel Langhorne Clemens (Mark Twain) transcended them all. A native of Missouri, he was forced to work at age twelve, becoming first a printer and then a Mississippi riverboat pilot. When the Civil War shut down the river traffic, he briefly joined a Confederate militia company, then left with his brother for Nevada, where he wrote for a local newspaper. He moved on to California in 1864 and first gained widespread notice with his tall tale of the gold country, "The Celebrated Jumping Frog of Calaveras County" (1865). With the success of *Roughing It* (1871), an account of his western years, he moved to Hartford, Connecticut, and was able to set up as a full-time author and hilarious lecturer.

Clemens was the first significant American writer born and raised west of the Appalachians. His early writings accentuated his western background, but for his greatest books he drew heavily upon his boyhood in the border slave state of Missouri and the tall-tale tradition of southwestern humor. In *The Adventures of Tom Sawyer* (1876) he evoked the prewar Hannibal, Missouri, where his own boyhood was cut so short. Its story of childhood adventures is firmly etched on the American memory. *Life on the Mississippi* (1882), based on articles written eight years before, drew upon what Clemens remembered as his happiest days as a young riverboat pilot before the war. His pseudonym, "Mark Twain," was in fact derived from a phrase that referred to the depth of the river.

Clemens's masterpiece, *The Adventures of Huckleberry Finn* (1884), created unforgettable characters in Huck Finn, his shiftless father, the runaway slave Jim, the Widow Douglas, the "King," and the "Duke." Huck Finn embodied the instinct of every red-blooded American boy to "light out for the territory" whenever polite society set out to civilize him. Huck's effort to help his friend Jim escape bondage expressed well the moral dilemmas imposed by slavery on everyone. One of Clemens's foremost supporters was his close friend William Dean Howells, who wrote "Clemens was sole, incomparable, the Lincoln of our literature."

During the half century after the Civil War, Howells dominated the American literary scene. As editor of the influential *Atlantic Monthly* and later a columnist and critic for *Harper's Monthly,* Howells preached and practiced the new doctrine of realism, a literary rebellion against romantic idealism that sought to portray with scientific accuracy the contemporary social scene. He wrote that realism "was nothing more or less than the truthful treatment of . . . the motives, the impulses, the principles that shape the life of actual men and women."

To this end, Howells wrote novels, plays, travel books, criticism, essays, biography, and autobiography. Amid the varied output of a long and productive life, *The Rise of Silas Lapham* (1885) stands out as his most famous novel. In it Howells presented a sympathetic portrayal of a newly rich manufacturer from the West, and one of the earliest fictional treatments of an American businessman.

The third major literary figure of the times, Henry James, moved in a world far different from that of Clemens or Howells. Brother of the pragmatist philosopher William James and son of wealthy parents, Henry spent most of his adult life as a voluntary expatriate in London, where he produced elegant novels that for the first time explored the international society of Americans in Europe. In works such as *Portrait of a Lady* (1881), *The Ambassadors* (1903), and *The Golden Bowl* (1904), James explored the tensions that developed between direct, innocent, and idealistic Americans (most often young women) and sophisticated, devious Europeans. Unlike Clemens, James typically wrote of the cosmopolitan upper class, and his stories turned less on plot than on moral dilemmas. His intense exploration of the inner selves of his characters brought him the title of "father of the psychological novel."

LITERARY NATURALISM   Realism grew into a powerful literary movement during the 1880s, but during the 1890s it took on a new character in the writings of the so-called naturalists. This group of younger writers sought to integrate scientific determinism into literature. Having grown up in the era of Darwin and Spencer, they viewed humankind as prey to natural forces and internal drives without control or full knowledge of them. Frank Norris thus pictured in *McTeague* (1899) the descent of a San Francisco dentist and his wife into madness, driven by greed, violence, and lust. Stephen Crane in *Maggie: A Girl of the Streets* (1893) and *The Red Badge of Courage* (1895) portrayed people caught up in environmental situations beyond their control. *Maggie* depicted a tenement girl driven to prostitution and death amid scenes so grim and sordid that Crane had to finance publication himself. *The Red Badge of Courage,* his masterpiece, told the story of a young man going through his baptism of fire in the Civil War, and evoked fear, nobility, and courage amid the carnage of war.

Two of the naturalists, Jack London and Theodore Dreiser, achieved a degree of popular success. London was both a professed socialist and a believer in the German philosopher Friedrich Nietzsche's doctrine of the superman. In adventure stories such as *The Call of the Wild* (1903) and *The Sea Wolf* (1904), he celebrated the triumph of brute force and the will to survive.

Theodore Dreiser did not celebrate the overwhelming power of social and biological forces; he dissected them for the reader. The result was powerfully disturbing to readers accustomed to more genteel fare. Dreiser shocked the public probably more than the others with protagonists who sinned without remorse and without punishment. *Sister Carrie* (1900), for example, showed Carrie Meeber surviving illicit loves and going on to success on the stage.

SOCIAL CRITICISM   Behind their dogma of determinism, several of the naturalists harbored intense outrage at human misery. Their indignation was shared by an increasing number of journalists and social critics who addressed themselves more directly to protest and reform. One of the most influential of these reformers was Henry George, a journalist who vowed to seek out the cause of poverty in the midst of the industrial progress he saw around him. The basic social problem, George reasoned, was the unearned increment in wealth that came to those who owned the land. He wrote down the fruit of his thought in *Progress and Poverty* (1879), a thick, rambling, and difficult book whose earnest moralism and sympathetic tone helped it sell about 2 million copies in several languages.

George held that everyone had a basic right to the use of the land, since it was provided by nature to all. Nobody had a right to the increasing value that accrued from the land, since that was created by the community, not by its owner. Labor and capital, on the other hand, did have a just claim on the wealth they produced. He proposed simply to tax the unearned increment in the value of the land, or the rent. George's "single-tax" idea was intended to free capital and labor from paying tribute for the land, and to put to use lands previously held out of production by speculators. George's idea provoked much discussion and actually affected local tax policy here and there, but his influence on the thinking of the day came less from his "single-tax" panacea than from the paradox he posed in his title *Progress and Poverty,* and his plea for social cooperation and equality.

The journalist and freelance writer Henry Demarest Lloyd, son of a minister, addressed himself to what many found a more vital issue than Henry George's, not the monopoly in land but in industry. His best-known book, *Wealth Against Commonwealth* (1894), drew on more than a decade of studying the Standard Oil Company. Lloyd, like George and Lester Frank Ward, saw the key to social progress in cooperation rather than competition. Economic activities in their cooperative aspects demonstrated a civilizing process, he argued. The cooperative principle should be applied "to all toils in which private sovereignty has become through monopoly a despotism over the public." Where monopoly had developed, it should be transferred to public operation in the public interest. In 1903, just before his death, Lloyd joined the Socialist party.

Thorstein Veblen brought to his social criticism a background of formal training in economics and a purpose of making economics more an evolutionary or historical science. By all accounts he taught miserably, even inaudibly, and seldom held a job for long, but he wrote brilliantly. In his best known work, *The Theory of the Leisure Class* (1899), he examined the pecuniary values of the affluent and introduced phrases that have since become commonplace in our language: "conspicuous consumption" and "conspicuous leisure." With the advent of industrial society, Veblen argued, the showy display of money and property became the conventional basis of status. For the upper classes, moreover, it became necessary to spend time casually as evidence of the ability to afford a life of leisure.

THE SOCIAL GOSPEL

While novelists, journalists, and commentators were writing about the rising social tensions and injustices of late-nineteenth-century America, more and more people were addressing these problems through direct social action. Some reformers focused on legislative solutions to social problems; others stressed philanthropy or organized charity. A few militants promoted socialism or anarchism. Whatever the method or approach, however, social reformers were on the march at the turn of the century, and their activities gave to American life a new urgency and energy.

RISE OF THE INSTITUTIONAL CHURCH   The churches responded slowly to the mounting social criticism, for American Protestantism had become one of the main props of the established order. The Reverend Henry Ward Beecher, for instance, pastor of the fashionable Plymouth Congregational Church in Brooklyn, preached material success, Social Darwinism, and the unworthiness of the poor.

As the middle classes moved out to the streetcar suburbs, their churches followed. In the years 1868–1888, for instance, seventeen Protestant churches abandoned the areas south of Fourteenth Street in Manhattan. In the center of Chicago 60,000 residents had no church, Protestant or Catholic. Where churches became prosperous they fell under the spell of complacent respectability and do-nothing Social Darwinism. Some prominent clergymen expressed open disdain for the lower classes. De Witt Talmage, an outspoken Presbyterian minister in Brooklyn, stressed that he wanted no working men stinking up his church. "If you are going to kill the church thus with bad smells, I will have nothing to do with this work of evangelization." Not surprisingly, more and more working-class people felt out of place in churches where affluence was both worshipped and flaunted.

But gradually some religious leaders realized that Protestantism was in danger of losing its working-class constituency unless it reached out to the urban poor. Two organizations were created expressly for that purpose. The Young Men's Christian Association (YMCA) had entered the United States from England in the 1850s and grew rapidly after 1870; the Salvation Army, founded in London in 1876, entered the

United States four years later. Individual urban churches also began to develop institutional features that were more social than strictly religious in function. Church leaders acquired gymnasiums, libraries, lecture rooms, and other facilities in an effort to attract working-class people back to organized religion.

RELIGIOUS REFORMERS   Some church reformers who feared that Christianity was becoming irrelevant to the needs and aspirations of the working poor began preaching what came to be called the social gospel. One of the earliest, Washington Gladden of Columbus, Ohio, managed to profess the social gospel from the pulpit of a middle-class Congregational church. The new gospel in fact expressed the social conscience of the middle class. Gladden maintained that true Christianity resided not in rituals, dogmas, or even in the mystical experience of God, but in the principle that "Thou shalt love thy neighbor as thyself." Christian law should therefore govern the workplace, with laborer and employer united in serving each other's interest. The "law of greed and strife," he insisted, "is not a natural law; it is unnatural; it is a crime against nature; the law of brotherhood is the only natural law." He thus argued for labor's right to organize, supported maximum-hours laws and factory inspections, and endorsed antitrust legislation.

A Salvation Army group in Flint, Michigan, 1894.

THE CATHOLIC CHURCH   In the post–Civil War years Catholic social thought was initially quite conservative. Papal decrees declared erroneous such current ideas as progress, liberalism, rationalism, and socialism, and warned American Catholics against supporting the new social movements. The Vatican's outlook altered drastically in 1891, when Pope Leo XIII issued his encyclical, *Rerum novarum* ("Of modern things"). This new expression of Catholic social doctrine upheld private property as a natural right but condemned capitalism where it had imposed poverty and degradation on workers. It also affirmed the right of Catholics to join labor unions and socialist movements insofar as these were not antireligious. But American Catholics for the most part remained isolated from organized reform movements until the twentieth century, though they themselves were among the most abused victims of urban slums.

EARLY EFFORTS AT URBAN REFORM

THE SETTLEMENT HOUSE MOVEMENT   While preachers of the social gospel dispensed inspiration, other dedicated reformers attacked the problems of the slums from residential and community centers called settlement houses. By 1900 perhaps a hundred settlement houses existed in America, some of the best known being Jane Addams and Ellen Starr's Hull House in Chicago and Lillian Wald's Henry Street Settlement in New York.

The settlement houses were staffed mainly by idealistic middle-class young people, a majority of them college-trained women who had few other outlets for meaningful work. Settlement workers sought to broaden the horizons and improve the lives of slum dwellers in diverse ways. At Hull House, for instance, workers sought to draw the neighborhood children into clubs, kindergartens, and a nursery, which served the infant children of working mothers. Settlement houses were also meant to provide workingmen an alternative to the saloon as a place of recreation and an alternative to the political boss as a source of social services. Their programs gradually expanded to include health clinics, lectures, music and art studios, employment bureaus, men's clubs, training in skills such as bookbinding, gymnasiums, and savings banks.

Addams and other settlement house leaders realized, however, that the spreading slums made their work as effective as bailing out the ocean with a teaspoon. They therefore organized political support for housing laws, public playgrounds, juvenile courts, mothers' pensions, workers' compensation laws, and legislation against child labor. Julia Lathrop, another Hull House staffer, was appointed in 1912 the first head of the federal Children's Bureau, an agency designed to scrutinize the use and abuse of child labor.

WOMEN'S EMPLOYMENT AND SUFFRAGE　Settlement house workers, insofar as they were paid, made up but a fraction of all gainfully employed women. With rapid population growth in the late nineteenth century the number of employed women steadily increased, as did their percentage of the labor force. The greatest leaps forward came in the decades of the 1880s and the 1900s, both of which were also peak decades of immigration, a correlation that can be explained by the immigrants' need for income. The number of employed women doubled from 1880 to 1900 and then doubled again by 1910. Through all those years, domestic work remained the largest category of employment for women; teaching and nursing also remained among the leading fields. The main change was that clerical work (bookkeeping, stenographic work, and the like) and sales jobs became increasingly available to women.

Jane Addams.

These changes in occupational status had little connection with the women's rights movement, which increasingly focused on the issue of suffrage. Immediately after the Civil War, Susan B. Anthony, a seasoned veteran of the movement, demanded that the Fourteenth Amendment guarantee the vote for women as well as black males. She made little impression on the defenders of masculine prerogative, however, who insisted that women belonged solely in the home. "Their mission is at home, by their blandishments and their love to assuage the passions of men as they come in from the battle of life. . . ." said a New Jersey senator.

In 1869 the unity of the women's movement disintegrated in a manner reminiscent of the antislavery rift three decades before. The question once again was whether the movement should concentrate on one overriding issue or broaden its focus. Anthony and Elizabeth Cady Stanton founded the National Woman Suffrage Association to promote a woman suffrage amendment to the Constitution, but they looked upon suffrage as but one among many feminist causes to be promoted. Later that same year, Lucy Stone, Julia Ward Howe, and other leaders formed the American Woman Suffrage Association, which focused single-mindedly on the vote as the first and basic reform.

The long struggle for state legislation on the suffrage issue focused the women's cause even more on the primary objective of the vote. In 1890, after three years of negotiation, the rival groups united as the National American Woman Suffrage Association, with Elizabeth Cady Stanton as president for two years, followed by Susan B. Anthony until 1900. The work thereafter was carried on by a new generation led by Anna Howard Shaw and Carrie Chapman Catt. Over the years, the movement slogged its way to some local and some partial victories, as a few states granted woman suffrage in school board or municipal elections. In 1869 the Territory of Wyoming provided full suffrage to women, and after 1890 retained women's suffrage when it became a new state. Three other western states soon followed suit, but not until New York acted in 1917 did a state east of the Mississippi adopt universal suffrage.

Despite the focus on the vote, women did not confine their public work to that issue. In 1866 a Young Women's Christian Association, a parallel to the YMCA, appeared in Boston and spread elsewhere. The New England Women's Club, started in 1868 by Julia Ward Howe and

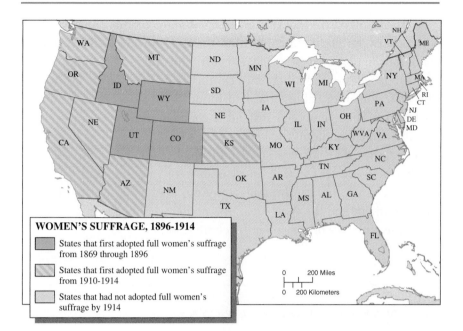

WOMEN'S SUFFRAGE, 1896-1914

States that first adopted full women's suffrage from 1869 through 1896

States that first adopted full women's suffrage from 1910-1914

States that had not adopted full women's suffrage by 1914

others, was an early example of the women's clubs that then prolifer-ated to the extent that a General Federation of Women's Clubs tied them together in 1890. Many women's clubs confined themselves to "literary" and social activities, but others became deeply involved in charities and reform. The New York Consumers League, formed in 1890, and the National Consumers League, established nine years later, sought to make the buying public, chiefly women, better aware of degrading labor conditions.

TOWARD A GENERAL WELFARE STATE Even without the support of voting women in most places, the states adopted rudimen-tary measures to regulate big business and labor conditions in the pub-lic interest. They passed laws to regulate railroads and working condi-tions, but the laws were generally poorly enforced or overturned by the courts. In the meantime, it was often urban machines that stepped in to help those who were suffering. While local and federal governments lacked a bureaucracy to relieve those who had fallen on hard times, the urban machines supplied temporary jobs, food, or other necessities as needed. As such, the machines were the precursor to the modern wel-fare state.

As the turn of the century neared, opinion in the country stood poised between conservative rigidities and a growing sense that new conditions impose new personal and governmental responsibilities. The last two decades of the nineteenth century had already seen a slow erosion of free-market values that had found their most secure home in the courts. There emerged instead a concept of the general-welfare state, which called upon the government to act on behalf of the whole society rather than allow rugged individualism to run rampant. The conflict between this notion and laissez-faire values spilled over into the new century, but by the mid–twentieth century, after the progressive movement and the New Deal, the nation would be firmly committed to the premises of the general-welfare state.

MAKING CONNECTIONS

- As the next chapter shows, the presidential election of 1896 was in many ways a contest between the new urban values discussed in this chapter and those of a more traditional rural American society.

- The reform impulse you've read about in this chapter finds voice again in the discussion of the progressive movement in Chapter 23.

- The nativist thinking discussed in this chapter fueled the immigration restriction laws enacted in the 1920s (Chapter 25).

FURTHER READING

The best survey of urbanization remains Charles N. Glaab and A. Theodore Brown's *A History of Urban America* (3rd ed., 1983). Gunther P. Barth discusses the emergence of a new urban culture in *City People:*

The Rise of Modern City Culture in Nineteenth Century America (1980). Urban politics is surveyed in Jon C. Teaford's *The Unheralded Triumph: City Government in America, 1870–1900* (1994). Oliver E. Allen's *The Tiger: The Rise and Fall of Tammany Hall* (1994) assesses the significance of New York's famous political machine.

John Bodnar provides a synthesis of the urban immigrant experience in *The Transplanted: A History of Immigrants in Urban America* (1985). Walter Nugent's *Crossings: The Great Transatlantic Migrations, 1870–1914* (1992) provides a wealth of demographic information and insight. John Higham's *Strangers in the Land: Patterns of American Nativism, 1860–1925* (2nd ed., 1988) examines how old-stock residents reacted to the influx of newcomers.

For the growth of urban leisure and sports, see Roy Rosenzweig's *Eight Hours for What We Will: Workers and Leisure in an Industrial City, 1870–1920* (1983) and Steven A. Riess's *City Games: The Evolution of American Urban Society and the Rise of Sports* (1989). Steven A. Riess's *Touching Base: Professional Baseball and American Culture in the Progressive Era* (1980) and Dominick Cavallo's *Muscles and Morals: Organized Playgrounds and Urban Reform, 1880–1920* (1981) link athletics to new forms of organization and socialization.

Richard Hofstadter's *Social Darwinism in American Thought* (rev. ed., 1992) and Cynthia E. Russett's *Darwin in America* (1976) examine the impact of the theory of evolution. On the rise of realism in thought and the arts during the second half of the nineteenth century, see David Shi's *Facing Facts: Realism in American Thought and Culture, 1850–1920* (1995).

William L. O'Neill's *Everyone Was Brave: The Rise and Fall of Feminism in America* (1969) and Eleanor Flexner's *Century of Struggle: The Woman's Rights Movement in the United States* (rev. ed., 1975) survey the condition of women in the late nineteenth century.

21 ⌒ GILDED-AGE POLITICS
AND AGRARIAN REVOLT

CHAPTER ORGANIZER

This chapter focuses on:

- political developments in the Gilded Age.

- problems, both real and perceived, affecting American farmers.

- the rise of the agrarian revolt and the Populists.

- the significant election of 1896.

*I*n 1873 Mark Twain and Charles Dudley Warner created an enduring label for the post–Civil War era when they collaborated on a novel entitled *The Gilded Age*. The book depicted an age of widespread political corruption, personal greed, and social vulgarity. Perspectives on the times would eventually change, but generations of political scientists and historians have since reinforced the two novelists' judgment. As a young college graduate in 1879, Woodrow Wilson described the state of the American political system: "No leaders, no principles; no principles, no parties."

PARADOXICAL POLITICS

Throughout the last third of the nineteenth century, political inertia reigned on the national level. A fairly even division between Republicans and Democrats created a sense of stalemate. Neither party was willing to embrace controversial issues or take bold initiatives because their relative strength was so precarious. Many observers then and since considered this a time of political mediocrity in which the parties refused to confront "real issues" such as the runaway growth of an unregulated economy and its attendant social injustices.

Voters of the time nonetheless thought politics was very important. Voter turnout during the Gilded Age was commonly about 70 to 80 percent, even in the South, where the disenfranchisement of blacks was not yet complete. (By contrast, the turnout for the 1996 presidential election was barely 50 percent.) The paradox of such high voter participation in the face of the inertia at the national political level raises an obvious question: How was it that leaders who failed to address the "real issues" of the day presided over the most highly organized and politically active electorate in American history?

The answer is partly that the politicians and the voters believed that they *were* dealing with crucial issues: the tariff, monopolies, the currency, civil service reform, and immigration. But the answer also reflects the extreme partisanship of the times and the essentially local nature of political culture during the Gilded Age. While people expected little from their national government, they demanded much from their local and state officials.

PARTISAN POLITICS Most Americans after the Civil War were intensely loyal to one of the two major parties, Democratic or Republican. In the midst of the social and economic disruptions caused by the second industrial revolution, the political parties gave people an anchor of activity and loyalty in an unstable world. Local party officials took care of those who voted their way, and they distributed appointive public offices and other favors to party loyalists. These "city machines" used patronage and favoritism to get and keep the loyalty of business supporters, while providing jobs or food or fuel to working-class voters who had fallen on hard times.

The political parties were also a key source of fun and entertainment for activist and ordinary voters. The party faithful marched and drilled and eagerly took part in rallies and picnics, deriving a sense of camaraderie as well as recreation that offered a welcome relief from their usual workday routine. In a time before movies and television, election campaigns filled the days with excitement and gave male citizens a chance to share rituals, express their loyalties, and carouse in a purely male sphere. In urban neighborhoods throughout the country, saloons served more than alcohol; they also provided gathering places for local political organizations.

Party loyalties and voter turnout in the late nineteenth century reflected religious and ethnic divisions as well as geographic differences. The Republican party attracted mainly Protestants of British descent. Their native seat was New England, and their other strongholds were New York and the upper Middle West, both of which were populated with Yankee stock. Legitimate heirs to the abolitionist tradition, Republicans drew to their ranks a host of reformers and moralists, spiritual descendants of the perfectionists who championed the revivals and the reform movements of the antebellum years. The party's heritage of anti-Catholic nativism would also make a comeback in the 1880s. And the Republicans, the party of Lincoln, could also rely on the votes of blacks and Union veterans of the Civil War.

The Democrats, by contrast, tended to be a heterogeneous, often unruly coalition embracing southern whites, immigrants and Catholics of any origin, Jews, freethinkers, skeptics, and all those repelled by the "party of morality." As one Chicago Democrat explained, "A Republican is a man who wants you t' go t' church every Sunday. A Democrat says if a man wants to have a glass of beer on Sunday he can have it."

In the Midwest, especially, tensions over religious and social issues, such as Sunday closing laws and liquor prohibition, created intense political allegiances. Republicans pressed nativist causes, calling for restrictions on immigration and on the employment of foreigners, and greater emphasis on the teaching of the "American" language in the schools. Prohibitionism revived along with nativism in the 1880s. Among the immigrants who crowded into the growing cities were many Irish, Germans, and Italians who enjoyed alcoholic beverages. Republicans increasingly saw saloons as the central social evil around which all others revolved, including vice, crime, political corruption, and neglect of families, and they associated these ethnic groups with the problem.

POLITICAL STALEMATE AT THE NATIONAL LEVEL Between 1869 and 1913, from the presidencies of Ulysses S. Grant to William Howard Taft, Republicans monopolized the White House except during the two nonconsecutive terms of Grover Cleveland, but Republican domination was more apparent than real. Between 1872 and 1896, no president won a majority of the popular vote. In each of those presidential elections, sixteen states invariably voted Republican and fourteen voted Democratic, leaving a pivotal six states whose results might change. The important swing-vote role that two of these states, New York and Ohio, played helps explain the election of seven presidents from these states from 1870 to 1912.

Deferential presidents also contributed to the political stalemate. No chief executive between Lincoln and Theodore Roosevelt could be described as a "strong" president. None seriously challenged the prevailing view that Congress, not the White House, should formulate policy. Senator John Sherman of Ohio expressed the widely held notion that the legislative branch should take initiative in a republic: "The President should merely obey and enforce the law."

While Congress was evenly divided between representatives and senators from the two parties, Republicans controlled the Senate, and Democrats controlled the House during the Gilded Age. Only during 1881–1883 and 1889–1891 did a Republican president have a Republican Congress, and only between 1893 and 1895 did a Democratic president enjoy a Democratic Congress.

Political stasis thus led Congress to postpone making major decisions or launching new programs and to concentrate instead on partisan maneuvering over procedural issues. The almost equal strength of the parties in Congress and the fear in each party of alienating key factions worked against any vigorous new initiatives in Congress. Because most bills required bipartisan support to pass both houses, and legislators tended to vote along party lines, the Democrats and Republicans pursued a policy of evasion on the national issues of the day. Only the tariff provoked clear-cut divisions between protectionist Republicans and low-tariff Democrats, but there were individual exceptions even on that. On the important questions of the currency, regulation of big business, farm problems, civil service reform, and immigration, the parties differed very little. As a result, they primarily became vehicles for seeking office and dispensing patronage in the form of government jobs and contracts.

STATE AND LOCAL INITIATIVES   Unlike today, people during the Gilded Age expected little direct support from the federal government. Most of the significant political activity occurred at the state and local levels. In the Western territories, prior to their receiving statehood, people were largely forced to fend for themselves rather than to rely on federal authorities. They formed towns, practiced vigilante justice, and made laws on their own. Once incorporated into the Union, these former territories retained much of their autonomy.

Much more than the national Congress, state governments after the Civil War were dynamic centers of political activity and innovation. Over 60 percent of the nation's spending and taxing were exercised by state and local authorities. Then, unlike today, the large cities spent far more on local services than did the federal government. And three-fourths of all public employees worked for state and local governments. Local issues such as prohibition, Sunday closing laws, and parochial school funding generated far more excitement than complex debates over tariffs and monetary policies.

It was state and local governments rather than the national government that first sought to curb the power and restrain the abuses of corporate interests. The states groped toward rudimentary measures to regulate big business and labor conditions in the public interest. By the turn of the century, nearly every state had provided for the regulation of railroads, if not always effectively, and had moved to supervise banks and insurance companies. Between 1887 and 1897, by one count, the states and territories passed over 1,600 laws relating to conditions of work, which limited the hours of labor, provided special protection for women, limited or forbade child labor, required regular wage payments in cash, called for factory inspections, and outlawed blacklisting or the importation of "Pinkerton men." Nearly all states had boards or commissioners of labor, and some had boards of conciliation and arbitration.

Initially, the courts upheld state and local laws regulating corporations, although conservative judges often limited the practical impact of such laws. In *Munn* v. *Illinois* (1877), the Supreme Court upheld the right of state and local governments to regulate industry essential to the public welfare. In the 1880s, however, while the Court continued to oppose monopolies, it wanted to protect interstate corporations from excessive local regulation, which might interfere with the conduct of business. Thus in *Stone* v. *Farmers Loan and Trust Company* (1886) the Court recognized the authority of Mississippi to regulate railroad rates, but it also declared that there might be cases in which the Court could review the rates: "Under pretense of regulating fares and freights, the State cannot require a railroad corporation to carry persons or property without reward." And in *Wabash* v. *Illinois* (1886), the Court ruled that a state could not regulate rates in interstate commerce.

In 1890, in *Chicago, Milwaukee and St. Paul Railway Company* v. *Minnesota,* the justices declared unconstitutional a state law that forbade judicial review of rates set by a railroad commission. "The question of the reasonableness of a rate of charge . . . is eminently a question for judicial investigation," the Court ruled, "requiring due process of law for its determination." This was a direct reversal of the ruling in *Munn* v. *Illinois* that regulation is a legislative prerogative. Now fears over regulation depriving a company of its property took precedence over protection of the public welfare. It remained only for the Court to overturn rates set directly by a state legislature. That it did when it struck down a Nebraska law in *Smyth* v. *Ames* in 1898, on the grounds that the state had set the rates so low as to be unreasonable.

In thwarting new attempts by states to regulate corporations, the Supreme Court used a revised interpretation of the Fourteenth Amendment clauses forbidding the states to "deprive any person of life, liberty or property without due process of law" or to deny any person the "equal protection of the law." The justices reasoned that corporations could be considered "artificial persons" with the right to own property, buy and sell, sue and be sued like natural persons. The Court also moved away from the old view that "due process" referred only to correct procedures and turned toward a doctrine of "substantive due process," which meant that the courts could review the substance of a law and decide if the law was so extreme that it deprived the person (here, the corporation) of property to an unreasonable degree.

States attempted to regulate how corporations treated their workers, but their efforts were also overturned by the courts. The Supreme Court derived a new doctrine of "liberty of contract," which it used to protect corporations' tangible and intangible property from actual and potential danger. It said that in going to work for a corporation, an employee contracted to work even under the most oppressive conditions without interference from the state. Using this reasoning, the Pennsylvania Supreme Court in 1886 overturned a state law protecting workers against payment in commodities instead of in cash, with the court declaring the law "an insulting attempt to put the laborer under a legislative tutelage, which is not only degrading to his manhood, but subversive of his rights as a citizen of the United States." And the high court of West Virginia in 1889 condemned a similar law as an attempt to "foist upon the people a paternal government of the most objectionable character, because it assumes that the employer is a knave, and the laborer an imbecile."

CORRUPTION AND REFORM

While the courts were overturning state regulation of corporations, a close alliance between business and political leaders characterized the period. This was not necessarily perceived by the public as inappropriate, since many politicians favored business interests out of conviction. Nor were people as sensitive to conflicts of interest as they would later become. Congressman James G. Blaine of Maine, for example, and many of his supporters, saw nothing wrong in his accepting stock certificates from an Arkansas railroad after helping it win a land

The Bosses of the Senate. *This 1889 cartoon bitingly portrays the alliance between big business and politics in this period.*

grant from Congress. Railroad passes, free entertainment, and a host of other favors were freely provided politicians, editors, and other leaders in positions to influence public opinion or affect legislation.

On the local level, the exchange of favors for votes was not perceived as improper either. People voted for their party because of their intense partisan loyalty. Although they looked to their parties to supply them with favors, entertainment, and even jobs, they did not see themselves as "selling their votes." This was simply the practice of patronage democracy, in which local party officials awarded party loyalists with contracts and public jobs such as heads of the customs houses and post offices.

Both Republican and Democratic leaders squabbled over the "spoils" of office. These were the appointive offices that were available on both the local and national levels. After each election, it was expected that the party that had won would throw out the appointees from the defeated party and appoint their own men to office in their stead. Each party had its share of corrupt officials willing to buy and sell government appointments or congressional votes, yet each also witnessed the emergence of factions promoting honesty in government. This struggle for clean government soon became one of the foremost issues of the day.

HAYES AND CIVIL SERVICE REFORM In the aftermath of Reconstruction, Rutherford B. Hayes admirably embodied the "party of morality." Hayes brought to the White House in 1877 a new style of uprightness, a sharp contrast to the graft and corruption of the Grant administration. The son of an Ohio farmer, Hayes became one of the early Republicans, was wounded four times in the Civil War, and was promoted to major-general. Elected governor of Ohio in 1867, he served three terms. Honest and respectable, competent and dignified, he lived in a modest style with his wife, who was nicknamed "Lemonade Lucy" because of her refusal to serve alcohol at White House functions.

Yet Hayes's tenure as president suffered from the manner of his defeat of Tilden in the 1876–1877 election. Snide references to him as "His Fraudulence" dogged his steps and denied him any chance at a second term, which he renounced from the beginning. Hayes's own party was split between so-called Stalwarts and Half-Breeds, led respectively by Senators Roscoe Conkling of New York and James G.

Blaine of Maine. The difference between these Republican factions was murkier than that between the parties. The Stalwarts generally supported Grant, a Radical southern policy, and the spoils system. The Half-Breeds took a contrary view on the first two and even vaguely supported civil service reform.

For the most part, the Stalwart and Half-Breed factions were loose alliances designed to advance the careers of Conkling and Blaine. The two men could not abide one another. Blaine once referred to Conkling as displaying a "majestic, supereminent, overpowering, turkey-gobbler strut." He was right. Tall and lordly, with a pointed beard, thick, auburn hair, and upturned jaw and nose, Conkling boasted good looks, fine clothes, and an arrogant manner. He dressed and lived flamboyantly, sporting pastel bow ties, silk scarves, moon-colored vests, and patent leather shoes. Yet for all his sartorial splendor and glamorous facade, he was always a ruthless power broker. Conkling viewed politics as a brute struggle for control, and he believed its arena was no place for faint hearts. Politics "is a rotten business," he declared. "Nothing counts except to win."

Hayes thought otherwise, and he aligned himself with the growing public discontent over the corruption that had prevailed under Grant. In promoting the cause of civil service reform, he issued an Executive Order in 1877 declaring that those already in office would be dismissed only for the good of the government and not for political reasons. His cabinet tried to carry out the new policy. Secretary of the Treasury John Sherman revealed that both customs collector Chester A. Arthur and naval officer Alonzo Cornell were guilty of "laxity" and of using the New York Customs House for political management on behalf of Conkling's organization. Hayes removed Arthur and Cornell, and thereby won Conkling's lasting hatred.

For all his efforts to clean house, Hayes retained a limited vision of government's role. On the economic issues of the day he held to a conservative line that would guide his successors for the rest of the century. His solution to labor troubles, demonstrated during the Great Railroad Strike of 1877, was to send in troops and break the strike. A financial conservative, he denied the demands of farmers and debtors for an expansion of the currency by vetoing the Bland-Allison Act, which required a limited expansion of silver currency through the government's purchase for coinage of $2 million to $4 million worth of silver per month. The bill was passed when Congress overrode Hayes's veto.

GARFIELD AND ARTHUR   With Hayes unavailable for a second term, the Republicans were forced to look elsewhere in 1880. The Stalwarts, led by Conkling, brought Grant forward for a third time, still a strong contender despite the tarnish of his administration's scandals. For two days the Republican convention in Chicago was deadlocked, with Grant holding a slight lead over Blaine and John Sherman. On the thirty-fifth ballot, Wisconsin suddenly switched sixteen votes to former House Speaker (now Senator-elect) James A. Garfield, Sherman's campaign manager. Garfield rose to protest but was ruled out of order, and on the next ballot the convention stampeded to the dark-horse candidate. As a sop to the Stalwarts, the convention tapped Chester A. Arthur, of Customs House notoriety, for vice-president.

The Democrats named Winfield Scott Hancock, a Union commander at Gettysburg, to counterbalance the Republicans' Brigadier-General Garfield and thus ward off "bloody-shirt" attacks on their party as the vehicle of secession. The election turned out to be the closest of the century. Garfield eked out a plurality of only 39,000 votes with 48.5 percent of the vote, but with a comfortable margin of 214 to 155 in the electoral college.

On July 2, 1881, President Garfield was leaving on a vacation when, as he walked through the Washington, D.C., rail station, a deranged office seeker named Charles Guiteau shot him in the back. "I am a Stalwart," Guiteau shouted to the arresting officers. "Arthur is now President of the United States." Guiteau's announcement would prove crippling to the Stalwarts and his attack fatal to Garfield, who died after a two-month struggle. Garfield had been president for a little over six months.

Chester Arthur, one of the chief henchmen of Stalwart leader Roscoe Conkling, was now president. Little in Arthur's past suggested that he would rise above spoils politics. But Arthur, a wealthy, handsome widower who loved fine wines and sported a lavish wardrobe and billowing sideburns, demonstrated surprising leadership qualities as president. He distanced himself from Conkling and the Stalwarts and established a genuine independence, almost a necessity after Guiteau's announcement. As Arthur noted, "For the vice-presidency I was indebted to Mr.

Conkling, but for the presidency of the United States my debt is to the Almighty."

Most startling of all was Arthur's emergence as something of a civil service and tariff reformer. Stalwarts had every reason to expect him to oppose such changes, but instead he allied himself with the reformers. While the assassin Guiteau had unwittingly added a certain urgency to the public support of reform, the defeat of a reform bill in 1882 sponsored by "Gentleman George" Pendleton, Democratic senator from Ohio, aroused public opinion further. The Pendleton Civil Service Act finally passed in 1883, setting up a three-member Civil Service Commission independent from the regular cabinet departments, the first such federal agency established on a permanent basis. About 14 percent of all government jobs would now be filled on the basis of competitive examinations rather than political connections. What was more, the president could enlarge the class of affected jobs at his discretion, as many other presidents later did.

Meanwhile the tariff continued to be the most controversial national political issue. The high protective tariff, a heritage of the Civil War, had by the early 1880s raised revenues to the point that the government actually enjoyed a surplus that drew money into the Treasury and out of circulation, thus impeding economic growth. Some argued that lower tariff rates would reduce prices and the cost of living, and at the same time leave more money in circulation. In 1882 Arthur named a special commission to study the problem. The Tariff Commission recommended a 20 to 25 percent rate reduction, which gained Arthur's support, but Congress's effort to enact the proposal was marred by logrolling (the trading of votes to benefit different legislators' local interests). The result was the "Mongrel Tariff" of 1883, so called because of its diverse percentages for different commodities. Overall the tariff provided for a slight rate reduction, but it actually raised the duty on some articles.

SCURRILOUS CAMPAIGN   As the 1884 election neared, Arthur's record might have commended him to the voters, but it did not please the leaders of his party. The Republicans dumped Arthur and turned to the majestic Senator James G. Blaine of Maine, leader of the Half-Breeds. Blaine was the consummate politician. He never forgot a name or a face, he inspired the party faithful with his ora-

Senator James G. Blaine of Maine.

tory, and at the same time he knew how to wheel and deal in the back rooms.

Back in 1876 Blaine had been nominated for the presidency by a Republican official who, in an eloquent flight of oratory, had announced: "Like an armed warrior, like a plumed knight, James G. Blaine marched down the halls of American Congress and threw his shining lance full and fair against the brazen forehead of the defamers of his country and maligners of his honor." To his followers in 1884 Blaine remained the "plumed knight," with a strikingly long, pale face animated by dark eyes and anchored in a silvery beard. But Democratic newspapers portrayed him as the plumed knave who had engaged in corrupt dealings with Arkansas railroad barons, selling his votes on measures favorable to their interests. Such charges were based on references contained in the so-called Mulligan letters.

During the campaign, more letters surfaced with disclosures embarrassing to Blaine. For the reform element of the Republican party, this was too much, and many bolted the ticket. Party regulars scorned the idealists as "goo-goos"—the "good-government" crowd who ignored partisan realities—and one editor jokingly tagged them Mugwumps, after an Algonquian word meaning a great chieftain. To the party regulars, in what soon became a stale joke, Mugwumps were unreliable Republicans who had their "mugs" on one side of the fence and their "wumps" on the other.

The rise of the Mugwumps, however, influenced the Democrats to nominate Stephen Grover Cleveland as a reform candidate. Elected mayor of Buffalo in 1881, Cleveland first attracted national attention for effectively battling graft and corruption in that city. In 1882 the Democrats elected him as governor of New York, and he continued to build a reform record by fighting New York's corrupt Tammany Hall organization. As mayor and as governor, he repeatedly vetoed what he considered special-privilege bills serving selfish interests. A stocky 250-pound man with a droopy mustache, Cleveland seemed the stolid opposite of Blaine. He possessed little charisma, but he impressed the public with his stubborn integrity. Cleveland was a crusader against government and corporate corruption, and as such he drew to him many of those making up the growing chorus of reformers. One supporter said: "We love him for the enemies he has made."

Then a scandal erupted when the *Buffalo Evening Telegraph* revealed that bachelor Cleveland had had an affair during the early 1870s with a tall, attractive Buffalo widow, Maria Halpin. Mrs. Halpin had named Cleveland as the father of a boy born to her in 1874. Cleveland took responsibility and provided financial help when the child was placed in an orphanage. When supporters asked Cleveland what to say about the affair, he answered with typical candor: "Tell the truth." The respective personal escapades of Blaine and Cleveland provided the 1884 campaign with some of the most colorful battle cries in American political history. "Blaine, Blaine, James G. Blaine, the continental liar from the state of Maine," Democrats chanted. Republicans countered with "Ma, ma, where's my pa? Gone to the White House, ha, ha, ha!"

Near the end of the campaign, Blaine and his supporters committed two fateful blunders. The first occurred at New York's fashionable Delmonico's restaurant, where Blaine attended a lavish fund-raising dinner with a clutch of millionaire bigwigs, including robber barons. Cartoons and accounts of this "Belshazzar's Feast" festooned the opposition press for days.

The second fiasco cost Blaine much of the Irish vote when a Protestant minister visiting Republican headquarters in New York insolently referred to the Democrats as the party of "rum, Romanism, and rebellion." A Cleveland campaign worker heard the remark and rushed back to his headquarters. Blaine, who was present, let it pass and perhaps failed to catch the implied insult to Irish Catholics—a fatal oversight, since he had always cultivated Irish-American support with his anti-British talk and public reminders that his mother was Catholic. Democrats spread word that he had let the insult pass, even that he had made it himself.

The two incidents may have tipped the election. The electoral vote in Cleveland's favor stood at 219 to 182, although the popular vote ran far closer; Cleveland's plurality was fewer than 30,000 votes.

CLEVELAND AND THE SPECIAL INTERESTS   For all of Cleveland's hostility to the spoils system and politics as usual, he represented no sharp break with the conservative policies of his Republican predecessors, except in opposing governmental favors to business. He held to a strictly limited view of government's role in both economic and social matters, a rigid philosophy illustrated by his 1887 veto of a bill to aid drought-stricken farmers. Back to Congress it went with a lecture on the need to limit the powers and functions of government—"though the people support the government, the government should not support the people," Cleveland asserted.

Despite his strong convictions, Cleveland had a mixed record on the civil service. He harbored good intentions, but he also headed a party hungry for partisan appointments to government jobs, with the first Democratic president since the election of James Buchanan in 1856. Before his inauguration he repeated his support for the Pendleton Act, and he pledged not to remove able government workers on partisan grounds. But party pressures gradually forced Cleveland's hand. To a friend he remarked: "The damned everlasting clatter for office continues . . . and makes me feel like resigning." When he left office about two-thirds of the federal officeholders were Democrats, but at the same time Cleveland had almost doubled the number of jobs subject to civil service regulation. He thereby satisfied neither Mugwumps nor spoilsmen; indeed, he managed to antagonize both.

Cleveland incurred the wrath of many Union military veterans by his firm stand against expanded pensions. Congress had passed the first Civil War pension law in 1862 to provide for Union veterans disabled in service and for the widows, orphans, and dependents of veterans. By 1882 the Grand Army of the Republic, an organization of Union veterans and a powerful pressure group, was trying to get pensions paid for any disability, no matter how it was incurred. Meanwhile, many veterans succeeded in getting legislators to pass private pension bills. Insofar as time permitted, Cleveland examined such bills critically and vetoed the dubious ones. Although he signed more than any of his predecessors, he also vetoed more. The issue climaxed in 1887 when Cleveland vetoed a new Dependent Pension bill containing more liberal benefits and qualifications. Cleveland argued that it would become a refuge for frauds rather than a "roll of honor."

About the middle of his term, Cleveland set out after new special interests by advocating an important new policy, railroad regulation. Since the late 1860s, state after state had adopted railroad regulatory laws, and from the early 1870s Congress had debated federal legislation. In 1886 a Supreme Court decision finally spurred action. Reacting to *Wabash Railroad* v. *Illinois,* in which the Court had ruled that a state could not regulate rates on interstate traffic, Cleveland urged that since this "important field of control and regulation [has] thus been left entirely unoccupied," Congress should act.

It did, and in 1887 Cleveland signed into law an act creating the Interstate Commerce Commission (ICC), the first such independent federal regulatory commission. The law required that all freight and passenger railroad rates be "reasonable and just," and it empowered the ICC to investigate carriers and prosecute violators. Railroads were also forbidden to grant secret rebates to preferred shippers, discriminate against persons, places, and commodities, or enter into pools (agreements to fix rates). The commission's actual powers, however, proved to be weak when first tested in the courts. Though creating the ICC seemed to conflict with Cleveland's fear of big government, it accorded with his wariness of big business. The Interstate Commerce Act, to his mind, was a legitimate exercise of sovereign power.

THE TARIFF ISSUE   Cleveland's most dramatic challenge to special interests focused on tariff reform. Why was the tariff such an important and controversial issue? By the late nineteenth century, many observers had concluded that the formation of huge corporate "trusts" was not a natural development of a maturing capitalist system. Instead, they charged that government policies had fostered big business at the expense of small producers and retailers. Among those policies was an excessively high protective tariff. "The mother of all trusts is the tariff bill," proclaimed one leading business executive. By shielding American manufacturers from foreign competition, the tariff, critics argued, made it easier for them to combine into ever-larger entities. High tariff

*Grover Cleveland made the issue of
tariff reform central to the politics of
the late 1880s.*

rates also enabled big corporations to restrict production and fix prices. "The heart of the trust problem is in our tariff system of plunder," declared the head of the New England Free Trade League. "The quickest and most certain way of reaching the evils of trusts is not by direct legislation against them, or by constitutional amendment, but by the abolition of tariff duties."

Cleveland agreed. Having decided that the rates were too high and included many inequities, he devoted his entire annual message in 1887 to the subject. He did so in full knowledge that he was walking onto a political minefield on the eve of an election year. "What is the use of being elected if you don't stand for something?" he asked skeptical advisers.

Cleveland's message noted that tariff revenues had bolstered the federal surplus, making the Treasury "a hoarding place for money needlessly withdrawn from trade and the people's use." The high tariff pushed up prices for everybody and benefited only a few politically powerful manufacturing interests. The wise solution was to spur Congress to look at the more than 4,000 items on the tariff list with an eye to eliminating as many as possible and lowering all the remaining duties.

The House soon passed a bill calling for modest tariff reductions from an average level of about 47 percent of the value of imported goods to about 40 percent. But the bill stalled in the Republican Senate and finally died a lingering death in committee. If Cleveland's tariff proposal accomplished his purpose of drawing party lines more firmly, it also confirmed the fears of his advisers. The election of 1888 for the first time in years highlighted a sharp difference between the major parties on an issue of substance.

THE ELECTION OF 1888 Cleveland was the nominee of his party, whose platform endorsed "the views expressed by the President in his last message to Congress." The Republicans passed up old warhorses such as Blaine and Sherman and turned to the obscure Benjamin Harrison, who had all the attributes of availability. Grandson of a former president, Harrison was a flourishing lawyer in Indiana, which was a pivotal state. He also boasted a good war record, and there was little in his political record to offend any voter. The Republican platform accepted Cleveland's challenge to make the protective tariff the chief issue, and promised generous pensions to veterans.

The campaign thus became the first waged mainly on the tariff issue. As insurance against tariff reduction, manufacturers obligingly filled up Harrison's campaign fund, which was used to denounce Cleveland's un-American "free-trade" stance and his pension vetoes.

On the eve of the election, Cleveland suffered a devastating blow from a dirty campaign trick. Posing as an English immigrant and using the false name Charles F. Murchison, a California Republican had written British minister Sir Lionel Sackville-West and asked his advice on how to vote. Sackville-West hinted in reply that he should vote for Cleveland. Published two weeks before the election, the "Murchison letter" aroused a storm of protest against foreign intervention and further linked Cleveland to British free-traders.

Still, the outcome in 1888 was very close. Cleveland won the popular vote by 5,538,000 to 5,447,000, but that was poor comfort. The distribution was such that Harrison, with the key states of Indiana and New York on his side, carried the electoral college by 233 to 168. For the first time since John Quincy Adams's election in 1824, the country had not only a minority president, but one who lacked even a plurality in the popular vote.

REPUBLICAN REFORM UNDER HARRISON As president, Benjamin Harrison became a competent and earnest figurehead, overshadowed by his secretary of state, James G. Blaine. His first step was to reward those responsible for his victory. He owed a heavy debt to the old-soldier vote, which he discharged by naming the head of the veterans' group to the office of pension commissioner. "God help the surplus," the new commissioner reportedly exclaimed. He proceeded to approve pensions with such abandon that the secretary of the interior removed him six months and several million dollars later. In 1890 Congress passed, and Harrison signed, the Dependent Pension Act, substantially the same measure that Cleveland had vetoed three years earlier. Any veteran unable to make a living by manual labor for whatever reason was granted a monthly pension. The pension rolls almost doubled by 1893.

During the first two years of Harrison's term, the Republicans controlled the presidency and both houses of Congress for the only time in the twenty years between 1875 and 1895. They made the most of their clout. During 1890, several significant pieces of legislation made their way to the White House for Harrison's signature. In addition to the Dependent Pension Act, Congress and the president approved the Sherman Anti-Trust Act, the Sherman Silver Purchase Act, the McKinley Tariff, and the admission of Idaho and Wyoming as new states, following admission of the Dakotas, Montana, and Washington in 1889.

Both parties had pledged themselves to address the growing power of trusts and monopolies. The Sherman Anti-Trust Act, named for Senator John Sherman, chairman of the committee that drafted it, forbade contracts, combinations, or conspiracies in restraint of trade or in the effort to establish monopolies in interstate or foreign commerce. A broad consensus put the law through, but its passage turned out to be largely symbolic. During the next decade, successive administrations expended little effort on the act's enforcement. From 1890 to 1901, the Justice Department instituted only eighteen antitrust suits, and four of those were against labor unions.

Congress meanwhile debated currency legislation against the backdrop of growing distress in the farm regions of the West and South. Hard-pressed farmers were now agitating for an increased coinage of silver to inflate the currency supply, which would raise commodity prices, making it easier for farmers to earn the money with which to pay their debts. The silverite forces were also strengthened, especially in the Senate, by members from those new western states that had silver-mining interests. Congress thus passed the Sherman Silver Purchase

Act of 1890, replacing the Bland-Allison Act of 1878. It required the Treasury to purchase 4.5 million ounces of silver each month and to issue in payment Treasury notes redeemable in either gold or silver. But the act failed to satisfy the demands of the silverites. Although it doubled the amount of silver purchased, that was still too little to have much inflationary impact on the economy. The stage was thus set for the currency issue to eclipse all others during the financial panic that swept the country three years later.

Republicans took their victory over Cleveland as a mandate not just to maintain the protective tariff but to raise it. Piloted through by the prominent Ohio senator William McKinley, the McKinley Tariff of 1890 raised duties on manufactured goods to an average of about 49.5 percent, the highest to that time.

The absence of a public consensus for higher tariffs became clearly visible in the 1890 midterm elections. The November congressional election returns suggested that the voters had repudiated the Republican-sponsored McKinley tariff with a landslide of Democratic votes. In the new House, Democrats outnumbered Republicans by almost a three to one margin; in the Senate, the Republican majority was reduced to eight. One of the election casualties was McKinley himself. But there was more to the election than the tariff. Voters also reacted against the baldly partisan measures of the Harrison administration and against its extravagant expenditures on pensions and other programs.

The large Democratic vote in 1890 may have also been a reaction to Republican efforts on a local level to legislate against alcohol and government-supported Catholic (parochial) schools. In many districts with a high percentage of Catholic constituents, local Democratic legislators had defied the principle of separation of church and state by allocating tax revenues to help support parochial schools. In 1889 Wisconsin Republicans pushed through a law that struck at parochial schools, and turned large numbers of outraged Catholic immigrants into Democratic activists. Between 1880 and 1890, sixteen out of twenty-one states outside the South held referenda on constitutional prohibition of alcoholic beverages (although only six states actually voted for prohibition). With this assault on drinking, Republicans were playing a losing game, arousing wets (anti-prohibitionists) on the Democratic side. In 1890 the Democrats swept state after state.

The Farm Problem and Agrarian Protest Movements

The 1890 election returns reflected more than a reaction against the Republican tariff, patronage politics, extravagant spending, and moralizing. The returns revealed a deep-seated unrest in the farming communities of the South and West. As the Democrats took power, the beginnings of an economic crisis appeared on the horizon. Farmers' debts mounted as crop prices plummeted.

Frustrated by the unwillingness of Congress to meet their demands and ease their plight, disgruntled farmers began to organize for political action. Like so many of their counterparts laboring in urban factories, they realized that social change could be provoked only by demonstrations of power, and power lay in numbers. But unlike labor unions, farm organizations faced a more complex array of economic variables affecting their livelihood. They had to deal with more than just management; bankers, processors, railroad and gain elevator operators, as well as the world commodities market, all affected the agricultural sector. So too did the unpredictable forces of nature: droughts, blizzards, insects, and erosion.

There were also many important obstacles to collective action by farmers. The deeply ingrained agrarian tradition of rugged individualism and physical isolation made communication and organization especially difficult. American farmers had long prided themselves on their self-reliant hardihood, and many balked at sacrificing their independence. Another hurdle was the fact that after the Civil War agricultural interests had diverged and in some cases conflicted with one another. In the Great Plains, for example, the railroads were the largest landowners. In addition, there were large absentee landowners, some foreign, who leased out vast tracts of land. There were also huge "bonanza" farms that employed hundreds of seasonal workers. Yet the majority of farmers were simple rural folk in the South and West who were moderate-size landowners, small land speculators, small landowners, tenant farmers, and hourly wage workers. It was the middle-size landowners who experienced rapidly rising land values and rising indebtedness. Such farmers were concerned with land values and crop prices, while tenants or sharecroppers or farm hands supported land distribution schemes that would give them access to their own land.

Given such a diversity of interests, farm activists discovered that it was often difficult to develop and maintain a cohesive organization. Yet, for all the difficulties, they persevered, and the results were dramatic, if not completely successful. Thus, for example, the deep-seated unrest in the farming communities of the South and West began to find voice in the Granger movement, the Alliance movement, and in the new People's party, agrarian movements of considerable political and social significance.

ECONOMIC CONDITIONS   For some time, farmers in the South and Midwest had been subject to worsening economic and social conditions. The source of their problems was a long-term decline in commodity prices from 1870 to 1898, the product of domestic increases in production and growing international competition for world markets. Considerations of abstract economic forces, however, puzzled many farmers. How could one speak of overproduction when so many remained in need? Instead, many assumed, there must be a screw loose somewhere in the system.

The railroads and the processors and bankers who handled the farmers' products were seen as the villains. Farmers resented the high railroad rates that prevailed in farm regions with no alternative forms of transportation. Individual farmers could not get the rebates the industrial shippers could extract from railroads, nor could they exert the political influence wielded by the railroad lobbies. In other ways farmers found themselves with little bargaining power either as buyers or sellers. When they went to sell wheat or cotton, the buyer set the price; when they went to buy a plow point, the seller set the price.

High tariffs operated to the farmers' disadvantage because they protected manufacturers against foreign competition, allowing them to raise the prices of factory goods on which farmers depended. Farmers, however, had to sell their wheat, cotton, and other staples in foreign markets, where competition lowered prices. Tariffs inflicted a double blow on farmers because insofar as they hampered imports, they indirectly hampered exports by making it harder for foreign buyers to get the necessary American currency or exchange to purchase American crops.

Debt, too, had been a perennial agricultural problem. After the Civil War, farmers grew ever more enmeshed in debt: western farmers incurred mortgages to cover the costs of land and machinery, while south-

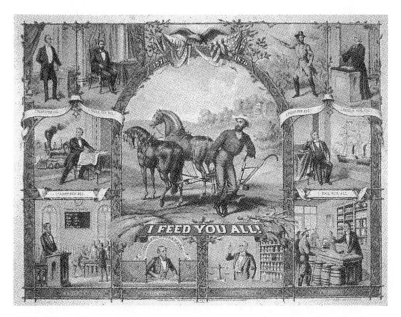

"I Feed You All," a poster showing the farmer at the center of society, first published in Prairie Farmer *in 1869.*

ern farmers were forced to use crop liens to the local merchant. As commodity prices dropped, the debt burden grew because farmers had to cultivate more wheat or cotton to raise the same amount of money. By growing more they furthered the vicious cycle of surpluses and price declines.

THE GRANGER MOVEMENT When the Department of Agriculture sent Oliver H. Kelley, a former Minnesota farmer and post office clerk, on a tour of the postbellum South in 1866, it was the farmers' isolation that most impressed him. Resolving to do something about it, Kelley in 1867 founded the Patrons of Husbandry, better known as the Grange (an old word for granary). In the next few years, the Grange mushroomed, reaching a membership as high as 1.5 million by 1874. While the Grange started out as a social and educational response to the isolation of farm folk, as it grew it began to promote farmer-owned cooperatives for buying and selling. Their ideal was to free farmers from the conventional marketplace.

The Grange soon became indirectly involved in politics through independent third parties, especially in the Midwest during the early 1870s. The Grangers' chief political goal was state regulation of the rates charged by railroads and warehouses. In five states they brought about the passage of "Granger Laws," which provoked court challenges. In a key case involving warehouse regulation, *Munn* v. *Illinois* (1877), the Supreme Court affirmed that the state under its "police powers" had the right to regulate property where that property was clothed with a public interest.

The Granger movement gradually declined (but never vanished) as members' energies were drawn off into cooperatives, many of which failed, and into political action. Out of the independent political movements of the time there grew, in 1875, a party known as the Greenback party, which favored expansion of the currency with more paper money. In the 1878 midterm elections it polled over 1 million votes and elected fifteen congressmen. But in 1880 the party's fortunes declined, and it disintegrated after 1884.

FARMERS' ALLIANCES   As the Grange lost energy, other farm organizations grew in size and significance: the Farmers' Alliances. Like the Grange, the Farmers' Alliances offered social and recreational opportunities, but they also emphasized political action. Farmers throughout the South and Midwest, where tenancy rates were highest, rushed to join the Alliance movement. They saw in collective action a way to seek relief from the hardships created by chronic indebtedness, declining prices, and devastating droughts. Unlike the Grange, which was a national organization and tended to attract larger and more prosperous farmers, the Alliance was a grassroots local organization representing marginal farmers.

The Alliance movement absorbed existing farm groups and organized new locals. It swept the cotton belt and established strong positions in Kansas and the Dakotas. In 1886, a white minister in Texas, which had one of the largest and most influential Alliance movements, responded to the appeals of black farmers and organized the Colored Alliance. The white leadership of the Alliance movement in Texas endorsed this development because the Colored Alliance stressed that its objective was economic justice, not social equality. By 1890, the Alliance movement had members from New York to California numbering about 1.5 million, and the Colored Farmers' Alliance claimed over 1 million members.

A powerful attraction for many isolated, struggling farmers and their families was the sense of community provided by the Alliance. An Alliance gathering resembled what one observer described as "a religious revival . . . a pentecost . . . in which the tongue of flame sat upon every man, and each spake as the spirit gave him utterance."

The Alliance movement welcomed rural women and men over sixteen years old who displayed a "good moral character," believed in God, and demonstrated "industrious habits." One North Carolina woman expressed her appreciation for the "grand opportunities" the Alliance provided women to emerge from traditional domesticity. "Drudgery, fashion, and gossip," she declared, "are no longer the bounds of woman's sphere." One of the Alliance publications made the point explicitly: "The Alliance has come to redeem woman from her enslaved condition, and place her in her proper sphere." The number of women in the Alliance movement grew rapidly, and many assumed key leadership roles.

The Alliance movement sponsored an ambitious social and educational program, and about 1,000 affiliated newspapers. But unlike the Grange, the Alliance also proposed from the start an elaborate economic program. In 1890 Alliance agencies and exchanges in some eighteen states claimed a business of $10 million, but they soon went the way of the Granger cooperatives, victims of discrimination by wholesalers, manufacturers, railroads, and bankers, and also of their own inexperienced management and overextended credit.

FARM POLITICS   In the late 1880s, the Alliance movement turned to politics to help farmers. In Texas, in 1886, a devastating drought brought matters to a head. When President Grover Cleveland vetoed a bill to aid Texas farmers, Alliance leaders resolved to challenge the Democratic party at the polls. Although conservative members whose primary allegiance was to the Democratic party left the movement, many members remained who were ready to carry out the fight both locally and nationally.

In 1887 Charles W. Macune, the new Alliance president, announced his intention to exert pressure on Congress to assist southern farmers. In addition, he proposed that Texas farmers create their own Alliance Exchange in an effort to free themselves from their dependence on processors and banks. Members of the Exchange would sign joint notes, borrow money from banks, and purchase their goods and supplies from a new corporation created by the Alliance in Dallas. The Exchange would also build its own warehouses to store and market the crops of members. While their crops were being stored, member farmers could obtain credit from the warehouse cooperative so they could buy goods and supplies.

This grand "cooperative" scheme collapsed when the Texas banks refused to accept the joint notes from Alliance members. This led Macune and others to focus their energies on what Macune called a "subtreasury plan." Under this plan, farmers would be able to store their crops in new government warehouses and obtain government loans for up to 80 percent of their crops' value at 1 percent interest. Besides providing immediate credit, the plan would allow the farmer the leeway to hold a crop for a better price later, since he would not have to sell it immediately at harvest time to pay off debts. The plan would also promote inflation because these loans to farmers would be made in new legal-tender notes.

The subtreasury plan went before Congress in 1890 but was never adopted. Its defeat as well as setbacks to other proposals convinced many farm leaders that they needed political power to secure railroad regulation, currency inflation, state departments of agriculture, antitrust laws, and farm credit.

In the West where hard times had descended after the blizzards of 1887, farmers were ready for third-party action. In the South, however, white Alliance members hesitated to bolt the Democratic party, seeking instead to influence or control it. Both approaches gained startling success. Independent parties under various names upset the political balance in western states, almost electing a governor under the banner of the People's party (also known as the Populist party) in Kansas (a Populist was elected governor in 1892) and taking control of one house of the legislature there and both houses in Nebraska. In South Dakota and Minnesota, Populists gained a balance of power in the legislatures, while Kansas and South Dakota sent Populists to the Senate.

The farm movement produced colorful leaders, especially in Kansas, where Mary Elizabeth Lease advised farmers "to raise less corn and more hell." Born in Pennsylvania to parents who were political exiles from Ireland, she eventually migrated to Kansas, taught school, raised a family, and finally failed at farming in the mid-1880s. She then studied law for a time, "pinning sheets of notes above her wash tub," and

Mary Elizabeth Lease, 1890.

through strenuous effort became one of the state's first female lawyers. At the same time, she took up public speaking on behalf of various causes ranging from Irish nationalism to temperance to women's suffrage. By the end of the 1880s, Lease had joined the Alliance as well as the Knights of Labor, and she soon applied her gifts as a fiery speaker to the cause of free silver. A tall, proud, and imposing woman, Lease drew attentive audiences. "The people are at bay," she warned in 1894, "let the bloodhounds of money beware."

"Sockless Jerry" Simpson was an equally colorful farm leader. Born in Canada, Simpson eventually moved to Kansas, where he tried and failed at farming and cattle-raising. Simpson's difficulties led him to the Alliance movement, and in 1890 he campaigned for Congress. A shrewd, witty, and intelligent man with huge, calloused hands and pale blue eyes, Simpson simplified the complex economic and political issues of the day. "Man must have access to the land," he maintained, "or he is a slave." He warned Republicans: "You can't put this movement down by sneers or by ridicule, for its foundation was laid as far back as the foundation of the world. It is a struggle between the robbers and the robbed." His Republican opponent for Congress, a wealthy railroad lawyer, conducted his campaign from a private rail car, and this gave Simpson a perfect foil. Simpson dismissed him as a pawn of the corporations whose "soft white hands" and "silk hosiery" betrayed his true priorities. His outraged opponent thereupon shouted that it was better to have silk socks than none at all, providing Simpson with an endearing

Tom Watson.

nickname. "Sockless Jerry" Simpson won a seat in Congress, and so too did many other farmers' advocates.

In the South the Alliance won equal if not greater success by forcing the Democrats to nominate candidates pledged to their program. In 1890 the southern states elected four pro-Alliance governors, seven pro-Alliance legislatures, forty-four pro-Alliance congressmen, and several senators. Among the most respected of the southern Alliance leaders was Tom Watson of Georgia. The son of prosperous slaveholders who lost everything during and after the Civil War, he attended Mercer University for two years before running out of funds, and eventually became a successful lawyer and charismatic orator on behalf of the Alliance cause. He took the lead in appealing to black tenants and sharecroppers to join with their white counterparts in ousting the Bourbon white political elite. "You are kept apart," he told black and white farmers, "that you may be separately fleeced of your earnings."

THE POPULIST PARTY AND THE ELECTION OF 1892 As economic conditions worsened, many insurgents began promoting the formation of a new national political party. In 1891 delegates from farm, labor, and reform organizations met in Cincinnati to discuss the creation of a People's party. Few southerners attended, but many endorsed the third-party idea after their failure to win over the Democratic party to the subtreasury plan. In 1892 a larger meeting at St. Louis proposed a national convention of the People's party at Omaha to adopt a platform and choose national candidates.

The platform focused on issues of finance, transportation, and land. Its financial program demanded the subtreasury plan, free and unlimited coinage of silver, an increase in the amount of money in circulation, and a graduated income tax. As to transportation, the government should nationalize the railroads, and the telephone and telegraph systems as well. It should also reclaim from railroads and other corporations lands "in excess of their actual needs," and forbid land ownership by illegal aliens. Finally, the platform endorsed the eight-hour workday and immigration restriction laws, taking these positions to win support from the urban workers, whom Populists looked upon as fellow "producers."

The party's platform turned out to be more exciting than its candidate, Iowa's James B. Weaver. Though an able, prudent man, Weaver carried the stigma of his defeat on the Greenback ticket twelve years before. To balance Weaver, a former Union general, the party named a former Confederate general for vice-president.

The Populist party was the startling new feature of the 1892 campaign. The major parties renominated Grover Cleveland and Benjamin Harrison. The tariff remained the chief issue between them. The outcome, however, was different. Both major candidates polled over 5 million votes, but Cleveland carried a plurality of the popular votes and a majority of the electoral college. Weaver gained over 1 million votes, which was 10 percent of the total vote, and carried Colorado, Kansas, Nevada, and Idaho, for a total of twenty-two electoral votes.

THE ECONOMY AND THE SILVER SOLUTION

While the farmers were funneling their discontent into politics and businessmen were consolidating their holdings, a fundamental weakness in the economy would soon manifest itself in a major economic collapse.

AN INADEQUATE CURRENCY The nation's money supply in the late nineteenth century lacked the flexibility to grow along with America's expanding economy. From 1865 to 1890, the amount of currency in circulation per capita decreased about 10 percent. Currency deflation then contributed to the cost of borrowing money, as a tight money supply caused bankers to hike interest rates on loans.

Metallic currency dated from the Mint Act of 1792, which authorized free and unlimited coinage of silver and gold at a ratio of 15 to 1. The ratio meant that the amount of precious metal in a silver dollar weighed fifteen times as much as that in a gold dollar. This reflected the relative values of gold and silver at the time. The phrase "free and unlimited coinage" simply meant that owners of precious metals could have any quantity of their gold or silver coined free, except for a nominal fee to cover costs.

A fixed ratio of values, however, could not reflect fluctuations in the market value of the metals. When gold rose to a market value higher than that reflected in the official ratio, owners ceased to present it for coinage. The country was actually on a silver standard until 1837, when Congress changed the ratio to 16 to 1, which soon reversed the situation. Silver became more valuable in the open market than in coinage, and the country drifted to a gold standard. This state of affairs prevailed until 1873, when Congress passed a general revision of the coinage laws and dropped the then-unused provision for the coinage of silver.

This occurred, however, just when silver production began to increase, reducing its market value through the growth in supply. Under the old laws, this would have induced owners of silver to present it at the mint for coinage. Soon advocates of currency inflation began to denounce the "crime of '73," which they had scarcely noticed at the time. Gradually suspicion grew that bankers and merchants had conspired in 1873 to ensure a scarcity of money. But the silverites had little more legislative success than the advocates of greenback inflation. The Bland-Allison Act of 1878 and the Sherman Silver Purchase Act of 1890 provided for some silver coinage, but too little in each case to offset the overall contraction of the currency.

THE DEPRESSION OF 1893 Just before Cleveland started his second term, one of the most devastating business panics in history erupted when the Philadelphia and Reading Railroad declared bankruptcy and set off a panic on Wall Street. Not only business was affected, but also entire farm regions were devastated by the spreading depression. One-quarter of the cities' unskilled workers lost their jobs, and by the fall of 1893 over six hundred banks had closed. By 1894 the economy had reached bottom. That year some 750,000 workers went out on strike; millions found themselves unemployed; railroad construction workers, laid off in the West, began tramping east and talked of marching on Washington.

Few of them made it to the capital. One group that did was "Coxey's Army," led by Jacob S. Coxey, a wealthy Ohio quarry owner turned Populist who demanded that the federal government provide unemployed people with meaningful work. Coxey, his wife, and their son, Legal Tender Coxey, rode in a carriage ahead of some 400 hardy protesters who finally straggled into Washington. There Coxey was arrested for walking on the grass. Although his ragtag army dispersed without any violent incidents, its march on Washington as well as the growing political strength of populism struck fear into the hearts of many Americans. Critics portrayed Populists as "hayseed socialists" whose election would endanger property rights.

The 1894 congressional elections took place amid this climate of anxiety. The elections amounted to a severe setback for the Democrats, who paid politically for the economic downturn, and the Republicans were the chief beneficiaries. The Populists emerged with six senators and seven representatives. They had polled 1.5 million votes for their congressional candidates and still expected the festering discontent to carry them to national power in 1896.

SILVERITES VS. GOLDBUGS The course of events, however, would dash that hope. In the mid-1890s events conspired to focus all concerns on the currency issue. One of the causes of the 1893 depression had been the failure of a major British bank, which led many British investors to unload their American holdings in return for gold. Soon after Cleveland's inauguration, the gold reserve fell below $100 million. To plug this drain on the Treasury, the president sought repeal of the Sherman Silver Purchase Act to stop the issuance of silver notes redeemable in gold. Cleveland won the act's repeal in 1893, but at the cost of irreparable division in his own party. One embittered silver Democrat labeled the president a "Benedict Arnold."

Western silver interests now escalated their demands for silver coinage, which presented a strategic dilemma for Populists: Should the party promote the long list of varied reforms it had originally advocated, or should it try to ride the silver issue into power? The latter seemed the practical choice. As a consequence, the Populist leaders decided, over the protest of more radical members, to hold their 1896 convention last, confident that the two major parties would at best straddle the silver issue and that the Populists would then reap a harvest of bolting silverite Republicans and Democrats.

THE ELECTION OF 1896 Contrary to these expectations, the major parties took clear and opposing positions on the currency issue. The Republicans, as expected, chose William McKinley on a gold-standard platform. McKinley had a magisterial appearance. His high forehead, sharply cut mouth, and Roman nose looked presidential, and then, as now, looks were important in national politics. On the Democratic side, the pro-silver forces gathered to wrest control of the party from Cleveland and the fiscal conservatives. A reporter covering the convention recognized the shift of power: "All the silverites need is a Moses. They have the principle, they have the grit . . . and they have the howl and the hustle." They also soon had their Moses, who emerged this time not from the bullrushes but from the Nebraska plains.

In William Jennings Bryan, the silver Democrats found a crusading, charismatic leader. A fervent Baptist and advocate of the free coinage of silver, Bryan was a two-term congressman from Nebraska who had been defeated in the senatorial race in 1894. At the 1896 convention the self-assured Bryan delivered a galvanizing speech that had most of the 20,000 delegates on their feet and many in tears. Much like a revivalist at a camp meeting, he drew the audience with the emotion of his appeal. Bryan spoke for silver and the new West, for the "hardy pioneers" and against the "financial magnates" of the urban East. "Burn down

William Jennings Bryan, whose "Cross of Gold" speech at the 1896 Democratic convention roused the delegates and secured him the party's presidential nomination.

your cities and leave our farms [untouched]," he predicted, "and your cities will spring up again as if by magic; but destroy our farms and the grass will grow in the streets of every city in the country." He then directly challenged Republicans as well as Cleveland and the gold Democrats with a compelling metaphor: "You shall not press down upon the brow of labor this crown of thorns. You shall not crucify mankind upon a cross of gold!"

The next day the heroic Bryan was nominated on the fifth ballot, and in the process the Democratic party was fractured beyond repair. Disappointed pro-gold Democrats walked out of the convention and nominated their own candidate, who then announced: "Fellow Democrats, I will not consider it any great fault if you decide to cast your vote for William McKinley."

When the Populists met in St. Louis two weeks later, they faced an impossible choice. "If we fuse [with the Democrats]," one Populist admitted, "all the silver men we have will leave us for the more powerful Democrats." But if they named their own candidate, they would divide the silver vote with Bryan and give the election to McKinley. "Sockless Jerry" Simpson advised merger: "I care not for party names; it is substance we are after, and we have it in William J. Bryan." In the end the delegates agreed. They backed Bryan, but chose their own vice-presidential candidate, Georgia's Tom Watson, and invited the Democrats to drop their vice-presidential nominee—an action that Bryan refused to countenance.

The thirty-six-year-old Bryan launched a whirlwind campaign. He crisscrossed the country, exploiting his spellbinding eloquence and radiating honesty, sincerity, and energy. McKinley, meanwhile, conducted a "front-porch campaign," receiving selected delegations of supporters at his home in Canton, Ohio, and giving only prepared responses. His campaign manager, Mark Hanna, shrewdly portrayed Bryan as a radical whose "communistic spirit" would ruin the capitalist system. Many observers agreed with the portrait. The editor of the *New York Tribune* denounced Bryan as a "wretched rattle-pated boy, posing in vapid vanity and mouthing resounding rottenness." A factory owner told his employees: "Men, vote as you please, but if Bryan is elected . . . the whistle will not blow Wednesday morning."

By preying upon such fears, Hanna raised a huge campaign chest and financed an army of Republican speakers who stumped the country in

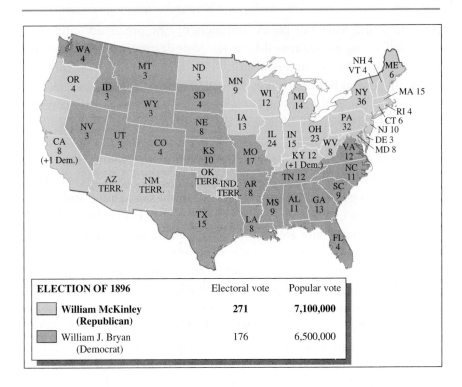

ELECTION OF 1896	Electoral vote	Popular vote
William McKinley (Republican)	271	7,100,000
William J. Bryan (Democrat)	176	6,500,000

support of McKinley. In the end, the Democratic-Populist-Silverite candidates were overwhelmed. McKinley won the popular vote by 7.1 million to 6.5 million and the electoral college vote by 271 to 176.

Bryan carried most of the West and the South below the border states, but garnered little support in the metropolitan centers east of the Mississippi and north of the Ohio and Potomac Rivers. Urban workers simply saw little to gain from the inflation promoted by Bryan and the silverites. Factory workers in the cities found it easier to identify with McKinley's "full dinner pail" than with Bryan's free silver. Moreover, in the critical midwestern battleground, from Minnesota and Iowa eastward to Ohio, Bryan carried not a single state. Many ethnic voters, normally drawn to the Democrats, were repelled by Bryan's Baptist evangelical style. Farmers in the East and Midwest, moreover, were hurting less than those in the wheat and cotton belts. There was less tenancy and a greater diversity of crops in those farm regions, and the prospering farmers therefore saw little attraction in agrarian radicalism.

A NEW ERA

The election of 1896 was a climactic political struggle between rural and metropolitan America, and metropolitan America won. Anticipating Bryan's defeat and the collapse of the Populist vision, Mark Hanna telegraphed McKinley on election night, "God's in his Heaven, all's right with the world!"

The values of urban-industrial America had indeed taken firm hold of the political system. As its first important act the McKinley administration called a special session of Congress to raise the tariff again. The Dingley Tariff of 1897 became the highest to that time. By 1897, prosperity was returning, helped along by inflation of the currency, which bore out the arguments of greenbackers and silverites. But the inflation came, in one of history's many ironies, not from silver but from a new flood of gold onto the market and into the mints. During the 1880s and 1890s, new discoveries of gold in South Africa, Canada, and the Yukon led to spectacular new gold rushes, a return to the gold standard, and an end to the free silver movement. To compound the irony, most of the Populist platform, which seemed so radical in 1892, would nevertheless take effect within two decades.

Amid the new prosperity, the old issues of tariffs and currency policy gave way to international concerns. "The Spanish War finished us," said Populist Tom Watson. "The blare of the bugle drowned the voice of the Reformer."

MAKING CONNECTIONS

- This chapter concludes with the suggestion that the Spanish-American War, a major event on the horizon, marked the end of the reform spirit of the Populists.

- The laissez-faire policies of the Gilded Age were challenged by Progressive reform activists, discussed in Chapter 23.

- William Jennings Bryan was one of the most prominent figures in American politics and political culture over some thirty years.

FURTHER READING

For overviews of the Gilded Age see Robert H. Wiebe's *The Search for Order, 1877–1920* (1967), John A. Garraty's *The New Commonwealth, 1877–1890* (1968), and Vincent P. DeSantis's *The Shaping of Modern America, 1877–1920* (2nd ed., 1989). Nell Painter's *Standing at Armageddon: The United States, 1877–1919* (1987) focuses on the experience of the working classes.

Party politics is the emphasis of H. Wayne Morgan's *From Hayes to McKinley: National Party Politics, 1877–1896* (1969) and Richard J. Jensen's *The Winning of the Midwest: Social and Political Conflict, 1888–1896* (1971). Public participation in politics is explained in Paul Kleppner's *Who Voted? The Dynamics of Electoral Turnout, 1870–1980* (1982).

On the Gilded-Age presidents, see William S. McFeely's *Grant: A Biography* (1981), Allan Peskin's *Garfield: A Biography* (1978), Thomas C. Reeves's *Gentleman Boss: The Life of Chester Alan Arthur* (rev. ed., 1991), and Lewis L. Gould's *The Presidency of William McKinley* (1980).

Scholars have also examined various Gilded-Age issues and interest groups. John G. Sproat's *The Best Men: Liberal Reformers in the Gilded Age* (1968) and Gerald W. McFarland's *Mugwumps, Morals, and Politics, 1884–1920* (1975) examine the issue of reforming government service. Tom E. Terrill's *The Tariff, Politics, and American Foreign Policy, 1874–1901* (1973) lends clarity to that complex issue. The finances of the Gilded Age are covered in Irwin Unger's *The Greenback Era: A Social and Political History of American Finance, 1865–1879* (1964) and Walter T. K. Nugent's *Money and American Society, 1865–1880* (1968).

One of the most controversial works on populism is Lawrence Goodwyn's *The Populist Movement: A Short History of the Agrarian Revolt in America* (1978). Goodwyn's emphasis on the cooperative nature of agrarian protest and his criticism of the western branch as a sham movement contradicted the prevailing interpretations. A more judicious account is Robert C. McMath, Jr.'s *American Populism: A Social History, 1877–1898* (1993). Jeffrey Ostler's *Prairie Populism: The Fate of Agrarian Radicalism in Kansas, Nebraska, and Iowa, 1880–1892* (1993) minimizes the role of the financial panic in stimulating the grassroots movement.

PART SIX

MODERN
AMERICA

POLITICAL	**GLOBAL**
1900	
William McKinley is reelected president (1900)	Hay-Pauncefote Treaty establishes mutual consent of Britain and U.S. to building canal across Central America (1901)
Government promotes efficiency, regulations, and reform legislation (1900–1917)	Panama wins independence from Colombia with support of U.S. troops (1903); U.S. constructs Panama Canal (1903–1914)
Commission system of municipal government implemented for 1st time (1901)	
McKinley is assassinated; Theodore Roosevelt becomes president (1901–1909)	Russo-Japanese War (1904–1905)
Government reforms continue as more states adopt direct primaries and elections (1900s–1920s)	Roosevelt Corollary to the Monroe Doctrine aims to curtail European interference in the Americas (1904)
	U.S. accepts Japanese control of Korea with Taft-Katsura Agreement (1905)
	Bloody Sunday massacre leads to revolution in Russia (1905)
	U.S.'s Great White Fleet circles the globe brandishing American naval might (1907–1909)
Manager plan of municipal government implemented for 1st time (1908)	Root-Takahira Agreement reaffirms Open Door Policy in China (1908)
William Howard Taft becomes president (1909–1913)	U.S. troops intervene in Honduras (1907, 1911, 1924)
1910 Ballinger-Pinchot controversy over conservation leads to reform of committee system in House (1910)	Revolution in China (1911)
Roosevelt forms Bull Moose party after split with Taft (1912)	U.S. troops occupy Nicaragua (1912–1925; 1926–1933)
17th Amendment ratified, calling for direct election of senators (1913)	
Woodrow Wilson becomes president (1913–1921)	Panama Canal opens (1914)
	Wilson sends troops to Mexico, Haiti, and Dominican Republic (1914–1917)
	Serbian nationalists murder Austrian Archduke Franz Ferdinand, precipitating WWI (1914)
	German U-boat sinks British liner *Lusitania* (1915)
	Einstein publishes "The Foundations of the General Theory of Relativity" (1916)
U.S. enters WWI on side of Britain, France, and Russia (1917)	Bolsheviks seize power in Russian Revolution (1917)
Espionage and Sedition Acts outlaw criticism of government leaders and war policies (1917, 1918)	
Wilson delivers his Fourteen Points to Congress (1918)	Russians withdraw from war after separate peace with Germany in Treaty of Brest-Litovsk (1918)
Congress rejects Wilson's Fourteen Points and the League of Nations (1919)	Treaty of Versailles ends WWI (1919)
Secretary of State Mitchell Palmer leads witch-hunts against suspected liberals, launching the 1st Red Scare in U.S. (1919)	

SOCIAL	ECONOMIC	
Muckrakers continue to use the press to engage America's social conscience (1900s)	Discovery of Texas's Spindletop gusher brings oil rush to Southwest (1901)	1900
Baseball's 1st world series takes place (1903)	Roosevelt's intervention (1902) leads to settlement of coal strike (1903)	
	Congress creates Department of Commerce and Labor (1903)	
National Child Labor Committee founded to combat employment of young children (1904)	Northern Securities Co. is broken up in 1st of 25 successful antitrust suits of the Roosevelt administration (1904)	
	Industrial Workers of the World (Wobblies) is established (1905)	
	Swift & Co. v. U.S. establishes "stream of interstate commerce" doctrine, making meat packers subject to federal legislation (1905)	
Upton Sinclair's The Jungle depicts horrors of meat-packing industry (1906)	Hepburn Act, Meat Inspection Act, and Pure Food and Drug Act increase federal regulatory authority over the economy (1906)	
Gentlemen's Agreement halts influx of Japanese laborers to U.S. (1907)		
Angel Island is established as reception center for Asian immigrants (1910)	Mann-Elkin Act extends federal regulation to telephone and telegraph industries (1910)	1910
Black leaders establish NAACP (1910)	Supreme Court dissolves Standard Oil and the American Tobacco Company (1911)	
Triangle Shirtwaist fire leads to increased regulation of the workplace (1911)		
Frederick W. Taylor publishes The Principles of Scientific Management (1911)	AFL union increases 37% (1913–1918)	
	16th Amendment creates income tax (1913)	
	Federal Reserve Act creates regional reserve banks (1913)	
	Underwood-Simmons Tariff reduces average duty from 37% to 29% (1913)	
	Federal Trade Commission is created to prevent unfair trade practices (1914)	
	Clayton Antitrust Act tightens 1890 Sherman Antitrust Act (1914)	
	War in Europe causes economic boom in U.S. (1915)	
Government drafts 4 million men; women, blacks, and other ethnic minorities employed in factories (1916–1919)	War mobilization results in widespread rationing (1916–1919)	
	Federal Highways Act provides funds for national road network (1916)	
"Great Migration" of southern blacks to northern cities (1916–1919)	War Industries Board sets priorities and plans industrial production (1917)	
Spanish flu kills 500,000 Americans (1918–1919)	Widespread strikes partially paralyze U.S. economy (1919)	
Nationwide race riots result in hundreds of dead and injured (1919)		
18th Amendment launches Prohibition (1919)		

	POLITICAL	GLOBAL
1920	Women win right to vote with 19th Amendment (1920)	League of Nations (1920–1946)
	Warren G. Harding becomes president (1921–1923)	Washington Armaments Conference attempts to ward off conflicts in the Pacific (1921)
	National Woman's party proposes Equal Rights Amendment (1923)	Benito Mussolini seizes power in Italy (1922)
	Harding administration plagued with corruption; Teapot Dome Scandal (1923–1924)	
	Progressive party is organized, nominates Robert La Follette for president (1924)	Kellogg-Briand Treaty renounces war as "an instrument of national policy" (1928)
	Calvin Coolidge becomes president when Harding dies in office (1923–1929)	Nationalists rule in China under Chiang Kai-shek (1928–1949)
	Herbert Hoover becomes president (1929–1933)	Japanese occupy Chinese Manchuria (1931)
1930	Hoover signs Emergency Relief and Construction Act to provide funds to states to relieve suffering (1932)	U.S. and Soviet Union renew diplomatic relations after 16 years (1933)
	Franklin D. Roosevelt becomes president (1933–1945)	Hitler becomes Chancellor of Germany (1933)
	FDR pushes through New Deal relief measures to combat Great Depression (1933)	U.S. withdraws American troops from Nicaragua, Haiti, and Cuba as part of the "Good Neighbor" policy (1934)
	FDR's stalemate with Congress brings New Deal legislation to a halt (1935)	Spanish Civil War (1936–1939)
	FDR launches his 2nd New Deal to break stalemate with Congress and radicals (1935)	Chinese and Japanese troops begin full-scale war in the Pacific (1937)
		Germany annexes Austria (1938)
		France and Britain abandon Czechoslovakia at Munich Conference (1938)
		Germany invades Czechoslovakia (1939)
		Germany signs nonaggression pact with Soviets, then invades Poland, which leads to World War II in Europe (1939)
1940		Japan, Italy, and Germany sign the Tripartite Pact, a defensive alliance (1940)
		Nazi troops begin *blitzkrieg* (1940)
		Germany invades Russia (1941)
	FDR proposes Lend-Lease Bill to Congress, pledging to make America "the arsenal for democracy" (1941)	Atlantic Charter sets forth Allied war aims (1941)
	U.S. funds Manhattan Project, which builds atomic bomb (1942–1945)	Japanese attack Pearl Harbor; U.S. enters the war (1941)
		Allies take control of North Africa, then attack Italy (1943)
		D-day invasion (1944)
	FDR elected to 4th term (1944)	Allies "leapfrog" toward Japan (1944–1945)
		Soviets set up puppet regimes in eastern Europe (1944–1945)
1945		Big Three meet at Yalta to discuss the postwar world (1945)
	Harry S. Truman becomes president when FDR dies (1945–1953)	Germans surrender (1945)
		U.S. drops atomic bombs on Hiroshima and Nagasaki, ending the war (1945)
		50 million people die in WWII (1939–1945)

SOCIAL	ECONOMIC	

Marcus Garvey promotes "Negro nationalism" (1920s)

Gangsters make fortunes illegally producing and distributing alcohol (1920s)

KKK leads nativist campaign (1920s)

Rise of jazz music (1920s)

Modernist literary movement includes F. Scott Fitzgerald, Ernest Hemingway, Thomas Wolfe, William Faulkner (1920s–1930s)

Harlem Renaissance epitomizes black cultural movement (1920s–1930s)

Scopes "monkey trial" debates teaching of evolution in public schools (1925)

23,000 movie theaters attended by 95 million persons weekly (1930)

Unemployed veterans demonstrate in Washington, D.C. (1932)

800,000 "Dust Bowl" migrants flee to California (1932–1935)

21st Amendment ends Prohibition (1933)

Poverty delays 800,000 marriages in 1930s; total marriages decline by 1/4 (1930s)

John Steinbeck and Richard Wright write about displacement and racism during the Great Depression (1930s–1940s)

15 million Americans serve in WWII (1939–1945)

NAACP membership rises from 50,000 to 450,000 during the war (1941–1945)

1/3 of all eligible Native American males (25,000) serve in the war (1941–1945)

6 million women enter labor force during the war (1941–1945)

FDR orders internment of Japanese Americans (1942)

Bracero program brings 200,000+ Mexican farm workers to U.S. (1942–1945)

1920

Non-farmer wages increase 20% while wages for farmers increase only 10% (1921–1928)

Union membership in U.S. declines from 5 million to 3.5 million (1920–1929)

McNary-Haugen bill calls for tariffs to protect farmers (1924)

Speculative investment in stocks and real estate sets stage for depression (1925–1929)

Stock market crashes (1929)

In Great Depression personal income plummets, unemployment rises from 3% to 25%; 9,000 banks close, and run on banks occurs (1929–1933)

1930

Hawley-Smoot Tariff establishes high rates on imports (1930)

Roosevelt declares a 4-day banking holiday and establishes the Emergency Banking Relief Act (1933)

FERA, AAA, NIRA, and CCC are some of "Hundred Days" measures enacted under the New Deal (1933)

Johnson Debt Default Act prohibits private loans to countries that have defaulted on their WWI debts (1934)

Wagner Act legalizes collective bargaining for labor (1935)

AFL expels CIO unions (1936)

Social Security Act (1935)

1940

Office of Price Administration enacts wartime rationing (1942)

Servicemen's Readjustment Act earmarks $13 billion for veterans (1944)

National Security Industrial Association forges permanent peacetime alliance between industry and military (1944)

1945

National debt reaches $260 billion, 6 times what it was in 1941 (1945)

The United States entered the twentieth century in a state of flux. Since the election of Thomas Jefferson in 1800, the country had seen itself relentlessly transformed. A rural, agrarian society largely detached from the concerns of international affairs turned into a highly industrialized, urban culture with a growing involvement in world politics and commerce. In other words, the United States in 1900 was on the threshold of modernity.

The prospect of modernity both excited and scared Americans. Old truths and beliefs clashed with unsettling new scientific discoveries and social practices. People debated the legitimacy of Darwinism, the existence of God, the dangers of jazz, and the federal effort to prohibit alcoholic beverages. The automobile, airplane, and radio helped shrink the distances of time and space and accelerate a national consciousness. In the process, the United States began to emerge from its isolationist shell.

Noninvolvement in foreign wars and nonintervention in the internal affairs of foreign governments formed the pillars of American foreign policy until the end of the century. During the 1890s, however, expanding commercial interests around the world led Americans to extend the horizons of their concerns. Imperialism was the order of the day among the great European powers, and a growing number of American expansionists demanded that the United States also adopt a global ambition and join in the hunt for new territories and markets. Such motives helped spark the Spanish-American War of 1898 and justify the resulting acquisition of American colonies outside the continental United States. Entangling alliances with European powers soon followed.

The outbreak of the Great War in Europe in 1914 posed an even greater challenge to the American tradition of isolation and nonintervention. The prospect of a German victory over the French and British threatened the European balance of power, which had long ensured the security of the United States. By 1917, it appeared that Germany might emerge triumphant and begin to menace the Western Hemisphere. Woodrow Wilson's crusade to use American intervention in World War I to transform the world order in accordance with his idealistic principles severed American foreign policy from its isolationist moorings. It also spawned a prolonged debate about the role of the United States in world affairs, a debate that World War II would resolve for a time on the side of internationalism.

At the same time that the United States was entering the world stage as a great military power, it was also becoming a great industrial power. Cities and factories sprouted across the landscape. An abundance of new jobs served as a magnet attracting millions of immigrants from every corner of the globe. They were not always welcomed, nor were they readily assimilated. Ethnic and racial strife, as well as labor agitation, increased at the turn of the century. In the midst of such social turmoil and unparalleled economic development, American reformers made their first sustained attempt to adapt their political and social institutions to the realities of the industrial age. The worst excesses and injustices of urban-industrial development—corporate monopolies, child labor, political corruption, hazardous working conditions, urban ghettos—were finally addressed in a comprehensive way. During the Progressive Era (1900–1917), local, state, and federal governments sought to rein in the excesses of industrial capitalism and develop a more rational and efficient public policy.

A conservative Republican resurgence challenged the notion of the new regulatory state during the 1920s. Free enterprise and corporate capitalism witnessed a dramatic revival. But the stock market crash of 1929 helped propel the United States and many other nations into the worst economic downturn in history. The unprecedented severity of the Great Depression renewed public demands for federal government programs to protect the general welfare. "This nation asks for action," declared President Franklin D. Roosevelt in his 1933 inaugural address. The many New Deal initiatives and agencies instituted by Roosevelt and his Democratic administration created the framework for a welfare state that has since served as the basis for American public policy.

The New Deal helped revive public confidence and put people back to work, but it did not end the Great Depression. It took a world war to restore full employment. The necessity of mobilizing the nation in support of the Second World War also served to accelerate the growth of the federal government. And the incredible scope of the war helped catapult the United States into a leadership role in world politics. The creation of a nuclear bomb to help end the war ushered in a new era of atomic diplomacy that held the fate of the world in the balance. For all of the new creature comforts associated with modern life, Americans in 1945 found themselves living amid an array of new anxieties.

22   AN AMERICAN EMPIRE

CHAPTER ORGANIZER

This chapter focuses on:

- the circumstances that led to America's "new imperialism."

- the causes of the Spanish-American War.

- Theodore Roosevelt's foreign policy in Asia and Latin America.

Throughout the nineteenth century, most Americans displayed what one senator called "only a languid interest" in foreign affairs. Indeed, the overriding concerns of the time were industrial development, western settlement, and domestic politics. Compared to these concerns, foreign relations simply were not important to the vast majority of Americans. After the Civil War, an isolationist mood swept across the United States as the country basked in its geographic advantages: wide oceans as buffers on either side, the British navy situated between America and the powers of Europe, and militarily weak neighbors in the Western Hemisphere.

Yet the notion of America having a "Manifest Destiny" ordained by God to expand its territory and influence remained alive in the decades after the end of the Civil War. Several prominent political and business leaders argued that the rapid industrial development of the United

States required the acquisition of foreign territories to gain easier access to vital raw materials. In addition, as their exports grew, American companies and farmers would become increasingly intertwined in the world economy. This, in turn, would require an expanded naval presence to protect the shipping lanes. And a modern steam-powered navy needed bases to replenish the coal and water required for its ships. For these reasons and others, the United States during the last quarter of the nineteenth century began to expand its presence beyond the Western Hemisphere.

TOWARD THE NEW IMPERIALISM

European powers had already unleashed a new surge of imperialism in Africa and Asia, where they had seized territory, established colonies and protectorates, and had begun a systematic program of economic exploitation and Christian evangelism. Writing in 1902, the British economist J. A. Hobson declared that imperialism was "the most powerful factor in the current politics of the Western world."

IMPERIALISM IN A GLOBAL CONTEXT Western imperialism had economic roots, and the new imperialism was above all a quest for markets and raw materials. The second industrial revolution generated such dramatic increases in production that business leaders felt compelled to find new markets for their burgeoning supply of goods and new sources of investment for their growing supply of capital. Manufacturers, on the other hand, were eager to find new sources of raw materials to supply their expanding needs. At the same time, the aggressive nationalism (called "jingoism" at the time) and bitter rivalries of the European powers made all of them compete with the others as they expanded their empires.

The result was a widespread process of imperial expansion into Africa and Asia, often with brutal consequences for the indigenous peoples. Beginning in the 1880s, the British, French, Belgians, Italians, Dutch, Spanish, and Germans used military force and political guile to conquer and subjugate regions of Africa and Asia. As a British nationalist explained such global ambitions, "Today, power and domination rather than freedom and independence are the ideas that appeal to the imagination of the masses—and the national ideal has given way to the imperial." Unfortunately, this imperial outlook also set in motion clashes among the Western powers that would lead to unprecedented conflict in the twentieth century.

AMERICAN IMPERIALISM   As the European nations expanded their control over much of the rest of the world, Americans also began to acquire territories outside the continental United States. This reflected the country's growing international power and prestige. It also mirrored the efforts of the European nations to acquire colonial possessions.

Most Americans became increasingly aware of world markets as developments in transportation and communication quickened the pace of commerce and diplomacy. From the first, agricultural exports had been the basis of economic growth. Now the conviction grew that American manufacturers had matured to the point that they could outsell foreign goods in the world market. But should the expansion of markets lead to territorial expansion as well? Or to intervention in the internal affairs of other countries? On such points Americans disagreed, but a small yet vocal and influential group of public officials embraced the idea of overseas possessions, regardless of the implications. These expansionists included Senators Albert J. Beveridge of Indiana and Henry Cabot Lodge of Massachusetts, Theodore Roosevelt, and not least of all, naval Captain Alfred Thayer Mahan.

During the 1880s, Captain Mahan became a leading advocate of sea power and Western imperialism. In 1890 he published *The Influence of Sea Power upon History, 1660–1783,* in which he argued that national greatness and prosperity flowed from sea power. To Mahan, modern economic development called for a powerful navy, a strong merchant marine, foreign commerce, colonies, and naval bases. Mahan championed America's "destiny" to control the Caribbean, build an isthmian canal, and spread Western civilization in the Pacific. His ideas were widely circulated in popular journals and within the American government.

Even before Mahan's writings became influential, a gradual expansion of the American navy had begun. In 1880 the nation had fewer than a hundred seagoing vessels, many of them rusting or rotting at the docks. By 1896, eleven powerful new battleships had been built or authorized.

IMPERIALIST THEORY   Certain intellectual concepts bolstered the new imperialist spirit and buttressed claims of racial superiority. Spokesmen in each country, including the United States, used the arguments of Social Darwinism to justify economic exploitation. Among nations as among individuals, expansionists claimed, the fittest survive and prevail. John Fiske, the historian and popular lecturer on Darwinism, developed racial corollaries from Darwin's ideas. In *American Political Ideas* (1885), he stressed the superior character of "Anglo-Saxon" institutions and peoples. The English "race," he argued, was destined to dominate the globe in the institutions, traditions, language, even in the blood of the world's peoples.

Josiah Strong, a Congregationalist minister, added the sanction of religion to theories of racial and national superiority. In his book *Our Country: Its Possible Future and Its Present Crisis* (1885), Strong asserted that "Anglo-Saxons" embodied two great ideas: civil liberty and "a pure spiritual Christianity." The Anglo-Saxon was "divinely commissioned to be, in a peculiar sense, his brother's keeper." Moreover, each of the imperial nations, including the United States, dispatched Christian missionaries to convert the subject peoples. By 1900, some 18,000 Christian missionaries were scattered around the world.

Expansion in the Pacific

For expansionists, Asia especially offered an alluring temptation. President Andrew Johnson's secretary of state, William H. Seward, believed that the United States must inevitably exercise commercial domination "on the Pacific Ocean, and its islands and continents." Eager for American manufacturers to exploit Asian markets, Seward believed the United States first had to remove all foreign interests from the northern Pacific coast and gain access to that region's valuable ports. To that end, Seward cast covetous eyes on the British crown colony of British Columbia, sandwiched between Russia's possessions in Alaska and Washington Territory.

Late in 1866, while encouraging annexation sentiment among the British Columbians, Seward learned of Russia's desire to sell Alaska because it had become unprofitable. He leaped at the opportunity, and in 1867 the United States bought Alaska for $7.2 million, less than 2 cents an acre. "Seward's folly" of buying the Alaskan "icebox" proved in time to be the biggest bargain for the United States, economically and strategically, since the Louisiana Purchase.

SAMOA AND HAWAII   Seward's successors at the State Department sustained his expansionist vision, and the Pacific Ocean remained the major field of overseas activity. During the post–Civil War years, the United States sought coaling stations and trading posts in this area, and it laid claim to various small islands and coral atolls of the mid-Pacific. Two of these islands were especially strategic: Samoa and Hawaii (also known as the Sandwich Islands).

American interest in these islands gradually deepened as commercial activity in the Pacific increased, and in 1878 the Samoans signed a treaty with the United States that granted a naval base at Pago Pago. The following year the German and British governments worked out similar arrangements on other islands of the Samoan group.

In Hawaii, the Americans had a clearer field. The islands, a united kingdom since 1795, hosted a sizable settlement of American missionaries and planters, and had long been a popular way station for whalers and traders. They were also strategically more important than Samoa to the United States, since their occupation by another major power might have posed a threat to American sugar interests and even to defense of the continent.

In 1875 the Hawaiians signed a reciprocal trade agreement under which their sugar entered the United States duty free. Twelve years later it was amended to grant the United States exclusive right to a fortified naval base at Pearl Harbor, near Honolulu. These agreements prompted a boom in sugar growing, and American settlers in Hawaii came to dominate the economy. In 1887 the Americans forced Hawaii's king to grant a constitutional government, which they controlled.

Hawaii's political climate changed sharply when the king's sister, Queen Liliuokalani, ascended the throne in 1891 and began efforts to reclaim power. Shortly before that, the McKinley Tariff had destroyed Hawaii's favored position in the sugar trade by putting the sugar of all countries on the free list and granting growers in the United States a two-cent subsidy per pound of sugar. The resultant economic crisis and discontent in Hawaii led the white population to revolt early in 1893 and to seize power. The American minister brought in marines to sup-

Queen Liliuokalani.

port the coup. As he cheerfully reported to Washington, "The Hawaiian pear is now fully ripe, and this is the golden hour for the United States to pluck it." Within a month, a committee of the new American-dominated government visited Washington and, in 1893, signed an annexation treaty.

This occurred just weeks before President Harrison left office, however, and Democratic senators blocked ratification. President Cleveland withdrew the treaty and sent a special commissioner to investigate. He recalled the American marines and reported that Americans on the islands had acted improperly. Most Hawaiians opposed annexation, said the commissioner, who thought the revolution had been engineered mainly by sugar planters hoping for annexation in order to get the new domestic sugar subsidy for sugar grown in the United States. Cleveland therefore proposed to restore the queen in return for amnesty to the revolutionists. The provisional government refused and on July 4, 1894, proclaimed the Republic of Hawaii, which had in its constitution a standing provision for American annexation.

When William McKinley became president in 1897, he was looking for an excuse to annex the Hawaiian Islands. This excuse was found when the Japanese, also hoping to take over the islands, sent warships to Hawaii. McKinley responded by sending American warships and asked the Senate to approve a treaty to annex Hawaii. When the Senate could not muster the two-thirds majority needed to approve the treaty,

McKinley used a joint resolution of the House and Senate to achieve his aims. This resolution passed by simple majorities in both houses, and the United States annexed Hawaii in the summer of 1898.

THE SPANISH-AMERICAN WAR

Until the 1890s, a certain ambivalence about overseas possessions had checked America's drive to expand. Suddenly, in 1898 and 1899, the inhibitions collapsed, but not in a quest for bases and trade. Rather, the chief motive was a sense of outrage at another country's imperialism.

"CUBA LIBRE" Throughout the second half of the nineteenth century, Cubans had repeatedly revolted against Spanish rule, only to be ruthlessly put down. At the same time, American investments in Cuba, mainly in sugar and mining, were steadily rising. The United States in fact traded more with Cuba than Spain did. The growing economic interest in their island neighbor made Americans sympathetic to the idea of Cuban independence. When insurrection broke out again on February 24, 1895, public feeling in the United States was with the rebels, and many Americans extended help to the Cuban Revolutionary party, which organized the revolt and waged an effective propaganda campaign from headquarters in New York.

In 1896 Spanish general Valeriano Weyler adopted a policy of gathering Cubans behind Spanish lines, often in detention (*reconcentrado*) centers so that no one could join the insurrections by night and appear peaceful by day. In some of these centers, poor food and unsanitary conditions soon brought a heavy toll of disease and death. The American press promptly christened the Spanish commander "Butcher" Weyler.

Events in Cuba supplied exciting copy for the popular press. William Randolph Hearst's *New York Journal* and Joseph Pulitzer's *New York World* were at the time locked in a monumental competition for readers. "It was a battle of gigantic proportions," one journalist wrote, "in which the sufferings of Cuba merely chanced to furnish some of the most convenient ammunition." The sensationalism practiced by both papers came to be called "yellow journalism," and Hearst emerged as the undisputed champion. His *New York Journal* excelled at invective against "Weyler the brute, the devastator of haciendas, the destroyer of men."

PRESSURE FOR WAR   American neutrality toward events in Cuba changed sharply when McKinley entered office. His platform had endorsed Cuban independence, as well as American control of Hawaii and the construction of an isthmian canal. Spain offered Cuba autonomy (self-government without formal independence) in return for peace. What the Cubans might once have welcomed, however, they now rejected as they sensed their growing power. Spain was impaled on the horns of a dilemma, unable to end the war and unready to give up Cuba.

Early in 1898 events moved rapidly to arouse opinion against Spain. On February 9, Hearst's *New York Journal* released the text of a letter from Spanish minister Depuy de Lôme to a friend in Havana. In the letter, which had been stolen from the post office by a Cuban spy, de Lôme called President McKinley "weak and a bidder for the admiration of the crowd." This was hardly more extreme than what McKinley's assistant secretary of the navy, Theodore Roosevelt, had said about him. As early as 1895 Roosevelt had written: "This country needs a war," and he had since become increasingly frustrated by McKinley's refusal to declare one. The "white-livered" president, Roosevelt groused, had "no more backbone than a chocolate eclair." But that comment had remained private. De Lôme's had not, and he resigned to prevent further embarrassment to his government.

Six days later, during the night of February 15, 1898, the American battleship *Maine* exploded in Havana Harbor and sank with a loss of 266 men, most of whom died in their hammocks. The ship's captain, one of only eighty-four survivors, scribbled a telegram to Washington: "*Maine* blown up in Havana Harbor at nine forty tonight and destroyed. Many wounded and doubtless more killed or drowned. . . . Public opinion should be suspended until further report." But those eager for a war with Spain saw no need to withhold judgment; they demanded an immediate declaration. Roosevelt called the sinking "an act of dirty treachery on the part of the Spaniards."

A naval court of inquiry reported that an external mine had sunk the ship. Lacking hard evidence, the court made no effort to fix the blame, but the yellow press had no need of evidence. The *New York Journal*

An American cartoon depicts the sinking of the Maine *in Havana Harbor. The uproar created by the incident and its coverage in the "yellow press" edged McKinley toward war.*

gleefully reported: "The Whole Country Thrills with War Fever." The jingoistic outcry against Spain rose in a crescendo with the words "Remember the *Maine!* To Hell with Spain!" Few of those promoting war wrestled with the obvious fact that the Spanish government was determined to *avoid* a confrontation with the United States and therefore had nothing to gain from sinking the *Maine*. A comprehensive study in 1976 concluded that the sinking of the *Maine* was an accident, the result of an internal explosion triggered by a fire in its coal bunker.

Under the mounting pressure of public excitement, McKinley tried to maintain a steady course. But the frazzled president was swayed by the weight of outraged public opinion and by militants in his own party such as Theodore Roosevelt and Henry Cabot Lodge. As one congressman remarked, McKinley "keeps his ear to the ground so close that he gets it full of grasshoppers much of the time." On March 9, 1898, the president pushed through Congress a $50 million defense appropriation. Still, he sought to avoid war, as did most business spokesmen. Such caution infuriated Roosevelt. "We will have this war for the freedom of Cuba," he fumed on March 26, "in spite of the timidity of the commercial interests."

The Spanish government, sensing the growing militancy in the United States, announced a unilateral cease-fire in early April 1898. On April 10, the Spanish minister gave the State Department a message that amounted to a surrender. But the message came too late. The following day McKinley sent Congress his war message. He asked for the power to use armed forces in Cuba to protect American property and trade. On April 20 a joint resolution of Congress went beyond endorsing the use of the armed forces: it declared Cuba independent and demanded withdrawal of Spanish forces. The Teller Amendment, added on the Senate floor, disclaimed any American designs on Cuban territory. McKinley signed the resolution and sent a copy to the Spanish government. On April 22 the president announced a blockade of Cuba, under international law an act of war. Rather than give in to an ultimatum, the Spanish government declared war on April 24. Congress then, determined to be first, declared war the next day but made it retroactive to April 21, 1898.

Why such a rush into war after the message from Spain indicated that it was ready for an armistice? No one knows for sure, but it seems apparent that too much momentum and popular pressure had already built up for a confidential message to change the course of events. Also, leaders of the business community, which tolerates uncertainty poorly, were demanding a quick resolution of the problem. Many lacked faith in the willingness or ability of the Spanish government to carry out a moderate policy in the face of a hostile public opinion. Still, it is fair to ask why McKinley did not take a stand for peace, knowing what he did. He might have defied Congress and public opinion, but in the end he deemed the political risk too high. The ultimate blame for war, if blame must be levied, belongs to the American people for letting themselves be whipped up into such a hostile frenzy.

DEWEY TAKES MANILA The war itself lasted only four months. The American victory marked the end of Spain's once-great New World empire, which had begun with Christopher Columbus, and the emergence of the United States as a world power. But if American participation saved many lives by ending the insurrection in Cuba, it also led to American involvement in another insurrection, in the Philippines, and it created a host of commitments in the Caribbean and the Pacific that would haunt American policy makers during the twentieth century.

The war was barely under way before the navy produced a spectacular victory in an unexpected quarter—Manila Bay. While public attention centered on Cuba, Roosevelt focused on the Philippines. As assistant secretary of the navy, he had Commodore George Dewey appointed commander of the small American squadron in Asia and ordered him to engage Spain's ships in the Philippines in case of war. President McKinley had approved those orders.

Arriving late on April 30, 1898, Dewey's squadron destroyed or captured all the Spanish warships in Manila Bay. Dewey, without an occupation force, was now in awkward possession of Manila Bay. Promised reinforcements, he stayed while foreign warships loomed about the scene like watchful vultures, ready to take over the Philippines if the United States did not do so. Army troops finally arrived, and with the help of Filipino insurrectionists under Emilio Aguinaldo, Dewey's forces liberated Manila from Spanish control on August 13.

THE CUBAN CAMPAIGN While these events transpired halfway around the world, the war reached a surprisingly quick climax closer to home. American ships blockaded the Spanish fleet at Santiago. Although the U.S. navy was fit, the army could muster only an ill-assorted guard of 28,000 regulars and about 100,000 militiamen. The armed forces suffered badly from both inexperience and maladministration, with the result that far more American troops died from disease than from enemy action. The United States's salvation was that Spanish forces were even worse off.

An invasion force of some 17,000 American troops was hastily assembled at Tampa, Florida. One significant element of that force was the so-called "Rough Riders," best remembered because Lieutenant-Colonel Theodore Roosevelt was second in command. Eager to get "in on the fun," and "to act up to my preachings," Roosevelt had quit the Navy Department after war was declared. He ordered a custom-fitted, fawn-colored uniform with yellow trim from Brooks Brothers, grabbed a dozen pairs of spectacles, and rushed to help organize a colorful volunteer regiment of Ivy League athletes, leathery ex-convicts, Indians, and southwestern sharpshooters.

Land and sea battles around Santiago, port for the Spanish fleet,

Lieutenant-Colonel Theodore Roosevelt posing with his "Rough Riders" after the Battle of San Juan, 1898.

broke Spanish resistance. The major land action of the Cuban campaign occurred on July 1. While a much larger American force attacked Spanish positions at San Juan Hill, a smaller unit, including the dismounted Rough Riders—most of whose horses were still in Florida—and two crack black regiments, seized the enemy position atop nearby Kettle Hill. In the midst of the fray, Roosevelt satisfied his blood lust by seeing a Spaniard he shot double up "neatly as a jackrabbit." He later claimed that he "would rather have led that charge than served three terms in the U.S. Senate." A friend wrote to Roosevelt's wife that her husband was "revelling in victory and gore."

The two battles put American forces atop heights from which they could bring Santiago and the Spanish fleet under siege. On July 3 the Spanish ships made a gallant run for it, but the aging vessels were little match for the newer American fleet. The casualties were one-sided: 474 Spanish were killed and wounded and 1,750 were taken prisoner, while only one American was killed and one wounded. Santiago surrendered with a garrison of 24,000 on July 17. On July 25, an American force also moved into the Spanish-held island of Puerto Rico.

The next day the Spanish government sued for peace. After discussions lasting two weeks, negotiators signed an armistice on August 12, 1898, less than four months after the war's start and the day before Americans entered Manila. The peace protocol specified that Spain should give up Cuba, and that the United States should annex Puerto Rico and should occupy the city, bay, and harbor of Manila pending disposition of the Philippines.

And so the "splendid little war," as the future secretary of state, John Hay, called it in a letter to his friend Roosevelt, officially ended. It was splendid only in the sense that its cost was relatively slight. Among more than 274,000 Americans who served during the war and the ensuing demobilization, 5,462 died, but only 379 in battle. Most succumbed to malaria, typhoid, dysentery, or yellow fever. At such a cost the United States was launched onto the world stage as a great power, with all the benefits—and burdens—of that new status.

THE DEBATE OVER ANNEXATION The United States and Spain signed the Treaty of Paris on December 10, 1898. Disposition of the Philippines posed the key question, indeed one of the biggest decisions to face United States foreign policy to that time, and one that caught the country unprepared for sober reflection. McKinley, who claimed that at first he himself could not locate the Philippines on a map, gave ambiguous signals to the peace commission, which itself was divided.

There had been no demand for annexation of the Philippines or other Spanish possessions before the war, but Dewey's victory quickly kindled expansionist fever. Business leaders began thinking of the commercial possibilities in the nearby continent of Asia, such as oil for the lamps of China and textiles for its millions of people. "If this be commercialism," cried Republican Senator Mark Hanna, then "for God's sake let us have commercialism." Missionary societies yearned to save the "little brown brother." Although these Filipino candidates for conversion were already largely Catholic, the word went forth to take the Philippines for the sake of their souls. Spanish negotiators raised the delicate point that American forces had no claim by right of conquest, and had even taken Manila after the armistice. American negotiators finally offered the Spanish $20 million as compensation for possession of the Philippines as well as Puerto Rico in the Caribbean and Guam in the Pacific.

Meanwhile, Americans had taken other giant steps in the Pacific.

Hawaii had been annexed in the midst of the war. The United States also claimed Wake Island (1898), which would be a vital link in a future trans-Pacific cable line. And in 1899, after another outbreak of fighting over the royal succession in Samoa, Germany and the United States agreed to partition the Samoan Islands. The United States annexed the easternmost islands; Germany took the rest, including the largest island.

The Treaty of Paris was opposed by most Democrats and Populists, and some Republicans. Anti-imperialists argued that acquisition of the Philippines would undermine democracy. They appealed to traditional isolationism, American principles of self-government, the inconsistency of liberating Cuba and annexing the Philippines, the involvement in foreign entanglements that would undermine the logic of the Monroe Doctrine, and the danger that the Philippines would be expensive if not impossible to defend. The prospect of incorporating so many alien peoples into American life was not the least of some people's worries. "Bananas and self-government cannot grow on the same piece of land," one senator claimed.

"Well, I Hardly Know Which to Take First." *At the end of the nineteenth century it seemed that Uncle Sam had developed a considerable appetite for foreign territory.*

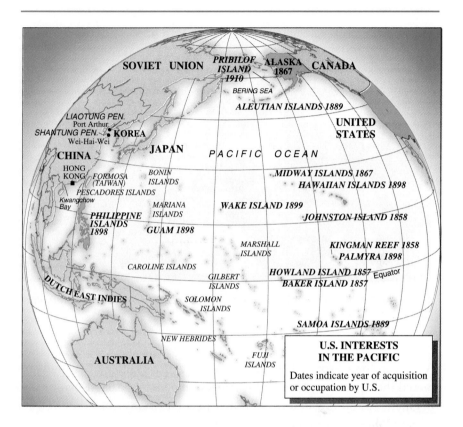

U.S. INTERESTS
IN THE PACIFIC

Dates indicate year of acquisition
or occupation by U.S.

The opposition may have been strong enough to kill the treaty had not the populist Democrat William Jennings Bryan influenced the vote for approval. A formal end to the war, he argued, would open the way for the future independence of Cuba and the Philippines. Ratification finally came on February 6, 1899.

By this time Americans had already clashed with Filipino insurrectionists near Manila. The Filipino rebel leader, Emilio Aguinaldo, had been in exile until Commodore Dewey brought him back to Luzon to make trouble for the Spanish. Since Aguinaldo's forces were more or less in control of the islands outside Manila, what followed over the next two years was largely an American war of conquest. Organized Filipino resistance collapsed by the end of 1899, but even after the capture of Aguinaldo in 1901, sporadic guerrilla action lasted until mid-1902.

It was a sordid little war, with massacres and torture on both sides.

Emilio Aguinaldo (seated third from right) *and other leaders of the Filipino insurgents.*

American forces soon displayed the same callous outlook that had animated the Spanish in Cuba. One American colonel boasted that he and his men "would rawhide these bullet-headed Asians until they yell for mercy." They must be pacified, he added, in order to make way for the "bandwagon of Anglo-Saxon progress and decency."

Against the backdrop of this nasty guerrilla war the great debate over annexation continued. The treaty debates inspired a number of anti-imperialist groups, which united in 1899 as the American Anti-Imperialist League. The league attracted members representing many shades of opinion; the main thing they had in common was that most belonged to an older generation. Andrew Carnegie footed the bills, but on imperialism at least, labor leader Samuel Gompers was in agreement with him. The usually soft-spoken philosopher William James exploded in opposition: "God damn the United States for its vile conduct in the Philippine Isles!" The selfish proponents of imperialism, he declared, had caused the nation to "puke up its ancient soul."

ORGANIZING THE NEW ACQUISITIONS   Such criticism, however, did not faze the expansionists. Senator Beveridge boasted in 1900:

"The Philippines are ours forever. And just beyond the Philippines are China's illimitable markets. We will not retreat from either. . . . The power that rules the Pacific is the power that rules the world. That power will forever be the American Republic."

In the Philippines, McKinley quickly moved toward setting up a civil government. On July 4, 1901, military government ended, and under an act of Congress, Judge William Howard Taft became the civil governor. The Philippine Government Act, passed by Congress on July 1, 1902, made the Philippine Islands an "unorganized territory" and made the inhabitants citizens of the Philippines. In 1934 the Tydings-McDuffie Act offered independence after a tutelary period of ten more years. Independence finally took effect on July 4, 1946.

Puerto Rico had been acquired in part to serve as an American outpost guarding the approaches to the Caribbean and any future isthmian canal. In 1900 the Foraker Act established a civil government on the island. Residents of the island were citizens of Puerto Rico but not of the United States until 1917, when they were granted United States citizenship. In 1952 Puerto Rico became a commonwealth with its own constitution and elected officials, a unique status. Like a state, Puerto Rico is free to change its constitution insofar as it does not conflict with the United States Constitution.

American authorities soon learned that liberated Cuba posed problems at least as irksome as those in the new possessions. After the American forces had restored order, started schools, and improved sanitary conditions, they began turning over the reins of power to the Cubans. The Platt Amendment to the Army Appropriations Bill passed by Congress in 1901, however, sharply restricted the new government's independence. The amendment required Cuba never to impair its independence by treaty with a third power, to maintain its debt within the government's power to repay out of ordinary revenues, and to acknowledge the right of the United States to intervene for the preservation of Cuban independence and the maintenance of "a government adequate for the protection of life, property, and individual liberty." Finally, Cuba was called upon to sell or lease to the United States lands to be used for coaling or naval stations—a proviso that led to an American naval base at Guantanamo Bay, which remains in existence.

IMPERIAL RIVALRIES IN EAST ASIA

CHINA AND THE "OPEN DOOR"   During the 1890s, not only the United States but also Japan emerged as a world power. Commodore Matthew Perry's voyage of 1853–1854 had opened Japan to Western ways, and the island nation began modernization in earnest after the 1860s. Flexing its new muscles, Japan defeated China's stagnant empire in the Sino-Japanese War (1894–1895) and, as a result, acquired the island of Taiwan (renamed Formosa). China's weakness, demonstrated in the war, led Russia, England, France, and Germany to renew their scramble for "spheres of influence" on that remaining frontier of imperialist expansion.

The possibility that these competing powers would carve up China and erect tariff barriers in their own spheres of influence dimmed the bright prospect of American trade with China. The British had much to lose in a tariff war though, for they already enjoyed substantial trade with China. Fearful of such a development, the British suggested in 1899 that the United States join them in preserving China's commercial and territorial integrity. The State Department agreed that something must be done, but Secretary of State John Hay preferred to act alone rather than in concert with the British.

In its origins and content, what came to be known as the Open Door Policy resembled the Monroe Doctrine. In both cases the United States proclaimed unilaterally a hands-off policy that the British had earlier proposed as a joint statement. The policy outlined in Hay's Open Door Note, dispatched in 1899 to London, Berlin, and St. Petersburg, and a little later to Tokyo, Rome, and Paris, proposed to keep China open to trade with all countries on an equal basis. None except Britain accepted Hay's principles, but none rejected them either, so Hay blandly announced that all powers had accepted the policy.

The Open Door Policy was rooted in the self-interest of American businessmen eager to exploit the markets of China. Yet it also tapped the deep-seated sympathies of those who opposed imperialism, especially as it endorsed China's territorial integrity. But it had little more legal standing than a pious affirmation. When the Japanese, concerned about Russian pressure in Chinese Manchuria, asked how the United States intended to enforce the Open Door Policy, Hay replied that the United States was "not prepared" to do so. So it would remain for forty years, a hollow but dangerous commitment, until continued Japanese expansion would bring war with America in 1941.

THE BOXER REBELLION A new crisis arose in 1900, when a group of Chinese nationalists known to the Western world as Boxers rebelled against foreign involvement in China. The Boxers surrounded the foreign embassies in Peking (Beijing). The British, Germans, Russians, Japanese, and Americans quickly mounted a military expedition to relieve the embassy compound. Hay, fearful that the intervention might become an excuse to dismember China, seized the chance to further refine his Open Door Policy. The United States, he declared in a circular letter of July 3, 1900, sought a solution that would "preserve Chinese territorial and administrative integrity" as well as "equal and impartial trade with all parts of the Chinese Empire." Six weeks later, the expedition reached Peking and broke the Boxer Rebellion.

ROOSEVELT'S BIG STICK DIPLOMACY

More than any other American political leader of his time, Theodore Roosevelt helped transform the role of the United States in world affairs. The nation had emerged from the Spanish-American War a world power, and he insisted that this entailed major new responsibilities. To ensure that the country accepted such international obligations, Roosevelt stretched both the Constitution and executive power to the limit. In the process, he pushed a reluctant nation onto the center stage of world affairs.

ROOSEVELT'S RISE In the fall elections of 1898 Republicans benefited from the euphoria of military victory and increased their majority in Congress. That hardly amounted to a mandate for imperialism, however, since the election preceded most of the debates on the issue. In 1900 the Democrats turned once again to William Jennings Bryan, who sought to make imperialism the "paramount issue" of the campaign. The Democratic platform condemned the Philippine conflict as "an unnecessary war" that had "placed the United States, previously known . . . throughout the world as the champion of freedom, in the false and un-American position of crushing with military force the efforts of our former allies to achieve liberty and self-government." The Republicans welcomed the issue. They renominated McKinley, and named as his running mate Theodore Roosevelt, who had been elected governor of New York after his role in the Spanish-American War.

The trouble with Bryan's idea of a solemn referendum on imperialism was the near impossibility of making any presidential contest so simple. Bryan himself complicated his message by insisting once again on the free coinage of silver, and the tariff became an issue again too. The Republicans' biggest advantage was probably the return to prosperity, which they were fully ready to take credit for. So those who opposed imperialism but also opposed free silver or tariff reduction faced a bewildering choice.

The outcome was a victory for McKinley greater than his last, by 7.2 million to 6.4 million in the popular vote and by 292 to 155 in the electoral vote. There had been no clear-cut referendum on annexations, but the question was settled nonetheless, although it would take yet another year and a half to subdue the Filipino rebels. The job would be finished, however, under the direction of another president.

On September 6, 1901, while McKinley attended a reception at the Pan American Exposition in Buffalo, a fanatical anarchist named Leon Czolgosz approached him with a gun and fired at point-blank range. McKinley died six days later, suddenly elevating Theodore Roosevelt to the White House. "Now look," Mark Hanna erupted. "That damned cowboy is President of the United States!"

Six weeks short of his forty-third birthday, Roosevelt was the youngest man ever to take charge of the White House, but he brought to it more experience in public affairs than most and more vitality than any. Born in 1858, the son of a wealthy New York merchant and a Georgia belle, Roosevelt grew up in Manhattan in cultured comfort, visited Europe as a child, spoke German fluently, and graduated Phi Beta Kappa from Harvard in 1880. A sickly, scrawny boy, he built himself up by sheer force of will into a uniquely blended physical and intellectual athlete who became a lifelong practitioner of the "strenuous life." Boxer, wrestler, and outdoorsman, he was also an omnivorous reader, renowned historian and essayist, and outspoken moralist.

After Harvard, Roosevelt read law briefly and within two years of graduation won election to the New York State legislature. That same year he published *The Naval War of 1812*, the first of a number of historical, biographical, and other writings to flow from his pen. He seemingly had the world at his feet—and then disaster struck. In 1884 his beloved mother, only forty-eight years old, died. Eleven hours later, in the same house, his twenty-two-year-old wife died in his arms, soon after giving birth to their only child. That night Roosevelt drew a large cross over the entry in his diary: "The light has gone out of my life." The double funeral was so wrenching that the officiating minister wept throughout his prayer.

In an attempt to recover from this "strange and terrible fate," Roosevelt sold the family house and moved west to take up the cattle business on the Dakota frontier. Adorned in a buckskin shirt, silver spurs, and alligator boots, he told a relative he was "having a glorious time here." The blue-blooded New Yorker relished hunting, leading roundups, capturing outlaws, fighting Indians—and reading Tolstoy by the campfire. Although his western career was brief, he never quite got over being a cowboy.

Back in New York City, the charming, earnest Roosevelt remarried, and ran for mayor and lost. He later served six years as civil service commissioner in Washington, D.C., and two years as New York City's police commissioner. In the latter capacity he loved to don a black cloak and broad-brimmed hat and patrol the streets at midnight. When he came upon a sleeping policeman, Roosevelt would rap the man with his nightstick. Such devotion to duty led McKinley to appoint him assistant secretary of the navy in 1897, and Roosevelt did all he could to promote the war with Spain over Cuba. "A just war," he insisted, "is in the long run far better for a man's soul than the most prosperous peace."

As a public servant Roosevelt quickly developed a reputation as a prodigious worker renowned for his pristine integrity and infectious sense of humor. Indeed, Teddy Roosevelt was an American original of seismic magnitude. His glittering spectacles and glistening teeth, along with his captivating grin and overflowing gusto, were a godsend to the cartoonists, who added another trademark when he pronounced the adage "Speak softly, and carry a big stick."

Roosevelt combined his boundless energy with an unshakable righteousness and a tendency to cast every issue in moral and patriotic terms. He saw the presidency as his "bully pulpit," and he was eager to preach fist-smacking sermons on the virtues of honesty, civic duty, and the strenuous life to his national flock. But appearances were deceiving. His nervous energy left a false impression of impulsiveness, and the talk of morality actually cloaked a cautious pragmatism. Roosevelt could get carried away on occasion, but as he said of his foreign policy steps, this was likely to happen only when "I am assured that I shall be able eventually to carry out my will by force."

BUILDING THE PANAMA CANAL   After the Spanish-American War the United States became more deeply involved than ever in the Caribbean area, where one issue overshadowed every other: the Panama Canal. The narrow isthmus of Panama had excited dreams of an interoceanic canal ever since Balboa's crossing in 1513. After America's victory over Spain, Secretary of State John Hay commenced talks with the British ambassador to gain Britain's consent to an American plan to build a canal. These negotiations led to the Hay-Pauncefote Treaty of 1901, in which Britain gave its consent to the American plan.

Other obstacles remained, however. From 1881 to 1887, a French

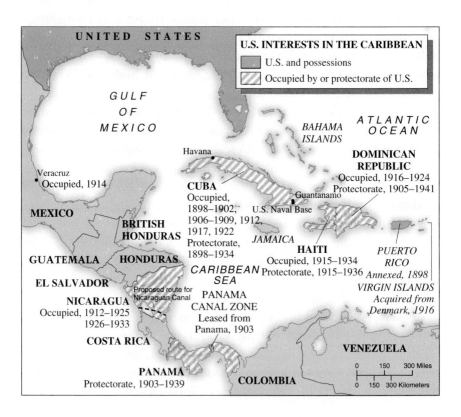

company had spent nearly $300 million and sacrificed some 20,000 lives to dig less than a third of a canal through Panama. The company now offered to sell its holdings to the United States. Meanwhile Secretary Hay had opened negotiations with Ambassador Thomas Herrán of Colombia to build a canal across Panama, which was then a reluctant province of Colombia. In return for a Canal Zone six miles wide, the United States agreed to pay $10 million in cash and a rental fee of $250,000 a year. The United States Senate ratified the Hay-Herrán Treaty in 1903, but the Colombian Senate held out for $25 million in cash. Incensed by the "foolish and homicidal corruptionists at Bogotá," Theodore Roosevelt flew into a rage punctuated by references to "dagoes" and "contemptible little creatures."

Colombia's rejection of the treaty heightened the desire of Panamanian rebels for independence. Recognizing this development, an employee of the French canal company then hatched a plot in collusion with the company's representative, Philippe Bunau-Varilla. He visited Roosevelt and Hay and, apparently with inside information, informed the Panamanian rebels that the U.S.S. *Nashville* would call at Colón in Panama on November 2, 1903.

An army of some 500 Panamanians revolted against Colombian rule the next day. Colombian troops, who could not penetrate the overland jungle, found American ships blocking the sea lanes. On November 4 the rebel commander addressed his victorious forces. "The world is astounded at our heroism. President Roosevelt has made good." A few days later the Roosevelt administration indeed made good on its collusion with the revolutionaries by recognizing Panama's independence, and on November 18 Roosevelt and the new Panamanian ambassador, who happened to be Bunau-Varilla, signed a treaty extending the Canal Zone from six to ten miles in width. For $10 million down and $250,000 a year the United States received "in perpetuity the use, occupation and control" of the canal zone. "I took Panama," Roosevelt would later boast.

In essence he had. Colombia eventually got its $25 million from the Harding administration in 1921, but only after America's interest in Colombian oil had lubricated the wheels of diplomacy. There was no apology, but the payment was made to remove "all misunderstandings growing out of the political events in Panama, November, 1903." The canal opened on August 15, 1914, less than two weeks after the outbreak of World War I in Europe. It was a tribute to American engineering and a boon to American commerce and the Panamanian economy.

THE ROOSEVELT COROLLARY   Even without the canal, the United States would have been concerned about the stability of the Caribbean area, and particularly with the activities of any hostile power in the region. A prime excuse for intervention in those days was to force the collection of debts owed to foreigners. In 1904 a crisis over the Dominican Republic's debts gave Roosevelt an opportunity to formulate American policy. In his annual address to Congress in 1904, he set forth what came to be known as the Roosevelt Corollary to the Monroe Doctrine: the principle, in short, was that since the Monroe Doctrine prohibited European intervention in the region, the United States was justified in intervening first to forestall the actions of outsiders. Roosevelt suggested that the United States could exercise an "international police power" in its own sphere of influence. As put into practice by mutual agreement with the Dominican Republic in 1905, the Roosevelt

The World's Constable. *Theodore Roosevelt, shown here as the world's policeman, wields the "big stick" symbolizing his approach to diplomacy.*

Corollary called for the United States to install and protect a collector of customs, who would apply a portion of the revenues to debt payments. The principle, applied peaceably in 1905, became the basis for military interventions later.

THE RUSSO-JAPANESE WAR   In East Asia, meanwhile, the Open Door policy received a serious challenge when tensions between Russia and Japan flared into a fight over China and Korea. On February 8, 1904, war broke out when the Japanese launched a surprise attack that devastated the Russian fleet. The Japanese then occupied Korea and drove the Russians back into Manchuria. But neither side could score a knockout blow, and neither relished a prolonged war. When the Japanese signaled President Roosevelt that they would welcome a negotiated settlement, he agreed to sponsor a peace conference in Portsmouth, New Hampshire. In the Treaty of Portsmouth (1905), the concessions all went to the Japanese. Russia acknowledged Japan's "predominant political, military, and economic interests in Korea" (Japan would annex the kingdom in 1910), and both powers agreed to evacuate Manchuria.

AMERICA'S RELATIONS WITH JAPAN   Japan's show of strength in the war with Russia raised doubts about the security of the Philippines. During the Portsmouth talks, Roosevelt sent Secretary of War William Howard Taft to meet with the Japanese foreign minister in Tokyo. The two men arrived at the Taft-Katsura Agreement of July 29, 1905, in which the United States accepted Japanese control of Korea and Japan disavowed any designs on the Philippines. Three years later, the Root-Takahira Agreement, negotiated by Secretary of State Elihu Root and the Japanese ambassador, endorsed the status quo, promised to respect the other's possessions, and reinforced the Open Door Policy by supporting "the independence and integrity of China" and "the principle of equal opportunity for commerce and industry in China."

Behind the diplomatic facade of goodwill, however, lay simmering mutual distrust. For many Americans, the Russian threat in East Asia now gave way to distrust of Japan's "yellow peril" (a term coined by Germany's Kaiser Wilhelm II). Racial animosities on the West Coast helped sour relations with Japan. In 1906 the San Francisco school board ordered students of Chinese, Japanese, and Korean descent to attend a separate public school. The Japanese government sharply protested such prejudice, and President Roosevelt managed to talk the school board into changing its mind. For its part Japan then agreed to limit sharply its issuance of passports to the United States. This "Gentleman's Agreement" of 1907, the precise terms of which have never been revealed, halted the influx of Japanese immigrants and brought some respite to racial agitations in California.

THE UNITED STATES AND EUROPE   During these years of expansionism abroad, the United States cast its gaze mainly westward and southward. But events in Europe also required attention. While Roosevelt was mediating the Russo-Japanese War in 1905, another dangerous crisis began heating up in Morocco, where the Germans and French fought for control. Roosevelt felt that the United States had something at stake in preventing the outbreak of a major war. At the kaiser's behest, he talked the French and British into attending an international conference at Algeciras, Spain, with American delegates present. Roosevelt then maneuvered the Germans into accepting his lead. The Act of Algeciras, signed in 1906, affirmed the independence of Morocco and guaranteed an open door for trade there. Roosevelt received the Nobel Peace Prize in 1906 for his work at Portsmouth and Algeciras. For all his bellicosity on other occasions, he had earned it.

Before Roosevelt left the White House in March 1909, he celebrated America's rise to world power with one great flourish. In late 1907 he sent the entire United States Navy, by then second in strength only to the British fleet, on a grand tour around the world. At every port of call the "Great White Fleet" set off rousing celebrations. It was the first such display of American naval might in the Pacific, and many feared the reaction of the Japanese, for whose benefit Roosevelt had in fact staged the show. They need not have worried, for in Japan the flotilla got the greatest welcome of all. Thousands of schoolchildren turned out waving tiny American flags and singing "The Star-Spangled Banner" in English. The triumphal procession continued home by way of the Mediterranean and steamed back into American waters in 1909, just in time to close out Roosevelt's presidency on a note of success.

But that note would not resonate for long. In time, the mixed consequences of Roosevelt's policies in Latin America and Asia would catch up to the United States.

MAKING CONNECTIONS

- The Spanish-American War marked a turning point in American foreign policy. America's emergence as a global power is a central theme in the twentieth century.

- Theodore Roosevelt's foreign policy displayed an activist approach to the presidency. In the next chapter, we see the connections between his foreign policies and his approach to domestic affairs.

FURTHER READING

An excellent survey of the diplomacy of the era is Charles Campbell's *The Transformation of American Foreign Relations, 1865–1900* (1976). For background to the events of the 1890s, see Walter LeFeber's *The American Search for Opportunity, 1865–1913* (1993) and David Healy's *U. S. Expansionism: The Imperialist Urge in the 1890s* (1970). The dispute over American policy concerning Hawaii is covered in Thomas J. Osborne's *"Empire Can Wait": American Opposition to Hawaiian Annexation, 1893–1898* (1981).

Ivan Musicant's *Empire by Default: The Spanish-American War and the Dawn of the American Century* (1998) is the most comprehensive volume on the conflict. Frank Freidel's *The Splendid Little War* (1958) shows what the war was like for those who fought it. Gerald F. Linderman's *The Mirror of War: American Society and the Spanish-American War* (1974) discusses the war at home. For the war's aftermath in the Philippines, see Stuart C. Miller's *"Benevolent Assimilation": American Conquest of the Philippines, 1899–1903* (1982). Robert L. Beisner's *Twelve Against Empire: The Anti-Imperialists, 1898–1900* (1985) handles the debate over annexation.

A good introduction to American interest in China is Michael H. Hunt's *The Making of a Special Relationship: The United States and China to 1914* (1983). Also useful is Marilyn B. Young's *The Rhetoric of*

Empire: America's China Policy, 1893–1901 (1968). Kenton J. Clymer's *John Hay: The Gentleman as Diplomat* (1975) examines the role of this key secretary of state in forming policy.

For American policy in the Caribbean and Central America, see Walter LeFeber's *Inevitable Revolutions: The United States in Central America* (1983) and Bruce J. Calder's *The Impact of Intervention: The Dominican Republic During the U.S. Occupation of 1916–1924* (1984). David McCullough's *The Path between the Seas: The Creation of the Panama Canal, 1870–1914* (1977) presents the fullest account of how the United States secured the Panama Canal.

23 ⬨ THE PROGRESSIVE ERA

CHAPTER ORGANIZER

This chapter focuses on:

- the social bases of progressivism.

- the basic elements of progressive reform.

- the presidencies of Theodore Roosevelt, William H. Taft, and Woodrow Wilson.

- the significance of the election of 1912.

---

heodore Roosevelt's emergence as a national leader coincided with the onset of what historians have labeled the Progressive Era (1900–1917). The so-called progressive movement arose in response to many causes, the most powerful of which was the devastating depression of the 1890s and its attendant social unrest. The depression brought hard times to the cities and provoked both the fears and consciences of the rapidly growing middle and upper-middle classes. By the turn of the century, so many outraged activists were at work seeking to improve social conditions and political abuses that people began to speak of a "Progressive Era, "a time of fermenting idealism, moral fervor, and constructive social, economic, and political change.

ELEMENTS OF REFORM

Progressivism was a reform movement so varied and comprehensive in its goals and motives that it almost defies definition. Political progressives crusaded against the abuses of urban political bosses and corporate robber barons. Their goals were greater democracy, honest and efficient government, more effective regulation of big business and "special interests," and greater social justice for working people. One paradox in the movement was that in some cases the regulation of business was proposed by business leaders. They preferred the stability afforded by a regulated market to the chaos and uncertainty of unrestrained competition.

The progressive movement represented the common spirit of an age rather than a single organized group or party. What reformers shared was a common assumption that the complex social ills and tensions generated by the urban-industrial revolution required expanding the scope of local, state, and federal government authority so as to elevate the public interest over private greed.

The "real heart of the movement," declared one reformer, was "to use the government as an agency of human welfare." Governments were now called upon to extend a broad range of direct services: schools, good roads (a movement propelled first by cyclists and then by automobilists), conservation of natural resources, public health and welfare, care of the handicapped, farm loans and demonstration agents, among other things. Such initiatives represented the first tentative steps toward what would become known during the 1930s and after as the welfare state.

ANTECEDENTS TO PROGRESSIVISM The progressive impulse began at the local level in the 1880s as a response to problems caused by industrialization and urbanization, and only gradually emerged on the national level. Beginning in the large cities of the East and Midwest, private citizens promoted reform as a form of charity. Private-sector reformers worked to improve basic public services that had been implemented quickly and often shoddily. They wished to improve sewers, housing, and transportation. Reformers of local government believed in greater efficiency, less favoritism, and tighter organization. They wanted to reorder government itself through budgets, audits, and a more rationalized new structure of government offices. Early efforts to improve public health, education, and factory conditions grew out of a desire to improve the administration and enforcement of local and state laws.

The Mugwumps, those gentlemen reformers who had fought the spoils system and promoted a civil service based on merit, supplied the progressive movement with an important element of its thinking, the "good-government" ideal. Over the years, their ranks had been supplemented and the good-government outlook broadened by leaders who confronted such old and new urban problems as crime, vice, and the efficient provision of gas, electricity, water, sewers, mass transit, and garbage collection.

Finally, another significant force in fostering the spirit of progressivism was the growing prominence of socialist critiques of living and working conditions. The Socialist party of the time, small but earnest and vocal, served as the left wing of progressivism. Most progressives found socialist remedies unacceptable, and the main progressive reform impulse grew in part from a desire to counter the growing appeal of socialist doctrines.

THE MUCKRAKERS Poverty, unsafe working conditions, epidemics, and child labor in unhealthy factories were complex social issues; remedying them would take more than an idealistic desire to effect change in government and public health and working conditions. Public consciousness needed to be raised. This required a publicizing of scandals and festering problems. A group of journalists dubbed "muckrakers" rose to the challenge. These writers who thrived on exposing scandal got their name when Theodore Roosevelt compared them to a character in John Bunyan's *Pilgrim's Progress:* "A man that could look no way but downwards with a muckrake in his hands." The muckrakers were "often indispensable to . . . society," Roosevelt said, "but only if they know when to stop raking the muck."

Henry Demarest Lloyd is sometimes cited as the first of the muckrakers for his critical examination of the Standard Oil Company and other monopolies in his book, *Wealth Against Commonwealth* (1894). Lloyd exposed the growth of corporate giants responsible to none but themselves, able to corrupt if not control governments. Lincoln Steffens likewise revealed the prevalence of municipal corruption in a series of articles later collected into a book, *The Shame of the Cities* (1904).

Another early muckraker was Jacob Riis, a Danish immigrant who, as an influential New York journalist, exposed slum conditions in *How the Other Half Lives* (1890). The chief outlets for social critics were the popular middle-class magazines that began to flourish in the 1890s, such as *The Arena* and *McClure's Magazine. McClure's* also published Ida M. Tarbell's *History of the Standard Oil Company* (1904). Tarbell provided a more detailed treatment than the earlier book by Lloyd, and it was all the more damaging in its detail.

Without the muckrakers, progressivism would never have achieved the popular support it had. In feeding a growing public appetite for facts about the new urban-industrial society, the muckrakers demonstrated one of the salient features of the progressive movement, and one of its central failures. The progressives were stronger on diagnosis than on remedy. They harbored a naive faith in the power of democracy. Show the people the facts, expose corruption, and bring government closer to the people, they assumed, and the correction of evils would follow automatically. The cure for the ills of democracy was, to progressive reformers, simply a more enlightened democracy. As Senator Robert M. La Follette declared, progressivism sought to make "our government represent with more fidelity the will of the people."

THE MAIN FEATURES OF PROGRESSIVISM

DEMOCRACY   The most important progressive reform intended to democratize government was the direct primary, in which candidates would be nominated by the vote of all party members rather than by a few political bosses. After South Carolina adopted the first statewide primary in 1896, the concept spread within two decades to nearly every other state.

The primary was but one expression of a broad movement for greater public participation in the political process. In 1898 South Dakota became the first state to adopt the initiative and referendum, procedures that allowed voters to enact laws directly. If a designated number of voters petitioned to have a measure put on the ballot (the initiative), the electorate could then vote it up or down (the referendum). Oregon also adopted a whole spectrum of reform measures, including a voter registration law (1899), the initiative and referendum (1902), the direct primary (1904), a sweeping corrupt-practices act (1908), and the recall (1910), whereby public officials could be removed by petition and vote. By 1920, nearly twenty states had adopted the initiative and referendum and nearly a dozen the recall. The direct election of senators by the people, rather than by the state legislatures, was another progressive political reform. The popular election of senators required a constitutional amendment, and by 1912 the Senate finally agreed to the Seventeenth Amendment, which was ratified by the states in 1913.

EFFICIENCY   A second major theme of progressivism was the "gospel of efficiency." In the business world at the turn of the century and after, Frederick W. Taylor, the original "efficiency expert," developed an array of scientific management techniques designed to cut costs and enhance productivity. "Taylorism," as scientific management came to be known, promised to reduce waste through the careful analysis of labor processes. By breaking down the production process into separate steps and by meticulously studying the time it took each worker to perform a task, Taylor sought to discover the optimal technique for the average worker and to establish performance standards for each job classification. The promise of higher wages, he believed, would motivate workers to exceed the "average" expectations.

As they incorporated Taylor's theories and "time-and-motion studies" into their operations, corporate executives highlighted the quest for efficiency and order that characterized the Progressive Era. But many workers resented Taylor's innovations. They saw in scientific management a tool for employers to make them work faster than was healthy or fair. Yet Taylor's system brought concrete improvements in productivity—especially among those industries whose production processes were highly standardized and where jobs were rigidly defined. "In the future," Taylor predicted in 1911, "the system [rather than the individual workers] will be first."

In government, the efficiency movement called for "experts" to replace bureaucrats and demanded the reorganization of agencies to prevent overlapping, to establish clear lines of authority, and to fix responsibility. Two new ideas for making municipal government more efficient gained headway in the first decade of the new century. The commission system was first adopted by Galveston, Texas, in 1901, when local government there collapsed in the aftermath of a devastating hurricane that killed 6,000 people and destroyed half the town. It placed ultimate authority in a board composed of elected administrative heads of city departments— commissioners of sanitation, police, utilities, and so on. By 1914 more than 400 towns and small cities across the country had adopted the commission system. The more durable idea, however, was the city-manager plan, under which a professional administrator ran the government in accordance with policies set by the elected council and mayor. Staunton, Virginia, first adopted the plan in 1908. By 1914 the National Association of City Managers heralded the arrival of a new profession.

By the early twentieth century, it was apparent that many functions of government and business now required greater expertise than in preindustrial America. This principle's most ardent disciple was Wisconsin governor Robert M. ("Fighting Bob") La Follette, who established a Legislative Reference Bureau staffed by professors and specialists to provide research, advice, and help in the drafting of legislation designed to curb the power of special interests and promote social justice. This "Wisconsin Idea" of efficient government was widely publicized and copied by other states. Born in a log cabin and educated at the Univer-

Robert M. La Follette.

sity of Wisconsin, the short, muscular La Follette possessed an abiding faith in grassroots democracy, in the power and judgment of the people. He worked passionately for reforms such as the direct primary, stronger railroad regulation, the conservation of natural resources, and workers' compensation.

Progressive counterparts to La Follette also appeared in other states. As counsel to a legislative committee in New York, Charles Evans Hughes became a national figure by uncovering spectacular insurance frauds, and won the New York governorship in 1906. Hiram Johnson was elected governor of California in 1910 on the promise of reining in the railroads.

REGULATION Of all the problems facing American society at the turn of the century, one engaged a greater diversity of reformers and elicited more controversial solutions than any other: the regulation of giant corporations, which became a third major theme of progressivism. Beginning in the 1870s, states had tried to regulate the rates of railroads and the working conditions in other businesses, only to be thwarted by Supreme Court rulings. The judges declared that only the federal government could regulate companies involved in interstate commerce. By the 1890s, the growth of monopolistic corporations spurred reformers to act on a national level. While some progressives believed that the problems of economic power and its abuses should be left to business to work out for itself, a policy known as laissez-faire, others advocated a policy of trust-busting in the belief that restoring old-fashioned competition would best prevent economic abuses. The Sherman Anti-Trust Act of 1890 had aimed for this, but the act turned out to be a paper tiger.

Efforts to restore the competitiveness of small firms proved unworkable in part because breaking up large corporations was complex and difficult. Consequently, the main thrust of progressive reform over the years was toward regulation, rather than dissolution, of big businesses. To some extent, regulation and "stabilization" won acceptance among businessmen who, whatever respect they paid to competition in principle, preferred not to face it in practice. As time passed, however, regulatory agencies often came under the influence or control of those they were supposed to regulate. Railroad executives, for instance, generally had more intimate knowledge of the intricate details involved in their

Kohinore Mine, Pennsylvania, *1891. Child labor was rampant until the progressive National Child Labor Committee spearheaded a movement to prohibit employing young children.*

business, giving them the advantage over the outsiders who might be appointed to the Interstate Commerce Commission.

SOCIAL JUSTICE   A fourth important feature of the progressive spirit was the impulse toward social justice, which motivated diverse actions from private charity drives to campaigns against child labor and liquor. The settlement house movement of the late nineteenth century had spawned a corps of social workers and genteel reformers devoted to the uplift of slum dwellers. But with time it became apparent that social evils extended beyond the reach of private charities and demanded governmental intervention.

Labor legislation was perhaps the most significant reform to emerge from the drive for social justice. It emerged first at the state level. The National Child Labor Committee, organized in 1904, led a movement for state laws banning the still widespread employment of young children. Within ten years, the committee helped foster new laws in most states banning the labor of underage children (the minimum age varied from twelve to sixteen) and limiting the working hours of older children.

Closely linked with the child-labor reform movement was a concerted effort to regulate the hours of work for women. Spearheaded by Florence Kelley, the head of the National Consumers League, this progressive crusade promoted the passage of state laws addressing the distinctive hardships that long working hours imposed on women who were wives and mothers.

The Supreme Court pursued a curiously erratic course in ruling on such state labor laws. In *Lochner* v. *New York* (1905), the Court voided a ten-hour-day law because it violated workers' "liberty of contract" to accept any terms they chose. Then in *Muller* v. *Oregon* (1908), the high court upheld a ten-hour law for women largely on the basis of sociological data that attorney Louis D. Brandeis presented regarding the adverse effects of long hours on the health and morals of women. In *Bunting* v. *Oregon* (1917), the Court accepted a ten-hour workday for both men and women, but held out for twenty more years against state minimum-wage laws.

Legislation to protect workers against avoidable accidents gained momentum from disasters such as the 1911 fire at the Triangle Shirtwaist Company in New York City in which 146 people, mostly young women,

Triangle Shirtwaist Company Fire, New York City, 1911.

died for want of adequate exits. The victims were either trapped on the three upper floors of a ten-story building, or they plunged to the street below. Stricter building codes and factory inspection acts followed.

PROHIBITION For many progressive activists, the cause of liquor prohibition was the foremost concern. The Women's Christian Temperance Union had been battling the sale of alcoholic beverages since 1874, but the most successful political action followed the formation in 1893 of the Anti-Saloon League, an organization that pioneered the strategy of the single-issue pressure group. In 1913 the league endorsed an amendment to the Constitution prohibiting all alcoholic beverages, which was adopted by Congress that year. By the time it was ratified six years later, state and local action already had dried up areas occupied by nearly three-fourths of the nation's population.

ROOSEVELT'S PROGRESSIVISM

While most progressive initiatives were started at the state and local levels, calls for national progressive efforts began to appear around 1900. Theodore Roosevelt brought to the White House in 1901 an expansive vision of the presidency that was admirably suited to the cause of progressive reform. In one of his first addresses to Congress, he stressed the need for a new political approach. When the Constitution was first drafted, he explained, the nation's social and economic conditions were quite unlike those at the dawn of the twentieth century. "The conditions are now wholly different and wholly different action is called for."

More than any other president since Lincoln, Roosevelt possessed an activist bent. Still, his initial approach to reform was cautious. He sought to avoid the extremes of socialism on the one hand and laissez-faire individualism on the other. A skilled political maneuverer, he cultivated party leaders in Congress and steered away from such divisive issues as the tariff and regulation of the banks. And when he did approach the explosive issue of the trusts, he always took care to reassure the business community. For him, politics was the art of the possible. Unlike the more radical progressives and the doctrinaire "lunatic fringe," as he called them, he would take half a loaf rather than none at all.

Theodore Roosevelt as an apostle of prosperity (top) and as a Roman tyrant (bottom). Roosevelt's energy, spirit, righteousness, and impulsiveness led people to have distinct reactions to his personality.

THE TRUSTS On the issue of huge business trusts, Roosevelt endorsed the "sincere conviction that combination and concentration should be, not prohibited, but supervised and within reasonable limits controlled." In 1902, he proposed a "square deal" for all, calling for enforcement of existing antitrust laws and stricter controls on big business. Roosevelt believed that wholesale trust-busting was too much like trying to unscramble eggs. Effective regulation, he insisted, was better than a futile effort to restore small business, which might be achieved only at a cost to the efficiencies of scale gained in larger operations.

Because Congress balked at regulatory legislation, Roosevelt sought to force the issue by a more vigorous federal prosecution of the Sherman Anti-Trust Act (1890). He chose his target carefully. In the case against the Sugar Trust (*United States v. E.C. Knight and Company,* 1895), the Supreme Court had declared manufacturing a strictly *intrastate* activity. Most railroads, however, were beyond question engaged in *interstate* commerce and thus subject to federal authority. Consequently, in 1902 Roosevelt moved against the Northern Securities Company, a holding company controlling the Great Northern and Northern Pacific Railroads. When Roosevelt attacked the new trust, J. P. Morgan invited him to "send your man to my man and they can fix it up." The president refused, and in 1904 the Supreme Court ordered the combination dissolved in *U.S. v. Northern Securities Company.* Roosevelt continued to use his executive powers to enforce the Sherman Anti-Trust Act, but he avoided conflict in Congress by not proposing any further antitrust legislation. Altogether his administration brought about twenty-five antitrust suits.

The most notable victory against a trust came in *Swift and Company v. United States* (1905), a decision against the "beef trust" through which most of the meat packers had avoided competitive bidding in the purchase of livestock. In this decision, the Supreme Court put forth the "stream-of-commerce" doctrine, which overturned its previous holding that manufacturing was strictly intrastate. Since both livestock and the meat products of the meat packers moved in the stream of interstate commerce, the Court reasoned, they were subject to federal regulation. This interpretation of the interstate commerce power would be broadened in later years until few enterprises would remain beyond the reach of federal regulation.

THE 1902 COAL STRIKE   Support for Roosevelt's use of the "big stick" against corporations was strengthened by the stubbornness of mine owners in the anthracite coal strike of 1902. On May 12 the United Mine Workers (UMW) walked off the job in West Virginia and Pennsylvania. They demanded a 20 percent wage increase, a reduction in daily working hours from ten to nine, and formal management recognition of their union. The operators dug in their heels against concessions and shut down the mines in an effort to starve out the miners. As one of them asserted, "The miners don't suffer—why, they can't even speak English."

Facing the real prospect of a national coal shortage, Roosevelt called both sides to a conference at the White House. The mine owners, led by George F. Baer, president of the Reading Railroad, attended but refused even to speak to the UMW leaders. The "extraordinary stupidity and temper" of the "wooden-headed" owners outraged Roosevelt. The president wanted to grab Baer "by the seat of his breeches" and "chuck him out" a White House window.

After the conference ended in an impasse, Roosevelt threatened to take over the mines and run them with the army. When a congressman questioned the constitutionality of such a move, an exasperated Roosevelt roared: "To hell with the Constitution when the people want coal!" Militarizing the mines would indeed have been an act of dubious legality, but the owners feared that Roosevelt might actually do it and that public opinion would support him.

The coal strike ended in October 1902 with an agreement to submit the issues to an arbitration commission named by the president. The agreement enhanced the prestige of both Roosevelt and the union's leader, although it produced only a partial victory for the miners. By the arbitrators' decision in 1903, the miners won a nine-hour workday but only a 10 percent wage increase and no union recognition.

AN EXPANDING GOVERNMENT   In 1903 Congress strengthened both antitrust enforcement and governmental regulation by creating the Department of Commerce and Labor and by passing the Elkins Act, which made it illegal for corporations to take as well as to give secret rebates to their preferred customers. The Bureau of Corporations, a new federal agency within the new department, had no direct regulatory powers, but it did have a mandate to study and report on the activities of interstate corporations. Its findings could lead to antitrust suits, but its purpose was rather to help corporations correct malpractices and avoid the need for lawsuits. Many companies cooperated, but others held back. When Standard Oil refused to turn over records, the government brought an antitrust suit that resulted in its dissolution in 1911. The Supreme Court ordered the American Tobacco Company broken up at the same time.

ROOSEVELT'S SECOND TERM

Roosevelt's policies built a coalition of progressive- and conservative-minded voters that assured his election in his own right in 1904. The Democrats, having twice lost with Bryan, turned to Alton B. Parker who, as chief justice of New York's state supreme court, had upheld labor's right to the closed shop (requiring that all employees be union members) and the state's right to limit hours of work. Despite Parker's liberal record, party leaders presented him as a safe conservative, and his acceptance of the gold standard as "firmly and irrevocably established" bolstered such a view. Yet the effort to portray their Democratic candidate as more conservative than Roosevelt proved a futile gesture for the party that had twice nominated Bryan. Despite Roosevelt's trust-busting, most business leaders, according to the *New York Sun,* preferred the "impulsive candidate of the party of conservatism to the conservative candidate of the party which the business interests regard as permanently and dangerously impulsive." Even financial titans J. P. Morgan and E. H. Harriman contributed handsomely to Roosevelt's campaign chest.

An invincible popularity and the sheer force of his personality swept Roosevelt to an impressive victory of 7.6 million votes to Parker's 5.1 million, and 336 electoral votes for Roosevelt against 140 for Parker. Parker carried only the Solid South of the former Confederacy and two border states, Kentucky and Maryland. On election night, Roosevelt announced that he would not run again, a statement he later would regret.

LEGISLATIVE LEADERSHIP   Elected in his own right, Roosevelt approached his second term with heightened confidence and a stronger commitment to progressive reform. In late 1905 he devoted most of his annual message to the need for greater regulation and control of business. This irked his corporate contributors. Said steel baron Henry Frick, "We bought the son of a bitch and then he did not stay put." The independent Roosevelt took aim at the railroads first.

Roosevelt asked Congress to extend the authority of the Interstate Commerce Commission (ICC) and to give it effective control over railroad rates. He had to mobilize all the pressure and influence at his disposal to push through the bill introduced by Representative Peter Hepburn of Iowa. Enacted in 1906, the Hepburn Act gave the ICC power to set maximum freight rates. The commission no longer had to go to court to enforce its decisions. The Hepburn Act also extended the ICC's regulatory reach beyond railroads to pipelines, freight companies, sleeping-car companies, bridges, and ferries.

On the very day after passage of the Hepburn Act, a growing movement for the regulation of meat packers, food processors, and makers of drugs and patent medicines reached fruition. Discontent with abuses in these fields had grown rapidly as a result of the muckrakers' disclosures. The chief chemist of the Agriculture Department, for example, supplied telling evidence of harmful additives used in the preparation of "embalmed meat" and other food products. Others reported on dangerous ingredients in some patent medicines.

Perhaps the most telling blow against such abuses was struck by Upton Sinclair's novel *The Jungle* (1906), which graphically portrayed the filthy conditions in Chicago's meat-packing industry. In the storage rooms, Sinclair wrote, "a man could run his hand over these piles of meat and sweep off handfuls of the dried dung of rats. These rats were nuisances, and the packers would put poisoned bread out for them, they would die, and then rats, bread, and meat would go into the hoppers together." Roosevelt read *The Jungle*—and reacted quickly. He sent two federal agents to Chicago to investigate, and their report confirmed all that Sinclair had said. Soon he and the Congress were hammering out a bill to address the problem.

The Meat Inspection Act of 1906 required federal inspection of meats destined for interstate commerce and empowered officials in the Agriculture Department to impose sanitary standards. The Pure Food and Drug Act, enacted the same day, placed restrictions on the makers of prepared foods and patent medicines, and forbade the manufacture, sale, or transportation of adulterated, misbranded, or harmful foods, drugs, and liquors.

With the achievements of 1903 and 1906, Theodore Roosevelt's campaign for regulatory legislation reached its chief goals and in the process moved the federal government a great distance from the laissez-faire policies that had prevailed before the turn of the century.

CONSERVATION   One of the most enduring legacies of the Roosevelt years was the president's energetic support for the budding conservation movement. Concern for protecting the environment grew with the rising awareness that exploitation of natural resources was despoiling the frontier. As early as 1872, Yellowstone National Park had been set aside as a public reserve, and in 1881, Congress had created a Division of Forestry in the Department of Agriculture. Roosevelt, an ardent hiker, camper, hunter, and bird watcher, strove to halt the unchecked destruction of the nation's natural resources and wonders by providing a barrier of federal regulation and protection. His appointment of Gifford Pinchot as chief forester resulted in vigorous new scientific management of public lands. Roosevelt added fifty federal wildlife refuges, approved five new national parks, and initiated the system of designating national monuments, such as the Grand Canyon. He also used the Forest Reserve Act (1891) to exclude from settlement or harvest some 172 million acres of timberland. Lumber companies were irate, but Roosevelt held firm, bristling, "I hate a man who would skin the land."

FROM ROOSEVELT TO TAFT

Toward the end of his second term, Roosevelt crowed: "I have had a great time as president." But he was ready to move on, and he held to his 1904 decision not to run again. Instead he sought to have his secretary of war, William Howard Taft, replace him, and the Republican convention ratified the choice on its first ballot in 1908. The Democrats, whose conservative strategy had backfired in 1904, decided to give William Jennings Bryan one more chance. Still vigorous at forty-eight, Bryan retained a faithful following, but once again it was not enough. In the end, the voters opted for Roosevelt's chosen successor, leaving

Bryan only the southern states plus Nebraska, Colorado, and Nevada. The real surprise of the election was the strong showing of the Socialist party candidate, labor hero Eugene V. Debs. He attracted over 400,000 votes, illustrating the mounting intensity of working-class unrest.

Born to a prominent Cincinnati family, Taft boasted more experience in public service than any other president since Van Buren. After graduating second in his class at Yale, he progressed through appointive offices, from assistant prosecutor, tax collector, and judge in Ohio, to solicitor in the Justice Department, federal judge, governor-general in the Philippines, and secretary of war. The presidency was the only elective office he ever held. Later he would be appointed Chief Justice of the Supreme Court (1921–1930), a job more suited to his temperament.

Taft was a jovial man who loved playing golf or poker but detested politics. "Politics, when I am in it," he admitted, "makes me sick." Taft never felt comfortable in the White House. He once observed that whenever someone said "Mr. President," he looked around for Roosevelt. The political dynamo in the family was his wife, Nellie, who had wanted the presidency more than he. One of the major tragedies of Taft's presidency was that Helen "Nellie" Taft suffered a debilitating stroke soon after they entered the White House, and for most of his term, she remained unable to serve as his political adviser.

William Howard Taft.

TARIFF REFORM   Once a student of the Social Darwinist William Graham Sumner, Taft had absorbed the laissez-faire views of his mentor and had since differed with orthodox Republican protectionism. Against Roosevelt's advice, he had promised a tariff reduction during the campaign, and true to his word, he called a special session of Congress eleven days after his inauguration. But if in pressing an issue that Roosevelt had skirted Taft seemed bolder, he proved less adroit in shepherding legislation.

A reduced tariff passed the House with surprising ease. But before the Senate passed the bill, it made more than 800 changes, most of which raised rates. Outraged by such obvious catering to special interests, a group of ten progressive Republicans joined the Democrats in an unsuccessful effort to defeat the bill. Taft at first agreed with them, but then, fearful of a party split, he backed the majority and agreed to an imperfect bill. He only made matters worse by calling the tariff the best "that the Republican party ever passed." Temperamentally conservative, inhibited by scruples about interfering too much with the legislative process, Taft drifted into the orbit of the Republican Old Guard and quickly alienated the progressive wing of his party, whom he tagged "assistant Democrats."

BALLINGER AND PINCHOT   In 1910 Taft's policies drove the wedge deeper between the Republican factions. What came to be known as the Ballinger-Pinchot controversy made Taft appear to be a less reliable custodian of Roosevelt's conservation policies than he actually was. The controversy arose after Taft's secretary of the interior, Richard A. Ballinger, turned over coal-rich government lands in Alaska to a group of investor friends. Apparently without Ballinger's knowledge, this group had already agreed to sell part of the lands to a mining syndicate. When Chief of Forestry Gifford Pinchot revealed the scam, Taft fired him for insubordination. A joint congressional investigation later exonerated Ballinger from all charges of fraud or corruption, but conservationist suspicions created such pressures that he resigned in 1911.

In firing Pinchot, Taft acted on the strictly legal view that his training had taught him to value. But the unsavory circumstances surrounding the incident tarnished Taft's public image. He had been elected to carry out the Roosevelt policies, his opponents said, and he *was* carrying them out—"on a stretcher." And it did not take long for Roosevelt, who was in Europe after completing an African safari ("Let every lion do his duty," J. P. Morgan had wished when Roosevelt left for Africa), to learn of Taft's apparent change of principles.

Events had conspired to cast Taft in a conservative role at a time when progressive sentiment was riding high. The result was a sharp setback for the president in the congressional elections of 1910, first by the widespread defeat of pro-Taft candidates in the Republican primaries, then by the election of a Democratic majority in the House and of enough Democrats in the Senate that progressive Republicans could wield the balance of power.

TAFT AND ROOSEVELT   In 1910 Roosevelt had returned from his travels abroad. As news accounts highlighted the Taft "betrayal" of Roosevelt's programs, his followers urged him to take action. After hesitating for several months, Roosevelt again entered the political arena, having concluded that Taft had "sold the Square Deal down the river." At a speech in Kansas in 1910, he gave a catchy name to his latest principles, the "New Nationalism," declaring that he intended to put the national interest above any "sectional or personal advantage." Roosevelt then issued a stirring call for an array of new federal regulatory laws, a social-welfare program, and new measures of direct democracy, including the old populist demands for the initiative, recall, and referendum. His purpose was not to revolutionize American life but to save it from the threat of revolution. "What I have advocated," he explained a few days later, "is not wild radicalism. It is the highest and wisest kind of conservatism."

Thereafter, Roosevelt intensified his criticism of the administration. Equally critical of Taft was Senator Robert La Follette of Wisconsin, who in 1911 helped organize the National Progressive Republican League and soon became its leading candidate for the Republican party nomination. A militant reformer fiercely committed to greater government regulation of business and civil rights for *all* Americans, La Follette was more of a crusader than a politician. Sensing Taft's weakness, Roosevelt officially threw his hat in the ring in 1912. Even though many of La Follette's supporters rushed to embrace the ex-president, the Wisconsin idealist stubbornly refused to give way to Roosevelt. He felt that Roosevelt was not genuinely committed to the sweeping reforms necessary for a truly progressive America.

The rebuke implicit in Roosevelt's decision to run against Taft, his chosen successor, was in many ways undeserved. During Taft's first year in office, one political tempest after another had left his image irreparably damaged. The three years of solid achievement that followed could not restore its luster or reunite his divided party. Taft had at least attempted tariff reform, which Roosevelt had never dared. And in the end his administration set aside more public lands for conservation in four years than Roosevelt's had in nearly eight and brought more antitrust suits, by a score of eighty to twenty-five. Taft also established the Bureau of Mines and the Federal Children's Bureau (1912). He supported both the Sixteenth Amendment (1913), which authorized a federal income tax, and the Seventeenth Amendment (1913), which provided for the popular election of senators.

Despite Taft's "progressive" record, Roosevelt now hastened Taft's demise. Brusquely pushing aside La Follette's claim to the "progressive" Republican mantle, Roosevelt won most of the Republican primaries in 1912, even in Taft's Ohio. But such popular support was no match for Taft's advantages as president and party leader. The Taft forces nominated their man by the same "steamroller" tactics that had nominated Roosevelt in 1904. Outraged at such "naked theft," the Roosevelt delegates issued a call for a Progressive party convention, which assembled in Chicago on August 5. The new third-party supporters were a curious

A skeptical view of Roosevelt, the Bull Moose candidate in 1912.

mixture of social gospel clergymen and laymen, college presidents, professors, journalists, liberal businessmen, and social workers. Roosevelt told the group he felt "fit as a bull moose" in accepting their nomination. Now it was the Democrats' turn.

WILSON'S PROGRESSIVISM

WILSON'S RISE   The emergence of Thomas Woodrow Wilson as the Democratic nominee in 1912 climaxed a political rise even more rapid than that of Grover Cleveland. In 1910, before his election as governor of New Jersey, Wilson had been president of Princeton University, but had never run for public office. Born in Staunton, Virginia, in 1856, the son of a "noble-saintly mother" and a stern Presbyterian minister, he had grown up in Georgia and the Carolinas during the Civil War and Reconstruction. From the beginning, he was a reconstructed southerner. As he once stressed, "*because* I love the South, I rejoice in the failure of the Confederacy."

Driven by a sense of destiny and duty, Wilson was resolute, humane, rigid, and self-exacting to a fault. He nurtured a righteous commitment to principle. When a friend once insisted that there were two sides to every question, Wilson replied: "Yes, a right side and a wrong side." His fits of tenacious inflexibility would prove to be his Achilles heel.

Running as a reform candidate, Wilson was elected governor of New Jersey in 1910. After his election, he promoted progressive measures and pushed them through the legislature. He pressured New Jersey lawmakers to enact a workers' compensation law, a corrupt-practices law, measures to regulate public utilities, and ballot reforms. Such strong leadership in a state known as the "home of the trusts" for its lenient corporation laws brought Wilson to national attention.

In the spring of 1911 a group of southern Democrats in New York opened a Wilson presidential campaign headquarters, and Wilson set forth on strenuous tours into all regions of the country, denouncing special privilege and political bossism. Wilson believed that the president of the country should be as active in directing legislation as in the administration and enforcement of laws. In calling for a strong presidency, Wilson expressed views closer to those of Roosevelt than to those of Taft. He likewise shared Roosevelt's belief that politicians should pro-

Democratic candidate Woodrow Wilson speaking from a train platform during the election of 1912.

mote the general welfare rather than narrow special interests. And, like Roosevelt, he was critical of big business, organized labor, socialism, and agrarian radicalism.

Despite a fast start, by convention time the Wilson campaign seemed headed for defeat. House Speaker Bennett Champ Clark of Missouri seemed destined to win the nomination. On the fourteenth ballot, however, Bryan, having decided that party conservatives were behind Clark, went over to Wilson; others followed, and Wilson captured the nomination.

THE ELECTION OF 1912 The 1912 presidential election involved four candidates: Wilson and Taft represented the two major parties, while Eugene Debs ran as a Socialist, and Roosevelt headed the Progressive party ticket. No sooner did the campaign open than Roosevelt's candidacy almost ended. While stepping into a car in Milwaukee, he was shot by a crazed fanatic. The bullet went through his overcoat, spectacles case, folded speech, then fractured a rib before lodging just below his right lung. Jolted, he reeled backward, coughed, and then righted himself. "Stand back, don't hurt the man," he yelled at the crowd as they mobbed the attacker. Roosevelt then demanded that he be driven to the auditorium to deliver his speech. His dramatic sense unhampered, he showed the audience his bloodstained shirt and punctured text and vowed: "It takes more than this to kill a bull moose." He apologized for his halting delivery, but, bullet and all, he gave his speech.

Roosevelt was soon shooting verbal bullets at Taft and Wilson. He called Taft a "fathead" with "brains less than those of a guinea pig." Taft, deeply wounded by the sharp rhetoric of his "closest friend," fought back, branding Roosevelt a "demagogue" and "a dangerous egotist." But it quickly became clear that in a three-man race Taft was out of the running. "There are so many people in the country who don't like me," he lamented.

After the initial name-calling, the campaign settled down to a debate over the competing ideologies of the two front-runners: Roosevelt's "New Nationalism" and Wilson's "New Freedom." The fuzzy ideas that Roosevelt fashioned into his New Nationalism had first been presented systematically in *The Promise of American Life* (1909), a widely influential book by Herbert Croly, a New York journalist. Its central point was that progressives must give up Jeffersonian prejudices against big government and use the power of government to achieve democratic ends in the public interest.

The old nationalism had been used "by the sinister . . . special interests," Roosevelt claimed. His New Nationalism would enable government to promote social justice and enact reforms such as graduated income and inheritance taxes, workers' compensation for disabling injuries or illnesses, regulation of the labor of women and children, and a stronger Bureau of Corporations. These and more went into the platform of his Progressive party, which called for a federal trade commission with sweeping authority over business and a tariff commission to set rates on a "scientific basis."

Before the end of his administration, Wilson would be swept into the current of such new nationalism too, but initially he adhered to the decentralizing antitrust traditions of his party. Before the start of the campaign, Wilson conferred with Louis D. Brandeis, a progressive lawyer from Boston who focused Wilson's thought much as Croly had focused Roosevelt's. Brandeis's design for the New Freedom differed from Roosevelt's New Nationalism in its belief that the federal government should restore competition rather than regulate monopolies. This required eliminating *all* trusts, lowering tariffs, and breaking up the concentration of financial power on Wall Street. Brandeis and Wilson also dreamed of turning over most social programs to the states and cities. In this sense, they saw the vigorous expansion of federal power as only a temporary necessity, not a permanent condition. Having restored competition and the diffusion of power and programs, the national government would revert to its aloof heritage. Roosevelt, who was convinced that both corporate concentration and an expanding federal government were permanent developments, dismissed the New Freedom as mere nostalgia.

The Republican schism between Taft and Roosevelt opened the way for Woodrow Wilson to win by 435 electoral votes to 88 for Roosevelt and 8 for Taft. The Republican Taft and the former Republican Roosevelt were now private citizens. During the 1920s, Taft was appointed Chief Justice of the Supreme Court and served there for nine years with distinction. Even his liberal jurist associates afforded him the highest respect. "It's very difficult for me to understand," Louis Brandeis later wrote, "why a man who is so good as Chief Justice . . . could have been so bad as President."

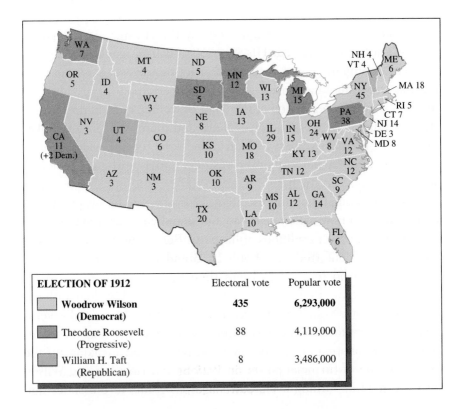

ELECTION OF 1912	Electoral vote	Popular vote
Woodrow Wilson (Democrat)	**435**	**6,293,000**
Theodore Roosevelt (Progressive)	88	4,119,000
William H. Taft (Republican)	8	3,486,000

The 1912 election was significant in a number of respects. First, it was a high-water mark for progressivism. The candidates debated the basic issues in a campaign unique for its focus on vital alternatives and for its high philosophical tone. And the Socialist party, the left wing of progressivism, polled over 900,000 votes for Eugene V. Debs, about 6 percent of the total vote, its highest proportion ever.

Second, the election brought the Democrats back into effective national power for the first time since the Civil War. For two years during the second Cleveland administration, 1893–1895, they had held the White House and majorities in both houses of Congress, but they had quickly fallen out of power during the most severe depression in American history to that time. Now, under Wilson, the Democrats again held the presidency, and enjoyed majorities in the House and Senate.

Third, Wilson's election brought southerners back into the orbit of national and international affairs in a significant way for the first time since the Civil War. Five of Wilson's ten cabinet members were born in the South, and William Jennings Bryan, the secretary of state, was an idol of the southern masses. At the president's right hand, and one of the most influential members of the Wilson circle, was Colonel Edward M. House of Texas. Southern legislators, by virtue of their seniority, held most committee chairmanships. As a result, much of the progressive legislation of the Wilson era would bear the names of the southerners who guided the bills through Congress.

WILSONIAN REFORM   Wilson's 1913 inaugural address vividly expressed the ideals of economic reform that inspired many progressives. "We have been proud of our industrial achievements," he observed, "but we have not hitherto stopped thoughtfully enough to count the human cost." He promised specifically a lower tariff and a new banking system. "This is not a day of triumph; it is a day of dedication. Here muster, not the forces of party, but the forces of humanity."

Whereas Roosevelt had been a strong president by force of personality, Wilson became a strong president by force of conviction. The president, he argued, must become the dynamic voice in national affairs. Wilson courted popular support, but he also courted members of Congress through personal contacts, invitations to the White House, and visits to the Capitol. He used patronage power to reward friends and punish enemies. Though he might have acted through a bipartisan progressive coalition, he chose instead to rely on party loyalty.

THE TARIFF   The new president's leadership met its first test on the issue of tariff reform. Wilson summoned Congress into special session and addressed it in person—the first president to do so since John Adams. In response to Wilson's request for lower tariff duties to promote competition, Congress voted for tariff reductions, with only four Democrats bolting the party line as the bill passed the House easily. The opposition centered in the Senate, the traditional graveyard of tariff reform. Swarms of lobbyists got so thick in Washington, Wilson noted, that "a brick couldn't be thrown without hitting one of them." The president turned the tables with a public statement that focused the spotlight on the "industrious and insidious" tariff lobby. In the end, Louisiana's two "sugar senators" were the only Democrats to vote against the bill. The Underwood-Simmons Tariff of 1913 reduced the overall average duty from about 37 percent to about 29 percent. The act lowered tariffs but raised internal revenues with the first federal income tax levied under the newly ratified Sixteenth Amendment.

THE FEDERAL RESERVE ACT   Before the new tariff had cleared the Senate, the administration proposed the first major banking and currency reform since the Civil War. The Glass-Owen Federal Reserve Act of 1913 created a new banking system with twelve regional Federal Reserve Banks, each owned by member banks in its district. All national banks became members of the new Federal Reserve system; state banks could join if they wished. Each member bank had to subscribe 6 percent of its capital to the Federal Reserve Bank and deposit a portion of its reserve there, the amount depending on the size of the community.

These "bankers' banks" dealt chiefly with their members, not with individuals. Along with other banking functions, the chief service to member banks was to take over their outstanding loans in exchange for Federal Reserve Notes (paper currency), which member banks might then use to make further loans. This arrangement made it possible to expand both the money supply and bank credit in times of high business activity, or as the level of borrowing increased. A Federal Reserve Board exercised general supervision over the activities of the member banks and adjusted interest rates to fight inflation or stimulate business. It is hard to exaggerate the significance of the passage of the Federal Reserve Act. Through Wilson's skillful leadership, the Congress took a major step in providing the nation with a sound yet flexible currency system and at the same time helped decentralize the money supply.

ANTITRUST LAWS   Wilson had made trust-busting the central focus of the New Freedom because the concentration of economic power had continued to grow despite the Sherman Anti-Trust Act and the watchdog agency, the Bureau of Corporations. During the summer of 1914, Wilson decided to make a strong Federal Trade Commission the cornerstone of his antitrust program. Created in 1914, the five-member commission replaced Roosevelt's Bureau of Corporations and assumed new powers to define "unfair trade practices" and to issue "cease and desist" orders when it found evidence of unfair competition.

Having now embraced the principle of "controlled competition," Wilson seemed to lose interest in the antitrust bill drafted by Henry D. Clayton (D-Ala.) of the House Judiciary Committee. The Clayton Antitrust Act, passed in 1914, outlawed such practices as price discrimination (charging different customers different prices for the same goods), "tying" agreements that limited the right of dealers to handle the products of competing manufacturers, and corporations' acquisition

Mr. Wilson Taking Charge of the School. *A cartoon depicting the professorial president taking on big business.*

of stock in competing corporations. In every case, however, conservative forces in the Senate qualified these provisions by tacking on the weakening phrase "where the effect may be to substantially lessen competition" or words of similar effect. And conservative southern Democrats and northern Republicans amended the act to allow for broad judicial review of the Federal Trade Commission's decisions, thus further weakening its freedom of action. In accordance with the president's recommendation, however, corporate officials were made personally responsible for any violations.

Agrarian reformers, in alliance with organized labor, won a stipulation in the Clayton Act that declared farm and labor organizations not to be, per se, unlawful combinations in restraint of trade. Injunctions in labor disputes, moreover, were not to be handed down by federal courts unless "necessary to prevent irreparable injury to property." Though hailed by Samuel Gompers as labor's "Magna Carta," these provisions were actually little more than pious affirmations, as later court decisions would demonstrate. Wilson himself remarked that the act did little more than affirm the right of unions to exist by forbidding their dissolution for being in restraint of trade.

Administration of the antitrust laws generally proved disappointing to the more vehement progressives under Wilson. The Justice Department offered advice to business owners interested in arranging matters so as to avoid antitrust prosecutions. The appointment of conservatives to the Interstate Commerce Commission and the Federal Reserve Board won plaudits from the business world and profoundly disappointed progressives.

SOCIAL JUSTICE   Wilson had in fact never been a strong progressive of the social-justice persuasion. He had carried out his promises to lower the tariff, reorganize the banking system, and strengthen the antitrust laws, but he was not inclined to go much further. The New Freedom was now complete, he wrote late in 1914; the future would be "a time of healing because a time of just dealing."

The sweep of events and the pressures of more far-reaching progressives pushed Wilson beyond where he intended to go on some points. Yet Wilson retained several social blind spots. Although he endorsed state action for women's suffrage, he declined to support a suffrage amendment because his party platform had not. He withheld support from federal child-labor legislation because he regarded it as a state matter, and he opposed a bill providing federal loans for strapped farmers on the grounds that it was "unwise and unjustifiable to extend the credit of the government to a single class of the community."

PROGRESSIVISM FOR WHITES ONLY   Like many other progressives, Woodrow Wilson showed little interest in the plight of African Americans. In fact, he shared many of the racist attitudes prevalent at the time. Although Wilson never joined the Ku Klux Klan, and he denounced its "reign of terror," he sympathized with its motives to restore white rule in the postwar South and to relieve whites of the "ignorant and hostile" power of the black vote. As a student at Princeton, Wilson had declared that "universal suffrage is the foundation of every evil in this country." He opposed giving the vote to uneducated whites, and he detested the enfranchisement of blacks, arguing that Americans of Anglo-Saxon origin would always resist domination by "an ignorant and inferior race." He believed that white resistance to black rule was "unalterable."

Later, as a politician, Wilson courted black voters, but he rarely consulted African-American leaders and repeatedly avoided opportunities to associate with them in public. Many of the southerners he appointed to his cabinet were uncompromising racists who systematically began segregating the employees in their agencies, even though the agencies had been integrated for over fifty years. Workplaces were segregated by race, as were toilets and drinking fountains. When black leaders protested these actions, Wilson replied that such racial segregation was intended to eliminate "the possibility of friction" in the federal workplace.

PROGRESSIVE RESURGENCE   The need to weld a winning coalition in 1916 pushed Wilson back on the road of reform. Progressive Democrats were restless, and after war broke out in Europe in 1914, further divisions in the party arose over defense and foreign policy. At the same time, the Republicans were repairing their own rift. The Progressive party showed little staying power in the 1914 midterm election, and Roosevelt showed little will to preserve it. Most observers recognized that Wilson could shape a majority only by courting progressives of all parties. In 1916 Wilson scored points with them when he nominated Louis D. Brandeis to the Supreme Court. Conservatives waged a vigorous battle against Brandeis, but Senate progressives rallied to win confirmation of the social-justice champion as the first Jewish member of the Supreme Court.

Wilson meanwhile began to embrace the broad program of farm and labor reforms he had earlier spurned. On the issue of federal farm credit, he reversed himself abruptly, supporting a proposal to set up land banks to sponsor farm loans. With this boost, the Federal Farm Loan Act became law in 1916. It created twelve Federal Land Banks that paralleled the Federal Reserve Banks and offered low-interest loans to farmers.

The dream of cheap rural credit, sponsored by a generation of populists, had come to fruition. Democrats never embraced the populist subtreasury plan, but they made a small step in that direction with the Warehouse Act of 1916. This measure authorized federal licensing of private warehouses, and federal backing made their receipts for stored produce more acceptable to local bankers as collateral for short-term loans to farmers. Other concessions to farm demands included the Smith-Lever Act of 1914 and the Smith-Hughes Act of 1917, both of which passed with little controversy. The first provided federal grants-in-aid for farm demonstration agents to show farmers new planting techniques, fertilizers, and equipment. The second measure funded agricultural and mechanical education in the high schools.

Farmers with automobiles had more than a passing interest as well in the Federal Highways Act of 1916, which provided dollar-matching contributions to states with highway departments that met certain federal standards. The measure authorized distribution of $75 million over five years, and marked a sharp departure from Jacksonian opposition to internal improvements at federal expense, just as the Federal Reserve System departed from Jacksonian banking principles. Although the argument that highways were one of the nation's defense needs had weakened constitutional scruples against the act, the Highways Act still restricted support to "post roads" used for the delivery of mail. A renewal act in 1921 would mark the beginning of a systematic network of numbered U.S. highways.

The progressive resurgence of 1916 broke the logjam on labor reforms as well. Advocates of child-labor legislation persuaded Wilson to overcome doubts of its constitutionality and sign the Keating-Owen Child Labor Act, which excluded from interstate commerce goods manufactured by children under fourteen. But the Supreme Court soon ruled it unconstitutional on the grounds that regulation of interstate commerce could not extend to the conditions of labor. On the other hand, the Supreme Court upheld the Adamson Act of 1916, which mandated the eight-hour workday for railroad workers.

In Wilson's first term, progressive government reached its zenith. It set a framework within which American politics and society would still function, by and large, near the end of the century. Progressivism had conquered the old premise that the government is best which governs least, whatever political rhetoric might be heard to the contrary, and left the more extreme doctrines of limited government as dead as Grover Cleveland. Progressivism, an amalgam of agrarian, business, governmental, and social reform, amounted in the end to a movement for active government on behalf of the public interest.

THE LIMITS OF PROGRESSIVISM

Like all great historic movements, progressivism contained elements of paradox and irony. Despite all the talk of greater democracy at the turn of the century, it was also the age of disenfranchisement for southern blacks and xenophobic reactions to "new" immigrants. The initiative and referendum, supposedly democratic reforms, proved subject to manipulation by well-financed publicity campaigns. And much of the public policy of the time came to be formulated by experts and members of appointed boards, not by broad segments of the population. There is a fine irony in the fact that the drive to increase the political role of ordinary people moved parallel with efforts to strengthen executive leadership and to exalt professional expertise. This age of much-ballyhooed efficiency and bureaucracy, in business as well as government, generated a situation in which more and more key decisions were made by faceless policy makers.

Progressivism was largely a middle-class movement in which the poor and unorganized had little influence. It is surprising that a movement so dedicated to democratic rhetoric should experience so steady a decline in voter participation. In 1912, the year of the Bull Moose campaign, voting dropped off by almost 7 percent. The new politics of issues and charismatic leaders proved to be less effective in turning out voters than party organizations and bosses had been. And by 1916 the optimism of an age that looked to infinite progress was already confronted by a vast slaughter. Europe had stumbled into war, and America would soon be drawn in. The twentieth century, which had dawned with such bright hopes, held in store episodes of unparalleled horror.

MAKING CONNECTIONS

- Many of the progressive reforms described in this chapter—particularly business regulation and the growth of the welfare state—provided the seeds for the New Deal reforms of the 1930s (Chapter 27).

- The progressive impulse carried on after World War I, but was transformed by the new political and social conditions of postwar America. Progressive reforms such as prohibition and women's suffrage were enacted after the war, but the moralistic strain in progressivism took an ugly turn in the Red Scare and immigration restriction.

- The next chapter shows how Wilson's foreign policy in Latin America and Europe reflected the same moralism that guided his domestic policy.

FURTHER READING

A splendid introduction to the topic of progressivism can be found in Arthur S. Link and Richard L. McCormick's *Progressivism* (1983). Progressivism has been interpreted in many ways. Robert H. Wiebe's *The Search for Order, 1877–1920* (1967) presents the organizational model for reform. Richard Hofstadter's *The Age of Reform: From Bryan to F. D.R.* (1955) examines an emerging middle-class consensus as the basis of reform. Gabriel Kolko sees the reform movement as a means of social control in *The Triumph of Conservatism* (1963). Dewey W. Grantham's *Southern Progressivism: The Reconciliation of Progress and Tradition* (1983) shows the distinctiveness of reform in that region. See also Alan Dawley's *Struggles for Justice: Social Responsibility and the Liberal State* (1991).

Biographers of the three progressive presidents, Roosevelt, Taft, and Wilson, elaborate on the complexity of reform. Edmund Morris's *The Rise of Theodore Roosevelt* (1979) and H. W. Brands's *T.R.: The Last Romantic* (1997) offer compelling portraits. For the Taft years, see Paolo E. Coletta's *The Presidency of William Howard Taft* (1973). Arthur S. Link's multivolume biography *Wilson (1947–1965)*—particularly *The New Freedom* (1956)—is the place to start on that president. John Milton Cooper, Jr., compares Roosevelt and Wilson in *The Warrior and the Priest* (1983).

The evolution of government policy toward business is examined in Martin J. Sklar's *The Corporate Reconstruction of American Capitalism, 1890–1916: The Market, the Law, and Politics* (1988). Roy Lubove's *The Progressives and the Slums* (1962), Mina Carson's *Settlement Folk: Social Thought and the American Settlement Movement, 1885–1930* (1990), and Jack M. Holl's *Juvenile Reform in the Progressive Era* (1971) examine the problem of urban decay.

Robert Kanigel's *The One Best Way: Frederick Winslow Taylor and the Enigma of Efficiency* (1997) highlights the role of efficiency in the Progressive Era. Samuel P. Hays's *Conservation and the Gospel of Efficiency: The Progressive Conservation Movement, 1890–1920* (rev. ed., 1969) and Harold T. Pinkett's *Gifford Pinchot: Private and Public Forester* (1970) cover conservation and the Ballinger-Pinchot controversy.

An excellent study of the role of women in progressivism's emphasis on social justice is Kathryn Kish Sklar's *Florence Kelley and the Nation's Work: The Rise of Women's Political Culture, 1830–1900* (1995).

24 ❦ AMERICA AND THE GREAT WAR

CHAPTER ORGANIZER

This chapter focuses on:

- Wilson's foreign policy toward Mexico.

- the causes and early years of the Great War in Europe.

- America's entry into and role in the Great War.

- Wilson's efforts to promote his peace plan.

- the aftermath of the war.

Throughout the nineteenth century, the United States reaped the benefits of its geographic distance from the wars that plagued Britain and Europe. The Atlantic Ocean provided a welcome buffer. During the early twentieth century, however, events combined to end the nation's comfortable isolation. Spectacular industrial development and ever-expanding world trade entwined American interests with the fate of Europe. In addition, the development of steam-powered ships and submarines meant that foreign navies could threaten American security. At the same time, the election of Woodrow Wilson brought to the White House a stern moralist determined to impose his standards for right conduct on renegade nations. This combination of circumstances would transform the outbreak of war in Europe in 1914 into a profound crisis for Americans, a crisis that in the end would transform the nation's role in international affairs.

WILSON AND FOREIGN AFFAIRS

Woodrow Wilson brought to the presidency little background in the study or conduct of foreign relations. The former college professor admitted before taking office that it "would be an irony of fate if my administration had to deal chiefly with foreign affairs." But events in Latin America and Europe were to make the irony all too real. From 1914 on, foreign relations increasingly preoccupied Wilson's attention.

Although lacking in international experience, Wilson did not lack ideas or convictions in this area. He saw himself as a man of destiny who would help create a new world order governed by morality and idealism rather than by greed and crass national interests. He believed that his election had put him on a course charted "by no plan of our conceiving, but by the hand of God who led us into this way." Both he and his pious secretary of state, William Jennings Bryan, believed that America had been called to promote democracy and moral progress in the world. "When properly directed," Wilson maintained in 1914, "there is no people not fitted for self-government." How to promote such democratic idealism and self-determination abroad, however, remained a thorny issue, as Wilson soon discovered in responding to rapidly changing events in Mexico.

INTERVENTION IN MEXICO   For most of the thirty-five years from 1876 to 1911, President Porfirio Díaz had dominated Mexico. As military dictator he had suppressed opposition and showered favors on his followers and on foreign investors, who piled up holdings in Mexican mines, petroleum, railroads, and agriculture. But eventually the dictator's hold slipped, and in 1910 popular resentment boiled over in revolt. A year later, revolutionary armies had occupied Mexico City, and Díaz had fled.

The leader of the rebellion, Francisco I. Madero, a charismatic dreamer, proved unable to manage the tough customers attracted to the revolt by the scramble for power. In 1913 General Victoriano Huerta assumed power, and Madero was murdered soon afterward. Wilson challenged the legitimacy of Huerta's violent coup. "I will not recognize a government of butchers," he insisted privately. At the same time, he expressed sympathy with a new revolutionary movement led by Venustiano Carranza and began to put diplomatic pressure on Huerta. "I am going to teach the South American republics to elect good men," he vowed to a British diplomat.

Early in 1914 Wilson removed an embargo on arms to Mexico in order to help Carranza's forces, and he stationed warships off Veracruz to halt foreign arms shipments to Huerta. On April 9, 1914, several American sailors, gathering supplies ashore at Tampico, strayed into a restricted area and were arrested. The Mexican officials quickly released them and sent an apology to the American naval commander. There the incident might have ended, but the naval officer demanded that the Mexicans salute the American flag. Wilson backed him up and won from Congress authority to use force to bring Huerta to terms. Before the Tampico incident could be resolved, Wilson sent a naval force to Veracruz. American marines and sailors went ashore on April 21, 1914, and they forcibly occupied the town at a cost of nineteen killed. The Mexicans lost at least 200 killed.

In Mexico the American occupation aroused the opposition of all factions, and Huerta tried to rally support against foreign invasion. At this juncture, Wilson accepted a mediation offer by the ABC powers (Argentina, Brazil, and Chile). In 1914 they proposed withdrawal of United States forces, the removal of Huerta, and installation of a provisional government. Huerta refused, but the moral effect of the proposal, his isolation abroad, and the growing strength of his foes forced him to leave office. The Carranzistas entered Mexico City, and the Americans left Veracruz. Wilson's "missionary diplomacy" seemed to have worked. "With the retirement of Huerta," one editor predicted, "prospects are bright for the triumph of President Wilson's moral-suasion peace policy." In 1915 the United States and several Latin American governments recognized Carranza as president of Mexico.

But no sooner had the Carranzistas taken power than they began to squabble among themselves for the spoils of office. The most incendiary confrontation occurred between Carranza and his foremost general, the charismatic Pancho Villa, a violent former bandit who shrewdly

Pancho Villa (center) *and his followers rebelled against the president of Mexico and antagonized the United States with violent attacks against "gringos."*

claimed to represent "the people" behind the revolution. Such a public stance attracted Wilson's sympathy, and he initially threw American support behind Villa. This turned out to be a colossal blunder. As fighting erupted in 1915, the Villistas suffered several serious defeats. The Wilson administration, confused and frantic, thereupon shifted its stance to that of strict neutrality, with the president announcing that the Mexicans should be allowed to determine their own fate without outside interference.

Critics, however, charged that Wilson was a bungler and a coward. The always militant Theodore Roosevelt, for example, attacked the president's earlier support of the revolution and called for American military intervention to restore order. Responding to such pressure, Wilson warned the two Mexican factions to stop fighting or risk the involvement of American troops. Villa then requested an armistice, but Carranza, sensing his military dominance, rejected Wilson's right to intrude in Mexico's affairs. This led Wilson to grumble that he had "never known a man more impossible to deal with on human principles than this man Carranza."

By the fall of 1915, however, relations between Carranza and Wilson improved, as the United States formally recognized his claim as the *de facto* leader of the Mexican nation. This enraged Villa, and his naturally violent tendencies now came to the fore. In early 1916 Villa's men stopped a train and murdered sixteen American mining engineers in a deliberate attempt to provoke American intervention, discredit Carranza, and build Villa up as an opponent of the "Gringos." Two months later, Villa's band of renegades entered Columbus, New Mexico, burned the town, and killed seventeen Americans.

Outraged, Wilson asked Carranza to allow American forces to pursue the attackers into Mexico. Carranza agreed, but he grew understandably alarmed when Wilson sent General John J. Pershing and a force of some 11,000 men deep inside Mexico. For nearly a year, Pershing's troops chased Villa through northern Mexico but, missing their quarry, they returned home in 1917. Carranza then pressed his own war against the bandits and put through a new liberal constitution in 1917. Mexico was by then well on the way to a more orderly government, almost in spite of Wilson's actions rather than because of them.

PROBLEMS IN THE CARIBBEAN In the Caribbean, Wilson found it as hard to act on his ideals as in Mexico. During President Taft's term (1909–1913), refinements of Roosevelt's interventionist policy had earned from its opponents the less exalted—if fairly accurate—title of "dollar diplomacy." The policy so tagged had its origin in China in 1909, when President Taft personally cabled the Chinese government on behalf of American investors interested in an international consortium to finance railroad lines in China. In Latin America "dollar diplomacy" worked differently and with somewhat more success. The idea was to encourage American bankers to help prop up the finances of shaky Caribbean governments.

One of the first applications of Wilsonian idealism to foreign policy came when the president renounced dollar diplomacy. The government, he declared, was not supporting any "special groups or interests." Despite Wilson's public stand against using military force to back up American investments, however, he kept the marines in Nicaragua, where they had been sent by Taft in 1912, to prevent renewed civil war. There they would stay almost continuously through 1933. Then in 1915 Wilson dispatched more marines to Haiti after two successive revolutions and subsequent disorders. The American forces stayed until 1934.

Turmoil in the Dominican Republic brought American marines to that country in 1916, where they remained until 1924. The presence of American military force in the region only worsened the already prevalent irritation at "Yankee imperialism."

AN UNEASY NEUTRALITY

Problems in Mexico and Central America loomed larger in Wilson's thinking than the gathering storm in Europe. When the thunderbolt of war struck Europe in the summer of 1914, it struck most Americans, one North Carolinian wrote, "as lightning out of a clear sky." Whatever the troubles in Mexico, whatever disorders and interventions agitated other countries, it seemed unreal that civilized Europe could

EUROPE AT WAR, 1914
- Central Powers (Triple Alliance)
- Allied Powers (Triple Entente)
- Neutral countries

descend into such an orgy of destruction. But the assassination of Austrian archduke Franz Ferdinand by a Serbian nationalist, Austria-Hungary's determination to punish Serbia, and Russia's military mobilization in sympathy with its Slavic brothers in Serbia suddenly triggered a conflict between a European system of alliances: the Triple Alliance or Central Powers (Germany, Austria-Hungary, and Italy) and the Triple Entente or Allied Powers (France, Great Britain, and Russia). The sequence of decisions leading to World War I unfolded with little thought of their consequences. When Russia refused to stop its mobilization, Germany, which backed Austria-Hungary, declared war on Russia on August 1, 1914, and on Russia's ally France two days later. Germany then invaded Belgium to get at France, which brought Great Britain into the war on August 4. Japan, eager to seize German holdings in the Pacific, declared war on August 23, and Turkey entered on the side of the Central Powers a week later. Although allied with the Central Powers, Italy initially stayed out of the war, and struck a bargain under which it joined the Allied Powers in 1915.

As the fighting unfolded, it quickly became apparent that the First World War was unlike any previous conflict in its scope and horrors because military tactics had not kept up with military technology. Over 61 million men served in the armed forces on both sides, and millions lost their lives. New and enhanced military technologies produced unprecedented carnage. Machine guns, high-velocity rifles, aerial bombing, poison gas, flame throwers, land mines, long-range artillery, and armored tanks changed the nature of warfare and produced massive casualties and widespread destruction. Over 9 million combatants were killed in action. Another 19 million were wounded.

The battlefields of World War I were surrealistic in their horrors. During the Battle of Verdun in France, lasting from February to December 1916, some 32 million artillery shells were fired—1,500 shells for every square meter of the battlefield. Such devastating firepower turned farm land and forests into wasteland. Flying over the battlefield, American pilot Edwin Parsons, a volunteer for France, saw how nature "had been ruthlessly murdered. Every sign of humanity had been swept away. Roads had vanished, and forests were fire-blackened stumps."

Trench warfare gave the First World War its lasting character. Most of the great battles of the war involved hundreds of thousands of men crawling out of their trenches and then crossing "no-man's-land" to attack enemy positions, only to be pushed back themselves a day or a week later. The 475 miles of trenches provided protection and living space as well as a jumping-off point for large- and small-scale attacks by day or night. Trenches were laid out in zigzag patterns to present the most difficult targets and to allow "enfilading fire" (fire from the flanks) on attackers. Trenches were heavily guarded by aprons of barbed wire and land mines; the gaps in the wire were covered by machine guns.

Life in the trenches was miserable. In addition to the dangers of enemy fire, soldiers on both sides were forced to deal with flooding and diseases such as trench fever and trench foot, which could lead to amputation. Lice and rats were constant companions. The stench was unbearable. Soldiers on both sides ate, slept, and fought among the dead, and amid the reek of death. A French soldier described the situation: "We had no communication with the rear for three days and nights because the bombardment did not let up. We were not even able to get our rations and we only ate biscuits and chocolate and there was almost nothing to drink; finally we were able to get our rations but with a lot of difficulty; therefore, we're glad to get out of here because we've been completely brutalized by the bombardment; one has

A gun crew firing on entrenched German positions.

to have a strong heart to endure such a martyrdom. This is not war, it's a massacre."

AMERICA'S INITIAL REACTIONS As the trench war along the Western Front in Belgium and in France stalemated, the casualties mounted and pressure for American intervention increased. On the first day of the Battle of the Somme, on July 1, 1916, 20,000 British soldiers were killed and 40,000 others were wounded—all in less than twenty-four hours. Shock in the United States over the sudden outbreak of war in Europe gave way to gratitude that an ocean stood between America and the killing fields. "Our isolated position and freedom from entangling alliances," said the *Literary Digest,* "inspire our press with cheering assurance that we are in no peril of being drawn into the European quarrel." President Wilson repeatedly urged the American people to be "neutral in thought as well as in action."

That was more easily said than done. In the 1910 U.S. population of 92 million, more than 32 million were first- or second-generation immigrants who retained close ties to their old countries. Among the more than 13 million from the countries at war, the 8 million German Americans were by far the largest group, and the 4 million Irish Americans harbored a deep-rooted enmity to Britain. These groups instinctively leaned toward the Central Powers.

Old-line Americans, largely of British origin, supported the Allied Powers. If, as has been said, Britain and the United States were divided by a common language, they were united by ties of culture and tradition. Americans identified also with France, which had contributed to American culture and ideas, and to independence itself. Britain and France, if not their ally Russia, seemed the custodians of democracy, while Germany more and more seemed the embodiment of autocracy and militarism. If not a direct threat to the United States, Germany would pose at least a potential threat if it destroyed the balance of power in Europe. High officers of the United States government were pro-British in thought from the outset. Robert Lansing, first counselor of the State Department, Walter Hines Page, ambassador to London, and Colonel Edward House, Wilson's closest adviser, saw in German militarism a potential danger to America.

What effect the propaganda of the warring powers had on American opinion is unclear. The Germans and the British were most active, but

German propaganda, which played on American dislike of Russian autocracy and anti-Semitism, fell mainly upon barren ground. Only German Americans and Irish Americans responded to a "hate England" theme. From the outset, the British had one supreme advantage in this area. Once they had cut the direct telegraph cable from Germany early in the war, nearly all news from the battlefronts had to clear through London.

A STRAINED NEUTRALITY   At first the war brought a slump in American exports and the threat of a depression, but by the spring of 1915 the Allies' demand for supplies generated a wartime boom. France and Britain bought so much that they soon needed loans to continue their purchases. Early in the war, Secretary of State Bryan argued that loans to any warring nation were "inconsistent with the true spirit of neutrality." Technically he was correct, but Wilson, for all his public professions of neutrality, was in fact determined to aid Great Britain. He quietly began approving credits to sustain trade with the Allies. American investors would advance over $2 billion to the Allies before the United States entered the war, and only $27 million to Germany.

The administration nevertheless clung to its official stance of neutrality through two and a half years of warfare in Europe and tried to uphold the traditions of "freedom of the sea," which had guided American policy since the Napoleonic Wars. Trade on the high seas assumed a new importance as the German drive through Belgium and toward Paris finally ground down into the stalemate of trench warfare. In a war of attrition, survival depended on access to supplies, and in such a war British naval power counted for a great deal. With the German fleet outnumbered and bottled up almost from the outset, the war in many ways assumed the pattern that in 1812 had led America into war with Britain.

In November 1914 the British declared the whole North Sea a war zone and sowed it with mines. Four months later, they announced that they would seize ships carrying goods of presumed enemy destination, ownership, or origin. British policies of search and seizure caused extended delays in shipping, sometimes running into months. Britain also ordered its ships to stop vessels carrying German goods via neutral ports. When the State Department protested, Britain reminded the United States that this was the same doctrine of continuous voyage on which the United States had acted in the 1860s to keep British goods out of the Confederacy.

NEUTRAL RIGHTS AND SUBMARINES   British actions, which included blacklisting companies that traded with the enemy and censoring the mails, raised some old issues of neutral rights, but the German reaction introduced an entirely new question. In the face of the British blockade, only German submarines could venture out to harass the enemy. On February 4, 1915, in response to the "illegal" British blockade, the German government proclaimed a war zone around the British Isles. Enemy merchant ships in those waters were liable to sinking by submarines, the Germans declared. As the chief advantage of U-boat (*Unterseeboot*) warfare was in surprise, it violated the established international procedure of stopping enemy vessels on the high seas and providing for the safety of passengers and crews before sinking the vessel. Since the British sometimes flew neutral flags as a ruse, neutral ships in the zone would also be in danger.

The United States pronounced the German policy "an indefensible violation of neutral rights" and warned that Germany would be held to "strict accountability" for any destruction of American lives and property. On March 28, 1915, one American drowned when the Germans sank a British steamer in the Irish Sea. The following May an American tanker went down with a loss of two lives. The administration was divided on the proper course of action. Bryan wanted to warn American citizens that they entered the war zone at their own risk; his counselor, Robert Lansing, and Colonel House wanted to threaten a possible break in diplomatic relations with Germany.

As Wilson pondered the alternatives, the sinking of the majestic British liner *Lusitania* provoked a crisis. On May 7, 1915, a German U-boat torpedoed the *Lusitania,* which exploded and sank within eighteen minutes. Before the ship's departure from New York, bound for Liverpool, the German embassy had published warnings in the American press against travel to the war zone, but among the 1,198 persons lost were 128 Americans.

Americans were outraged. The sinking was an act of piracy, Theodore Roosevelt declared. To quiet the uproar, Wilson urged patience: "There is such a thing as a man being too proud to fight. There is such a thing as a nation being so right that it does not need to convince others by

"All the News That's Fit to Print."

The New York Times.

THE WEATHER
Fair today and tomorrow; fresh to strong southeast to east winds.

VOL. LXIV...NO. 20,923.　　NEW YORK, SATURDAY, MAY 8, 1915.—TWENTY-FOUR PAGES.　　ONE CENT

LUSITANIA SUNK BY A SUBMARINE, PROBABLY 1,000 DEAD;
TWICE TORPEDOED OFF IRISH COAST; SINKS IN 15 MINUTES;
AMERICANS ABOARD INCLUDED VANDERBILT AND FROHMAN;
WASHINGTON BELIEVES THAT A GRAVE CRISIS IS AT HAND

THE LOST CUNARD STEAMSHIP LUSITANIA

Americans were outraged when a German torpedo sank the Lusitania *on May 7, 1915.*

force that it is right." But his previous demand for "strict accountability" forced him to make a strong response. On May 13 Secretary of State Bryan reluctantly signed a note demanding that the Germans abandon unrestricted submarine warfare, disavow the sinking, and pay reparations. The Germans responded that the passenger ship had been armed (which it was not) and carried a secret cargo of small arms and ammunition (which it did). A second note on June 9 repeated American demands in stronger terms. Bryan, unwilling to risk war over the issue, resigned in protest and joined the peace movement as a private citizen. His successor, Robert Lansing, signed the note.

In response to the uproar over the *Lusitania,* the German government had secretly ordered U-boat captains to avoid sinking large passenger vessels. When, despite the order, two American lives were lost in the sinking of the British liner *Arabic,* bound for New York, the German ambassador demanded and got from Berlin a public assurance, which he delivered on September 1, 1915: "Liners will not be sunk by our submarines without warning and without safety of the lives of non-combatants, provided that the liners do not try to escape or offer resistance."

With this *Arabic* pledge, Wilson's resolute stand seemed to have won a victory for his policy.

THE DEBATE OVER PREPAREDNESS The *Lusitania* incident, and more generally the quarrels over neutral commerce, contributed to a growing demand for a stronger American army and navy. After the *Lusitania* sinking, the outcry from preparedness advocates grew into a clamor, and Theodore Roosevelt stood at the forefront of the movement. As journalist William Allen White recognized, "Social and industrial justice no longer interested Colonel Roosevelt. He had a war, a war greater than he ever realized it would be, to engage his talents."

In his annual message in 1915, Wilson alerted Congress to his plans for war preparedness. The response was far from unanimous. Progressives and pacifists, especially in the rural South and West, opposed military expansion. Jane Addams and suffragist Carrie Chapman Catt organized a Women's Peace party. Bryan, La Follette, and other leaders also lent their voices to the peace movement.

Wilson eventually accepted a compromise between advocates of an expanded force under federal control and advocates of a traditional citizen army. The National Defense Act of 1916 expanded the regular army from 90,000 to 175,000 and permitted a gradual enlargement to 223,000. It also authorized a National Guard of 440,000. The bill for an increased navy had less trouble because of the general feeling expressed by Secretary Josephus Daniels that there was "no danger of militarism from a relatively strong navy such as would come from a big standing army." The Naval Construction Act of 1916 authorized between $500 and $600 million for a three-year shipbuilding program.

Forced to relent on preparedness, progressive opponents determined that the financial burden should rest on the wealthy people they held responsible for the military buildup. The income tax became their weapon. Supported by a groundswell of popular support, they wrote into the Revenue Act of 1916 changes that doubled the basic income tax from 1 to 2 percent, lifted the surtax on incomes over $2 million to 13 percent, added an estate tax graduated up to a maximum of 10 percent, levied a 12.5 percent tax on gross receipts of munitions makers, and added a new tax on corporations. The new taxes amounted to the most clear-cut victory of radical progressives in the entire Wilson period, a victory that Wilson supported in preparation for the election of 1916.

THE ELECTION OF 1916   As the 1916 election approached, Republicans hoped to regain their normal electoral majority, and Roosevelt hoped to be their leader again. But in 1912 he had committed the deadly sin of bolting his party and, what was more, he now expressed a bellicosity on war issues that would scare off voters. Needing somebody who would draw Bull Moose progressives back into the fold, the Republican regulars turned to Justice Charles Evans Hughes, a progressive governor of New York from 1907 to 1910. On the Supreme Court since then, he had neither endorsed a candidate in 1912 nor spoken out on foreign policy.

The Democrats, as expected, chose Wilson once again, and in their platform endorsed a program of social legislation, neutrality, and reasonable preparedness. The party further commended women's suffrage to the states, denounced groups that placed the interests of other countries above those of the United States, and pledged support for a postwar League of Nations to enforce peace with collective security measures against aggressors. The Democrats found their most popular issue, however, in Wilson's commitment to neutrality. The peace theme, re-

Peace with Honor. *Wilson's neutral policies proved popular in the 1916 campaign.*

fined into the slogan "He kept us out of war," became the rallying cry of the campaign, one that had the merit of taking credit without making any promises for the future.

In the end, Wilson's twin pledges of peace and progressivism, a unique combination of issues forged in the legislative and diplomatic crucibles of 1916, brought victory. The final vote showed a Democratic sweep of the Far West and South, enough for victory in the electoral college by 277 to 254, and in the popular vote by 9 million to 8.5 million. Wilson also carried many social-justice progressives who in 1912 had supported the Bull Moose campaign.

LAST EFFORTS FOR PEACE   Immediately after the election, Wilson began to plan another peace move, whereupon the German government announced its readiness to discuss peace terms. Wilson sent identical notes to all the belligerent powers, asking each to state its war aims. The Germans responded promptly that they would state theirs only to a conference of the belligerents at a neutral site (although it soon became clear that they intended to seize new territory along the Baltic Sea, in the Congo of Africa, and in France, Belgium, and Luxembourg). In early 1917 the Allies made it plain that they intended to exact reparations, break up the Austro-Hungarian and Ottoman Empires, and destroy German power. Wilson then decided to make one more appeal, in the hope that public opinion would force the hands of the warring governments. Speaking before the Senate, he asserted the right of the United States to share in laying the foundations for a lasting peace. This would have to be a "peace without victory," for only a "peace among equals" could endure.

Although Wilson did not know it, he was already too late. Exactly two weeks before he spoke, German military leaders had decided to wage unrestricted submarine warfare. Faced with weakening resources in a war of attrition, the Germans took the calculated risk of provoking American anger in the hope of scoring a quick knockout. On January 31, 1917, Germany announced the new policy, effective the next day: all vessels in the war zone, belligerent or neutral, would be sunk without warning. "Freedom of the seas," said the *Brooklyn Eagle,* "will now be enjoyed by icebergs and fish."

On February 3, 1917, Wilson informed a joint session of Congress that the United States had broken diplomatic relations with the German government. He added that he still did not believe the Germans would do what they said they felt at liberty to do—only overt acts would persuade him that they actually intended to sink neutral ships. In case of such acts, he would take measures to protect American seamen and citizens.

Then, on March 1, news of the so-called Zimmermann Telegram broke in the American press. The British had intercepted and decoded an important message from German foreign secretary Arthur Zimmermann to his minister in Mexico. The note instructed the envoy to offer an alliance and financial aid to Mexico in case of war between the United States and Germany. In return for diversionary action against the United States, Mexico would recover "the lost territory in Texas, New Mexico, and Arizona." All this was contingent on war with the United States, but an electrified public read in it an aggressive intent. Later in March another bombshell burst when a revolution overthrew Russia's czarist government and established the provisional government of a Russian Republic. The fall of the czarist autocracy allowed Americans the illusion that all the major Allied Powers were now fighting for constitutional democracy. Not until November 1917 was this illusion shattered, when the Bolsheviks seized power in Russia.

AMERICA'S ENTRY INTO THE WAR

In March 1917, German submarines sank five American merchant vessels. On March 20, Wilson's cabinet unanimously endorsed a declaration of war, and the following day the president called a special session of Congress. When it met on April 2, Wilson asked Congress to recognize the war that imperial Germany was already waging against the United States, then turned to a discussion of the issues. The German government had revealed itself as a natural foe of liberty, and, Wilson argued in the rhetoric of progressivism, "The world must be made safe for democracy." The war resolution passed the Senate by a vote of 82 to 6 on April 4. The House concurred, 373 to 50, and Wilson signed the measure on April 6.

How had it come to this, less than three years after Wilson's proclamation of neutrality? Prominent among the various explanations of America's entrance into the war were the effects of British propaganda and America's deep involvement in trade with the Allies, which some observers then and later credited to the intrigues of war profiteers and munitions makers. Some Americans thought German domination of Europe would be a threat to American security, especially if it meant the destruction or capture of the British navy. Whatever the influence of such factors, they likely would not have been decisive without the issue of submarine warfare. This issue need not have become decisive, either, since such neutrals as Norway, Sweden, and Denmark took relatively heavier losses and yet stayed out of the war. But once Wilson had taken a stand for the traditional rights of neutrals and noncombatants, he was to some extent at the mercy of decisions by the German high command. Wilson was then led step by step into a war over what to a later generation would seem a rather quaint, if noble, set of principles.

AMERICA'S EARLY ROLE   The scope of America's role in the European land war remained unclear for a time. Few on either side of the Atlantic expected more from the United States than a token military effort. Despite Congress's preparedness measures, the army remained small and rudimentary. The navy also was largely undeveloped. This began to change, however, when Rear Admiral William S. Sims assumed command of American ships in European waters. He systematically built up the United States Navy and started sending American destroyers to Ireland. Sims also persuaded the Allies to adopt a convoy system of escorting merchant ships in groups, resulting in an impressive decrease in Allied shipping losses.

Within a month of America's declaration of war, the British and French requested money for supplies, a request Congress had already anticipated in the Liberty Loan Act, which added $5 billion to the national debt in "Liberty Bonds." Of this amount, $3 billion could be loaned to the Allied Powers. The United States was also willing to furnish naval support, credits, supplies, and munitions. But to raise and train a large army, equip it, and send it across a submarine-infested ocean seemed out of the question.

The United States agreed to send a token army force to bolster Anglo-French morale, and on June 26, 1917, the first American contingent, about 14,500 men commanded by General John J. Pershing, began to disembark on the French coast. After reaching Paris, Pershing decided that the war-weary Allies would be unable to mount an offensive by themselves. He therefore requested that Wilson send a million American troops by the following spring, and the president obliged.

When the United States entered the war, the combined strength of the regular army and National Guard was only 379,000; at the end it would be 3.7 million. The need for such large numbers of troops converted Wilson to the idea of conscription. Under the Selective Service Act of May 18, 1917, all men aged twenty-one to thirty (later, from eighteen to forty-five) had to register for service. By July 1917, when the first lottery was held to determine who would actually be drafted to fight in the war, almost 24 million men were registered. In the course of the war, about 2 million Americans crossed the Atlantic and about 1.4 million of them saw some combat.

Training of the soldiers went on in thirty-two camps, half of them located in the South for reasons of climate. The example of the Spanish-American War was well learned: the camps were for the most part sanitary and equipped with modern plumbing, hospitals, and recreation centers. Many saw the mobilization of hundreds of thousands of young men as an opportunity for social engineering. They aimed to improve the recruits' character and outlook, inculcating middle-class "progressive" virtues and values into recruits when they were undergoing their military training. To this end, they developed sex education programs to prevent the spread of venereal diseases, worked with local authorities to police "red-light" districts near the military bases and to arrest prostitutes, and sponsored sporting events and entertainment programs, as well as dances and religious services.

MOBILIZING A NATION   Complete economic mobilization on the home front was also necessary to conduct the war efficiently. Still, a lingering lack of coordination among public and private officials made wartime mobilization less efficient than it should have been. It was not the Wilson administration's finest hour.

In 1916 Congress had created a Council of National Defense, which in turn set up other wartime agencies. The United States Shipping Board, organized in 1917, within two years was constructing more than forty steel and ninety wooden ships monthly. In 1917 Congress created both a Food Administration, headed by Herbert Hoover, a future president, and a Fuel Administration. Hoover, a mining engineer and former head of the Commission for Relief in Belgium, had the responsibility of

Food Will Win the War, *the slogan of the Food Administration, appears over the entrance of this "real Bohemian Grill."*

raising crop production while reducing civilian use of foodstuffs. "Food will win the war" was the slogan. Hoover directed a propaganda campaign that "Hooverized" the country with "Meatless Tuesdays," "Wheatless Wednesdays," "Porkless Saturdays," the planting of victory gardens, and the use of leftovers. The Fuel Administration introduced the country to Daylight Saving Time and "heatless Mondays" to save fuel.

The War Industries Board (WIB) was established in 1917, and it soon became the most important of all the mobilization agencies. Wilson summoned Bernard Baruch, a brilliant Wall Street investor, to head the board, giving him a virtual dictatorship over the economy. The WIB could allocate raw materials, tell manufacturers what to produce, order construction of new plants, and, with presidential approval, fix prices.

A NEW LABOR FORCE   The closing off of foreign immigration and the movement of almost 4 million men into the armed services created a labor shortage. To meet it, women, blacks, and other ethnic minorities were encouraged to enter industries and agricultural activities heretofore dominated by white males. Northern businesses sent recruiting agents into the Deep South to find workers for their factories and mills, and over 400,000 southern blacks began the "Great Migration" northward during the war years, a mass movement that continued unabated through the 1920s. Mexican Americans followed the same migratory pattern. Recruiting agents and newspaper editors portrayed the North as the "land of promise" for southern blacks suffering from their region's depressed agricultural economy and rising racial intimidation and violence. The African-American newspaper *Chicago Defender* exclaimed: "To die from the bite of frost is far more glorious than at the hands of a mob." By 1930, the number of African Americans living in the North had tripled from 1910 levels.

But the newcomers were not always welcomed above the Mason-Dixon line. Many native white workers resented the new arrivals, and racial tensions sparked riots in cities across the country. In 1917 over forty African Americans and nine whites were killed during a riot over employment in a defense plant in East St. Louis. Two years later the toll of a Chicago race riot was nearly as high, with twenty-three black and fifteen white deaths. In these and other incidents of racial violence the pattern was the same. Whites angered by the influx of blacks into their communities would seize upon an incident to rampage through black neighborhoods, killing, burning, and looting, while white policemen looked the other way or encouraged the mobs.

American intervention in World War I also had a significant impact on women. Initially, females supported the war effort in traditional ways. They helped organize war-bond and war-relief drives, conserved foodstuffs and war-related materials, supported the Red Cross, and joined the Army nurse corps. But as the scope of the war widened, both government and industry sought to mobilize women workers for service on farms, loading docks, and railway crews, as well as in armaments industries, machine shops, steel and lumber mills, and chemical plants. Many women leaders saw such opportunities as a real breakthrough. "At last, after centuries of disabilities and discrimination," said a speaker at a Women's Trade Union League meeting in 1917, "women are coming into the labor and festival of life on equal terms with men." A black woman who exchanged her job as a live-in servant for work in a factory declared: "I'll never work in nobody's kitchen but my own any more. No indeed, that's the one thing that makes me stick to this job."

In fact, however, war-generated changes in female employment were limited and brief. About a million women participated in "war work," but most of them were young, single, and already working outside the home. Most returned to their previous jobs once the war ended. In fact, male-dominated unions encouraged women to revert to their stereotypical domestic roles after the war ended. The Central Federated Union of New York baldly insisted that "the same patriotism which induced women to enter industry during the war should induce them to vacate their positions after the war." The anticipated gains of women in the workforce failed to materialize. In fact, by 1920 the 8.5 million working women made up a smaller percentage of the labor force than they had in 1910. Still, one tangible result of women's contributions to the war effort was Woodrow Wilson's decision to endorse female suffrage. In the fall of 1918 he told the Senate that giving women the vote was "vital to the winning of the war."

The wartime emergency placed organized labor in a position to make solid advances in employment and wages, despite the rise in consumer prices. A newly created United States Employment Service placed some 4 million workers in war-related jobs. Labor unions benefited from expanded employment, the increased demand for labor, and government policies favorable to collective bargaining. From 1913 to 1918, AFL membership increased by 37 percent.

WAR PROPAGANDA   The exigencies of winning the war led the government to mobilize more than economic life: the progressive gospel of efficiency suggested mobilizing public opinion as well. On April 14, 1917, eight days after the declaration of war, Wilson established the Committee on Public Information. Its executive director, George Creel, a Denver journalist, sold Wilson on the idea that the best approach to influencing public opinion was "expression, not repression"—propaganda instead of censorship. Creel organized a propaganda machine to convey the Allies' war aims to the people, and above all to the enemy, where it might encourage the forces of moderation.

CIVIL LIBERTIES   By arousing public opinion to such a frenzy, however, the war effort channeled the zeal of progressivism into grotesque campaigns of "Americanism" and witch-hunting. Wilson had foreseen such consequences. "Once lead this people into war," he told an editor, "and they'll forget there even was such a thing as tolerance." Popular prejudice equated anything German with disloyalty. Schools even dropped German language courses.

While mobs hunted spies and chased rumors, the federal government stalked bigger game, with results often as absurd. The Espionage and Sedition Acts of 1917 and 1918 effectively outlawed criticism of government leaders and war policies. These laws led to more than 1,500 prosecutions and 1,000 convictions. Such repression disillusioned many progressives. Senator La Follette declared that those engaged in such a "witch-hunt" were trying "to throw the country into a state of terror, to coerce public opinion, stifle criticism, suppress discussion of the issues of the war, and put a quietus on all opposition. It is time for the American people to assert and maintain their rights."

The impact of these acts fell with most severity upon radicals. In Chicago over 100 leaders of the Industrial Workers of the World went on trial for opposing the war effort. All were found guilty, and the IWW never fully recovered from the blow. The same fate befell members of the Socialist party. Eugene V. Debs, who had polled over 900,000 votes as the Socialist candidate for president in 1912, ardently opposed American intervention, declaring that "I am opposed to every war but one; I am for that war heart and soul, and that is the worldwide revolution." He repeatedly urged men to refuse to serve in the military, even though he knew he could be prosecuted for such remarks under the Espionage Act. "I would a thousand times rather be a free soul in jail than a sycophant and a coward in the streets." He received his wish. Debs was arrested and eventually sentenced to twenty years in prison for encouraging draft resistance. In 1920, still in jail, he polled nearly 1 million votes for president.

In an important decision just after the war, the Supreme Court upheld the Espionage and Sedition Acts. *Schenck v. United States* (1919) sustained the conviction of a man for circulating antidraft leaflets among members of the armed forces. In this case Justice Oliver Wendell Holmes observed: "Free speech would not protect a man in falsely shouting fire in a theater, and causing a panic." The act applied where there was "a clear and present danger" that free speech in wartime might create evils Congress had a right to prevent.

"THE DECISIVE POWER"

American troops played little more than a token role in the European fighting until the end of 1917, when the Allied position turned desperate. In October the Italian lines collapsed in the face of the Austrian offensive. In November, having suffered some 5.5 million casualties and widespread food and ammunition shortages, the Russian provisional republican government succumbed to a revolution led by Vladimir Lenin and his Bolshevik party, which promised the Russian people "Peace, Land, and Bread." With German troops then deep in Russian territory, and with armies of "White" Russians organizing to resist the Bolsheviks, Lenin concluded a separate peace with the Germans in the Treaty of Brest-Litovsk (March 3, 1918). The Central Powers were now free to concentrate their forces on the Western Front, and the American war effort became a "race for France" to restore the balance of strength in that arena. French premier Georges Clemenceau appealed to the Americans to accelerate their mobilization: "A terrible blow is imminent," he predicted to an American journalist. "Tell your Americans to come quickly."

THE WESTERN FRONT   On March 21, 1918, Clemenceau's prediction came true when the Germans began the first of several offensives to try to end the war before the Americans arrived in force. On the Somme River they broke through at the juncture of British and French sectors and penetrated thirty-five miles, nearly to Amiens. Farther north, the Germans struck in Flanders, where the Allies still held a corner of Belgium. At this critical point, on April 14 the Allies made French general Ferdinand Foch the supreme commander of all Allied forces.

On May 27 the Germans began their next drive along the Aisne River, took Soissons, and pushed on to the Marne River along a forty-mile front. By May 1918 there were a million fresh American troops in Europe, and for the first time they made a difference. In a counterattack, American forces retook Cantigny on May 28 and held it. A week later, on June 2–3, a marine brigade blocked the Germans at Belleau Wood. American army troops took Vaux and opposed the Germans at Château-Thierry. Though these actions had limited military significance, their effect on Allied morale was immense. Each was a solid American success, and together they reinforced Pershing's demand for a separate American army.

Before that could come to pass, the Second Battle of the Marne (July 15, 1918) erupted, and it proved to be the turning point in the western campaign. On both sides of Reims, the Germans commenced their push

THE WESTERN FRONT, 1918
- - - The Western Front, March 1918
······ German offensive, spring 1918
→ Allied counteroffensive
—— The Western Front, November 1918

against the French lines. Within three days, however, they had stalled, and the allies, mainly with American troops, went on the offensive.

Soon the British, French, and American forces began to roll the German front back into Belgium. On September 12, an army of more than 500,000 staged the first strictly American offensive of the war, aimed at German forces at St. Mihiel. Within three days the Germans had pulled back. Two weeks later, the massive Meuse-Argonne offensive employed American divisions in a drive toward the rail center at Sédan, which supplied the entire German front. The largest American action of the war, it cost 117,000 American casualties, including 26,000 dead. All along the front from Sédan to Flanders the Germans were in retreat. "America," wrote a German commander, "thus became the decisive power in the war."

Fresh troops moving to an advanced position near the front, France.

Meanwhile, in an effort to prevent stockpiled Allied supplies from falling into German hands, and to encourage the counter-revolutionary Russian "Whites" in their civil war against the "Reds," fourteen Allied nations sent troops into eastern Russia. On August 2, 1918, some 8,000 Americans joined the expedition and remained on Russian soil until April 1920. But the Allied intervention in Russia was a colossal failure. The Bolsheviks were able to consolidate their power, defeat the "Whites," and withdraw from World War I. The Russians therefore did not participate in the peace settlement. Even more importantly, Lenin and the Soviets never forgave the West for attempting to thwart their revolution.

THE FOURTEEN POINTS   As the conflict was ending, the question of war aims arose again. Neither the Allies nor the Central Powers, despite Wilson's prodding, had stated openly what they hoped to gain through the bloodletting. Wilson insisted that the Americans had no selfish ends. "We desire no conquest, no dominion," he stressed in his war message. Unfortunately for his purpose, the Bolsheviks later published copies of secret treaties in which the Allies had promised territorial gains in order to win Italy, Romania, and Greece to their side. When an Interallied Conference in Paris late in 1917 failed to agree on a statement of aims, Wilson formulated his own.

With advice from a panel of experts, Wilson drew up a statement that would be labeled the Fourteen Points. These he delivered to a joint session of Congress on January 8, 1918, "as the only possible program" for peace. The first five points called for open diplomacy, freedom of the seas, removal of trade barriers, armaments reduction, and an impartial adjustment of colonial claims based on the interests of the populations involved. Most of the remainder called on the Central Powers to evacuate occupied lands and to allow self-determination for various nationalities, a crucial principle for Wilson. Point 14, the capstone in Wilson's thinking, called for the formulation of a "league of nations" to guarantee the independence and territorial integrity of all countries, great and small.

Wilson sincerely believed in the Fourteen Points, but they also served important political purposes. One of their aims was to keep Russia in the war by a more liberal statement of purposes—a vain hope, as it turned out. Another was to reassure the Allied peoples that they were involved in a noble cause. A third was to drive a wedge between the governments of the Central Powers and their peoples by the offer of a reasonable peace. But the chaos into which central Europe descended in 1918, as both Germany and Austria-Hungary verged on starvation and experienced socialist uprisings, took matters out of Wilson's hands.

THE END OF THE WAR   On September 29, 1918, German general Erich Ludendorff advised his government to seek the best peace terms possible. On October 3, a new chancellor made the first German overtures for peace on the basis of the Fourteen Points. The Allies, after a month of diplomatic fencing, accepted the Fourteen Points as a basis of peace but with two significant reservations: they reserved the right to discuss freedom of the seas further, and they demanded reparations (financial compensation to the victors) for war damages.

Meanwhile, German morale plummeted, culminating in a naval mutiny. Germany's allies, Bulgaria, Turkey, and Austria-Hungary, dropped out of the war during the early fall of 1918. On November 9 the kaiser, head of the German Empire, abdicated, and a German Republic was proclaimed. Two days later, on November 11, 1918, an armistice was signed, ceasing the hostilities. Under the Armistice, the Germans agreed to evacuate occupied territories, pull back behind the Rhine River, and surrender their navy, railroad equipment, and other materials. The Germans were assured that the Fourteen Points would be the basis for the peace conference.

During its nineteen months of participation in the war, the United States saw 114,000 of its servicemen killed. Germany's war dead totaled over 2 million; France and Russia lost over 1.7 million each. In France alone in 1918 there were 630,000 war widows. The new Europe emerging from the conflagration would be much different: darker, more violent, more polarized, more cynical, less sure of itself, and less capable of decisive action. The United States, for good or ill, would be sucked into the vacuum of power created by the destructiveness of the Great War.

THE FIGHT FOR PEACE AT HOME AND ABROAD

DOMESTIC UNREST Wilson made a fateful decision to attend in person the Paris Peace Conference, which convened on January 18, 1919, and would last almost six months. A president had never left the

On his way to the Paris Peace Conference, Wilson was welcomed as a hero in Europe. Here he reviews a line of troops in Calais.

country for so long, but doing so dramatized all the more Wilson's messianic vision and his desire to ensure his goal of a lasting peace. From one viewpoint it was a shrewd move, for his prestige and determination made a difference in Paris. But he lost touch with developments at home, where his political coalition was already unraveling under the pressures of wartime discontent (a state of war officially existed until 1921). Western farmers complained about the government's control of wheat prices, while Eastern business leaders chafed at revenue policies designed, according to the *New York Sun,* "to pay for the war out of taxes raised north of the Mason and Dixon Line." Organized labor, despite real gains, groused about inflation and the problems of reconversion to a peacetime economy.

In the midterm elections of 1918, Wilson made matters worse with a partisan appeal for a Democratic Congress to ensure support of his foreign policies. Republicans, who for the most part had supported his war measures, took affront. So too did many voters. In elections held a week before the Armistice, the Democrats lost control of both houses of Congress. With an opposition majority in the new Congress, Wilson further weakened his standing by failing to include a single prominent Republican in the American delegation headed for Paris and the treaty negotiations. Humorist Will Rogers joked that Wilson was telling the Republicans, "I tell you what, we will split 50–50. I will go and you fellows can stay." Former President Taft suggested that Wilson's real intention in going to Paris was "to hog the whole show."

When Wilson reached Europe in December 1918, enthusiastic demonstrations greeted him in Paris. At the conference table, however, Wilson had to deal with some tough-minded statesmen. The Paris conference included delegates from all countries that had declared war or broken diplomatic relations with Germany. But it was dominated by the Big Four: the prime ministers of Britain, France, and Italy, and the president of the United States. David Lloyd George of England was a gifted politician fresh from electoral victory on the slogan "Hang the Kaiser." Italy's Vittorio Orlando was there to pick up the spoils promised his country in the secret Treaty of London (1915). French premier Georges Clemenceau, a stern realist, insisted on severe measures to weaken Germany and guarantee French security. He scorned Wilson's idealism. "God gave us the Ten Commandments and we broke them," he sneered. "Wilson gave us the Fourteen Points—we shall see."

THE LEAGUE OF NATIONS   Wilson insisted that his cherished League of Nations must come first in the conference and in the treaty. Whatever compromises he might have to make, whatever mistakes might result, Wilson believed that such a permanent peace agency would maintain international stability.

Wilson presided over the commission to draft a charter for the League. Article X of the charter, which he called "the heart of the League," pledged members to consult on military and economic sanctions against aggressors. The use of arms would be a last resort. The League structure allowed each member an equal voice in the Assembly; the Big Five (Britain, France, Italy, Japan, and the United States) and four other rotating members would make up the Council; the administrative staff in Geneva would make up the Secretariat; and finally, a Permanent Court of International Justice (set up in 1921 and usually called the World Court) could "hear and determine any dispute of an international character."

On February 14, 1919, Wilson delivered the finished draft of the League charter and departed the next day for a month-long visit home. Already he faced rumblings of opposition. Republican Henry Cabot Lodge, chairman of the Senate Foreign Relations Committee, claimed that the League was unacceptable "in the form now proposed." His statement of March 4 bore the signatures of thirty-nine Republican senators or senators-elect, more than enough to block ratification.

TERRITORY AND REPARATIONS   Back in Paris, Wilson grudgingly conceded to French demands for territorial concessions and reparations from Germany. He clashed sharply with Clemenceau, but after the president threatened to leave the conference, they agreed that the Allies would occupy a demilitarized German Rhineland for fifteen years, and that the League of Nations would administer Germany's coal-rich Saar Basin. France could use Saar mines for fifteen years, after which the region's voters would determine their status.

In other territorial matters Wilson had to compromise his principle of national self-determination. There was in fact no way to make boundaries correspond to ethnic divisions, because the folk wanderings of centuries had left mixed populations scattered through central Europe. In some areas, moreover, national self-determination yielded to other interests such as trade and defense. The result was a reorganized map

EUROPE AFTER VERSAILLES
········ 1914 boundaries
New nations
Plebiscite areas
Occupied area

of central Europe in which portions of the former Austro-Hungarian Empire became independent, most notably Czechoslovakia and Yugoslavia, and portions became attached to Poland, Romania, and Italy. Ethnic and nationalist tensions continued, and would contribute to the crisis that culminated in World War II.

The discussion of reparations was among the longest and most bitter at the conference. Despite a pre-Armistice agreement that Germany would be liable only for civilian damages, Clemenceau and Lloyd George proposed reparations for the entire cost of the war. On this point Wilson made perhaps his most fateful concessions. He agreed to a clause in the treaty by which Germany accepted responsibility for starting the war and for its entire costs. The "war guilt" clause offended all Germans and provided a source of persistent bitterness.

On May 7, 1919, the victorious powers presented the treaty to the

German delegates, who returned three weeks later with 443 pages of criticism protesting that the terms violated the Fourteen Points. A few small changes were made, but when the Germans still refused to sign, Marshal Ferdinand Foch prepared to move his French army across the Rhine River. Finally, on June 28, 1919, the Germans signed the treaty at Versailles.

WILSON'S LOSS AT HOME   Wilson returned home with the Versailles Treaty on July 8, 1919. Two days later he called on the Senate to accept "this great duty." The force of Wilson's idealism struck deep, and he returned amid a great clamor of popular support. A third of the state legislatures had endorsed the League, as had thirty-three of forty-eight governors.

Senator Henry Cabot Lodge, however, harbored serious reservations. He did not wish the United States to withdraw from world affairs, but he doubted that the Paris negotiators could make "mankind suddenly virtuous by a statute or written constitution." A powerful Republican who nourished an intense dislike for Wilson, Lodge relished a fight. "I never thought I could hate a man as I hate Wilson," he confessed. Lodge knew the undercurrents already stirring up opposition to the treaty: the resentment felt by German, Italian, and Irish groups, the disappointment of liberals at Wilson's compromises on reparations and boundaries, the distractions of demobilization and resulting domestic problems, and the revival of isolationism. Lodge's close friend, Theodore Roosevelt, still a popular figure, lambasted the League, noting that he keenly distrusted a "man who cares for other nations as much as his own."

Others agreed. In the Senate a group of "irreconcilables," fourteen Republicans and two Democrats, opposed American participation in the League on any terms. They were mainly western or midwestern progressives who feared that new foreign commitments would threaten domestic programs and reforms. The irreconcilables would be useful to Lodge's purpose, but he belonged to a larger group of "reservationists." They were ready to compromise with Wilson but insisted on limiting American involvement in the League and its actions. Wilson said that he had already amended the covenant to these ends, pointing out that with a veto in the League Council the United States could not be obligated to do anything against its will.

Lodge, who set more store by the old balance of power than by the new idea of collective security, offered a set of amendments, or reservations. Wilson responded by agreeing to interpretive reservations, but to nothing that would reopen the negotiations with Germany and the Allies. He especially opposed the amendments weakening Article X, which provided for collective action by the signatory governments against aggression.

By September, with momentum for the treaty slackening, Wilson decided to go directly to the people. Against the advice of doctors and friends he set forth on a tour through the Midwest to the West Coast, pounding out speeches on his typewriter between stops. In all he traveled 6,000 miles in twenty-two days, gave thirty-two major addresses, refuted his opponents, and voiced dire warnings.

For a while Wilson seemed to be regaining the initiative, but then his body rebelled. On October 2, 1919, he suffered a severe stroke and paralysis on his left side, leaving him an invalid for the rest of his life. For more than seven months his protective wife kept him isolated from all but the most essential business. The illness intensified his stubbornness. He might have done better to have secured the best compromise possible, but he refused to yield anything. As he scoffed to an aide, "Let Lodge compromise."

Lodge was determined to amend the treaty before it was ratified. Between November 7 and 19, the Senate adopted fourteen of Lodge's

Three Senators Refuse the Lady a Seat. *Americans reacted against the Senate's defeat of the Versailles peace treaty.*

reservations to the Versailles Treaty, most having to do with the League. Wilson refused to make any compromises or concessions. As a result, the Wilsonians found themselves thrown into an unlikely combination with irreconcilables who opposed the treaty under any circumstances. The Senate vote on the treaty with Lodge's reservations was 39 for and 55 against. On the question of taking the treaty without reservations, irreconcilables and reservationists combined to defeat ratification again, with 38 for and 53 against.

In the face of strong public criticism, however, the Senate voted to reconsider. But the stricken Wilson remained adamant: "Either we should enter the League fearlessly . . . or we should retire as gracefully as possible from the great concert of powers by which the world was saved." On March 19, 1920, twenty-one Democrats deserted Wilson and joined the reservationists, but the treaty once again fell short of a two-thirds majority by a vote of 49 yeas and 35 nays. The real winners were the smallest of the three groups in the Senate, neither the Wilsonians nor the reservationists but the irreconcilables.

When Congress declared the war at an end by joint resolution on May 20, 1920, Wilson vetoed the action; it was not until after he left office, on July 2, 1921, that a joint resolution officially ended the state of war with Germany and Austria-Hungary. Peace treaties with Germany, Austria, and Hungary were ratified on October 18, 1921, but by then Warren Gamaliel Harding was president of the United States.

LURCHING FROM WAR TO PEACE

The Versailles Treaty, for all the time it took in the Senate, was but one issue clamoring for public attention in the turbulent period after the war. Demobilization of the armed forces and the government's war effort proceeded without plan, indeed without much sense that a plan was needed once the war ended. The War Industries Board closed shop on January 1, 1919, and the sudden cancellation of war contracts left workers and business leaders to cope with reconversion on their own. Wilson's leadership was missing. He had been preoccupied by the war and the League, and once broken by his illness, he became strangely grim and peevish. His rudderless administration floundered through rough waters during its last two years.

THE SPANISH FLU   Amid the initial confusion of postwar life, many Americans confronted a virulent menace that produced far more casualties than the war itself. It became known as the Spanish flu, and its contagion spread around the globe. Erupting in the spring of 1918 and lasting a year, the pandemic killed more than 22 million people throughout the world, twice as many as the number who had died in World War I. In the United States alone the flu accounted for over 500,000 deaths, five times the number of combat deaths in France.

American servicemen returning from France brought the flu with them, and it raced through the congested army camps and naval bases. Still, no one seemed alarmed, for the flu remained a common if severe ailment. But then the hospitalized men started dying by the dozens, and it became obvious that this was no ordinary flu virus. Some 43,000 American servicemen died of influenza in 1918.

By September 1918 the epidemic had spread to the civilian population. In that month alone 10,000 Americans died from the disease. Municipal health officers began fining people for spitting on the sidewalks or for sneezing without a handkerchief. Millions of people began wearing surgical masks to work. Phone booths were locked up, as were other public facilities such as dance halls, poolrooms, and theaters. Even churches and saloons in many communities were declared off limits. Still the death toll rose. From September 1918 to June 1919, a quarter of the population had contracted the illness.

Yet by the spring of 1919 the pandemic had run its course. It ended as suddenly—and as inexplicably—as it had begun. Although another outbreak occurred in the winter of 1920, the population had grown more resistant to its assaults. No disease, plague, war, famine, or natural catastrophe in world history had killed so many people in such a short time.

THE ECONOMIC TRANSITION   The problems of postwar readjustment were worsened by widespread labor unrest. Prices continued to rise steeply after the war, and discontented workers, released from wartime constraints, were more willing to strike for their demands. In 1919, more than 4 million workers walked out in thousands of disputes. After a general strike in Seattle, public opinion began to turn hostile toward militant workers.

The most celebrated postwar labor confrontation was the Boston

Police Strike, which inadvertently launched a presidential career. On September 9, 1919, most of Boston's police force went out on strike, demanding recognition of their union. Massachusetts governor Calvin Coolidge mobilized the National Guard to arrest looters and restore order. After four days the strikers were ready to return, but the police commissioner fired them all. When labor leader Samuel Gompers appealed for their reinstatement, Coolidge responded in words that suddenly turned him into a national figure: "There is no right to strike against the public safety by anybody, anywhere, anytime."

RACIAL FRICTION The summer of 1919 also brought a season of violent race riots, both in the North and South. Whites invaded the black section of Longview, Texas, in search of a teacher who had allegedly accused a white woman of a liaison with a black man. They burned shops and houses and ran several blacks out of town. A week later, in Washington, D.C., reports of attacks on white women aroused white mobs, and for four days gangs of white and black rioters waged race war in the streets until soldiers and driving rains ended the fighting.

These were but preliminaries to the Chicago riot of late July, in which 38 people were killed, 537 injured, and a thousand left homeless. It all started when a black youth's raft drifted into the white beach area, and whites started stoning him. The climactic disorders of the summer occurred in the rural area around Elaine, Arkansas, where black tenant farmers tried to organize a union. According to official reports, 5 whites and 25 blacks were killed in the violence, but whites told one reporter in the area that in fact more than 100 blacks died. Altogether twenty-five race riots took place in 1919, and more threatened.

THE RED SCARE Public reaction to the wave of labor strikes and race riots was influenced by the impact of Russia's Bolshevik Revolution. A minority of radicals thought America's domestic turbulence, like that in Russia, was the first scene in a drama of revolution. A much larger public was persuaded that they might be right. After all, Lenin's tiny faction in Russia had exploited confusion to impose its will on the entire nation. Wartime hysteria against all things German was thus readily transformed into a postwar Red Scare.

Fears of revolution might have remained latent except for the actions of a lunatic fringe. In April 1919 the postal services intercepted nearly forty bombs addressed to prominent citizens. One slipped through and blew off the hands of a Georgia senator's maid. In June another destroyed the front of Attorney-General A. Mitchell Palmer's house in Washington. Such random violence led many Americans to see Red on all sides and to condone attacks on all minorities in retaliation.

Soon the government itself was promoting witch-hunts. Attorney-General Palmer harbored a bitter distrust of aliens and a strong desire for the presidency. In June 1919 the Justice Department decided to deport radical aliens, and Palmer set up as the head of the department's new General Intelligence Division the young J. Edgar Hoover, who began to collect an index file on radicals. Raids began on November 7, 1919, when agents swooped down on the Union of Russian Workers in twelve cities. Many of those arrested were deported without a court hearing. On January 2, 1920, police raids in dozens of cities swept up some 5,000 suspects, many taken from their homes without search warrants. About half of those seized were kept in custody. That same month the New York legislature expelled five duly elected Socialist members.

Basking in popular approval, Palmer continued to warn of the Red menace, but like other fads and alarms, the ugly mood of intolerance passed. By the summer of 1920, the Red Scare had begun to evaporate. Communist revolutions in Europe died out, leaving Bolshevism isolated in Russia; bombings tapered off; the wave of strikes and race riots receded. The reactionary attorney-general began to seem more threatening to civil liberties than a handful of radicals were to the social order. By September 1920, when a bomb explosion at the corner of Broad and Wall Streets in New York killed thirty-eight people, Americans were ready to take it for what it was, the work of a crazed mind and not the start of a revolution.

The Red Scare nevertheless left a lasting mark on American life. Part of its legacy was the continuing crusade for "100 percent Americanism" and restrictions on immigration. It also left a stigma on labor unions (already weakened by their own internal ethnic and racial tensions) and contributed to the anti-union open-shop campaign—the "American Plan," its sponsors called it. But for many thoughtful Americans the chief residue of the Great War and its chaotic aftermath was a profound disillusionment.

MAKING CONNECTIONS

- The Red Scare at the end of World War I led to a wave of nativism and immigration restriction, outlined in the next chapter.

- This chapter ends by noting the "profound disillusionment" Americans felt with efforts to reform the world. The political aspect of that disillusionment—the return to "normalcy" of the 1920s—is discussed in Chapter 26.

- The treaty ending World War I was designed to cripple Germany's military strength. But as Chapter 28 shows, within two decades Adolf Hitler was leading a rebuilt German military force into World War II.

FURTHER READING

Frederick S. Calhoun's *Power and Principle: Armed Intervention in Wilsonian Foreign Policy* (1986) surveys one aspect of Wilsonian diplomacy. For the Mexican intervention, consult John S. D. Eisenhower's *Intervention!: The United States and the Mexican Revolution, 1913–1917* (1993). A lucid and thoughtful overview of events covered in this chapter is Daniel M. Smith's *The Great Departure: The United States and World War I, 1914–1920* (1965).

A number of scholars have concentrated on the neutrality issue. Arthur S. Link, Wilson's greatest biographer, is sympathetic to the ideals of the president in *Woodrow Wilson: Revolution, War, and Peace* (1979). For a more critical view, see Ross Gregory's *The Origins of American Intervention in the First World War* (1971). A notable biography is August Heckscher's *Woodrow Wilson: A Biography* (1991).

Edward M. Coffman's *The War to End All Wars: The American Military Experience in World War I* (1968) is a detailed presentation of America's military involvement. The best survey of the war from the European perspective is John Keegan's *The First World War* (1999).

David M. Kennedy's *Over Here: The First World War and American Society* (1980) surveys the impact of the war on the home front. Maurine Weiner Greenwald's *Women, War, and Work: The Impact of World War I on Women Workers in the United States* (1980) discusses the role of women. Ronald Schaffer's *America in the Great War: The Rise of the War Welfare State* (1991) shows the effect of war mobilization on business organization. Richard Polenberg's *Fighting Faiths: The Abrams Case, the Supreme Court, and Free Speech* (1987) examines prosecutions under the 1918 Sedition Act.

How American diplomacy fared in the making of peace has received considerable attention. In addition to the Link book on Wilson, the role of the president is treated in Robert H. Ferrell's *Woodrow Wilson and World War I, 1917–1921* (1985), Arno J. Mayer's *Politics and Diplomacy in Peacemaking: Containment and Counterrevolution at Versailles, 1918–1919* (1967), and N. Gordon Levin, Jr.'s *Woodrow Wilson and World Politics: America's Response to War and Revolution* (1968). Thomas J. Knock interrelates domestic affairs and foreign relations in his explanation of Wilson's peacemaking in *To End All Wars: Woodrow Wilson and the Quest for a New World Order* (1992).

The problems of the immediate postwar years are chronicled by a number of historians. On the Spanish flu, see Alfred W. Crosby's *America's Forgotten Pandemic: The Influenza of 1918* (1990). Labor tensions are examined in David E. Brody's *Labor in Crisis: The Steel Strike of 1919* (1965) and Francis Russell's *A City in Terror: 1919, the Boston Police Strike* (1975). On racial strife, see William Tuttle, Jr.'s *Race Riot: Chicago in the Red Summer of 1919* (1970). The fear of Communists is analyzed in Robert K. Murray's *Red Scare: A Study in National Hysteria, 1919–1920* (rev. ed., 1980).

25 ✧ THE MODERN TEMPER

CHAPTER ORGANIZER

This chapter focuses on:

- the reactionary strains of the 1920s.

- the social ferment of the 1920s.

- the influence of modernism in American culture.

The horrors of World War I dealt a shattering blow to the widespread belief that Western civilization was steadily progressing, a myth that had dominated the public consciousness for a century and that had been so powerful a stimulus to progressivism. The editors of *Presbyterian Magazine* announced in 1919 that the "world has been convulsed . . . and every field of thought and action has been disturbed. . . . The most settled principles and laws of society . . . have been attacked."

The war's unimaginable carnage produced a postwar disillusionment among young intellectuals that challenged traditional values. A new "modernist" sensibility emerged among artists, writers, and journalists. At once a mood and a movement, modernism emerged first in Europe at the end of the nineteenth century and became a pervasive international force by 1920. It arose out of a widespread recognition that Western civilization had entered an era of bewildering change. New technologies, new modes of transportation and communication, and new scientific discoveries such as quantum mechanics and relativity theory combined to rupture perceptions of reality and generate new forms of artistic expression. "One must never forget," declared Gertrude Stein, the experimentalist poet, "that the reality of the twentieth century is not the reality of the nineteenth century, not at all." Modernism introduced a whole series of intellectual and artistic movements: impressionism, futurism, dadaism, surrealism, Freudianism. As the French painter Paul Gauguin acknowledged, the upheavals of modernism produced "an epoch of confusion."

At the same time that the war provided an accelerant for modernism, it also stimulated social tensions and political radicalism. The postwar wave of strikes, bombings, anti-Communist hysteria, and race riots convinced many that America had entered a frightening new era of diversity and change. Defenders of tradition located the germs of radicalism in the polyglot cities teeming with immigrants and foreign ideas. The defensive mood of the 1920s fed on a growing tendency to connect American nationalism with nativism, Anglo-Saxon racism, and militant Protestantism.

REACTION IN THE TWENTIES

NATIVISM   The foreign connections of so many political radicals strengthened the suspicion that the seeds of sedition were foreign born. In the early 1920s, over half the white men and a third of the white women working in manufacturing and mechanical industries were foreign born, most of them from central or eastern Europe. That socialism and anarchism were prevalent in these regions made such immigrant workers especially suspicious in the eyes of "old stock" Americans.

The most celebrated case of nativist prejudice involved two Italian-born anarchists, Nicola Sacco and Bartolomeo Vanzetti. Arrested in 1920 for a robbery and murder in South Braintree, Massachusetts, they were tried by a judge who privately referred to the defendants as "anarchist bastards." Whether or not the two men were guilty is still disputed. Many then and since have insisted that Sacco and Vanzetti were sentenced more for their political beliefs and their ethnic origins than for any crime they had committed. The case became a great radical and liberal cause of the 1920s, but despite pleas for mercy and worldwide demonstrations on behalf of the two men, Sacco and Vanzetti were sent to the electric chair in 1927.

The surging postwar nativism generated new efforts to restrict immigration. Congress, alarmed at the influx of new foreigners after 1919, passed the Emergency Immigration Act of 1921, which restricted new European arrivals each year to 3 percent of the foreign-born of any nationality as shown in the 1910 census. A new quota law in 1924 reduced the number to 2 percent based on the 1890 census, which included fewer of the "new" immigrants from southern and eastern Europe. This law set a permanent limitation, which became effective in 1929, of slightly over 150,000 immigrants per year based on the "national origins" of the American people as of 1920. In signing the law, President Coolidge pledged: "America must be kept American."

However inexact the quotas, their purpose was clear: to tilt the balance in favor of the old immigration from northern and western Europe, which was assigned about 85 percent of the total. The law completely excluded people from East Asia. Yet it left the gate open to new arrivals from Western Hemisphere countries, so that an ironic consequence was a great increase in the Hispanic Catholic population. People of Latin American descent (chiefly Mexicans, Puerto Ricans, and Cubans) became the fastest growing ethnic minority in the country.

THE KLAN   During the postwar years, the nativist tradition took on a new form, a revived Ku Klux Klan modeled on the group founded during Reconstruction. But now the new Klan was devoted to "100 percent Americanism" rather than to the old Confederacy, and it restricted its membership to native-born white Protestants. The new Klan was determined to protect its warped notion of the American way of life not only from blacks, but also from Roman Catholics, Jews, and immigrants. America was no melting pot, its founder, the failed Methodist minister William J. Simmons, warned: "It is a garbage can! . . . When the hordes of aliens walk to the ballot box and their votes outnumber yours, then that alien horde has got you by the throat." In going nativist, the new Klan spread far outside the South. Its appeal reached areas as widely scattered as Oregon and Maine. It thrived in small towns and cities in the North, and especially in the Midwest. And it was preoccupied with

In 1925 the Ku Klux Klan staged a 40,000-man parade down Pennsylvania Avenue in Washington, D.C.

the defense of white ("native") women and Christian morals. The Klan's spooky robes and flaming crosses brought drama into the dreary routine of a thousand communities.

For all its own exotic ritual, the Klan represented a vicious reflex against the strange and alien, against shifting moral standards, the declining influence of churches, and the social permissiveness of cities and colleges. In the Southwest, the Klan became more than anything else a moral crusade. "It is going to drive the bootleggers forever out of this land," declared a Texan. "It is going to bring clean moving pictures . . . clean literature . . . break up roadside parking . . . enforce the laws . . . protect homes." The Klan used intimidation and floggings to achieve its goals. Estimates of its peak membership, probably inflated, range from 3 million to 8 million, but the Klan's influence diminished as quickly as its numbers grew. For one thing, the Klan suffered from a decline in nativist excitement after passage of the 1924 immigration law. For another, it suffered recurrent factional quarrels and schisms. And its willing use of violence tarnished its moral pretensions.

FUNDAMENTALISM While the Klan saw a threat mainly in the "alien menace," many adherents of the old-time religion saw threats from modernism in the churches: new ideas that the Bible should be studied in the light of modern scholarship (the "higher criticism"), or that it could be reconciled with scientific theories of evolution. Fearing that such "modernist" notions had infected schools and even pulpits, fundamentalism, grounded in a literal interpretation of the Bible, took on a new militancy.

Among the rural fundamentalist leaders only William Jennings Bryan had the following, prestige, and eloquence to make the movement a popular crusade. By 1920, Bryan was showing signs of age: paunchy, balding, his face lined with deepening creases, he had lost his commanding physical presence. But he remained as silver-tongued as ever. In 1921 Bryan sparked a drive for laws to prohibit the teaching of Darwinian evolution in the public schools. Anti-evolution bills began to appear in legislatures, but the only victories came in the South—and there were few of those. Some officials took direct action without legislation. Governor Miriam "Ma" Ferguson of Texas outlawed textbooks upholding Darwinism. "I am a Christian mother . . ." she declared, "and I am not going to let that kind of rot go into Texas schoolbooks."

The climax came in Tennessee, where in 1925 the legislature outlawed the teaching of evolution in public schools and colleges. A young teacher at a high school in Dayton, Tennessee, John T. Scopes, accepted an offer from the American Civil Liberties Union to defend a test case. It soon was a case heard round the world. Before the opening day of the "monkey trial," the streets of Dayton swarmed with "holy rollers," publicity hounds, curiosity-seekers, professional evangelists and professional atheists, hot-dog and soda-pop hucksters, and a mob of reporters.

The two stars of the show were Bryan, who led the prosecution of Scopes for teaching evolution in violation of Tennessee law, and Clarence Darrow, renowned Chicago trial lawyer and confessed agnostic, who defended Scopes by challenging the anti-evolution law. The trial quickly became a debate between fundamentalism and mod-

Courtroom Scene during the Scopes Trial. *The media, food vendors, and other assorted characters flocked to Dayton to hear the case against John Scopes, the teacher who taught evolution.*

ernism. When the judge (a practicing evangelist) damaged Darrow's case by ruling out scientific testimony on evolution, most observers assumed the trial was over.

But the defense rebounded by calling Bryan as an expert witness on biblical interpretation. Darrow, who had once supported Bryan, now relentlessly entrapped the elderly statesman in literal-minded interpretations and exposed Bryan's ignorance of biblical history and scholarship. Bryan insisted that a "great fish" actually swallowed Jonah, that Joshua literally made the sun stand still, that the world was created in 4004 B.C.—all, according to Darrow, "fool ideas that no intelligent Christian on earth believes." It was a bitter scene. At one point the two men, their patience exhausted in the broiling summer heat, lunged at one another, shaking their fists, leading the judge to adjourn the court.

The next day the testimony ended. The only issue before the court, the judge ruled, was whether Scopes had in fact taught evolution. He was found guilty, but the Tennessee Supreme Court, while upholding the law, overruled the $100 fine on a legal technicality. The chief prosecutor accepted the higher court's advice against "prolonging the life of this bizarre case" and dropped the issue. With more prescience than he knew, Bryan had described the trial as a "duel to the death." A few days after it closed, he died suddenly of a heart condition aggravated by heat and fatigue. After Dayton, the fundamentalists—their fury spent for the moment—went dormant.

PROHIBITION Prohibition offered another example of reforming zeal channeled into a drive for moral righteousness and conformity. American moralists had been campaigning against excessive drink since the eighteenth century. Around 1900, however, the leading temperance organizations, the Women's Christian Temperance Union and the Anti-Saloon League, shifted their efforts from reforming individuals to campaigning for legal prohibition. The Anti-Saloon League became one of the most effective pressure groups in American history, mobilizing Protestant churches behind its single-minded battle to elect "dry" candidates.

The 1916 elections finally produced two-thirds majorities in both houses of Congress for a prohibition amendment to the Constitution. Soon the wartime spirit of sacrifice, the need to use grain for food, and wartime hostility to German-American brewers transformed the cause virtually into a test of patriotism. On December 18, 1917, Congress sent to the states the Eighteenth Amendment, which, one year after ratification on January 16, 1919, banned nationwide the manufacture, sale, or transport of intoxicating liquors.

But determined Americans kept drinking. Congress never supplied adequate enforcement, if such were even possible given the public thirst, the spotty support of local officials, and the profits to be made in bootlegging. In Detroit, across the river from Ontario, Canada, where booze was still legal, the liquor industry during the Prohibition Era was second in size only to the auto industry. Speakeasies, hip flasks, and cocktail parties were among the social innovations of the Prohibition Era, along with increased drinking by women.

It would be too much to say that prohibition gave rise to organized crime, for organized vice, gambling, and extortion had long been practiced, and often tied in with the saloons. But prohibition supplied ruthless and flamboyant criminals, such as "Scarface" Al Capone, with a new source of enormous income, while the automobile and the submachine gun provided greater mobility and firepower. Gangland leaders showed remarkable gifts for exploiting loopholes in the law, when they did not simply bribe policemen and politicians.

Capone was by far the most celebrated criminal of the 1920s. In 1927 he pocketed $60 million from his bootlegging, prostitution, and gambling empire, and he took pains to flaunt his wealth as well as his open disregard for legal authorities. The son of Italian immigrants, Capone rapidly worked his way up from nightclub bouncer to syndicate crime boss. He wore expensive suits and silk pajamas, rode in a custom-upholstered and bulletproof Cadillac, surrounded himself with an entourage of bodyguards, lavishly supported city charities, and insisted that he was merely providing the public with the goods and services it demanded. "I've given people light pleasures," he once complained, "and all I get is abuse." He neglected to say that he had also bludgeoned to death several conspiring police lieutenants and ordered the execution of dozens of his criminal competitors. Law-enforcement officials began to smash his bootlegging operations in 1929, but they were unable to pin anything on Capone until a Treasury agent infiltrated his gang and uncovered evidence that convicted him later that year for tax evasion. He was sentenced to eleven years in prison.

In the light of the illegal activities of Capone and other organized crime members, it came as no great surprise in 1931 when a commis-

Al Capone (center) *in 1929.*

sion reported evidence that enforcement of prohibition had broken down. Still, the commission voted to extend prohibition, and President Herbert Hoover chose to stand by what he called the "experiment, noble in motive and far-reaching in purpose."

THE ROARING TWENTIES

In many ways the defensive temper of the 1920s and the repressive movements to which it gave rise seemed the dominant trends of the decade. But they arose in part as reactions to disruptive social and intellectual currents. During those years, a new cosmopolitan, urban America confronted an old provincial, small-town and farm America, and cultural conflict reached new levels of tension.

The smart set of the sophisticated metropolis developed an active disdain for the old-fashioned values of the hinterlands. Sinclair Lewis's novel *Main Street* (1920) caricatured the stifling life of the prairie town, depicting a "savorless people, gulping tasteless food, and sitting afterward, coatless and thoughtless, in rocking chairs prickly with inane decorations, listening to mechanical music, saying mechanical things about the excellence of Ford automobiles, and viewing themselves as the greatest race in the world." The banality of small-town life became a pervasive theme in much of the literature of the time, and the heartland responded with counterimages of alien cities infested with vice, crime, corruption, and foreigners.

THE JAZZ AGE   Writer F. Scott Fitzgerald dubbed the postwar era the "Jazz Age" because young people were willing to experiment with new forms of recreation and sexuality. The new jazz music bubbling up in New Orleans, Kansas City, Memphis, New York City, and Chicago blended African and European musical traditions into a distinctive sound characterized by improvisation, "blue notes," and polyrhythms. Its leading performers included King Oliver, Jelly Roll Morton, Louis Armstrong, and Bessie Smith. The syncopated rhythms of jazz were immensely popular among rebellious young adults and helped spawn carefree new dance steps such as the Charleston and Black Bottom, gyrations that shocked guardians of morality.

If people were not listening to "ragtime" or "jazz" music or to the fam-

Frankie "Half Pint" Jackson and His Band at the Sunset Cafe, Chicago, 1920s. *Jazz emerged during this period as an especially American expression of the modernist spirit. Black artists bent musical conventions to give fuller rein to improvisation.*

ily radio shows that became the rage in the 1920s, they were frequenting movie theaters. By 1930 there were more than 23,000 of them around the country, and they drew more than 95 million customers each week. In Muncie, Indiana, a small city of 35,000 people, there were nine movie theaters operating seven days a week. Movies were by far the most popular form of mass culture in the twenties, and films became even more favored after the introduction of sound in 1927. *The Jazz Singer,* starring Al Jolson, was the first feature-length "talkie."

THE NEW MORALITY Much of the shock to traditionalists during the Jazz Age came from the changes in manners and morals evidenced first among young people, and especially on college campuses. In *This Side of Paradise* (1920), a novel of student life at Princeton, F. Scott Fitzgerald wrote of "the great current American phenomenon, the 'petting party.'" None of the Victorian mothers, he said, "had any idea how casually their daughters were accustomed to be kissed." From such novels, and also from magazines and movies, many Americans learned about the cities' wild parties, bathtub gin, promiscuity, and speakeasies.

Writers also informed the nation about the "new woman" eager to exercise new freedoms. These independent females discarded corsets, sported bobbed hair, heavy makeup, and skirts above the ankles; they smoked cigarettes and drank beer, drove automobiles, and in general, defied old Victorian expectations for womanly behavior.

Sex came to be discussed with surprising frankness during the 1920s. Much of the talk derived from a spreading awareness of Dr. Sigmund Freud, the Viennese father of psychoanalysis. When in 1909 Freud visited Clark University in Massachusetts, he was surprised to find himself so well known "even in prudish America." By the 1920s, his ideas had begun to percolate into the popular awareness, and the talk spread in society and literature about libido, inhibitions, Oedipus complexes, sublimation, and repression. The writer Sherwood Anderson recalled in his memoirs: "Freud had been discovered at the time and all the young intellectuals were busy analyzing each other and everyone they met." Freudian themes also penetrated popular culture. Radio singers during the 1920s belted out songs with titles such as "Hot Lips," "I Need Lovin'," and "Burning Kisses." Movie ads promised kisses on screen "where heart, and soul, and sense in concert move, and the blood is lava, and the pulse is ablaze."

Fashion also reflected the rebellion against prudishness and a loosening of inhibitions. In 1919 women's skirts were typically six inches above the ground; by 1927 they were at the knees, and the "flapper," with her bobbed hair, rolled stockings, cigarettes, lipstick, and sensuous dancing, was providing a shocking model of the new feminism. The name "flapper" derived from the way female rebels allowed their galoshes to "flap" about their ankles. Conservative moralists saw the flappers as just another sign of a degenerating society. Others saw in the "new woman" an expression of rugged American individualism. "By sheer force of violence," explained the *New York Times* in 1929, the flapper has "established the feminine right to equal representation in such hitherto masculine fields of endeavor as smoking and drinking, swearing, petting, and upsetting the community peace."

By 1930, however, the thrill of rebellion was waning; the revolution against Victorian morality had run its course. Its extreme expressions in time aroused doubts that the indulgence of lust equaled liberation. And

The cartoonist John Held's depiction of the modern coed, June 1926.

the much-discussed revolution in morals was also greatly exaggerated. The twenties "roared" for only a small proportion of the population. F. Scott Fitzgerald reminded Americans in 1931 that the "jazz age" was jazzy only for the "upper tenth of [the] nation." Still, some new folkways had come to stay. In the late 1930s a survey disclosed that among college women almost half had had sexual relations before marriage.

THE WOMEN'S MOVEMENT   At the same time that many women were embracing new sexual mores, all women were being liberated politically. The suffrage movement, which had been in the doldrums since 1896, sprang back to life in the second decade of the new century. In 1912 Alice Paul, a Quaker social worker, returned from an apprenticeship with the militant suffragists of England to become chair of the National American Woman Suffrage Association's Congressional Committee. Paul told female activists to picket state legislatures, target and "punish" politicians who failed to endorse suffrage, chain themselves to public buildings, provoke police into arresting them, and undertake hunger strikes. By 1917 Paul and her followers were picketing the White House and deliberately inviting arrest, after which they went on hunger strikes in prison.

In 1915 Carrie Chapman Catt had once again become head of the National Suffrage Association and through her gift for organization had spurred the final campaigns for voting rights. For several years President Wilson had evaded the issue of a suffrage amendment, but he supported a plank in the 1916 Democratic platform endorsing state action for woman suffrage. He addressed the National Suffrage Organization that year, and thereafter he worked closely with its leaders. On June 4, 1919, the Senate finally adopted the Nineteenth Amendment by a bare two-thirds majority, and after an agonizing fourteen months, the states finally ratified the women's suffrage amendment on August 21, 1920, the climactic achievement of the Progressive Era.

Women thereafter entered politics in growing numbers, but this did not suddenly release women from deeply embedded social customs and legal discrimination. The new women voters tended to vote like men on most issues. What was more, the suffrage victory left the broader women's movement prey to a letdown that lasted for a generation. A few years after the triumph, Catt wrote that suffragists were disappointed "because they miss the exaltation, the thrill of expectancy, the vision which stimulated them in the suffrage campaign. They find none of these appeals to their aspiration in the party of their choice."

One group, however, wanted something more. Alice Paul set a new

The march for women's suffrage, 1915.

goal, first introduced in Congress in 1923: an Equal Rights Amendment that would eliminate any remaining legal distinctions between the sexes—including the special legislation for the protection of working women put on the books in the previous fifty or so years. It would be another fifty years before Alice Paul would see Congress adopt her amendment in 1972; she did not live, however, to see it fall short of ratification.

The sharp increase in the number of women in the workforce during World War I proved short-lived, but in the longer view a steady increase in the numbers of employed women occurred in the 1920s and, surprisingly, continued through the depression decade of the 1930s. Still these women remained concentrated in traditional occupations: they were mostly domestics, office workers, teachers, clerks, salespeople, dressmakers, milliners, and seamstresses. On the eve of World War II, women's work was little more diversified than it had been at the turn of the century, but by 1940 it would be on the eve of a great transformation.

THE "NEW NEGRO" The discriminations that have befallen blacks and women display many parallels, and the loosening of restraints for both have frequently coincided. The most significant development in African-American life during these years was the Great Migration northward. Competition for jobs from foreign immigrants was prevented first by the war and then by legal restrictions on immigration. The movement of blacks from the South to the North began in 1915–1916, when rapidly expanding war industries were experiencing a labor shortage, leaving openings for blacks in the North. Altogether, between 1910 and 1920, the Southeast had lost some 323,000 blacks, or 5 percent of the 1920 native black population, and by 1930 it had lost another 615,000 or 8 percent of the native black population. With the migration north, a slow but steady growth in black political influence set in. African Americans were freer to speak and act in a northern setting, and they gained political leverage by concentrating in large cities located in states with many electoral votes.

Along with political activity came a bristling spirit of protest among blacks, a spirit that received cultural expression in a literary and artistic movement labeled the Harlem Renaissance. Claude McKay, a Jamaican immigrant, was the first significant writer of the movement, which sought to rediscover black folk culture. Poems collected in McKay's *Harlem Shadows* (1922) expressed defiance in such titles as "If We Must Die" and "To the White Fiends." Other emergent black writers included Langston Hughes, Zora Neale Hurston, Countée Cullen, and James Weldon Johnson. Perhaps the greatest single creation of the time was Jean Toomer's novel *Cane*, which portrayed the lives of simple folk in rural Georgia and the sophisticated inhabitants of Washington's African-American middle class.

The spirit of the "New Negro" also found an outlet in what came to be called "Negro nationalism," which exalted blackness, black cultural expression, and, at its most extreme, black exclusiveness. The leading spokesman for such views was the flamboyant Marcus Garvey. Racial bias, Garvey said, was so ingrained in whites that it was futile to appeal to their sense of justice. Garvey told American blacks to liberate themselves from the surrounding white culture. "We have outgrown slavery," he declared, "but our minds are still enslaved to the thinking of the Master Race."

Garvey saw every white person as a "potential Klansman" and therefore endorsed the "social and political separation of all peoples to the

Marcus Garvey, founder of the United Negro Improvement Association and a leading spokesman for "Negro nationalism" in the 1920s.

extent that they promote their own ideals and civilization." Such a separatist message appalled other black leaders. W. E. B. Du Bois, for example, labeled Garvey "the most dangerous enemy of the Negro race." Garvey and his aides created their own black version of Christianity, organized their own fraternal lodges and community cultural centers, started their own businesses, and published their own newspaper. Garvey's message of racial pride and self-reliance appealed to many blacks who had arrived in the northern cities during the Great Migration and had grown frustrated and embittered with the hypocrisy of American democracy during the postwar economic slump. Garvey declared that the only lasting hope for blacks was to flee America and build their own republic in Africa.

In 1916 Garvey brought to New York the United Negro Improvement Association (UNIA), which he had started in his native Jamaica two years before. He quickly enlisted half a million members in his association, and claimed as many as 6 million by 1923. As one of his followers remarked, Garvey gave "my people backbone where they had wishbone." At the peak of his popularity, however, Garvey was convicted of mail fraud. He was imprisoned in 1925 and remained so until President Calvin Coolidge pardoned him and deported him to Jamaica in 1927. Garvey died in obscurity in London in 1940, but the memory of his movement kept alive an undercurrent of racial pride that would reemerge later under the slogan of "black power."

Even more influential in promoting black rights was the National Association for the Advancement of Colored People (NAACP). Founded in 1910, it was led by northern white liberals and black leaders such as Du Bois. Its main strategy focused on enforcing the Fourteenth and Fifteenth Amendments. One early victory came with *Guinn v. United States* (1915), in which the Supreme Court struck down Oklahoma's grandfather clause, which had been part of the state's attempt to disenfranchise blacks.

In 1919 the NAACP launched a campaign against lynching, still a common atrocity in many parts of the country. An anti-lynching bill making mob murder a federal offense passed the House in 1922, but in the Senate it lost to a filibuster by southern senators. Nonetheless, the bill stayed before the House until 1925, and the continued agitation of the issue helped to reduce lynchings, which declined to a third of what they had been the previous decade.

The Culture of Modernism

Changes in the realms of science and social thought were perhaps even more dramatic than those affecting women and blacks in the interwar years. As the twentieth century advanced, the easy faith in progress and reform expressed by progressives fell victim to a series of frustrations and disasters, including the Great War, the failure of the League of Nations, Woodrow Wilson's physical and political collapse, and the failure of prohibition. Startling new findings in physics further shook prevailing assumptions of order and certainty.

SCIENCE AND SOCIAL THOUGHT   Physicists of the early twentieth century altered the image of the cosmos in ways that seemed almost a conspiracy against common sense. Since Isaac Newton, conventional wisdom had held the universe to be governed by laws that the scientific method could ultimately uncover. A world of such certain order had bolstered hopes of infinite progress in human knowledge.

This world of order and certainty disintegrated at the turn of the century when Albert Einstein, a young German physicist, announced his theory of relativity, which maintained that space, time, and mass were not absolutes but relative to the location and motion of the observer. Isaac Newton's eighteenth-century mechanics, according to Einstein's relativity theories, worked well enough at relatively slow speeds, but the more nearly one approached the velocity of light (about 186,000 miles per second) the more all measuring devices would change accordingly, so that yardsticks would become shorter, clocks and heartbeats would slow down, even the aging process would ebb.

Certainty dissolved the farther one reached out into the universe and the farther one reached down into the minute world of the atom. The discovery of radioactivity in the 1890s showed that atoms were not irreducible units of matter but that some of them emitted particles of energy. This meant, Einstein noted, that mass and energy were not separate phenomena but interchangeable.

Meanwhile, the German physicist Max Planck had discovered that electromagnetic emissions of energy, whether as electricity or light, came in little bundles that he called quanta. The development of quantum theory suggested that atoms were far more complex than once believed and, as another pioneering German physicist, Werner Heisenberg, stated in his uncertainty principle in 1927, ultimately indescribable. One could never know both the position and the velocity of an electron, Heisenberg concluded, because the very process of observation would inevitably affect the behavior of the particle, altering its position or velocity.

Heisenberg's thesis meant that human knowledge had limits. "The physicist thus finds himself in a world from which the bottom has dropped clean out," a Harvard mathematician wrote in 1929. He had to "give up his most cherished convictions and faith. The world is not a world of reason, understandable by the intellect of man, but as we penetrate ever deeper, the very law of cause and effect, which we had thought to be a formula to which we could force God Himself to subscribe, ceases to have any meaning." Hard for the public to grasp, such findings proved too troubling even for Einstein, who spent much of the rest of his life in quest of an explanation that would unify the relativity and quantum theories. "I shall never believe that God plays dice with the world," Einstein asserted.

Just as Enlightenment thinkers drew on Isaac Newton's laws of gravitation two centuries before to formulate their views on the laws governing society, the ideas of relativity and uncertainty in the twentieth century provoked people to deny the relevance of absolute values in any sphere of society, which undermined the concepts of personal responsibility and absolute standards. Anthropologists aided the process by transforming the word "culture," which had before meant refinement, into a term for the whole system of ideas, folkways, and institutions within which any group lived. Even the most primitive groups had cultures and, all things being relative, one culture should not impose its value judgments on another. Two anthropologists, Ruth Benedict and Margaret Mead, were especially effective in spreading this viewpoint.

MODERNIST ART AND LITERATURE The cluster of scientific ideas associated with Darwin and Einstein helped inspire a "modernist" revolution in the minds of many intellectuals and creative artists during the early twentieth century. The modernist world was one in which, as Karl Marx said, "All that is solid melts into air." Modernism arose out of a widespread recognition that Western civilization was entering an era of bewildering change. New technologies, new modes of transportation and communication, and new scientific discoveries combined to transform the nature of everyday life and to generate dramatic new forms of artistic expression.

Where nineteenth-century writers and artists took for granted an accessible world that could be readily observed and accurately represented, self-willed modernists viewed the "real" as something to be created rather than copied, expressed rather than reproduced. As a consequence, they concluded that the subconscious regions of the psyche were more interesting and potent than reason, common sense, and logic.

In the various arts, such concerns resulted in abstract painting, atonal music, free verse in poetry, stream-of-consciousness narrative, and interior monologues in stories and novels. Writers showed an intense concern with new forms in language in an effort to violate expectations and shock their audiences.

The chief American prophets of modernism were living in Europe: Ezra Pound and T. S. Eliot in London and Gertrude Stein in Paris. All were deeply concerned with creating new and often difficult styles of modernist expression. Pound, as foreign editor for *Poetry,* served as the conduit through which many American poets achieved publication in America and Britain. At the same time he became the leader of the imagist movement, a revolt against the ornamental verbosity of Victorian poetry in favor of the concrete image.

Pound's brilliant protégé was the St. Louis-born Harvard graduate, T. S. Eliot, who in 1915 contributed to *Poetry* his first major poem, "The Love Song of J. Alfred Prufrock," the musings of an ineffectual man who "after tea and cakes and ices" could never find "the strength to force the moment to its crisis." Eliot went to Oxford in 1913 and soon decided to make England his home and poetry his career. Skeptical of the Western notion of social progress through scientific advance and horrified by the slaughter of the Great War, he rejected the nineteenth century's "cheerfulness, optimism, and hopefulness." He rejected as well the traditional notion of poetry as the representation of a beautiful world. The modern poet, he insisted, must "be able to see beneath both beauty and ugliness; to see the boredom, and the horror and the glory." Eliot's *The Waste Land* (1922) made few concessions to readers in its obscure allusions, its juxtaposition of unexpected metaphors, its deep sense of postwar disillusionment and melancholy, and its suggestion of a burned-out civilization. But it became for an alienated younger generation almost the touchstone of the modern temper.

Gertrude Stein, another voluntary exile, settled in Paris in 1903 and became an early champion and collector of modern art. Long regarded as no more than the literary eccentric who wrote "A rose is a rose is a rose is a rose," she would later be recognized as one of the chief originators of the modernist prose style. At the time she was known chiefly through her influence on such 1920s expatriates as Sherwood Anderson and Ernest Hemingway, whom she told: "All of you young people who served in the war, you are the lost generation."

The earliest chronicler of that "lost" generation, F. Scott Fitzgerald, blazed up brilliantly and then quickly flickered out, like all the tinseled, carefree, sad young people of his novels. Successful and famous at age twenty-four with the publication of *This Side of Paradise* (1920), he, along with his wife, Zelda, experienced and depicted the "greatest, gaudiest spree in history," and then both had their crack-ups during the Great Depression. What gave depth to the best of Fitzgerald's work was what a character in *The Great Gatsby* (1925), his finest novel, called "a sense of the fundamental decencies" amid all the surface gaiety—and almost always a sense of impending doom.

Hemingway suffered even more from a psychic wound inflicted by an uncaring world. For him literature was a means of defense, a way to strike back, and in the process find a meaning for himself rather than accept one imposed by society. Hemingway's first novel, *The Sun Also Rises* (1926), pictures a desperate search for life by a group of American expatriates, chasing about frantically from the bistros of Paris to the bullrings of Spain. Young Jake Barnes, emasculated by a war wound, explains his postwar outlook toward the world: "I did not care what it was all about. All I wanted to know was how to live in it." Hemingway's second novel, *A Farewell to Arms* (1929), is based on his own experience as a volunteer in the ambulance corps in northern Italy during World War I. It describes the love affair of a driver and a nurse who abandon the war for Switzerland, where the young woman dies in childbirth. Hundreds of writers tried to imitate Hemingway's terse style, but few had his gift, which lay less in what he had to say than in the way he said it.

THE SOUTHERN RENAISSANCE As modernist literature arose as a response to the changes taking place in Western civilization, so did southern literature of the twenties reflect a world in the midst of rebirth. A southern renaissance in writing emerged from the conflict between the dying world of tradition and the modern, commercial world struggling to be born in the aftermath of the Great War. While in the South the conflict of values aroused the Ku Klux Klan and fundamentalist furies that tried desperately to bring back the world of tradition, it also inspired the vitality and creativity of the South's young writers.

Two of the most notable of these young new southern writers were Thomas Wolfe and William Faulkner. Fame rushed in first on Wolfe and his native Asheville, North Carolina, which he wrote about in his first novel, *Look Homeward, Angel*. "Against the Victorian morality and the Bourbon aristocracy of the South," Wolfe had "turned in all his fury," newspaper editor Jonathan Daniels, a former classmate, wrote. Yet, for all his lust for experience and knowledge, his demonic drive to escape the encircling hills for the "fabled" world outside, his agonized search for some "lost lane-end into heaven," Wolfe never completely severed his roots in the South.

William Faulkner's achievement, more than Wolfe's, was rooted in the coarsely textured social world that produced him. Born near Oxford, Mississippi, he grew up there and transmuted his hometown into the fictional Jefferson, Yoknapatawpha County. After a brief stint with the Royal Canadian Air Force, he passed the postwar decade in what seemed to fellow townspeople an aimless drifting, until he finally returned to Oxford. There, in writing *Sartoris* (1929), he began to discover that his "own little postage stamp of native soil was worth writing about" and that he "would never live long enough to exhaust it." With *Sartoris* and the creation of his mythical land of Yoknapatawpha, Faulkner kindled a blaze of creative energy. Next, as he put it, he wrote his gut into *The Sound and the Fury* (1929). It was one of the triumphs of the modernist style, but most early readers, taking their cue from the title instead of the critics, found it signified nothing.

Modernism and the southern literary renaissance, both of which emerged from the crucible of the Great War and its aftermath, were products of the twenties. But the studied alienation of the artists of the 1920s did not survive the decade. The onset of the Great Depression in 1929 seemed to spark a renewed sense of commitment and affirmation in the arts, as if people could no longer afford the art-for-art's-sake affectations of the 1920s. Alienation would give way to social purpose in the decade to come.

MAKING CONNECTIONS

- The next chapter discusses the growing consumer culture of the 1920s, an economic aspect of the "Roaring Twenties" described here.

- Chapter 27 describes changes in American literary culture wrought by the Great Depression—from the modernism discussed in this chapter to a return of social significance and the cultural "rediscovery of America" in the 1930s.

- The status of women in the workforce remained stable in the 1920s, despite the successes of the women's movement. That status changed, at least temporarily, during World War II. Chapter 29 traces the rise of "Rosie the Riveter."

FURTHER READING

For a standard survey of the interwar period, start with William E. Leuchtenburg's *The Perils of Prosperity, 1914–1932* (rev. ed., 1993). The best introduction to the culture of the 1920s remains Loren Baritz's *The Culture of the Twenties* (1970). See also Lynn Dumenil's *The Modern Temper: American Culture and Society in the 1920s* (1995). Paula S. Fass's *The Damned and the Beautiful: American Youth in the 1920s* (1977) describes the social attitudes of youth.

John Higham's *Strangers in the Land: Patterns of American Nativism, 1860–1925* (rev. ed., 1988) details the story of immigration restriction. Paul Avrich's *Sacco and Vanzetti: The Anarchist Background* (1991) treats the famous case. For analysis of the revival of Klan activity, see Nancy MacLean's *Behind the Mask of Chivalry: The Making of the Second Ku Klux Klan* (1994). Two contrasting views of prohibition are Andrew Sinclair's *Prohibition: The Era of Excess* (1962) and Norman H. Clark's *Deliver Us from Evil: An Interpretation of American Prohibition* (1976).

Women's suffrage is treated extensively in Eleanor Flexner's *Century of Struggle: The Women's Rights Movement in the United States* (rev. ed., 1975). See Charles F. Kellogg's *NAACP: A History of the National Association for the Advancement of Colored People* (1967) for his analysis of the pioneering court cases against racial discrimination. Nathan I. Huggins's *Harlem Renaissance* (1971) assesses the cultural impact of the Great Migration in New York. On the migration to Chicago, see James R. Grossman's *Land of Hope: Chicago, Black Southerners, and the Great Migration* (1989). Nicholas Lemann's *The Promised Land* (1991) is a fine exposition of the changes brought about by the Great Migration in both the South and North.

Much of our treatment of "modernism" comes from Daniel J. Singal's *The War Within: From Victorian to Modernist Thought in the South, 1919–1945* (1982). Stanley Coben's *Rebellion Against Victorianism: The Impetus for Cultural Change in 1920s America* (1991) surveys the appeal of "modernism" among writers, artists, and intellectuals. On developments in physics, see Stanley Goldberg's *Understanding Relativity: Origin and Impact of a Scientific Revolution* (1984). Nathan G. Hale, Jr.'s *Freud and the Americans* (1971) examines the impact of psychoanalysis.

26 REPUBLICAN RESURGENCE AND DECLINE

CHAPTER ORGANIZER

This chapter focuses on:

- the conservatism in the presidencies of Harding, Coolidge, and Hoover.

- growth in the American economy in the 1920s.

- the causes of the Great Depression.

*T*he progressive political coalition that reelected Woodrow Wilson in 1916 proved to be quite fragile, and by 1920 it had fragmented. It began to show signs of fissure during the war when radicals and other reformers grew disaffected with America's involvement. After the war, Wilson's support continued to erode. Organized labor resented the administration's unsympathetic attitude toward the strikes of 1919–1920, and farmers complained that wartime price controls had discriminated against them. While prominent intellectuals grew disillusioned with the popular support for prohibition and religious fundamentalism, many among the middle class lost interest in political activism. They instead channeled their energies into building a new business civilization based upon mass production and mass consumption, greater leisure, and the introduction of labor-saving electrical appliances in the home. Moreover, progressivism's final triumphs at the national level were already pretty much foregone conclusions before the war's end: the Eighteenth Amendment, which outlawed alcoholic beverages, was ratified in 1919, and the Nineteenth Amendment, which extended women's suffrage to the entire country, became law a year later.

Progressivism, however, did not completely disappear in the 1920s. Reformers remained active in Congress during much of the decade even while the White House was in conservative Republican hands. The progressive impulse for "good government" and extended public services still remained strong, especially at the state and local levels, where movements for good roads, education, public health, and social welfare all gained momentum during the decade. At the same time, however, the reactionary temper of the times gave rise to the drive for moral righteousness and conformity animating the Ku Klux Klan and the fundamentalist and prohibitionist movements.

"NORMALCY"

HARDING'S ELECTION   After World War I, most Americans had grown weary of idealistic crusades and suspicious of leaders promoting reform. Woodrow Wilson himself recognized this fact. "It is only once in a generation," he remarked, "that a people can be lifted above material things. That is why conservative government is in the saddle two-thirds of the time."

When the Republicans met in Chicago in 1920, the Old Guard party regulars found their man in Ohio senator Warren Gamaliel Harding, who had set the tone of his campaign when he told a Boston audience: "America's present need is not heroics, but healing; not nostrums, but normalcy; not revolution, but restoration; not agitation, but adjustment; not surgery, but serenity; not the dramatic, but the dispassionate; not experiment, but equipoise; not submergence in internationality, but sustainment in triumphant nationality." His prose was clumsy, but Harding caught the mood of the times—a longing for "normalcy" and contentment with the status quo. So too did his running mate, Massachusetts governor Calvin Coolidge, who had gained national attention with his stern opposition to the Boston Police Strike.

Harding's promise of a "return to normalcy" reflected his own conservative values and folksy personality. The son of an Ohio farmer, he described himself as not an intellectual or a crusader but "just a plain fellow" who was "old-fashioned and even reactionary in matters of faith and morals." But such a description suggests a certain puritan regimen that Harding never practiced. Far from being an old-fashioned moralist in his personal life, he drank bootleg liquor in the midst of prohibition, smoked and chewed tobacco, relished weekly poker games, and actively sought sexual satisfaction from women other than his austere and matronly wife, whom he called "Duchess." The general public, however, remained unaware of Harding's self-indulgence and weak character. Instead the voters saw him as a handsome, charming, gregarious, and lovable politician. A man of self-confessed limitations in vision, leadership, and intellectual power, he once admitted that "I cannot hope to be one of the great presidents, but perhaps I may be remembered as one of the best loved."

The Democrats hoped that Harding would not be president at all. James Cox, former newsman and former governor of Ohio, won the nomination of an increasingly fragmented party on the forty-fourth ballot. For vice-president the convention named Franklin D. Roosevelt, who as assistant secretary of the navy occupied the same position his Republican cousin Theodore Roosevelt had held before him.

The Democrats suffered from the breakup of the Wilsonian coalition and the conservative postwar mood. In the words of progressive journalist William Allen White, Americans in 1920 were "tired of issues, sick at heart of ideals, and weary of being noble." The country voted overwhelmingly for Harding's promised "return to normalcy." Harding got 16 million votes to 9 million for Cox, who carried no state outside the Solid South.

EARLY APPOINTMENTS AND POLICY Harding in office had much in common with Ulysses Grant. His cabinet, like Grant's, mixed some of the best men in the party with some of the worst. Charles Evans Hughes became a distinguished secretary of state. Herbert Hoover in the Commerce Department, Andrew W. Mellon in Treasury, and Henry A. Wallace in Agriculture were also efficient and forceful figures. Of the others, Secretary of the Interior Albert B. Fall landed in prison and Attorney-General Harry M. Daugherty only narrowly escaped prosecution. Many lesser offices went to members of the soon notorious "Ohio Gang," headed by Daugherty, a group of Harding's old Ohio friends with whom the president met regularly for poker games lubricated with illegal liquor.

Until he became president, Harding had loved politics. He was the complete party hack, "bloviating" (a verb of his own making, which meant speaking with gaseous eloquence) on the stump, jollying it up in the clubhouse and cloakroom, hobnobbing with the great and near-great in Washington. As president, however, Harding was simply in over his head, and self-doubt overwhelmed him. "I don't think I'm big enough for the Presidency," he confided to a friend. Alice Roosevelt Longworth, Theodore Roosevelt's oldest daughter, recognized Harding's limitations. "Harding wasn't a bad man," she noted. "He was just a slob."

Harding and his friends set about dismantling or neutralizing as many of the social and economic components of progressivism as they could. Harding's four appointments to the Supreme Court were all conservatives, including Chief Justice William Howard Taft, who announced that he had been "appointed to reverse a few decisions." Dur-

Warren Harding "bloviating" on the stump.

ing the 1920s, the Taft Court struck down a federal child-labor law and a minimum wage law for women, issued numerous injunctions against striking unions, and issued rulings limiting the powers of federal regulatory agencies.

The Harding administration established a pro-business tone reminiscent of the McKinley White House. To sustain economic growth, Secretary of the Treasury Mellon promoted government spending cuts and federal tax reduction. Mellon insisted that tax cuts should go mainly to the rich, on the assumption that wealth in the hands of the few would promote the general welfare through increased capital investment.

In Congress a group of western Republicans and southern Democrats fought a dogged battle to preserve the graduated scale built into wartime taxes, but Mellon, in office through the 1920s, eventually won out. At his behest, Congress first repealed the wartime excess-profits tax and lowered the maximum rate on personal income from 65 to 50 percent. Subsequent revenue acts eventually lowered the maximum rate to 20 percent. The Revenue Act of 1926 extended further benefits to high-income groups by lowering estate taxes and repealing the gift tax. Much of the tax money released to wealthy people by these acts seems to have fueled the speculative excess of the late 1920s as much as it boosted consumer spending and entrepreneurial activity. Mellon, however, did balance the federal budget for a time. Governmental expenditures fell, as did the national debt.

In addition to tax cuts, Mellon favored the time-honored Republican policy of high tariffs. So too did spokesmen for several emerging new industries. Wartime innovations in chemical and metal processing revived the argument for protection of infant industries from foreign competition. The Fordney-McCumber Tariff of 1922 dramatically increased rates on chemical and metal products as a safeguard against the revival of German industries that had previously commanded the field. To please the farmers, the new act further extended the duties on imported farm products.

Higher tariffs, however, had unexpected consequences. During the war, the United States had been transformed from a debtor to a creditor nation. In former years foreign capital had flowed into the United States, playing an important role in fueling economic expansion. But the private and public credits given the Allies during the war had reversed the pattern. Mellon now insisted that the European powers must repay all that they had borrowed during the war. The tariff walls erected against imports, however, made it all the harder for other nations to sell in the United States and thereby acquire the dollars with which to repay their war debts. For nearly a decade, further extensions of American loans and investments sent more dollars abroad, postponing the reckoning.

Rounding out the Republican economic program was a more lenient attitude toward government regulation of corporations. Neither Harding nor his successor, Coolidge, could dissolve the regulatory agencies created by progressivism, but they named commissioners who sought to make them more effective for a business constituency that now saw advantages in "friendly" government regulation. Harding appointed advocates of big business to the Interstate Commerce Commission, the Federal Reserve Board, and the Federal Trade Commission. One senator characterized the new appointments as "the nullification of federal law by a process of boring from within." Senator Henry Cabot Lodge agreed, noting: "We have torn up Wilsonism by the roots."

A CORRUPT ADMINISTRATION   Republican conservatives such as Lodge, Mellon, Coolidge, and Hoover were at least operating out of philosophical conviction. The crass members of Harding's "Ohio Gang," however, used White House connections to line their own pockets. In 1923 Harding learned that the head of the Veterans Bureau was systematically looting the government's medical and hospital supplies. The corrupt administrator resigned and fled to Europe. Harding's general counsel then committed suicide.

Not long afterward, a close crony of Attorney-General Daugherty also shot himself. The man held no federal appointment, but he had set up an office in the Justice Department from which he peddled influence for a fee. Daugherty himself was implicated in the fraudulent handling of German assets seized after the war. When this was discovered, he refused to testify on the grounds that he might incriminate himself. Twice brought to court, he was never indicted; possibly the lack of evidence resulted from his destruction of pertinent records. These were but the most visible among many scandals that touched the Justice Department, the Prohibition Bureau, and other agencies under Harding.

But one major scandal rose above all others. Teapot Dome, like the Watergate break-in fifty years later, became the catchword for an era of government corruption. An oil deposit on federal land in Wyoming, Teapot Dome had been set aside to be administered by the Interior Department under Albert B. Fall. He let private companies exploit the deposits, arguing that such contracts were in the government's interest. Yet Fall acted in secret, without allowing competitive bids.

Suspicion grew when Fall's own standard of living suddenly skyrocketed. It turned out that he had taken "loans" of about $400,000 (which came in "a little black bag") from oil executives. For the rest of his life, Fall insisted that the loans were unrelated to the oil leases, and that he had contrived a good deal for the government, but at best the questionable circumstances revealed his fatal blindness to impropriety.

Harding himself avoided public disgrace. How much he knew of the scandals swirling around him remains unclear, but he knew enough to become visibly troubled. "My God, this is a hell of a job!" he confided to a journalist. "I have no trouble with my enemies, I can take care of my enemies all right. But my damn friends, my God-damn friends . . . they're the ones that keep me walking the floor nights!" In 1923 Harding left on what would be his last journey, a western speaking tour and a

Juggernaut. *This 1924 cartoon shows the dimensions of the Teapot Dome scandal.*

trip to the Alaska territory. In Seattle he suffered an attack of food poisoning, recovered briefly, then died in a San Francisco hotel.

Not since the death of Lincoln had there been such an outpouring of grief for a "beloved President," for the kindly, ordinary man who found it in his heart (as Wilson had not) to pardon the former Socialist candidate Eugene Debs, who had been jailed for opposing U.S. intervention in World War I. As the funeral train moved toward Washington, then back to Ohio, millions stood by the tracks to honor their lost leader.

Eventually, however, grief yielded to scorn and contempt. For nearly a decade after Harding's death, scandalous revelations concerning his administrative officials were paraded before congressional committees and then courts. Harding's extramarital affairs with several mistresses also came to light. As a result of such amorous detours and corrupt associates, Harding's foreshortened administration came to be widely viewed as one of the worst in American history. More recently, however, scholars have suggested that the scandals obscured several real accomplishments. Some historians credit Harding with leading the nation out of the turmoil of the postwar years and creating the foundation for the decade's remarkable economic boom. They also stress that he was a hardworking president who played a far more forceful role in shaping administrative economic and foreign policies than was previously believed. Still, even Harding's foremost scholarly defender admits that he lacked good judgment and "probably should never have been president."

"SILENT CAL" The news of Harding's death came when Vice-President Calvin Coolidge was visiting his father in the mountain village of Plymouth, Vermont, his birthplace. There at 2:47 on the morning of August 3, 1923, by the light of a kerosene lamp, Colonel John Coolidge administered the oath of office to his son. The rustic simplicity of Plymouth, the very name itself, evoked just the image of traditional roots and solid integrity that the country would long for amid the wake of the slimy Harding scandals.

Coolidge brought to the White House a clear conviction that the presidency should revert to its passive stance of the Gilded Age and defer to the leadership of Congress. One editor observed that Coolidge "aspired to become the least President the country ever had; he attained his desire." Coolidge insisted on twelve hours of sleep and an afternoon nap. Satirist H. L. Mencken asserted that Coolidge "slept more than any other president, whether by day or by night. Nero fiddled, but Coolidge only snored."

Americans took to their hearts the unflappability of "Silent Cal," his long midday naps, and the pictures of him fishing, pitching hay, and wearing Indian warbonnets while primly clad in business suit and necktie. His pinched facial expression and dry personality provoked affectionate satire. One wit, commenting on Coolidge's seemingly dour facial expression, suggested that he must have been weaned on a pickle. Another popular story reported that a dinner guest had bet Coolidge she could make him say three words. "You lose," he replied. The image of "Silent Cal," however, has been overdrawn; he may have been a man of few words, but he was not as bland or as dry as critics claimed.

As Herbert Hoover once stressed, Coolidge was a "real conservative, probably the equal of Benjamin Harrison. He was a fundamentalist in religion, in the economic and social order, and in fishing, too." (He used live worms for bait.) Even more than Harding, Coolidge embraced the orthodox creed of business. "The chief business of the American people is business," he intoned. "The man who works there worships there." Where Harding had sought to balance the interests of labor, agriculture, and industry, Coolidge focused on industrial development at the expense of the other two areas. He sought to unleash the free enterprise system, and, even more than Harding, he sought to end government regulation. One of his appointees to the Federal Trade Commission openly scorned its regulatory purposes, declaring that he would make it "a bulwark [of business] instead of an oppressor." Business mergers skyrocketed during the 1920s. Coolidge's pro-business stance led the *Wall Street Journal* to exult: "Never before, here or anywhere else, has a government been so completely fused with business."

THE 1924 ELECTION Coolidge successfully distanced himself from the Harding scandals and put two lawyers of undoubted integrity in charge of the prosecutions. He also quietly took control of the Republican party machinery and seized the initiative in the campaign for the 1924 nomination, which he won with only token opposition.

The Coolidge luck held as the Democrats fell victim to continuing internal dissensions, which were enough to prompt humorist Will Rogers's classic statement: "I am a member of no organized political party. I am a Democrat." The party's divisions reflected the deep alienation growing up between the new urban culture of the twenties and the more traditional hinterland, a gap that the Democratic party could not bridge. It took 103 ballots to bestow the party's tarnished nomination on John W. Davis, a Wall Street lawyer from West Virginia who could hardly outdo Coolidge in conservatism.

While the Democrats fumbled, a new farm-labor coalition mobilized a third-party effort. Meeting in Cleveland on July 4, 1924, farm and labor groups reorganized the Progressive party and nominated Wisconsin senator Robert M. La Follette for president. La Follette also won the support of the Socialist party and the American Federation of Labor.

In the campaign, Coolidge chose to focus on La Follette, whom he called a dangerous radical who would turn America into a "communistic and socialistic state." The country preferred to "keep cool with Coolidge," who swept both the popular and electoral votes by decisive majorities. Davis took only the Solid South, and La Follette carried only his native Wisconsin.

THE NEW ERA

Business executives interpreted the Republican victory as a vindication of their leadership, and Coolidge saw in the decade's surging prosperity a confirmation of his pro-business philosophy. In fact, the prosperity and technological achievements of the time known as the New Era, had much to do with Coolidge's victory over the Democrats and Progressives. Those in the large middle class who before had formed an important part of the progressive coalition were now absorbed instead into the new corporate and consumer world created by advances in communications, transportation, and business organization. As more and more commentators stressed, the United States seemed to be entering a "new era" of advanced capitalism.

A GROWING CONSUMER CULTURE   The American economy was changing markedly during the 1920s. Dramatic increases in productive efficiency flooded the marketplace with new consumer delights. Goods once available only to the wealthy were now made accessible to the general public: hand cameras, wristwatches, cigarette lighters, vacuum cleaners, washing machines. But such enticing new goods threatened to produce economic havoc unless people abandoned traditional notions of frugality and went on a buying spree. Hence, business leaders, salespersons, and public relations experts began a concerted effort to eradicate what was left of the original Protestant ethic's emphasis on plain living. "People may ruin themselves by saving instead of spending," warned one economist. A newspaper editorial was even more blunt. It insisted that the American's "first importance to his country is no longer that of citizen but that of consumer. Consumption is a new necessity."

The public had to be taught the joys of carefree consumerism, and the new industry of mass advertising obliged. By portraying impulse buying as a therapeutic measure to help self-esteem, advertisers shrewdly helped undermine notions of simple living. In his popular novel *Babbitt,* Sinclair Lewis recognized advertising's impact upon middle-class life: "These standard advertised wares—toothpastes, socks, tires, cameras, instantaneous hot water heaters—were the symbols and proofs of excellence."

Inventions in communications, such as motion pictures, radio, and telephones, were also transforming social life and creating a more homogeneous national culture. By 1905 the first movie house opened in Philadelphia, and within three years there were nearly 10,000 nationwide. During the next decade, Hollywood became the center of movie production, spinning out Westerns and the timeless comedies of Mack Sennett's Keystone Studios, where slapstick comedians, most notably Charlie Chaplin, perfected their art into a powerful form of social criticism. By the mid-1930s, every large American city and most small towns had movie theaters, and films replaced oratory as the chief mass entertainment, growing into a multi-million-dollar industry that catered to the working poor as well as to the affluent. In the mid-1920s, motion pictures were attracting 50 million people weekly, equal to half the national population.

Radio broadcasting had an even more spectacular growth. The first radio commercial aired in 1922. By the end of that year, there were over 500 stations and some 3 million receivers in action. In 1927 Congress established a Federal Radio Commission to regulate the industry; in 1934 it became the Federal Communications Commission, with authority over other forms of communication as well.

Radio Broadcast, *mid-1920s. Radios gained such popularity that within a decade millions would tune into newscasts, soap operas, sporting events, and church services.*

A nationwide mass culture now started to replace the local and regional economies of the nineteenth century. The leading advertising agency explained in 1926 that the advent of nationally circulated magazines, chain stores, syndicated news features, motion pictures, national brand names, and radio programs was creating "a nation which lives to [the same] pattern everywhere." Nonetheless, even though working-class folk could buy brand goods, phonographs, and radios, as well as movie tickets, the new consumer culture did not erase social distinctions. "Participating in mass culture," as one historian stressed, "made them feel no more mainstream or middle class, no less ethnic, religious, or working class than they already felt." And poor rural folk were the least involved with the new consumer culture. As late as 1930, some 45 million farm dwellers had no indoor plumbing and almost no electricity. They relieved themselves in chamber pots and outhouses, cooked and heated with wood stoves, and used oil lamps.

AIRPLANES, AUTOMOBILES, AND THE ECONOMY While most of society was being transformed by mass culture, startling advances in transportation were also laying the basis for a transformation of the economy and a narrowing of the distances that separated people. Wilbur and Orville Wright of Dayton, Ohio, owners of a bicycle shop, built and flew the first airplane at Kitty Hawk, North Carolina, in 1903, but the use of planes advanced slowly until the outbreak of war in Europe in 1914. An American aircraft industry developed during the war but foundered in the postwar demobilization. In 1925 the government began to subsidize the industry through airmail contracts, and, the following year, it started a program of federal aid to air transport and navigation, including funds for constructing airports.

Aviation received a psychological boost in 1927 when Charles A. Lindbergh, Jr., flew the first transatlantic solo flight from New York to Paris in thirty-three hours and thirty minutes. To accomplish the heroic deed, which won him a prize of $25,000, he flew through a dense fog and at times dropped to within ten feet of the water before sighting the Irish coast and regaining his bearings. The scope of the New York City parade honoring Lindbergh surpassed even the celebration of the Armistice.

Four years later New York City honored another pioneering American aviator—Amelia Earhart. In 1931 she became the first woman to fly solo across the Atlantic Ocean. Born in Kansas in 1897, she made her first solo flight in 1921. Soon thereafter she bought her own plane and began working as a barnstorming stunt pilot at air shows across the country. A tall, thin, grey-eyed young woman with short, tousled blond hair and a "boyish" smile, she looked remarkably like Lindbergh. Earhart's popularity soared after her own transatlantic solo flight from Newfoundland to Northern Ireland. The fifteen-hour feat led Congress to award her the Distinguished Flying Cross, and she was named Outstanding American Woman of the Year.

Caught up in the fervor of the time for such dramatic exploits, Earhart began preparing in 1935 for "just one more long flight." Two years later she and a male navigator left Miami, Florida, and headed east on a round-the-world flight. The trip went smoothly until July 2, 1937, when they attempted the most difficult leg: from New Guinea to a tiny atoll in the Pacific 2,556 miles away. A Coast Guard vessel anchored near the island picked up weakening signals indicating that Earhart's plane was losing fuel. The plane disappeared, and despite extensive searches, no trace of it or the aviators was ever found. It remains the most intriguing mystery in aviation history. The accomplishments of

Earhart and Lindbergh helped catapult the aviation industry into prominence. By 1930 there were forty-three American airline companies in operation.

By far the most significant transportation development of the time was the automobile. The first motor car had been manufactured for sale in 1895, but the founding of the Ford Motor Company in 1903 revolutionized the industry. Ford's reliable Model T (the celebrated "tin lizzie") appeared in 1908 at a price of $850 (in 1924 it would sell for $290). Ford aimed "to democratize the automobile. When I'm through everybody will be able to afford one, and about everyone will have one." He was right. In 1916 the number of cars manufactured passed 1 million; by 1920 more than 8 million were registered, and in 1929 more than 23 million. The production of automobiles stimulated the whole economy by consuming large portions of steel, rubber, glass, and textiles. It gave rise to a gigantic market for oil products just as the Spindletop gusher (1901) in Texas heralded the opening of vast southwestern oilfields. The automotive revolution also quickened the movement for good roads, introduced efficient mass-production assembly-line techniques to other industries, speeded transportation and tourism, encouraged the sprawl of suburbs, and sparked real-estate booms in California and Florida.

Ford Motor Company's Highland Park Plant, *1913. Gravity slides and chain conveyors aided the mass production of automobiles.*

STABILIZING THE ECONOMY   During the 1920s, the efficiency craze, which had been a prominent feature of the progressive impulse, powered the wheels of mass production and consumption and became a cardinal belief of Republican leaders. Herbert Hoover, who served as secretary of commerce through the Harding-Coolidge years, was himself an engineer who had made a fortune in far-flung mining operations in Australia, China, Russia, and elsewhere. During World War I, he was a brilliant manager of the Belgian relief program and the Food Administration. When young Franklin D. Roosevelt met Hoover in 1919, he labeled him "a wonder." Roosevelt then added with what would become prophetic irony: "I wish we could make him President of the United States. There could not be a better one."

As Harding's and Coolidge's dynamic secretary of commerce, Hoover transformed the trifling Commerce Department into the most active agency of two Republican administrations. During a period of governmental retrenchment, he promoted expansion. Hoover sought out new markets for business and sponsored more than a thousand conferences on product design, production, and distribution. He also continued the wartime emphasis on standardization of everything from automobile tires and paving bricks to bedsprings and toilet paper.

Most of all Hoover endorsed the burgeoning trade-association movement. The organization of business trade associations became his favorite instrument for "stabilization" to avoid the waste inherent in competition. Through such associations, executives in a given field would gather and disseminate information on sales, purchases, shipments, production, and prices. This information allowed them to plan with more confidence, the advantages of which included predictable costs, prices, and markets, as well as more stable employment and wages. Sometimes abuses crept in as trade associations skirted the edge of legality by engaging in price-fixing and other monopolistic practices, but the Supreme Court in 1925 held the practice of sharing information as such to be within the law.

THE BUSINESS OF FARMING   During the Harding and Coolidge administrations, agriculture remained the weakest sector in the economy, in many ways as weak as it had been during the 1890s, when cities flourished and agriculture languished. For a brief time after the war, the farmers' hopes soared on wings of prosperity. The wartime boom lasted into 1920, and then commodity prices collapsed as European farmers began to resume high levels of production. Low prices persisted into 1923, especially in the wheat and corn belts, and after that improvement was spotty. A bumper cotton crop in 1926 resulted only in a price collapse and an early taste of depression in much of the South, where foreclosures and bankruptcies spread.

In some ways farmers shared the business outlook of the so-called New Era. Many farms, like corporations, were getting larger, more efficient, and more mechanized. By 1930 about 13 percent of all farmers had tractors, and the proportion rose even higher on the western plains. Better plows and other new machines were part of the mechanization process that accompanied improved crop yields, fertilizers, and animal breeding.

Farm organizations of the 1920s moved away from the proposed alliance with urban labor that had marked the Populist Era and toward a new view of farmers as profit-conscious business owners. During the postwar farm depression, the idea of marketing cooperatives emerged as the farmer's equivalent to the businessman's trade-association movement. Farm groups formed regional commodity-marketing associations that enabled them to negotiate ironclad contracts with producers for the delivery of their crops over a period of years. These associations also brought order to the marketing of farm products, requiring uniform standards and grades, efficient handling and advertising, and a businesslike organization with professional technicians and executives.

But if concern with marketing co-ops and other businesslike approaches drew farmers farther away from populist traditions, nagging farm problems still invited political solutions. The most effective political response to the collapse of farm prices of the early 1920s was the formation of the farm bloc, a congressional coalition of western Republicans and southern Democrats that put through an impressive, if fairly moderate, program of legislation from 1921 to 1923. During that period, the farm bloc passed bills exempting farm cooperatives from antitrust laws and creating new credit banks that could lend to cooperative producing and marketing associations.

In the spring of 1924 Senator Charles L. McNary of Oregon and Representative Gilbert N. Haugen of Iowa introduced a bill to secure "equality for agriculture in the benefits of the protective tariff." Their plan sought to dump American farm surpluses on the world market in order to raise commodity prices in the home market. The goal was to achieve "parity"–that is, to raise domestic farm prices to a point where farmers would have the same purchasing power relative to other commodity prices that they had enjoyed between 1909 and 1914, a time viewed in retrospect as a golden age of American agriculture. A McNary-Haugen bill finally passed both houses of Congress in 1927 and again a year later, only to be vetoed both times by President Coolidge. He criticized the measure as an unsound effort at price-fixing, and as un-American and unconstitutional to boot. Nonetheless, the bill catapulted the farm problem into the arena of national debate and defined it as a problem of crop surpluses, as well as reviving the political alliance between the South and West.

SETBACKS FOR UNIONS   Urban workers shared more than farmers in the affluence of the times. "A workman is far better paid in America than anywhere else in the world," a French visitor wrote in 1927, "and his standard of living is enormously higher." Non-farm workers gained about 20 percent in real wages between 1921 and 1928, while farm income rose only 10 percent. The benefits of this rise, however, were distributed unevenly. Miners and textile workers suffered a decline in real wages. In these and other trades, technological unemployment followed the introduction of new methods and machines, because technology eliminated as well as created jobs.

Organized labor, however, did no better than organized agriculture in the 1920s. In fact, unions suffered a setback after the growth years of the war as the Red Scare and strikes of 1919 left the uneasy impression that unions practiced political subversion. The brief postwar depression of 1921 further weakened the unions, as did the popularity of open-shop associations. While the open shop in theory implied only the employer's right to hire anyone, in practice it meant discrimination against unionists and refusal to recognize unions even in shops where most of the workers belonged to one.

To suppress unions, employers used intimidation and repression. They often required "yellow-dog" contracts that forced workers to agree to stay out of unions, used labor spies, exchanged blacklists, and resorted to other forms of coercion. Some employers tried to kill the unions with kindness. They introduced programs of "industrial democracy" guided by company unions or various schemes of "welfare capital-

The Cash Register Chorus *sings of its ties to Coolidge in this 1924 cartoon.*

ism" such a profit-sharing, bonuses, pensions, health programs, recreational activities, and the like. The benefits of such programs were often considerable. Prosperity, propaganda, welfare capitalism, and active hostility combined to cause union membership to drop from about 5 million in 1920 to 3.5 million in 1929.

PRESIDENT HOOVER, THE ENGINEER

HOOVER VS. SMITH   On August 2, 1927, while on vacation in the Black Hills of South Dakota, President Coolidge passed out to reporters slips of paper with the curious statement: "I do not choose to run for President in 1928." Exactly what he meant puzzled observers then and since. Apparently he at least half hoped for a convention draft, but his statement cleared the way for Herbert Hoover to mount an active campaign for the Republican nomination. Well before the 1928 Republican convention in Kansas City, Hoover was too far in the lead to be stopped. The party platform took credit for postwar prosperity, debt and tax reduction, and the protective tariff that had been in operation since 1922 ("as vital to American agriculture as it is to manufacturing"). It rejected the McNary-Haugen program, but promised a farm board to manage crop surpluses more efficiently.

The Democratic nomination went to Governor Alfred E. Smith of New York. The Democratic party had had its fill of factionalism in 1924, and all remained fairly harmonious until Smith revealed in his acceptance speech a desire to liberalize prohibition. Hoover by contrast had pronounced the outlawing of alcoholic beverages "a great social and economic experiment, noble in motive and far-reaching in purpose," and he called for improved enforcement.

The two candidates projected sharply different images. Hoover was the Quaker son of middle America, the successful engineer and businessman from rural Iowa, the architect of Republican prosperity, a simple man who dressed plainly, spoke tersely, and followed his strong conscience. Smith was the prototype of those things that rural and small-town America distrusted: the son of Irish immigrants, Catholic, and a critic of prohibition. Outside the large cities such qualities were handicaps he could scarcely surmount, for all his affability and wit.

In the election Hoover won in the third consecutive Republican landslide, with 21 million popular votes to Smith's 15 million, and an even more top-heavy electoral majority of 444 to 87. Hoover even cracked the Solid South, leaving Smith only a hard core of six Deep South states plus Massachusetts and Rhode Island. The election was above all a vindication of Republican prosperity, but the shattering defeat of the Democrats concealed a major realignment in the making. Smith had nearly doubled the vote for the Democratic candidate of four years before. Smith's image, though a handicap in the hinterlands, swung big cities back into the Democratic column. In the farm states of the West there were signs that some disgruntled farmers had switched over to the Democrats. A coalition of urban workers and unhappy farmers was in the making.

HOOVER IN CONTROL   The milestone year of 1929 dawned with high hopes. Business seemed solid, incomes were rising, and the chief architect of Republican prosperity was about to enter the White House. "I have no fears for the future of our country," Hoover told his inauguration audience. "It is bright with hope."

Forgotten in the rush of later events would be Hoover's credentials as a progressive and humanitarian president. Over the objection of Treasury Secretary Mellon, he announced a plan for tax reductions in the low-income brackets. He shunned corrupt patronage practices, and he

"I have no fears for the future of our country," Herbert Hoover told his audience at his inauguration in 1929.

refused to countenance "Red hunts" or interference with peaceful picketing of the White House. He also defended his wife's right to invite prominent blacks to the White House, and he sought more money for all-black Howard University.

Hoover showed greater sympathy than Coolidge for the struggling agricultural sector. In 1929 he pushed through a special session of Congress the Agricultural Marketing Act, which established both a Federal Farm Board with a revolving loan fund of $500 million to help farm cooperatives market major commodities and a program in which the Farm Board could set up "stabilization corporations" empowered to buy surpluses off the market. To open up glutted markets, he also proposed higher tariffs on imported farm products. After fourteen months of struggle with competing interests, however, Hoover settled for a general upward revision of tariffs on manufactures as well as farm goods. The Hawley-Smoot Tariff of 1930 carried duties to a new high. Average rates went from about 32 to 40 percent. More than 1,000 economists petitioned Hoover to veto the bill because, they predicted, it would raise prices to consumers, damage the export trade and thus hurt farmers, promote inefficiency, and provoke foreign reprisals. Events proved them right, but Hoover felt that he had to go along with his party in an election year. This proved to be a disastrous mistake, for it only exacerbated the growing economic depression.

THE ECONOMY OUT OF CONTROL   Depression? Most Americans had come to assume during the 1920s that there would never be another depression. This misguided optimism proved to be an important factor in generating the economic free-fall after 1929. Throughout the 1920s, the idea grew that American business had entered a New Era of *permanent* growth. Such naive talk helped promote an array of get-rich-quick schemes. Speculative mania fueled the Florida real-estate boom, which got under way when the combination of Coolidge prosperity and Henry Ford's "tin lizzies" made Florida an accessible playground.

The Florida real-estate boom collapsed in 1926, but the stock market took up the slack. Until 1927 stock values had risen with profits, but then they began to soar on wings of fanciful speculation. Mellon's tax reductions had released money which, with the help of aggressive brokerage houses, found its way to Wall Street. One could now buy stock on margin—that is, make a small down payment (usually 10 percent) and borrow the rest from a broker who held the stock as security against a down market. If the stock price fell and the buyer failed to provide more cash, the broker could sell the stock to cover his loan.

Gamblers in the market ignored warning signs. By 1927 residential construction and automobile sales were catching up to demand, business inventories rose, and the rate of consumer spending slowed. By mid-1929 production, employment, and other gauges of economic activity were declining. Still the stock market rose, driven by excessive confidence and perennial greed.

By 1929 the stock market had become a fantasy world. Conservative financiers and brokers who counseled caution went unheeded. Hoover worried too, and he sought to discourage speculation, but to no avail. On September 4, stock prices wavered, and the next day they dropped. The Great Bull Market staggered on into October, trending downward but with enough good days to keep hope alive. On October 22 a leading bank president told reporters: "I know of nothing fundamentally wrong with the stock market or with the underlying business and credit structure."

THE CRASH AND ITS CAUSES   The next day prices tumbled, and the day after that a wild scramble to unload stocks lasted until word arrived that leading bankers had formed a pool to stabilize prices. For the rest of the week, stock prices steadied, but after a weekend to think the situation over, stockholders began to unload their portfolios. On Tuesday, October 29, the most devastating single day in the market's history to that point, the index dropped another 43 points, almost 13 percent. The plunge in prices fed on itself as brokers sold the shares they held for buyers who failed to come up with more cash. During October, the value of stocks on the New York Exchange fell by an average of 37 percent.

Business and government leaders initially expressed hope. According to President Hoover, "the fundamental business of the country" was sound. Some speculators who got out of the market went back in for bargains but found themselves caught in a slow erosion of values. By 1933, the value of stocks on the New York Exchange was less than 20 percent of the value at the market's 1929 peak.

Caution was now the watchword for consumers and business leaders. Buyers held out for lower prices, orders fell off, wages fell or ceased altogether, and the decline in purchasing power brought further cutbacks in business activity. From 1929 to 1932, Americans' personal incomes declined by more than half, from $82 million to $40 million. Unemployment continued to rise exponentially, from 1.6 million in 1929 to 12.8 million in 1933, from 3 percent to 25 percent of the labor force. Farmers, already in trouble, faced catastrophe as commodity prices fell by half. More than 9,000 banks closed during the period, hundreds of factories and mines shut down, entire towns were abandoned, and thousands of farms were sold to pay debts.

The crash had revealed the economy's structural problems. Too many businesses during the boom years had maintained prices and taken profits while holding down wages. As a result, about one-third of the nation's personal income went to only 5 percent of the population. By plowing profits back into expansion, business brought on a growing imbalance between rising productivity and declining purchasing power. As the demand for goods declined, the rate of investment in new plants and equipment also began to decline. For a time the softness of purchasing power was concealed by greater use of installment buying, and the deflationary effects of high tariffs were concealed by the volume of loans and investments abroad, which supported foreign demand for American goods. But the flow of American capital abroad began to dry up when the stock market became a more attractive investment. Swollen profits and dividends enticed the rich into market speculation. When trouble came, the bloated corporate structure collapsed.

Governmental policies also contributed to the debacle. Mellon's tax reductions brought oversaving, which helped diminish demand for consumer goods. The growing money supply fed the fever of speculation by lowering interest rates. Hostility toward unions discouraged collective bargaining and may have worsened the prevalent imbalances in income. High tariffs discouraged foreign trade. Lax enforcement of antitrust laws encouraged concentration, monopoly, and high prices.

Another culprit was the gold standard. The world monetary system remained fragile throughout the 1920s. When economic output, prices, and savings began dropping in 1929, policy makers—certain that they had to keep their currencies tied to gold at all costs—either did nothing or tightened money supplies, thus exacerbating the downward spiral. The only way to restore economic stability within the constraints of the gold standard was to let prices and wages continue to fall. The best policy, Andrew Mellon advised, would be to "liquidate labor, liquidate stocks, liquidate the farmers, liquidate real estate," allowing the downturn to "purge the rottenness out of the system." Such passivity helped turn a recession into the world's worst depression.

THE HUMAN TOLL OF DEPRESSION   The devastating collapse of the economy caused immense social hardships. By 1933, there were over 13 million people out of work and many more found themselves working fewer hours. Blacks and Mexicans were usually the first laid off. As factories shut down, banks closed, and farms went bankrupt, millions of people found themselves not only jobless, but also homeless and penniless. Hungry people lined up at churches and soup kitchens; others rummaged through trash cans behind restaurants. Local welfare agencies were swamped with appeals for charity and quickly ran out of funds. Many of the destitute slept on park benches or in back alleys. Others congregated in makeshift shelters in vacant lots. Thousands of men in search of jobs "rode the rails." These "hobos" or "tramps," as they were derisively called, sneaked onto empty railway cars and rode from town to town looking for work. During the winter, homeless people wrapped themselves in newspapers to keep warm, referring to them sarcastically as "Hoover blankets." Some grew weary of their grim fate and ended their lives. Suicide rates soared during the 1930s.

HOOVER'S EFFORTS AT RECOVERY   Not only did the policies of public officials help bring on economic collapse, but few political or economic leaders acknowledged the severity of the crisis: all that was needed, they thought, was a slight correction of the market. Those who held to the theory of laissez-faire, such as Andrew Mellon, thought the economy would cure itself. Hoover, however, was unwilling to sit by and let events take their course. In fact, he did more than any previous president in such dire economic circumstances. Still, his own philosophy, now hardened into dogma, set strict limits to action by the federal government, and he refused to set it aside even to meet an emergency.

Hoover believed that the country's main need was confidence. In speech after speech, he exhorted the public to keep up hope. On May 1, 1930, he told the U.S. Chamber of Commerce that "we have passed the worst and with continued effort we shall rapidly recover." To that end, he asked business and labor leaders to keep the mills and shops open, maintain wage levels, and spread the work to avoid layoffs—in short, to let the shock fall on corporate profits rather than on purchasing power. In return, union leaders, who had little choice, agreed to refrain from wage demands and strikes.

While reassuring the American public, Hoover also accelerated the building of public projects in order to provide jobs, but state and local cutbacks more than offset new federal spending. At Hoover's demand the Federal Reserve returned to an easier credit policy, and Congress passed a modest tax reduction to put more purchasing power in people's pockets. The high Hawley-Smoot Tariff, proposed at first to help farmers, brought reprisals abroad, devastating foreign trade.

As always, depression hurt the political party in power, and the floundering president was easy game. Near the city dumps and along railroad tracks, the dispossessed huddled in shacks of tarpaper and galvanized iron, in old packing boxes and abandoned cars. These squalid settlements were labeled "Hoovervilles"; a "Hoover flag" was an empty pocket turned inside out. Such scornful labels reflected the quick erosion of Hoover's political support. In 1930 the Democrats gained their first national victory since 1916, winning a majority in the House and enough gains in the Senate to control it in coalition with western agrarians.

"Hoovervilles" in New York's Central Park, 1931.

In the first half of 1931 economic indicators rose, renewing hope for an upswing. Then, as recovery beckoned, another shock jolted public confidence. In 1931 the failure of Austria's largest bank triggered a financial panic in central Europe. To halt the domino effect of spreading defaults, President Hoover proposed a one-year moratorium on both reparations and war-debt payments. The major European nations accepted the moratorium and later also a temporary "standstill" on settlement of private obligations between banks. The general shortage of monetary exchange drove Europeans to withdraw their gold from American banks and dump their American securities. One European nation after another abandoned the gold standard and devalued its currency. All these foreign developments worsened the collapse of the American economy, which slid into the third bitter winter of depression.

CONGRESSIONAL INITIATIVES With a new Congress in session, demands for federal action impelled Hoover to stretch his governmental philosophy to its limits. He was ready now to use governmental resources at least to shore up the financial institutions. In early 1932 the new Congress responded to pleas from the banking sector and set up the Reconstruction Finance Corporation (RFC) with $500 million (and authority to borrow $1.5 billion more) for emergency loans to banks, life insurance companies, building and loan societies, farm mortgage associations, and railroads. The RFC staved off some bankruptcies, but Hoover's critics charged that it favored business at the expense of workers. The RFC nevertheless remained a key agency through the decade and during World War II.

Further help to the financial structure came with the Glass-Steagall Act of 1932, which eased the availability of commercial loans. It also released about $750 million in gold formerly used to back Federal Reserve notes, countering the effect of foreign withdrawals and domestic hoarding of gold at the same time that it enlarged the supply of credit. For homeowners the Federal Home Loan Bank Act of 1932 created with Hoover's blessing a series of discount banks for home mortgages. They provided savings and loan associations a service much like that which the Federal Reserve System provided to commercial banks.

Hoover's critics argued that all these measures reflected a dubious "trickle-down" theory. If government could help banks and railroads, asked New York senator Robert G. Wagner, "is there any reason why we should not likewise extend a helping hand to that forlorn American, in every village and every city of the United States, who has been without wages since 1929?" The contraction of credit devastated debtors such as farmers and those who made purchases on the "installment plan" or who held "balloon" mortgages whose monthly payments increased over time. By 1932 members of Congress were filling the hoppers with bills to provide federal relief for distressed individuals. At that point, Hoover might have pleaded "dire necessity," taken the leadership of the relief movement, and salvaged his political fortunes.

Instead he held back and only grudgingly edged toward federal relief. On July 21, 1932, Hoover signed the Emergency Relief and Construction Act, which avoided a direct federal dole (cash payments to individuals) but gave the RFC $300 million for relief loans to the states, authorized loans of up to $1.5 billion for state and local government construction projects, and appropriated $322 million for federal public works.

Government relief for farmers had long since been abandoned. In mid-1931 the government quit buying surpluses and helplessly watched prices slide. In 1919 wheat had fetched $2.16 a bushel; by 1932 it had sunk to 38¢. Cotton had reached a high of 41.75¢ a pound in 1919; before the 1932 harvest it went to 4.6¢. Other farm prices declined comparably. Between 1930 and 1934, the titles of nearly a million farms passed from their owners to the mortgage holders.

FARMERS AND VETERANS IN PROTEST   Faced with total loss, some desperate farmers began to defy the law. Angry mobs stopped foreclosures and threatened to lynch bankers and judges. In Nebraska farmers burned corn to keep warm; dairy farmers dumped milk into roadside ditches in an effort to raise prices. Like voluntary efforts to reduce acreage, these strikes generally failed, but they vividly dramatized the farmers' frustration and anger.

Fears of organized disorder arose when unemployed World War I veterans converged on Washington in the spring of 1932. The "Bonus Expeditionary Force" grew quickly to more than 15,000. Their purpose was to get immediate payment of the cash bonus to war veterans that Congress had voted in 1924. It took the form of life insurance payable in 1945 (earlier to heirs of deceased veterans). The House approved a bonus bill, but when the Senate voted it down, most of the veterans went home. The rest, having no place to go, camped in vacant government buildings and in a shantytown within sight of the Capitol.

The chief of the Washington police gave the squatters a friendly welcome and won their trust, but a fearful White House fretted. Eager to disperse the destitute veterans, Hoover convinced Congress to vote funds to buy their tickets home. More left, but others stayed even after Congress adjourned, hoping at least to meet with the embattled president.

Late in July the administration ordered the shantytown razed. In the ensuing melee, one policeman panicked, fired into the crowd, and killed two veterans. The secretary of war then dispatched about 700 soldiers under General Douglas MacArthur, aided by junior officers Dwight D. Eisenhower and George S. Patton, Jr. The soldiers easily drove out the unarmed veterans and their families, and burned the shacks. MacArthur self-righteously explained in his report that when dealing with "riotous elements" a show of "obvious strength gains a moral ascendancy." The one fatality—from tear gas—was an eleven-week-old boy, born in one of the shanties.

General MacArthur said the "mob," spurred by "the essence of revo-

Unemployed veterans, members of the "Bonus Expeditionary Force," clash with Washington, D.C., police at Anacostia Flats, July 1932.

lution," was about to seize control of the government. The administration insisted that the Bonus Army consisted mainly of Communists and criminals, but neither a grand jury nor the Veterans Administration could find evidence to support the charge. The spectacle of army troops using tanks to dislodge unarmed veterans did not help Hoover's eroding image. To most Americans, the Bonus Army was more pathetic than threatening. One observer wrote before the incident: "There is about the lot of them an atmosphere of hopelessness, of utter despair, though not of desperation. . . . They have no enthusiasm whatever and no stomach for fighting."

Their mood, and the mood of the country, echoed that of Hoover himself. He worked hard, but took no joy from his labors. "I am so tired," he sometimes sighed, "that every bone in my body aches." As the months passed, presidential news conferences were more strained and less frequent. When friends urged Hoover to seize the reins of leadership, he replied, "I can't be a Theodore Roosevelt," or "I have no Wilsonian qualities." His gloom and growing sense of futility were apparent to the country. In a mood more despairing than rebellious, people waited to see what another presidential campaign would bring forth.

MAKING CONNECTIONS

- This chapter discusses setbacks for labor unions during the Republican administrations of the 1920s. In the next chapter, unions win new protections under Franklin Roosevelt's New Deal.

- An element of the "normalcy" discussed in this chapter was American isolationism from global affairs. Chapter 28 discusses that isolationism in the context of the coming of World War II.

- Compare the characteristics of 1920s American society with the postwar society and culture of the 1950s, discussed in Chapter 31.

FURTHER READING

A fine synthesis of events immediately following the First World War is Ellis W. Hawley's *The Great War and the Search for a Modern Order: A History of the American People and Their Institutions, 1917–1933* (1979).

For an introduction to Harding, see Francis Russell's *The Shadow of Blooming Grove: Warren G. Harding in His Times* (1968). Robert K. Murray's *The Harding Era: Warren G. Harding and His Administration* (1969) is more favorable to Harding. On Coolidge, see Donald R. McCoy's *Calvin Coolidge: The Silent President* (1967). Studies on Hoover include Joan Hoff Wilson's *Herbert Hoover: Forgotten Progressive* (1975) and George Nash's multivolume work, *The Life of Herbert Hoover* (1983–1987). Other works on politics include Burl Noggle's *Teapot Dome: Oil and Politics in the 1920s* (1962) and David Burner's *The Politics of Provincialism: The Democratic Party in Transition, 1918–1932* (1968).

The impact of transportation is gauged in Reynold M. Wik's *Henry*

Ford and Grassroots America (1972). Roland Marchand's *Advertising the American Dream: Making Way for Modernity, 1920–1940* (1985) covers the development of national advertising in the 1920s. Susan J. Douglas's *Inventing American Broadcasting, 1899–1922* (1989) is a cultural history of the formative years of radio. Motion pictures are the subject of Robert Sklar's *Movie-Made America: A Cultural History of American Movies* (1975) and Lary May's *Screening out the Past: The Birth of Mass Culture and the Motion Picture Industry* (1980).

Overviews of the depressed economy are found in Charles P. Kindleberger's *The World in Depression, 1929–1939* (rev. ed., 1986) and Peter Fearon's *War, Prosperity and Depression: The U.S. Economy, 1917–1945* (1987). John Kenneth Galbraith details the fall of the stock market in *The Great Crash, 1929* (1955). A different interpretation is given in Peter Temin's *Did Monetary Forces Cause the Great Depression?* (1976).

John A. Garraty's *The Great Depression: An Inquiry into the Causes, Course, and Consequences of the Worldwide Depression of the Nineteen Thirties* (1986) describes how people survived the depression. First-hand accounts of the Great Depression can be found in Tom E. Terrill and Jerrold Hirsch's *Such As Us: Southern Voices of the Thirties* (1978), Studs Terkel's *Hard Times* (1970), Robert S. McElvaine's *Down and Out in the Great Depression: Letters from the Forgotten Man* (1983), and *"Slaves of the Depression": Workers' Letters about Life on the Job* (1989), edited by Gerald Markowitz and David Rosner.

27 ⟨∞⟩ NEW DEAL AMERICA

CHAPTER ORGANIZER

This chapter focuses on:

- the social effects of the Great Depression and Roosevelt's efforts at relief, recovery, and reform.

- criticism of the New Deal, from both the right and the left.

- how the New Deal greatly expanded the federal government's authority and responsibilities.

- the change in cultural direction in the 1930s.

On June 14, 1932, while the ragtag Bonus Army was still encamped in Washington, Republicans gathered in Chicago to renominate Hoover. The delegates went through the motions in a mood of defeat. The Democrats, in contrast, converged on Chicago late in June confident that they would nominate the next president. New York governor Franklin D. Roosevelt already had lined up most of the delegates, and he won the nomination on the fourth ballot.

In a bold gesture, Roosevelt appeared before the convention in person to accept the nomination instead of awaiting formal notification. He told the expectant delegates: "I pledge you, I pledge myself to a new deal for the American people." What the New Deal would be in practice Roosevelt had little idea as yet, but he was much more flexible and willing to experiment than Hoover. What was more, his upbeat personality communicated joy and hope—as did his campaign song, "Happy Days Are Here Again."

FROM HOOVERISM TO THE NEW DEAL

FDR'S ELECTION   Born in 1882 into a wealthy family, educated by governesses and tutors at Springwood, his father's rambling Hudson River Valley estate, young Franklin led the cosmopolitan life of a young patrician. After attending Groton, an elite Connecticut boarding school, he earned degrees from Harvard and Columbia University Law School. While a law student, he married Anna Eleanor Roosevelt, the niece of President Theodore Roosevelt, his own distant cousin.

Franklin Roosevelt began work with a prominent Wall Street law firm, but he soon lost interest in legal affairs and decided to enter politics. In 1910 he won a Democratic seat in the New York State Senate. As a freshman legislator he displayed the contradictory qualities that would always characterize his political career: an aristocrat with a sincere affinity for common folk; a traditionalist with a penchant for experiment; an affable charmer with a luminous smile and upturned chin who also harbored profound convictions; and a skilled political tactician with a shrewd sense of timing and a distinctive willingness to listen to and learn from others.

Tall, handsome, and athletic, Roosevelt seemed destined for great achievement. In 1912 he backed Woodrow Wilson, and for both of Wilson's terms he served as his assistant secretary of the navy. Then, in 1920, largely on the strength of his name, he gained the vice-presidential nomination. Political defeat was followed by personal crisis when in 1921, at the age of thirty-nine, Roosevelt contracted polio, which left him permanently crippled, unable to stand or walk without braces. But his prolonged struggle with this handicap transformed the once snobbish young aristocrat into one of the century's most outgoing political figures. A friend recalled that Roosevelt emerged from his struggle with polio "completely warm-hearted, with a new humility of spirit" that led him to identify with the poor and suffering.

For seven years, aided by his talented wife Eleanor, Roosevelt strengthened his body to compensate for his disability, and in 1928, he ran for governor of New York and won. Reelected by a whopping majority of 700,000 in 1930, he became the Democratic front-runner for the presidency in 1932. Behind the public facade of a cheery and self-confident politician, Roosevelt was also at times a crass manipulator of people and power. Obsessed with gaining the highest office in the land, he was willing to sacrifice all else in his life—marriage, health, staff, friends—to that end. Roosevelt occasionally inflated his own accomplishments and took credit for those of others, but his own strengths and achievements were considerable. A born leader, he had a talent for surrounding himself with capable people and getting the most out of them. Most important, however, was his bulldog determination to succeed, to overcome all obstacles, to triumph over despair and adversity, and in the process achieve greatness.

THE 1932 CAMPAIGN Partly to dispel doubts about his health, Roosevelt set forth on a grueling campaign tour in 1932. He blamed the depression on Hoover and the Republicans, and he began to define what he meant by his New Deal. Like Hoover, Roosevelt made the requisite pledge to balance the budget, but he left open the loophole that

Governor Franklin D. Roosevelt, the Democratic nominee, campaigning in Topeka, Kansas. Roosevelt's confidence inspired voters.

he would incur short-term deficits to prevent starvation. He was evasive on the tariff, and on farm policy he offered several options pleasing to farmers but ambiguous enough not to alarm city dwellers. He did come out unequivocally for strict regulation of utilities, and he consistently stood by his party's pledge to repeal the prohibition amendment. Perhaps most important, he recognized that a mature economy would require imaginative national planning. "The country needs, and, unless I mistake its temper, the country demands bold, persistent experimentation." What came across to voters, however, was less the content of his speeches than the confidence and irrepressible buoyancy of the man.

The dour Hoover, by contrast, had no confidence. Democrats, he argued, ignored the international causes of the depression. Roosevelt's reckless proposals, Hoover warned, "would destroy the very foundations of our American system." But few were listening. Mired in the persistent depression, the country wanted a new course, a new leadership, a new deal.

Some voters took a dim view of both major candidates. Those who believed that only a truly radical departure would suffice went over to

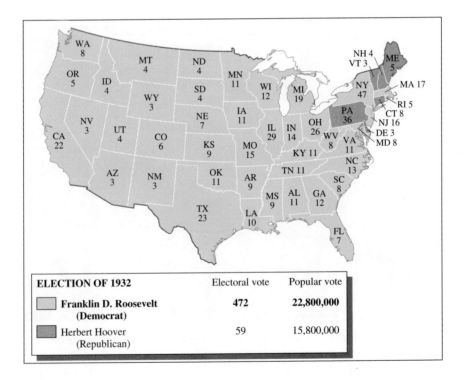

ELECTION OF 1932	Electoral vote	Popular vote
Franklin D. Roosevelt (Democrat)	472	22,800,000
Herbert Hoover (Republican)	59	15,800,000

the Socialist Norman Thomas, who polled 882,000 votes, and a few went on to support the Communist party candidate, who won 103,000 votes. The wonder is that a desperate people did not turn in greater numbers to such radical alternatives. Instead they swept Roosevelt into office by a whopping margin.

THE INAUGURATION For the last time, the country waited four months, until March 4, for a new president and Congress to take office. The Twentieth Amendment, ratified on February 6, 1933, provided that the president would thereafter take office on January 20 and the newly elected Congress on January 3.

Amid spreading destitution and misery, unemployment continued to rise during the bleak winter of 1932–1933, and panic struck the banking system. As bank after bank announced they were closing and did not have adequate cash to repay depositors, people rushed to their own banks to remove their deposits. Many discovered that they, too, were caught short. The "run" on the banks exacerbated the crisis and paralyzed the economy. When the Hoover administration left office, four-fifths of the nation's banks were closed, and the country was on the brink of economic paralysis.

The profound crisis of confidence that prevailed when Roosevelt took office on March 4, 1933, gave way to a mood of expectancy. The new president exploited both with a spirit of assurance that conveyed a confident sense of vigorous action. First, he asserted "that the only thing we have to fear is fear itself." He would not merely exhort, he promised: "This nation asks for action, and action now!" It was exactly what a distraught nation wanted to hear. One citizen wrote Roosevelt that the speech was "the finest thing this side of heaven. It seemed to give the people, as well as myself, a new hold on life."

COMPETING SOLUTIONS When Roosevelt and the New Dealers arrived in Washington, they were confronted by three major challenges: reviving the devastated economy, relieving the human misery brought on by the Great Depression, and alleviating the desperate plight of farmers and their families. Roosevelt's "brain trust" of advisers developed conflicting opinions about how best to turn the economy around. Some promoted vigorous enforcement of the antitrust laws as a means of restoring competition; others argued just the opposite, saying that antitrust laws should be suspended so as to enable large corporations to collaborate with the federal government in "managing" the economy. Still others called for a massive expansion of welfare programs and a prolonged infusion of government spending to address the profound human crisis and revive the economy.

For his part, Roosevelt vacillated among these three schools of thought. He was willing to try elements of each without embracing one approach completely. In part, this reflected the political reality that conservative southern Democrats controlled most of the major congressional committees, and Roosevelt could not risk alienating these party elders who were committed to states' rights and balanced budgets. Roosevelt's inconsistencies also reflected his own outlook. When asked by a reporter to label his philosophy, Roosevelt replied: "Philosophy? I am a Christian and a Democrat—that's all." His willingness to act, to be decisive, and to experiment with new programs and policies set his presidency apart from most others. Nevertheless, for all his energy and daring, Roosevelt brought to the White House no concrete agenda or long-range plan. He was a pragmatist rather than an ideologue. As he once explained, "Take a method and try it. If it fails admit it frankly and try another." He liked to say "I have no expectation of making a hit every time I come to bat. What I seek is the highest possible batting average." Roosevelt's New Deal, therefore, would take the form of a series of trial-and-error actions.

Roosevelt and his lieutenants initially settled on a three-pronged strategy as their first attempt at addressing the problems facing the nation. First, they sought to remedy the financial crisis and to provide short-term emergency relief for the jobless. Second, they tried to promote industrial recovery through increased federal spending and cooperative agreements between management and organized labor. Third, they attempted to raise commodity prices (and thereby farm income) by paying farmers to reduce crops and herds. By reducing the overall supply of farm products, prices would rise. None of these initiatives worked perfectly, but their combined effect was to restore hope and energy to a nation paralyzed by fear and uncertainty.

STRENGTHENING THE MONETARY SYSTEM The first order of business for the new administration was to free up the channels of finance. On his second day in office, Roosevelt displayed his activist bent by calling for a special session of Congress, and he then declared a four-day banking holiday. It took Congress only seven hours to pass the Emergency Banking Relief Act, which permitted sound banks to reopen and provided managers for those still in trouble. On March 12, 1933, in the first of his radio "fireside chats," the president insisted that it was safer to "keep your money in a reopened bank than under the mattress." The following day, deposits in reopened banks exceeded withdrawals, and by March 15, banks controlling nine-tenths of the nation's banking resources were once again open. Having decisively ended the bank panic, Roosevelt next slashed military pensions and government payrolls and then urged Congress to pass the Twenty-first Amendment, which ended prohibition.

These measures were but the beginning of an avalanche of executive and legislative action. Between March 9 and June 16, the so-called Hundred Days, Congress passed more than a dozen of Roosevelt's major proposals, legislation whose scope was unprecedented in American history. Said one legislator, Roosevelt's New Deal "reads like the first chapter of Genesis."

With the banking crisis over, there still remained an acute debt problem for farmers and homeowners and a lingering distrust of the banks, which might be aroused again. By early 1933, banks were foreclosing on farm mortgages at the rate of 20,000 per month. By executive de-

The Galloping Snail. *A vigorous Roosevelt drives the Congress to action in this* Detroit News *cartoon, March 1933.*

cree, Roosevelt reorganized all farm credit agencies into the Farm Credit Administration (FCA). Congress authorized the extensive refinancing of farm mortgages at lower interest rates. The Home Owner's Loan Act provided a similar service to city dwellers through the new Home Owner's Loan Corporation (HOLC)—something which, incidentally, Hoover had vainly urged on Congress in 1931. The HOLC refinanced mortgage loans at lower monthly payments for strapped homeowners. This helped slow the rate of foreclosures. The Glass-Steagall Banking Act further shored up confidence in the banking system by creating the Federal Deposit Insurance Corporation (FDIC) to insure personal bank deposits up to $5,000. It also required commercial banks to separate themselves from investment brokerages.

Roosevelt and Congress also tightened the regulation of Wall Street. The Federal Securities Act required that new stock and bond issues register with the Federal Trade Commission and later with the Securities and Exchange Commission (SEC), a new agency that regulated the stock and bond markets.

Throughout 1933 Roosevelt tinkered with devaluation of the currency as a way to raise stock and commodity prices and ease the debt burden on strapped investors and farmers. On April 19 the government achieved this by officially abandoning the gold standard, which infuriated fiscal conservatives. One fumed that Roosevelt's decision "can't be defended except as mob rule." Yet the consequent decline in the value of the dollar increased the prices of commodities and stocks at home.

RELIEF MEASURES   Another urgent priority in 1933 was relieving the widespread personal distress caused by the depression. Hoover had steadfastly resisted using the federal government to provide direct relief for the unemployed. Roosevelt had fewer qualms. As he once remarked, the "test of our progress is not whether we add to the abundance of those who have much. It is whether we provide enough for those who have too little." Congress took a first step toward such relief with the creation of the Civilian Conservation Corps (CCC), which was designed to provide useful jobs for young working-class men aged eighteen to twenty-five with little educational or vocational background.

Between 1931 and 1932, nearly 3 million CCC workers took to the woods to perform a variety of jobs in forests, parks, recreational areas, and soil conservation projects. They built roads, bridges, camping facilities, and fish hatcheries, planted trees, taught farmers how to control soil erosion, and fought fires. Directed by army officers and foresters, they worked under military discipline and provided perhaps the most direct analogue of war in the whole New Deal. Like the military at the time, the CCC camps were racially segregated. In Texas, African Americans were initially told that the camps were for whites only, and this falsehood helps explain the low number of blacks enrolled. Only 400 black Texans, less than 5 percent of the total number of men enrolled, participated in the program.

The Federal Emergency Relief Administration (FERA) addressed the broader problems of human distress. Designed as a shared undertaking between the federal government and the state and city governments, it was in fact shaped and directed by the Roosevelt administration. Harry L. Hopkins, a tireless social worker from Iowa who had earlier directed Roosevelt's state relief program in New York, headed the new effort and became the second most powerful figure in the administration. He pushed the FERA with a boundless energy, spending $5 million within two hours of taking office. FERA funds supported state construction of over 5,000 public buildings and 7,000 bridges, organized adult literacy programs, financed college education for poor students, and set up day-care centers for low-income families. The agency also helped local agencies dispense food and clothing for the needy.

The first large-scale experiment with *federal* work relief, which put people directly on the government payroll at competitive wages, came with the formation of the Civil Works Administration (CWA). Created in 1933, when it had become apparent that the state-sponsored programs under the FERA would not prevent widespread privation, the CWA provided federal jobs and wages to those unable to find work that winter. It was hastily conceived and implemented, but during its four-month existence, it put to work over 4 million people. In Chicago alone, some 70,000 people gathered before sunrise to register for the CWA on its opening day. The agency spent over $900 million (mostly in wages) for a variety of useful projects, from making highway repairs to constructing or improving more than 1,000 airports and 40,000 schools, to providing 50,000 teaching jobs that helped keep rural schools open. As the number of people employed by the CWA soared, the program's costs skyrocketed to over a billion dollars. Roosevelt balked at such high expenditures, and he worried that people would become dependent on federal jobs. "We must not take the position," Roosevelt stressed, "that we are going to have a permanent Depression in this country." He ordered the CWA dissolved in the spring of 1934. By April some 4 million workers were again unemployed.

Roosevelt, however, continued to favor work relief over the dole (direct cash payment to individuals); he thought the dole was an addictive "narcotic, a subtle destroyer of the human spirit." In 1935 he asked Congress for an array of new federal job programs, and it responded by passing a $4.8 billion bill providing work relief for the jobless. To manage these programs, Roosevelt created the Works Progress Administration (WPA), headed by Harry L. Hopkins, to replace the FERA. Hopkins was told to provide millions of jobs quickly, and as a result some of the new jobs appeared to be make-work or mere "leaning on shovels." But before the WPA died during World War II, it left permanent monuments on the landscape in the form of buildings, bridges, hard-surfaced roads, airports, and schools.

The WPA also employed a wide range of talents in the Federal Theatre Project, the Federal Art Project, and the Federal Writers' Project. Talented writers such as Ralph Ellison, John Cheever, and Saul Bellow found work writing travel guides to the United States, and Orson Welles directed Federal Theatre productions. The National Youth Administration (NYA), under the WPA, provided part-time employment to students, set up technical training programs, and aided jobless youth. Twenty-seven-year-old Lyndon Johnson was director of an NYA program in Texas, and Richard Nixon, a penniless Duke University law student, found work through the local NYA at thirty-five cents an hour. Although the WPA took care of only about 3 million out of some 10 million jobless at any one time, in all it helped some 9 million clients weather desperate times before it expired in 1943.

RECOVERY THROUGH REGULATION

In addition to rescuing the banks and providing relief for the unemployed, Roosevelt and his advisers promoted the recovery of the agricultural and industrial sectors. Roosevelt's "brain trust" of university-trained experts, lawyers, and professors initially felt that the trend toward economic concentration was inevitable. They also believed that the mistakes of the 1920s showed that the only way to operate an integrated economy at full capacity and in the public interest was through stringent regulation and organized central planning in cooperation with big business, not through trust-busting. The success of centralized economic planning on a national scale during World War I reinforced such ideas. New farm and industrial recovery programs sprang from their beliefs and experiences.

AGRICULTURAL RECOVERY: THE AAA The sharp decline in crop prices after 1929 meant that many farmers could not afford to plant or harvest their crops. The Agricultural Adjustment Act (AAA) of 1933 sought to help raise commodity prices by paying farmers for voluntary cutbacks in production. The money for the benefits payments made to farmers would be raised from a "processing tax" levied on the businesses (such as cotton gins, flour mills, and meat-packing plants) that processed farm products for sale.

As a complement to the AAA, Roosevelt created the Commodity Credit Corporation (another CCC!), which extended loans to farmers above the market price of their crops, which were kept in federal warehouses and off the market until crop prices rose. In principle, if not in form, it was a revival of the old Farmers' Alliance–Populist subtreasury plan. If crop prices rose over time, the farmers could repay the loans, retrieve their crops, and sell them. If prices did not rise, the government kept the crops in storage, and the farmers kept the loaned money.

By the time Congress acted, the growing season was already advanced, and the prospect of another bumper cotton crop created an urgent problem. The AAA reluctantly sponsored a plow-under program. To destroy a growing crop was a "shocking commentary on our civilization," Agriculture Secretary Henry A. Wallace lamented. "I could tolerate it only as a cleaning up of the wreckage from the old days of unbalanced production." In addition to plowing under ripening crops, the AAA encouraged farmers to destroy young livestock as a means of raising prices. Critics thereafter labeled Wallace the "assassin of little pigs."

Despite the controversy, for a while these farm measures worked. By the end of 1934, Wallace could report significant declines in wheat, cotton, and corn production and a simultaneous increase in commodity prices. Farm income increased by 58 percent between 1932 and 1935. The AAA, however, was only partially responsible for such gains. The

Dust Storm Approaching, *1930s. When a dust storm blew in, it would bring complete darkness as well as sand and grit that would soon cover every surface, both inside and out.*

devastating drought that settled over the Great Plains between 1932 and 1935 played a major role in reducing production and creating the epic "dust bowl" migrations so poignantly evoked in John Steinbeck's *Grapes of Wrath.* Many of these migrant families had actually been driven off the land by AAA benefit programs that encouraged large farmers to take the lands worked by tenants and sharecroppers out of cultivation first.

Although it created unexpected problems, the AAA achieved real successes in boosting the overall farm economy. Then the Supreme Court in *United States* v. *Butler* (1936) ruled the AAA's processing tax unconstitutional because farm production was intrastate and thus beyond the reach of federal power. The administration hastily devised a new plan to achieve crop reduction indirectly in the Soil Conservation and Domestic Allotment Act (1936), which it pushed through Congress in six weeks. The new act omitted processing taxes and acreage quotas, but it provided benefit payments to farmers who engaged in soil conservation practices and cut back on soil-depleting staple crops. Since the money to pay benefits came out of general funds and not from taxes, this approach was not vulnerable to lawsuits.

The act was an almost unqualified success as an engineering and educational project because it went far to heal the scars of erosion and the plague of dust storms. But soil conservation nevertheless failed as a device for limiting production. With their worst lands taken out of production, farmers cultivated their fertile acres more intensively. In response, Congress passed the second Agricultural Adjustment Act (1938), which reestablished the earlier programs but left out the processing taxes. Benefit payments would come from general funds. Increasingly, federal farm programs came to dominate the nation's agricultural economy. As the novelist William Faulkner recognized, "Our economy is not agricultural any longer. Our economy is the federal government. We no longer farm in Mississippi cotton fields. We farm now in Washington corridors and Congressional committee rooms."

INDUSTRIAL RECOVERY: THE NRA   The industrial counterpart to the AAA was the National Industrial Recovery Act (NIRA), passed in 1933. The NIRA had two major components. One part created the Public Works Administration (PWA) with $3.3 billion for public buildings, highway programs, flood control, bridges, tunnels, and aircraft carriers. Under the direction of Interior Secretary Harold L. Ickes, the PWA indirectly served the purpose of work relief. Ickes directed it toward well-planned permanent improvements rather than the provision of hasty make-work jobs, and he used private contractors rather than placing workers directly on the government payroll. PWA workers built Virginia's Skyline Drive, New York's Triborough Bridge, the Overseas Highway from Miami to Key West, and Chicago's subway system.

The more controversial and ambitious part of the NIRA created the National Recovery Administration (NRA), headed by the colorful former army general, Hugh S. Johnson. Modeled after the War Industries Board of 1917–1918, its purposes were essentially twofold: first, to stabilize the business sector by reducing competition through the implementation of codes that set wages and prices, and second, to generate more purchasing power by providing jobs, defining labor standards, and raising wages. The NRA also enlisted trade union hopes for protection of basic hour and wage standards and raised liberal hopes for comprehensive government planning for the economy.

In each industry, committees representing management, labor, and government drew up the fair practice codes. The labor standards were quite progressive. Every code set a forty-hour workweek and minimum weekly wages of $13 ($12 in the South, where living costs were considered lower), which more than doubled earnings in some cases. Child labor under the age of sixteen was prohibited.

As the drafting of other codes governing particular industries began to drag, the NRA launched a crusade to whip up popular support for its efforts. The public responded, proudly displaying the NRA symbol of compliance, the "Blue Eagle," on signs and in stores. Some 2 million employers signed a much-publicized "We Do Our Part" pledge affirming their support for the NRA codes.

Labor unions, already hard pressed by the economic downturn and the loss of members, however, were understandably concerned about the NRA's efforts to reduce competition by allowing businesses to cooperate in fixing wages and prices as well as production levels. To gain their support, the NRA included a provision (Section 7a) that guaranteed the right of workers to organize unions. But while prohibiting employers from interfering with labor organizing efforts, the NRA did not create adequate enforcement measures, not did it require employers to bargain in good faith with labor representatives.

For a time the NRA worked, perhaps because a new air of confidence had overcome the depression blues and the downward spiral of wages and prices had subsided. But as soon as economic recovery began, the honeymoon ended. Charges mounted that the larger companies dominated the code negotiations, that they used the codes to stifle competition by dividing up markets and entrenching their own positions, and that price-fixing robbed small producers of the chance to compete. The NRA wage codes also excluded agricultural and domestic workers—three out of every four employed blacks. The effort to develop codes for every industry in the nation proved an administrative nightmare, and the daily annoyances of code enforcement inspired growing hostility among business executives.

By 1935 the NRA had developed more critics than friends. A full economic recovery was nowhere in sight. In 1935, when the Supreme Court declared the NRA unconstitutional, few mourned. Yet, while generally deemed a failure, the NRA experiment left an enduring mark. With dramatic suddenness, the codes had set new standards, such as the forty-hour workweek and the end of child labor, from which it proved hard for management to retreat. The NRA's endorsement of collective bargaining also spurred union growth.

REGIONAL PLANNING: THE TVA   The wide-ranging philosophy of the New Deal embraced more than the restrictive approaches of the NRA. The creation of the Tennessee Valley Authority (TVA) was a truly bold venture, the product neither of a single imagination nor of a single concept, but of an unfolding progression of purposes. In 1916 the government started electric power and nitrate (for dynamite) plants at Muscle Shoals, Alabama, to strengthen national defense. New objectives unfolded in succession: the plants could produce nitrate fertilizers as well as nitrate explosives, promote general industrial development, and provide cheap public power to be used as a "yardstick" for private utility rates. Water-power development led in turn to improved flood control, and to conservation of soil and forests to prevent silting. The chain of connections led ultimately to the concept of overall planning for an entire regional watershed, which included a total drainage area in the Southeast of 41,000 square miles overlapping parts of seven states.

Through the 1920s, Nebraska senator George W. Norris had fought off efforts to sell the Alabama project to private developers, but he never marshaled sufficient support for his goal of a federal project to provide electricity for the public. In 1932, however, Norris won the new president's support for a vast enlargement of the Muscle Shoals project.

On May 18, 1933, Congress created the TVA as a multipurpose public corporation. By 1936, the TVA board had six dams completed or under way, and had developed a master plan to build nine high dams on the Tennessee River, which would create the "Great Lakes of the South," and other dams on the tributaries. The agency, moreover, opened the rivers for navigation, fostered soil conservation and forestry, experimented with fertilizers, drew new industry to the region, and sent cheap power pulsating through the valley.

The TVA's success at generating greater power consumption and lower rates awakened private utilities to the mass consumer markets. It also transported farmers of the valley from the age of kerosene to the age of electricity. "The women went around turning the switches on and off," reported a Farm Bureau man who witnessed the transition. "The light and wonder in their eyes was brighter than that from the lamps."

Through loans of more than $321 million to rural cooperatives, the Rural Electrification Administration (REA) paved the way to the electrification of the nation's farms.

THE HUMAN COST OF THE DEPRESSION

Although New Deal programs helped ease the devastation wrought by the depression, they did not restore prosperity or end the widespread human suffering. The depression continued to take a toll on ordinary Americans—factory workers, farmers, bankers, professionals remained in the throes of a shattered economy that only slowly was working its way back to health.

CONTINUING HARDSHIPS   As late as 1939, some 9.5 million workers (17 percent of the labor force) remained unemployed. Prolonged economic hardship continued to create personal tragedies and tremendous social strains. Poverty led desperate people to do desperate things. Petty theft soared during the 1930s, as did street-corner begging and prostitution. In Pittsburgh an unemployed father, desperate to feed his starving children, stole a loaf of bread from a neighbor, was arrested, and hanged himself in shame. Although the divorce rate dropped during the decade, in part because couples could not afford to live separately or pay the legal fees to obtain divorces, all too often husbands down on their luck simply deserted their wives. In 1940 a survey revealed that 1.5 million husbands had left home. A California woman reported to a friend that her husband "went north about three months ago to try his luck. The first month he wrote pretty regularly. . . . For five weeks now we have had no word from him. . . . Don't know where he is or what he is up to."

Many couples decided to postpone marriage because of hard times. Some 800,000 marriages were delayed during the 1930s, and the total number of marriages declined by one-fourth compared to the previous decade. With their own future uncertain, married couples often decided not to have children; the birthrate plummeted during the depression. Those with children sometimes could not support them. In 1933 the Children's Bureau reported that one out of every five children was not getting enough to eat. Often, struggling parents sent their children to live with relatives or friends. Some 900,000 other children simply left home and joined the army of homeless "tramps."

DUST BOWL MIGRANTS   Uprooted farmers and their families formed a migratory stream rushing from the South and Midwest toward California, buoyed by currents of hope and desperation. One couple claimed they had heard "how much money a man could make out there and we wanted to go."

Although frequently lumped together as "Okies," most of the dust bowl refugees were actually from cotton-belt communities in Arkansas, Texas, and Missouri, as well as Oklahoma. During the 1930s and 1940s, some 800,000 people left those four states and headed to the Far West. Not all were farmers; many were professionals, white-collar workers, retailers, and farm implement salesmen whose jobs had been tied to the health of the agricultural sector. Most of the dust bowl migrants were white, and most were young adults in their twenties and thirties who re-located with spouses and children. Some traveled on trains or buses, others hopped a freight or hitched a ride; most rode in their own cars, the trip taking four to five days on average.

Most of the dust bowl migrants who had come from cities gravitated to California's urban areas—Los Angeles, San Diego, or San Francisco. Half of the newcomers, however, moved into the San Joaquin Valley, the agricultural heartland of the state. There they discovered that Cali-fornia was no paradise. Only a few of the migrants could afford to buy land. Most (men and women) found themselves competing with local Hispanics and Asians for seasonal work as pickers in the cotton fields or orchards of large corporate farms. Living in tents or crude cabins and frequently on the move, they suffered from exposure and from poor sanitation.

They also felt the sting of social prejudice. John Steinbeck explained that "Okie us'ta mean you was from Oklahoma. Now it means you're a dirty son-of-a-bitch. Okie means you're scum. Don't mean nothing in itself, it's the way they say it." Such hostility drove a third of the "Okies" to return to their home states. Most of the farm workers who stayed tended to fall back upon their old folkways rather than assimi-late themselves into their new surroundings. These gritty "plain folk" brought with them their own prejudices against blacks and ethnic mi-norities as well as a potent tradition of evangelical Protestantism and a distinctive style of music variously labeled "country," "hillbilly," or "cow-boy." This "Okie" subculture remains a vivid part of California society today.

MINORITIES AND THE NEW DEAL   The depression was especially traumatic for the most disadvantaged groups in American society.
However progressive Roosevelt was on social issues, he failed to assault
long-standing patterns of racism and segregation for fear of alienating
southern Democrats. As a result, many of the New Deal programs were
for whites only. The Federal Housing Administration (FHA), for example, refused to guarantee mortgages on houses purchased by blacks in
white neighborhoods. The Civilian Conservation Corps and the Tennessee Valley Authority both practiced racial segregation.

The efforts of the Roosevelt administration to raise crop prices by reducing production proved especially devastating for blacks and Chicanos. To earn the federal payments for reducing crops as provided by
the AAA and other New Deal agricultural programs, many farm owners
would first take out of cultivation the marginal lands worked by tenants
and sharecroppers. This would drive the landless off farms and cost the
jobs of many migrant workers. Over 200,000 black tenant farmers nationwide were displaced by the AAA.

Mexican Americans suffered even more. Thousands of Mexicans had
migrated to the United States during the 1920s, most of them settling
in California, New Mexico, Arizona, Colorado, Texas, and the midwestern states. But because many Mexican Americans were unable to prove
their citizenship, either out of ignorance of the regulations or because
their migratory work hampered their ability to meet residency requirements, they were denied access to the many new federal relief programs under the New Deal. As economic conditions worsened, government officials called for the deportation of Mexican-born Americans to
avoid the costs of providing them with public services and relief. By
1935, over 500,000 Mexican Americans and their American-born children had returned to Mexico. The state of Texas alone returned over
250,000 people.

Deportation became such a popular solution in part because of the
rising level of involvement of Mexican-American workers in union
activities. In 1933 Mexican-American women in El Paso, Texas, formed
the Society of Female Manufacturing Workers to protest wages as low
as 75¢ a day. In the same year, some 18,000 cotton pickers went on
strike in California's San Joaquin Valley. Police crushed the strike by
burning the workers' camps.

Native Americans were especially devastated by the Great Depression. They initially were encouraged by Roosevelt's appointment of John Collier as the commissioner of the Bureau of Indian Affair (BIA). Collier steadily increased the number of Native Americans employed by the BIA and lobbied strenuously with the heads of New Deal agencies to ensure that Indians gained access to the various relief programs. Collier's primary objective, however, was passage of the Indian Reorganization Act. He wanted the new legislation to replace the provisions of the Dawes General Allotment Act (1887), which had sought to "Americanize" the Indians by breaking up their tribal lands and allocating them to individuals. Collier insisted that the Dawes Act had produced only widespread poverty and demoralization among the Indians. Collier hoped to reinvigorate traditional Indian cultural traditions by restoring land to tribes, granting Indians the right to charter business enterprises and establish self-governing constitutions, and providing federal funds for vocational training and economic development. The act that Congress finally passed, however, was a much diluted version of Collier's original proposal, and the "Indian New Deal" brought only a partial improvement in the lives of Native Americans.

CULTURE IN THE THIRTIES

In view of the celebrated—if exaggerated—alienation of writers, artists, and intellectuals rebelling against the materialistic world of the 1920s, one might have expected the onset of the Great Depression to deepen the despair of such cultural leaders. Instead it brought a renewed sense of militancy and affirmation, as if people could no longer afford the art-for-art's sake outlook of the 1920s. Said one writer early in 1932: "I enjoy the period thoroughly. The breakdown of our cult of business success and optimism, the miraculous disappearance of our famous American complacency, all this is having a tonic effect."

In the early 1930s the "tonic effect" of commitment sometimes took the form of allegiance to revolution. By the summer of 1932, even the "golden boy" of the lost generation, F. Scott Fitzgerald, declared that "to bring on the revolution, it may be necessary to work within the Communist party." But few remained Communists for long. Being a notoriously independent lot, most writers rebelled at demands to hew to a shifting party line. And many abandoned communism upon learning that Soviet leader Joseph Stalin practiced a tyranny more horrible than anything under the czars.

LITERATURE AND THE DEPRESSION   Among the writers who addressed themes of immediate social significance two novelists deserve special notice: John Steinbeck and Richard Wright. The single piece of fiction that best captured the ordeal of the depression, Steinbeck's *The Grapes of Wrath* (1939), avoided political formula to treat workers as people. Steinbeck had taken the trouble to travel with displaced "Okies" driven from the Oklahoma dust bowl by bankers and farm combines to pursue the illusion of good jobs in the fields of California's Central Valley. The story focused on the Joad family as they made their painful journey west from Oklahoma. Met chiefly with contempt and rejection, Ma Joad strove to keep hope alive. At the end, even as the family was breaking up under the pressure, she grasped at a broader loyalty: "Use 'ta be the fambly was fust. It ain't so now. It's anybody. Worse off we get, the more we got to do."

Among the most talented new young novelists emerging in the thirties was Richard Wright, a black writer born on a plantation near Natchez, Mississippi. The son of a matriarch whose husband deserted the family, Wright grew up in the course of moving from town to town, ended his formal schooling with the ninth grade (as valedictorian of his class), worked in Memphis, and greedily devoured books he borrowed on a white friend's library card, all the while saving up to go North to escape the racism of the segregated South. In Chicago, where he arrived on the eve of the depression, the Federal Writers' Project gave him a chance to perfect his talent. His period as a Communist from 1934 to 1944 gave him an intellectual framework that did not, however, overpower his fierce independence. His autobiographical *Black Boy* (1945) revealed in its rebellion against racial injustice his ties to the South, for, he wrote, "there had been slowly instilled into my personality and consciousness, black though I was, the culture of the South."

Native Son (1940), Wright's masterpiece, was set in the Chicago he had come to know before moving on to New York. It was the story of Bigger Thomas, a product of the black ghetto, a man hemmed in and finally impelled to murder by forces beyond his control. "They wouldn't let me live and I killed," he says unrepentently at the end. Somehow

Wright managed to sublimate into literary power his bitterness and rage at what he called "The Ethics of Living Jim Crow."

POPULAR CULTURE DURING THE DEPRESSION   While many of America's most talented writers and artists dealt directly with the human suffering and social tensions provoked by the Great Depression, the more popular cultural outlets such as radio programs and movies provided patrons with a welcome "escape" from the decade's grim realities.

By the 1930s, radio had become a major source of family entertainment. More than 10 million families owned a radio, and by the end of the decade the number had tripled. "There is radio music in the air, every night, everywhere," reported a San Francisco newspaper. "Anybody can hear it at home on a receiving set which any boy can put up in an hour."

Millions of housewives listened to radio "soap operas" during the day. The shows lasted fifteen minutes and derived their name from their sponsors, soap manufacturers. The recipe for a successful soap opera, noted one writer, was to provide "twelve minutes of dialogue, add predicament, villainy, and female suffering in equal measure, throw in a dash of nobility, sprinkle with tears, season with organ music, cover with a rich announcer sauce, and serve five times a week." The soap operas provided struggling people with distractions as well as a sense of comparative well-being. As one female listener explained, "I can get through the day better when I hear they have sorrows, too."

Late afternoon radio programs were directed at children home from school. In the evening after supper, families would gather around the radio to listen to newscasts, comedies such as *Amos 'n Andy* and the husband-and-wife team of George Burns and Gracie Allen, adventure dramas such as *Superman, Jack Armstrong, The Lone Ranger, Dick Tracy,* and *The Green Hornet,* and "big band" musical programs, all interspersed with commercials. On Sundays, most radio stations broadcast church services. Fans could also listen to baseball and football games or boxing matches. Franklin Roosevelt was the first president to take full advantage of the popularity of radio broadcasting. He hosted sixteen "fireside chats" to generate public support for his New Deal initiatives.

In the late 1920s, what had been "silent" films were transformed by the introduction of sound. The "talkies" made the movie industry by far the most popular form of entertainment during the 1930s—much more popular than today. The introduction of double features in 1931 and the construction of outdoor drive-in theaters in 1933 also boosted interest and attendance. More than 60 percent of the population—70 million people—saw at least one movie each week. Adults paid a quarter and children a dime for their tickets. "The immense influence of Hollywood in our national life," declared a writer in 1936, " . . . seems to be accepted as a matter of fact. Manners, clothes, speech, tastes, all are affected by the actors and actresses of the motion picture screen as they never were by the popular figures of the stage or by any of our popular idols."

Films of the 1930s rarely dealt directly with hard times. Exceptions were film versions of *Gone with the Wind* (1939) and *The Grapes of Wrath* (1940) and the classic documentaries by Pare Lorenz entitled *The River* (1937) and *The Plow That Broke the Plains* (1936). Much more common were movies intended for pure entertainment; they transported viewers into the realm of adventure, spectacle, and fantasy. People relished "shoot 'em up" gangster films, Walt Disney's animated cartoons, spectacular musicals, "screwball" comedies, and classic horror films such as *Dracula* (1931), *Frankenstein* (1931), *The Werewolf* (1932), and *The Mummy* (1932).

The appeal of gangster films perhaps reflected public sympathy with gritty characters determined to succeed whatever the consequences. *Little Caesar* (1930), *Public Enemy Number One* (1931), and *Scarface* (1932) portrayed the rise and fall of brutal mobsters and in the process made stars of "tough guys" Edward G. Robinson, James Cagney, and Paul Muni. Dozens of similar films followed.

By the time Roosevelt was inaugurated in 1933, theatrical dance musicals choreographed and directed by Busby Berkeley had also captured the popular imagination. Flamboyant, if inane, movie musicals such as *42nd Street* (1933), *The Gold Diggers* (1933), and *Dames* (1934) reinforced Roosevelt's upbeat assurance that "happy days are here again!" Berkeley used elaborate sets, multiple cameras, flocks of chorus girls, and huge orchestras to produce entertainment extravaganzas.

But the best way to escape the daily troubles of the depression was to watch one of the zany comedies perfected by the Marx Brothers, former vaudeville performers. As one Hollywood official explained, the movies during the 1930s were intended to "laugh the big bad wolf of the de-

Frankenstein. *Popular 1930s movies included the gangster, horror, and animation genres that provided the viewer with pure entertainment and often relieved them from the burdens of the Depression.*

pression out of the public mind." *Cocoanuts* (1929), *Animal Crackers* (1930), and *Monkey Business* (1931) introduced Americans to the anarchic antics of Chico, Groucho, Harpo, and Zeppo Marx. These madcap comedians combined slapstick humor with verbal wit to create plotless masterpieces filled with irreverent satire.

THE SECOND NEW DEAL

During Roosevelt's first year in office his programs and his personal charms aroused massive support. The president's travels and speeches, his twice-weekly press conferences, and his "fireside chats" over the radio generated vitality and warmth from a once-remote White House. In the congressional elections of 1934, the Democrats actually increased their strength in both the House and the Senate, an almost unprecedented midterm victory for the party in power. When it was over, only seven Republican governors remained in office throughout the country.

ELEANOR ROOSEVELT One of the reasons for Roosevelt's unprecedented popularity was his wife, Eleanor, who had increasingly become an enormous political asset and would prove to be one of the most influential and revered leaders of her time. From an early age, Eleanor had channeled her energies into social service. As a teen, she had volunteered in a New York settlement house, doing what she could to help the poor and suffering. As an adult, she remained ardently concerned about issues of human welfare and rights for women and blacks. Her compassion resulted in part from the loneliness she had experienced as she was growing up and in part from the sense of betrayal she had felt when she discovered in 1918 that her husband was engaged in an extramarital affair with Lucy Mercer, her personal secretary. "The bottom dropped out of my own particular world," she recalled. Upon learning of the affair, she had asked Franklin if he wanted a divorce. Absolutely not, he replied, in part because his mother threatened to disown him, and he promised Eleanor that he would end his relationship with Mercer (he did not).

In the face of personal setbacks, Eleanor Roosevelt "lived to be kind." Compassionate without being maudlin, more stoical than sentimental, she exuded warmth and sincerity, and she challenged the complacency of the comfortable and the affluent. "No woman," observed a friend, "has ever so comforted the distressed or so distressed the comfortable."

An intelligent, principled, and candid woman, First Lady Eleanor Roosevelt became a political figure in her own right. Here she is waving to delegates at the Democratic convention in 1940.

A Maine fisherman described her uniquely endearing qualities: "She ain't stuck up, she ain't dressed up, and she ain't afraid to talk."

After FDR's election, Eleanor could not be satisfied with the traditionally passive role of First Lady. She was an activist who redefined the role of presidential spouse. She was the first woman to address a national political convention, to write a nationally syndicated column, and to hold regular press conferences. One of her key functions was to keep the president from being isolated from the public. She served, he said, as his "eyes and ears," as well as his conscience, and she relished traveling around the country visiting with common people. Journalists dubbed her "Eleanor Everywhere."

A tireless advocate and agitator, Eleanor crisscrossed the nation, representing the president and the New Deal, defying local segregation ordinances to meet with black leaders, supporting women's causes, highlighting the plight of unemployed youth, and imploring Americans to live up to their egalitarian and humanitarian ideals. An opinionated and outspoken woman who occasionally used her syndicated column to criticize Franklin's policy decisions, she was especially forceful in prodding officials to ease racial discrimination in federal programs and housing.

Eleanor Roosevelt also became her husband's most visible and effective liaison with many liberal groups, bringing labor leaders, women activists, and black spokesmen into the White House after hours, and serving to deflect criticism of the president by taking progressive stands and running political risks he himself dared not. He was the politician, she once remarked, she was the agitator.

CRITICISM OF THE NEW DEAL Public criticism of the New Deal during 1933 was muted or reduced to helpless carping. But as the sense of crisis passed, the spirit of unity relaxed. The depression's downward slide had been halted, but unemployment remained high (10 million in 1935, more than 20 percent of the workforce) and prosperity remained elusive. Even more unsettling to some was the dramatic growth of executive power and the emergence of welfare capitalism, whereby workers developed a sense of entitlement to federal support programs. In 1934 a group of conservative businessmen and politicians, including Al Smith and John W. Davis, two previous Democratic presidential candidates, formed the American Liberty

League to oppose New Deal measures as violations of personal and property rights.

More potent threats to Roosevelt came from the hucksters of social panaceas, old and new. The most flamboyant of the group was Louisiana's "Kingfish," Senator Huey P. Long, Jr. A short, strutting man, Long sported pink suits and pastel shirts, red ties, and two-toned shoes. He seemed like a clown to some observers, and he loved to make people think he was a country bumpkin. But underneath all the carefully designed hoopla was a shrewd lawyer and consummate politician. First as Louisiana governor, then as political boss of the state, Long had delivered to its citizens tax favors, roads, schools, free textbooks, charity hospitals, and better public services. That he had become a sort of state dictator in the process, using bribery, physical intimidation, and blackmail to achieve his ends seemed irrelevant to many of his ardent supporters.

In 1933 Long joined Roosevelt in Washington as a Democratic senator. He initially supported the New Deal but quickly grew suspicious of the NRA's collusion with big business. He also had grown jealous of Roosevelt's mushrooming popularity, having himself developed aspirations for the Oval Office. Promoting himself as a radical egalitarian, a true, if self-indulgent, friend of the people, Long had his own plan for dealing with the Great Depression.

Long's Share Our Wealth program was tantalizingly generous and

The "Kingfish," Huey Long, governor of Louisiana.

simple. In one version he proposed to confiscate large personal fortunes, guarantee every family a cash grant of $5,000, every worker an annual income of $2,500, provide pensions to the aged, reduce working hours, pay veterans' bonuses, and assure a college education for every qualified student. It did not matter to him that his figures failed to add up or that his program offered little to promote an economic recovery. As he told a group of distressed Iowa farmers, "Maybe somebody says I don't understand it. Well, you don't have to. Just shut your damn eyes and believe it. That's all." Whether he had a workable plan or not, by early 1935 the charismatic Long was claiming 7.5 million supporters. He was also successful in arousing the concern and ire of the Roosevelt administration. Interior Secretary Harold Ickes growled that Long suffered from "halitosis of the intellect."

Another popular social scheme was hatched by a gray-haired California doctor, Francis E. Townsend. Outraged by the sight of three haggard old women raking through garbage cans in Long Beach, Townsend proposed government pensions for the aged. In 1934 he began promoting the Townsend Plan of paying $200 a month to every citizen over sixty who retired from employment and who promised to spend the money within the month. The plan had the lure of providing both financial security for the aged and job openings for the young. Critics noted that the cost of his program for 9 percent of the population would be more than half the national income. Yet Townsend was indifferent to such factors. "I'm not in the least interested in the cost of the plan," he blandly told a House committee.

A third huckster of panaceas, Father Charles E. Coughlin, the Roman Catholic "radio priest," founded the National Union for Social Justice in 1934. In broadcasts over the CBS network, he promoted schemes for the coinage of silver and made attacks on bankers that carried growing overtones of anti-Semitism.

Coughlin, Townsend, and Long drew support largely from desperate lower-middle-class Americans. Of the three, Long had the widest following. A 1935 survey showed that he could draw 5 to 6 million votes as a third-party candidate for president in 1936, perhaps enough to undermine Roosevelt's chances of reelection. Beset by pressures from both ends of the political spectrum, Roosevelt hesitated for months before deciding to "steal the thunder" from the left by instituting new programs of reform and social security. "I'm fighting Communism, Huey

Longism, Coughlinism, Townsendism," Roosevelt told a reporter in early 1935. He needed "to save our system, the capitalist system," from "crackpot ideas." Political pressures impelled Roosevelt to move left, but so did the growing influence within the administration of Supreme Court Justices Louis Brandeis and Felix Frankfurter. These powerful advisers urged Roosevelt to be less cozy with big business and to push for restored competition and heavy taxes on large corporations.

OPPOSITION FROM THE COURT   A series of Supreme Court decisions finally galvanized the president into action. On May 27, 1935, the Court killed the National Industrial Recovery Act by unanimous vote. In *Schechter Poultry Corporation* v. *United States,* quickly tagged the "sick chicken" case, the defendants had been convicted of selling an "unfit chicken" and violating other NRA code provisions. The high court ruled that Congress had delegated too much power to the executive branch when it granted the code-making authority to the NRA, and Congress had exceeded its power under the commerce clause by regulating *intrastate* commerce. The poultry in question, the Court decided, had "come to permanent rest within the state," although it earlier had been moved across state lines. In a press conference soon afterward, Roosevelt fumed: "We have been relegated to the horse-and-buggy definition of interstate commerce." The same line of reasoning, he warned, might endanger other New Deal programs.

LEGISLATIVE ACHIEVEMENTS OF THE SECOND NEW DEAL   To rescue his legislative program from such judicial and political challenges, Roosevelt in 1935 ended the stalemate in Congress and launched the so-called Second New Deal. He demanded several pieces of "must" legislation, most of which were already pending. During the next two months, Congress passed another cluster of significant—and quite controversial—legislation.

The National Labor Relations Act, often called the Wagner Act for its sponsor, New York senator Robert Wagner, gave workers the right to bargain through unions of their own choice and prohibited employers from interfering with union activities. A National Labor Relations Board of five members could supervise plant elections and certify unions as bargaining agents where a majority of the workers approved. The board could also investigate the actions of employers and issue "cease and desist" orders against specified unfair practices.

The Social Security Act of 1935, Roosevelt announced, was the New Deal's "cornerstone" and "supreme achievement." Indeed, it has proven to be the most significant and far-reaching of all the New Deal initiatives. The concept was by no means new. Progressives during the early 1900s had proposed a federal system of social security for the aged, indigent, disabled, and unemployed. Other nations had already enacted such programs, but the United States remained steadfast to its tradition of individual self-reliance. The Great Depression, however, revived the idea, and Roosevelt masterfully guided the legislation through Congress.

The Social Security Act included three major provisions. Its centerpiece was a pension fund for retired people over the age of sixty-five and their survivors. Beginning in 1937, workers and employers contributed payroll taxes to establish the fund. Benefit payments started in 1940 and averaged $22 per month, a quite modest sum even for those depressed times. Roosevelt knew this, and he stressed that the pension program was not intended to guarantee a comfortable retirement; it was

"Yes, You Remembered Me."
The social legislation of the Second New Deal prompted this depiction of FDR as the friend of "The Forgotten Man."

designed to supplement other sources of income and protect the elderly from some of the "hazards and vicissitudes of life." Only later did American voters and politicians come to perceive Social Security as the *primary* source of retirement income for most of the aged. By 1998, the average monthly payment was about $1,000.

The Social Security Act also set up a shared federal-state unemployment insurance program, financed by a payroll tax on employers. In addition, the new legislation committed the national government to a broad range of social welfare activities based on the assumption that "unemployables"—people who were unable to work—would remain a state responsibility, while the national government would provide work relief for the able-bodied. To that end, the law inaugurated federal grants-in-aid for three state-administered public assistance programs—old age assistance, aid for dependent children, aid for the blind—and further aid for maternal, child welfare, and public health services.

Relatively speaking, the new federal program was quite conservative. It was the only government pension program in the world financed by taxes on the earnings of current workers. Most other countries funded such programs out of general revenues. The Social Security payroll tax was also a regressive tax in that it entailed a single fixed rate for all, regardless of income level. It thus hurt the poor more than the rich, and it also hurt Roosevelt's efforts to revive the economy because it removed from circulation a significant amount of money. The new Social Security tax took money out of workers' pockets and placed it into a trust fund, thus exacerbating the shrinking money supply that was one of the main causes of the depression. By taking discretionary income away from workers, the government blunted the sharp increase in public consumption needed to restore the health of the economy. In addition, the Social Security system initially excluded 9.5 million workers who needed it the most: farm laborers, domestic servants, and the self-employed, a disproportionate percentage of whom were black.

Roosevelt recognized and regretted such limitations, but he knew that they were necessary compromises in order to see the Social Security Act through Congress and to enable it to withstand court challenges. As he replied to an aide who criticized funding the pension program through employee contributions, "I guess you're right on the economics, but those taxes were never a problem of economics. They are politics all the way through. We put those payroll contributions there so as to give the contributors a moral, legal, and political right to collect their pensions and their unemployment benefits. With those taxes in there, no damn politician can ever scrap my Social Security program."

The last of the major bills making up the "Second New Deal" was the Revenue Act of 1935, sometimes called the Wealth Tax Act, but popularly known as the "Soak-the-Rich" tax. The Revenue Act raised tax rates on incomes above $50,000. Estate and gift taxes also rose, as did the corporate tax on all but small corporations (those with less than $50,000 annual income).

Business leaders fumed over Roosevelt's tax and spending policies. The wealthy resented their loss of status and the growing power of government and labor. They railed against the New Deal and Roosevelt, whom they called "a traitor to his own class." Visitors at the home of J. P. Morgan, Jr., were cautioned not to mention Roosevelt's name lest it raise his blood pressure.

By "soaking" the rich, Roosevelt stole much of the thunder from the political left, as he claimed, although the results fell short of the promise. The new "soak the rich" tax failed to increase federal revenue significantly, nor did it result in a significant redistribution of income. Still, the prevailing view was that Roosevelt had moved in a radical direction. Newspaper editor William Randolph Hearst growled that the Wealth Tax was "essentially communism. This bastard proposal should be ascribed to a composite personality which might be labeled Stalin Delano Roosevelt."

The extent of the new departure taken by the Second New Deal is easy to exaggerate. Such measures as Social Security, utility regulation, and higher taxes on the wealthy had long been in the works in Congress and had already been adopted by most other industrial nations. Roosevelt himself stressed his own basic conservatism and asserted that he had no love for socialism. "I am fighting communism. . . . I want to save our system, the capitalistic system." Yet he added that to save it from revolutionary turmoil required a more equal "distribution of wealth."

ROOSEVELT'S SECOND TERM

THE 1936 ELECTION   The popularity of Roosevelt and the New Deal impelled the Republican convention in 1936 to avoid candidates too closely identified with the "hate-Roosevelt" contingent. The party chose Governor Alfred M. Landon of Kansas, a former Bull Moose Progressive. A fiscal conservative, Landon had nevertheless endorsed many New Deal programs. He was probably more liberal than most of his backers, and clearly more so than the party's platform, which accused the New Deal of usurping power.

The Republicans hoped that the followers of Long, Coughlin, Townsend, and other dissidents would combine to draw enough votes away from Roosevelt to throw the election to them. But that possibility faded when an assassin, the son-in-law of a Louisiana judge whom Long had sought to remove, gunned down the "Kingfish" in 1935. Coughlin, Townsend, and a remnant of the Long movement supported Representative William Lemke of North Dakota on a Union party ticket, but it was a forlorn effort that polled only 882,000 votes.

In 1936 Roosevelt forged a new electoral coalition that would affect national politics for years to come. While holding the support of most traditional Democrats North and South, FDR made strong gains among beneficiaries of the AAA farm program in the West. In the northern cities, he held on to the ethnic groups helped by New Deal welfare measures and afforded greater recognition in government appointments. Middle-class voters, whose property had been saved by New Deal measures, flocked to Roosevelt's support, along with intellectuals stirred by the ferment of new governmental ideas. The revived labor movement threw its support to Roosevelt, and in the most profound new departure of all, black voters for the first time cast the majority of their ballots for a Democratic president. "My friends, go home and turn Lincoln's picture to the wall," a black Pittsburgh journalist told black Republicans. "That debt has been paid in full." The final vote tally revealed that 81 percent of those with incomes under a thousand dollars a year opted for Roosevelt, as did 79 percent of those earning one to two thousand dollars. By contrast, only 46 percent of those earning five thousand dollars voted for FDR.

In his acceptance speech to the Democratic convention, Roosevelt dropped efforts to reassure corporate leaders. As the Americans of 1776 had sought freedom from political autocracy, he noted, the Americans of 1936 sought freedom from the "economic royalists." Roosevelt campaigned with tremendous buoyancy, and he wound up carrying every state except Maine and Vermont, with a popular vote of 27.7 million to

Landon's 16.7 million. Democrats would also dominate Republicans in the new Congress, by 77 to 19 in the Senate and 328 to 107 in the House.

THE COURT-PACKING PLAN   Soon after his reelection, Roosevelt found himself deluged in a sea of troubles. His second inaugural address, delivered on January 20, 1937, suggested that he was ready to move toward even greater reforms. The challenge to American democracy, he maintained, was that millions of citizens "at this very moment are denied the greater part of what the very lowest standards of today call the necessities of life. . . . I see one-third of a nation ill-housed, ill-clad, ill-nourished." The election of 1936 had been a mandate for even more extensive governmental action, he argued, and the overwhelming Democratic majorities in Congress ensured their passage. But one major roadblock stood in the way: the Supreme Court.

By the end of the 1936 term, the Court had ruled against New Deal laws in seven of the nine major cases it reviewed. Suits against the Social Security and Wagner Labor Relations Acts were also pending. Given the established trend of rulings, the Second New Deal seemed in danger of being nullified like the first.

For that reason, Roosevelt resolved to change the Court's philosophy by enlarging it, a move for which there was ample precedent and power. Congress, not the Constitution, determines the size of the Court, which at different times had numbered six, seven, nine, and ten justices, and in 1937 numbered nine. On February 5 Roosevelt sent his plan to Congress, without having consulted congressional leaders. He wanted to create up to fifty new federal judges, including six new Supreme Court justices, and to diminish the power of the judges who had served ten or more years or reached the age of seventy.

But the "court-packing" maneuver, as opponents quickly tagged it, backfired on Roosevelt. It was a shade too contrived, much too brazen, and far too political. By implying that some judges were impaired by senility, Roosevelt affronted the elder statesmen of Congress and the Court, especially Justice Louis D. Brandeis, who was both the oldest and the most liberal of the Supreme Court judges. It also ran headlong into a deep-rooted public veneration of the courts and aroused fears that another president might use the precedent for quite different purposes.

As it turned out, unforeseen events blunted Roosevelt's drive to change the Court. A sequence of Court decisions during the spring of 1937 reversed previous judgments in order to uphold the Wagner Act and the Social Security Act. In addition, a conservative justice resigned, and Roosevelt named to the vacancy one of the most consistent New Dealers, Senator Hugo Black of Alabama.

Roosevelt later claimed he had lost the battle but won the war. The Court had reversed itself on important New Deal legislation, and Roosevelt was able to appoint justices in harmony with the New Deal. But the episode created dissension in his party and blighted Roosevelt's prestige. For the first time, Democrats in large numbers deserted the "champ," and the Republican opposition found a powerful issue. During the first eight months of 1937, the momentum of Roosevelt's great 1936 victory was lost. As Henry Wallace later remarked, "The whole New Deal really went up in smoke as a result of the Supreme Court fight."

A NEW DIRECTION FOR LABOR   Rebellions meanwhile erupted on other fronts. Under the impetus of the New Deal, the labor movement stirred anew. John L. Lewis rebuilt the United Mine Workers from 150,000 members to 500,000 within a year. Spurred by the mine workers' example, Sidney Hillman of the Amalgamated Clothing Workers and David Dubinsky of the International Ladies Garment Workers joined Lewis in promoting a campaign to organize workers in the mass-production industries. As leaders of some of the few industrial unions (made up of all workers) in the American Federation of Labor (AFL), they found the smaller, more restrictive, craft unions (made up of male workers, with each limited to a single skilled trade) to be obstacles to organizing the basic industries.

In 1934 these leaders persuaded the AFL and its president William Green to charter "industrial unions" in the unorganized industries. But Green and other craft unionists saw these "federal" unions as temporary pools from which to draw members into the crafts. Lewis and the industrial unionists saw them as a chance to organize on a massive scale. In 1935, with passage of the Wagner Act, action began in earnest. The industrial unionists formed a Committee for Industrial Organization (CIO), and craft unionists began to fear submergence by the mass unions. Jurisdictional disputes spread among the unions, and in 1936 the AFL expelled the CIO unions, which then formed a permanent structure called after 1938 the Congress of Industrial Organizations. The rivalry spurred both groups to greater unionizing efforts.

The CIO's major organizing drives in the automobile and steel industries began in 1936, but they were thwarted by management's use of blacklisting, private detectives, labor spies, vigilante groups, and intimidation. Early in 1937 automobile workers spontaneously adopted a new technique, the "sit-down strike," in which workers refused to leave the shop until employers granted collective bargaining rights.

Led by the fiery young autoworker and union organizer Walter Reuther, thousands of employees at General Motors' assembly plants in Flint, Michigan, occupied the factories and stopped all production. Women workers supported their male counterparts by picketing at the plant entrances. The wives, daughters, and mothers of the strikers formed a Women's Auxiliary to feed the workers who slept at the plants. Management refused to recognize the union efforts. Company officials called in police to harass the strikers, sent spies to union meetings, and threatened to fire the workers. They also pleaded with Roosevelt to dispatch federal troops. He refused, while at the same time expressing his displeasure with the sit-down strike. The standoff lasted over a month. Then, on February 11, the company relented and signed a contract recognizing the United Auto Workers (UAW). Other automotive companies soon followed suit. And the following month, United States Steel capitulated to the Steel Workers Organizing Committee (later the United Steelworkers of America), granting it recognition, a 10 percent wage hike, and a forty-hour workweek.

Having captured two giants of heavy industry, the CIO went on in the next few years to organize much of industrial America: rubber, oil, electronics, and a good part of the textile industry, in which unionists had to fight protracted struggles to organize scattered plants. The slow pace of labor organizing in textiles denied the CIO a major victory in the South comparable to its swift conquest of autos and steel in the North, but even down South a labor movement appeared that was at last something more than a vehicle for sporadic revolt. Union membership in the United States grew from under 3 million in 1933 to 8.5 million in 1940.

A SLUMPING ECONOMY   The years 1935 and 1936 had seen steady economic improvement, achieved largely through government spending. On top of relief and public-works outlays, Congress in 1936 provided cash payments of veterans' bonuses upon demand. By the spring of 1937, economic output had moved above the 1929 level. But worried about deficits and rising inflation, Roosevelt now decided to order sharp cuts in federal spending. At the same time, the Treasury began to reduce disposable income by collecting $2 billion in Social Security from employee paychecks. Private spending could not fill the gap left by reductions in government spending, and big business still lacked the faith to risk large investments.

The result was the slump of 1937, which was sharper than that of 1929 but which the press called a "recession" to distinguish it from the "depression." By the end of 1937, an additional 4 million people had been thrown out of work; grim scenes of the earlier depression reappeared. Secretary of the Interior Harold Ickes noted in his diary that Roosevelt "is plainly worried. It looks to me as if all the courage has oozed out of the President. He has let things drift. There is no fight and no leadership."

The recession provoked a fierce debate within the administration. One group, led by Treasury Secretary Henry Morgenthau, Jr., favored less federal spending and a balanced budget. The other group, which included Harry Hopkins and Harold Ickes, argued for renewed government spending and stricter enforcement of antitrust laws.

ECONOMIC POLICY AND LATE REFORMS   Roosevelt seemed bewildered by the recession, but he eventually endorsed the ideas of the spenders. In the spring of 1938, he asked Congress to adopt a large-scale spending program intended to increase mass purchasing power, and Congress voted almost $3.3 billion, mainly for public works. In a short time, the increase in spending reversed the economy's decline, but the recession and Roosevelt's reluctance to adopt massive, sustained government spending forestalled the achievement of full recovery. Only the massive and prolonged crisis of World War II would return the American economy to full production and full employment.

The 1937 recession helped further erode Roosevelt's prestige and dissipate the mandate of the 1936 elections. Only a few major new reforms were enacted for the benefit of the "ill-housed, ill-fed, and ill-clad." They included the Wagner-Steagall National Housing Act, the Bankhead-Jones Farm Tenant Act, and the Fair Labor Standards Act.

The Housing Act set up the United States Housing Authority (USHA) in the Department of the Interior, which extended long-term loans to local agencies willing to assume part of the cost for slum clearance and public housing. The agency also subsidized rents for low-income residents.

Congress in 1937 also passed the Farm Tenant Act, administered by a new agency, the Farm Security Administration (FSA). The program made available loans to prevent marginal farmers from sinking into tenancy. It also offered loans to tenants to help them purchase their own farms. But the idea of small homesteads by the late 1930s was doomed to failure. American mythology still exalted the family farm, but in reality the ever-larger agricultural unit predominated. In the end the FSA proved to be little more than another relief operation that tided a few farmers over difficult times. A more effective answer to the problem, sadly, awaited mobilization for war, which took many tenants off into the military services or defense industries, broadened their horizons, and taught them new skills that enabled them to leave the farm altogether.

The Fair Labor Standards Act of 1938 applied to employees in enterprises that operated in or affected interstate commerce. It set a minimum wage of 40¢ an hour and a maximum workweek of forty hours, to be put into effect over several years. The act also prohibited child labor under the age of sixteen, and in hazardous occupations under eighteen. Southern congressmen howled in opposition to the bill because it would have the effect of raising wages in their region and thus increasing employers' expenses.

THE LEGACY OF THE NEW DEAL

SETBACKS FOR THE PRESIDENT Although critics were unable to defeat the Fair Labor Standards Act, their stiff resistance revealed that an effective opposition to the New Deal was emerging within the president's own party, especially in the southern wing. Southern Democrats were at best uneasy bedfellows with organized labor and blacks, and more and more of them drifted toward closer cooperation with conservative Republicans. By the end of 1937, a formidable anti–New Deal bloc had developed.

In 1938 the bipartisan conservative opposition stymied a bill granting Roosevelt authority to reorganize the executive branch amid cries that it would lead to dictatorship. The House of Representatives also set up a Committee on Un-American Activities chaired by Martin Dies of Texas. Dies launched a crusade against Communists, and soon he began to brand New Dealers as Red dupes. "Stalin baited his hook with a 'progressive' worm," Dies wrote in 1940, "and New Deal suckers swallowed bait, hook, line, and sinker."

As the political season of 1938 advanced, Roosevelt unfolded a new idea as momentous as his Court-packing plan—a proposal to reshape the Democratic party in the image of the New Deal. He announced his purpose to campaign in Democratic primaries as the party leader, "charged with the responsibility of carrying out the definitely liberal declaration of principles set forth in the 1936 Democratic platform." He wanted his own supporters nominated. Instead of succeeding, however, the effort to shape the elections backfired and broke the spell of presidential invincibility, or what was left of it. As in the Court fight, Roosevelt had risked his prestige while handing his adversaries persuasive issues. His opponents tagged his intervention in the primaries an attempted "purge"; the word evoked visions of Adolf Hitler and Joseph Stalin, tyrants who had purged their Nazi and Communist parties in blood.

The elections of November 1938 handed the administration another setback, a result caused in part by the friction among Democrats. Their majority in the House fell from 229 to 93, in the Senate from 56 to 42. The margins remained large, but the president headed an increasingly divided party. In his State of the Union message in 1939, Roosevelt for the first time proposed no new reforms, but he spoke of the need "to *preserve* our reforms." Roosevelt did manage, however, to put through his plan to reorganize the executive branch. Under the Administrative Reorganization Act of 1939, the president could "reduce, coordinate, consolidate, and reorganize" the agencies of government. With that, Roosevelt's domestic innovations feebly ended.

A HALFWAY REVOLUTION   The New Deal had lost momentum, but it had wrought several enduring changes. By the end of the 1930s, the power of the national government was vastly enlarged over what it had been in 1932, and hope had been restored to people who had grown fatalistic. But the New Deal entailed more than just bigger government and revived public confidence. It also constituted a significant change from the older liberalism embodied in the progressivism of Theodore Roosevelt and Woodrow Wilson. Those earlier reformers, despite their sharp differences, had assumed that the function of progressive government in the American republic was to ensure through aggressive regulation that the people had equal opportunity to pursue their notions of happiness.

Franklin Roosevelt and the New Dealers went beyond this regulatory-state concept by insisting that the government should not simply *respond* to social crises but take positive steps to *avoid* them. To this end, the New Deal's various welfare and benefit programs conferred on government the responsibility to ensure a minimum level of well-being for all Americans. The New Deal had established minimum qualitative standards for labor conditions and public welfare and helped middle-class Americans hold on to their savings, their homes, and their farms. The protection afforded by bank deposit insurance, unemployment pay, and Social Security pensions would come to be universally accepted as a safeguard against future depressions.

The old progressive formulation of regulation versus trust-busting was now superseded by the rise of the "broker state," a powerful federal government that mediated among major interest groups. Government's role was to act as an honest broker protecting a variety of interests, not just business but workers, farmers, consumers, small business, and the unemployed.

In implementing his domestic program, Roosevelt steered a zigzag course between the extremes of laissez-faire capitalism and socialism. The first New Deal had experimented for a time with a managed economy under the NRA, but had abandoned that experiment for a turn toward enforcing competition and priming the economy with increased government spending. This finally produced full employment during World War II.

Roosevelt himself, impatient with political theory, was indeed a pragmatist in developing policy: he kept what worked and discarded what did not. The result was, paradoxically, both profoundly revolutionary and profoundly conservative. Roosevelt sharply increased the regulatory functions of the federal government and laid the foundation for what would become an expanding welfare state. But despite what his critics charged, his initiatives fell far short of socialism; they left the basic cap-italistic structure in place. In the process of such bold experimentation and dynamic preservation, the New Deal represented a "halfway revolu-tion" that permanently altered the social and political agenda.

MAKING CONNECTIONS

- In the mid-1930s, just as Roosevelt was getting the New Deal into place, the growing conflict in Europe began to assume more and more of his (and America's) attention; Chapter 28 shows how Roosevelt went from combating the depression to leading the United States into World War II.

- Harry Truman, Roosevelt's successor in the White House, tried unsuccessfully to expand the idea of the New Deal into new areas (national health insurance and federal aid to education, for example), topics covered in Chapter 30.

FURTHER READING

The best recent interpretive survey of the 1930s is David M. Kennedy's *Freedom from Fear: The American People in Depression and War, 1929–1945* (1999). An engaging introduction to the decade of the New Deal is Anthony J. Badger's *The New Deal: The Depression Years, 1933–1940* (1989). Van L. Perkins's *Crisis in Agriculture* (1969) and Sidney Baldwin's *Poverty and Politics: The Rise and Decline of the Farm Security Administration* (1969) look at agricultural reforms. Michael E. Parrish's *Securities Regulation and the New Deal* (1970) and Ellis W. Hawley's *The New Deal and the Problem of Monopoly: A Study in Economic Ambivalence* (1966) analyze government attempts to forestall an-other market crash.

Alan Brinkley's *The End of Reform: New Deal Liberalism in Recession and War* (1995) suggests that the New Deal reformers did not go far enough in their efforts to curb big business. Bernard Bellush's *The Failure of the NRA* (1977) studies government relations with business. William R. Brock's *Welfare, Democracy, and the New Deal* (1988) describes the development of welfare policy.

For scholarship about the various groups involved in the New Deal, consult Lois Scharf's *To Work and to Wed: Female Employment, Feminism, and the Great Depression* (1980), on women; Nancy J. Weiss's *Farewell to the Party of Lincoln: Black Politics in the Age of FDR* (1983) and Harvard Sitkoff's *A New Deal for Blacks* (1978), on blacks; and John M. Allswang's *A House of All Peoples: Ethnic Politics in Chicago, 1890–1936* (1971), on immigrants. On Roosevelt's prominent wife, see Blanche Wiesen Cook's *Eleanor Roosevelt* (2 vols.; 1998–1999).

Works on the critics of the New Deal include T. Harry Williams's *Huey Long* (1969) and Alan Brinkley's *Voices of Protest: Huey Long, Father Coughlin, and the Great Depression* (1982). For leftist reactions to reform, see Harvey Klehr's *The Heyday of American Communism: The Depression Decade* (1984) and David Shannon's *The Socialist Party of America* (1955).

One interest group that both supported and criticized New Deal policies was organized labor. See Sidney Fine's *Sit-down: The General Motors Strike of 1936–1937* (1969) and Lizabeth Cohen's *Making a New Deal: Industrial Workers in Chicago, 1919–1939* (1990).

The most complete introduction to the New Deal in the South remains the relevant chapters in George B. Tindall's *The Emergence of the New South, 1913–1945* (1967). How southern farmers fared is examined in David E. Conrad's *The Forgotten Farmers: The Story of the Sharecroppers in the New Deal* (1965). Dan T. Carter provides an insightful analysis of the influence of reform on race relations in the 1930s in his *Scottsboro: A Tragedy of the American South* (1969).

James M. Gregory's *American Exodus: The Dust Bowl Migration and Okie Culture in California* (1989) describes the migratory movement's effect on American culture. For the cultural impact of the New Deal, consult Richard H. Pells's *Radical Visions and American Dreams: Cultural and Social Thought in the Depression Years* (1973) and Richard D. McKinzie's *The New Deal for Artists* (1973). The best analysis of the end of the New Deal is Alan Brinkley's *The End of Reform: New Deal Liberalism in Recession and War* (1995).

28 ∞ FROM ISOLATION
TO GLOBAL WAR

CHAPTER ORGANIZER

This chapter focuses on:

- isolationism and peace movements between the two World Wars.

- America's response to German aggression in Europe.

- how events in Asia led to Japan's attack on Pearl Harbor and America's entry into the global war.

*I*n the late 1930s the winds of war swept across Asia and Europe, abruptly shifting the focus of American politics from domestic to foreign affairs. Another Democratic president had to turn his attention from social and economic reform to military preparedness and war. And the public again had to wrestle with the painful choice between involving the country in volatile world affairs or remaining aloof and officially neutral.

POSTWAR ISOLATIONISM

THE LEAGUE AND THE UNITED STATES Between Woodrow Wilson and Franklin Roosevelt lay two decades of relative isolation from foreign entanglements. The postwar mood of 1920 set the pattern. The voters expressed their resistance to international commitments, and President-elect Harding lost little time in disposing of American membership in the League of Nations. The spirit of isolation found other expressions as well: the higher tariff walls, the Red Scare, the rage for "100 percent Americanism," and restrictive immigration laws by which the nation all but shut the door to any more newcomers.

The United States may have felt the urge to insulate itself from a wicked world, but it could hardly stop the world and get off. American business, despite the tariff walls, now had worldwide connections. Investments and loans abroad put in circulation the dollars that purchased American exports. America's overseas possessions, moreover, directly involved the country in world affairs, especially in the Pacific. Even the League of Nations was too great an organization to ignore entirely. After 1924 the United States gradually entered into joint efforts with the League on such matters as policing the international trade in drugs and arms, and on a variety of economic, cultural, and technical conferences.

WAR DEBTS AND REPARATIONS   Probably nothing did more to heighten American isolationism during the 1920s and 1930s—or anti-American feeling in Europe—than the war-debt tangle. When in 1917 the Allies had begun to exhaust their sources of private credit in the United States, the American government advanced them funds, first for the war effort and then for postwar reconstruction. To Americans the repayment of the war debts seemed a simple matter of obligation, but Europeans commonly had a different perception.

The French and British insisted that they could pay America only as they collected reparations from defeated Germany. Twice during the 1920s the resulting strain on Germany brought the structure of international payments to the verge of collapse, and both times the Reparations Commission called in American bankers to work out rescue plans.

The whole structure finally did collapse during the Great Depression. In 1931 President Hoover negotiated a moratorium on both German reparations and Allied payment of war debts. At the end of 1932, after Hoover's debt moratorium ended, most of the European countries defaulted on their war debts to the United States. In retaliation, Congress passed the Johnson Debt Default Act of 1934, which prohibited private loans to any such government.

ATTEMPTS AT DISARMAMENT   Yet for all the isolationist senti- ment of the time, Wilsonian internationalism persisted during the 1920s and after. A lingering doubt, tinged with guilt, haunted many Americans about their rejection of the League of Nations. Before long the Harding administration hit upon a happy substitute—disarmament. The conviction had grown after World War I that the armaments race had caused the war, and that arms limitation would therefore bring last- ing peace. The United States had no intention of maintaining a large army, but under the naval building program begun in 1916, it had con- structed a fleet second only to that of Britain.

Neither the British nor the Americans relished a naval armaments race, but both shared a common concern about the alarming growth of Japanese military power. Since 1914 Japanese-American relations had grown increasingly strained, as the United States objected to continued Japanese encroachments in Asia. During World War I, Japan had quickly taken China's Shantung Peninsula and the islands of Microne- sia from its enemy, Germany. In 1917, after the United States entered the war, Viscount Kikujiro Ishii visited Washington to secure American recognition of Japan's expanded position in Asia, dropping hints that Germany had several times tried to get Japan to quit the war. To fore- stall the loss of an ally in the war, Secretary of State Robert Lansing signed an ambiguous agreement saying that "Japan has special interests in China." Americans were unhappy with the Lansing-Ishii Agreement, but it was viewed as the only way to keep Japan in the war.

After the war ended, Japanese-American relations grew more tense. To address the problem, President Warren Harding invited countries to an armaments conference at which Pacific and East Asian affairs would also be discussed. The Washington Armaments Conference of 1921 opened with a surprise announcement by the American secretary of state, Charles Evans Hughes, who told the delegates that "the way to disarm is to disarm." It was one of the most dramatic moments in Amer- ican diplomatic history. In less than fifteen minutes, one reporter said, Hughes had destroyed more tonnage "than all the admirals of the world have sunk in a cycle of centuries."

Delegates from the United States, Britain, Japan, France, and Italy

The Washington Armaments Conference, *1921. The Big Five at the confer-ence were* (from left): *Prince Tekugawa (Japan), Arthur Balfour (Great Britain), Charles Evans Hughes (United States), M. Briand (France), and H. E. Carlo Sanchez (Italy).*

signed a Five-Power Naval Treaty (1922) incorporating Hughes's plan for tonnage limits and a moratorium of ten years during which no bat-tleships would be built. These powers also agreed to refrain from fur-ther fortification of their Pacific possessions. The agreement in effect partitioned the world: United States naval power became supreme in the Western Hemisphere, Japanese power in the western Pacific, British power from the North Sea to Singapore.

Two other major agreements emerged from the Washington Confer-ence. With the Four-Power Treaty, the United States, Britain, Japan, and France agreed to respect each other's possessions in the Pacific and to refer any disputes or any outside threat to consultation. The Nine-Power Treaty for the first time formally pledged the signers to support the principle of the Open Door enunciated by Secretary of State John Hay at the turn of the century. The Open Door enabled all nations to compete for trade and investment opportunities in China on an equal footing rather than allow individual nations to create economic monop-olies in particular regions of that country. The signers of the Nine-Power Treaty also promised to respect the territorial integrity of China. The powers, in addition to those signing the Five-Power Treaty, were China, Belgium, Portugal, and the Netherlands.

With these agreements in hand, President Harding's supporters could boast of a brilliant diplomatic stroke that relieved American tax-payers of the need to pay for an enlarged navy and that defused potential conflicts in the Pacific. Yet the agreements were uniformly without obligation and without teeth. The signers of the Four-Power Treaty agreed only to consult, not to help each other. The formal endorsement of the Open Door in the Nine-Power Treaty was just as ineffective, for the United States remained unwilling to use force to uphold the principle. Moreover, the naval disarmament treaty set limits only on battle-ships; the race to build cruisers, destroyers, submarines, and other smaller craft continued.

THE KELLOGG-BRIAND PACT   During and after World War I, the fanciful ideal of simply abolishing war altogether seized the American imagination. Peace societies thrived, and the glorious vision of ending war by the stroke of a pen culminated in the Kellogg-Briand Pact of 1928. This unique treaty originated when French foreign minister Aristide Briand proposed to Coolidge's secretary of state, Frank B. Kellogg, an agreement that the two countries would never go to war with each other. Kellogg countered with a scheme to have all nations sign the pact, an idea all the more acceptable to peace organizations.

The Pact of Paris (its official name) solemnly declared that the signatories "condemn recourse to war . . . and renounce it as an instrument of national policy." Eventually sixty-two powers joined the pact, but all explicitly or tacitly reserved "self-defense" as an escape hatch. The United States Senate included a reservation declaring the Monroe Doctrine necessary to America's self-defense, and then ratified the agreement by a vote of 85 to 1. A Virginia senator who voted for "this worthless, but perfectly harmless peace treaty" wrote a friend that he feared it would "confuse the minds of many good people who think that peace may be secured by polite professions of neighborly and brotherly love."

THE "GOOD NEIGHBOR" POLICY   In Latin America the spirit of peace and noninvolvement helped allay resentments against the United States, which had freely intervened in the Caribbean during the first two decades of the century. In 1924 American marines left the Dominican Republic after an eight-year occupation. American troops left Nicaragua a year later, but returned in 1926 with the outbreak of disorder and civil war. In 1927 the Coolidge administration negotiated an agreement for American-supervised elections, but one rebel leader, César Augusto Sandino, held out, and the U.S. marines stayed until 1933. The unhappy legacies of this intervention were public bitterness toward the United States and a Nicaraguan National Guard, created to keep order after the marines left, but used in 1936 to set up the dictatorship of Anastasio Somoza.

The troubles in Nicaragua increased strains with Mexico. Relations were already threatened by repeated Mexican threats to take over American oil properties. In 1928, however, the American ambassador to Mexico negotiated an agreement protecting American economic rights. It lasted until 1938, when the Mexican government expropriated U.S.-owned properties, promising to reimburse American owners.

In 1928 President-elect Hoover improved America's image in Latin America by permitting publication of a memorandum that denied that the Monroe Doctrine justified American intervention in Latin America. It stopped short of repudiating intervention on any grounds, but that fine point hardly blunted the celebration in Latin America. Although Hoover never endorsed this so-called Clark Memorandum, he never ordered American military intervention in the region. Before he left office, steps had already been taken to withdraw American forces from Nicaragua and Haiti.

Franklin D. Roosevelt likewise embraced "the policy of the good neighbor" and soon advanced it in practice. In 1933 at the Seventh Pan-American Conference, the United States supported a resolution that affirmed: "No state has the right to intervene in the internal or external affairs of another." Under Roosevelt the marines completed their withdrawals from Nicaragua and Haiti, and in 1934 the president negotiated with Cuba a treaty that abrogated the Platt Amendment (1901), which had given America a formal right to intervene in Cuba.

WAR CLOUDS

JAPANESE INCURSIONS IN CHINA The lessening of irritants in the Western Hemisphere during the 1930s proved an exception in an otherwise dismal world scene, as war clouds darkened over Europe and Asia. Actual conflict erupted first in Asia, where unsettled social and political conditions in China had attracted foreign encroachments since before the turn of the century. In 1929 Chinese nationalist aspirations and China's subsequent clashes with Russia convinced the Japanese that their own extensive rights in Manchuria, including the South Manchurian Railway, were in danger.

Japanese military occupation of Manchuria began with the Mukden Incident of 1931, when an explosion destroyed a section of railway track near that city. The Japanese "Kwantung Army," based in Manchuria to guard the railway, blamed the incident on the Chinese and used it as a pretext to begin its occupation, which it extended during the winter of 1931–1932 to all of Manchuria. In 1932 the Japanese converted Manchuria into the puppet empire of "Manchukuo."

The Manchuria Incident, as the Japanese called their undeclared war, flagrantly violated the Nine-Power Treaty, the Kellogg-Briand Pact, and Japan's pledges as a member of the League of Nations. But when China asked the League and the United States for help, neither obliged. President Herbert Hoover refused to invoke either military or economic sanctions.

In early 1932, Japan's indiscriminate bombing of civilians in Shanghai, China's great port city, aroused Western indignation, but provoked no action. When the League of Nations condemned Japanese aggression in 1933, Japan withdrew from the League. Thereafter, hostilities in Manchuria gradually subsided and ended with a truce. An uneasy peace settled upon East Asia for four years, during which time Japan's military leaders further extended their political sway at home.

ITALY AND GERMANY   The rise of the Japanese militarists paralleled the rise of warlike dictators in Italy and Germany. In 1922 Benito Mussolini had seized power in Italy after organizing the fascist movement, which was based on a composite of superheated nationalism and socialism. The party's program, and above all Mussolini's promise to restore order and pride in a country fragmented by dissension and self-doubts, enjoyed a wide appeal. Once in power, Mussolini largely abandoned the socialist part of his platform and gradually suppressed all opposition. By 1925 he wielded dictatorial power as Il Duce (the leader).

There was always something ludicrous about the strutting Mussolini. Italy, after all, was a minor European power. But Germany was another matter, and most Americans were not amused, even at the beginning, by Il Duce's counterpart, Adolf Hitler. Hitler's National Socialist (Nazi) party duplicated the major features of Italian fascism, including the ancient Roman salute. Hitler capitalized both on the weakness of Germany's postwar government, especially in the face of world depression, and on festering German resentment toward the Versailles Treaty.

Named chancellor on January 30, 1933, Hitler swiftly intimidated the opposition, won dictatorial powers, and in 1934 assumed the title of Reichsführer (national leader). The Nazi police state cranked up the engines of tyranny, persecuting Jews, whom Hitler blamed for all Germany's troubles, and rearming in defiance of the Versailles Treaty. Hitler flouted international agreements, pulled Germany out of the League of Nations in 1933, and proclaimed that he meant to extend control over all German-speaking peoples. Despite one provocation after another, the European democracies lacked the will to resist.

RUSSIAN RECOGNITION Isolationist sentiment in the United States grew even more potent during the early 1930s, but one significant exception to American insularity was Roosevelt's decision to favor official recognition of Soviet Russia. By 1933 the reasons for American refusal to recognize the Bolshevik regime had grown stale. Seen as an expansive market for American goods, Russia stirred fantasies of an American trade boom, much as China had at the turn of the century.

Mussolini and Hitler in Munich, Germany, June 1940.

Japanese expansionism in Asia, moreover, gave the Soviet Union and the United States a common foreign policy concern. Given an opening by the shift of opinion, Roosevelt invited the Soviet commissar for foreign affairs to visit Washington. After nine days of talks, a formal exchange of notes on November 16, 1933, signaled the renewal of diplomatic relations. The Soviet commissar promised that his country would abstain from propaganda in the United States, extend religious freedom to Americans in the Soviet Union, and reopen the question of prerevolutionary Russian debts to the United States.

THE MARCH OF AGGRESSION   After 1932 a catastrophic chain of events in Asia and Europe sent the world hurtling toward disaster. In 1934 Japan renounced the Five-Power Naval Treaty. The next year Mussolini commenced Italy's conquest of Ethiopia. That same year a referendum in Germany's Saar Basin, held in accordance with the Versailles Treaty, delivered that coal-rich region into the hands of Hitler. In 1936 Hitler reoccupied the Rhineland with armed forces, in violation of the Versailles Treaty but without any forceful response from the French.

The year 1936 also brought the Spanish Civil War, which began with an uprising of the Spanish armed forces in Morocco, led by General Francisco Franco, against the democratically elected Spanish Republic. Over the next three years, Franco established a fascist dictatorship with help from Hitler and Mussolini while the Western democracies left the Spanish Republic to its fate.

On July 7, 1937, Japanese and Chinese troops clashed at the Marco Polo Bridge near Peking (Beijing), and the incident quickly developed into a full-scale war. It was the beginning of World War II in Asia, two years before fighting erupted in Europe. That same year Japan joined Germany and Italy in establishing an alliance known as the Rome-Berlin-Tokyo "Axis."

By 1938 the peace of Europe trembled in the balance. Having rebuilt German military force, Hitler forced the *Anschluss* (union) of Austria with Germany in March 1938. Six months later Germany took the mountainous Sudetenland, largely German in population, which had been given to Czechoslovakia at the Versailles Peace Conference in 1919 because of its strategic importance to that new nation's defense. Hitler's latest aggression came shortly after a conference at Munich, where British and French leaders sought to appease Hitler by agreeing to abandon Czechoslovakia, a country that had probably the second strongest army in central Europe.

After promising that the Sudetenland would be his last territorial demand, Hitler in 1939 brazenly broke his pledge. He occupied the remainder of Czechoslovakia and seized former German territory from Lithuania. In quick succession the Spanish Republic finally collapsed on March 28, and Mussolini seized the kingdom of Albania on April 7. Finally, on September 1, 1939, Hitler launched his conquest of Poland. A few days before, he had signed a nonaggression pact with Soviet Russia. Having deserted Czechoslovakia, Britain and France now honored their commitment to go to war if Poland were invaded.

DEGREES OF NEUTRALITY During these years of deepening crisis, the Western democracies seemed paralyzed, hoping in vain that

each concession would appease the appetites of fascist dictators. Americans retreated more deeply into isolation.

A lengthy Senate inquiry into the origins of American involvement in World War I reinforced the desire to stay out of Europe's conflicts. Under Senator Gerald P. Nye of North Dakota, a progressive Republican, the committee sat from 1934 to 1937 and concluded that bankers and munitions makers had made scandalous profits from the war. Although Nye never proved that greed for profit had actually impelled President Woodrow Wilson into war, he did insist that the administration had been duped by the "merchants of death." If the United States wanted to remain neutral in the current world crisis, therefore, it would have to keep Americans out of war zones, keep belligerents' vessels out of American ports, embargo arms shipments, and set quotas on the export of contraband. Such ideas became official policy as war enveloped Asia and Europe.

Like generals who are said to be always preparing for the last war, Congress occupied itself with keeping out of the last war. Neutrality laws of the 1930s moved the United States toward complete isolation from the quarrels of Europe. But while Americans wanted to keep out of war, their sympathies were more strongly than ever with the Western democracies, and the triumph of fascist aggression aroused growing fears for national security.

The Neutrality Act of 1935 forbade the sale of arms and munitions to all belligerents whenever the president proclaimed that a state of war existed. Americans who traveled on belligerents' ships thereafter did so at their own risk. Roosevelt would have preferred discretionary authority to levy an embargo only against aggressors, but he reluctantly accepted the act because it was to be effective for only six months, and for the time being it met "the need of the existing situation." That is, it would likely be enforced against Italy, which was then threatening war with Ethiopia.

On October 3, 1935, Italy invaded Ethiopia and Roosevelt invoked the Neutrality Act. When Congress reconvened in 1936, it extended the arms embargo and added a provision forbidding loans to belligerents. Then in July 1936, while Italian troops mopped up the last resistance in Ethiopia, the Spanish Civil War broke out. Roosevelt now became more isolationist than some of the isolationists. Although the Spanish Civil War involved a fascist uprising against a recognized, democratic government, Roosevelt accepted the French and British position

A 1938 cartoon showing U.S. foreign policy entangled by the serpent of isolationism.

that only their nonintervention would localize the fight and keep it from spreading to the rest of Europe. There existed, moreover, a strong bloc of pro-Franco Catholics in America who feared that the liberal Spanish Republic was influenced by the Communists and therefore posed a threat to the church. Intrigues by Spanish Communists did prove divisive, and the Soviet Union did supply aid to the Republic, but nothing like the quantity of German and Italian aid to Franco.

Roosevelt asked for a "moral embargo" on the arms trade, and he encouraged Congress to extend the neutrality laws to cover civil wars. Congress did so in 1937 with only one dissenting vote. The Western democracies then stood witness while German and Italian soldiers, planes, and armaments supported Franco's overthrow of Spanish democracy.

In the spring of 1937 isolationist sentiment in the United States peaked. A Gallup poll found that 94 percent of its respondents preferred efforts to keep out of war over efforts to prevent war. That same spring Congress passed yet another neutrality law, which continued restraints on arms sales and loans, forbade Americans to travel on belligerents' ships, and prohibited the arming of American merchant ships trading with belligerents. The new law also empowered the president to require that goods other than arms or munitions exported to belligerents be placed on a cash-and-carry basis (that is, the nation purchasing the goods would have to pay in cash and then deliver the cargo in its own ships). This was an ingenious scheme to preserve a profitable trade without running the risk of war.

The new law had its first test in July 1937, when Japanese and Chinese forces clashed at the Marco Polo Bridge. Since neither side declared war, Roosevelt was able to avoid invoking the neutrality law, which would have favored the Japanese, since China had greater need of American arms but few means to get supplies past the Japanese navy. A flourishing trade in munitions to China flowed around the world as ships carried American military equipment across the Atlantic to England, where it was reloaded onto British ships bound for Hong Kong. Roosevelt, by inaction, had challenged strict isolationism.

Roosevelt soon ventured a step further. In Chicago on October 5, 1937, he denounced the "reign of terror and international lawlessness" in which 10 percent of the world's population threatened the peace of the other 90 percent. He called for a "quarantine" against those nations "creating a state of international anarchy and instability from which there is no escape through mere isolation or neutrality." On the whole, public reaction to the speech was mixed, but the president nevertheless quickly backed off from its implications and refused to spell out any specific program for dealing with aggression.

The continuing Japanese war against China brought public outrage and protests from Secretary of State Cordell Hull. In 1938, after nearly a year of war in China, the State Department notified domestic aircraft manufacturers and exporters that it opposed sales to those guilty of attacks on civilian populations. To have imposed an outright embargo would have violated a commercial treaty of 1911 with Japan, but after another year, on July 26, 1939, the United States gave six months' notice of the termination of the treaty—thus clearing the way for an embargo on all war materials to Japan.

After the German occupation of Czechoslovakia, Roosevelt no longer pretended impartiality in the impending European struggle. He urged Congress to repeal the embargo and permit the United States to sell arms on a cash-and-carry basis to Britain and France, but to no avail. "You haven't got the votes," Vice-President Garner told him, "and that's all there is to it." When the Germans attacked Poland on September 1,

1939, Roosevelt proclaimed official neutrality, but in a radio talk stressed that he did not, like Woodrow Wilson, ask Americans to remain neutral in thought because "even a neutral has a right to take account of the facts."

Roosevelt summoned Congress into special session and asked it again to amend the Neutrality Act. "I regret the Congress passed the Act," he confessed. "I regret equally that I signed the Act." Under the Neutrality Act of 1939, the Allies could buy supplies with cash and take away in their own ships arms or anything else they wanted. American ships, on the other hand, were excluded from belligerent ports and from specified war zones. Roosevelt then designated as a war zone the Baltic Sea and the waters around Great Britain and Ireland, from Norway south to the coast of Spain. One unexpected effect of this move was to relieve Hitler of any inhibitions against using unrestricted submarine warfare to blockade Britain.

American attitudes toward the European conflict continued to vacillate. When the war crisis first developed, an isolationist policy prevailed. Once the great democracies of western Europe faced war, American public opinion, appalled at Hitler's tyranny, came to support measures short of war to help their cause. For a time it seemed that the Western Hemisphere could remain insulated from the war. After Hitler overran Poland in less than a month, the war settled into an uneasy stalemate that began to be called the "phony war." What lay ahead, it seemed, was a long war of attrition—much like World War I—in which Britain and France would have the resources to outlast Hitler. This illusion lasted from October 1939 through the winter of 1940.

THE STORM IN EUROPE

BLITZKRIEG   In the spring of 1940 the long winter lull in the fighting suddenly erupted into *Blitzkrieg*—lightning war. At dawn on April 9, without warning, Nazi troops entered Denmark and disembarked along the Norwegian coast. Denmark fell in a day; Norway within a few weeks. On May 10 Hitler unleashed his dive bombers and tank divisions on neutral Belgium and the Netherlands. On May 21 German troops moving down the valley of the Somme reached the English Channel, cutting off a British force sent to help the Belgians and French. A desperate evacuation from the beaches at Dunkirk enlisted every available boat, from warship to tug. Some 338,000 men, about a third of them French, escaped to England.

Having outflanked France's heavily fortified defense perimeter, the Maginot Line, the German forces rushed ahead, cutting the French armies to pieces and spreading panic by strafing refugees in a deliberate policy of terror. On June 10 Italy entered the war as Germany's ally. "I need only a few thousand dead to enable me to take my seat . . . at the peace table," Il Duce said. On June 14 the swastika flew over Paris.

AMERICA'S GROWING INVOLVEMENT Britain now stood alone, but its new prime minister, Winston Churchill, breathed defiance. "We shall go on to the end," he pledged; "we shall never surrender." Despite such grim resolution, America itself seemed suddenly vulnerable as Hitler unleashed his air force against Britain. President Roosevelt, who in his annual budget had requested $1.9 billion for defense, now asked for more, and he called for the production of 50,000 combat planes a year. In 1940 Congress voted more than $17 billion for defense. In response to Churchill's appeal for American military supplies, the War and Navy Departments began releasing stocks of arms, planes, and munitions to the British.

French refugees fleeing German troops, June 1940.

The summer of 1940 brought the desperate Battle of Britain, in which the Royal Air Force finally forced the Germans to give up plans to invade the British Isles. Submarine warfare meanwhile strained the resources of the battered Royal Navy. To relieve the pressure, Churchill urgently requested the transfer of American destroyers. Secret negotiations led to an executive agreement under which fifty "overaged" destroyers went to the British in return for ninety-nine-year leases on naval and air bases in Newfoundland, Bermuda, and islands in the Caribbean. Roosevelt disguised the action as being necessary for hemispheric defense. Two weeks later, on September 16, 1940, Congress adopted the first peacetime conscription in American history. All men aged twenty-one to thirty-five were required to register for a year's military service within the United States.

The new state of affairs prompted vigorous debate between "internationalists," who believed national security demanded aid to Britain, and isolationists, who charged that Roosevelt was drawing the United States into a needless war. In 1940 the nonpartisan Committee to Defend America by Aiding the Allies was organized, drawing its strongest support from the East and West Coasts and the South. Two months later, isolationists formed the America First Committee. Before the end of 1941, the committee had about 450 chapters around the country, but probably two-thirds of its members lived within a 300-mile radius of Chicago. The isolationists argued that a Nazi victory, while distasteful, would pose no threat to American national security.

A THIRD TERM FOR FDR   In the midst of these profound developments, the quadrennial presidential campaign came due. Isolationist sentiment was strongest in the Republican party, yet their nominee took a different stance. Wendell L. Willkie was a former Democrat who had voted for Roosevelt in 1932. An Indiana farm boy whose disheveled charm inspired strong loyalty, he openly supported aid to the Allies.

The Nazi victory also ensured another nomination for Roosevelt. The president cultivated party unity behind his foreign policy and kept a sphinx-like silence about his intentions. The world crisis reconciled southern conservatives to the man whose foreign policy, at least, they supported. At the convention in Chicago, Roosevelt won nomination for a third term with only token opposition. For his new running mate, Roosevelt tapped his secretary of agriculture, Henry Wallace, a devoted supporter who would appeal to farm voters.

Through the summer, Roosevelt assumed the role of a man above the political fray, busy rather with urgent matters of defense and diplomacy. Willkie was reduced to attacking New Deal red tape and promising to run the programs better. In the end, however, as his campaign languished, he switched to an attack on Roosevelt's conduct of foreign policy: "If you re-elect him you may expect war in April, 1941." To this Roosevelt responded, "I have said this before, but I shall say it again and again and again: Your boys are not going to be sent into any foreign wars." Neither man distinguished himself with such hollow claims, since each knew the risk of the all-out aid to Britain, which they both supported.

Roosevelt won the election by a comfortable margin of 27 million votes to Willkie's 22 million, and a wider margin of 449 to 82 in the electoral college. Though the popular vote was closer than any presidential election since 1916, the dangerous world situation convinced a majority of voters to back the Democrats' slogan: "Don't switch horses in the middle of the stream."

THE ARSENAL OF DEMOCRACY   Bolstered by the mandate for an unprecedented third term, Roosevelt moved quickly to provide greater aid to Britain. Soon after the election, Churchill informed him that British cash was fast running out. Since direct government loans would arouse memories of earlier war-debt defaults—the Johnson Act of 1934 forbade such loans anyway—the president created an ingenious device to bypass that issue and yet supply British needs: the "lend-lease" program.

In a fireside chat, Roosevelt told the nation that it must become "the great arsenal of democracy" to help prevent Britain's fall. In his annual message to Congress on January 6, 1941, he warned that only the British navy stood between America and the peril of attack. Greater efforts to bolster British defenses were therefore in order. The Lend-Lease Bill, introduced in Congress on January 10, authorized the president to sell, transfer, exchange, lend, lease, or otherwise dispose of arms and other equipment and supplies to "any country whose defense the President deems vital to the defense of the United States."

For two months a bitter debate over the lend-lease bill raged in Congress and around the country. Isolationists saw it as the point of no return. Administration supporters denied that lend-lease would lead to

American involvement in the war, but it did indeed increase the risk. Lend-lease became law in early 1941, and Britain and China were the first beneficiaries.

While the nation debated, the war intensified. In late 1940, as the American presidential campaign approached its climax, Mussolini launched attacks on Greece and, from Italian-controlled Libya, assaulted the British in Egypt. But his forces had to fall back in both cases, and in the spring of 1941 German forces under General Erwin Rommel joined the Italians in Libya, forcing the British, whose resources had been drained to help Greece, to withdraw into Egypt. In April 1941 Nazi armored divisions overwhelmed Yugoslavia and Greece, and by the end of May airborne forces subdued the Greek island of Crete, putting Hitler in a position to menace the entire Middle East.

With Hungary, Romania, and Bulgaria forced into the Axis fold, Hitler controlled nearly all of Europe. Then, on June 22, 1941, he suddenly fell upon the Soviet Union, his ally, hoping to eliminate the potential threat on his rear with another lightning stroke. The Nazis moved on a 2,000-mile front from the Arctic to the Black Sea with seeming invincibility until, after four months, the Russian soldiers and civilians rallied in front of Leningrad, Moscow, and Sevastopol. During the winter of 1941–1942, Hitler began to learn the bitter lesson the Russians had taught Napoleon and his French invaders in 1812.

Winston Churchill had already decided to provide British support to the Soviet Union in case of such an attack. Roosevelt adopted the same policy, offering American aid two days after the German invasion. Stalinist Russia, so long as it held out, ensured Britain's survival. American aid was now indispensable to Europe's defense, and the logic of lend-lease led to deeper American involvement. To deliver aid to Britain, American goods had to be maneuvered through the German U-boat "wolf packs" in the North Atlantic. So on April 11, 1941, Roosevelt informed Churchill that the United States Navy would extend its patrol areas in the North Atlantic nearly all the way to Iceland.

In August 1941 Roosevelt and Churchill held a secret naval rendezvous off Newfoundland. There they drew up a statement of principles known as the Atlantic Charter. In effect it amounted to a joint declaration of war aims, its eight points a mixture of the idealistic goals of the New Deal and Wilson's Fourteen Points. It called for the self-determination of all peoples, economic cooperation, freedom of the seas, and a new international system of collective security. The Soviet Union later endorsed the statement.

Having entered into a joint statement of war aims with the anti-Axis powers, the United States soon became involved in shooting incidents in the North Atlantic. The first attack on an American warship occurred on September 4, when a German submarine fired two torpedoes at a destroyer. A week later the president ordered American ships to "shoot on sight" any German or Italian raiders ("rattlesnakes of the Atlantic") that ventured into American defensive waters. Five days later the United States Navy announced it would convoy merchant ships all the way to Iceland.

Further attacks hastened Congress into making changes in the Neutrality Act already requested by the president. On November 17 Congress removed the bans on arming merchant vessels and allowed them to enter combat zones and belligerent ports. Step by step the United States was giving up neutrality and embarking on naval warfare against Germany. Still, the American people hoped to avoid taking the final step into all-out war. The decision for war would come in an unexpected quarter—the Pacific.

THE STORM IN THE PACIFIC

JAPANESE AGGRESSION   After the Nazi victories in the spring of 1940, America's relations with Japan also took a turn for the worse. Japanese militarists, bogged down in the vastness of China, now eyed new temptations in South Asia (French Indochina, the Dutch East Indies, British Malaya, and Burma). They wanted to incorporate into their "Greater East Asia Co-Prosperity Sphere" the oil, rubber, and other strategic materials that their crowded homeland lacked. As it was, Japan depended on the United States for important supplies, including 80 percent of its oil.

During the summer of 1940, Japan forced the helpless French government to permit the construction of Japanese airfields in northern Indochina and to sever the rail line into South China, thus cutting off Western supplies to the Chinese. The United States responded with a loan to China and the Export Control Act of July 2, 1940, which autho-

rized the president to restrict the export of arms and other strategic materials to Japan. Gradually Roosevelt extended embargoes on aviation gas, scrap iron, and other supplies to Japan.

On September 27, 1940, the Tokyo government signed a Tripartite Pact with Germany and Italy, by which each pledged to declare war on any nation that attacked any of them. The Germans hoped to persuade Japan to enter Siberia when Nazi forces entered the Soviet Union from the west. The Soviet presence in Siberia did inhibit the Japanese impulse to move southward into Indochina, but on April 13, 1941, while the Nazis were sweeping through the Balkans, Japan signed a nonaggression pact with the Soviet Union and, once the Nazis invaded Russia in June, the Japanese were freed of any threat from the north.

In July 1941 Japan announced that it was assuming a protectorate over all of French Indochina. Responding to this latest act of aggression, Roosevelt froze all Japanese assets in the United States; he restricted exports of oil to Japan; and he took the armed forces of the Philippines into the Army of the United States and put their commander, General Douglas MacArthur, in charge of all American forces in the Far East. By September the oil restrictions had tightened into a complete embargo. Forced to secure oil supplies elsewhere, the Japanese army and navy began to plan attacks on the Dutch and British colonies in Southeast Asia.

Actions by both sides put the United States and Japan on the path to a war neither wanted. In his regular talks with the Japanese ambassador, Secretary of State Cordell Hull insisted that Japanese withdrawal from Indochina and China was the price of renewed trade with the United States. A more flexible position might have strengthened the moderates in Japan. Premier Fumimaro Konoye, however, while known as a man of liberal principles who preferred peace, caved in to pressures from the militants. Perhaps he had no choice.

The Japanese warlords, for their part, seriously misjudged the United States. The desperate wish of Americans to stay out of war might still have enabled the Japanese to conquer the British and Dutch colonies before an American decision to act. But the warlords decided that they dared not leave the American navy intact and the Philippines untouched on the flank of their new lifeline to the south.

TRAGEDY AT PEARL HARBOR   Thus a tragedy began to unfold with a fatal certainty mostly out of sight of the American people, whose attention was focused on the war in the Atlantic. Late in August 1941 Premier Konoye proposed a personal meeting with President Roosevelt. Hull advised Roosevelt not to meet unless agreement on fundamentals could be reached in advance. On September 6, a Japanese imperial conference approved preparations for a surprise attack on Hawaii and gave Premier Konoye six more weeks to reach a settlement.

The Japanese emperor's clear displeasure with the risk of an attack afforded the premier one last chance to pursue a compromise, but the presence of Japanese troops in China remained a stumbling block to any American agreement. In October Konoye urged War Minister Hideki Tojo to consider withdrawal while saving face by keeping some troops in North China. Tojo responded with his "maximum concession" that Japanese troops would stay in China no longer than twenty-five years if the United States stopped aiding the Chinese.

Faced with this rebuff and with Tojo's threat to resign and bring down the cabinet, Konoye himself resigned on October 15. Tojo became premier the next day. The war party was now in complete control of the government.

On the very day that Tojo became premier, a special Japanese envoy conferred with Hull and Roosevelt in Washington. His arrival was largely a cover for Japan's war plans, although neither he nor Japan's ambassador to the United States knew that. On November 20 they presented Tojo's final proposal to Hull: Japan would occupy no more territory if the United States would cut off aid to China, restore trade with Japan, and help the Japanese get supplies from the Dutch Indies. In that case Japan would pull out of southern Indochina immediately and abandon the remainder once peace had been established with China—presumably on Japanese terms. Tojo expected the United States to refuse such demands. On November 26 Hull repeated that Japan must withdraw altogether from China. That same day a Japanese naval force began heading across the North Pacific toward Pearl Harbor, Hawaii.

Washington officials already knew that war was imminent. Reports of Japanese troop transports moving south from Formosa prompted Washington to send warnings to Pearl Harbor and Manila, and to the British government. The massive Japanese movements southward clearly signaled attacks on the British and the Dutch. American leaders had every reason to expect war in the southwest Pacific, but none expected that Japan would commit most of its aircraft carriers to another attack 5,000 miles away at Pearl Harbor.

On the morning of December 7, 1941, Americans decoded the last part of a secret Japanese message breaking off the negotiations in Washington. Tojo instructed Japan's ambassador to deliver the message at 1:00 P.M. (7:30 A.M. in Honolulu), about a half hour before the blow fell, but delays held up delivery until more than an hour later than scheduled. The War Department sent out an alert at noon that something was about to happen, but the message, which went by commercial wire because radio contacts were broken, arrived in Hawaii eight and a half hours later. Even so, the decoded Japanese message did not mention Pearl Harbor specifically, and American military leaders there would probably have assumed the attack was to come in Southeast Asia.

It was still a sleepy Sunday morning when the first Japanese planes roared down the west coast and the central valley of Oahu to begin their assault. At 7:53 A.M. the flight commander sounded the cry "Tora! Tora! Tora!" (Tiger! Tiger! Tiger!), the signal that the attackers had taken the American navy by surprise. For nearly two hours the Japanese planes kept up their fierce attack. Of the eight U.S. battleships in Pearl Harbor, three were sunk and the others were badly battered. Altogether nineteen ships were sunk or disabled. At the airfields on the island the Japanese destroyed about 150 planes. Before it was over the raid had killed more than 2,400 American servicemen and civilians.

The surprise attack fulfilled the dreams of its planners, but it fell short of total success in two ways. The Japanese ignored oil storage tanks, without which the surviving ships might have been forced back to the West Coast, and they missed the American aircraft carriers that had fortuitously left port a few days earlier. In the naval war to come, these carriers would be decisive.

Later the same day (December 8 in the western Pacific), Japanese forces began assaults on the Philippines, Guam, and Midway, and on British forces in Hong Kong and the Malay Peninsula. With one stroke, the Japanese had silenced America's debate on neutrality, and a suddenly unified and vengeful nation resolutely prepared for the struggle. A Michigan man recalled his reactions to the Japanese attack: "First it

The Attack on Pearl Harbor. *The view from an American airfield shows the destruction and confusion brought on by the surprise attack.*

was indignation, then it turned to anger, and by the time one went to work the following morning it was determination: 'They can't do that to us.'"

The day after the attack President Roosevelt told Congress that December seventh was "a date which will live in infamy," and he asked for a declaration of war. It was approved unanimously, with the sole exception of Representative Jeanette Rankin, a pacifist who was unable in good conscience to vote for war in 1917 or 1941. On December 11, Germany and Italy declared war on the United States. The separate wars in Asia and Europe had become one global conflict—and American isolationism was cast aside.

MAKING CONNECTIONS

- The United States tried to stake out a neutral position in the growing world conflict. Compare this to earlier American attempts at neutrality, from the Napoleonic Wars era of Jefferson's administration onward.

- The American alliance with the Soviet Union described in this chapter proved to be temporary; after the war, the Americans and the Soviets would be adversaries in a great cold war, the beginnings of which are outlined in Chapter 30.

- The Japanese conquest of French Indochina (Vietnam) would play an important role in the events leading to American involvement in the region, a topic discussed in Chapter 32.

FURTHER READING

The best overview of interwar diplomacy remains Selig Adler's *The Uncertain Giant: American Foreign Policy between the Wars* (1965). Joan Hoff Wilson's *American Business and Foreign Policy, 1920–1933*

(1971) highlights the efforts of Republican administrations during the 1920s to promote international commerce. Robert Dallek's *Franklin D. Roosevelt and American Foreign Policy, 1932–1945* (1979) provides a judicious assessment of Roosevelt's foreign policies during the 1930s.

Other scholars have concentrated on particular diplomatic issues of the 1920s. Thomas H. Buckley's *The United States and the Washington Conference, 1921–1922* (1970) examines disarmament. For a study of the Kellogg-Briand Pact, see Robert H. Ferrell's *Peace in Their Time: The Origins of the Kellogg-Briand Pact* (1968). Relations between the United States and Europe are covered in Frank Costigliola's *Awkward Dominion: American Political, Economic, and Cultural Relations with Europe, 1919–1933* (1984). A comprehensive analysis of American responses to Nazi aggression is Arnold Offner's *American Appeasement: United States Foreign Policy and Germany, 1933–1938* (1969).

For American relations in East Asia during the period, see Akira Iriye's *After Imperialism: The Search for a New Order in the Far East, 1921–1931* (1965) and the relevant chapters in Walter LaFeber's *The Clash: A History of U.S.-Japan Relations* (1997). More specific studies are Warren I. Cohen's *America's Response to China: An Interpretive History of Sino-American Relations* (2nd ed., 1981) and Jonathan G. Utley's *Going to War with Japan, 1937–1941* (1985). For relations with Latin America, see Irwin F. Gellman's *Good Neighbor Diplomacy: United States Policies in Latin America, 1933–1945* (1979).

The best general account of the onset of World War II is Donald Watt's *How War Came: The Immediate Origins of the Second World War, 1938–1939* (1990). A noteworthy study of America's entry into World War II is Waldo Heinrichs's *Threshold of War: Franklin D. Roosevelt and American Entry into World War II* (1988). Other interpretations include Robert A. Divine's *The Reluctant Belligerent* (2nd ed., 1979) and Patrick Hearden's *Roosevelt Confronts Hitler: America's Entry into World War II* (1986). Bruce M. Russett's *No Clear and Present Danger* (1972) provides a critical account of American actions. American relations with Great Britain are detailed in David Reynolds's *The Creation of the Anglo-American Alliance, 1937–1941* (1981).

On Pearl Harbor, see Gordon W. Prange's *Pearl Harbor: The Verdict of History* (1986). The Japanese perspective is given in Robert J. C. Butow's *Tojo and the Coming of War* (1961).

29 ⟡ THE SECOND
WORLD WAR

CHAPTER ORGANIZER

This chapter focuses on:

- the social and economic effects of World War II, especially in the West.

- how the Allied forces won the war.

- the efforts of the Allies to shape the postwar world.

The Japanese attack on Pearl Harbor ended a period of uneasy neutrality for the United States. Even more important, of course, it launched America into an epochal world event that would transform the nation's social and economic life as well as its position in international affairs. The Second World War would become the most destructive and far-reaching war in history. It was a conflict so terrible and capricious, so surreal in its intensity and obscene in its cruelties, that it altered the image of war itself. Devilish new instruments of destruction were invented—plastic explosives, flame throwers, proximity fuses, rockets, jet airplanes, and atomic weapons—and systematic genocide emerged as an explicit war aim of the Nazis. Racist propaganda flourished on both sides, and intense hatred of the enemy caused many military and civilian prisoners to be executed. Over 50 million deaths were attributed to the war, and the physical destruction was incalculable. Whole cities were leveled, nations dismembered, and societies transformed. Latin America was the only region to escape the war's fury. The world is still struggling to cope with the consequences of the Second World War.

AMERICA'S EARLY BATTLES

SETBACKS IN THE PACIFIC In early December 1941, American military leaders focused on halting the Japanese advance and mobilizing the whole nation for war. For months after Pearl Harbor, the news from the Pacific was "all bad," as President Roosevelt confessed. A string of Allied outposts surrendered in the three months after December 1941: Guam, Wake Island, the Gilbert Islands, Hong Kong, Singapore, and Java. The Japanese capture of Rangoon, Burma, in March 1942 cut off the Burma Road, the main supply route to China.

In the Philippines, where General Douglas MacArthur, commander of U.S. forces in the Far East, abandoned Manila on December 27, the main American forces, outmanned and outgunned, held out tenaciously

American prisoners of war, captured by the Japanese in the Philippines, 1942.

on Bataan Peninsula until April 9, and then on the fortified island of Corregidor. MacArthur himself had slipped away in March, when he was ordered to Australia to take command of Allied forces in the Southwest Pacific. By May 6, when American forces surrendered Corregidor, Japan controlled a new empire that stretched from Burma eastward through the Dutch Indies and extended to Wake Island and the Gilbert Islands.

The Japanese might have consolidated an almost impregnable empire with the resources they had seized. But the Japanese navy succumbed to what one of its admirals later called "victory disease." Its leaders decided to push farther into the South Pacific, isolate Australia, and strike again at Hawaii. Japanese planners hoped to destroy the American navy before the productive power of the United States could be brought to bear on the war effort.

CORAL SEA AND MIDWAY American forces finally halted the Japanese advances in two decisive naval battles. The Battle of the Coral Sea (May 7–8, 1942) stopped a fleet convoying Japanese troop transports toward New Guinea. Planes from the *Lexington* and *Yorktown* sank one Japanese aircraft carrier, damaged another, and destroyed smaller ships. American losses were greater, and included the carrier *Lexington,* but the Japanese designs on Australia were thwarted.

Less than a month after the Coral Sea engagement, Admiral Isoruku Yamamoto, the Japanese naval commander, forced a showdown in the central Pacific. With nearly every ship under his command, he headed for Midway Island, from which he hoped to render Pearl Harbor helpless. This time it was the Japanese who were the victims of surprise. American cryptanalysts had by then broken the Japanese naval code, and Admiral Chester Nimitz, commander of the central Pacific, knew their plan of attack. He reinforced Midway with planes and the carriers *Enterprise, Hornet,* and *Yorktown.*

The first Japanese foray against Midway, on June 4, 1942, severely damaged the American installation on the island, but at the cost of about a third of the Japanese planes. Before another attack could be mounted, American torpedo planes and dive bombers had caught three of the four Japanese carriers in the process of servicing their planes. Dive bombers sank three of them during the first assault. Later the Japanese lost another carrier, but not before its planes disabled the *Yorktown.* The only other major American loss was a destroyer.

The Japanese defeat at Midway was the turning point of the Pacific war.

SETBACKS IN THE ATLANTIC Early Allied setbacks in the Pacific were matched by losses in the Atlantic. Since the *Blitzkrieg* of 1940, German submarine "wolf packs" had wreaked havoc in the North Atlantic. In 1942, after an ominous lull, German U-boats suddenly appeared off American shores and began to sink coastal shipping, much of it tankers. Nearly 400 ships were lost in American waters before effective countermeasures brought the problem under control. The naval command hastened the building of small escort vessels, meanwhile pressing into patrol service all kinds of surface craft and planes, some of them civilian. During the second half of 1942, these efforts reduced losses to a negligible number.

MOBILIZATION AT HOME

The Pearl Harbor attack ended not only the long debate between isolation and intervention but also the long economic depression that had ravaged the country in the 1930s. The war effort required all of America's huge productive capacity and full employment of the workforce. For 1942 alone the government ordered 60,000 planes, 45,000 tanks, and 8 million tons of merchant shipping. The next year's goals were even higher. Soon after Pearl Harbor, British prime minister Winston Churchill recalled that someone had compared the United States to a gigantic boiler: "Once the fire is lighted under it, there is no limit to the power it can generate."

Mobilization was in fact already farther along than preparedness had been in 1916–1917. The draft had been in effect for more than a year, and the army had grown to more than 1.4 million men by July 1941. Congress quickly extended the term of military service to last until six months after the war's end. Men between eighteen and forty-five now became subject to service. Altogether more than 15 million American men and women would serve in the armed forces during the war.

ECONOMIC CONVERSION The economy, too, was already partially mobilized by lend-lease and defense efforts. Congress had authorized the president to reshuffle government agencies and to allot materials and facilities as needed for defense, with penalties for those who failed to comply. The War Production Board (WPB), created in 1942, directed the conversion of private industries to war production. The Office of Scientific Research and Development mobilized thousands of scientists to create and modify radar, sonar, the proximity fuse, the bazooka, and the many other innovations that contributed to the war effort.

The pressure of wartime needs and the stimulus of government spending doubled the gross national product between 1940 and 1945. Government expenditures during the war years soared. The total was about 10 times what America spent in World War I and 100 times the expenditures during the Civil War. The massive infusion of government capital into the economy also encouraged greater centralization and consolidation in private industry. The larger companies tended to win the most government contracts, and the more they won the larger they became. Conversely, those without government contracts withered and died. In 1942 alone 300,000 businesses shut down.

FINANCING THE WAR   To cover the war's huge cost, the president preferred taxes to borrowing, but Congress, dominated by fiscal conservatives, feared taxes more than deficits and refused to go more than halfway with Roosevelt's fiscal prudence. As a result, the government covered about 45 percent of its 1939–1946 costs with tax revenues; the rest was borrowed from the public. War-bond drives induced citizens to put aside more than $150 billion in bonds. Financial institutions picked up most of the rest of the government's debt. In all, the national debt grew by the end of the war to $260 billion, about six times its size at the time of the attack on Pearl Harbor.

America's basic economic problem during the war years was no longer creating jobs but finding workers for the booming shipyards, aircraft factories, and munitions plants. Millions of people, especially women, who had lived on the margin of the economic system, were now brought fully into the workforce. Stubborn poverty did not disappear, but for most civilians the war spelled neither severe hardship nor suffering but a better life than ever before, despite shortages and rationing of consumer goods. Labor unions benefited directly from the dramatic growth of the civilian workforce. Union membership increased significantly during the war years, from about 11 million to 15 million.

ECONOMIC CONTROLS Increased incomes and spending during the war raised the specter of inflation. Some of the available money went into taxes and war bonds, but even so, more purchasing power was sent chasing civilian goods just as production was converting to war needs. Consumer durables such as cars, washing machines, and nondefense housing in fact ceased to be produced at all. Only strict restraints would keep prices of scarce goods from soaring out of sight. In 1941 Roosevelt created the Office of Price Administration (OPA), and the following year Congress authorized it to set price ceilings. With prices frozen, goods had to be allocated through rationing, which began with tires and was gradually extended to other scarce items such as sugar, coffee, meat, and gasoline.

At first, however, wages and farm prices were not controlled, and this complicated matters. War prosperity offered farmers a chance to recover from two decades of distress, and farm-state legislators raised both floors and ceilings on farm prices. Higher food prices reinforced worker demands for higher wages. To relieve this inflationary pressure, the president won new authority to control wages and farm prices. Both business and workers chafed at the new controls, and on occasion the government was forced to seize industries threatened by strike. The coal mines and railroads were both nationalized for a short time in 1943. Despite these problems, the government's program to stabilize the war economy succeeded. By the end of the war, consumer prices had risen about 31 percent, a far better record than the World War I rise of 62 percent.

To make the economic controls work, the government launched a program to encourage conservation of resources. As one popular slogan had it, "Use it up, wear it out, make it do or do without." The public collected scrap metal and grew their own food in backyard "victory gardens." In 1942, when the war plants faced a rubber shortage, Roosevelt asked citizens to turn in "old tires, old rubber raincoats, old garden hoses, rubber shoes, bathing caps, gloves—whatever you have that is made of rubber."

DOMESTIC CONSERVATISM Despite the government's efforts to encourage the public to make sacrifices for the war effort, discontent with price controls, labor shortages, rationing, and a hundred other petty vexations spread. The result was a reaction against Roosevelt liberalism at the polls that indicated a growing political conservatism. In 1942 the congressional elections registered a national swing against the New Deal. Republicans gained forty-six seats in the House and nine in the Senate, chiefly in the farm areas of the midwestern states. Democratic losses outside the South strengthened the southern delegation's position within the party, and the delegation itself reflected conservative victories in southern primaries. A coalition of conservatives proceeded to eviscerate "nonessential" New Deal agencies. In 1943 Congress abolished the Works Progress Administration, the National Youth Adminstration, and the Civilian Conservation Corps. It also began to dismantle the Farm Security Administration, and it liquidated the National Resources Planning Board.

Organized labor, despite substantial gains during the war, felt the impact of the conservative trend. In the spring of 1943, when John L. Lewis led the coal miners out on strike, widespread public resentment prompted Congress to pass the Smith-Connally War Labor Disputes Act, which authorized the government to seize plants useful to the war. In 1943 a dozen states adopted laws variously restricting picketing and other union activities, and in 1944 Arkansas and Florida set in motion a wave of "right-to-work" legislation that outlawed the closed shop (requiring that all employees be union members).

SOCIAL EFFECTS OF THE WAR

MOBILIZATION AND THE DEVELOPMENT OF THE WEST The dramatic expansion of defense production after 1940 and the mobilization of millions of men into the armed forces accelerated economic development and the population boom in the western states. Nearly 8 million people moved into the states west of the Mississippi River between 1940 and 1950. The states witnessing the largest population growth during the war were California, Oregon, Washington, Nevada, Utah, Texas, and Arizona. Most of this expansion occurred in metropolitan centers. Indeed, the Far West experienced the fastest rate of urban growth in the country. Small cities such as Phoenix and Albuquerque mushroomed, while Seattle, San Francisco, Los Angeles, and San Diego witnessed dizzying growth. San Diego's population, for example, increased by 147 percent between 1941 and 1945.

Abundant defense-related jobs at high wages enticed people to the western states. California alone garnered 10 percent of all the defense contracts during the war years. In Texas, manufacturing employment almost doubled between 1940 and 1945. Los Angeles, which in 1939 was the seventh largest manufacturing center in the nation, had by 1943 become second only to Detroit in industrial activity. City services could not keep up with the influx of workers and military personnel. Employees at Seattle's shipyards and the huge Boeing airplane plant lived in tents because of a housing shortage. To address the problem, Congress passed the Lanham Act, which authorized the federal government to finance over a million new temporary housing units across the country. Yet this federal housing program did not meet the demand. Some women workers at a San Diego defense plant lived eight to a room in a company dormitory.

The migration of workers to new defense jobs in the West had significant demographic effects. Communities with few African Americans witnessed an influx of blacks. Lured by news of job openings and higher wages, African Americans from Texas, Oklahoma, Arkansas, and Louisiana headed west. During the war years, Seattle's black population jumped from 4,000 to 40,000, Portland's from 2,000 to 15,000.

CHANGING ROLES FOR WOMEN The war marked an important watershed in the changing status of women. From 1910 to 1940, the proportion of women working outside the home had barely altered, but with millions of men going into military service, the demand for labor shook up old prejudices about sex roles in the workplace—and in the military. Nearly 200,000 women went into the Women's Army Corps (WAC) and the navy's equivalent, Women Accepted for Volunteer Emergency Service (WAVES). Lesser numbers joined the Marine Corps, the Coast Guard, and the Army Air Force.

Even more significant were the 6 million women who entered the workforce during the war, an increase in general of over 50 percent and in manufacturing alone of some 110 percent. By 1944 over a third of all American women were in the labor force. Old barriers fell overnight as women became toolmakers, machinists, riveters, crane operators, lumberjacks, stevedores, blacksmiths, and railroad workers. Desperate for laborers, the government launched an intense public-

Women Workers. *These women took the place of men in constructing airplanes for use in the war.*

ity campaign to draw women into traditional male jobs. "Do your part, free a man for service," one ad pleaded. "Rosie the Riveter," a beautiful model dressed in overalls, served as the cover girl for the recruiting campaign.

One striking feature of the wartime economy was the larger proportion of older, married women in the workforce. In 1940 about 15 percent of married women went into gainful employment; by 1945 it was 24 percent. In the workforce as a whole, married women for the first time outnumbered single women.

There were many vocal opponents to this new trend. One disgruntled legislator asked what would happen to traditional domestic tasks if married women worked in factories: "Who will do the cooking, the washing, the mending, the humble homey tasks to which every woman has devoted herself; who will rear and nurture the children?" Many women, however, were eager to get away from the grinding routine of domestic life. One female welder remembered that her wartime job "was the first time I had a chance to get out of the kitchen and work in industry and make a few bucks. This was something I had never dreamed would happen." And it was something that many women did not want to relinquish after the war.

EXPANDED PARTICIPATION OF BLACKS The most volatile issue ignited by the war was that of black participation in the defense effort. From the start, black leaders demanded full civil rights in the armed forces and defense industries. Eventually about a million African Americans served in the armed forces, in every branch and every theater. But most served in segregated units. Every army camp had its separate facilities and its periodic racial "incidents." The most important departure from this pattern came in a 1940 decision to give up segregation in officer candidate schools, except those for air force cadets. A separate military flight school at Tuskegee, Alabama, trained about 600 black pilots, many of whom later distinguished themselves in combat.

War industries were even less accessible to black influence and pressure, although government policy in theory opposed discrimination. In 1941 A. Philip Randolph, the brilliant head of the Brotherhood of Sleeping Car Porters, organized a March on Washington Movement to demand

Tuskegee Airmen, 1942. *One of the last segregated military training schools, the flight school at Tuskegee trained African-American men for combat during World War II.*

an end to racial discrimination in defense industries. The administration, alarmed at the prospect of a mass descent on Washington, struck a bargain. The Randolph group called off its march in return for an executive order prohibiting discrimination in defense work and training programs.

Blacks quickly broadened their drive for wartime participation into a more inclusive and open challenge to all kinds of discrimination, including racial segregation itself. Membership in the NAACP soared during the war from 50,000 to 450,000. Blacks could look forward to greater political participation after the Supreme Court, in *Smith v. Allwright* (1944), struck down Texas's whites-only primary on the grounds that Democratic primaries were part of the election process and thus subject to the Fifteenth Amendment.

Growing black militancy aroused antagonism from some whites. Racial violence did not approach the level of that in World War I, but rising tensions on a hot summer afternoon in Detroit sparked two days of fighting in 1943, until federal troops arrived on the second evening. Twenty-five blacks and nine whites had been killed.

HISPANICS IN THE LABOR FORCE   As rural folk moved to the western cities, the farm counties experienced a labor shortage. In an ironic about-face, local and federal government authorities who before the war strove to force Mexican alien laborers back across the border now recruited them to harvest crops. The Mexican government, however, first insisted that the United States ensure certain minimum work and living conditions before it would assist in providing the needed workers. The result was the creation of the *bracero* program in 1942. Mexico agreed to provide seasonal farm workers in exchange for a promise by the American government not to draft them into military service. The workers were hired on year-long contracts that offered wages at the prevailing rate, and American officials provided transportation from the border to their job sites. Under this *bracero* program, some 200,000 Mexican farm workers entered the western United States. At least that many more crossed the border as illegal aliens.

The influx of people created new tensions. The rising tide of Mexican Americans in Los Angeles provoked a growing stream of anti-Hispanic editorials and incidents. Event though Mexican Americans fought in the war with greater valor, earning seventeen Congressional Medals of

Honor, there was constant conflict between servicemen and Mexican-American gang members and teenage "zoot-suiters" in southern California. "Zoot suits" were the flamboyant clothes worn by some young Chicano men. In 1943, several thousand off-duty sailors and soldiers, joined by hundreds of local white civilians, rampaged through downtown Los Angeles streets, assaulting Hispanics, blacks, and Filipinos. The violence lasted a week and came to be labeled the "zoot suit" riots.

NATIVE AMERICANS AND THE WAR EFFORT Indians may have supported the war effort more fully than any other group in American society. Almost a third of eligible Native American men, over 25,000 people, served in the armed forces. Another one-fourth worked in defense-related industries. Thousands of Indian women volunteered as nurses or joined the Women's Voluntary Service. As was the case with African Americans, Indians benefited from the broadening experiences afforded by the war. Those who left reservations to work in defense plants or to join the military gained new vocational skills aswell as a greater awareness of opportunities available in the larger American society.

Why did Native Americans so eagerly fight for a nation that had stripped them of their lands and decimated their heritage? Some felt that they had no choice. Mobilization for the war effort ended many New Deal programs that had provided Indians with jobs. Reservation Indians thus faced the necessity of finding new jobs elsewhere. Many viewed the Nazis and Japanese warlords as threats to their own homeland. Others saw in the war an opportunity to revitalize the warrior tradition. Joseph Medicine Crow remembered that, while fighting in Europe, he "never thought" about the traditional requirements for a young Crow male to earn his status as a warrior, but "afterwards, when I came back and went through this telling of the war deeds ceremony, why, I told my war deeds, and lo and behold I completed the four requirements to become a chief." The most common sentiment animating Indian involvement in the war effort, however, seems to have been a genuine sense of patriotism.

Whatever the reasons, Indians distinguished themselves in the military during the war. Unlike their African-American counterparts, Indian servicemen were integrated within the regular units. Perhaps the most distinctive activity performed by Indians was their service as "code talkers." Every military branch used Indians—Oneidas, Chippewas, Sauks, Foxes, Comanches, and Navajos—to encode and decipher messages so as to prevent enemy discovery. The Dineh (Navajo) developed their own specialized dictionary to convey idiomatic military terms. For example, a submarine became an "iron fish" and a machine gun was a "fast shooter."

INTERNMENT OF JAPANESE AMERICANS The record on civil liberties during World War II was on the whole better than that during World War I, if only because there was virtually no opposition to the war effort after the attack on Pearl Harbor. Neither German Americans nor Italian Americans faced the harassments meted out to their counterparts in the previous war; few had much sympathy for Hitler or Mussolini. The shameful exception to an otherwise improved record was the treatment given to Americans of Japanese descent. Few, if any, were disloyal, but all were victims of fear and racial prejudice.

This was especially the case in the months following the attack on Pearl Harbor. One California barbershop offered "free shaves for Japs" but noted that it was "not responsible for accidents." Others were even blunter. Idaho's governor declared: "A good solution to the Jap problem would be to send them all back to Japan, then sink the island. They live like rats, breed like rats, and act like rats." Such attitudes were regrettably widespread, and the government finally succumbed to demands that it force all Japanese, citizens or not, into "War Relocation Camps" in the interior. Caught up in the war hysteria and racial prejudice provoked by the attack on Pearl Harbor, President Roosevelt initiated the removal of Japanese Americans when he issued Executive Order 9066 on February 19, 1942. More than 60 percent of the internees were U.S. citizens; a third were under the age of nineteen. Forced to sell their farms and businesses at great losses, the internees lost not only their liberty but also their property. More than 100,000 were eventually removed from their homes and businesses in this sorry episode. As one Japanese American poignantly complained, "What really hurts most is the constant reference to us evacuees as 'Japs.' 'Japs' are the guys we are fighting. We're on this side and we want to help. Why won't America let us?" Not until 1983 did the government finally acknowledge the injustice of the internment policy. Five years later, Congress voted to give

$20,000 and an apology to each of the 60,000 former internees who were still living.

The Allied Drive toward Berlin

In mid-1942 the "home front" began to get news from the war fronts that some of the lines were holding at last. By midyear a fleet of American air and sea sub-chasers was ending six months of happy hunting for German U-boats off the Atlantic coast. This was promising because Allied war plans called for the defeat of Germany first.

WAR AIMS AND STRATEGY There were many reasons for giving top priority to defeating Hitler: Nazi forces in western Europe and the Atlantic posed a more direct threat to the Western Hemisphere; German war potential exceeded Japan's; and, German science was more likely to come up with some devastating new weapon. Lose in the Atlantic, General George Marshall grimly predicted, and you lose everywhere. Yet Japanese attacks involved Americans directly in the Pacific war from the start, and as a consequence, during the first year of fighting more Americans went to the Pacific than across the Atlantic.

The Pearl Harbor attack brought Winston Churchill quickly to Washington for talks about a common war plan. Thus began a wartime alliance between the United States and Great Britain, a partnership marked almost as much by disagreement and suspicion as it was by common purposes. As Churchill later remarked, "There is only one thing worse than fighting with allies, and that is fighting without them." Although he and Roosevelt admired each other, they disagreed about military strategy and the likely makeup of the postwar world. They often pursued the interests of their own country at the expense of the military alliance; they occasionally deceived each other; in a few cases, they lied to each other. Roosevelt worried about Churchill's excessive drinking, and Churchill worried about Roosevelt's "naive" understanding of Soviet behavior and his innocent faith in Stalin's integrity.

Initially, at least, such differences of opinion and outlook were masked by the need to make basic decisions related to the conduct of the war. The meetings in Washington in 1942 affirmed the priority of first winning the war against Germany. Agreement on war aims, however, did not bring agreement on strategy. When Roosevelt and Churchill met at the White House again in 1942, they could not agree on where to hit first. American strategists wanted to strike German-held France directly across the English Channel before the end of 1942. With vivid memories of the last war, the British feared a mass bloodletting in trench warfare if they struck prematurely. The Soviets, bearing the brunt of the German attack in the east, insisted that the Western Allies must do something to relieve the pressure along the Russian front. Finally, the Americans accepted Churchill's proposal to invade French North Africa.

THE NORTH AFRICA CAMPAIGN On November 8, 1942, Anglo-American forces under the command of General Dwight D. Eisenhower landed in Morocco and Algeria. Completely surprised, French forces under the Vichy government (which collaborated with the Germans) had little will to resist. Farther east, British forces were pushing German armies back across Libya. Before spring, the Germans were caught in a gigantic pincers. By April the British had linked up with American forces. Hammered from all sides, unable to retreat across the Mediterranean, an army of 275,000 Germans surrendered on May 13, 1943, leaving all of North Africa in Allied hands.

While this battle of Tunisia was still unfolding, Roosevelt, Churchill, and the Combined Chiefs of Staff met at Casablanca, Morocco. Stalin declined to leave beleaguered Russia for the meeting but continued to press for the opening of a second front in Europe. The Anglo-American planners, however, decided to postpone the cross-Channel invasion and to carry out Churchill's scheme to attack what he called the "soft underbelly of the Axis" by invading Sicily and then Italy. They also authorized an American offensive in the Pacific islands. Top priority, however, went to an antisubmarine campaign in the Atlantic.

Before leaving Casablanca, Roosevelt announced, with Churchill's endorsement, that the war would end only with the "unconditional surrender" of all enemies. This demand was designed to reassure Stalin that the Western Allies would not negotiate separately with the Germans. The West desperately needed Soviet cooperation in defeating Germany, and Roosevelt and Churchill were eager to reassure Stalin of their good intentions.

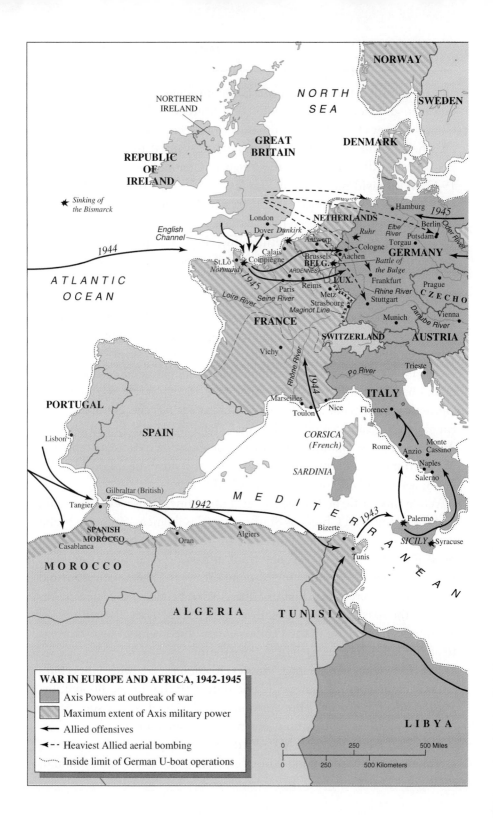

NORWAY

SWEDEN

NORTHERN
IRELAND

*NORTH
SEA*

GREAT
BRITAIN

DENMARK

REPUBLIC
OF
IRELAND

★ *Sinking of
the Bismarck*

Hamburg *1945*

London

NETHERLANDS

Elbe
River

Berlin

*English
Channel*

Dover *Dunkirk*

Ruhr

Potsdam

Oder River

1944

Calais

Antwerp

Cologne

Torgau

GERMANY

St.Lô
Normandy

Compiègne

Brussels

Aachen

*Battle of
the Bulge*

ATLANTIC

1945

BELG.

Prague

OCEAN

ARDENNES

LUX.

Frankfurt

CZECHO

Paris
Seine River

Reims

Rhine River

Loire River

Metz
Strasbourg
Maginot Line

Stuttgart

Vienna

Munich

Danube River

FRANCE

SWITZERLAND

AUSTRIA

Vichy

Rhône River

Po River

Trieste

PORTUGAL

1944

ITALY

Marseilles

Florence

Toulon

Nice

SPAIN

Lisbon

CORSICA
(French)

Rome

Anzio

Monte
Cassino

SARDINIA

Naples

Salerno

M E D I T E

Gilbraltar (British)

Tangier

1942

R

1943

Palermo

SPANISH
MOROCCO

Oran

Algiers

Bizerte

SICILY

Syracuse

Casablanca

Tunis

A N E A N

MOROCCO

ALGERIA

TUNISIA

LIBYA

WAR IN EUROPE AND AFRICA, 1942-1945

Axis Powers at outbreak of war

Maximum extent of Axis military power

← Allied offensives

◄- - Heaviest Allied aerial bombing

.... Inside limit of German U-boat operations

0		250		500 Miles

0	250	500 Kilometers

FINLAND

BALTIC SEA

Leningrad

ESTONIA

1944

LATVIA

Moscow

LITHUANIA

Danzig

Dnieper River

SOVIET UNION

Volga River

EAST
PRUSSIA

Vistula R.

1943

Warsaw

1945

Stalingrad

POLAND

1942

CASPIAN
SEA

SLOVAKIA

Budapest

HUNGARY

ROMANIA

Sevastopol

Yalta

1944

BLACK SEA

Belgrade

*Danube
River*

Bucharest

YUGOSLAVIA

BULGARIA

Sofia

ALBANIA

Ankara

GREECE

TURKEY

Athens

CYPRUS
(British)

SYRIA

CRETE

RHODES

IRAQ

S   E   A

PALESTINE
(British)

TRANS-
JORDAN

Tobruk

Alexandria

*Suez
Canal*

SAUDI
ARABIA

1943

El Alamein,
1942

EGYPT

RED SEA

The announcement also reflected Roosevelt's determination to see that "every person in Germany should realize that this time Germany is a defeated nation." This dictum was later criticized for having stiffened enemy resistance, but it probably had little effect; in fact neither the Italian nor Japanese surrender would be totally unconditional. But the decision virtually assured eventual Soviet control of eastern Europe because it required Soviet armies to pursue Hitler's forces all the way to Germany. And as they liberated the countries of eastern Europe, the Soviets created puppet governments they could easily control.

THE BATTLE OF THE ATLANTIC While fighting raged in North Africa, the more crucial Battle of the Atlantic reached its climax on the high seas. Several factors brought success to the Allied effort. Scientists perfected a variety of new detection devices: radar, which the British had already used to advantage in the Battle of Britain, bounced radio waves off objects above the surface and registered their positions on a screen; sonar gear detected sound waves from submerged U-boats, and sonobuoys, dropped from planes, radioed back their findings; advanced magnetic equipment enabled aircraft to detect objects under water. New escort aircraft carriers ("baby flat-tops") and improvements in depth charges added to the effectiveness of convoys.

By early 1943, there were in the western half of the North Atlantic at any one time an average of thirty-one convoys with 145 escorts and 673 merchant ships, and a number of heavily escorted troopships. None of the troopships going to Britain or the Mediterranean was lost, although submarines sank three en route to Greenland and Iceland. The U-boats kept up the Battle of the Atlantic until the war's end; but their commander later admitted that the Battle of the Atlantic was lost by the end of May 1943. He credited the difference largely to radar. What he did not know then was that the Allies had a secret weapon. By early 1943 their cryptanalysts were routinely decoding secret messages and telling their sub-hunters where to look for German U-boats.

SICILY AND ITALY After the Allied victory in the North African campaign, on July 10, 1943, about 250,000 British and American troops landed on Sicily, scoring a complete surprise. The German-Italian collapse in Sicily ended Mussolini's twenty years of fascist rule. On July 25, 1943, Italy's king notified the dictator of his dismissal as premier.

A new regime startled the Allies when it offered not only to surrender but to switch sides in the war. Unfortunately, mutual suspicions prolonged talks until September 3, while the Germans poured reinforcements into Italy and seized key points. In the confusion the Italian army disintegrated, although most of the navy escaped to Allied ports. A few army units later joined the Allied effort, and many of the Italian soldiers joined bands of partisans who fought behind the German lines. Mussolini, plucked from imprisonment by a daring German airborne raid, became head of a shadowy puppet government in northern Italy.

The Allied assault on the Italian mainland therefore did not turn into an easy victory. The main landing at Salerno on September 9 encountered heavy German resistance. The Americans, joined by British troops, nevertheless secured beachheads within a week and soon captured Naples. Rome was the next objective, but mountainous country stood in the way. Fighting stalled through the winter of 1943–1944 in some of the most miserable, muddy, and frigid conditions of the war. After a five-month siege, the Americans finally took Rome on June 4, 1944. Yet they enjoyed only a brief moment of glory, for the long-awaited cross-Channel landing in France began two days later.

STRATEGIC BOMBING OF EUROPE Behind the long-postponed landings on the Normandy beaches lay months of preparation. While waiting, the United States Army Air Force and the Royal Air Force (RAF) carried the battle into Hitler's "Fortress Europe." By 1943 American strategic bombers were full-fledged partners of the RAF in the effort to pound Germany into submission. Yet, despite the widespread damage it caused, the strategic air offensive ultimately failed to cut severely into German production or, as later studies found, to break civilian morale. German war production in fact increased until the last few weeks of the war, and German fighter planes downed more and more Allied bombers. By the end of 1943, however, new jettisonable gas tanks permitted Allied escort fighters to fly as far as Berlin and back. Thereafter, heavy losses of both planes and pilots forced the German Luftwaffe to conserve its strength and cease challenging every Allied mission.

With air supremacy assured, the Allies were free to concentrate on their primary urban and industrial targets, and, when the time came, to provide cover for the Normandy landings. On April 14, 1944, General Dwight D. Eisenhower assumed control of the Strategic Air Forces for use in the Normandy landings, less than two months away. On D-Day he told the troops: "If you see fighting aircraft over you, they will be ours."

THE TEHERAN MEETING By the summer of 1943, the buildup of American forces in Britain, combined with successes in the Battle of the Atlantic and the strategic bombing of Europe, finally convinced Churchill to support a cross-Channel invasion. Late in November he and Roosevelt met with Stalin in Teheran, Iran, to coordinate plans for the invasion of France and a Soviet offensive from the east. After Churchill and Roosevelt assured Stalin that a cross-Channel invasion was finally coming, the Soviet premier in return promised to enter the war against Japan after Germany's defeat. The Allied leaders also agreed to begin plans for a new international peacekeeping organization and for the occupation of postwar Germany.

Earlier, in November 1943, while on the way to the Teheran meeting with Stalin, Churchill and Roosevelt had met with China's Generalissimo Chiang Kai-shek in Cairo, Egypt. The resulting Declaration of Cairo affirmed that war against Japan would continue until its unconditional surrender, that all Chinese territories taken by Japan would be restored to China, and that "in due course Korea shall become free and independent."

D-DAY AND AFTER In early 1944 General Eisenhower arrived in London to take command at Supreme Headquarters, Allied Expeditionary Forces (SHAEF). Already battle-tested in North Africa and the Mediterranean, he now faced the supreme test of planning and conducting Operation "Overlord," the cross-Channel assault on Hitler's "Atlantic Wall." By early 1944, over a million American soldiers were training along England's southern coast for the cross-Channel invasion.

Of course, Hitler had been preparing for such an assault as well. German forces using captive Europeans for laborers had created what seemed to be a series of impregnable fortifications along the French coastline. Huge concrete blockhouses protected their artillery, and trenches and camouflage shielded their machine-gun nests. The Germans also used forced laborers to sow the beaches with 4 million mines interlaced with barbed wire and antitank obstacles.

General Dwight D. Eisenhower instructing paratroopers just before they board their airplanes to launch the D-Day assault.

The prospect of an amphibious assault against such defenses in a single huge battle unnerved some of the Allied planners. Churchill worried about "Channel tides running red with Allied blood." As D-Day approached, Eisenhower's chief of staff predicted only a 50-50 chance of success. Ike had his doubts as well. He kept in his wallet a message for the press in case the invasion failed. It read: "My decision to attack at this time and place was based upon the best information available. If any blame or fault attaches to the attempt, it is mine alone."

On the evening of June 5, Eisenhower visited some of the 16,000 American paratroopers preparing to land in France behind the German lines to create chaos and disrupt communications. The men noticed his look of concern and tried to lift his spirits. "Now quit worrying, General," one of them said, "we'll take care of this thing for you." After the planes took off, Eisenhower returned to his car with tears in his eyes. "Well," he said quietly to his driver, "it's on."

The day before, Eisenhower's German counterpart, Field Marshal Erwin Rommel, left his headquarters along the French coast to go to Berlin to see his family and meet with Hitler. As he departed, he confidently asserted that "there's not going to *be* an invasion. And if there is, then they won't even get off the beaches." When the American public learned that the invasion had been launched, routine activities gave way to anxious listening over the radio for reports from the front. Stores closed, baseball games and horse races were canceled, and church bells tolled across the country.

Operation Overlord surprised the Germans. Eisenhower fooled Hitler's generals into believing that the invasion would come at Pas de Calais, on the French-Belgian border, where the English Channel was narrowest. Instead, the landings occurred in Normandy, about 200 miles south. Airborne forces dropped behind the beaches during the night while planes and battleships pounded the coastal defenses.

At dawn on June 6, 1944, D-Day, the invasion fleet of some 4,000 ships and 150,000 men (57,000 Americans) filled the horizon off the Normandy coast. Overhead, thousands of Allied planes supported the invasion force. Sleepy German soldiers awoke to see the vast armada arrayed before them. Lieutenant Hans Heinze, a twenty-one-year-old vet-

The array of Allied forces at Normandy, June 1944.

eran of the Russian front, could not believe his eyes. Wiping off his binoculars, he peered through the lifting fog and shouted to his messenger: *"Sie kommen!"* [They are coming!] He then scribbled a note for his headquarters and handed it to his messenger, thinking "They'll never believe it." Nearby, another German lookout peered through his binoculars and muttered, "That's not possible! That's not possible!" His aide retreated into their bunker to pray.

For several hours, the local German commanders refused to believe that this was the actual invasion. They interpreted the Normandy landings as merely a diversion for the "real" attack at Pas de Calais. When Hitler learned of the Allied landings, he boasted that "the news couldn't be better. As long as they were in Britain, we couldn't get at them. Now we have them where we can destroy them."

Despite Eisenhower's meticulous planning and the imposing array of Allied troops and firepower, the D-Day invasion almost failed. Cloud cover and German antiaircraft fire caused many of the paratroopers and glider pilots to miss their landing zones. Oceangoing landing craft delivered their troops to the wrong locations. Low clouds also led the Allied planes assigned to soften up the seaside defenses to drop their bombs too far inland. The naval bombardment was equally ineffective. Moreover, rough seas caused many of the soldiers to become seasick and dozens of landing craft to capsize. Over a thousand men drowned. Waterlogged radios failed to work, and the deafening noise of the artillery and gunfire made oral communication impossible.

On Utah Beach the American invaders made it in against relatively light opposition, but farther east, on a four-mile segment designated Omaha Beach, bombardment had failed to take out German defenders and the Americans were caught in heavily mined water. They then had to make it across a fifty-yard beach exposed to crossfire from concrete pillboxes before they could huddle under a seawall and begin to root out the defenders. In just ten minutes, one rifle company had 197 (out of a unit of 205) men killed or wounded, including every officer and sergeant. Still farther east, British forces had less difficulty on Gold, Juno, and Sword Beaches, but found themselves subjected to bitter counterattack by German forces. By nightfall there were some 5,000 killed or wounded Allied soldiers strewn across Normandy beaches.

German losses were even more incredible. Entire units were decimated or captured. Operation Overlord was the greatest military invasion in the annals of warfare and the climactic battle of World War II. With the beachhead secured, the Allied leaders knew that victory was now in their grasp. "What a plan!" Churchill exclaimed to the British parliament. Stalin, who had been clamoring for the cross-Channel invasion for years, applauded the Normandy operation and heaped praise on the Allies. He declared that the "history of warfare knows no other like undertaking from the point of view of its scale, its vast conception and its orderly execution."

Within two weeks after D-Day, the Allies had landed a million troops, 556,000 tons of supplies, and 170,000 vehicles. They had seized a beachhead sixty miles wide and five to fifteen miles deep. They continued to pour men and supplies onto the beaches and to edge inland through the Normandy marshes and hedgerows. On July 19, 1944, General Omar Bradley's troops took St. Lô, a transportation hub for roads and railroads into the heart of France. The German commanders advised withdrawal to defenses behind the Seine River, but a stubborn Hitler issued disastrous orders to contest every inch of land. Field Marshal Erwin Rommel, convinced that all was lost, began to intrigue for a separate peace. Other like-minded German officers, convinced that the war was hopeless, tried to kill Hitler at his headquarters on July 20, 1944, but the Führer survived the bomb blast, and hundreds of conspirators and suspects were tortured to death. Rommel was granted the option of suicide, which he took.

Meanwhile, Hitler's tactics brought calamity to the German forces in western France. On July 25 American forces broke out westward into Brittany and eastward toward Paris. On August 15 a joint American-French invasion force landed on the French Mediterranean coast and raced up the Rhône Valley. German resistance in France collapsed. A Free French division, aided by American forces, had the honor of liberating Paris on August 25. Hitler's forces retreated toward the German border, and by mid-September most of France and Belgium were cleared of enemy troops. By this time, the Americans were in Aachen, the old seat of Charlemagne's empire, the first German town to fall.

Leapfrogging to Tokyo

Even in the Pacific, relegated to lower priority, Allied forces had brought the war within reach of the enemy homeland by the end of

1944. The war's first American offensive in fact had been in the south-west Pacific. There the Japanese, stopped at Coral Sea and Midway, had thrust into the southern Solomons, and were building an airstrip on Guadalcanal from which they could attack Allied transportation routes to Australia. On August 7, 1942, two months before the North Africa landings, the American First Marine Division landed on Guadalcanal. Japanese reinforcements poured in, and the opposing navies challenged each other in a confusing series of night battles that battered both badly. But while the Americans suffered heavy losses, they so devastated the Japanese carrier groups that the Japanese navy remained on the defensive for the rest of the war. The marines, helped by reinforcements, finally cleared Guadalcanal of Japanese soldiers six months later.

MACARTHUR IN NEW GUINEA Meanwhile, American and Australian forces under General Douglas MacArthur had begun to push the Japanese out of their positions on New Guinea's northern coast. These costly battles, fought through some of the hottest, most humid and mosquito-infested swamps in the world, secured the eastern tip of New Guinea by the end of January 1943.

At this stage, American war planners made a critical decision. MacArthur proposed to move his forces westward along the northern coast of New Guinea toward the Philippines and ultimately to Tokyo. Admiral Chester Nimitz argued for a sweep through the islands of the central Pacific toward Formosa and China. The Combined Chiefs of Staff agreed to MacArthur's plan, but they also ordered Nimitz to undertake his sweep in order to protect MacArthur's northern flank. Another consideration in this decision was pitifully political: to keep both leaders satisfied, as well as the two rival armed services they represented.

A new tactic expedited the movement. During the air Battle of the Bismarck Sea (March 2–3, 1943), American bombers sank eight Japanese troopships and ten warships bringing reinforcements. Thereafter the Japanese dared not risk sending transports to points under siege, making it possible to use the tactic of neutralizing Japanese strongholds with air and sea power, and moving on, leaving them to die on the vine. Some called it "leapfrogging," and it was a major cause of Allied victory. By the end of 1943, MacArthur's forces controlled the northern coast of New Guinea.

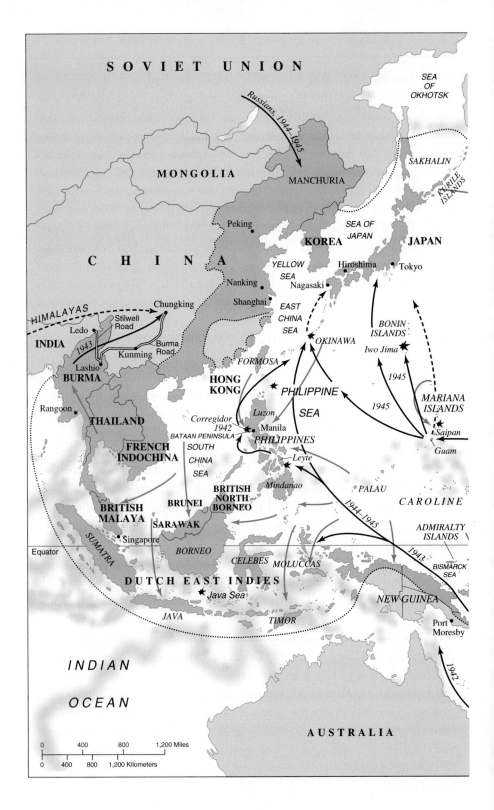

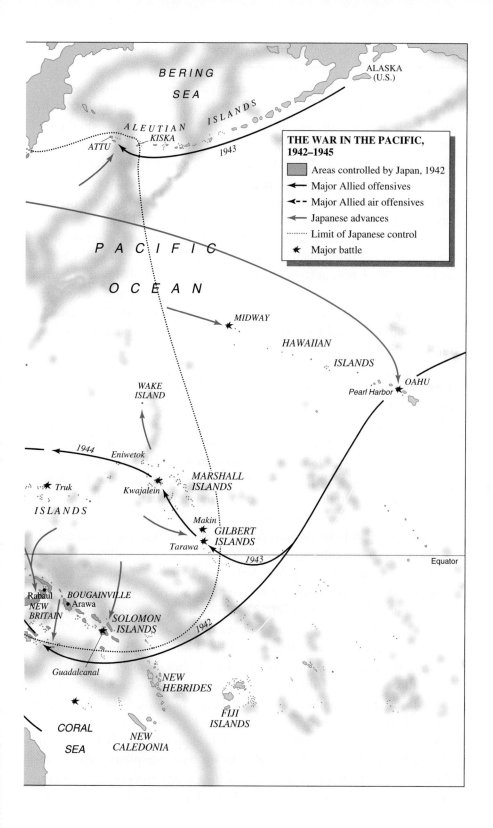

BERING
SEA

ALASKA
(U.S.)

ALEUTIAN ISLANDS

KISKA

ATTU

1943

**THE WAR IN THE PACIFIC,
1942–1945**

Areas controlled by Japan, 1942
Major Allied offensives
Major Allied air offensives
Japanese advances
Limit of Japanese control
★ Major battle

P A C I F I C

O C E A N

MIDWAY

HAWAIIAN

ISLANDS

WAKE
ISLAND

OAHU
Pearl Harbor

1944   Eniwetok

★ Truk

MARSHALL
ISLANDS

Kwajalein

ISLANDS

Makin

GILBERT
ISLANDS

Tarawa

1943

Equator

Rabaul
NEW
BRITAIN

BOUGAINVILLE
Arawa

SOLOMON
ISLANDS

1942

Guadalcanal

NEW
HEBRIDES

★

FIJI
ISLANDS

CORAL

SEA

NEW
CALEDONIA

NIMITZ IN THE CENTRAL PACIFIC   Admiral Nimitz's advance through the central Pacific had as its first target Tarawa in the Gilbert Islands. Tarawa was one of the most heavily protected islands in the Pacific. There nearly 1,000 American soldiers, sailors, and marines lost their lives rooting out 4,000 Japanese who refused to surrender. The Gilberts provided airfields from which the Seventh Air Force began softening up strong points in the Marshall Islands to the northwest. Japanese planes completely abandoned the region.

In the Battle of the Philippine Sea, fought mostly in the air on June 19 and 20, 1944, the Japanese lost three more carriers, two submarines, and over 300 planes, at the cost of only 17 American planes. The battle secured the Marianas, and soon large B-29 bombers were winging their way to the first systematic bombing of the Japanese homeland. Defeat in the Marianas finally convinced General Tojo that the war was lost. On July 18, 1944, he and his entire cabinet resigned.

THE BATTLE OF LEYTE GULF   With New Guinea and the Marianas all but conquered, President Roosevelt met with General MacArthur and Admiral Nimitz in Honolulu to decide the next major step. Previous plans had marked China as the essential springboard for invading Japan, but a Japanese offensive in April 1944 had taken most of the South China airfields from which American air power had operated. This strengthened MacArthur's opinion that the Philippines would provide a safer staging area. He also had a personal desire to recapture the islands he and his American troops had earlier defended. Sentimental and political considerations, as well as military factors, tipped the decision his way. MacArthur made his move into the Philippines on October 20, 1944, landing first on the island of Leyte. Wading ashore behind the first landings, he issued an emotional announcement: "People of the Philippines: I have returned."

The Japanese, knowing that loss of the Philippines would cut them off from the essential resources of the East Indies, brought in fleets from three directions. The three encounters that resulted on October 25 came to be known collectively as the Battle of Leyte Gulf, the largest naval engagement in history. The Japanese lost most of their remaining sea power and the ability to defend the Philippines. The battle also included the first use of suicide attacks by Japanese pilots, who crash-dived into American carriers, thereby killing themselves but also sinking or putting out of commission the Allied ships. The "Kamikaze" units, named for the "Divine Wind" that centuries before had saved Japan from Mongol invasion, inflicted substantial damage on the American navy.

A NEW AGE IS BORN

ROOSEVELT'S FOURTH TERM In 1944, war or no war, the calendar dictated another presidential election. This time the Republicans turned to the former crime-fighter and New York governor, Thomas E. Dewey, as their candidate. Once again no Democratic challenger rose high enough to contest Roosevelt, but a fight did develop over the second spot on the ticket. Vice-President Henry Wallace had aggravated both southern conservatives and northern city bosses who feared his ties with organized labor, so Roosevelt finally chose the relatively unknown Missouri senator Harry S. Truman.

Dewey ran under the same handicap as Alf Landon and Wendell Willkie before him. He did not propose to dismantle Roosevelt's programs, rather he argued that it was time for younger men to replace the tired old leaders of the New Deal. The problem was that, even though considerably younger than Roosevelt, Dewey showed few signs of vitality. Though blessed with a silky voice and a stylish wardrobe, he was ill at ease in public, stiff, formal, seemingly arrogant, and worst of all— dull. "How can we be expected to vote for a man who looks like the bridegroom on a wedding cake?" one Washington veteran asked. Roosevelt betrayed distinct signs of illness and exhaustion, but nevertheless carried the contest to the opposition. On November 7, 1945, he was once again elected, this time by a popular margin of 25.6 million to 22 million and an electoral vote of 432 to 99.

CONVERGING FRONTS The war in Europe was not going as well; final victory remained elusive. After the quick sweep across France, the Allies lost momentum in the fall of 1944 and settled down to slugging it out on the frontiers of Germany. The armies fought along this line all winter.

Then the Germans sprang a surprise in the rugged Ardennes Forest, where the Allied line was thinnest. On December 16, 1944, the Nazis advanced along a fifty-mile bulge in the Allied lines in Belgium and Luxembourg (hence the name, the Battle of the Bulge) before they stalled at Bastogne. Reinforced by the Allies just before it was surrounded, Bastogne held out for six days against all the Germans could bring against it. On December 22 American general "Tony" McAuliffe gave his memorable answer to the German demand for surrender: "Nuts." His situation remained desperate until the next day when the clouds lifted, allowing Allied air power both to drop in supplies and to attack the Germans. On December 26, the besieged American army at Bastogne was relieved, but it would be mid-January 1945 before the previous lines were restored.

Germany's sudden thrust upset Eisenhower's timetable and made continued coordination with the Soviet army even more crucial. The Nazi counterattack in the west had weakened their defense of the eastern front, and in January 1945 the Soviets began their final offensive. The destruction of Hitler's last reserve units at the Battle of the Bulge also left open the door to Germany's heartland. The western offensives started in February, and by early March Allied forces were pouring across the Rhine River. By this time the Soviet offensive had also reached Germany itself.

With the British and American armies racing across western Germany and the Soviets moving in from the east, the attention of the war planners turned to Berlin. Churchill had grown suspicious of the Soviets and worried that if they arrived in Berlin first, they would gain dangerous leverage in deciding the postwar map of Europe. He told Eisenhower of his concerns and urged him to get to Berlin first. Eisenhower, however, refused to mix politics with military strategy. Berlin, he said, no longer was of military significance. His purpose remained the destruction of the enemy's ground forces. Churchill disagreed and appealed to Roosevelt, but the American leader, now seriously ill, left the decision to the Supreme Commander. Eisenhower then asked General Omar Bradley to predict what it would take to liberate Berlin before the Soviets. Bradley estimated that it would cost 100,000 Allied casualties, which he described as a "pretty stiff price to pay for a prestige objective." Eisenhower agreed, and they left Berlin for the Soviets to conquer.

YALTA AND THE POSTWAR WORLD As the final offensives got under way, the Big Three leaders met again in early February 1945 at Yalta, a resort in southern Russia. While the focus at Teheran in 1943 had been on wartime strategy, it was now on the shape of the postwar

The Yalta Conference, *February 1945. Stalin* (right), *FDR* (center), *and Churchill* (left) *confer on the shape of the postwar world.*

world. Two aims loomed large in Roosevelt's thinking. One was the need to ensure that the Soviet Union join the war against Japan. The other was based on the lessons he drew from the previous world war. Chief among the mistakes to be remedied were the failures of the United States to join the League of Nations and of the Allies to maintain a united front in negotiations with the German aggressors.

The Yalta meeting thus began by calling for a conference to create a new world organization called the United Nations. The conferees also decided that substantive decisions in the new organization's Security Council would require the agreement of its five permanent members: the United States, Britain, the Soviet Union, France, and China.

GERMANY AND EASTERN EUROPE With Hitler's "Thousand-Year Reich" stumbling to its doom, the leaders at Yalta had to make arrangements for the postwar governance of Germany. The war map dictated the basic pattern of occupation zones: the Soviet Union would control the east and the Western Allies would control the rich industrial areas of the west. Berlin, isolated within the Soviet zone, would be jointly occupied. Churchill and Roosevelt insisted that liberated France receive a zone along its border with Germany and also in Berlin. Austria was similarly divided, with Vienna, like Berlin, under joint occupation within the Soviet zone. Russian demands for reparations of $20 billion to the Allies, half of which would go to the Soviet Union, were referred to a Reparations Commission. The commission never reached agreement, although the Soviets took untold amounts of machinery and equipment from their occupation zone.

With respect to eastern Europe, where Soviet forces were advancing on a broad front, there was little the Western Allies could do to influence events. Poland became the main focus of Western concern. Britain and France had gone to war in 1939 to defend Poland, and now, six years later, the course of the war had ironically left Poland's fate in the hands of the Soviets. Events had long foreshadowed the outcome. When they entered Poland in 1944, the Soviets placed civil administration under a puppet regime in Lublin. The Soviets refused to recognize the legitimacy of Poland's government-in-exile in London, formed by officials who had fled the country following Hitler's invasion in September 1939. With Soviet troops at the gates of Warsaw, the underground resistance in the city rose against the Nazi occupiers. The Polish underground, however, supported Poland's government-in-exile in London. The Soviets then stopped their offensive for two months while the Nazis in Warsaw wiped out thousands of Poles, potential rivals to the Soviets' Lublin puppet government.

Hope that postwar cooperation between the Soviets and Americans could survive such events was a triumph of optimism over experience. The Western Allies found at Yalta that they could do no more than acquiesce or stall. On the Soviet proposal to expand the Lublin Committee into a provisional government together with representatives of the London Poles, they acquiesced. On the issue of Poland's boundaries, they stalled. The Soviets proposed to keep eastern Poland, offering land taken from Germany as compensation. Roosevelt and Churchill accepted the proposal, but they considered Poland's new western boundary at the Oder–Western Neisse Rivers only provisional. Yet the peace conference at which Poland's western boundary was to be settled never took place because of later disagreements. The presence of the London Poles in the provisional government only lent a tone of legitimacy to a regime dominated by the Communists, who soon ousted their rivals.

The Big Three also promised to sponsor free elections, democratic governments, and constitutional safeguards of freedom throughout the rest of Europe. The Yalta Declaration of Liberated Europe reaffirmed faith in the principles of the Atlantic Charter and the United Nations, but in the end it made little difference. It may have postponed Communist takeovers in eastern Europe for a few years, but before long Communist members of coalition governments had their hands on the levers of power and purged the opposition. Russia, twice invaded by Germany in the twentieth century, was determined to create buffer states between it and the Germans.

YALTA'S LEGACY Critics later attacked the Yalta agreements for "giving" eastern Europe over to Soviet domination. Some argued that Roosevelt's declining health caused him to buckle under Stalin's insistent demands. But the course of the war shaped the actions at Yalta, not personal diplomacy. The Red Army had the upper hand in eastern Europe. Perhaps the most bitterly criticized of the Yalta understandings was a secret agreement on the Far East, not made public until after the war. The Joint Chiefs of Staff still estimated that Japan could hold out for eighteen months after the defeat of Germany. Costly campaigns thus lay ahead, and the atomic bomb was still an expensive and untested gamble.

Roosevelt felt that he had no choice but to accept Stalin's demands on postwar arrangements in the Far East, subject technically to later agreement by Chiang Kai-shek. Stalin wanted continued Soviet control of Outer Mongolia through its puppet People's Republic there, acquisition of the Kurile Islands from Japan, and recovery of rights and territory lost after the Russo-Japanese War of 1905. Stalin in return promised to enter the war against Japan two or three months after the German defeat, to recognize Chinese sovereignty over Manchuria, and to conclude a treaty of friendship and alliance with the Chinese Nationalists. Roosevelt's concessions would later appear in a different light, but given their geographical advantages in Asia as in eastern Europe, the Soviets were in a position to get what they wanted in any case.

THE THIRD REICH COLLAPSES The collapse of Nazi resistance was imminent by early 1945, but President Roosevelt did not live to join the celebrations. All through 1944 his health had been declining, and on April 12, 1945, while he was drafting a speech, he suffered a cerebral hemorrhage, which brought sudden death.

Hitler's Germany collapsed less than a month later. The Allied armies rolled up almost unopposed to the Elbe River, where they met advance detachments of Soviets on April 25. Three days later Italian partisans captured and brutally killed Mussolini and his mistress as they tried to flee. In Berlin, which was under siege by the Soviets, Hitler married his mistress, Eva Braun, in an underground bunker on the last day of April, just before killing her and himself. On May 2 Berlin fell to the Soviets. That same day German forces in Italy surrendered. On May 7 the Germans signed an unconditional surrender in Allied headquarters at Reims.

Massive victory celebrations on V-E Day, May 8, 1945, were tempered by the tragedies that had engulfed the world: mourning for the lost president and the death and mutilation of untold millions. Most shocking was the revelation of the Nazi Holocaust, scarcely believable until the Allied armies discovered the death camps in which Nazis had sought to apply their "final solution" to the Jewish "problem": the

A Russian soldier raises the Soviet flag over the Reichstag after the conquest of Berlin, May 1945.

wholesale extermination of some 6 million Jews along with more than 1 million others from occupied countries.

During the war, reports from Red Cross and underground sources had amassed growing evidence of Germany's systematic genocide against European Jews. Stories appeared in major American newspapers as early as 1942, but they were nearly always buried on inside pages. And reports of such horror seemed beyond belief. American government officials, even some Jewish leaders, dragged their feet on the question for fear that relief efforts for Jewish refugees might stir latent anti-Semitism at home. Finally, Roosevelt set up a War Refugees Board in 1944, but with few resources at its disposal. It nevertheless managed to rescue about 200,000 European Jews and some 20,000 others. But more might have been done. The Allies rejected the bombing of rail lines into the largest death camp, Auschwitz in Poland, although American planes hit industries five miles away. Moreover, few refugees were accepted into the United States. The Allied handling of the Holocaust was inept at best and disgraceful at worst.

A GRINDING WAR AGAINST JAPAN The sobering thought that Japan must still be defeated cast a further pall over the victory celebrations. American forces continued to penetrate and disrupt the Japanese Empire in the early months of 1945, but at heavy cost. On February 19, 1945, American marines invaded Iwo Jima, a volcanic island 750 miles from Tokyo. The island was needed to provide fighter escort for bombers over Japan and as a landing strip for disabled B-29s. It took nearly six weeks to secure Iwo Jima from defenders hiding in an underground labyrinth, and the cost was high: more than 20,000 American casualties, including 7,000 dead.

The fight for Okinawa, beginning on Easter Sunday, April 1, was even bloodier. The island was large enough to afford a staging area for the invasion of the Japanese islands, and its capture required the largest amphibious operation of the Pacific war, involving some 300,000 troops. Desperate Japanese counterattacks inflicted heavy losses. Kamikaze planes attacked by the hundreds. The Japanese sent the battleship *Yamato* and nine other ships—the remnant of a great navy—to aid the fighters. American seaplanes intercepted them and sank the *Yamato* and two other ships and badly damaged the rest, thereby destroying the remains of the Japanese navy. The battle for Okinawa raged until late June, when the bloody attrition destroyed any further Japanese ability to resist. The fighting brought nearly 50,000 American casualties. The Japanese lost an estimated 140,000 dead. Casualties included about 42,000 Okinawans. When resistance on Okinawa collapsed, the Japanese emperor instructed his new premier to seek peace terms. Washington decoded Japanese messages that suggested either an effort to avoid unconditional surrender or perhaps just a stall.

THE ATOMIC BOMB By the summer of 1945, however, word of a new weapon had changed all strategic calculations: President Truman learned of the first successful test of an atomic bomb. In 1939, Albert Einstein had alerted President Roosevelt to German research on nuclear fission. In 1940 the president diverted some army and navy funds into research that grew ultimately into the $2 billion top-secret Manhattan Project, involving over 120,000 workers.

A group of physicists directed by Dr. J. Robert Oppenheimer worked out the scientific and technical problems of bomb construction in a laboratory at Los Alamos, New Mexico. On July 16, 1945, the first atomic fireball rose from the desert. The test explosion broke windows 125 miles away, and a blind woman saw the flash. Oppenheimer said later that in the observation bunker, "A few people laughed, a few people cried, most people were silent." After learning of the successful test, President Truman wrote in his diary: "We have discovered the most terrible bomb in the history of the world."

How to use this awful new weapon posed unique problems. Some scientists favored a demonstration explosion for the Japanese in a remote area, but this was vetoed because only two bombs were available, and even those might misfire. The choice of targets received more consideration. Four Japanese cities had been reserved from conventional bombing as potential targets for the new weapon. After deciding against Kyoto, Japan's ancient capital and repository of many national and religious treasures, priority went to Hiroshima, a port city of 400,000 people in southern Japan, which was a center of war industries, headquarters of the Second General Army, and command center for the homeland's defenses. This target met Truman's guidelines. He had written that only military personnel and installations, not "women and children" should be targeted. He had no idea that the bomb would destroy virtually an entire city.

On July 25, 1945, President Truman, then at the Big Three Conference in Potsdam, Germany, ordered the bomb dropped if Japan did not surrender before August 3. Although an intense scholarly debate has emerged over the decision to drop the atomic bomb, Truman never considered not using it at the earliest opportunity. He later stressed: "Let there be no mistake about it. I regarded the bomb as a military weapon and never had any doubt that it should be used." He was convinced that using the atomic bomb would in the end save lives by avoiding an American invasion against defenders who would fight like "savages, ruthless, merciless, and fanatic."

The ferocious Japanese defense of Okinawa had convinced American military planners that an amphibious invasion of Japan itself, scheduled to begin on November 1, 1945, could cost as many as 250,000 Allied casualties and even more Japanese losses. Moreover, some 100,000 Allied prisoners of war being held in Japan were to be executed whenever an invasion began. It is important to remember as well that the bombing of cities and the consequent killing of civilians had become accepted military practice during 1945. Once the Japanese navy was destroyed, American ships were able to roam the Japanese coastline, shelling targets on shore. American planes bombed at will and mined the waters of the Inland Sea. Tokyo, Nagoya, and other major cities were devastated by firestorms created by incendiary bombs. The prevalence of wooden structures in earthquake-prone Japan made the incendiary raids even more deadly. The firebomb raids on Tokyo on a single night in March 1945 killed 100,000 civilians and left over a million people homeless. By July more than sixty of Japan's largest cities had been firebombed, resulting in 500,000 deaths and 13 million civilians left homeless. The use of atomic bombs on Japanese cities was thus seen as a logical next step in an effort to end the war without an invasion of Japan. As it turned out, American scientists greatly underestimated the physical effects of the atomic bomb. They predicted that 20,000 people would be killed.

On July 26 the heads of the American, British, and Chinese governments issued the Potsdam Declaration demanding that Japan surrender or face "prompt and utter destruction." The deadline passed, and at 8:15 in the morning, flying at 31,600 feet, the *Enola Gay* released the five-ton uranium bomb nicknamed "Little Boy." Forty-three seconds later, as the *Enola Gay* turned sharply to avoid the blast, the bomb tum-

A charred watch marks the moment of nuclear conflagration in Hiroshima, August 6, 1945.

bled to an altitude of 1,900 feet, where it exploded as planned with the force of 15,000 tons of TNT. A blinding flash of light was followed by a fireball towering to 40,000 feet. The tail gunner on the *Enola Gay* described the scene: "It's like bubbling molasses down there . . . the mushroom is spreading out . . . fires are springing up everywhere . . . it's like a peep into hell."

The shock wave, firestorm, cyclonic winds, and radioactive rain killed some 80,000 people, including thousands of Japanese soldiers assigned to the Second General Army headquarters and 23 American prisoners of war housed in the city. Dazed survivors wandered the streets, so badly burned that their skin began to peel in large strips. By the end of the year, the death toll had reached 140,000 as the effects of radiation burns and infection took their toll. In addition, 70,000 buildings were destroyed, and four square miles of the city turned to rubble.

In the United States, Americans greeted the first news with elation: it promised a quick end to the long nightmare of war. "No tears of sympathy will be shed in America for the Japanese people," the *Omaha World Herald* predicted. "Had they possessed a comparable weapon at Pearl Harbor, would they have hesitated to use it?" Others were more circumspect. "Yesterday," journalist Hanson Baldwin wrote in the *New York Times*, "we clinched victory in the Pacific, but we sowed the whirlwind." Only later would people realize that it marked the start of a more enduring nightmare, the nuclear arms race.

Two days after the Hiroshima bombing, an opportunistic Soviet Union hastened to enter the war. On August 9, a second American atomic bomb exploded over the port city of Nagasaki, a shipbuilding and torpedo-factory center, killing 36,000 more people. That night the emperor urged his cabinet to accept the inevitable and surrender on the sole condition that he remain as sovereign. The next day the United States government, to facilitate surrender and an orderly transition, announced its willingness to let him keep the throne, but under the authority of an Allied Supreme Commander. Frantic exchanges ended with Japanese acceptance on August 14, 1945, when the emperor himself broke precedent to record a radio message announcing the surrender to his people. Even then a last-ditch palace revolt had to be squashed. On September 2, 1945, General MacArthur and other Allied representatives accepted Japan's formal surrender on board the battleship *Missouri*.

THE FINAL LEDGER

Thus ended the most deadly conflict in human history. No effort to tabulate a ledger of death and destruction can ever take the full measure of the suffering caused by the war, nor hope to be more than a rough guess as to the numbers involved. One estimate has it that 70 million in all fought in the war, at a cost of some 50 million military and civilian dead. Material costs were also enormous, perhaps $1 trillion in military expenditures and twice that in property losses. The Soviet Union suffered the greatest losses of all, over 13 million military deaths, more than 7 million civilians dead, and at least 25 million left homeless. World War II was more costly for the United States than any other of the country's foreign wars: 292,000 battle deaths and 114,000 other deaths. But in proportion to population, the United States suffered a loss far smaller than any of the major Allies or enemies, and American territory escaped the devastation inflicted on so many other parts of the world.

World War II had profound effects on American life and society. Mobilization for war stimulated a phenomenal increase in American productivity and brought full employment, thus ending the Great Depression and laying the foundation for a new era of unprecedented prosperity. New technologies and products developed for military purposes—radar, computers, electronics, plastics and synthetics, jet engines, rockets, atomic energy—soon began to transform the private sector as well. And new opportunities for women as well as for blacks and other minorities set in motion changes that would culminate in the civil rights movement of the 1960s and the feminist movement of the 1970s.

The Democratic party benefited from the war effort by solidifying its control of both the White House and Congress. The dramatic expansion of the federal government occasioned by the war continued after 1945. Presidential authority and prestige increased enormously at the expense of congressional and state power. The isolationist sentiment in foreign relations that had been so powerful in the 1920s and 1930s fell into disrepute as the United States emerged from the war with global responsibilities and interests. Thus the war's end opened a new era for the United States in the world arena. It accelerated the growth of American power while devastating all other world powers, leaving the United States economically and militarily the strongest nation on earth.

MAKING CONNECTIONS

- Compare the impact of World War II on the home front to that of World War I, especially the effects of war on race and gender relations.

- The growing domestic conservatism of the war years continued into the 1950s, a topic discussed in the next chapter.

- Dwight D. Eisenhower's success as American general and Allied leader led to his nomination and election as president in 1952. Compare Eisenhower's political experience to those of Ulysses S. Grant and other American military leaders.

FURTHER READING

John Keegan's *The Second World War* (1990) surveys the European conflict in its entirety, while Charles B. MacDonald's *The Mighty Endeavor: The American War in Europe* (rev. ed., 1992) concentrates on American involvement. Roosevelt's wartime leadership is analyzed in Eric Larrabee's *Commander in Chief: Franklin Delano Roosevelt, His Lieutenants and Their War* (1987).

Books on specific campaigns in Europe include Stephen E. Ambrose's *D Day, June 6, 1944: The Climactic Battle of World War II* (1994) and Charles B. MacDonald's *A Time for Trumpets: The Untold Story of the Battle of the Bulge* (rev. ed., 1997).

For the war in the Far East, see John Costello's *The Pacific War, 1941–1945* (1983), Ronald H. Spector's *Eagle against the Sun: The American War with Japan* (1984), John Dower's award-winning *War Without Mercy: Race and Power in the Pacific War* (1986), and Dan van der Vat's *The Pacific Campaign: The U.S.–Japanese Naval War, 1941–1945* (1992).

An excellent overview of the war's effects on the home front is Michael C. C. Adams's *The Best War Ever: America and World War II* (1993). The government's effort to use movies to influence public opinion is described in Clayton R. Koppes and Gregory D. Black's *Hollywood Goes to War: How Politics, Profits and Propaganda Shaped World War II Movies* (1987).

Susan M. Hartmann's *The Home Front and Beyond: American Women in the 1940s* (1982) and Karen Anderson's *Wartime Women: Sex Roles, Family Relations, and the Status of Women during World War II* (1981) treat the new working environment for women. Neil Wynn looks at the participation of blacks in *The Afro-American and the Second World War* (rev. ed., 1993). The story of the oppression of Japanese Americans is told in Peter Irons's *Justice at War* (1983) and David J. O'Brien and Stephen S. Fugita's *The Japanese American Experience* (1993).

A sound introduction to American diplomacy during the conflict can be found in Gaddis Smith's *American Diplomacy during the Second World War, 1941–1945* (2nd ed., 1985). To understand the role that Roosevelt played in policy making, consult Warren F. Kimball's *The Jug-

gler: Franklin Roosevelt as Wartime Statesman (1991). Diane Shaver Clemens is critical of Roosevelt in *Yalta* (1970).

The issues and events that led to the deployment of atomic weapons are addressed in Gregg Herken's *The Winning Weapon: The Atomic Bomb in the Cold War, 1945–1950* (1980) and Martin J. Sherwin's *A World Destroyed: The Atomic Bomb and the Grand Alliance* (1975). Gar Alperovitz's *Atomic Diplomacy: Hiroshima and Potsdam* (2nd ed., 1995) details how the bomb helped shape American postwar policy.

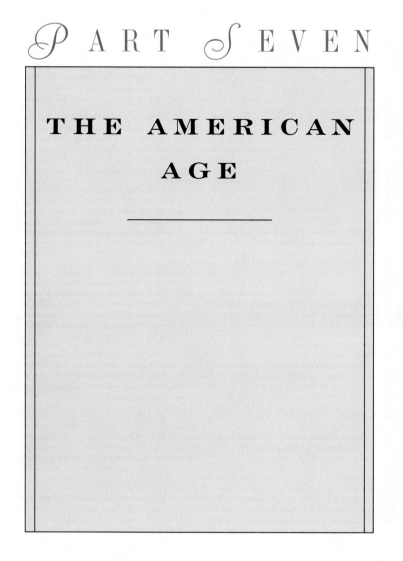

PART SEVEN

THE AMERICAN
AGE

POLITICAL	GLOBAL

1945

Truman becomes president (1945–1953)

George Kennan outlines the rationale of containment in *Foreign Affairs* (1947)

National Security Act makes permanent the Joint Chiefs of Staff, creates the Central Intelligence Agency and the National Security Council (1947)

Truman Doctrine establishes plan to help postwar Europe (1947)

Dixiecrats nominate J. Strom Thurmond for president; Truman unexpectedly wins reelection (1948)

House Un-American Activities Committee keeps lists on possible subversives, eventually fueling the outbreak of the 2nd Red Scare (1940s–1950s)

11 top Communist party leaders convicted under Smith Act (1949)

United Nations is created (1945)

Communists take over governments in eastern Europe (1946–1948)

Civil War in Greece (1946–1947)

Indian independence (1947)

Marshall Plan funnels $13 billion to Europe (1948–1951)

Soviets blockade West Berlin; U.S. and Allies respond with Berlin Airlift (1948)

State of Israel declared; Arabs begin war to destroy Israel (1948)

Soviets lift blockade of Berlin; create German Democratic Republic (1949)

NATO is created (1949)

Soviets explode atomic bomb (1949)

Communists led by Mao Tse-tung win civil war in China; Nationalists under Chiang Kai-shek flee to Formosa (Taiwan) (1949)

1950

Alger Hiss convicted for lying about espionage; Congress passes McCarren Internal Security Act; Senator Joseph McCarthy begins witch-hunt for Communists (1950)

22nd Amendment limits presidents after Truman to 2 terms (1951)

Dwight D. Eisenhower becomes president (1953–1961)

U.S. executes Julius and Ethel Rosenberg for espionage (1953)

McCarthy hearings; Congress votes to censure McCarthy (1954)

Civil Rights Acts (1957, 1960) do little to achieve equality for black citizens

Korean War (1950–1953)

U.S. helps overthrow governments of Iran (1953) and Guatemala (1954)

Communist Viet Minh defeat French at Dien Bien Phu; Geneva Accords create North Vietnam and South Vietnam (1954)

U.S. sends funds and military advisers to South Vietnam (1954)

Warsaw Pact confirms military alliances of Communist eastern European countries with the Soviet Union (1955)

Egypt nationalizes the Suez Canal Company, causing the Suez War (1956)

Soviet forces crush a liberation movement in Hungary (1956)

Soviets launch Sputnik (1957); U.S. launches Explorer I (1958)

Fidel Castro leads a successful revolution in Cuba (1959)

1960

John F. Kennedy becomes president (1961–1963)

Black employment in the upper ranks of federal civil service increases 88% (1961–1963)

Lyndon B. Johnson becomes president following JFK's assassination (1963–1969)

Johnson defeats Goldwater in landslide (1964)

Voting Rights Act ends literacy tests in the South (1965)

Johnson decides not to run for reelection; Democratic convention in Chicago turns violent (1968)

Martin Luther King and Robert Kennedy killed by assassins (1968)

Soviet Uri Gagarin orbits earth; American Alan Shepard reaches space (1961)

U.S. launches Alliance for Progress and Peace Corps (1961)

Plot to overthrow Castro fails at Bay of Pigs in Cuba (1961)

Cuban missile crisis (1962)

U.S. presence in Vietnam escalates after Gulf of Tonkin Resolution (1964)

Cultural Revolution in China (1966–1969)

Tet Offensive turns U.S. public opinion against the war in Vietnam (1968)

Soviets occupy Czechoslovakia, ending "Prague Spring" (1968)

Student riots in Paris (1968)

SOCIAL	ECONOMIC	

| | | |

Women leave the workforce to make room for returning soldiers (1945)

College enrollment quadruples (1945–1970)

Nearly 50% of all adult Americans own homes (1945–1960)

Benjamin Spock publishes *Common Sense Book of Baby and Child Care* (1946)

Baby boom increases U.S. population by 30% (40 million) (1946–1960)

Number of television sets in U.S. increases from 7,000 to 50 million (1946–1960)

Jackie Robinson becomes 1st black player in major league baseball (1947)

Truman bans racial discrimination in federal hiring and orders desegregation of armed forces (1948)

Returning servicemen use GI bill to pay for college or job training or to buy homes (1945–1949)

Strikes by auto and steel workers lead to wage and price increases, fueling inflation and leading to a 6% rise in the cost of living (1945–1946)

Car production soars from 2 million to 8 million (1946–1950s)

Greater availability of discretionary income and credit leads to purchases of homes, cars, televisions, and washing machines (1946–1950s)

Technological advances lead to agricultural surpluses (1940s–1970s)

Taft-Hartley Act curbs power of labor unions (1947)

Congress funds construction of 79,000 miles of highways (1947–1956)

Rise of the suburbs (1950s)

A religious revival castes prosperity and conformity in a moral light (1950s)

Beat poets rebel against middle-class life and conformity (1950s)

Brown v. *Board of Education* prohibits segregation in public schools, overruling "separate but equal" doctrine (1954)

Rosa Parks inspires Montgomery Bus Boycott (1955)

Arthur Miller, Edward Albee, and Tennessee Williams write plays portraying alienation (1950s–1960s)

Martin Luther King establishes SCLC to combat racism (1957)

Arkansas prevents blacks from entering Little Rock's Central High School; Eisenhower sends federal troops to enforce desegregation (1957)

Gap between incomes of blacks and whites continues to increase (1950s)

Eisenhower approves joint U.S.-Canadian development of St. Lawrence Seaway (1954)

Amendments to Social Security Act extend benefits to professionals (1954, 1956)

Government raises minimum wage from 75¢ to $1 per hour (1955)

Eisenhower submits to Congress largest peacetime budget in history (1957)

Government makes agriculture surpluses available to poor Americans through use of food stamps (1959)

Social Security benefits increase 7% (1959)

César Chavez organizes the United Farm Workers (1962)

Betty Friedan's *The Feminine Mystique* is published (1963)

200,000 demonstrators join Dr. King's March on Washington (1963)

Bracero program ends (1964)

Civil Rights Act outlaws segregation in public facilities and discriminatory employment practices (1964)

LBJ's "war on poverty" leads to Great Society legislation (1964–1965)

Student activists protest Vietnam War (1964–1970s)

Immigration Act of 1965 liberalizes nation's immigration policies (1965)

Separatist black power movement leads to founding of Black Panthers (1966)

Redevelopment Act earmarks $400 million for "distressed areas" (1961)

Kennedy makes available $4.9 billion to cities for mass transit and housing (1962)

Tariff Expansion Act leads to tariff cuts between U.S. and Common Market (1963)

Federal allocation of billions of dollars for education, medical care, and housing fuels economic growth (1964)

Government establishes Department of Housing and Urban Development (1966)

POLITICAL	GLOBAL
1970 Richard Nixon becomes president (1969–1974)	American Neil Armstrong is 1st man to walk on moon (1969)
26th Amendment gives 18-year-olds the right to vote in all elections (1971)	
Watergate break-in (1972)	Nixon reopens Communist China (1972)
War Powers Act passes (1973)	U.S. and Soviets sign SALT, and begin détente (1972)
Spiro Agnew resigns vice-presidency after accepting bribes (1973)	Last U.S. combat troops pulled out of Vietnam (1973)
House impeaches Nixon for his role in Watergate (1974)	South Vietnam falls to Communists (1975)
Nixon resigns (1974); Gerald Ford becomes president (1974–1977)	
Ford pardons Nixon (1974)	Mao Tse-tung dies (1976)
Jimmy Carter becomes president (1977–1981)	Panama Canal Treaties (1977)
	Israel and Egypt sign Camp David Accords (1978)
	U.S. signs SALT II with the Soviets (1979)
	Soviets invade Afghanistan (1979)
	Iranian hostage crisis (1979–1980)
1980 Moral Majority becomes political force (1980s)	Iran-Iraq War (1980)
Ronald Reagan becomes president (1981–1989)	
Iran-Contra scandal cripples Reagan Presidency (1986)	U.S. supports Contras and anti-Communist regimes in Central America (1980s)
	U.S. begins development of Strategic Defense Initiative ("Star Wars") (1983)
	Mikhail Gorbachev promotes *glasnost* and *perestroika* in Soviet Union (1985–1989)
	U.S. and Soviets sign the INF Treaty eliminating intermediate-range missiles (1987)
George Bush becomes president (1989–1993)	Soviets pull out of Afghanistan; Berlin Wall falls; Soviet empire collapses (1989)
	Government kills Chinese student protesters in Tiananmen Square (1989)
1990	Germany is reunited (1990)
	U.S. and Soviets sign agreement to reduce number of long-range missiles (1990)
	Soviet Union dissolves into 12 autonomous republics (1991)
	Operation Desert Storm (1991)
William J. Clinton becomes president (1993–2001)	Former Yugoslavia erupts in violent ethnic conflict between Serbs, Croats, and Bosnian Muslims (1991–1995)
Republican-dominated Congress attempts to enact "Contract with America," passing 26 bills, but only 4 become law (1995)	Apartheid ends in South Africa (1992)
1999 House impeaches Clinton as a result of Lewinsky scandal; Senate does not vote to convict him (1999)	NATO intervention against Serbs restores Muslim refugees to Kosovo (1999)

SOCIAL	ECONOMIC	
Affirmative action programs encourage hiring of women and members of racial minorities (1960s–1980s)	Inflation rises from 3% to 12% (1967–1974)	**1970**
Revival of evangelical religion (1970s–1980s)	Clean Air Act allocates funds for cleaning up air and water pollution (1970)	
	Stock market contraction leads to "Nixon recession"; Nixon freezes wages and prices (1971)	
In *Roe* v. *Wade,* Supreme Court legalizes abortions during first trimester (1973)	Energy crisis in U.S. due to Arab oil boycott and OPEC price increases (1973)	
Percentage of those living below poverty level increases (1979–1983)		
90% of nation's population growth occurs in Sunbelt southwestern states (1980s)	Inflation reaches 18%; mortgage rates reach 15%, and interest rates peak at 20% (1980)	**1980**
Culture of consumerism characterized by rampant spending and less personal savings (1980s)	Economic Recovery Tax Act lowers taxes and leads to mounting deficit (1981)	
Most immigrants to U.S. come from Asia and Latin America (1980s–1990s)	Unemployment reaches 10.4% in worst recession since 1930s (1981–1982)	
Computer technology revolutionizes the way people live and work (1980s–1990s)	Federal deficit for 1983 higher than all previous deficits combined (1983)	
Rise of right to life movement (1980s–1990s)	Union participation decreases (1980s)	
	Federal debt soars to $1.4 trillion (1987)	
	Stock market crashes 22.6% (1987)	
	Savings & Loan crisis resolved by $500 billion federal bailout (1989)	
		1990
Militia movements spread throughout America, culminating with tragedies at Ruby Ridge, Waco, and Oklahoma City (1992–1996)	NAFTA links economies of Mexico, the U.S., and Canada (1993)	
Federal courts limit affirmative action programs (1996)	Major federal welfare programs turned over to states (1996)	
	Record-setting productivity and profits; gap widens between rich and poor (1990s)	
	1st federal surplus in 30 years (1998)	
Internet and e-mail spark commercial and communications revolutions (1990s)	Dow Jones industrial average increases from 3,500 to 11,000+ (1993–1999)	**1999**

The United States emerged from World War II the preeminent military and economic power in the world. Americans had a monopoly over the atomic bomb and enjoyed a commanding position in international trade. While much of Europe and Asia struggled to recover from the horrific physical devastation of the war, the United States was virtually unscathed, its economic infrastructure intact and operating at peak efficiency. By 1955 the United States, with only 6 percent of the world's population, was producing well over half of the world's goods. In Europe, Japan, and elsewhere, American products and forms of entertainment and fashion attracted excited attention.

Yet the specter of the "cold war" cast a pall over the buoyant revival of the American economy after World War II. The ideological contest with the Soviet Union and Communist China produced numerous foreign crises and sparked a domestic witch-hunt for Communists that far surpassed earlier episodes of political and social repression in the nation's history. There was widespread acceptance in both major political parties of the geopolitical assumptions embedded in the ideological cold war with international communism. Both Republican and Democratic presidents affirmed the need to "contain" the spread of Communist influence around the world.

This bedrock assumption eventually embroiled the United States in a tragic war in Southeast Asia that destroyed Lyndon Johnson's presidency and revived neo-isolationist sentiments. The Vietnam War also was the catalyst for a countercultural movement in which young idealists of the "baby-boom" generation sought alternatives to a government and a society that in their eyes had become oppressive and corrupt. The youth revolt provided energy for many overdue social reforms, including the civil rights and environmental movements, but it also contributed to an array of social ills, from street riots to drug abuse to sexual promiscuity. The social upheavals of the 1960s and early 1970s provoked a conservative backlash that overreached itself as well. In their efforts to restore "law and order," mayors failed to protect civil liberties in their cities. Richard Nixon's paranoid reaction to his critics led to the destruction of his presidency as a result of the Watergate investigations.

Through all of this turmoil, however, the basic premises of welfare state capitalism that Franklin Roosevelt had instituted with his New Deal programs remained essentially intact. With only a few exceptions, both Republicans and Democrats after 1945 came to accept the notion that the *federal government must assume greater responsibility for the welfare of individuals than had heretofore been the case. Even Ronald Reagan, a sharp critic of liberal social-welfare programs, recognized the need for the federal government to provide a "safety net" for those who could not help themselves.*

Yet this fragile consensus about public policy began to disintegrate in the late 1980s amid stunning international events and less visible domestic developments. The internal collapse of the Soviet Union and the disintegration of European communism surprised observers and sent policy makers scurrying to respond to a post–cold war world in which the United States remained the only legitimate superpower. After forty-five years, American foreign policy was no longer centered on a single adversary, and world politics lost its bipolar quality. During the early 1990s, the European Community finally coalesced, the two Germanys reunited, apartheid in South Africa finally ended, and Israel and the Palestinians signed a heretofore unimaginable peace treaty.

At the same time, American foreign policy began to focus less on military power and more on economic competition and technological development. In those arenas, Japan and a reunited Germany challenged the United States for preeminence. By reducing the public's fear of nuclear annihilation, the ending of the cold war also reduced public interest in foreign affairs. The presidential election of 1992 was the first since 1936 in which foreign policy issues played virtually no role. This was an unfortunate development, for post–cold war world affairs remained volatile and dangerous. The implosion of Soviet communism unleashed a series of ethnic, nationalist, and separatist conflicts throughout Eurasia. In the face of inertia among other governments and pleas for assistance, the United States found itself being drawn into crises in faraway locations such as Bosnia, Rwanda, Somalia, Chechnya, and Kosovo.

As the new multipolar world careened toward the end of a century and the start of a new millennium, fault lines began to appear in the American social and economic landscape. A gargantuan federal debt and rising annual deficits threatened to bankrupt a nation that was becoming top-heavy with retirees. Yet by the end of the century, a prolonged period of economic growth, low inflation, budget surpluses, and a record-setting stock market revived the myth of perennial prosperity.

30 ◌◌ THE FAIR DEAL
AND CONTAINMENT

---

*N*o sooner did the Second World War end than a cold war began. The uneasy wartime alliance between the United States and the Soviet Union collapsed completely by the fall of 1945. The two strongest nations to emerge from the carnage of World War II could not bridge their ideological differences over basic issues such as essential human rights, individual liberties, and religious beliefs. Mutual suspicion and a race to gain influence and control over the so-called Third World countries further polarized the two nations. The defeat of Japan and Germany created power vacuums that sucked America and the Soviet Union into an unrelenting war of words fed by clashing strategic interests. At the same time, the destruction of western Europe and the exhaustion of its peoples led to anticolonial uprisings in Asia and Africa that threatened to strip Britain and France of their once-great empires. The postwar world was thus an unstable one in which international tensions shaped the contours of domestic politics and culture as well as foreign adventures.

DEMOBILIZATION UNDER TRUMAN

TRUMAN'S UNEASY START "Who the hell is Harry Truman?" Roosevelt's chief of staff asked the president in the summer of 1944. The question was on more lips when, after less than twelve weeks as vice-president, Harry Truman took the presidential oath on April 12, 1945. Clearly he was not as charismatic or as magisterial as Franklin Roosevelt and that was one of the burdens he would bear. Roosevelt, a journalist wrote years later, "looked imperial, and he acted that way, and he talked that way. Harry Truman, for God's sake—looked and acted and talked like—well, like a failed haberdasher"—which he was.

Roosevelt and Truman came from quite different backgrounds. For Truman there had been no inherited wealth, no early contact with the great and near-great, no European travel, no Groton, no Harvard—indeed, no college at all. Born in 1884 in western Missouri, Truman grew up in Independence, outside of Kansas City. Too nearsighted to join in the activities of other boys, Truman became bookish and introverted. After high school, however, he spent a few years working in Kansas City banks and grew into an outgoing young man.

During World War I, Truman served in France as captain of an artillery battery. Afterward, he and a partner went into the clothing business, but it failed during the recession of 1922, and Truman then entered politics. Elected county judge in 1922, he was defeated in 1924 and elected once again in 1926. In 1934 Missouri sent him to the United States Senate, where he remained fairly obscure until he became chairman of the committee to investigate corruption in defense industries during World War II.

Something about Harry Truman evoked the spirit of Andrew Jackson: his decisiveness, his feisty character, his family loyalty. But that was a side of the man that the American people came to know only as he settled into the presidency. On his first full day as president, as the war in Asia ground on, he remained awestruck. "Boys, if you ever pray, pray for me now," he told a group of reporters. "I don't know whether you fellows ever had a load of hay fall on you, but when they told me yesterday what had happened, I felt like the moon, the stars and all the planets had fallen on me."

Truman favored much of the New Deal and was even prepared to extend its scope, but at the same time he was uneasy with many of the most ardent New Deal reformers. Within ninety days he had replaced much of the Roosevelt cabinet with his own choices. On the whole, his cabinet was more conservative in outlook and included several mediocrities. Truman suffered the further handicap of seeming to be a caretaker for the remainder of Roosevelt's term. Few expected him to run on his own in 1948.

Truman gave one significant clue to his domestic policies on September 6, 1945, when he sent Congress a comprehensive peacetime program that in effect proposed to continue and enlarge the New Deal. Its twenty-one points included expansion of unemployment insurance, a higher minimum wage, a permanent Fair Employment Practices Commission, slum clearance and low-rent housing projects, regional development of the nation's river valleys, and a public works program. "Not even President Roosevelt asked for so much at one sitting," charged the House Republican leader. "It's just a plain case of out-dealing the New Deal." Beset by other problems, Truman soon saw his new domestic proposals mired down in disputes over the transition to a peacetime economy.

CONVERTING TO PEACE The raucous celebrations that greeted Japan's surrender signaled the habitual American response to victory: a rapid demobilization and a return to more carefree pursuits. The public demanded that the president and Congress bring the boys home as soon as possible. By 1947 the total armed forces were down to 1.5 million from a wartime high of almost 12 million. In his memoirs Truman termed this "the most remarkable demobilization in the history of the world, or 'disintegration' if you want to call it that." By early 1950 the army had shrunk to 600,000.

The military veterans returned to schools, new jobs, wives, and babies. Population growth, which had dropped off sharply in the depres-

The Eldridge General Store, Fayette County, Illinois. *Postwar America quickly demobilized, turning its attention to the pursuit of abundance.*

sion decade, now soared: the population increase of 9 million during the 1930s exploded to a growth of 19 million in the 1940s. Americans born during this postwar period comprised what came to be known as the baby-boom generation, a population cohort that continues to exercise a disproportionate influence on American life.

The end of the war, with its sudden demobilization and reconversion to a peacetime economy, generated a wave of labor unrest and strikes but not the postwar depression that many feared. Several shock absorbers cushioned the economic impact of demobilization: unemployment pay and other Social Security benefits; the Servicemen's Readjustment Act of 1944, known as the "GI Bill of Rights," under which $13 billion was spent for veterans on education, vocational training, medical treatment, unemployment insurance, and loans for building houses or going into business; and, most important, the pent-up demand for consumer goods that was fueled by wartime shortages. Instead of sinking into depression after the war, the economy enjoyed a spurt of private investment in new industrial plants and equipment.

CONTROLLING INFLATION The most acute economic problem facing Truman was not depression but inflation. Released from wartime restraints, the demands of businesses for higher prices and of workers for higher wages conspired to frustrate Truman's efforts to "continue stabilization of the economy." He endorsed "reasonable" wage increases, which he thought businesses could absorb without raising prices, and which he considered necessary to sustain consumer purchasing power. Management, however, did not agree. Within six weeks of the war's end, corporations refused union demands for higher wages and better benefits, and a series of strikes followed in the automotive, steel, mining, petroleum, and railroad industries.

Truman, miffed at what he considered to be excessive union demands, including a 30 percent wage boost, used powers granted the chief executive during wartime to seize the mines and threaten to draft striking railroad workers into the armed forces. In a staff meeting, Truman asked what organized labor "wanted to do—run the country?" A strike in the steel industry finally gave rise to a formula for settling most of the disputes. President Truman suggested a pay raise of 18½¢ per hour, which the Steel Workers accepted but management refused. To break the logjam, the administration in 1946 agreed to let the steel companies increase their prices. That pattern then became the basis for settlements in other industries, and also set a dangerous precedent of price-wage spirals that would plague consumers in the postwar world.

The wartime Office of Price Administration maintained some restraint on price increases while gradually ending the rationing of most goods, and Truman asked for a one-year renewal of its powers. But during the late winter and spring of 1946, business lobbyists mounted a massive campaign against price controls, and Truman allowed them to end. Congress finally extended controls in July, but by then the cost of living had already risen by 6 percent. After the 1946 congressional elections, Truman gave up the battle against inflationary prices, ending all price controls except on rents, sugar, and rice.

PARTISAN CONFLICT As congressional elections approached in the fall of 1946, public discontent ran high, most of it directed against the administration. Truman caught the blame for labor problems from both sides. Union supporters tagged Truman "the No. 1 strikebreaker," while much of the public, angry at striking unions, blamed the White House for the strikes. In 1946 Truman fired Henry A. Wallace as secretary of commerce in a disagreement over foreign policy, thus offending the Democratic left. At the same time, Republicans charged that Communists had infiltrated the government. Critics of the administration had a field day coining slogans. "To err is Truman" was credited to Martha Taft, the wife of Senator Robert Taft. But most effective was the simple "Had enough?" attributed to a Boston ad agency: their message was that the Democrats had simply been in power too long. In the end, Republicans won majorities in both houses of Congress in 1946 for the first time since 1928.

With momentum building up against organized labor, the new Republican Congress quickly passed the Taft-Hartley Act of 1947 to curb the power of unions. It banned the closed shop (in which nonunion workers could not be hired) but permitted a union shop (in which workers newly hired were required to join the union), except where banned by state law. The anti-union legislation included provisions against "unfair" union practices such as "featherbedding" (pay for work not done), refusal to bargain in good faith, and contributing to political campaigns. Unions' political action committees were allowed to function only on a voluntary basis, and union leaders had to take oaths that they were not members of the Communist party. Employers were permitted to sue unions for breaking contracts and to speak freely during union campaigns. The act forbade strikes by federal employees, and imposed a "cooling-off" period of eighty days on any strike that the president found to be dangerous to the national health or safety.

Truman vetoed the Taft-Hartley bill, which unions called the "slave-labor act." This restored his credit with labor and brought many unionists who had voted Republican in 1946 back to the Democratic fold. But the bill passed over Truman's veto. Its most severe impact probably was on "Operation Dixie," a drive to win for unions a more secure foothold in the South. By 1954 fifteen states, mainly in the South, had used the Taft-Hartley Act's authority to pass "right-to-work" laws forbidding the union shop. These laws also eroded union strength in the North as many firms began to migrate to "right-to-work" states in the South.

Truman clashed with the Republicans on other domestic issues, including a tax reduction. Congress passed a tax cut but it was vetoed by Truman on the principle that in times of high production and employment the federal debt should be reduced. In 1948, however, Congress overrode his veto of a $5 billion tax cut at a time when government debt still ran high.

These conflicts between Truman and Congress obscured the high degree of bipartisan cooperation marking matters of governmental reorganization and foreign policy. In 1947 a bipartisan majority in Congress passed the National Security Act. It created a national military establishment, headed by a secretary of defense with subcabinet departments of army, navy, and air force, and a new National Security Council (NSC), which included the president, heads of the defense departments, and the secretary of state, among others. The act made permanent the Joint Chiefs of Staff, which had been a wartime innovation, and established the Central Intelligence Agency (CIA), to coordinate intelligence-gathering abroad.

THE COLD WAR

BUILDING THE U.N. The hope that the wartime alliance would carry over into the postwar world proved but another great illusion. The pragmatic Roosevelt had shared no such illusion. He expected that the Great Powers in the postwar world would have geographic spheres of influence, but felt he had to temper such *Realpolitik* with an organization "which would satisfy widespread demand in the United States for new idealistic or universalist arrangements for assuring the peace."

On April 25, 1945, two weeks after Roosevelt's death and two weeks before the German surrender, delegates from fifty nations at war with the Axis met in San Francisco to draw up the charter of the United Nations (U.N.). Additional members could be admitted by a two-thirds vote of the General Assembly. This body, one of the two major agencies set up by the charter, included delegates from all member nations and was to meet annually in regular session to approve the budget, receive annual reports from U.N. agencies, and choose members of the Security Council and other bodies.

The Security Council, the other major charter agency, would remain in permanent session and would have "primary responsibility for the maintenance of international peace and security." Its eleven (after 1965, fifteen) members included six (later ten) members elected for two-year terms and five permanent members: the United States, the Soviet Union, Britain, France, and China. Each permanent member could veto any question of substance. The Security Council might investigate any dispute, recommend settlement or reference to another U.N. body—the International Court of Justice at the Hague, in the Netherlands—and take measures, including a resort to military force. The United States Senate, in sharp contrast to the reception it gave the League of Nations, ratified the U.N. charter by a vote of 89 to 2.

DIFFERENCES WITH THE SOVIETS Since the end of World War II, historians have debated which side was more responsible for the onset of the cold war. The conventional or "orthodox" view declares that the Soviets, led by a paranoid dictator, tried to dominate the globe, and the United States had no choice but to stand firm in defense of democratic capitalist values.

By contrast, those scholars known as "revisionists" argue that Truman and American economic imperialists were the culprits. Instead of maintaining Roosevelt's efforts to collaborate with Stalin and ensure the survival of the alliance after the war, these scholars assert, Truman adopted an unnecessarily belligerent stance and activist foreign policy that itself sought to create American spheres of influence around the world. He and his military advisers exaggerated the Soviet threat, in part to justify an American military buildup. Their provocative policies thus crystallized the tensions between the two countries. Yet such an interpretation fails to recognize that Truman inherited a deteriorating relationship with the Soviets. Events of 1945 made compromise and conciliation more and more difficult, whether for Roosevelt or Truman.

There were signs of trouble in the grand alliance as early as the spring of 1945, as the Soviet Union moved to set up compliant governments in eastern Europe, violating the Yalta promises of democratic elections. On February 1 the Polish Committee of National Liberation, a puppet group of the Soviets already claiming the status of provisional government, moved from Lublin to Warsaw. In March the Soviets installed a puppet premier in Romania. Protests against such actions led to Soviet counterprotests that the British and Americans were negotiating German surrender in Italy "behind the back of the Soviet Union." A few days before his death, Roosevelt responded to Stalin: "I cannot avoid a feeling of resentment toward your informers . . . for such vile misrepresentations."

Such was the atmosphere when Truman entered the White House. A few days before the San Francisco conference to organize the U.N., he gave Soviet foreign minister Vyacheslav M. Molotov a dressing down in Washington on the Polish situation. "I have never been talked to like that in my life," Molotov protested. "Carry out your agreements," Truman snapped, "and you won't get talked to like that."

On May 12, 1945, four days after victory in Europe, Winston Churchill sent Truman a telegram: "What is to happen about Europe? An iron curtain is drawn down upon [the Russian] front. We do not know what is going on behind [it]. . . . Surely it is vital now to come to an understanding with Russia, or see where we are with her, before we weaken our armies mortally." Nevertheless, as a gesture of goodwill, and over Churchill's protest, the American forces withdrew from the occupation zone in Germany assigned to the Soviet Union at Yalta. Americans still hoped that the Yalta agreements would be carried out, and they were even more eager to have Soviet help against Japan.

Although the Soviets admitted British and American observers to their sectors of eastern Europe, there was little the Western powers could have done to prevent Soviet control of the region even if they had kept up their military strength. The presence of Soviet armed forces frustrated the efforts of non-Communists to gain political influence. Opposition leaders were either exiled, silenced, executed, or imprisoned.

Secretary of State James F. Byrnes, who took office in 1945, struggled on through 1946 with the problems of postwar settlements. In early 1947, the Council of Foreign Ministers finally produced treaties for Italy, Hungary, Romania, Bulgaria, and Finland. The treaties in effect confirmed Soviet control over eastern Europe, which in Russian eyes seemed but a parallel to American control in Japan and Western control over most of Germany and all of Italy. The Yalta guarantees of democracy in eastern Europe had turned out much like the Open Door Policy in China, little more than pious rhetoric sugar-coating the realities of power and national interest.

Byrnes's impulse to brandish the atomic bomb only added to the irritations, intimidating no one. As early as April 1945, he had suggested to

Truman that possession of the new weapon "might well put us in a position to dictate our own terms at the end of the war." After becoming secretary of state, he tried on several occasions to threaten Soviet diplomats with America's growing arsenal of nuclear weapons. But they paid little notice, and such attempts at intimidation were soon dropped.

The United States still enjoyed exclusive possession of atomic weapons and, together with Britain and Canada (partners in developing the atomic bomb), proposed in 1946 to internationalize the control of atomic energy. Under the plan presented to the U.N. Atomic Energy Commission, an International Atomic Development Authority would have a monopoly of atomic explosives and atomic energy. The Soviets, fearing Western domination of the agency, proposed instead simply to outlaw the manufacture and use of atomic bombs, with enforcement vested in the Security Council and thus subject to a veto. Later they conceded the right of international inspection, but they still refused to give up the veto. The American government rejected the arrangement, which it considered a compromise of international control.

CONTAINMENT By the beginning of 1947, relations with the Soviet Union had become even more troubled. The year before, Stalin had already pronounced international peace impossible "under the present capitalistic development of the world economy." His statement impelled George F. Kennan, counselor of the American Embassy in Moscow, to send an 8,000-word dispatch to the State Department in which he sketched the roots of Soviet policy and warned that the Soviet Union was "committed fanatically to the belief that it is desirable and necessary that the internal harmony of our society be disrupted, our traditional way of life be destroyed, the international authority of our state be broken, if Soviet power is to be secure."

More than a year later, Kennan, now back at the State Department in Washington, spelled out his ideas for a proper response to the Soviets in a 1947 article published anonymously in *Foreign Affairs*. Kennan signed himself "X" so that readers would not mistake the article for an official State Department position. He did not offer a cohesive strategy or an operational plan but instead provided a psychological analysis of historic Soviet insecurity and postwar intentions. He predicted that the Soviets would try to fill "every nook and cranny available . . . in the basin of world power." Yet their insecurity also meant that, in general, they would act cautiously and seek to reduce their risks. Therefore, he insisted, the United States must pursue "a long-term, patient but firm and vigilant *containment* of Russian expansive tendencies."

Kennan's "containment" concept lay behind the new departure in foreign policy that America's political leaders had already decided to take. Containment reflected a growing fear that Soviet aims reached beyond eastern Europe, posing dangers in the eastern Mediterranean, the Middle East, and western Europe itself. The Soviet Union was indeed looking for a breakthrough into the Mediterranean region, long important to Russia for purposes of trade and defense. After the war, the Soviet Union began to press Turkey for territorial concessions and the right to build naval bases on the Bosporus, an important gateway between the Black Sea and the Mediterranean. In 1946 civil war broke out in neighboring Greece between a British-backed government and a Communist-led faction that held the northern part of Greece. In 1947 the British ambassador informed the American government that the British could no longer bear the economic and military burden of aiding Greece and suggested that the United States assume the responsibility.

THE TRUMAN DOCTRINE AND THE MARSHALL PLAN On March 12, 1947, Truman asked Congress for $400 million in economic and military aid to both Greece and Turkey. In his speech to Congress, the president announced what quickly became known as the Truman Doctrine. Although intended as a response to a specific crisis, its rhetoric was dangerously universal. "I believe," Truman declared, "that it must be the policy of the United States to support free peoples who are resisting attempted subjugation by armed minorities or by outside pressures." In 1947 Congress passed the Greek-Turkish aid bill, and by 1950 had spent $659 million on the program. Turkey achieved economic stability, and Greece defeated the Communist insurrection in 1949.

But such immediate gains created long-term problems. The Truman Doctrine marked the beginning of a contest that stock market whiz Bernard Baruch labeled "a cold war." Greece and Turkey were but the front lines of an ideological struggle for world power and influence between East and West. That struggle quickly focused on western Europe, where wartime damage had devastated factory production, and a severe drought in 1947, followed by a harsh winter, had destroyed crops. Coal shortages in London left only enough fuel to heat and light homes for a few hours each day. In Berlin, people were freezing or starving to death. The transportation system in Europe was in shambles. Bridges were out, canals clogged, and rail networks destroyed. Amid the chaos, the Communist parties of France and Italy were flourishing.

In the spring of 1947, George C. Marshall, who had replaced James Byrnes as secretary of state, called for a program of massive aid to rescue western Europe from disaster and possible Communist subversion. The retired chairman of the Joint Chiefs of Staff who orchestrated the Allied victories over Germany and Japan, Marshall had been the highest-ranking army general during World War II. "He is the great one of the age," said Truman. Marshall used the occasion of the Harvard graduation ceremonies in 1947 to outline his plan for the reconstruction of Europe. "Our policy," he pledged, "is directed not against country or doctrine, but against hunger, poverty, desperation, and chaos." Marshall offered aid to all European countries, including the Soviet Union, but Moscow refused to participate in the "imperialist" scheme.

In late 1947 Truman submitted his proposal for the European Recovery Program to Congress. Two months later, a Communist coup d'état in Czechoslovakia ended the last remaining coalition government in eastern Europe. The Communist seizure of power in Prague assured congressional passage of the Marshall Plan, which from 1948 until 1951 provided $13 billion to promote European recovery.

DIVIDING GERMANY The breakdown of the wartime alliance left the problem of postwar Germany unsettled. The German economy had stagnated, requiring the American army to carry a staggering burden of relief. Slowly, occupation zones evolved into functioning governments. In 1948 the British, French, and Americans merged their zones, and the West Germans then elected delegates to a federal constitutional convention.

Soviet reactions to the Marshall Plan and the unification of West Germany were antagonistic and quickly focused on Berlin, situated deep in the Soviet occupation zone. In April 1948 the Soviets began to restrict the flow of traffic into West Berlin; on June 23 they stopped all traffic. The Soviets hoped the blockade would force the Allies to give up either Berlin or the plan to unify West Germany. But the American commander in Germany proposed to stand firm. "If we mean . . . to

hold Europe against communism," he told his superiors at the Pentagon, "we must not budge."

Truman agreed, and after considering the use of armed convoys to supply West Berlin, he opted for a massive airlift. At the time this seemed an enormous and perhaps impossible task. By quick work, however, the Allied air forces brought in planes from around the world, and soon they were flying in nearly 5,000 tons of food and coal a day. Altogether, from June 1948 to mid-May 1949, the Berlin Airlift provided more than 1.5 million tons of supplies, or well over a half ton for each of the 2.2 million West Berliners.

Finally, on May 12, 1949, after extended talks, the Soviets lifted the blockade. Before the end of the year, the German Federal Republic in West Germany had a functioning government. At the end of May 1949,

The Berlin Airlift. *An American airplane arrives in West Berlin with much-needed supplies, 1948.*

a German "Democratic" Republic arose in the Soviet-dominated eastern zone, dividing Germany into two independent states.

BUILDING NATO As relations between the Soviets and western Europe chilled, transatlantic unity ripened into an outright military alliance. On April 4, 1949, diplomats signed the North Atlantic Treaty in Washington. Twelve nations were represented: the United States, Britain, France, Belgium, the Netherlands, Luxembourg, Canada, Denmark, Iceland, Italy, Norway, and Portugal. Greece and Turkey joined the alliance in 1952, West Germany in 1955, and Spain in 1982. The treaty pledged that an attack against any one of the signers would be considered an attack against all, and provided for a council of the North Atlantic Treaty Organization (NATO), which could establish other necessary agencies. In 1950 the council decided to create an integrated defense force for western Europe. Five years later the Warsaw Treaty Organization appeared as the eastern European counterpart to NATO.

The eventful year 1948 produced one other foreign policy decision with long-term consequences. Late in 1947 the U.N. General Assembly voted to partition Palestine into Jewish and Arab states. Despite fierce

Arab opposition, Jewish leaders proclaimed the independence of the new state of Israel on May 14, 1948. President Truman, who had been in close touch with Jewish leaders, ordered immediate recognition of the new state—the United States was the first nation to do so.

The neighboring Arab states thereupon went to war against Israel, which, however, held its own. U.N. mediators gradually worked out truce agreements with Israel's Arab neighbors that restored an uneasy peace by May 11, 1949, when Israel was admitted as a member of the United Nations. But the mutual hatred and intermittent warfare between Israel and the Arab states have festered ever since, complicating American foreign policy, which has tried to maintain friendship with both sides while insisting on the legitimacy of the Israeli nation.

HARRY GIVES 'EM HELL

CIVIL RIGHTS DURING THE 1940S The social tremors triggered by World War II and the onset of the cold war transformed America's racial landscape. The vicious racism of the German Nazis, Italian fascists, and Japanese imperialists focused attention on the need for the United States to improve its own race relations and to provide for equal rights under the law. As a *New York Times* editorial explained in early 1946, "This is a particularly good time to campaign against the evils of bigotry, prejudice, and race hatred because we have witnessed the defeat of enemies who tried to found a mastery of the world upon such cruel and fallacious policy."

For most of his political career, Harry Truman had shown little concern about the plight of African Americans. He had grown up in western Missouri assuming that both blacks and whites preferred to be segregated from one another. As president, however, he began to reassess his convictions. A recent biographer of Truman concludes that he "was magnificently right on what may have been the two most important issues of his time: civil rights and the Soviet challenge."

In the fall of 1946 Truman hosted a delegation of civil rights activists from the National Emergency Committee Against Mob Violence. The visitors graphically described incidents of torture and intimidation against blacks in the South. Truman was aghast. "My God," he exclaimed. "I had no idea it was as terrible as that. We've got to do something." Two months later, he appointed a Committee on Civil Rights to investigate violence against African Americans and to recommend preventive measures. The committee recommended the renewal of the Fair Employment Practices Committee (FEPC) and the creation of a permanent civil rights commission to investigate abuses. It also argued that federal aid be denied to any state that mandated segregated schools and public facilities.

On July 26, 1948, Truman banned racial discrimination in the hiring of federal employees. Four days later, he issued an Executive Order ending racial segregation in the armed forces. The air force and navy quickly complied, but the army dragged its feet until the early 1950s. By 1960 the armed forces were the most racially integrated of all American organizations. Desegregating the military was, Truman claimed, "the greatest thing that ever happened to America."

Meanwhile, racial segregation was being confronted in a much more public field of endeavor—professional baseball. In April 1947, as the baseball season opened, the National League's Brooklyn Dodgers included on their roster the first black player to cross the color line in major league baseball: Jackie Robinson. Born in Georgia but raised in California, Robinson was an army veteran and baseball player in the Negro leagues. He earlier had been a football, basketball, baseball, and track star at UCLA. Branch Rickey, president of the Dodgers, selected Robinson to integrate professional baseball, not only for his athletic potential but because of his willingness to control his temper in the face of virulent racism. Teammates and opposing players viciously baited Robinson, pitchers threw at him, base runners spiked him, and spectators booed and taunted him in every city. Hotels refused him rooms, and restaurants denied him service. Hate mail arrived by the bucket load. On the other hand, black spectators were electrified by Robinson's courageous example. They turned out in droves at baseball games to see him play.

What Branch Rickey called his "noble experiment" provided a public forum for people to confront the charged issue of segregation. The headline in the *Boston Chronicle* trumpeted: "Triumph of Whole Race Seen in Jackie's Debut in Major League Ball." Huge crowds flocked to see Robinson play, and he played well, doing everything necessary to help the Dodgers win games—bunt, sacrifice, draw walks, steal bases, hit for average and for power. His success earned him the Rookie of the

Jackie Robinson, *1949. Racial discrimination remained widespread through the postwar period. In 1947 Jackie Robinson of the Brooklyn Dodgers became the first black to play major league baseball.*

Year Award in 1947. Leo Durocher, manager of the Dodgers, declared that Robinson "didn't just come to play. He come to beat ya."

As time passed, Robinson won over many fans and opposing players through his quiet courage, self-deprecating wit, and determined performance. Soon, other teams began to sign black players. Baseball's pathbreaking efforts also stimulated football and basketball to integrate their rosters. Jackie Robinson vividly demonstrated that racism, not inferiority, impeded African-American advancement in the postwar era and that segregation need not be a permanent condition of American life.

TRUMAN'S AGENDA Just as some of the owners of professional sports teams were slowly desegregating their teams, so Truman was also making efforts to desegregate the federal workforce. But while some people found his actions laudatory, others were appalled. Liberals felt his efforts were misdirected and that his solutions were too conservative. Southern conservative Democrats found him too radical and were very unhappy with his attempts to shake up the status quo.

After three years in the White House, Truman had yet to overcome the impression that he was not up to the job of leading the country. But he had a game plan for 1948. His advisers knew that to win another presidential term he needed the midwestern and western farm belts, and he enjoyed fairly strong support among farmers. In metropolitan areas he needed to carry the labor and the black vote, which Truman wooed by working closely with unions and pressing the cause of civil rights. Truman's advisers counted on the Solid South to stay in the Democratic column. With the South and West, Truman could afford to lose some New Deal strongholds in the East and still win. This strategy erred chiefly in underrating the rebellion that would take four Deep South states out of Truman's camp because of his support for civil rights.

Truman used his State of the Union message in 1948 to set the agenda for an election year. The speech offered something to nearly every group the Democrats hoped to win over. The first goal, Truman remarked, was "to secure fully the essential human rights of our citizens," and promised a special message later on civil rights. "To protect human resources," he proposed federal aid to education, increased and extended unemployment and retirement benefits, a comprehensive system of health insurance, more federal support for housing, and extension of rent controls. As one senator put it, the speech "raised all the ghosts of the old New Deal. . . ."

THE 1948 ELECTION The Republican majority in Congress for the most part spurned the Truman program, an action it would later regret. Scenting victory in November, Republican delegates again nominated Thomas Dewey, former New York governor. The platform endorsed most of the New Deal reforms as an accomplished fact and approved the administration's bipartisan foreign policy, but as Alf Landon had in 1936, Dewey promised to run things more efficiently.

In July a glum Democratic convention gathered in Philadelphia, expecting to do little more than go through the motions, only to find itself doubly surprised: first by the battle over the civil rights plank, and then by Truman's acceptance speech. To keep from stirring southern hostility, the administration sought a platform plank that opposed racial discrimination only in general terms. Activists, however, sponsored a plank that called on Congress for specific action and commended Truman

Truman's support of civil rights for African Americans had its political costs, as this 1948 cartoon suggests.

"for his courageous stand on the issue of civil rights." Speaking last in favor of the change, Minneapolis mayor Hubert H. Humphrey electrified the delegates and set off a ten-minute demonstration: "The time has arrived for the Democratic party to get out of the shadow of states' rights and walk forthrightly into the bright sunshine of human rights." Segregationist delegates from Alabama and Mississippi walked, instead, out of the convention.

After the convention had nominated Truman, the president delivered a rousing, combative address, unlike most of his earlier speeches, which he usually read in a flat drone. Near the end he dropped a bombshell. He would call Congress back into session "to get the laws the people need."

A group of rebellious southern Democrats, miffed by Truman's civil rights plank, met in Birmingham, Alabama, and nominated South Carolina governor J. Strom Thurmond on a States' Rights Democratic ticket, quickly dubbed the "Dixiecrat" ticket. The Dixiecrats sought to draw enough electoral votes to preclude a majority for either major party, throwing the election into the House, where they might strike a sectional bargain. A few days later, the left wing of the Democratic party gathered in Philadelphia to name Henry A. Wallace on a Progressive party ticket. These splits in the Democratic ranks seemed to spell the final blow to Truman. The special session of Congress petered out in futility.

But Truman, undaunted, set out on a 31,000-mile "whistle-stop" train tour during which he castigated the "do-nothing" Eightieth Congress, provoking cries from his audiences: "Pour it on, Harry!" and "Give 'em hell, Harry." Truman responded: "I don't give 'em hell. I just tell the truth and they think it's hell." Dewey, in contrast, ran a restrained campaign designed to avoid controversy. By so doing, he may have snatched defeat from the jaws of victory.

To the end, the polls and the pundits predicted a sure win for Dewey, and most speculation centered on his cabinet choices. But on election day Truman chalked up the biggest upset in American history, taking 24 million votes (49.5 percent) to Dewey's 22 million (45.1 percent) and winning a thumping 303 to 189 margin in the electoral college. Thurmond and Wallace each got more than a million votes, but the revolt of right and left worked to Truman's advantage. The Dixiecrat rebellion reassured black voters who had questioned the Democrats' commitment to civil rights, while the Progressive movement, which had received support from the Communist party, made it hard to tag Truman as "soft on communism." Thurmond carried four Deep South states, and his success started a momentous disruption of the Democratic Solid South. But Truman's victory also carried Democratic majorities into Congress.

The Man Who "Done His Damndest." Truman's victory in 1948 was a huge upset.

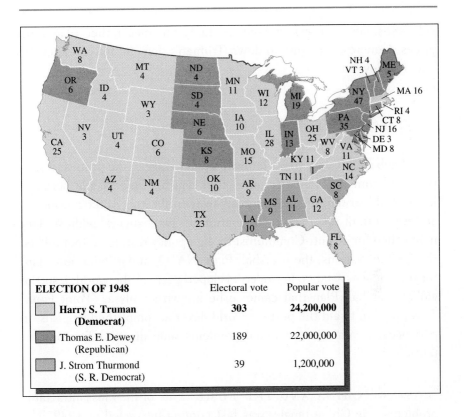

ELECTION OF 1948	Electoral vote	Popular vote
Harry S. Truman (Democrat)	**303**	**24,200,000**
Thomas E. Dewey (Republican)	189	22,000,000
J. Strom Thurmond (S. R. Democrat)	39	1,200,000

Truman viewed his upset victory as a vindication for the New Deal and a mandate for liberalism. His State of the Union message repeated the agenda he had set forth a year previously. "Every segment of our population and every individual," he stressed, "has a right to expect from his government a fair deal." Whether deliberately or not, he had invented a tag, the "Fair Deal," to set off his program from the New Deal.

Congress passed some of Truman's Fair Deal proposals, but they were mainly extensions or enlargements of New Deal programs already in place: a higher minimum wage, bringing more people under Social Security, extension of rent controls, farm price supports, a sizable slum-clearance and public housing program, and more money for the TVA, rural electrification, and farm housing. Despite Democratic majorities in Congress, however, the conservative coalition disdained any drastic new departures in domestic policy. Congress balked at civil rights bills, national health insurance, federal aid to education, and a plan to provide subsidies that would hold up farm incomes rather than farm prices. Congress also turned down Truman's demand for repeal of the Taft-Hartley Act.

THE COLD WAR HEATS UP

Global concerns, never far from center stage in the postwar world, plagued Truman's second term, as they had his first. People began to live in real fear that the Communists were infiltrating American society and were intent upon world domination. In his inaugural address, Truman called for an anti-Communist foreign policy resting on four pillars: the United Nations, the Marshall Plan, NATO, and a "bold new plan" for technical assistance to underdeveloped parts of the world, a sort of global Marshall Plan that came to be known simply as "Point Four." This program to aid the postwar world never accomplished its goals, in part because other international problems soon diverted Truman's attention.

"LOSING" CHINA AND THE BOMB One of the most intractable problems, the China tangle, was fast coming unraveled in 1949. The Chinese Nationalists (Kuomintang) of Chiang Kai-shek had been fighting Mao Tse-tung* and the Communists since the 1920s. The outbreak of war with Japan in 1937 halted the civil war, and both Roosevelt and Stalin believed that the Nationalists would organize China after the war.

The commanders of American forces in China during World War II, however, concluded that Chiang's government had become hopelessly corrupt, tyrannical, and inefficient. U.S. policy during and immediately after the war was to promote peace between the factions in China. But when the civil war resumed in 1945, American forces ferried nationalist armies back into the eastern and northern provinces as the Japanese withdrew.

---

* The traditional (Wade-Giles) spellings are used in this text. After Mao's death, the Chinese government adopted the "Pinyin" transliterations that are widely used today: Mao Tse-tung became Mao Zedong; and Peking became Beijing.

Mao Tse-tung on the march with Red Army troops in northern China, 1947.

It soon became a losing fight for the Nationalists, as the Communists radicalized the land-hungry peasantry. By late 1948, Mao's forces were in Peking and heading southward. A year later they had taken the port city of Canton, and the Nationalist government had fled to the island of Formosa, which it renamed Taiwan.

From 1945 through 1949, the United States funneled some $2 billion in aid to the Nationalists, to no avail. Administration critics asked bitterly: "Who lost China?" and a State Department report blamed Chiang for his failure to hold the support of the Chinese people. In fact it is hard to imagine how the United States government could have prevented the outcome short of military intervention, which would have been very risky, quite costly, and exceedingly unpopular. The United States continued to recognize the Nationalist government on Taiwan as the rightful government of China, delaying formal relations with Red China for thirty years. In an effort to shore up friendly governments in Asia, the United States in 1950 recognized the French-supported regime of Emperor Bao Dai in Vietnam and shortly afterward extended aid to the French in their battle against Ho Chi Minh's Vietnamese guerrillas.

As the Communists secured control in China, American intelligence in 1949 found evidence that the Soviets had set off an atomic explosion. The discovery of the Soviet bomb provoked an intense reappraisal of the strategic balance in the world, causing Truman in 1950 to order the construction of a hydrogen bomb, a weapon far more powerful than the Hiroshima bomb, lest the Soviets make one first. Another result was a National Security Council recommendation for rebuilding conventional military forces to provide options other than nuclear war. This represented a major departure from America's time-honored aversion to keeping large standing armies in peacetime, and was an expensive proposition. But the American public was growing more receptive to the nation's role as world leader, and an invasion of South Korea by Communist forces from the North clinched the issue for most.

WAR IN KOREA The Japanese had occupied Korea during World War II, and after their defeat and withdrawal, the victorious Allies faced the difficult task of creating a new nation. Complicating that task was the fact that Soviet troops had advanced into northern Korea and had accepted the surrender of Japanese forces above the 38th parallel, while American forces did the same south of the line. The Soviets quickly organized a Korean government along Stalinist lines, while the Americans set up a Western-style regime in the South.

Like the division of Germany, the division of Korea at the 38th parallel in 1945 began as a temporary expedient and ended as a permanent fact. With the onset of the cold war, it became clear that Soviet-American agreement on unification was no more likely in Korea than in Germany. By the end of 1948, separate regimes had appeared in the two sectors and occupation forces had withdrawn. The weakened state of the demobilizing American military contributed to the impression that South Korea was vulnerable. A growing body of evidence in Soviet archives reveals that Stalin encouraged the North Koreans to use force to unify their country and oust the Americans from the peninsula. The Soviets helped design and ultimately approved a war plan that called for North Korean forces to seize Seoul within three days and all of South Korea within a week.

North Korean forces crossed the boundary on June 25, 1950, and swept down the peninsula. President Truman responded decisively. He and his advisers assumed that the North Korean attack was directed by

Moscow and was a brazen indication of the aggressive designs of monolithic communism. "The attack upon Korea makes it plain beyond all doubt," Truman told Congress, "that communism has passed beyond the use of subversion to conquer independent nations and will now use armed invasion and war."

An emergency meeting of the U.N. Security Council quickly censured the North Korean "breach of peace." The Soviet delegate, who held a veto power, was at the time boycotting the council because it would not seat Communist China in place of Nationalist China. On June 27, its first resolution having been ignored, the Security Council called on U.N. members to "furnish such assistance to the Republic of Korea (ROK) as may be necessary to repel the armed attack and to restore international peace and security in the area."

Truman ordered American air, naval, and ground forces into action. Eventually American forces numbered over 350,000, while the South Koreans contributed 400,000. In all, some fourteen other U.N. members sent military units totaling about 50,000 men. Later, when the U.N. voted a unified command, it put General Douglas MacArthur in charge. The defense of South Korea remained chiefly an American affair, and one that set a precedent of profound consequence: war by order of the president rather than by vote of Congress. Yet it had the sanction of the U.N. Security Council and could technically be considered a "police action," not a war. Other presidents had ordered American troops into action without a declaration of war, but never on such a scale.

Truman's conviction that the invasion of South Korea was actually orchestrated by Stalin in Moscow led to two other decisions that had far-reaching consequences. Believing that the Korean action was actually a diversion for a Soviet advance into western Europe, Truman began a major expansion of American forces in NATO. By 1952 there were 261,000 American troops stationed in Europe, three times the number in 1950 and slightly more than the total number of American soldiers in Korea. While dispatching American forces to Korea and Europe, Truman also increased his assistance to the French in Indochina, creating the Military Assistance Advisory Group for Indochina. This was the start of America's deepening involvement in Vietnam.

For three months, the fighting went badly for the South Korean and U.N. forces. Soviet pilots battled American planes over South Korea. To

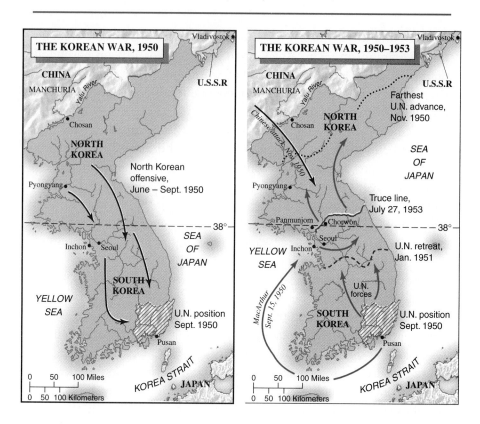

THE KOREAN WAR, 1950

THE KOREAN WAR, 1950–1953

mask their identity, the Soviets wore Chinese uniforms and used Chinese phrases over the radio. By September, the South Korean and U.N. forces were barely hanging on to the Pusan perimeter in the southeast corner of Korea. Then, in a brilliant ploy, on September 15, 1950, General MacArthur landed a new force to the North Korean rear at Inchon. Synchronized with a breakout from Pusan, the sudden blow stampeded the enemy back across the border.

At this point, MacArthur convinced Truman to allow him to push on and seek to reunify Korea. The Soviet delegate was now back in the Security Council, wielding his veto, so on October 7 the United States got approval for this course from the U.N. General Assembly, where the veto did not apply. American forces had already crossed the boundary into North Korea by October 1, and now continued northward against minimal resistance. President Truman, concerned over broad hints of Communist Chinese intervention, flew out to Wake Island for a conference with General MacArthur on October 15. There the general discounted chances that the Red Army would act, but if it did, he confidently predicted, "there would be the greatest slaughter."

That same day Peking announced that China "cannot stand idly by." On October 26, U.N. units reached the Yalu River border with China. MacArthur predicted total victory by Christmas, but on the night of November 25, thousands of Chinese "volunteers" counterattacked, and massive "human wave" attacks, with the support of tanks and planes, turned the tables on the U.N. forces, sending them into a desperate retreat just at the onset of winter. It had become "an entirely new war," MacArthur concluded. Soon he was reporting that the war dragged on because the administration refused to let him blockade the Chinese mainland and use Taiwanese Nationalists to invade the mainland. MacArthur seemed to have forgotten altogether his earlier reluctance to bog down the country in a major war on the Asian mainland.

Truman opposed leading the United States into the "gigantic booby trap" of a ground war with China, and the U.N. forces soon rallied. By January 1951, U.N. troops under General Matthew Ridgway finally secured their lines below Seoul, and then launched a counterattack that in some places carried them back across the 38th parallel in March.

U.N. forces recapture Seoul from the North Koreans, September 1950.

When Truman seized the chance and offered negotiations to restore the boundary, MacArthur undermined the move by issuing an ultimatum for China to make peace or be attacked. Truman decided then that he had no choice but to accept MacArthur's policy or fire him. Civilian control of the military was at stake, Truman later asserted, and he did not let it remain at stake very long. The Joint Chiefs of Staff all backed the decision, and on April 11, 1951, the president removed MacArthur from all his commands and replaced him with Ridgway.

Truman's action set off an uproar across the country, and a tumultuous reception greeted MacArthur upon his return home for the first time since 1937. His dramatic speech to a joint session of Congress provided the climactic event. "Once war is forced upon us," he maintained, "there is no alternative than to apply every available means to bring it to a swift end." A Senate investigation brought out the administration's arguments, best summarized by General Omar Bradley, chairman of the Joint Chiefs of Staff. The MacArthur strategy "would involve us in the wrong war at the wrong place at the wrong time and with the wrong enemy." Americans, nurtured on classic Western showdowns in which good always triumphed over evil, found the logic of limited war hard to swallow, but also found Bradley's logic persuasive.

On June 24, 1951, the Soviet representative at the United Nations proposed a cease-fire and armistice along the 38th parallel. A few days later Secretary of State Dean Acheson accepted in principle. China and North Korea responded favorably—at the time General Ridgway's "meat-grinder" offensive was inflicting severe losses. Truce talks started in July, only to drag out for another two years while the fighting continued. The chief snags were prisoner exchanges and the insistence of South Korea's president on unification.

By the time a truce was finally reached on July 27, 1953, Truman had relinquished the White House to Dwight D. Eisenhower. The truce line followed the front at that time, mostly a little north of the 38th parallel, with a demilitarized zone separating the forces; repatriation of prisoners would be voluntary, supervised by a neutral commission. No final peace conference ever took place, and Korea, like Germany, remained divided. The war had cost the United States more than 33,000 deaths and 103,000 wounded and missing. South Korean casualties, all told, were about 1 million, and North Korean and Chinese casualties totaled an estimated 1.5 million.

ANOTHER RED SCARE   In calculating the costs of the Korean War, one must add in the far-reaching consequences of the second Red Scare, which had grown since 1945 as the domestic counterpart to the cold war abroad and reached a crescendo during the Korean conflict. Since 1938, the House Un-American Activities Committee (HUAC) had kept up a barrage of accusations about subversives in government.

In 1947 HUAC subpoenaed nineteen prominent Hollywood actors, producers, and writers. It wanted to prove that Communist party members dominated the Screen Writers Guild, injected subversive propaganda into motion pictures, and that President Roosevelt had brought improper pressure to bear upon the industry to produce pro-Soviet films during the war. Only ten of the witnesses ended up testifying. The so-called Hollywood Ten jointly decided to use the First Amendment as a defense, and each of them refused to answer the question "Are you now or have you ever been a member of the Communist party?" All ten had been members of that party, but they would not answer the question as a matter of principle, claiming that party identification was their business—especially since the Communist party, at that time, was not illegal in the United States. They were all judged to be in contempt and were sentenced to a year in prison. But greater punishment awaited them. The movie industry blacklisted the Hollywood Ten, denying them any further work.

In the charged atmosphere of the postwar years, Truman decided that he too must become more vigilant in rooting out Communists from the government. On March 21, 1947, just nine days after he announced the Truman Doctrine, Truman signed an executive order setting up procedures for an employee loyalty program in the federal government. Designed partly to protect the president's political flank, it failed to do so, mainly because of disclosures of earlier Communist penetrations into government that were few in number but sensational in character.

The case most embarrassing to the administration involved Alger Hiss, president of the Carnegie Endowment for International Peace, who had served in several government departments, including the State Department. Whittaker Chambers, a former Soviet agent and later an editor of *Time* magazine, told the House Un-American Activities Committee in 1948 that Hiss had given him secret documents ten years earlier, when Chambers worked for the Soviets. Hiss sued for libel, and

Chambers produced microfilms of the State Department documents he claimed Hiss had passed on to him. Hiss denied the accusation, whereupon he was indicted for perjury and, after one mistrial, convicted in 1950. The charge was perjury, but he was convicted of lying about espionage—for which he could not be tried because the statute of limitations on the crime had expired.

Most damaging to the administration was the fact that President Truman, taking at face value the many testimonials to Hiss's integrity, called the charges against him a "red herring." Secretary of State Dean Acheson compounded the damage when, meaning to express compassion, he pledged not "to turn my back on Alger Hiss." The Hiss affair had another political consequence: it raised to national prominence a young California congressman, Richard M. Nixon, who doggedly insisted on pursuing the case and then exploited an anti-Communist stance to win election to the Senate in 1950.

More cases of Communist infiltration surfaced. In 1950 the government disclosed the existence of a British-American spy network that had fed information about the development of the atomic bomb to the Soviet Union. These disclosures led to the arrest of, among others, Julius and Ethel Rosenberg. The Rosenbergs, convicted of espionage in wartime, were executed in 1953.

MCCARTHY'S WITCH-HUNT Such revelations encouraged politicians in both parties to exploit public fears. If a man of such respectability as Hiss was guilty, many wondered, who then could be trusted? Early in 1950 the hitherto obscure Republican senator from Wisconsin, Joseph R. McCarthy, suddenly surfaced as the shrewdest and most ruthless exploiter of such anxieties. He took up the cause, or at least the pose, of anti-communism with a vengeance. He began with a speech in which he claimed that the State Department was infested with Communists and that he held in his hand a list of their names. Later there was confusion as to whether he had said 205, 81, 57, or "a lot" of names, and even whether the sheet of paper carried a list. But such confusion always pursued McCarthy's charges.

Challenged to provide names, McCarthy finally pointed to Owen Lattimore of the Johns Hopkins University, an Asia expert, as head of "the espionage ring in the State Department." A special Senate committee looked into the matter and pronounced McCarthy's charges "a fraud

Senator Joseph McCarthy (left) *and his aide Roy Cohn* (right) *exchange comments during testimony.*

and a hoax." McCarthy then turned, in what became his common tactic, to other charges, other names. McCarthy never uncovered a single Communist agent in government. But with the United States at war with Korean Communists in mid-1950, he continued to mobilize true believers behind his crusade. Republicans encouraged him to keep up the game. By 1951 he was riding so high as to list Generals George C. Marshall and Dwight D. Eisenhower among the disloyal. He kept up his campaign without successful challenge until the end of the Korean War.

Under the influence of the anti-Communist hysteria, the Congress in 1950 passed the McCarran Internal Security Act over President Truman's veto. The act required Communist and Communist-front organizations to register with the attorney-general. Aliens who had belonged to totalitarian parties were barred from admission to the United States, a provision that, ironically, also discouraged any temptation for lapsed Communists to defect to the United States.

ASSESSING THE COLD WAR In retrospect, the onset of the cold war takes on an appearance of terrible inevitability. America's preference for international principles, such as self-determination and democracy, conflicted with Stalin's preference for international spheres of influence. Russia, after all, had suffered two German invasions in the first half of the twentieth century, and Soviet leaders wanted tame buffer states on their borders for protection.

The people of eastern Europe, as usual, were caught in the middle. But the Communists themselves held to a universal principle: world revolution. And since the time of President Monroe, Americans had bristled at the thought of foreign intervention in their own sphere of influence, the Western Hemisphere. Thus, to create a defensive shield against the spread of communism, the United States signed mutual defense treaties. Under the Treaty of Rio de Janeiro, the nations of the Western Hemisphere agreed to aid any country in the region that was attacked. In 1951, the United States and Japan signed a treaty that permitted the United States to maintain military forces in Japan. That same year, American negotiators signed other mutual defense treaties with the Philippines, Australia, and New Zealand.

If international conditions set the stage for the cold war, the actions of political leaders and thinkers set events in motion. President Truman may have erred in suggesting that the United States must intervene anywhere in the world to stop the tide of Communist aggression. His loyalty program, following on the heels of the Truman Doctrine, may have spurred on the anti-Communist hysteria of the times.

The years after World War II were unlike any other postwar era in American history. Having taken on global burdens, the nation had become, if not a "garrison state," at least a country committed to a major and permanent national military establishment. By 1952 this newly entrenched sector of the government included the National Security Council, the Central Intelligence Agency, and the enormous National Security Agency, entrusted with the monitoring of media and communications for foreign intelligence.

The policy initiatives of the Truman years had led the country to abandon its long-standing aversion to peacetime alliances. It was a far cry from the world of 1796, when George Washington in his farewell address warned against "those overgrown military establishments which . . . are inauspicious to liberty" and advised his country "to steer clear of permanent alliances with any portion of the foreign world." But, then, Washington had warned only against participation in the "ordinary" combinations and collisions of Europe, and surely the postwar years had seen extraordinary events and unprecedented combinations.

> **MAKING CONNECTIONS**
>
> - The cold war had a major impact on American society; among
>   other things, it helped create the "conforming culture" described
>   in the next chapter.
>
> - The New Frontier and Great Society programs of Presidents
>   Kennedy and Johnson accomplished much of what Truman tried
>   to do through his Fair Deal policies. See Chapter 33.
>
> - The world seemed a dangerous place at the height of the cold war,
>   but when seen from the perspective of the post–cold war world of
>   the 1990s (see Chapters 35 and 36), it had a certain stability that
>   discouraged political violence.

FURTHER READING

The cold war remains a hotly debated topic. The traditional interpretation is best reflected in John L. Gaddis's *The United States and the
Origins of the Cold War, 1941–1947* (1972). Both superpowers, Gaddis
argues, were responsible for causing the cold war, but the Soviet Union
was more culpable. The revisionist perspective is represented by Gar
Alperovitz's *Atomic Diplomacy* (rev. ed., 1994). He places primary responsibility for the conflict on the United States. Also see H. W.
Brands's *The Devil We Knew: Americans and the Cold War* (1993),
Michael J. Hogan's *The End of the Cold War: Its Meaning and Implications* (1992), Melvyn P. Leffler's *A Preponderance of Power: National Security, the Truman Administration, and the Cold War* (1992), John Lewis
Gaddis's *The Long Peace: Inquiries Into the History of the Cold War* (rev.
ed., 1993), and Wilson D. Miscamble's *George F. Kennan and the Making of American Foreign Policy, 1947–1950* (1992).

Other scholars concentrate on more specific events in the buildup of
international tensions. Lynn Etheridge Davis's *The Cold War Begins:
Soviet-American Conflict over Eastern Europe* (1974) and Bruce Kuk-

lick's *American Policy and the Division of Germany* (1972) deal with initial tensions at the close of the war. For the Truman administration's reliance on the atomic bomb monopoly, see Michael Mandelbaum's *The Nuclear Question: The United States and Nuclear Weapons, 1946–1976* (1979) and Daniel Yergin's *Shattered Peace: The Origins of the Cold War and the National Security State* (1977).

For a positive assessment of Truman's leadership, see Alonzo Hamby's *Beyond the New Deal: Harry S. Truman and American Liberalism* (1973). The domestic policies of the Fair Deal are treated in William C. Berman's *The Politics of Civil Rights in the Truman Administration* (1970), Richard M. Dalfiumes's *Desegregation of the United States Armed Forces* (1969), and Maeva Marcus's *Truman and the Steel Seizure Case: The Limits of Presidential Power* (rev. ed., 1994). The most comprehensive biography of Truman is David McCullough's *Truman* (1992).

For an introduction to the tensions in Asia, see Akira Iriye's *The Cold War in Asia* (1974). For the Korean conflict, see Callum A. MacDonald's *Korea: The War before Vietnam* (1986) and Max Hasting's *The Korean War* (rev. ed., 1993). The high-command perspective is revealed in Michael Schaller's *Douglas MacArthur: The Far Eastern General* (1989).

The anti-Communist syndrome is surveyed in David Caute's *The Great Fear: The Anti-Communist Purge under Truman and Eisenhower* (1978). Thomas C. Reeves's *The Life and Times of Joe McCarthy* (1982) covers McCarthy himself. For a well-documented account of how the cold war was sustained by superpatriotism, intolerance, and suspicion, see Stephen J. Whitfield's *The Culture of the Cold War* (1990). See also Richard Fried's *Nightmare in Red: The McCarthy Era in Perspective* (1990).

31 ∾ THROUGH THE PICTURE WINDOW: SOCIETY AND CULTURE, 1945–1960

CHAPTER ORGANIZER

This chapter focuses on:

- the economic prosperity of America in the postwar period.

- the culture of the 1950s, with its strains of conformity and innovation.

- America's burgeoning consumer culture.

*A*mericans emerged from World War II elated, proud of their military strength and industrial might. As the editors of *Fortune* magazine proclaimed in 1946, "This is a dream era, this is what everyone was waiting through the blackouts for. The Great American Boom is on." So it was, from babies to Buicks to Admiral television sets. An American public that had known deprivation and sacrifice for the last decade and a half began to enjoy unprecedented prosperity. The postwar era enjoyed tremendous economic growth and seeming social contentment—at least on the surface.

Yet in the midst of such rising affluence and optimism, many social critics, writers, and artists expressed a growing sense of unease. Was postwar American society becoming too complacent, too conformist, too materialistic? These questions reflected the perennial tension in American life between idealism and materialism, a tension that arrived with the first settlers and remains with us today. Americans have always struggled to accumulate goods and cultivate goodness. During the post-war era, the nation tried to do both. For a while, at least, it appeared to succeed.

PEOPLE OF PLENTY

The dominant feature of post–World War II American society was its remarkable prosperity. After a surprisingly brief postwar recession, the economy soared to record heights. The gross national product (GNP) nearly doubled between 1945 and 1960, and the 1960s witnessed an even more spectacular expansion of the economy. By 1970, the gap between living standards in the United States and the rest of the world had become a chasm: with 6 percent of the world's population, Americans produced and consumed nearly two-thirds of the world's goods.

Such abundance generated a mood of giddy optimism. During the 1950s, government officials assured the citizenry that they should not fear another economic collapse. The leading economists of the postwar era agreed that the New Deal safeguards built into the economy would prevent another dramatic downturn. They and others led the public to believe that perpetual economic growth was possible, desirable, and, in fact, essential. The expectation of unending plenty thus became the reigning assumption of social thought in the two decades after 1945.

Several factors contributed to this sustained economic surge. The massive federal expenditures for military needs during World War II had catapulted the economy out of the depression. High government spending continued to drive the postwar economy, thanks to the tensions generated by the cold war and the increase in defense spending provoked by the Korean conflict. Military-related research also helped spawn the new glamour industries of the postwar era: chemicals, electronics, and aviation.

Most of the other major industrial nations of the world—England, France, Germany, Japan, the Soviet Union—had been physically devastated during the war, which meant that American manufacturers enjoyed a virtual monopoly over international trade. In addition, the widespread use of new and more efficient machinery and computers led to a 35 percent jump in the productivity of American workers between 1945 and 1955.

The major catalyst in promoting economic expansion after 1945, however, was the unleashing of pent-up consumer demand. During the war, Americans had postponed purchases of major items such as cars and houses, and in the process had saved over $150 billion. Now they were eager to buy. The United States after World War II thus experienced a purchasing frenzy.

THE GI BILL OF RIGHTS Part of the purchasing frenzy was financed by the federal government. People feared that a sharp drop in military spending and the sudden influx of veterans back into the civilian workforce would send the economy into a downward spiral and produce widespread unemployment. Such concerns led Congress to pass by a unanimous vote the Servicemen's Readjustment Act of 1944. Popularly known as the GI Bill of Rights (GI meant "government issue," a phrase stamped on military uniforms and also slang for a serviceman), it led to the creation of a new government agency, the Veterans Administration. The GI Bill also included provisions for mustering out pay, unemployment pay for one year, preference for veterans seeking civil service jobs, loans for home construction, access to government hospitals, and generous subsidies for college or professional training.

The infusion of funds into the economy provided by the GI Bill helped fuel the postwar prosperity. Almost 8 million veterans took advantage of $14.5 billion in GI Bill subsidies to attend college or to enroll in job training programs. Some 5 million people used additional monies from the GI Bill to buy new homes. These two programs combined to produce a social revolution.

The educational benefits of the GI Bill encouraged many people to consider pursuing higher education. Before World War II, approximately 160,000 Americans graduated from college each year. By 1950 the figure had more than tripled. In 1949 veterans accounted for 40 percent of all college enrollments, and the United States could boast the world's best-educated workforce.

The GI Bill also democratized higher education. It provided a generation of working-class Americans with an opportunity to earn a college degree for the first time. In turn, a college education served as a lever into the middle class and economic security. But while the GI Bill helped erode class barriers, it was less successful in dismantling racial barriers. Many black veterans could not take equal advantage of the education benefits. Most colleges and universities after the war remained racially segregated, either by regulation or by practice. Those blacks who did manage to gain admission to white colleges or universities were barred from playing on athletic teams, attending dances and other social events, and joining fraternities or sororities.

The historically black colleges, most of which were in the South, could not expand quickly enough to meet the demand. In 1940 black colleges enrolled 43,000 students; in 1950 the number had soared to 77,000. Yet over 20,000 were denied admission because of overcrowded facilities. As a result, most black veterans did not get into a college. In 1946 only one-fifth of the 100,000 who had applied for educational benefits had enrolled. In other cases, black veterans were inadequately prepared for college-level work. As late as 1950, some 70 percent of black adults in the southern states had only a seventh-grade education or less.

The return of some 12 million veterans to private life also helped generate the postwar "baby boom," which peaked in 1957. Between 1946 and 1964, America's total population grew by almost 40 million, a whopping 30 percent increase. Such a dramatic growth rate had a host of reverberating effects. Indeed, much of America's social history since the 1940s has been the story of the unusually large baby-boom generation and its progress through the stages of life. Initially the postwar baby boom created a massive demand for diapers, baby food, toys, medicines, schools, books, teachers, furniture, and housing. It also spurred the growth of new suburban communities as the burgeoning population moved from the cities into the countryside.

AN EXPANDING CONSUMER CULTURE Postwar America soon became a beehive of construction activity and prolific factory output of the tools and materials to build and furnish the new homes. The proportion of homeowners in the population increased by 50 percent between 1945 and 1960. And those new homes were increasingly filled with the latest electrical appliances—refrigerators, washing machines, sewing machines, vacuum cleaners, freezers, and mixers.

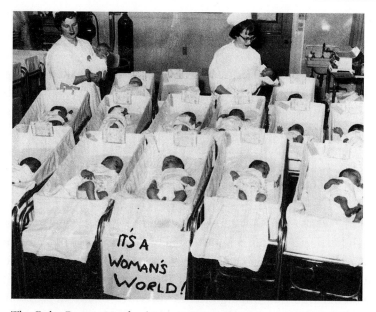

The Baby Boom. *Much of America's social history since the 1940s has been the story of the "baby-boom" generation.*

By far the most popular new household product was the television set. In 1946 there were only 7,000 primitive black-and-white TV sets in the country; by 1960 there were 50 million high-quality sets. Nine out of ten homes had one, and by 1970, 38 percent owned new color sets. *TV Guide* was the fastest-growing new periodical of the 1950s, and the new television culture had a transforming effect on the patterns of daily living. Time previously devoted to reading, visiting, playing, listening to the radio, or movie-going was now spent in front of the "electronic hearth."

What differentiated the affluence of the post–World War II era from earlier periods of prosperity was its ever-widening dispersion. Although pockets of rural and urban poverty persisted, destined to explode in the 1960s, during the 1950s few noticed such exceptions to the prevailing prosperity. After being sworn in as head of the AFL-CIO in 1955, George Meany proclaimed that "American labor never had it so good."

On the surface many blacks were also beneficiaries of the wave of prosperity that swept over postwar American society. By 1950, African Americans were earning on average more than four times their 1940 wages. One black journalist declared in 1951 that "the progressive improvement of race relations and the economic rise of the Negro in the

United States is a flattering example of democracy in action." While gains had been made, however, blacks and other minority groups lagged behind whites in their rate of improvement. Indeed, the gap between the average yearly income of whites and blacks widened during the decade of the 1950s. Yet such trends were rarely noticed amid the boosterism of the day. The need to present a united front against communism led commentators to ignore or gloss over issues of racial and economic injustice. Such corrosive neglect would fester and explode during the 1960s, but for now the emphasis was on consensus, conformity, and economic growth.

To perpetuate the postwar prosperity, economists repeated the basic marketing strategy of the 1920s: the public must be taught to consume more and expect more. Economists knew that people had more money than ever before. The average American had twice as much *real* income in 1955 as in the rosy days of the late 1920s before the crash. Still, many adults who had undergone the severities of the depression and the rationing required for the war effort had to be weaned from a decade and a half of imposed frugality in order to nourish the growing consumer culture. A motivational researcher told a business group that the fundamental challenge facing the modern capitalist economy was to demonstrate to the consumer that "the hedonistic approach to life is a moral, not an immoral one."

Advertising became a more crucial component of the consumer culture than ever before. TV advertising expenditures increased 1,000 percent during the 1950s. Such startling results led the president of the National Broadcasting Company (NBC) to claim in 1956 that the primary reason for the postwar economic boom was that "advertising has created an American frame of mind that makes people want more things, better things and newer things."

Paying for such "things" was no problem; the age of the credit card had arrived. Between 1945 and 1957, consumer credit soared 800 percent. Where families in other industrialized nations were typically saving 10 to 20 percent of their income, American families by the 1960s were saving only 5 percent. "Never before have so many owed so much to so many," *Newsweek* announced in 1953. "Time has swept away the Puritan conception of immorality in debt and godliness in thrift."

This consumer revolution had far-reaching cultural effects. Shopping, for instance, became a major recreational activity. In 1945 there were only eight shopping centers in the entire country; by 1960 there were almost 4,000. Much as life in a medieval town revolved around the cathedral, life in postwar suburban America seemed to center on the new giant shopping centers and malls.

Young Americans especially participated in this shopping culture. By the late 1950s, the baby-boom generation was entering its teens, and the disproportionate number of affluent adolescents generated a vast new specialized market for goods ranging from transistor radios, Hula Hoops, and "rock 'n' roll" records to cameras, surfboards, *Seventeen* magazine, and Pat Boone movies. Most teenagers had far more discretionary income and free time than previous generations. Teens in the postwar era knew nothing of depressions or rationing; they were immersed in abundance from an early age and took the notion of carefree consumption for granted.

THE SUBURBAN FRONTIER The population increase of the 1950s and 1960s was an urban as well as a suburban phenomenon. Dramatic new technological advances in agricultural production reduced the need for manual laborers and thereby led 20 million Americans to leave the land for the city between 1940 and 1970. Much of the urban population growth occurred in the South, the Southwest, and the West, in an arc that stretched from the Carolinas down through Texas and into California, diverse states that by the 1970s were being lumped together into the "Sunbelt." The dispersion of air conditioning throughout these warm regions dramatically enhanced their attraction to northerners. But the Northeast remained the most densely populated area; by the early 1960s, 20 percent of the national population lived in the corridor that stretched from Boston to Norfolk, Virginia.

While more concentrated in cities, Americans after World War II were simultaneously spreading out within metropolitan areas. In 1950 the Census Bureau redefined the term "urban" to include suburbs as well as central cities. During the 1950s, suburbs grew six times faster than cities. By 1970, more Americans lived in suburbs (76 million) than in central cities (64 million). "Suburbia," proclaimed the *Christian Century* in 1955, "is now a dominant social group in American life."

William Levitt, a brassy New York developer, led the suburban revolution. In 1947, on 1,200 acres of Long Island farmland, he built 10,600 houses that were immediately sold and inhabited by more than

40,000 people—mostly adults under thirty-five and their children. "Everyone is so young," one Levittowner noted, "that sometimes it's hard to remember how to get along with older people."

Within a few years, there were similar Levittowns in Pennsylvania and New Jersey, and other developers soon followed suit around the country. The federal government aggressively fostered this suburban revolution. "If it weren't for the government," a San Francisco developer explained, "the boom would end overnight." By insuring loans for up to 95 percent of the value of a house, the Federal Housing Administration made it easy for a builder to borrow money to construct low-cost homes. Military veterans were given added benefits. A veteran could buy a Levitt house with no down payment and monthly installments of $56. African Americans and other racial minorities, however, often were discriminated against when such housing loans were issued.

Expanded automobile production and highway construction also facilitated the rush to the suburbs, as more and more people were able to commute longer distances to work. Car production soared from 2 million in 1946 to 8 million in 1955, and a "car culture" soon emerged. As one commentator observed, the proliferation of automobiles "changed our dress, manners, social customs, vacation habits, the shape of our cities, consumer purchasing patterns, and common tastes." Widespread car ownership also necessitated an improved road network. Local and

Moving Day, *1953. A new subdivision opens its doors.*

state governments built many new roads, but the guiding force was the federal government. In 1947 Congress authorized the construction of 37,000 miles of highways, and nine years later it funded 42,000 additional miles of interstate expressways.

Such new roads provided access to the suburbs, and Americans—mostly young middle-class white Americans—rushed to take advantage of the new living spaces. Motives for moving to the suburbs were numerous. The availability of more spacious homes as well as greater security and better educational opportunities for children all played a role. Racial considerations were also a factor. After World War II, blacks migrated in record numbers from the rural South into the cities of the North, Midwest, and West. As they moved in, white residents moved out. Those engaged in "white flight" were usually eager to maintain residential segregation in their new suburban communities. Contracts for homes in Levittown, Long Island, for example, specifically excluded "members of other than the Caucasian race." Such discrimination, whether explicit or implicit, was widespread; the nation's suburban population in 1970 was 95 percent white.

THE GREAT BLACK MIGRATION World War II, like World War I, helped spur a mass migration of rural southern blacks to the cities of other regions. This second great migration was much larger in scope than the first, and its social consequences were much more dramatic. After 1945, more than 5 million southern blacks, mostly farm folk, left their native region in search of better jobs, higher wages, decent housing, and greater social equality. During the 1950s, for example, the black population of Chicago more than doubled. As many as 2,000 migrants a week arrived at the Illinois Central train station. The South Side of Chicago soon became known as the capital of black America. It remains the largest concentration of African Americans in the country. In its scope and effects, this internal migration of blacks from South to North was every bit as significant as the post–Civil War settlement of the West.

Most of these southern blacks were sharecroppers and farm laborers from the Mississippi Delta, the richest cotton-producing land in the world. For over a century, the Delta cotton culture had been dependent on black workers, first as slaves and then as sharecroppers and wage laborers. But a more efficient mechanical cotton picker invented in 1944 changed all that. The new machine could do the work of fifty people, thus making many farm workers superfluous. Displaced southern blacks, many of them illiterate and provincial, streamed northward in search of a new promised land, only to see many of their dreams dashed. The great writer Richard Wright, himself a migrant from the Delta to Chicago, observed that "never in history has a more utterly unprepared folk wanted to go to the city." In northern cities such as Chicago, Philadelphia, Newark, Detroit, New York, Boston, and Washington, D.C., blacks from the rural South confronted harsh new realities. Slumlords often gouged them for rent, employers refused to hire them, and some union bosses denied them membership. Soon the promised land had become for many an ugly nightmare of slum housing, joblessness, illiteracy, dysfunctional families, welfare dependency, street gangs, pervasive crime, and racism.

The unexpected tidal wave of black migrants severely taxed the resources of urban governments and the patience of white racists. Throughout the North, angry whites attacked blacks who dared move into their neighborhoods. For several nights during 1951, a white mob in a Chicago suburb assaulted a building into which a black family had moved. The National Guard had to quell the disturbance and disperse the crowd. Like other northern cities, Chicago sought to deal with the migrants and alleviate racial stress by constructing massive, all-black public housing projects to accommodate the newcomers. These overcrowded racial enclaves, however, were essentially segregated prisons. To be sure, many black migrants and their children did manage through extraordinary determination and ingenuity to "clear," that is, to climb out of the teeming ghettos and into the middle class. But most did not. As a consequence, the great black migration produced a web of complex social problems that in the 1960s would burgeon into a crisis.

A CONFORMING CULTURE

In the 1950s, American social commentators mostly ignored people and cultures outside the mainstream. As evidenced in many of the new look-alike suburbs sprouting up across the land, much of white middle-class social life during the two decades after the end of World War II exhibited an increasingly homogenized character. While fears generated by the cold war initially played a key role in encouraging orthodoxy, corporations and advertisers also came to play an increasingly important role in promoting homogeneity. Suburban life itself encouraged uniformity, as people felt a need for companionship and a sense of belonging as they moved into new communities of strangers. "Conformity," predicted an editor in 1954, "may very well become the central social problem of this age."

CORPORATE LIFE   During World War II, big business had grown bigger. The government had relaxed antitrust activity, and huge defense contracts had tended to promote corporate concentration and consolidation. In 1940, for example, 100 companies were responsible for 30 percent of all manufacturing output; three years later, they were producing 70 percent. After the war, fewer and fewer people were self-employed; many now worked for large corporations, with manual labor giving way to mental labor for a large part of the workforce. In the huge companies as well as in similarly large government agencies and universities, the working atmosphere began to take on a distinctive new cast. The traditional notion of the hardworking, strong-minded individual advancing by dint of competitive ability and creative initiative gave way to a new managerial personality and an ethic of collective cooperation and achievement. And being in a large corporation and on track to promotion led to conforming to corporate culture and saying and doing what the management of the corporation expected.

WOMEN'S "PLACE"   Increasing conformity in middle-class business and corporate life was mirrored in the middle-class home. A special issue of *Life* magazine in 1956 featured the "ideal" middle-class woman, a thirty-two-year-old "pretty and popular" suburban housewife, mother of four, who had married at age sixteen. Described as an excellent wife, mother, hostess, volunteer, and "home manager" who made her own clothes, she hosted dozens of dinner parties each year, sang in the church choir, worked with the PTA and Campfire Girls, and was devoted to her husband. "In her daily round," *Life* reported, "she attends club or charity meetings, drives the children to school, does the weekly grocery shopping, makes ceramics, and is planning to study French." She also exercised on a trampoline in order "to keep her size 12 figure."

The Ideal Woman. *A 1956* Life *magazine cover story pronounced the ideal woman a "pretty and popular" suburban housewife who "attends club or charity meetings, drives the children to school, does the weekly grocery shopping, makes ceramics, and is planning to study French."*

Life's ideal of the middle-class woman reflected a veritable cult of feminine domesticity that witnessed a dramatic revival in the postwar era. The soaring birthrate reinforced the deeply embedded notion that a woman's place was in the home as tender of the hearth and guardian of the children. "Of all the accomplishments of the American woman," the *Life* cover story proclaimed, "the one she brings off with the most spectacular success is having babies."

Even though millions of women had responded to wartime appeals and joined the traditionally male workforce, afterward they were encouraged—and even forced—to turn their jobs over to the returning veterans and resume their full-time commitment to home and family. An article in *House Beautiful* in 1945 lectured women on their postwar responsibilities. The ex-serviceman was "head man again. . . . Your part in the remaking of this man is to fit his home to him, understanding why he wants it this way, forgetting your own preferences." Throughout the postwar era, educators, politicians, ministers, advertisers, and other commentators exalted the cult of domesticity and castigated the few feminists who were encouraging women to broaden their horizons beyond crib and kitchen. Women were to forget any thoughts of continuing their own careers in the workplace. "Back to the kitchen" was the repeated refrain after 1945. Thus many married women, willingly or unwillingly, returned to their traditional domestic roles. Nonetheless, despite the ideal of women remaining in the home and the stigma associated with violating this norm, overall the percentage of women working outside the home increased during the 1950s.

SEARCH FOR COMMUNITY   Another illustration of the conformist tendency of middle-class life during the 1950s was the spiraling growth of membership in social institutions and organizations. This was in part because of the great mobility of Americans after World War II. Some 20 percent of the population changed their place of residence each year. One cause of such mobility was the standard policy of the largest corporations to relocate their sales and managerial employees. IBM executives told friends that the company initials actually stood for "I've Been Moved." As they moved from central cities to suburbs, from suburb to suburb, from farm to city, from state to state, Americans looked for a way to connect with the strangers they lived amidst. Subject to such flux, they searched for a sense of community and rootedness. Hence Americans, even more than usual, became joiners; they joined civic clubs, garden clubs, car pools, and babysitting groups.

Americans also joined churches and synagogues in record numbers. "One comes early to get a seat in suburban churches," a writer observed in 1956; "they overflow, and new ones are being built every day." The postwar era witnessed a massive renewal of religious participation. In 1940 less than half of the adult population belonged to churches; by 1960 over 65 percent were official communicants. Bible sales soared, and books, movies, and songs with religious themes were stunning commercial successes.

The prevailing tone of the popular religious revival during the 1950s was upbeat and soothing. Many ministers assumed that people were not interested in "fire-and-brimstone" harangues from the pulpit; they did not want their consciences overly burdened with a sense of personal sin or social guilt over issues such as segregation or inner-city poverty. Instead they wanted to be reassured that their own comfortable way of life was indeed God's will.

By far the best salesman of this gospel of reassuring "good news" was

Billy Graham Preaches to Thousands, 1955. *Encouraged by the president and Congress, radio, television, and billboard advertising, droves of Americans joined churches and synagogues and attended revival meetings.*

the Reverend Norman Vincent Peale, the impresario of "positive thinking" and feel-good theology. No speaker was more in demand during the 1950s, and no writer was more widely read. Peale's book *The Power of Positive Thinking* (1952) was a phenomenal best-seller throughout the decade—and for good reason. It offered a simple "how-to" course in personal happiness. "Flush out all depressing, negative, and tired thoughts," Peale advised. "Start thinking faith, enthusiasm, and joy." By following this simple formula for success, he pledged, the reader could become "a more popular, esteemed, and well-liked individual."

CRACKS IN THE PICTURE WINDOW

Many Americans found powerful reassurance in Peale's message of psychological security and material success. They were aware that the widely publicized evidence of middle-class prosperity masked festering poverty in rural areas and urban ghettoes. They were also profoundly anxious about the meaning of their lives and of life in general in the nuclear age. That tranquilizers were the fastest growing new medication suggested that considerable anxiety accompanied America's much-trumpeted affluence.

Although Norman Vincent Peale's positive message appealed to many Americans, others found his message shallow and misleading, lacking in genuine conviction and commitment. Reinhold Niebuhr, a brilliant preacher-professor at New York's Union Theological Seminary, led the "neo-orthodox" movement that lambasted the "undue complacency and conformity" settling over American life in the postwar era. Niebuhr deemed the popular religion of self-assurance and the psychology of material success promoted by Peale and his followers woefully inadequate prescriptions for the ills of modern society.

Thus one of the most striking aspects of postwar American life was the sharp contrast between Peale's message that everything was fine and for the best as long as people believed in God, the American Way, and themselves, and the increasingly bitter criticism of American life coming from intellectuals, theologians, novelists, playwrights, poets, and artists. As the philosopher and editor Joseph Wood Krutch recognized in 1960, "the gap between those who find the spirit of the age congenial and those who do not seems to have grown wider and wider."

THE LONELY CROWD The criticism of postwar American life and values began in the early 1950s and quickly gathered momentum among intellectuals, theologians, novelists, playwrights, poets, and artists. Social scientists, too, attacked the prevailing optimism of the time. In *The Affluent Society* (1958), for example, economist John Kenneth Galbraith warned that sustained economic growth would not necessarily solve chronic social problems. He reminded readers that for all of America's vaunted postwar prosperity, the nation had yet to confront, much less eradicate, the chronic poverty plaguing the nation's inner cities and rural hamlets.

Postwar cultural critics also questioned the supposed bliss offered by middle-class suburban life. John Keats, in *The Crack in the Picture Window* (1956), launched a savage assault on life in the huge new suburban developments. He ridiculed Levittown and other such mass-produced communities as having been "conceived in error, nurtured in greed, corroding everything they touch." In these rows of "identical boxes spreading like gangrene," commuter fathers were always at work and "mothers were always delivering children, obstetrically once and by car forever after." Locked into a deadly routine, hounded by financial insecurity, and engulfed by mass mediocrity, suburbanites, he concluded, were living in a "homogeneous, postwar Hell."

Social critics repeatedly cited the huge modern corporation as an equally important source of regimentation in American life. The most comprehensive and provocative analysis of the docile new corporate character was David Riesman's *The Lonely Crowd* (1950). Riesman, a social psychologist, detected a fundamental shift in the dominant American personality from what he called the "inner-directed" to the "other-directed" type. Inner-directed people, Riesman argued, possessed a deeply internalized set of basic values implanted by strong-minded parents or other elders. This core set of fixed principles, analogous to the traditional Protestant ethic of piety, diligence, and thrift, acted, in Riesman's words, like an internal gyroscope. Inner-directed people had a built-in stabilizer of fixed values that kept them on course.

Such an assured, self-reliant personality, Riesman claimed, had been dominant in American life throughout the nineteenth century. But during the mid–twentieth century a new, other-directed personality had displaced it. In the huge, hierarchical corporations that abounded in postwar America, employees who could win friends and influence people thrived; rugged individualists indifferent to personal popularity did not. The other-directed people who adapted to this corporate culture had few internal convictions and standards; they did not follow their conscience so much as adapt to the prevailing standards of the moment. They were more concerned with being well liked than being independent.

Riesman amassed considerable evidence to show that the other-directed personality was not just an aspect of the business world; its characteristics were widely dispersed throughout middle-class life. One source of this may have been Dr. Benjamin Spock's influential advice on raising children. Spock's popular manual, *The Common Sense Book of Baby and Child Care,* sold an average of 1 million copies a year between its first appearance in 1946 and 1960. Spock stressed that parents should foster in their children qualities and skills that would enhance their chances in what Reisman called the "popularity market." Riesman charged that this made the middle-class mother a "chauffeur and booking agent," determined to "cultivate all the currently essential talents, especially the gregarious ones. It is inconceivable to some that a child might prefer his own company or that of just another child."

YOUTH CULTURE AND DELINQUENCY Heeding Dr. Spock's advice, most parents of the 1950s tended to be permissive with their children, who occupied a distinctive place in postwar American life. One commentator described the American family in 1957 as a "child-centered anarchy."

The children of the postwar baby boom were becoming adolescents during the 1950s, and in the process, a distinctive "teen" subculture began to emerge. Living in such a prosperous era, teenagers had more money and free time than any previous generation. And as most adults in postwar American society were striving to get along and to conform to the values of the club or civic group or corporation, so too were most young people during the 1950s embracing the values of their parents and the capitalist system. This "silent generation" was generally content to cavort at proms or fraternity parties or "sock hops" before landing a job with a large corporation, marrying, and settling down into the routine of middle-class suburban life.

Yet such conformity and striving for popularity masked a great deal of turbulence. During the 1950s, a wave of juvenile delinquency swept across middle-class society. One sociologist went so far as to declare that "no social problem has wrought deeper concern in the United States." By 1956, over a million teens a year were being arrested. Car theft was the leading offense, but larceny, rape, and murder were not uncommon. A Boston judge announced that the entire city was being "terrorized" by juvenile gangs.

What was causing such delinquency? J. Edgar Hoover, the head of the FBI, insisted that the root of the problem was a lack of religious training in more and more households. Others pointed to the growing number of urban slums, whose "bad" and "brutish" environments could lead to criminality. Yet such factors failed to explain why so many middle-class kids from God-fearing families were becoming delinquents. One explanation may have been the unprecedented mobility of young people. Access to automobiles enabled teens to escape parental control, and in the words of a journalist, cars provided "a private lounge for drinking and for petting or sex episodes."

A Drive-in Movie, *1951. Accessibility to cars gave teenagers in the 1950s mobility and freedom from adult supervision—something that had eluded previous generations of adolescents.*

ROCK 'N' ROLL   Many concerned observers blamed the delinquency problem on a new form of music that emerged during the postwar era—rock 'n' roll. Indeed, when the film *The Blackboard Jungle* appeared in 1955, people drew a direct connection between the behavior of the film's juvenile gang members and the rock 'n' roll songs by Bill Haley and the Comets featured in the soundtrack. Rock music combined a strong beat with off-beat accents and repeated harmonic patterns to produce its distinctive sound, and the electric guitar was the basic instrument. By the mid-1950s it had captured the imagination of young Americans. In 1955 *Life* magazine published a long article about a mysterious new "frenzied teenage music craze," that was creating "a big fuss."

Alan Freed, a Cleveland disc jockey, had coined the term "rock 'n' roll" in 1951. While visiting a record store, he had noticed an interesting new musical trend: white teenagers were buying rhythm and blues (R & B) records that had heretofore been purchased only by African Americans and Chicanos. Freed wanted to take advantage of the new trend, but he realized that few white households would listen to a radio program featuring what was then called "race music." So he began playing R & B records but labeled the music rock 'n' roll (a phrase used in black communities to refer to dancing and sex) to surmount the racial barrier.

Freed's radio program was an immediate success, and its popularity helped bridge the gap between "white" and "black" music. African-American singers such as Chuck Berry, Little Richard, and Ray Charles, and Chicano performers such as Ritchie Valens (Richard Valenzuela) suddenly were the rage among young, white middle-class audiences eager to claim their own cultural style and message. Berry, for example, was distinctive for his biting guitar riffs, inventive vocals, and athletic showmanship. He sang about dating and school life, about alienated teens riding around in cars "with no particular place to go." Valens, whose meteoric career was cut short by his death at age seventeen in a plane crash in 1959 (Buddy Holly was killed in the same accident), wrote a hit song entitled "Donna" about a failed romance with an Anglo classmate whose father ordered her to stop dating "that Mexican" boy. At the same time, Elvis Presley, a young white truck driver and aspiring singer born in Tupelo, Mississippi, and raised in Memphis, Tennessee, began experimenting with "rockabilly" music, his own unique blend of gospel, country-and-western, and R & B rhythms and lyrics.

In 1956 the twenty-one-year-old Presley released his smash hit "Heartbreak Hotel," and over the next two years the sensual baritone garnered fourteen gold records and emerged as the most popular musical entertainer in American history. Presley appeared on numerous television variety shows, starred in movies, and by the end of the decade had captured the attention of the world. His long hair and sideburns, his knowing grins and disobedient sneers, his leather jacket and tight blue jeans—all shouted defiance against adult conventions. His sexually suggestive stage performances featuring twisting hips and a gyrating pelvis drove teenagers wild. Girls attending his performances went into a frenzy, often fainting or throwing themselves at Presley's feet.

Such hysterics prompted cultural conservatives to urge parents to confiscate and destroy Presley's records because they promoted "a pagan concept of life." A Catholic cardinal denounced Presley as a vile symptom of a new teen "creed of dishonesty, violence, lust and degeneration." Patriotic groups claimed that rock music was a tool of Communist insurgents designed to corrupt American youth. One anti-Communist book denounced rock 'n' roll disc jockeys as "Reds, left

Elvis Presley, 1956. *The teenage children of middle-class America made rock 'n' roll a thriving industry in the 1950s and Elvis its first star.*

wingers, or hecklers of social convention." A Buffalo disc jockey was fired for playing Presley's records. And a congressional report concluded that "the gangster of tomorrow is the Elvis Presley type of today."

Rock 'n' roll not only survived such assaults, it flourished as an exciting new musical idiom directed at young people experiencing the turbulence of puberty. It gave adolescents a self-conscious sense of being a unique social group with distinctive characteristics. And it represented an unprecedented intermingling of racial, ethnic, and class identities. As such, rock music would become one of the major vehicles of the youth revolt of the 1960s.

ALIENATION IN THE ARTS Dissatisfaction with the conventions and conformity of American society not only surfaced in rock 'n' roll, it was also manifested in literature in the 1950s as well as in some of the paintings of the times.

Many of the best novels and plays of the postwar period reinforced Riesman's image of modern American society as a "lonely crowd" of individuals, hollow at the core, groping for a sense of belonging and affection. Arthur Miller's much-celebrated play *Death of a Salesman* (1949) powerfully explored this theme. Willy Loman, an aging, confused traveling salesman in decline, centers his life and that of his family on the notion of material success through personal popularity, only to be abruptly told by his boss that he is in fact a failure. Loman insists that it is "not what you say, it's how you say it—because personality always wins the day," and he tries to raise his sons, Biff and Happy, in his own image, encouraging them to be athletic, outgoing, popular, and ambitious. As he instructs them: "Be liked and you will never want." Happy had followed his father's advice but was anything but happy: "Sometimes I sit in my apartment—all alone. And I think of the rent I'm paying. And it's crazy. But then, it's what I always wanted. My own apartment, a car, and plenty of women. And still, goddammit, I'm lonely."

Such vacant loneliness is the play's recurring theme. Willy, for all his puffery about being well liked, admits that he is "terribly lonely." He has no real friends; even his relations with his family are neither honest nor intimate. "He never knew who he was," Biff sighs. When Willy finally realizes that he has been leading a counterfeit existence, he yearns for a life in which "a man is not a piece of fruit," but eventually he is so dumbfounded by his predicament that he decides he can endow his life with meaning only by ending it.

Death of a Salesman and many other postwar plays written by Arthur Miller, Edward Albee, and Tennessee Williams portray a central theme of American literature and art during the postwar era: the sense of alienation experienced by sensitive individuals in the midst of an oppressive mass culture. In the aftermath of the horrors of World War II and the Holocaust, and in the midst of the nuclear terror, many of the country's foremost writers, painters, and poets refused to embrace the prevailing celebration of modern American life and values.

While millions were reading heartwarming religious epics such as *The Cardinal* (1950), *The Robe* (1953), and *Exodus* (1957), literary critics were praising the more disturbing and sobering novels of James Baldwin, Saul Bellow, John Cheever, Ralph Ellison, Joseph Heller, James Jones, Norman Mailer, Joyce Carol Oates, J. D. Salinger, William Styron, John Updike, and Eudora Welty. There were few happy endings here—and even fewer celebrations of contemporary American life. J. D. Salinger's *The Catcher in the Rye* (1951) was an unsettling exploration of a young man's search for meaning and self in a smothering society. Holden Caulfield finally decides that rebellion against conformity is useless. "If you want to stay alive," he concludes, "you have to say that stuff, like 'Glad to meet you' to people you are not at all glad to meet."

This brooding sense of resigned alienation dominated the best literature in the two decades after 1945. The characters in novels such as James Jones's *From Here to Eternity*, Ralph Ellison's *Invisible Man*, Saul Bellow's *Dangling Man* and *Seize the Day*, William Styron's *Lie Down in Darkness*, and John Updike's *Rabbit, Run*, among many others, tended to be like Willy Loman—restless, tormented, impotent individuals who are unable to fasten on a satisfying self-image and therefore can find neither contentment nor respect in an overpowering or impersonal world.

Many artists also explored the theme of desolate loneliness in urban-industrial American life. For example, virtually all of Edward Hopper's paintings depict isolated individuals, melancholy, anonymous, motionless. A woman undressing for bed, a diner seated at a counter in an all-night restaurant, a housewife in a doorway, a businessman at his desk, a lone passerby in the street—these are the characters in Hopper's world. The silence of his scenes is deafening, the monotony striking, the alienation absorbing.

A younger group of painters in New York City felt that postwar society was so chaotic that it denied any attempt at literal representation. As Jackson Pollock maintained, "the modern painter cannot express this age—the airplane, the atomic bomb, the radio—in the old form of the Renaissance or of any past culture. Each age finds its own technique."

The technique Pollock adopted came to be called abstract expressionism, and during the late 1940s and 1950s it dominated not only the American art scene but the international field as well. In addition to Pollock, the abstract artists included Robert Motherwell, Willem de Kooning, Arshile Gorky, Clyfford Still, Adolph Gottlieb, and Mark Rothko. "Abstract art," Motherwell declared, "is an effort to close the void that modern men feel."

In practice this meant that the *act* of painting was as important as the final result, and that art no longer had to represent one's visual surroundings. Instead it could unapologetically represent the painter's personal thoughts and actions. Wyoming-born Pollock, for example, placed his huge canvases flat on the floor and then walked around each side,

Jackson Pollock at Work. *Pollock poured paint from a can and then dripped and splattered it across the canvas with a stick to create his "action paintings."*

pouring and dripping his paints, all in an effort to "literally be *in* the painting." Such action paintings, with their commanding size, bold form, powerful color contrasts, and rough texture, conveyed the whole spectrum of aesthetic qualities: they were vibrant, frenzied, meditative, disorienting, provocative. Many among the general public found them simply provoking. One wit observed that "I suspect any picture I think I could have made myself."

THE BEATS The desire to liberate self-expression and reject middle-class conventions also animated a small but highly visible and contro-versial group of young writers, poets, painters, and musicians known as the Beats. These angry young men—Jack Kerouac, Allen Ginsberg, Gary Snyder, William Burroughs, and Gregory Corso, among others—rebelled against the mundane horrors of middle-class life. The Beats were not lost in despair, however; they strenuously embraced life. But it was life on their own terms, and their terms were shocking to most observers.

The Beats grew out of the bohemian underground in New York's

Greenwich Village. Kerouac was a handsome, athletic, working-class kid from Lowell, Massachusetts, who went to Columbia University on a football scholarship. Ginsberg was a skinny New Jersey boy with horn-rimmed glasses, an unstable mother, and an intense love for poetry and ideas. At age fourteen he had declared "I'll be a genius of some kind or another, probably in literature. Either I'm a genius, I'm eccentric, or I'm slightly schizophrenic. Probably the first two." Probably all three, some thought. Ginsberg also studied at Columbia, where a perplexed dean directed him to undergo psychotherapy. The moody poet chose William Burroughs as his therapist. Burroughs had graduated from Harvard in 1936, then studied medicine in Vienna. Later he would become a heroin addict, kill his wife while trying to shoot an apple off her head, and write the influential experimental novel *Naked Lunch* (1959).

This fervent threesome found its hero in Neal Cassady, a twenty-year-old ex-convict who arrived in New York from Denver hoping to enroll at Columbia. He was in their view a mythic cowboy turned "cool" hipster, utterly free and rootless because he defied both maturity and reason. Soon this quartet attracted others in quest of *real* life, and the Beat culture was born.

Essentially apolitical throughout the 1950s, the Beats sought personal rather than social solutions to their hopes and anxieties. As Kerouac insisted, his friends were not beat in the sense of beaten; they were "mad to live, mad to talk, mad to be saved." Their road to salvation lay in hallucinogenic drugs and alcohol, sex, a penchant for jazz and the street life of urban ghettos, an affinity for Buddhism, and a restless, vagabond spirit that took them speeding back and forth across the country between San Francisco and New York.

This existential mania for intense experience and frantic motion provided the subject matter for the Beats' writing. Ginsberg's long prose-poem *Howl* (1956) featured an explicit sensuality as well as an impressionistic attempt to catch the color, movement, and dynamism of modern life. Ginsberg howled at the "Robot apartments! invincible suburbs! skeleton treasuries! blind capitals! demonic industries!" Kerouac published his autobiographical novel *On the Road* a year later. In frenzied prose it portrayed the Beats' life of "bursting ecstasies" and maniacal traveling. At one point Dean Moriarty (Neal Cassady) has the following exchange with Sal Paradise (Kerouac): "We gotta go and never stop going till we get there." "Where we going, man?" "I don't know, but we gotta go."

Howl and *On the Road* provoked angry sarcasm from many reviewers, but the books enjoyed brisk sales, especially among young people. *On the Road* made the best-seller list, and soon the term "Beat Generation" or "beatnik" referred to almost any young rebel who openly dissented from the comfortable ethos of middle-class life. Defiant young actors such as James Dean and Marlon Brando were added to the pantheon of Beat "anti-heroes." In *The Wild One* (1954) a waitress asks Brando what he is rebelling against. He replies: "Whattaya got?" A young folk-singer from Minnesota named Bob Dylan was directly inspired by *Howl* and *On the Road*. In this sense the anarchic gaiety of the Beats played an important role in preparing the way for the more widespread youth revolt of the 1960s.

A PARADOXICAL ERA

For all their eccentricities and vitality, the Beats had little impact on the prevailing patterns of postwar social and cultural life. The same held for most of the other critics who attacked the smug conformity and excessive materialism they saw pervading their society. The public had become weary of larger social or political concerns in the aftermath of the depression and the war. Instead Americans eagerly focused their efforts on personal and family goals and material achievements.

Yet those achievements, considerable as they were, eventually created a new set of problems. The benefits of abundance were by no means equally distributed, and millions of Americans still lived in poverty. For those more fortunate, unprecedented affluence and security fostered greater leisure and independence, which in turn provided opportunities for pursuing more diverse notions of what the good life entailed. Yet the conformist mentality of the cold war era discouraged experimentation. By the mid-1960s, tensions between innovation and convention would erupt into open conflict. Many members of the baby-boom generation would become the leaders of the 1960s rebellion against the corporate and consumer cultures. Ironically, the person who would warn Americans of the 1960s about the mounting dangers of the burgeoning "military-industrial complex" was the president who had long symbolized its growth—Dwight D. Eisenhower.

MAKING CONNECTIONS

- The culture of the 1950s laid the groundwork for the counterculture of the 1960s. See Chapters 33 and 34.

- There are fruitful comparisons between American culture in the 1950s and the earlier postwar period, the 1920s. See Chapter 25.

- The women's movement of the 1970s, discussed in Chapter 34, was led by women who rejected the cult of domesticity described in this chapter.

- The baby boom of the postwar period would have continuing economic, social, political, and cultural significance as this generation moved through the life cycle. Follow along in coming chapters.

FURTHER READING

Two excellent overviews of social and cultural trends in the postwar era are William H. Chafe's *The Unfinished Journey: America Since World War II* (rev. ed., 1995) and William E. Leuchtenburg's *A Troubled Feast: America Since 1945* (rev. ed., 1983). For fascinating insights into the cultural life of the 1950s, see Douglas T. Miller and Marion Nowak's *The Fifties: The Way We Really Were* (1977), Jeffrey Hart's *When the Going Was Good: American Life in the Fifties* (1982), and David Halberstam's *The Fifties* (1993).

The baby-boom generation and its impact are vividly described in Paul C. Light's *Baby Boomers* (1988). Readers interested in economic trends should consult David P. Calleo's *The Imperious Economy* (1981). A comprehensive history of the advertising industry and its cultural implications can be found in Jackson Lears's *Fables of Abundance: A Cultural History of Advertising in America* (1994). The emergence and impact of the television industry are discussed in Erik Barnouw's *Tube of*

Plenty: The Evolution of American Television (1982) and Ella Taylor's *Prime-Time Families: Television Culture in Postwar America* (1989).

A comprehensive account of the process of suburban development is Kenneth Jackson's award-winning study *Crabgrass Frontier: The Suburbanization of the United States* (1985). Michael Danielson examines racial discrimination in the suburbs in *The Politics of Exclusion* (1976). For an analysis of the development of western cities in this century, see Carl Abbott's *The Metropolitan Frontier: Cities in the Modern American West* (1993).

The middle-class ideal of family life in the 1950s is examined in Elaine Tyler May's *Homeward Bound: American Families in the Cold War Era* (1988). Thorough accounts of women's issues in the twentieth century are found in William Chafe's *The American Woman: Her Changing Social, Economic, and Political Roles: 1920–1970* (rev. ed., 1988) and Wini Breines Young's *Young, White and Miserable: Growing up Female in the 1950s* (1992).

For an overview of the resurgence of religion in the 1950s, see George Marsden's *Religion and American Culture* (1990). For a treatment of one of the leading religious leaders, see Carol V. R. George's *God's Salesman: Norman Vincent Peale and the Power of Positive Thinking* (1992).

The origins and growth of rock 'n' roll music are surveyed in Carl Belz's *The Story of Rock* (1972). Thoughtful interpretive surveys of postwar American literature include Josephine Hendin's *Vulnerable People: A View of American Fiction Since 1945* (1978) and Malcolm Bradbury's *The Modern American Novel* (1984). The colorful Beats are brought to life in Steven Watson's *The Birth of the Beat Generation: Visionaries, Rebels, and Hipsters, 1944–1960* (rev. ed., 1998).

32 ◯◯ CONFLICT AND DEADLOCK: THE EISENHOWER YEARS

CHAPTER ORGANIZER

This chapter focuses on:

- Eisenhower's "dynamic conservatism."

- American foreign policy in the 1950s.

- the civil-rights movement in the 1950s.

- the background to the Vietnam War.

he New Deal political coalition established by Franklin Roosevelt and sustained by Harry Truman posed a formidable challenge to Republicans after World War II. To counter the unlikely but potent combination of "Solid South" white Democrats, blacks and ethnics, and organized labor, the Grand Old Party turned to General Dwight David Eisenhower, a military hero capable of attracting independent voters as well as tenuous Democrats. His commitment to a "moderate Republicanism" promised to slow the rate of federal government expansion while at the same time retaining many of the coveted social programs established by Roosevelt and Truman. His two terms as president are often characterized as representing a lull between two eras of Democratic activism. But Eisenhower wanted to restore the authority of state and local governments and restrain the executive branch from political and social "engineering." In the process, he sought to reinforce traditional virtues and inspire people with a vision of a brighter future.

"Time for a Change"

By 1952 the Truman administration had piled up a heavy burden of political liabilities. Its bold stand in Korea had brought a bloody stalemate abroad, renewed wage and price controls at home, reckless charges of subversion and disloyalty, and exposure of corrupt lobbyists and influence peddlers who rigged favors in Washington. The disclosure of government corruption led Truman to fire nearly 250 employees of the Bureau of Internal Revenue. But doubts lingered that he would ever finish the housecleaning.

EISENHOWER'S POLITICAL RISE   It was, in a slogan of the day, "time for a change," and Republicans saw public sentiment turning their way as the 1952 election approached. The Republican field quickly narrowed to two men, Ohio senator Robert A. Taft and General Dwight D. Eisenhower. The party wheelhorses turned instinctively to Taft, "Mr. Republican," long a faithful party worker. For all his experience and ability, however, Taft was a dull public figure. Eisenhower, the war hero, on the other hand, had the popular appeal that Taft lacked, and his unpretentious manner inspired widespread support.

Despite his roots in rural Kansas Republican conservatism, Eisenhower had initially supported Roosevelt and the New Deal, and he admired Roosevelt's wartime leadership. But during the Truman years Eisenhower reverted to the political party of his youth. In early 1952 he affirmed that he was a Republican and permitted his name to be entered in party primaries. Bumper stickers across the land announced simply, "I like Ike," and the immensely popular Eisenhower won the nomination on the first ballot. He then balanced the ticket with a youthful Californian, the thirty-nine-year-old Senator Richard M. Nixon, who had built a career on strenuous opposition to domestic "subversives."

THE 1952 ELECTION The Twenty-second Amendment, ratified in 1951, forbade any president to seek a third term. The amendment exempted the incumbent, but weary of the war in Korea, harassed by charges of subversion and corruption in his administration, and with his popularity declining, Truman chose to withdraw. In a wide-open Democratic race, he supported Illinois governor Adlai E. Stevenson, who aroused the Democratic convention delegates with an eloquent speech welcoming them to Chicago. On the third ballot, the convention drafted Stevenson.

The campaign matched two of the most magnetic personalities ever pitted against each other in a presidential contest, but the race was uneven from the start. Eisenhower, though a political novice, was a world hero who had been in the public eye for a decade. Stevenson was hardly known outside Illinois.

The genial Eisenhower, who disliked politics and politicians, pledged to clean up "the mess in Washington." To this he added a promise, late in the campaign, that as president-elect he would go to Korea to secure "an early and honorable" peace. Stevenson offered a keen intellect spiced with a quick wit, but his resolve to "talk sense" and "tell the truth to the American people" came across as a bit too aloof, a shade too intellectual. The Republicans labeled him an "egghead," in contrast to Eisenhower, the folksy man of the people, the man of decisive action. Eisenhower's running mate, Richard Nixon, savagely—and clumsily—tried to tar Stevenson with the brush of being "soft" on communism. Can such a man, Nixon asked the voters, be "trusted to lead our crusade against communism?" Stevenson replied: "If the Republicans will stop telling lies about us, we will stop telling the truth about them."

In the end, Stevenson's humor and intellect were no match for Eisenhower's popularity. The war hero triumphed in a landslide of 33.9 million votes to 27.3 million. The election marked a turning point in Republican fortunes in the South: for the first time since the 1850s the South was moving toward a two-party system. Stevenson carried only eight southern states plus West Virginia; Eisenhower picked up five states on the periphery of the Deep South: Florida, Oklahoma, Tennessee, Texas, and Virginia. The "nonpolitical" Eisenhower had made it respectable, even fashionable, to vote Republican in the South. Elsewhere, too, the general made inroads into the Democrats' New Deal

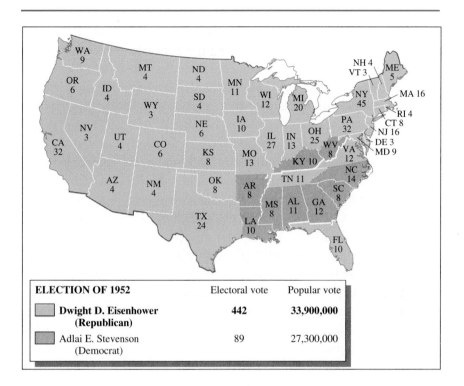

ELECTION OF 1952

	Electoral vote	Popular vote
Dwight D. Eisenhower (Republican)	**442**	**33,900,000**
Adlai E. Stevenson (Democrat)	89	27,300,000

coalition, attracting supporters among the ethnic and religious minorities in the major cities.

The voters, it turned out, liked Ike better than they liked his party. Democrats retained most of the governorships, lost control of the House by only eight votes, and broke even in the Senate. The congressional elections two years later would weaken the Republican grip on Congress, and Eisenhower would have to work with a Democratic Congress until he left office.

EISENHOWER'S "HIDDEN-HAND" PRESIDENCY

IKE Born in Denison, Texas, in 1890, Dwight David Eisenhower grew up in Abilene, Kansas. After finishing West Point, he spent nearly his entire adult life in the military service. As a general, he took command of American forces in the European theater and directed the invasion of

North Africa in 1942. In 1944 he assumed the post of supreme commander of Allied forces in preparation for the invasion of the continent. After the war, by then a five-star general, he became chief of staff and supreme commander of NATO forces, with a brief interlude in between as president of Columbia University.

Eisenhower's inauguration brought a change in style to the White House. The contrast in character between the feisty Truman and the genial Ike accompanied a contrast in philosophy and approach to the presidency. Eisenhower's military experience developed in him an instinct for methodical staff work. He met with the cabinet and the National Security Council nearly every week, and he relied heavily on them for advice.

Far from being a "do-nothing" president, as some have charged, Eisenhower was in fact an effective leader. The art of leadership, he once explained, did not require "hitting people over the head. Any damn fool can do that. . . . It's persuasion—and conciliation—and education—and patience. That's the only kind of leadership I know—or believe in—or will practice."

The public image of Ike was that of a man who rose above partisan politics. It was hard not to like the buoyant and modest war hero. Ike was warm, sincere, and unpretentious, an ardent golfer and bridge player, a common man who read little but Western novels, was uninformed about trends in intellectual and artistic life, and often gave folksy advice: "Everybody ought to be happy every day. Play hard, have fun doing it, and despise wickedness." As one diplomat observed: "He was the nation's number one Boy Scout."

Those who were close to Ike have presented another side to the man. When provoked, he could release a fiery temper and scalding profanity. While Ike talked with genuine feeling about such traditional virtues as duty, honesty, and thrift, he was not above a calculated dissimulation. One student of Eisenhower's techniques has spoken of a "hidden-hand presidency" in which Ike deliberately cultivated a public image of passivity to hide his active involvement in policy decisions.

"DYNAMIC CONSERVATISM" AT HOME Like Ulysses Grant, Eisenhower betrayed a weakness for hobnobbing with rich men. His cabinet, a journalist quipped, consisted of "eight millionaires and a plumber." The plumber, Secretary of Labor Martin Durkin, was gone in eight months, charging that the administration had reneged on a promise to change the Taft-Hartley Act. The president of General Motors became secretary of defense, and two auto distributors were appointed secretary of the interior and postmaster-general. The New Dealers, Adlai Stevenson wryly remarked, "have all left Washington to make way for the car dealers."

Eisenhower called his domestic program "dynamic conservatism," which meant being "conservative when it comes to money and liberal when it comes to human beings." Budget cutting was a high priority. Eisenhower warned repeatedly against the dangers of "creeping socialism," huge bureaucracies, and budget deficits. His administration ended wage and price controls and reduced farm price subsidies.

But though Eisenhower chipped away at New Deal programs, his presidency in the end served rather to legitimate the New Deal by keeping its basic structure and premises intact during an era of prosperity. In a letter to his brother in 1954, Eisenhower observed: "Should any political party attempt to abolish Social Security and eliminate labor laws and farm programs, you would not hear of that party again in our political history." He added that those conservative Republicans who sought to dismantle the New Deal in its entirety were "stupid." Essentially Eisenhower sought to leave the basic structure of the New Deal intact while preventing its costs from rising. This led Republican Senator Barry Goldwater to grouse that Ike was promoting a "Dime Store New Deal."

In some ways, moreover, the administration not only maintained the New Deal but extended its reach, especially after 1954, when it had the help of Democratic Congresses. Amendments to the Social Security Act in 1954 and 1956 brought coverage to millions in categories formerly excluded: professional people, domestic and clerical workers, farm workers, and members of the armed forces. The federal minimum wage rose in 1955 from 75¢ to $1 an hour. Federal expenditures for public health rose steadily in the Eisenhower years, and low-income housing continued to be built, although on a much reduced scale. Some farm-related aid programs were actually expanded during the Eisenhower years.

Despite Eisenhower's general disapproval of federal electric power programs, he continued to support public works for which he saw a legitimate need. Indeed, two such programs left major monuments to his presidency: the St. Lawrence Seaway and the interstate highways. The

St. Lawrence Seaway, opened in 1959 as a joint venture with Canada, made it possible for oceangoing ships to reach the Great Lakes. The Federal Highway Act of 1956 authorized the federal government to put up 90 percent of the cost of building 42,500 miles of limited-access interstate highways to serve the needs of commerce and defense, as well as private convenience. The states provided the remaining 10 percent. It was only afterward that people realized that the huge national commitment to the automobile might have come at the expense of America's railroad system, already in a state of advanced decay.

CONCLUDING AN ARMISTICE   America's new global responsibilities in the postwar world continued to absorb Eisenhower's attention. The most pressing problem when he entered office was the continuing, painful deadlock in the Korean peace talks. Many prisoners of war from North Korea wished to remain in South Korea. U.N. negotiators refused to return prisoners of war who did not want to go back to the North. The North Koreans and Red Chinese insisted that all prisoners be returned regardless of their wishes.

To break the stalemate, Eisenhower took a bold stand. In mid-May 1953 he stepped up aerial bombardment of North Korea, then had Secretary of State John Foster Dulles warn the Chinese of his willingness to use atomic bombs. Whether for that reason or others, negotiations then moved quickly toward an armistice along the established border just above the 38th parallel, and toward a complicated arrangement for prisoner exchange that allowed captives to decide whether to accept or refuse repatriation.

On July 26, 1953, Eisenhower announced the conclusion of the Korean armistice agreement. No one knows if he actually would have forced the issue with atomic weapons. Perhaps the more decisive factors in bringing about a settlement were the size of Chinese Communist losses, which they increasingly found unacceptable, and the new spirit of uncertainty and caution felt by Russian Communists after the death of Joseph Stalin on March 5, 1953—six weeks after Ike's inauguration.

CONCLUDING A WITCH-HUNT   The Korean armistice helped to end another dismal episode: the meteoric career of Senator Joseph R. McCarthy, which had flourished amid the anxieties of wartime. Con-

The Army-McCarthy Hearings, *June 1954. Joseph Welch* (hand on head) *listens dejectedly after McCarthy's attempt to smear one of Welch's associates.*

vinced that the government was thoroughly infested with Communists and spies, the Wisconsin senator launched a one-man crusade to root them out. In the process he and his aides lied, falsified evidence, and bullied or blackmailed witnesses. Eventually the logic of McCarthy's unscrupulous tactics led to his self-destruction, but not before he had left many careers and reputations in ruins. The Eisenhower Republicans thought their victory in 1952 would curb his recklessness, but McCarthy actually grew more outlandish in his charges and his investigative methods. Many Americans caught up in the anti-Communist hysteria viewed him as a heroic knight doing battle against the forces of darkness.

McCarthy finally overreached himself in 1954 when, as chairman of the Senate's Government Operations Committee, he made the absurd charge that the United States Army itself was "soft" on communism. The televised Army-McCarthy hearings displayed McCarthy at his worst, scowling at critics, bullying witnesses, dragging out lengthy irrelevancies, repeatedly calling "point of order." He became the perfect foil for the army's gentle but unflappable counsel, Joseph Welch, whose rapier wit repeatedly drew blood. When McCarthy tried to smear one of Welch's young associates, Welch exploded: "Until this moment, Senator, I think I never really gauged your cruelty or your recklessness. . . . Have you no sense of decency, sir, at long last?" When the audience, including press corps photographers, burst into applause, the confused and skulking senator was reduced to whispering, "What did I do?"

McCarthy descended into new depths of mean-spirited desperation, now directing charges at his own colleagues, calling one senator "senile" and another "a living miracle . . . the only man who has lived so long with neither brains nor guts." On December 2, 1954, the Senate voted 67 to 22 to "condemn" McCarthy for contempt of the Senate. McCarthy was finished and increasingly took to alcohol. Three years later, at the age of forty-eight, he was dead. For all his attacks and inquiries, he had never uncovered one Communist in government.

McCarthyism, Ike joked, had become McCarthywasm, though not for those whose reputations had been wrecked. To the end, Eisenhower kept his resolve not to "get down in the gutter with that guy" and sully the dignity of the presidency. He did work resolutely against McCarthy behind the scenes, but some scholars consider his "hidden hand" approach to have been ineffective at best and cowardly at worst. Eisenhower shared, nevertheless, the widely held conviction that espionage posed a real danger to national security. He denied clemency to Julius and Ethel Rosenberg, who had been convicted of passing atomic secrets to the Russians, on the grounds that they "may have condemned to death tens of millions of innocent people." The Rosenbergs were electrocuted at Sing Sing Prison in 1953.

INTERNAL SECURITY The anti-Communist crusade survived McCarthy's downfall. Even before 1954, Eisenhower stiffened the government security program that Truman had set up six years before. In 1953 he issued an executive order broadening the basis for firing government workers. It replaced Truman's criterion of "disloyalty" with the new category of "security risk." Under the new edict, federal workers could lose their jobs because of dubious associations or personal habits that might make them careless or vulnerable to blackmail. In 1953 the Atomic Energy Commission (AEC) removed the security clearance of physicist J. Robert Oppenheimer, the "father of the atomic bomb," on the grounds that he had expressed qualms about the hydrogen bomb in 1949–1950 and had associated with Communists or former Communists in the past. Lacking evidence of any disloyalty or betrayal, the

AEC nevertheless branded him a "security risk" because of "fundamental defects in his character."

The Supreme Court, however, modified some of the more extreme expressions of this new Red Scare. In 1953 Eisenhower appointed as chief justice former governor Earl Warren of California, a decision the president later pronounced the "biggest damnfool mistake I ever made." Warren, who had seemed safely conservative while in electoral politics, led an active Court on issues of civil rights and civil liberties. The Warren Court (1953–1969), under the chief justice's influence, became an important agency of social and political change through the 1960s. In connection with security programs and loyalty requirements, the Court veered back in the direction of traditional individual rights.

FOREIGN INTERVENTION

DULLES AND FOREIGN POLICY The Eisenhower administration promised new foreign policy departures under the direction of Secretary of State John Foster Dulles. Grandson of one secretary of state and nephew of another, Dulles pursued a lifetime career as an international lawyer and sometime diplomat. Son of a minister and himself an earnest Presbyterian, Dulles, in the words of the British ambassador, resembled those old zealots of the wars of religion who "saw the world as an arena in which the forces of good and evil were continuously at war." Tall, spare, and stooped, he gave the appearance of dour sternness and Calvinist righteousness. But he was also a man of immense energy, intelligence, and experience. As Eisenhower once said of Dulles, "There's only one man I know who has seen *more* of the world, and talked with more people and *knows* more than he does—and that's me."

The foreign policy planks of the 1952 Republican platform, which Dulles wrote, showed both the moralist and the tactician at work. Truman's policy of containment was needlessly defensive, Dulles thought. Containment implied contentment with the status quo. He saw no need for the United States to accept a permanent Soviet presence in eastern Europe. Americans instead should promote the "liberation" of sovereign nations from Soviet domination. This conviction meshed nicely with the conventional wisdom of the right wing that the Yalta Conference agreements were perhaps a betrayal, at best a blunder. The

1952 platform, therefore, promised to "repudiate all commitments . . . such as those of Yalta which aid Communist enslavement" and to end "the negative, futile and immoral policy of 'containment' which abandons countless human beings to a despotism and godless terrorism." A new policy of liberation, the platform promised, would help generate independence movements within the Communist bloc.

The policy verged perilously close to proclaiming a holy war, but Dulles stressed that he did not intend forcible liberation. Soon it became apparent that it was less a policy than a web of rhetoric to catch ethnic voters whose homelands had fallen captive to the Soviets. The hollowness of the policy became evident when the administration did nothing but deplore a Soviet crackdown on rebellious East German workers in 1953. For three years more Dulles assumed that his rhetoric was undermining the Communist hold on Eastern Europe—until ruthless Soviet suppression of the 1956 uprising in Hungary underscored the danger of stirring futile hopes among captive peoples.

Insofar as American interventions occurred abroad, they were covert operations by the Central Intelligence Agency (CIA) in countries outside the Soviet sphere. Under Eisenhower, Allen Dulles, brother of the secretary of state, rose from second in command to chief of the CIA. A veteran of the Office of Strategic Services (the CIA's predecessor, which had coordinated intelligence gathering and covert operations during the war), he had already helped enhance the CIA's capacity for cloak-and-dagger operations. In two cases early in the Eisenhower years this capability was actually used to overthrow governments believed hostile to American interests: in Iran (1953) and in Guatemala (1954).

BRINKSMANSHIP For all his talk of liberation, Dulles made no significant departure from the containment strategy created under Acheson and Truman. Instead he institutionalized containment in the rigid mold of his cold war rhetoric and extended it into the military strategy of deterrence. Dulles betrayed a fatal affinity for colorful phrases. In addition to "liberation" and "roll back," he added two major new contributions while in office: "massive retaliation" and "going to the brink."

"Massive retaliation" was an effort to get, in the slogan soon current, "more bang for the buck." Budgetary considerations lay at the root of the administration's military plans, for Eisenhower and his cabinet feared that in the effort to build a superior war power the country could

"Don't Be Afraid—I Can Always Pull You Back." *Secretary of State Dulles pushes a reluctant America to the brink of war.*

spend itself into bankruptcy. During 1953 the Joint Chiefs of Staff designed a new military posture. The heart of their so-called New Look was the assumption that nuclear weapons could be used in limited-war situations, which would allow reductions in conventional forces and thus budgetary savings. No longer would "the Communists nibble us " to death all over the world in little wars," Vice-President Nixon explained.

By this time, both the United States and the Soviet Union had exploded new hydrogen bombs. With the new policy of deterrence, what Winston Churchill called a "balance of terror" had replaced the old "balance of power." The threat of nuclear holocaust was terrifying, but the notion that the United States would risk such a disaster in response to local wars had little credibility.

Dulles's policy of "brinksmanship" depended for its strategic effect on those very fears of nuclear disaster. He argued in 1956 that in following a tough policy of confrontation with communism, a nation sometimes had to "go to the brink" of war. Such a firm stand had halted further aggression in Korea when America threatened in 1953 to use atomic weapons. Dulles also employed brinksmanship in Indochina in 1954, when American aircraft carriers moved into the South China Sea "both to deter any Red Chinese attack against [French] Indochina and to provide weapons for instant retaliation."

INDOCHINA: THE BACKGROUND TO WAR   Like the rest of the old colonial world of Asia and Africa, Indochina experienced a wave of nationalism in the years after World War II, damaging both the power and prestige of the colonial powers. By the early 1950s, most of British Asia was independent or on the way: India, Pakistan, Ceylon (now Sri Lanka), Burma (now Myanmar), and the Malay States (now Malaysia). The Dutch and French, however, were less willing to give up their colonies, which created a dilemma for American policy makers. Americans sympathized with colonial nationalists who sometimes invoked the example of 1776, but Americans also wanted Dutch and French help against the spread of communism. The Truman administration felt obliged to comply with the Dutch and French pleas for aid in reconquering areas that had passed from Japanese occupation into the hands of local patriots.

French Indochina, created in the nineteenth century out of the old kingdoms of Cambodia, Laos, and Vietnam, offered a variation on Third World nationalism. During World War II, opposition to the Japanese occupation of Indochina was led by the Viet Minh (Vietnamese League for Independence), nationalists who fell under the influence of Communists led by the magnetic rebel Ho Chi Minh. At the end of the war, the Viet Minh controlled part of northern Vietnam, and on September 2, 1945, Ho Chi Minh proclaimed a Democratic Republic of Vietnam, with its capital in Hanoi. American officers were on the reviewing stand in Hanoi, and American planes flew over the celebration. Ho had received secret American help against the Japanese during the war, but his bids for further aid after the war went unanswered. Vietnam took low priority in American diplomatic concerns, which at the time were focused on restoring western Europe and containing the spread of communism there.

In 1946 the French government recognized Ho's new government as a "free state" within the French colonial union. Before the year was out, however, Ho opposed French efforts to establish another regime in the southern provinces, and this clash soon expanded into the First Indochina War.

This was a troubling development for the American government. On the one hand, the United States resented France's determination to restore colonial rule. Yet Truman was even more determined to see France become a bulwark against communism in Europe. As a State

Ho Chi Minh.

Department report concluded in 1948, the United States had an "immediate and vital interest" in supporting the French government in order to further "our aims in Europe," and that goal must "take precedence over active steps looking toward the realization of our objectives in Indochina." As a result, the American government acquiesced in France's efforts to crush Vietnamese nationalism.

The Viet Minh movement thereafter became more completely dominated by Ho Chi Minh and his Communist associates, and more dependent on the Soviet Union and Red China for help. In 1950, with the outbreak of fighting in Korea, the struggle in Vietnam took on the appearance of a battleground in the cold war. When the Korean War ended, American aid to the French in Vietnam, begun by the Truman administration, escalated dramatically. By the end of 1953, the Eisenhower administration was paying about two-thirds of the cost of the French war effort, or about $1 billion annually.

But even with lavish American aid the French were unable to suppress the well-organized and tenacious Viet Minh. In 1954 a major French force had been sent to Dien Bien Phu in the northwest corner of Vietnam, near the Laos border, in the hope of luring Viet Minh guerrillas into the open and grinding them up with superior firepower. The French instead found themselves surrounded by a superior force that laid siege to their stronghold.

The French government requested an American air strike to relieve the pressure on Dien Bien Phu. Eisenhower seemed to endorse forceful action when he advanced his "domino theory" at a news conference on April 7, 1954. He implied that if Indochina fell to the Communists, the rest of Asia would be next. Eisenhower, however, opposed direct American military action unless the British lent support. When they refused, Eisenhower backed away from unilateral action, explaining that it would be a "tragic error to go in alone as a partner of France."

America's decision not to intervene sealed the fate of the besieged French garrison at Dien Bien Phu. On May 7, 1954, the Viet Minh launched massive attacks and finally overwhelmed the courageous, but vastly outnumbered, French resistance. It was the very eve of the day an international conference at Geneva took up the question of Indochina. Six weeks later, as French forces continued to suffer defeats in Vietnam, a new French government promised an early settlement. On July 20 representatives of France, Britain, the Soviet Union, the People's Republic of China, and the Viet Minh reached agreement on the Geneva Accords, and the next day produced their Final Declaration, which proposed to neutralize Laos and Cambodia and divided Vietnam at the 17th parallel. The Viet Minh would take power in the North, and the French would remain south of the line until elections in 1956 should reunify Vietnam. American and South Vietnamese representatives refused either to join in the accord or to sign the Final Declaration.

Dulles responded to the growing Communist influence in Vietnam by organizing mutual defense arrangements for Southeast Asia. On September 8, 1954, at a meeting in Manila, the United States joined seven other countries in an agreement the press quickly labeled the Southeast Asia Treaty Organization (SEATO). The impression that it paralleled NATO was false, for the Manila Defense Accord was neither a common defense organization like NATO nor was it primarily Asian. The signers agreed that in case of an attack on one, the others would act according to their "constitutional practices," and in case of threats or subversion they would "consult immediately."

The members of SEATO included only three Asian countries—the Philippines, Thailand, and Pakistan—together with Britain, France, Australia, New Zealand, and the United States. India and Indonesia, the two most populous countries in the region, refused to join. A special protocol added to the treaty extended coverage to Indochina. The treaty reflected what Dulles's critics called "pactomania," which by the end of the Eisenhower administration had contracted the United States to defend forty-three other countries.

Eisenhower announced that though the United States "had not itself been party to or bound by the decision taken at the [Geneva] Conference," any renewal of Communist aggression in Vietnam "would be viewed by us as a matter of grave concern." (He failed to note that the United States had agreed at Geneva to "refrain from the threat or use of force to disturb" the agreements.) Ho Chi Minh and his government in Hanoi quickly sought to consolidate control throughout the North. In the hinterlands, local Communists held kangaroo courts that tried and executed landowners and confiscated their lands. Residents of the North who wished to leave for southern Vietnam did so with American aid. Over 900,000 refugees, most of them Catholics, relocated to the South, causing staggering logistical problems for the struggling new government there.

Power in the South gravitated to a new premier: Ngo Dinh Diem, a Catholic nationalist who had opposed both the French and the Viet Minh. Diem took office during the Geneva talks after returning from exile at a Catholic seminary in New Jersey. In 1954 Eisenhower offered to assist Diem "in developing and maintaining a strong, viable state, capable of resisting attempted subversion or aggression through military means." In return the United States expected Diem to carry out "needed reforms." American aid took the form of CIA and military cadres charged with training Diem's armed forces and police.

Instead of instituting comprehensive reforms, however, Diem tightened his grip on the country, suppressing opposition on both right and left, offering little or no land distribution, and permitting widespread corruption. In 1956 he refused to join in the elections to reunify Vietnam, and the United States endorsed his decision. But Diem's efforts to eliminate all opposition only played into the hands of the Communists, who found more and more recruits among the discontented. By 1957 guerrilla forces in the South, known as the Viet Cong, had begun attacks on the Diem government, and in 1960 the resistance formed its own political arm, the National Liberation Front. As guerrilla warfare gradually disrupted South Vietnam, Eisenhower was helpless to do anything but "sink or swim with Ngo Dinh Diem."

REELECTION AND FOREIGN CRISES

As the United States continued to forge postwar alliances and to bring pressure to bear on foreign governments by practicing brinksmanship, a new presidential campaign unfolded. Despite having suffered a coronary seizure in the fall of 1955 and an operation for ileitis (an intestinal inflammation) in early 1956, Eisenhower decided to run for reelection. He retained the support and confidence of the public, although the Democrats controlled Congress. Meanwhile, new crises in foreign and domestic affairs required him to take decisive action.

A LANDSLIDE FOR IKE In 1956 the Republican convention renominated Eisenhower by acclamation and again named Nixon as the vice-presidential candidate. The party platform endorsed Eisenhower's "modern Republicanism." The Democrats turned again to Stevenson, with a platform that revived party issues: less "favoritism" to big business, repeal of the Taft-Hartley Act, increased aid to farmers, and tax relief for those in low-income brackets.

Neither candidate generated much excitement during the 1956 campaign. The Democrats focused their fire on the heir apparent, Richard Nixon, a "man of many masks." Stevenson aroused little enthusiasm for two controversial proposals: to drop military conscription and rely on an all-volunteer army, and to ban H-bomb tests by international agreement. Both involved military questions that put Stevenson at a disadvantage by pitting his judgment against that of a successful general. Voters handed Eisenhower a landslide victory. He lost one border state, Missouri, but in carrying Louisiana became the first Republican to win a Deep South state since Reconstruction; nationally, he carried all but seven states.

CRISIS IN THE MIDDLE EAST To forestall Soviet penetration into the Middle East, the Eisenhower-Dulles foreign policy sought to cultivate Arab friendship. In 1955 Dulles had completed his line of alliances across the "northern tier" of the Middle East. Under American sponsorship, Britain had joined Turkey, Iraq, Iran, and Pakistan in the Middle East Treaty Organization (METO), or Baghdad Pact, as the treaty was commonly called. By linking the easternmost NATO state (Turkey) to the westernmost SEATO state (Pakistan), METO had a certain superficial logic. But after Iraq, the only Arab member, withdrew in 1959, METO collapsed. Below the northern tier, moreover, the Arab states remained aloof from the organization. These were the states of the Arab League (Egypt, Jordan, Syria, Lebanon, and Saudi Arabia), which had warred on Israel in 1948–1949 and remained committed to its destruction.

The most fateful developments in the region turned on the rise of Egyptian general Gamal Abdel Nasser, who overthrew King Farouk in 1952. Nasser's nationalist regime soon pressed for the withdrawal of British forces guarding the Suez Canal, the crucial link between the Mediterranean Sea and the Indian Ocean. Eisenhower and Dulles supported Nasser's demand, and in 1954 an Anglo-Egyptian treaty provided for British withdrawal within twenty months. Ownership of the canal, however, remained with the Anglo-French Suez Canal Company.

Nasser, like other leaders of the Third World, remained unaligned in the cold war and sought to play both sides off against each other. The United States in turn courted Egyptian support by offering a loan to

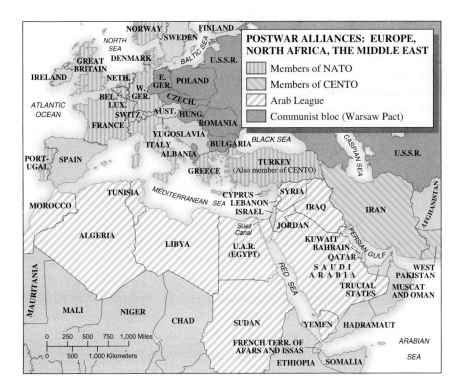

build a great hydroelectric plant at Aswan on the Nile River. From the outset, the administration's proposal was opposed by Jewish constituencies concerned with Egyptian threats to Israel, and by southern congressmen who feared the competition from Egyptian cotton. When Nasser then increased trade with the Soviet bloc and recognized Red China, Dulles abruptly canceled the loan offer in 1956.

The outcome was far from a triumph of American diplomacy. The chief victims, it turned out, were Anglo-French interests in the Suez. Unable to retaliate against the United States, Nasser nationalized the Anglo-French Suez Canal Company and earmarked its revenues for the Aswan project, thereby enhancing his prestige in the Arab world. The British and French reacted strongly. While negotiations dragged out, Israeli forces invaded the Gaza Strip and Sinai peninsula. Ostensibly their aim was to root out Arab guerrillas, but actually it was to synchronize with the British and French, who jointly began bombing Egyptian air bases and occupied Port Said. The British and French claimed that their actions were meant to protect the canal against the opposing belligerents.

The Suez War put the United States in a quandary. Either the administration could support its Western allies and see the troublesome Nasser crushed, or it could stand on the United Nations Charter and champion Arab nationalism against imperialistic aggression. Eisenhower opted for the latter course, with the unusual result that the Soviet Union sided with the United States. Once the threat of American embargoes had forced Anglo-French-Israeli capitulation, the Soviets capitalized on the situation by threatening to use missiles against the Western aggressors. This belated bravado won for the Soviet Union some of the credit in the Arab world for what the United States had actually accomplished.

REPRESSION IN HUNGARY In the Soviet Union, Nikita Khrushchev had come out on top in the post-Stalinist power struggles. In 1955, the Soviets had agreed to end the four-power occupation of Austria and to restore its independence as a neutral but Western-oriented state. Khrushchev had delivered a "secret speech" on the crimes of the Stalin era in 1956 before the Communist Party Congress and hinted at relaxed policies and suggestions that different countries might take "different roads to socialism." This new policy of "de-

Stalinization" put Stalinist leaders in the satellite countries of eastern Europe on the defensive and emboldened the more independent leaders to take action. Riots in the Polish city of Poznan led to the rise of Wladyslaw Gomulka, a Polish nationalist, to leadership of the Polish Communist party. Gomulka managed to win a greater degree of independence by avoiding an open break with the Soviets.

In Hungary, however, a similar movement got out of hand. On October 23, 1956, fighting broke out in Budapest, followed by the installation of Imre Nagy, a moderate Communist, as head of the government. Again the Soviets seemed content to let "de-Stalinization" follow its course, and on October 28 they withdrew their forces from Budapest. But Nagy's announcement three days later that Hungary would withdraw from the Warsaw Pact brought Soviet tanks back into Budapest. Although Khrushchev was willing to relax relations with the eastern European satellites, he refused to allow them to break with the Soviet Union or abandon their mutual defense obligations. The Soviets installed a more compliant leader, Janos Kadar, and hauled Nagy off to Moscow, where a firing squad executed him in 1958. It was a tragic ending to a movement that, at the outset, promised the sort of moderation that might have vindicated Kennan's policy of "containment," if not Dulles's notion of "liberation."

SPUTNIK   On October 4, 1957, the Soviets launched the first satellite, called *Sputnik,* an acronym for the Russian phrase "fellow traveler of earth." Americans, until then complacent about their technical superiority, suddenly discovered an apparent "missile gap." If the Soviets were so advanced in rocketry, then perhaps they could hit American cities just as Nazi rockets had hit London in 1944–1945. All along Eisenhower knew that the "missile gap" was more illusory than real, but he could not reveal that high-altitude American U-2 spy planes were gathering this information. Even so, American missile development floundered, with a tangle of agencies and committees engaged in waste and duplication. The launching of Explorer I, the first American satellite, on January 31, 1958, did not quiet the public outcry.

Soviet success with Sputnik frightened the United States and led to efforts to enlarge defense spending, to offer NATO allies intermediate-range ballistic missiles (IRBMs) pending development of long-range intercontinental ballistic missiles (ICBMs), to set up a new agency to coordinate space efforts, and to establish a crash program in science education. The "Sputnik syndrome," compounded by a sharp recession through the winter of 1957–1958, loosened the purse strings of frugal legislators, who added to the new budget more than Eisenhower wanted for both defense and domestic programs. In 1958 Congress created the National Aeronautics and Space Agency (NASA) to coordinate research and development in the space program. Before the end of the year, NASA had a program to put a manned craft in orbit, but the first manned flight, by Commander Alan B. Shepard, Jr., did not take place until May 5, 1961. Finally, in 1958 Congress enacted the National Defense Education Act, which authorized federal grants especially for training in mathematics, science, and modern languages, as well as for student loans and fellowships.

FESTERING PROBLEMS ABROAD

Once the Suez and Hungary crises faded from the front pages, Eisenhower enjoyed eighteen months of smooth sailing in foreign affairs. Nonetheless, a brief flurry occurred in 1958 over hostile demonstrations in Peru and Venezuela against Vice-President Nixon, who was on a goodwill tour of eight Latin American countries. Meanwhile, problems in the Middle East and Europe continued to fester, only to reemerge again with new force in 1958. The cold war would again be played out in the Middle East and in eastern Europe, as well as at America's back door, in Cuba.

THE MIDDLE EAST In 1958 the Middle East flared up again. By this time the president had secured from Congress authority for what came to be called the Eisenhower Doctrine, which promised to extend economic and military aid to Middle East nations, and to use armed forces if necessary to assist any such nation against military aggression from any Communist country.

Egypt's President Nasser meanwhile had emerged from the Suez crisis with heightened prestige, and in 1958 he created the United Arab Republic (UAR) by merger (a short-lived one) with Syria. Then a leftist coup in Iraq, supposedly inspired by Nasser and the Soviets, threw out the pro-Western government. Lebanon, already unsettled by internal conflict, appealed to the United States for support against a similar fate. Eisenhower immediately ordered 5,000 marines into Lebanon, where they limited themselves to the capital, Beirut, and its airfield. He proposed to go no farther because, he said later, if the government was not strong enough to hold out with such protection, then "we probably should not be there." Once the situation stabilized, and the Lebanese factions reached a compromise, American forces withdrew.

BERLIN The problem of Berlin being situated in East Germany continued to fester with little chance of a resolution for either side. Premier Khrushchev called it a "bone in his throat." West Berlin provided a "showplace" of Western democracy and prosperity in the middle of Communist East Germany, a listening post for Western intelligence, and a funnel through which news and propaganda from the West penetrated what Winston Churchill had called "the iron curtain." Although East Germany had sealed its western frontiers, refugees could still pass from East to West Berlin. On November 10, 1958, Khrushchev threatened to give East Germany control of East Berlin and the air lanes into West Berlin. After the deadline he set, May 27, 1959, Western occupation authorities would have to deal with the East German government, in effect recognizing it, or face the possibility of another blockade.

But Eisenhower refused to budge from his position on Berlin. At the same time, he refused to engage in saber-rattling or even to cancel existing plans to reduce the size of the army. Khrushchev, it turned out, was no more eager for confrontation than Eisenhower. Khrushchev's deadline passed almost unnoticed. In 1959, Premier Khrushchev visited the United States, going to New York, Washington, Los Angeles, San Francisco, and Iowa, and dropping in on Eisenhower at Camp David. In talks there Khrushchev endorsed "peaceful coexistence," and Eisenhower admitted that the Berlin situation was "abnormal." They agreed to hold a summit meeting in the spring.

THE U-2 SUMMIT The summit meeting, however, blew up in Eisenhower's face. On May 1, 1960, a Soviet rocket brought down an American U-2 spy plane on a mission over the Soviet Union. After a period of international jousting with Khrushchev, Eisenhower finally took personal responsibility for the incident—an unprecedented action for a head of state—and justified the action on grounds of national security. At a summit meeting in Paris five days later, Khrushchev called on the president to repudiate the U-2 flights, which had been going on for more than three years, and "pass severe judgment on those responsible." When Eisenhower refused, Khrushchev left the meeting.

CASTRO'S CUBA The greatest thorn in Eisenhower's side was the Cuban regime of Fidel Castro, which took power on January 1, 1959, after three years of guerrilla warfare against a right-wing dictator. In their struggle Castro's forces had the support of many Americans who hoped for a new day of democratic government in Cuba. But these hopes were dashed when American television reported trials and executions conducted by the victorious Castro. Staged before crowds of howling spectators, the trials offered little in the way of legal procedure or proof. Castro, moreover, opposed the widespread foreign control of the Cuban economy. When he began programs of land reform and nationalization of foreign-owned property, relations with the United States worsened. Some observers believed, however, that by rejecting Castro's requests for loans and other help, the American government lost a chance to influence the direction of the revolution. Some thought too that by acting on the assumption that Communists had the upper hand in his movement, the administration may have ensured that fact.

Castro, on the other hand, eagerly accepted the Communist embrace. In 1960 he entered a trade agreement to swap Cuban sugar for

Fidel Castro (center) *became Cuba's premier in 1959 after three years of guerrilla warfare against the Batista regime.*

Soviet oil and machinery. One of Eisenhower's last acts as president was to suspend diplomatic relations with Cuba. The president also secretly authorized the CIA to begin training a force of Cuban refugees (some of them former Castro stalwarts) for a new revolution. But the final decision on its use would rest with the next president, John F. Kennedy.

THE EARLY CIVIL RIGHTS MOVEMENT

While the cold war produced an uneasy stalement by the mid-1950s, race relations in the United States threatened to destroy the domestic tranquility masking years of injustice. Eisenhower entered office committed to civil rights in principle, and he pushed the issue in areas of federal authority. During his first three years, public services in Washington, D.C., were desegregated, as were navy yards and veterans' hospitals. Beyond that, however, two aspects of the president's philosophy inhibited vigorous action in enforcing the principle of civil rights: his preference for state or local action over federal involvement, and his doubt that laws could change racial attitudes. "I don't believe you can change the hearts of men with laws or decisions," he said. For the time, then, leadership in the civil rights field came from the judiciary more than from the executive or legislative branches of the government.

In the 1930s, the National Association for the Advancement of Colored People (NAACP) had resolved to test the "separate but equal" doctrine that had upheld racial segregation since the *Plessy* decision in 1896. Charles H. Houston, dean of the Howard University Law School, laid the plans, and his former student, Thurgood Marshall, served as chief NAACP lawyer. In *Sweatt v. Painter* (1950), the Supreme Court ruled that a separate black law school in Texas failed to measure up because of intangible factors, such as its isolation from most of the future lawyers with whom its graduates would interact.

THE *BROWN* DECISION By the early 1950s, challenges to state laws mandating segregation in the public schools were rising through the appellate courts. Five such cases, from Kansas, Delaware, South Carolina, Virginia, and the District of Columbia—usually cited by reference to the first, *Brown v. Board of Education of Topeka, Kansas*—came to the Supreme Court for joint argument by NAACP attorneys in 1952. Chief Justice Earl Warren wrote the opinion, handed down on May 17,

1954, in which a unanimous Court declared that "in the field of public education the doctrine of 'separate but equal' has no place." In support of its opinion, the Court cited current sociological and psychological findings—demonstrating that even if separate facilities were equal in quality, the mere fact of separating people by race engendered feelings of inferiority. A year later, after further argument, the Court directed "a prompt and reasonable start toward full compliance," ordering that the process should move "with all deliberate speed."

Eisenhower refused to take any part in leading white southerners toward compliance. Privately he maintained "that the Supreme Court decision *set back* progress in the South *at least fifteen years*. The fellow who tries to tell me you can do these things by *force* is just plain *nuts*." While token integration began as early as 1954 in the border states, hostility mounted in the Deep South and Virginia, led by the newly formed Citizens' Councils. The Citizens' Councils were middle- and upper-class versions of the Ku Klux Klan that spread quickly across the region and eventually included 250,000 members. Instead of physical violence and intimidation, the Councils used economic coercion to discipline blacks who crossed racial boundaries. African Americans who

Racial segregation continued in the South during the 1950s.

defied white supremacy would lose their jobs, have their insurance policies canceled, or be denied personal loans or home mortgages. The Citizens' Councils grew so powerful that membership in them became almost a prerequisite for an aspiring white politician.

Before the end of 1955, moderate sentiment in the South gave way to surly reaction against desegregation of the schools. Virginia senator Harry F. Byrd supplied a rallying cry: "Massive Resistance." State legislatures sought futilely to interpose their power between the courts and the schools. In 1956, 101 southern members of Congress signed a "Southern Manifesto," which denounced the Court's decision in the *Brown* case as "a clear abuse of judicial power." At the end of 1956, in six southern states, not a single black child attended school with whites.

THE MONTGOMERY BUS BOYCOTT The essential role played by the NAACP and the courts in providing a legal lever for the civil rights movement often overshadows the courageous contributions of individual African Americans who took great personal risks to challenge segregation. For example, in Montgomery, Alabama, on December 1, 1955, Mrs. Rosa Parks, a black seamstress tired after a day's work, was arrested for refusing to give up her seat on a city bus to a white man. "I'm going to have you arrested," the driver said. "You may do that," Parks replied. As was the case in many southern communities, Montgomery had a local ordinance that required blacks to give up their bus or train seat to a white when asked. The next night black community leaders met in the Dexter Avenue Baptist Church to organize a massive bus boycott under the aegis of the Montgomery Improvement Association.

In Dexter Avenue's twenty-six-year-old pastor, Martin Luther King, Jr., the movement found a charismatic leader. Born in Atlanta, the grandson of a slave and the son of a minister, King was endowed with intelligence, courage, and eloquence. After attending Morehouse College in Atlanta and then receiving a seminary degree, he earned a Ph.D. in philosophy from Boston University before accepting a call to preach in Montgomery. He brought the movement a message of nonviolent disobedience based on the Gospels, the writings of Henry David Thoreau, and the example of Mahatma Gandhi in India. "We must use the weapon of love," he told his people. "We must realize so many people are taught to hate us that they are not totally responsible for their hate." To his antagonists he said: "We will soon wear you down by our capacity

Martin Luther King, Jr., here facing arrest for leading a civil rights march, advocated nonviolent resistance to racial segregation.

to suffer, and in winning our freedom we will so appeal to your heart and conscience that we will win you in the process."

The bus boycott achieved a remarkable solidarity. For months blacks in Montgomery formed carpools, hitchhiked, or simply walked. But the white town fathers held out against the boycott and against the pleas of a bus company tired of losing money. The boycotters finally won a federal case they had initiated against bus segregation, and in 1956 the Supreme Court let stand without review an opinion of a lower court that "the separate but equal doctrine can no longer be safely followed as a correct statement of the law." The next day King and other blacks boarded the buses.

To keep alive the spirit of the bus boycott, King and a group of associates in 1957 organized the Southern Christian Leadership Conference (SCLC). Several days later, King found an unexploded dynamite bomb on his front porch. Two hours later, he addressed his congregation: "I'm not afraid of anybody this morning. Tell Montgomery they can keep shooting and I'm going to stand up to them; tell Montgomery they can keep bombing and I'm going to stand up to them. If I had to die tomorrow morning I would die happy because I've been to the mountain top and I've seen the promised land and its going to be here in Montgomery."

THE CIVIL RIGHTS ACT Despite Eisenhower's reluctance to take the lead in desegregating schools, he supported the right of blacks to vote. In 1956, hoping to exploit divisions between northern and southern Democrats and to reclaim some of the black vote for Republicans, Eisenhower proposed legislation that became the Civil Rights Act of 1957, the first civil rights law passed since Reconstruction. It finally got through the Senate, after a year's delay, with the help of Majority Leader Lyndon B. Johnson, who won southern acceptance by watering down the act. It established the Civil Rights Commission and a new Civil Rights Division in the Justice Department, which could seek injunctions to prevent interference with the right to vote. Yet, by 1959 the Civil Rights Act had not added a single southern black to the voting rolls. Neither did the Civil Rights Act of 1960, which provided for federal court referees to register blacks where a court found a "pattern and practice" of discrimination, and also made it a federal crime to interfere with any court order or to cross state lines to destroy any building. This bill, too, lacked teeth and depended upon vigorous presidential enforcement to achieve any real results.

DESEGREGATION IN LITTLE ROCK A few weeks after the Civil Rights Act of 1957 passed, Arkansas governor Orval Faubus called out the National Guard to prevent nine black students from entering Little Rock's Central High School under federal court order. A conference between the president and the governor proved fruitless, but on court order Faubus withdrew the National Guard. When the students tried to enter the school, an hysterical white mob forced their removal for their own safety. At that point Eisenhower, who had said two months before that he could not "imagine any set of circumstances that would ever induce me to send federal troops," ordered a thousand paratroopers to Little Rock to protect the students, and placed the National Guard on federal service. The soldiers stayed through the school year.

The following year Faubus closed the high schools of Little Rock rather than allow integration, and court proceedings dragged on into 1959 before the schools could be reopened. In that year, massive resistance to integration in Virginia collapsed when both state and federal courts struck down state laws that had cut off funds from integrated schools. Thereafter, massive resistance for the most part was confined to the Deep South where five states, from South Carolina west through Louisiana, still opposed even token integration.

ASSESSING THE EISENHOWER YEARS

Eisenhower entered office in 1953 after being elected in a land-slide and held high approval ratings for ending the Korean War and his strong handling of foreign crises. He won a second landslide election in 1956. Yet support for the president did not translate into support for his party. Eisenhower's decisive win failed to swing a congressional majority for Republicans in either house, leaving the country in the hands of a Republican president and a Democratic Congress. Eisenhower was thus the first president to face three successive Congresses controlled by the opposition party. This meant that he could manage few new ini-tiatives in domestic policy, although he did oversee the admission of the first states not contiguous to the continental forty-eight: Alaska became the forty-ninth state on January 3, 1959, and Hawaii became the fifti-eth on August 21, 1959.

During Eisenhower's second term, the country experienced an eco-nomic slump, a drop in tax revenues, and a large federal deficit. The country also suffered the embarrassment of the U-2 incident and of Cuba falling into the Communist orbit. Emotional issues such as civil rights and defense policy and corrupt aides also compounded Eisen-hower's troubles. As a result of domestic and foreign problems during his presidency, the Eisenhower administration did not draw much ac-claim. One observer called the Eisenhower years "the time of the great postponement," during which the president left domestic and foreign policies "about where he found them in 1953."

Yet opinion about Eisenhower's presidency has improved with time. Even critics now grant that Eisenhower succeeded in ending the war in Korea and settling the dust raised by McCarthy. If Eisenhower failed to end the cold war and in fact institutionalized global confrontation, he did sense the limits of American power and kept its application to low-risk situations. He also tried to restrain the arms race. If he took few initiatives in addressing social and racial problems that would erupt in the 1960s, he did sustain the major innovations of the New Deal. If he tolerated unemployment of as much as 7 percent at times, inflation re-mained minimal during his two terms.

Eisenhower's farewell address to the American people showed his re-markable foresight in his own area of special expertise, the military. Like George Washington, Eisenhower couched his wisdom largely in the form of warnings: that America's "leadership and prestige depend, not merely upon our unmatched material strength, but on how we use our power in the interests of world peace and human betterment"; that the temptation to find easy answers should take into account "the need to maintain balance in and among national problems"; and above all that Americans "must avoid the impulse to live only for today, plundering, for our own ease and convenience, the precious resources of tomorrow."

As a soldier, Eisenhower highlighted, perhaps better than anyone else could have, the dangers of a military establishment in a time of peace. "In the councils of government we must guard against the acquisition of unwarranted influence, whether sought or unsought, by the military-industrial complex. The potential for the disastrous rise of misplaced power exists and will persist." Eisenhower confessed that his great disappointment was his inability to affirm "that a lasting peace is in sight," only that "war has been avoided."

MAKING CONNECTIONS

- The civil rights movement of the 1950s aimed to achieve the racial integration of public services and equal access to political rights. This struggle would continue into the 1960s and then move in several new directions. See Chapter 33.

- American involvement in Vietnam grew in the 1950s, but remained limited to an advisory role. Escalation to an active fighting role came under Lyndon Johnson in 1965, a topic covered in Chapter 33.

- Eisenhower's "hands-off" approach to the presidency was reminiscent of the Gilded-Age presidencies and those of the 1920s. See Chapters 17, 21, and 26.

FURTHER READING

Scholarship on the Eisenhower years is extensive. A carefully balanced overview of the period is Chester Pach, Jr., and Elmo Richardson's *The Presidency of Dwight D. Eisenhower* (1991). For the manner in which Eisenhower conducted foreign policy, see Robert A. Divine's *Eisenhower and the Cold War* (1981).

The conservatism of the 1950s is documented in George H. Nash's *The Conservative Intellectual Movement in America* (1976) and Richard M. Fried's *Nightmare in Red: The McCarthy Era in Perspective* (1990). On links between business and government, see Louis Galambos and Joseph Pratt's *The Rise of the Corporate Commonwealth: United States Business and Public Policy in the Twentieth Century* (1988).

Several specialized studies are illuminating. See Robert A. Divine's *The Sputnik Challenge: Eisenhower's Response to the Soviet Satellite* (1993) and Tom Lewis's *Divided Highways: Building the Interstate Highways, Transforming American Life* (1997).

For the buildup of American involvement in Indochina, consult Lloyd C. Gardner's *Approaching Vietnam: From World War II through Dien Bien Phu, 1941–1954* (1988), and David L. Anderson's *Trapped by Success: The Eisenhower Administration and Vietnam, 1953–1961* (1991). (For more on foreign policy, see Stephen Ambrose and Douglas Brinkley's *Rise to Globalism: American Foreign Policy Since 1938* (rev. ed., 1997), James A. Bill's *The Eagle and the Lion: The Tragedy of American-Iranian Relations* (1988), and Stephen G. Rabe's *Eisenhower and Latin America: The Foreign Policy of Anticommunism* (1988).

Two introductions to the impact wrought by the Warren Supreme Court during the 1950s are Alexander Bickel's *The Supreme Court and the Idea of Progress* (1970) and Paul Murphy's *The Constitution in Crisis Times, 1918–1969* (1972). Also helpful is Archibald Cox's *The Warren Court: Constitutional Decision as an Instrument of Reform* (1968). A masterful study of the important Warren Court decision on school desegregation is Richard Kluger's *Simple Justice: The History of Brown v. Board of Education and Black America's Struggle for Equality* (1975).

For the story of the early civil rights movement, see Taylor Branch's *Parting the Waters: America in the King Years, 1954–1963* (1988), and Robert Weisbrot's *Freedom Bound: A History of America's Civil Rights Movement* (1990).

33 ∽ NEW FRONTIERS: POLITICS AND SOCIAL CHANGE IN THE 1960s

CHAPTER ORGANIZER

This chapter focuses on:

- Kennedy's New Frontier and Johnson's Great Society.

- the achievements of the civil rights movement and ensuing splinter movements.

- America's growing involvement in Vietnam and the rising opposition to it.

- Kennedy's efforts to combat communism in Cuba.

For those pundits who considered the social and political climate of the 1950s dull, the following decade would provide a striking contrast. The 1960s were years of extraordinary turbulence and innovation in public affairs—as well as sudden tragedy and trauma. Many social ills that had been simmering for decades suddenly forced their way onto the national agenda during the 1960s. At the same time, the deeply entrenched assumptions of cold war ideology led the country into the longest, most controversial, and least successful war in the nation's history.

THE NEW FRONTIER

KENNEDY VS. NIXON   In 1960 there was little sense of dramatic change on the horizon. The presidential election that year featured two candidates—Richard M. Nixon and John F. Kennedy—who initially seemed to symbolize the becalmed politics of the 1950s. Though better known than Kennedy because of his eight years as Eisenhower's vice-president, Nixon had also developed the reputation of a cunning chameleon, the "Tricky Dick" who concealed his duplicity behind a series of masks.

But Nixon possessed ability, tenacious energy, and a compulsive love for politics, the more combative the better. Born in suburban Los Angeles in 1913, he grew up amid a Quaker family struggling to make ends meet. After law school and service in the Pacific during World War II, Nixon jumped into the political arena in 1946 as a Republican and surprised observers by unseating a popular congressman in southern California. He arrived in Washington eager to reverse the tide of New Deal liberalism. "I was elected to smash the labor bosses," he explained. Four years later he won election to the Senate. In his campaigns, Nixon unleashed scurrilous personal attacks on his opponents, shrewdly manipulating the growing anti-Communist hysteria. Yet Nixon became both a respected and effective member of Congress, and by 1950 he was the most requested Republican speaker in the country. His rapid rise to political stardom led to his being offered the vice-presidential nomination in 1952 and 1956. He was an active, highly visible vice-president.

Kennedy lacked such experience and exposure. Despite an abundance of assets, including a widely publicized record of heroism in World War II, a glamorous young wife, a Harvard education, and a large, wealthy family, the handsome forty-three-year-old Kennedy lacked national prominence and political distinction. Kennedy's record in the Senate was mediocre. Author of a Pulitzer Prize–winning study of political leaders who had "made the tough decisions," entitled *Profiles in Courage* (1956), Kennedy, said critics, had shown more profile than courage during the McCarthy witch-hunts of the early 1950s and had a weak record on civil rights.

During his campaign for the Democratic nomination, Kennedy had shown that he had the energy to match his grace and ambition. As the first Catholic to run for the presidency since Al Smith, he strove to dispel the impression that his religion was a major political liability. By the time of the convention in 1960, he had traveled over 65,000 miles and made over 350 speeches. Hubert Humphrey, the buoyant liberal senator from Minnesota, was knocked out of the race in the West Virginia primary. In his acceptance speech Kennedy found the stirring rhetoric that would stamp the rest of his campaign and his presidency: "We stand today on the edge of a New Frontier—the frontier of unknown opportunities and perils—a frontier of unfulfilled hopes and threats."

The turning point in the presidential campaign came when Richard Nixon agreed to debate his less prominent opponent on television. During the first of four debates, some 70 million viewers saw Nixon, still weak from a recent illness, perspiring heavily and sporting a five-o'clock shadow. He looked haggard, uneasy, and even sinister before the camera. Kennedy, on the other hand, projected a cool poise that made him seem equal, if not superior, in his fitness for the office. Kennedy's popularity immediately shot up in the polls. Reporters discovered that he

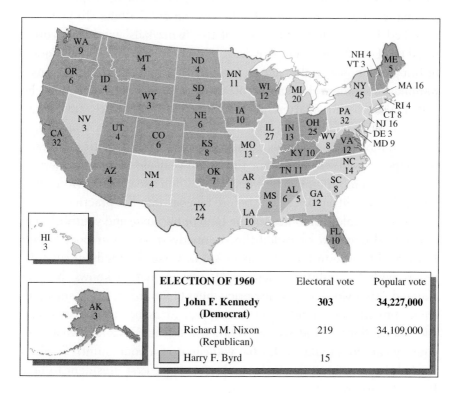

ELECTION OF 1960		Electoral vote	Popular vote
John F. Kennedy (Democrat)		303	34,227,000
Richard M. Nixon (Republican)		219	34,109,000
Harry F. Byrd		15	

had "charisma" and noted the giddy young people who now greeted his arrival at campaign stops. In the words of a bemused southern senator, Kennedy combined "the best qualities of Elvis Presley and Franklin D. Roosevelt."

When the votes were counted, Kennedy and his running-mate, Lyndon B. Johnson of Texas, had won the closest presidential election since 1888. The winning margin was only 118,574 votes out of the 68 million cast. Kennedy's wide lead in the electoral vote, 303 to 219, belied the paper-thin margin in several key states, especially Illinois, where Chicago mayor Richard Daley's Democratic machine appeared to have lived up to its legendary campaign motto: "In Chicago we tell our people to vote early and to vote often."

THE NEW ADMINISTRATION   Kennedy was the youngest person ever elected president, and his cabinet appointments put an accent on youth and "Eastern Establishment" figures. A self-described "idealist without illusions," Kennedy sought to attract the "best and the brightest" minds available, men who would inject a tough, dispassionate, pragmatic, and vigorous outlook into governmental affairs. To that end, he asked Robert McNamara, one of the "whiz kids" who had reorganized the Ford Motor Company with his "systems analysis" techniques, to bring his managerial magic to bear on the Department of Defense. Kennedy appointed Harvard professor McGeorge Bundy, whom he called "the second smartest man I know," as special assistant for national security affairs, and chose as his secretary of state Dean Rusk, a career diplomat and former Rhodes Scholar. When critics attacked the appointment of Kennedy's thirty-five-year-old brother Robert as attorney-general, the president quipped, "I don't see what's wrong with giving Bobby a little experience before he goes into law practice."

The inaugural ceremonies set the tone of elegance and youthful vigor that would come to be called the "Kennedy style." After poet Robert Frost paid tribute to the administration in verse, Kennedy dazzled listeners with his uplifting rhetoric. "Let every nation know," he proclaimed, "that we shall pay any price, bear any burden, meet any hardship, support any friend, oppose any foe, to assure the survival and success of liberty. And so, my fellow Americans: ask not what your country can do for you—ask what you can do for your country." Spines tingled; Kennedy, one journalist wrote, was the first president to be a Prince Charming.

Kennedy and his wife, Jacqueline, at the inauguration, January 20, 1961.

THE KENNEDY RECORD But for all of his idealistic rhetoric, Kennedy had a difficult time launching his New Frontier domestic program. Elected by a razor-thin margin, he did not have a popular mandate. Nor did he show much skill in dealing with a Democratic majority in Congress that remained in the grip of a conservative southern coalition. It blocked his efforts to increase federal aid to education, provide health insurance for the aged, and create a new Department of Urban Affairs.

Administration proposals, nevertheless, did win some notable victories in Congress. They included a new Housing Act that appropriated nearly $5 billion for urban renewal over four years, a raised minimum wage, and increased Social Security benefits. Just two months into his administration Kennedy launched the celebrated Peace Corps to supply volunteers for educational and technical service in underdeveloped countries. Kennedy also won support for an accelerated program to land astronauts on the moon before the end of the decade. Congress readily approved a series of broad foreign aid programs to help Latin American nations, dubbed the "Alliance for Progress." Another important Kennedy initiative was a bold tax-reduction bill intended to accelerate economic growth. Although it was not passed until 1964, after Kennedy's death, it provided a surprisingly potent boost to the economy. Perhaps Kennedy's most significant legislative accomplishment was the Trade Expansion Act of 1962, which eventually led to tariff cuts averaging 35 percent between the United States and the European Common Market.

THE WARREN COURT Under Chief Justice Earl Warren, the Supreme Court continued to be a decisive influence on American domestic life during the 1960s. The Court's decisions on civil liberties proved as controversial as its earlier decisions on civil rights. In 1962 the Court ruled that a school prayer adopted by the New York State Board of Regents violated the constitutional prohibition against an established religion. In *Gideon* v. *Wainwright* (1963), the Court required that every felony defendant be provided a lawyer regardless of the defendant's ability to pay. In 1964 the Court ruled in *Escobedo* v. *Illinois* that a person accused of a crime must also be allowed to consult a lawyer before being interrogated by police. Two years later, in *Miranda* v. *Arizona,* the Court issued perhaps its most bitterly criticized ruling when it ordered that an accused person in police custody must be informed of certain basic rights: the right to remain silent; the right to know that anything said can be used against the individual in court; and the right to have a defense attorney present during interrogation. In addition, the Court established rules for police to follow in informing suspects of their legal rights before questioning could begin.

EXPANSION OF THE CIVIL RIGHTS MOVEMENT

The most important development in American domestic life during the 1960s occurred in civil rights. Kennedy was initially reluctant to challenge conservative southern Democrats on the race issue. He also was never as personally committed to civil rights as his brother Bobby. Despite a few dramatic gestures of support toward black leaders, John Kennedy only belatedly grasped the moral and emotional significance of the most widespread reform movement of the decade. Eventually, however, his conscience was pricked by the grassroots civil rights movement led by Martin Luther King, Jr.

SIT-INS AND FREEDOM RIDERS After the Montgomery bus boycott of 1955, King's philosophy of "militant nonviolence" inspired thousands to challenge Jim Crow practices with direct action. At the same time, lawsuits to desegregate the schools activated thousands of parents and young people. The momentum generated the first genuine mass movement in the history of African Americans when four black college students sat down and demanded service at a "whites only" Woolworth's lunch counter in Greensboro, North Carolina, on February 1, 1960. Within a week, the "sit-in" movement had spread to six more towns in the state, and within two months, demonstrations had occurred in fifty-four cities in nine states.

In 1960 the student participants, black and white, formed the Student Nonviolent Coordinating Committee (SNCC), which worked with King's Southern Christian Leadership Conference (SCLC) to spread the movement. The sit-ins at restaurants became "kneel-ins" at churches and "wade-ins" at segregated public pools. Music provided a common source of inspiration and solace to the demonstrators. Drawing upon the tradition of slave spirituals, they developed freedom songs such as "Ain't Gonna Let That Sheriff Turn Me Around" and "We Shall Overcome." A participant in an organizational meeting at a church recalled that after the last speaker concluded, "tears filled the eyes of hard, grown men who had seen with their own eyes merciless atrocities committed. . . . Bertha told of spending Thanksgiving in jail . . . and when we rose to sing 'We Shall Overcome,' nobody could imagine what kept the church on four corners. . . . I threw my head back and closed my eyes as I sang with my whole body."

Words cannot do justice to the suffering, sacrifice, courage, and commitment of the young protesters. During the year after the Greensboro sit-ins, over 3,600 black and white activists spent some time in jail. In many communities they were struck with clubs, poked with cattle prods, pelted with rocks, burned with lighted cigarettes, and subjected to unending verbal abuse. In Orangeburg, South Carolina, officers used fire hoses against the demonstrators amid subfreezing temperatures. Nonetheless, everywhere they demonstrated, the protesters refused to retaliate.

In 1961 the Congress of Racial Equality (CORE) sent a group of black and white "freedom riders" on buses to test a federal ruling that had banned segregation on buses and trains, and in their depots. In Alabama, mobs attacked the young travelers with fists and pipes, burned one of the buses, and assaulted Justice Department observers, but the demonstrators persisted, drawing national attention and generating new support for their cause.

FEDERAL INTERVENTION IN 1962 Governor Ross Barnett of Mississippi, who believed that God made "the Negro different to punish him," defied a court order and refused to allow James H. Meredith to enroll at the University of Mississippi. Attorney-General Robert Kennedy thereupon dispatched federal marshals to enforce the law, but they were prevented by a violent white mob. Federal troops had to intervene, and Meredith was finally registered at "Ole Miss," but only after two deaths and many injuries.

Everywhere, it seemed, black activists and white supporters were challenging deeply entrenched patterns of segregation and prejudice. In 1963 Martin Luther King launched a series of demonstrations in Birmingham, Alabama, where Police Commissioner Eugene "Bull" Connor proved the perfect foil for King's tactic of nonviolent civil disobedience. Connor's policemen used dogs, tear gas, electric cattle prods, and fire hoses on the protesters while millions of outraged Americans watched the confrontations on television.

King, who was arrested and jailed during the demonstrations, then wrote his "Letter from a Birmingham Jail," a stirring defense of his non-

Eugene "Bull" Connor's police unleash attack dogs on civil rights demonstrators in Birmingham, Alabama, May 1963.

violent strategy that became a classic of the civil rights movement. "One who breaks an unjust law," he stressed, "must do so openly, lovingly, and with a willingness to accept the penalty." He also signaled a shift in his strategy for social change. Heretofore King had emphasized the need to educate southern whites about the injustice of segregation and other patterns of discrimination. Now he focused more on gaining federal enforcement and new legislation by provoking racists to display their violent hatreds in public. As King admitted in his "Letter," he sought through organized nonviolent protest to "create such a crisis and foster such a tension that a community which has constantly refused to negotiate is forced to confront the issue." This concept of civil disobedience did not set well with J. Edgar Hoover, the powerful head of the FBI, who labeled King "the most dangerous Negro of the future in this nation." He ordered agents to follow King and authorized the use of wiretaps on his telephones and in his motel rooms.

Southern traditionalists remained steadfast in opposing racial integration. In 1963, Governor George Wallace dramatically stood in the doorway of a building at the University of Alabama to block the enrollment of several black students, but he stepped aside in the face of insistent federal marshals. Later the same night NAACP official Medgar Evers was shot to death as he returned home in Jackson, Mississippi.

The high point of the integrationist phase of the civil rights movement occurred on August 28, 1963, when over 200,000 blacks and whites marched down the Mall in Washington, D.C., toward the Lincoln Memorial singing "We Shall Overcome." The March on Washington was the largest civil rights demonstration in American history. Standing in front of Lincoln's statue, King delivered one of the memorable public speeches of the century: "Even though we face the difficulties of today and tomorrow, I still have a dream. It is a dream chiefly rooted in the American dream . . . one day . . . the sons of former slaves and the sons of former slave-owners will be able to sit together at the table of brotherhood." That the time for such racial harmony had not yet arrived, however, became clear a little over two weeks later when a bomb exploded in a Birmingham church, killing four black girls who had arrived early for Sunday school.

Yet King's dream—shared and promoted by thousands of other activists—survived. The intransigence and violence that civil rights workers encountered won converts to their cause across the country. Persuaded by his brother Robert, a man of greater passion, compassion,

Martin Luther King, Jr. (second from left), *and other civil rights leaders at the head of the March on Washington for Jobs and Freedom, August 28, 1963.*

and vision, and by the pressure of events, President Kennedy finally decided that enforcement of existing statutes was not enough; new legislation was needed to deal with the race question. In 1963 he told the nation that racial discrimination "has no place in American life or law," and he then endorsed an ambitious civil rights bill intended to end discrimination in public facilities, desegregate the public schools, and protect black voters. But southern conservatives quickly blocked the bill in Congress.

FOREIGN FRONTIERS

EARLY SETBACKS Kennedy's record in foreign affairs was mixed, more spectacularly so than his domestic record. Upon taking office, he discovered that there was in the works a CIA operation designed to prepare 1,500 anti-Castro Cubans for an invasion of their homeland. The Joint Chiefs of Staff endorsed the plan; analysts reported that the invasion would inspire Cubans on the island to rebel against Castro. The scheme, poorly conceived and executed, had little chance of succeeding. When the invasion force landed at Cuba's Bay of Pigs on April 17, 1961, it was brutally subdued in two days, and over a thousand men were captured. A *New York Times* columnist lamented that the United States "looked like fools to our friends, rascals to our enemies, and incompetents to the rest."

Two months after the Bay of Pigs disaster, Kennedy met Soviet premier Nikita Khrushchev in Vienna, Austria. It was a tense confrontation during which Khrushchev tried to bully the young and inexperienced Kennedy. He threatened to limit Western access to Berlin, the divided city located deep within Communist East Germany. Kennedy was shaken by the aggressive Soviet stand. Upon his return home, he demonstrated American resolve by mobilizing Army Reserve and National Guard units. The Soviets responded by erecting the Berlin Wall, which cut off movement between East and West Berlin and became a symbol of the chill in relations between the Soviet Union and the United States.

THE CUBAN MISSILE CRISIS A year later, Khrushchev posed another serious challenge, this time just ninety miles south of Florida. Khrushchev granted Castro's request for nuclear missiles in Cuba to protect the island from future American-sponsored invasions, and to redress the strategic imbalance caused by the presence of American missiles in Turkey aimed at the Soviet Union. While such missiles would hardly alter the military balance, they would be placed in areas not covered by American radar systems and, if launched, would arrive too quickly for warning. More important to Kennedy was the psychological effect of American acquiescence to a Soviet presence on its doorstep. Khrushchev's purpose was apparently to demonstrate his toughness to both Chinese and Soviet critics of his earlier advocacy of peaceful coexistence. But he misjudged the American response.

On October 14, 1962, American intelligence flights discovered that Soviet missile sites were under construction in Cuba. The administration immediately decided that they had to be removed; the only question was how. In a series of secret meetings, the Executive Committee of the National Security Council debated between a "surgical" air strike and a naval blockade of Cuba. They opted for a blockade, but since this would technically represent an act of war, they called it a "quarantine" rather than a blockade. It offered the advantage of forcing the Soviets to shoot first, if it came to that, and it left open further options of stronger action. Monday, October 22, began one of the most anxious weeks in world history. On that day, the president announced to Congress and then to the public the discovery of the missile sites in Cuba; he also announced the naval quarantine.

Tensions grew as Khrushchev blustered that Kennedy had pushed humankind "to the abyss of a world nuclear-missile war." Soviet ships, he declared, would ignore the quarantine. But on Wednesday, October 24, five Soviet supply ships stopped short of the American ships. Two days later an agent of the Soviet embassy privately approached a television journalist with a proposal for an agreement: the Soviet Union would withdraw the missiles in return for a public pledge by the United States not to invade Cuba. Secretary of State Dean Rusk replied that the administration was interested, but told the journalist: "Remember, when you report this, that eyeball to eyeball, they blinked first." On Sunday, October 28, Khrushchev agreed to remove the missiles and added a conciliatory invitation "to continue the exchange of views on the prohibition of atomic and thermonuclear weapons, general disarmament, and other problems relating to the relaxation of international tension."

In the aftermath of the crisis, the United States took several symbolic steps to relax tensions: an agreement to sell surplus wheat to the Soviets, the installation of a "hot line" telephone between Washington and Moscow to provide instant contact between the heads of government, and the removal of obsolete American missiles from Turkey, Italy, and Britain. The United States also negotiated a treaty with Soviet and British representatives to stop nuclear testing in the atmosphere. The treaty, ratified in September 1963, did not provide for on-site inspection, nor did it ban underground testing, which continued, but it promised to end the dangerous pollution of the atmosphere with radioactivity. The test-ban treaty was an important move toward greater international cooperation on nuclear proliferation. Kennedy quoted the Chinese sage Confucius to suggest the treaty's significance: "A journey of a thousand miles begins with one step."

KENNEDY AND VIETNAM As tensions with the Soviet Union were easing, a crisis was growing in Southeast Asia that would become the greatest American foreign policy debacle of the century. During John Kennedy's "thousand days" in office, the turmoil of Indochina never preoccupied public attention for any extended period, but it dominated international diplomatic debates from the time the administration entered office.

The Geneva Accords of 1954 had declared the landlocked kingdom of Laos a neutral country, but thereafter a complex power struggle erupted between the Communist Pathet Lao insurgents and the Royal Laotian Army. There matters stood when Eisenhower left office and told Kennedy: "You might have to go in there and fight it out." The chairman of the Joint Chiefs of Staff argued in favor of a stand against the Pathet Lao, even if it meant direct intervention. After a lengthy consideration of alternatives, the Kennedy administration decided to back the formation of a neutralist coalition government including Pathet Lao representatives. This would preclude American military involvement in Laos, yet prevent a Pathet Lao victory. The Soviets, who were extending aid to the Pathet Lao, indicated a readiness to negotiate, and in May 1961 talks began in Geneva. After more than a year of tangled negotiations, the three factions in Laos agreed to a neutral coalition government.

Meanwhile, North Vietnam kept open the Ho Chi Minh Trail through eastern Laos, over which it supplied its Viet Cong allies fighting in South Vietnam. There the situation worsened under the leadership of the Catholic premier Ngo Dinh Diem, despite encouraging reports from the military commander of the American "advisers" in South Vietnam. At the time, the problem was less the scattered guerrilla attacks than Diem's failure to deliver social and economic reforms and his inability to rally popular support. His repressive tactics, directed not only against Communists but also against the Buddhist majority and other critics, played into the hands of his enemies.

In 1961 White House assistant Walt Rostow and General Maxwell Taylor became the first in a long line of presidential emissaries to South Vietnam's capital, Saigon. They proposed a major increase in the American military presence, but Kennedy refused, and instead continued to dispatch more military "advisers." When he took office, there had been 2,000 American troops in South Vietnam; by the end of 1963, there were 16,000, none of whom had been officially committed to battle. But the Diem regime continued to be its own worst enemy. By mid-1963, growing Buddhist demonstrations made the public discontent in

South Vietnam more plainly visible. The spectacle of Buddhist monks setting themselves on fire on Saigon streets in protest of Diem's iron-fisted rule shocked Americans but brought from Diem's sister-in-law only sarcasm about "barbecued monks."

By the fall of 1963, the Kennedy administration had decided that Diem was a lost cause. When dissident Vietnamese generals proposed a coup d'état, American ambassador Henry Cabot Lodge assured them that Washington would not stand in the way. On November 1 the insurgent military leaders seized the government and murdered Diem. Yet the generals provided no more stability than earlier regimes, as successive coups set South Vietnam spinning from one military leader to the other.

KENNEDY'S ASSASSINATION Kennedy now seemed to recognize the intractability of the situation in Vietnam. He spoke of the South Vietnamese: "In the final analysis it's their war. They're the ones who have to win it or lose it. We can help them as advisers but they have to win it." Some of his aides later argued that Kennedy would never have allowed a dramatic escalation of American military involvement in Vietnam. Others strongly disagreed.

The answer of course will never be known, for on November 22, 1963, while on a campaign swing through downtown Dallas, Kennedy was shot twice in the throat and head and died almost immediately. A few hours later Dallas police arrested Lee Harvey Oswald, a twenty-four-year-old ex-Marine drifter who had worked in the Texas Book Depository, the building from which the shots were fired at Kennedy. Investigators had several other reasons to suspect Oswald: he had recently returned from a prolonged stay in the Soviet Union, in recent years he had also visited Cuba, and his family had ties to a Mafia member who had made threats to kill Kennedy. Yet before Oswald could be thoroughly interrogated, he too was killed. Two days after Oswald's arrest, as television cameras covered his transfer to another jail, Jack Ruby, a Dallas nightclub owner, stepped from the crowd of onlookers and fatally shot Oswald in the abdomen.

Oswald's death ignited a controversy over the assassination that still simmers today. In December 1963 President Johnson appointed a commission to investigate Kennedy's murder. Headed by Chief Justice Earl Warren, it concluded that Oswald had acted alone. Yet many people were (and are) not convinced, and since 1963 dozens of conspiracy theories have been proposed. Some blame the CIA or the

Mafia, others point at Fidel Castro, whom the CIA had once tried to assassinate. Still others insist that Cuban exiles in Miami, angered by Kennedy's failure to rescue their comrades during the Bay of Pigs fiasco, were behind the assassination. In 1979 a House committee reported that more than one person had fired shots at Kennedy in Dallas, but FBI scientists discredited the theory. Books and movies setting forth various conspiracy theories have kept the controversy alive. Whatever the actual story of the assassination, Kennedy's tragic death enshrined him in the public imagination as a martyred leader cut down in the prime of his career.

LYNDON JOHNSON AND THE GREAT SOCIETY

Texan Lyndon Johnson took the oath as president of the United States on board the plane that took John Kennedy's body back to Washington from Dallas. At age fifty-five, Johnson had spent twenty-six years on the Washington scene and had served nearly a decade as Senate Democratic leader, where he had displayed the greatest gift for compromise since Henry Clay.

Johnson brought to the White House a marked change of style from his predecessor. A self-made man, he used gritty determination and shrewd manipulation to work his way out of a hardscrabble rural Texas background to become one of Washington's most powerful figures. Yet he had none of the Kennedy elegance or charisma. The first southern president since Woodrow Wilson, he harbored a sense of being the perpetual "outsider" despite his long experience with legislative power. And indeed he was so regarded by Kennedy "insiders."

Those who viewed Johnson as a stereotypical southern conservative ignored his long-standing admiration for Franklin Roosevelt, the depth of his concern for poor people, and his heartfelt commitment to the cause of civil rights. The day after the assassination he told an aide: "I am a Roosevelt New Dealer. As a matter of fact . . . Kennedy was a little too conservative to suit my taste." In foreign affairs Johnson was a novice. But in the domestic arena during the 1950s he was unsurpassed in his ability to shepherd legislation through the gauntlet of special-interest lobbyists and Congress. He once bragged that "Ike couldn't pass the Lord's Prayer in Congress without me."

THE JOHNSON MYSTIQUE   Lyndon Johnson was a baffling para-dox, capable of altering himself to fit any occasion. In one of his favorite stories, he told of an applicant for a teaching job who is asked by the school board whether the world is flat or round. The man replies: "I can teach it either way." Likewise, Johnson could assume the guise of a multitude of different characters at will. On the one hand, he was a compulsive worker and achiever, animated by greed, ambition, and an all-consuming lust for power, an overbearing man capable of ruthless-ness and deceit and driven by inner demons that required him to be the center of attention. On the other hand, he could be warm, caring, and gracious. He made friends easily and displayed genuine concern for the welfare of the disadvantaged. Overflowing with passions and self-doubts, eager for affection and attention, Johnson was both a loving husband and a philanderer.

Growing up poor, Johnson worked his way through Southwest Texas State Teachers College. In 1931 he was hired as an assistant to a South Texas congressman and moved to Washington, D.C., where he became an enthusiastic New Dealer. Johnson returned to Texas in 1935 as head of the National Youth Administration for Texas and was elected to Con-gress two years later. In 1941 he ran for a vacant Senate seat, but de-spite Roosevelt's support, he narrowly lost the fraudulent election. This defeat convinced him that to get elected a senator from Texas one had to bend the rules.

After a stint in the navy during World War II, which Johnson, like Kennedy, later exaggerated to appear more heroic than it was, he ran for the Senate again in 1948. This time he played the "Texas game," letting his lieutenants bribe local political bosses to "stuff" ballot boxes in their precincts. At the last minute Johnson was declared the winner by eighty-seven votes. He tried to deflect criticism by jokingly referring to himself as "Landslide Lyndon," but a cloud of suspicion hung over him as he assumed his Senate seat. During the early 1950s, Johnson kept his seat by engaging in the required "Red-baiting," catering to the oil and natural gas interests in Texas, and opposing civil rights legislation. "There's nothing more useless," he once observed, "than a dead liberal." In 1950, at age forty-four, he became the youngest Senate minority leader in Democratic party history.

After reelection in 1954 Johnson was elected Senate majority leader when the Democrats recaptured the upper house of Congress. During the next six years, he displayed a remarkable ability for manipulating others to get legislation passed, resorting to horse-trading and back-room deals in order to shepherd some 1,300 bills through the Senate. He engineered the censure of Joseph McCarthy and the passage of the Civil Rights Act of 1957. His accomplishments made him a natural contender for the presidency in 1960, but he was unable to project himself as anything more than a regional candidate. Having done all he could as a legislative leader, he eagerly accepted Kennedy's invitation to join the ticket as his vice-presidential running mate. The invitation resulted not from affection or admiration. Kennedy simply needed Johnson to help carry the South for him.

POLITICS AND POVERTY President Johnson established domestic politics as his first priority. He exploited the nation's grief after the assassination by declaring that Kennedy's legislative program, stymied in several congressional committees, would now be passed. Johnson loved the kind of political infighting and legislative detail that Kennedy had loathed. Recalcitrant congressmen and senators were brought to the White House for what became famous as "the Johnson Treatment." A

The Johnson Treatment. *Johnson used powerful body language and facial expressions to intimidate and manipulate anyone who dared to disagree with him.*

journalist described the technique: "He moved in close, his face a scant millimeter from his target, his eyes widening and narrowing, his eyebrows rising and falling. From his pockets poured clippings, memos, statistics. Mimicry, humor, and the genius of analogy made the Treatment an almost hypnotic experience and rendered the target stunned and helpless." The logjam in the Congress that had blocked Kennedy's program broke under Johnson's forceful leadership, and a torrent of legislation poured through.

At the top of Johnson's agenda were the stalled measures for tax reduction and civil rights. He then added to his "must" list a bold new idea that bore the LBJ brand: "This Administration today, here and now, declares unconditional war on poverty in America." The particulars of this "war on poverty" were to come later, the product of a task force already at work before Johnson took office.

Americans had suddenly rediscovered poverty in the early 1960s when the social critic Michael Harrington published a powerful exposé titled *The Other America* (1962). Harrington argued that while most Americans had been celebrating their rising affluence during the postwar era, some 40 to 50 million people were mired in a "culture of poverty" hidden from view and passed on from one generation to the other. Unlike the upwardly mobile immigrant poor at the turn of the century, these modern poor were impervious to hope. "To be impoverished," Harrington asserted, "is to be an internal alien, to grow up in a culture that is radically different from the one that dominates the society."

President Kennedy read a review of *The Other America* in 1963 and asked his advisers to investigate the problem and suggest a plan of attack. Upon taking office, Johnson announced that he wanted an antipoverty package that was "big and bold, that would hit the nation with real impact." Money for the program would come from the economic growth generated by the tax reduction of more than $10 billion passed in 1964.

The administration's "war on poverty" was embodied in an Economic Opportunity Bill that incorporated a wide range of programs: a Job Corps for inner-city youths, a Head Start program for disadvantaged preschoolers, work-study jobs for college students, grants to farmers and rural businesses, loans to those willing to hire the chronic unemployed, the Volunteers in Service to America (VISTA, a "domestic Peace Corps"), and the

Community Action Program, which would provide "maximum feasible participation" of the poor in directing neighborhood programs designed for their benefit. Speaking at Ann Arbor, Michigan, Johnson called for a "Great Society" resting on "abundance and liberty for all. The Great Society demands an end to poverty and racial injustice, to which we are fully committed in our time." In theory it was liberalism triumphant; in practice its considerable achievements were accompanied by administrative bungling, corruption, and misguided idealism.

THE 1964 ELECTION As the 1964 election approached, Johnson was conceded the Democratic nomination from the start. He chose as his running mate Hubert H. Humphrey of Minnesota, the prominent liberal senator with the seemingly permanent smile and inexhaustible supply of optimism and energy.

In the Republican party, conservatives charged that the party was falling into the hands of an "Eastern Establishment" that had given in to the same internationalism and big-government policies as liberal Democrats. Ever since 1940, so the theory went, the party had nominated "me-too" candidates who merely promised to run more efficiently the programs that Democrats promoted. Offer the voters "a choice, not an echo," they reasoned, and a truly conservative majority would assert itself.

By 1960 Arizona senator Barry Goldwater, a millionaire department-store owner, had emerged as the leader of the Republican right. A movement to draft Goldwater began as early as 1961, mobilizing conservative activists to capture party caucuses and contest primaries. In 1964 they took an early lead, and after Goldwater swept the all-important California primary, his forces controlled the Republican convention. "I would remind you," Goldwater told the delegates, "that extremism in the defense of liberty is no vice."

Goldwater displayed an unusual gift for frightening voters. Accusing the administration of waging a "no-win" war in Vietnam, he urged wholesale bombing of North Vietnam and left the impression of being trigger-happy. He also savaged Johnson's war on poverty and the New Deal tradition. At times he was foolishly candid. In Tennessee he proposed the sale of the TVA; in St. Petersburg, Florida, a major retirement community, he questioned the value of Social Security. He had voted against both the nuclear test ban and the Civil

Rights Act. Republican campaign buttons claimed: "In your heart, you know he's right." Democrats responded: "In your guts, you know he's nuts."

Johnson, on the other hand, moved to the center. He appealed to the middle of the political spectrum. In contrast to Goldwater's bellicose rhetoric on Vietnam, he made a pledge that won great applause at the time and much comment later: "We are not about to send American boys nine or ten thousand miles from home to do what Asian boys ought to be doing for themselves."

The election was a landslide. Johnson polled 61 percent of the total vote; Goldwater carried only Arizona and five states in the Deep South. Johnson won the electoral vote by a whopping 486 to 52. In the Senate the Democrats increased their majority by two (68 to 32) and in the House by thirty-seven (295 to 140).

LANDMARK LEGISLATION   Johnson took advantage of his new mandate to launch his Great Society program. It would, he promised, end poverty, renovate the decaying central cities, provide every young American with the chance to attend college, protect the health of the elderly, enhance cultural life, clean up the air and water, and make the highways safer and prettier.

To accomplish such goals, the Johnson administration pushed an array of new legislation through the Congress at a pace unseen since Roosevelt's Hundred Days. "Hurry, boys, hurry," Johnson told aides. "Get that legislation up to Capitol Hill and out. Eighteen months from now ol' Landslide Lyndon will be lame-duck Lyndon." Priority went to health insurance and aid to education, proposals that had languished since President Truman advanced them in 1945. The proposal for a comprehensive plan of medical insurance had long been stalled by the American Medical Association's ardent opposition. But now that Johnson had the votes, the AMA joined Republicans in boarding the bandwagon for a bill serving those over age sixty-five. The act not only created the Medicare insurance program for the aged, but added another program, Medicaid, which provided states with federal grants that would help cover medical payments for the indigent.

Five days after he submitted his Medicare program, Johnson sent to Congress his proposal for $1.5 billion in federal aid to elementary and secondary education. Such proposals had been ignored since the 1940s, blocked alternately by issues of segregation or separation of church and state. Now Johnson and congressional leaders devised a means of extending aid to "poverty-impacted" school districts, regardless of their public or parochial character.

The momentum generated by the passage of these measures had already begun to carry others along, and it continued through the following year. Altogether the tide of Great Society legislation carried 435 bills through the Congress. Among them was the Appalachian Regional Development Act of 1966, which allocated $1.1 billion for programs to enhance the standard of living of those in remote mountain coves. The Housing and Urban Development Act of 1965 provided for construction of 240,000 housing units and $2.9 billion for urban renewal. Rent supplements for low-income families followed in 1966, and in that year there began a new Department of Housing and Urban Development, headed by Robert C. Weaver, the first black cabinet member. Johnson had, in the words of one Washington reporter, "brought to harvest a generation's backlog of ideas and social legislation."

THE IMMIGRATION ACT Little noticed among the legislation flowing from the Congress was a major new immigration bill that had originated in the Kennedy White House. Johnson used his 1964 State of the Union address to endorse immigration reform in general and the Kennedy bill in particular. A modified version finally passed the Congress in the fall of 1965.

President Johnson signed the Immigration Act of 1965 in a ceremony held on Liberty Island in New York Harbor, with Ellis Island in the background. In his speech, Johnson stressed that the new law would redress the wrong done to those "from southern and eastern Europe" and the "developing continents" of Asia, Africa, and Latin America. It did so by abolishing the discriminatory quotas based on national origins that had governed immigration policy since the 1920s.

The new law, whose provisions were to take full effect in 1968, treated all nationalities and races equally. In place of national quotas it created hemispheric ceilings on visas issued: 170,000 for persons from outside the Western Hemisphere, 120,000 for persons from within. It also stipulated that no more than 20,000 people could come from any one country each year. The new act allowed the entry of immediate family members of American residents without limit. Most of the annual visas were to be given on a first-come-first-served basis to "other relatives" of American residents, and only a small proportion (about 10 percent) were allocated to those with special talents or job skills.

During the prosperous 1960s, few western Europeans sought to emigrate to the United States; those living in Communist-controlled eastern Europe could not leave. But Asians and Latin Americans flocked to American consulates in search of visas. And within a few years, the new arrivals in turn used the family-preference system to bring their family members as well. This so-called chain immigration quickly filled the annual quotas for nations such as the Philippines, Mexico, Korea, and the Dominican Republic, and Hispanics and Asians became the largest contingents of new Americans.

THE GREAT SOCIETY: SUCCESSES AND FAILURES The Great Society programs included several genuine success stories. The Highway Safety Act and the Traffic Safety Act established safety standards for automobile manufacturers and highway design, and the scholarships provided for college students under the Higher Education Act were quite popular. Many Great Society initiatives aimed at improving the health, nutrition, and education of poor Americans, young and old, made headway against these intractable problems. So, too, did efforts to clean up air and water pollution. But several ambitious programs were hastily designed and ill conceived, others were vastly underfunded, and many were mismanaged. Medicare, for example, removed any incentives for hospitals to control costs, and medical bills skyrocketed. Often funds appropriated for various programs never made it through the tangled bureaucracy to the needy. Widely publicized cases of welfare fraud placed a powerful weapon in the hands of those opposed to liberal social programs. By 1966 middle-class resentment over the cost and waste of the Great Society programs helped generate a strong conservative backlash.

FROM CIVIL RIGHTS TO BLACK POWER

CIVIL RIGHTS LEGISLATION Among the successes of the Great Society were several key pieces of civil rights legislation. After Kennedy's death, President Johnson called for passage of the long-stalled civil rights bill as a memorial to the fallen leader. The Civil Rights Act of 1964 was the most far-reaching civil rights measure ever enacted. It outlawed racial discrimination in hotels, restaurants, and other public accommodations. In addition, the attorney-general could now bring suits for school desegregation, relieving parents of a painful necessity. Federally assisted programs and private employers alike were required to eliminate discrimination. An Equal Employment Opportunity Commission administered a ban on job discrimination by race, religion, national origin, or sex.

Perhaps equally important, the Civil Rights Act gave new momentum to activists in the cause. Early in 1965 Martin Luther King, the recipient of the Nobel Peace Prize the year before, announced a voter-registration drive aimed at the 3 million blacks in the South who had not registered to vote. On March 7 civil rights protesters began a march for voting rights from Selma, Alabama, to Montgomery, only to be violently dispersed by state troopers and a mounted posse. A federal judge then agreed to allow the march, and President Johnson provided federal protection. By March 25, when the demonstrators reached Montgomery, they numbered 35,000, and King delivered a rousing address from the steps of the state capitol.

Several days before the march, President Johnson went before Congress with a moving plea for voting rights legislation. The resulting Voting Rights Act of 1965 was passed to ensure all citizens the right to vote. It authorized the attorney-general to dispatch federal examiners to register voters. In states or counties where fewer than half the adults had voted in 1964, the act suspended literacy tests and other devices commonly used to defraud citizens of the vote. By the end of the year, some 250,000 blacks were newly registered.

"BLACK POWER"   In the midst of success, however, the civil rights movement began to fragment. On August 11, 1965, less than a week after the passage of the Voting Rights Act, the predominantly black Watts area of Los Angeles exploded in a frenzy of riots and looting. When the uprising ended, there were thirty-four dead, almost 4,000 rioters in jail, and property damage exceeding $35 million. Liberal commentators were stunned, since the riots occurred in the wake of the greatest legislative victories for black Americans since Reconstruction.

But events did not stand still to await white liberal comprehension.

During the 1965 riots in Watts, Los Angeles, more than 800 armed guards were stationed on area streets to quell looting and violence.

The Watts upheaval marked the beginning of four "long hot summers" of racial conflagration. Riots in the summer of 1966 erupted in Chicago and Cleveland, along with forty other American cities. The following summer Newark and Detroit burst into flames. Detroit provided the most graphic example of urban violence, as tanks rolled through the streets.

In retrospect, it was understandable that the civil rights movement would begin to focus on the plight of urban blacks. By the middle 1960s, about 70 percent of America's black population lived in metropolitan areas, most of them in central-city ghettos that had been by-passed by the postwar prosperity. It seems clear, also in retrospect, that the nonviolent tactics that had worked in the rural South would not work in the northern cities. In the North, racial problems resulted from segregated residential patterns not amenable to changes in law. More-over, northern white ethnic groups did not have the cultural heritage that southern whites shared with blacks by virtue of their living to-gether in the South. A special Commission on Civil Disorders noted that, unlike earlier race riots that had been started by whites, the urban upheavals of the middle 1960s were initiated by blacks themselves in an effort to destroy what they could not stomach and what civil rights legislation seemed unable to change.

In the midst of such violence, a new philosophy of racial separatism began to emerge. By 1966 "black power" had become the rallying cry of young activists. Radical members of SNCC had become estranged from Martin Luther King's theories of nonviolence. When Stokely Carmichael, a twenty-five-year-old graduate of Howard University, became head of SNCC in 1966, he adopted a separatist philosophy of black power, and ousted whites from the organization. "We reject an American dream defined by white people and must work to construct an American reality defined by Afro-Americans," said a SNCC position paper. H. Rap Brown, who succeeded Carmichael as head of SNCC in 1967, even urged blacks to "get you some guns" and "kill the honkies." Meanwhile Carmichael had moved on to the Black Panther party, a self-professed group of urban black revolutionaries founded in Oakland, California, in 1966. Headed by Huey P. Newton and Eldridge Cleaver, the Black Panthers terrified the public by wearing bandoleras and carrying rifles. Eventually the Panthers fragmented in spasms of violence, much of which the FBI and local police officials helped to provoke.

The most articulate spokesman for black power was one of the earliest, Malcolm X (formerly Malcolm Little, with the "X" denoting his lost African surname). Malcolm had risen from a ghetto childhood involving narcotics and crime to become the chief disciple of Elijah Muhammad, the Black Muslim prophet who rejected Christianity as "the religion of white devils" and encouraged black culture and black pride. "Yes, I'm an extremist," Malcolm acknowledged in 1964. "You show me a black man who isn't an extremist and I'll show you one who needs psychiatric attention." By 1964 Malcolm had broken with Elijah Muhammad and founded his own organization, which was committed to the establishment of alliances between American blacks and the nonwhite peoples of the world. He also had begun to abandon his earlier separatist agenda and violent tactics. But just after the publication of his *Autobiography* in 1965, Malcolm was gunned down in Harlem by Black Muslim assassins. With him went the most effective voice for urban black militancy. What made the assassination of Malcolm X especially tragic was that he had just months before begun to abandon his strident antiwhite rhetoric and to preach a biracial message of social change.

Although widely publicized and highly visible, the "black power" movement never attracted more than a small minority of African Americans. Only about 15 percent of blacks labeled themselves separatists.

Malcolm X, influential spokesman for the Black Muslim movement.

The preponderant majority continued to identify with the philosophy of nonviolent integration promoted by Martin Luther King, Jr., and organizations such as the NAACP. King dismissed black separatism and the promotion of violent social change as a "nihilistic philosophy." He reminded his followers that "we can't win violently. We have neither the instruments nor the techniques at our disposal, and it would be totally absurd for us to believe we could do it."

Yet the black power philosophy, despite its hyperbole and violence, had two positive effects upon the civil rights movement. First, it helped African Americans take greater pride in their racial heritage. As Malcolm X often pointed out, prolonged slavery and institutionalized racism had eroded the self-esteem of many blacks in the United States. "The worst crime the white man has committed," he declared, "has been to teach us to hate ourselves." He and others helped blacks appreciate their African roots and their American accomplishments. In fact, it was Malcolm X who insisted that blacks call themselves African Americans as a symbol of pride in their roots and as a spur to learn more about their history as a people. As the popular singer James Brown urged, "Say it loud—I'm black and I'm proud."

Second, the black power phenomenon forced King and other mainstream black leaders and organizations to launch a new stage in the civil rights movement that would focus attention on the plight of poor inner-city blacks. Legal access to restaurants, schools, and other public accommodations, King pointed out, meant little to people mired in a culture of urban poverty. They needed jobs and decent housing as much as they needed legal rights. To this end, King began to emphasize the economic plight of poor inner-city blacks. The time had come for radical measures "to provide jobs and income for the poor." Yet as King and others sought to escalate the war on poverty at home, the war in Vietnam was taking more and more of America's resources and energies.

THE TRAGEDY OF VIETNAM

As violence was escalating in America's inner cities, the war in Vietnam reached new levels of intensity and destruction. At the time of President Kennedy's death, there were 16,000 American military "advisers" in Vietnam. Lyndon Johnson inherited a commitment to prevent a Communist takeover in South Vietnam along with a reluctance to assume the military burden for fighting the war. One president after another had done just enough to avoid being charged with having "lost" Vietnam. Johnson did the same, fearing that any other course would undermine his influence and endanger his Great Society programs in Congress. But this path took him and the United States inexorably deeper into intervention in Asia.

ESCALATION The official sanction for America's "escalation"—a Defense Department term coined in the Vietnam era—was the Tonkin Gulf Resolution, voted by Congress on August 7, 1964. Johnson reported in a national television address that two American destroyers had been attacked by North Vietnamese vessels on August 2 and 4 in the Gulf of Tonkin off the coast of North Vietnam. Although he described the attacks as unprovoked, in truth the destroyers had been monitoring South Vietnamese raids against two North Vietnamese islands—raids planned by American advisers. Even though there was no tangible evidence that the American ships had been attacked, the Tonkin Gulf Resolution authorized the president to "take all necessary measures to repel any armed attack against the forces of the United States and to prevent further aggression."

Three months after his landslide victory over Goldwater, Johnson made the crucial decisions that shaped American policy in Vietnam for the next four years. On February 5, 1965, Viet Cong guerrillas killed 8 and wounded 126 Americans at Pleiku. Further attacks on Americans later that week led Johnson to order operation "Rolling Thunder," the first sustained American bombings of North Vietnam, which were intended to stop the flow of soldiers and supplies into the South. Six months later, a task force concluded that the bombing had had little effect on the supplies pouring down the Ho Chi Minh Trail from North Vietnam through Laos. Still, the bombing continued.

In March 1965 the new American army commander in Vietnam, General William C. Westmoreland, requested and got the first installment of combat troops, ostensibly to defend American airfields. By the end of 1965, there were 184,000 American troops in Vietnam; in 1966 the troop level reached 385,000. As combat operations increased throughout South Vietnam, so did the list of American casualties, announced each week on the nightly news along with the "body count" of alleged enemy dead. "Westy's War," although fought with helicopter gunships, chemical defoliants, and napalm, became like the trench warfare of World War I—a grinding war of attrition.

THE CONTEXT FOR POLICY Johnson's decision to "Americanize" the Vietnam War, so ill-starred in retrospect, was entirely consistent with the foreign policy principles pursued by all American presidents after World War II. The version of the containment theory articulated in the Truman Doctrine, endorsed by Eisenhower and Dulles throughout the 1950s, and reaffirmed by Kennedy, pledged United States opposition to the advance of communism anywhere in the world. "Why are we in Vietnam?" Johnson asked rhetorically at Johns Hopkins University in 1965. "We are there because we have a promise to keep. . . . To leave Vietnam to its fate would shake the confidence of all these people in the value of American commitment." Secretary of State Dean Rusk repeated this rationale before countless congressional committees, warning that Thailand, Burma, and the rest of Southeast Asia would fall "like dominoes" to communism if American forces withdrew. Military intervention was thus a logical culmination of the assumptions widely shared by the foreign policy establishment and leaders of both political parties since the early days of the cold war.

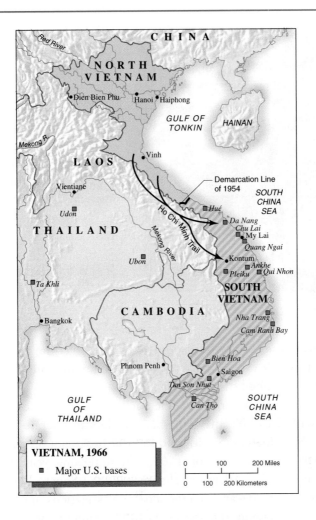

VIETNAM, 1966

■ Major U.S. bases

Nor did the United States blindly "stumble into a quagmire" in Vietnam, as some commentators maintained. Johnson insisted from the start that American military involvement must not reach levels that would provoke the Chinese or Soviets into direct intervention. He therefore exercised a tight rein over the bombing campaign, once boasting that "they can't even bomb an outhouse without my approval." Such a restrictive policy meant, in effect, that military victory in any traditional sense of the term was never possible. "It was startling to me to find out," the new secretary of defense, Clark Clifford, recalled in 1968, "that we had no military plan to end the war." America's goal was not to win the war in a conventional sense by capturing enemy territory,

"How deep do you figure we'll get involved, sir!" *Although American soldiers were first sent to Vietnam as noncombatant advisers, they soon found themselves involved in actual fighting.*

but to prevent the North Vietnamese and Viet Cong from winning. This meant that America would have to maintain a military presence as long as the enemy retained the will to fight.

As it turned out, American public support for the war eroded faster than the will of the North Vietnamese leaders to tolerate devastating casualties. Systematic opposition to the war broke out on college campuses with the escalation of 1965. The following year, Senator J. William Fulbright of Arkansas, chairman of the Senate Foreign Relations Committee, began congressional investigations into American policy. George Kennan, the architect of the containment doctrine, told Fulbright's committee that the doctrine was appropriate for Europe, but not for Southeast Asia. By 1967 antiwar demonstrations in New York and at the Pentagon were attracting massive support. Nightly television accounts of the fighting—Vietnam was the first war to receive extended television coverage, and hence has been dubbed the "living room war"—made the official optimism look fatuous. As Secretary of Defense McNamara admitted, "The picture of the world's greatest superpower killing or injuring 1,000 noncombatants a week, while trying to pound a tiny backward nation into submission on an issue whose merits are hotly disputed, is not a pretty one."

In a war of political will, North Vietnam had the advantage. Johnson and his advisers grievously underestimated the tenacity of North Vietnam's commitment to unify Vietnam and expel the United States. Ho Chi Minh had warned the French in the 1940s that "You can kill ten of my men for every one I kill of yours, but even at those odds, you will lose and I will win." He knew that in a battle of attrition, the Vietnamese Communists had the advantage, for they were willing to sacrifice all for their cause. While the United States fought a limited war for limited objectives, the Vietnamese Communists fought a total war for their very survival. Indeed, just as General Westmoreland was assuring Johnson and the American public that his forces in early 1968 were on the verge of gaining the upper hand, the Communists again displayed their cunning and tenacity.

THE TURNING POINT   On January 31, 1968, the first day of the Vietnamese New Year (Tet), the Viet Cong and North Vietnamese defied a holiday truce to launch a wave of surprise assaults on American and South Vietnamese forces throughout South Vietnam. The old capital city of Hué fell to the Communists, and Viet Cong units temporarily occupied the grounds of the American Embassy in Saigon. Within a few days, however, American and South Vietnamese forces organized a devastating counterattack. General Westmoreland justifiably proclaimed the Tet offensive a major defeat for the Viet Cong. But while Viet Cong casualties were enormous, the psychological impact of the offensive on the American public was more telling. *Time* and *Newsweek* soon ran antiwar editorials urging American withdrawal. Walter Cronkite, the dean of American television journalists, confided to his viewers that he no longer believed the war was winnable. "If I've lost Walter," Johnson was reported to say, "then it's over. I've lost Mr. Average Citizen." Polls showed that Johnson's popularity had declined to 35 percent, lower than any president since Truman in his darkest days. In 1968 the United States was spending $322,000 on every enemy soldier killed in Vietnam; the poverty programs at home received only $53 per person.

During 1968 Johnson grew increasingly isolated. The secretary of defense reported that a task force of prominent soldiers and civilians saw no prospect for a military victory; the war was hopelessly stalemated. Robert Kennedy was considering a run for the presidency in order to challenge Johnson's Vietnam policy, and Senator Eugene McCarthy of Minnesota decided to oppose Johnson in the Democratic primaries. With antiwar students rallying to his candidacy, McCarthy polled 42 percent of the vote to Johnson's 48 percent in New Hampshire's March primary. It was a remarkable showing for a little-known senator. Each presidential primary now promised to become a referendum on Johnson's Vietnam policy.

On March 31 Johnson announced a limited halt to the bombing of North Vietnam and fresh initiatives for a negotiated cease-fire. Then he added a dramatic postscript: "I have concluded that I should not permit the Presidency to become involved in the partisan divisions that are developing in this political year. Accordingly, I shall not seek, and I will not accept, the nomination of my party for another term as your President." Although American combat troops would remain in Vietnam for seven more years and the casualties would mount, the quest for military victory had ended. Now the question was how the most powerful nation in the world could extricate itself from Vietnam with a minimum of damage to its prestige. It would not be easy. When direct negotiations with the North Vietnamese finally began in Paris in May 1968, they immediately bogged down over North Vietnam's demand for an American bombing halt as a precondition for further discussion.

SIXTIES CRESCENDO

A TRAUMATIC YEAR History seemed to move at a fearful pace throughout the 1960s, but 1968 was a year of extreme turbulence even for that volatile decade. On April 4, only four days after Johnson's announced withdrawal from the presidential race, Martin Luther King, Jr., was gunned down while standing on the balcony of a motel in Memphis, Tennessee. The assassin had expressed hostility toward blacks, but debate still continues over whether he was a pawn in an organized conspiracy. King's death set off an outpouring of grief among whites and blacks. It also set off riots in over sixty American cities, with the most serious in Chicago and Washington, D.C.

Two months later, on June 6, Robert Kennedy was shot in the head by a young Palestinian who resented Kennedy's strong support of Israel. Kennedy died at the end of the day on which he had convincingly defeated Eugene McCarthy in the California Democratic primary, thereby assuming leadership of the antiwar forces in the race for the nomination for president.

CHICAGO AND MIAMI In August 1968 Democratic delegates gathered inside the convention hall at Chicago to nominate Vice-President Hubert Humphrey, while 24,000 police and National Guardsmen and a small army of television reporters stood watch over several thousand diverse protesters herded together miles away in a public park. Chicago mayor Richard Daley, who had given "shoot-to-kill" orders to police during the April riots protesting the King assassination, warned that he would not tolerate disruptions. Nonetheless, riots broke out in front of the Hilton Hotel and were televised nationwide. As police tear gas and billy clubs struck demonstrators, others chanted, "The whole world is watching."

The Democratic party's liberal tradition was clearly in disarray, a fact that gave heart to the Republicans who gathered in Miami to nominate Richard Nixon. Nixon's nomination represented a remarkable political comeback. His narrow loss to Kennedy in 1960 had been followed by a disastrous defeat in the California gubernatorial race two years later. In what he labeled his "last press conference," he bitterly lashed out at reporters, claiming that they had cost him the race. "You won't have Nixon to kick around any more," he defiantly pledged. Yet Nixon displayed his remarkable resilience by returning to national politics in 1964, when he crisscrossed the nation in support of Goldwater's candidacy. For the next several years he remained active, and in 1968 Nixon was ready to take advantage of Johnson's crumbling popularity. He offered a vision of stability and order that a majority of Americans—soon to be called "the silent majority"—wanted desperately.

But others were ready as well to challenge the Democratic party regulars. George Wallace, the Democratic governor of Alabama, ran as a third candidate in the campaign on the American Independent party ticket. Wallace had made his political reputation as a brazen defender of segregation, but in his campaign for national office in 1968 he moderated his position on the race issue. And he appealed even more candidly than Nixon to the fears generated by antiwar protesters, the welfare system, and the growth of the federal government. Wallace insisted that "liberals, intellectuals, and long-hairs have run the country for too long," and he pledged that when he took over in Washington, he would "throw all these phonies and their briefcases into the Potomac." Wallace's platform was compel-

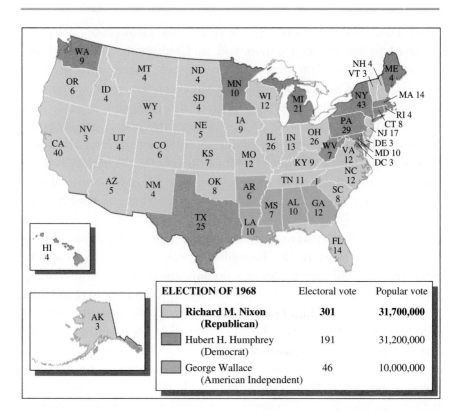

ELECTION OF 1968	Electoral vote	Popular vote
Richard M. Nixon (Republican)	**301**	**31,700,000**
Hubert H. Humphrey (Democrat)	191	31,200,000
George Wallace (American Independent)	46	10,000,000

ling in its simplicity: rioters would be shot, the war in Vietnam won, states' rights and law and order restored, open-housing laws repealed, and welfare cheats jailed.

Wallace's reactionary candidacy generated considerable appeal outside his native South, especially in white working-class communities where resentment against Johnson's Great Society liberalism was rife. Although never a possible winner, Wallace had to be taken seriously: he could deny Humphrey or Nixon an electoral majority and thereby throw the choice into the House of Representatives, which could provide an appropriate climax to a chaotic year.

NIXON AGAIN It did not happen that way. Nixon enjoyed an enormous early lead in the polls, which narrowed as the election approached. Wallace's campaign was hurt by his outspoken running mate, retired Air Force general Curtis LeMay, who suggested using nuclear weapons in Vietnam. In October 1968, Humphrey, tainted by his ties to

LBJ and the party bosses, announced that, if elected, he would stop bombing North Vietnam "as an acceptable risk for peace."

In the end, Nixon and his running mate, Governor Spiro Agnew of Maryland, eked out a narrow victory by roughly 500,000 votes, a margin of about 1 percentage point. The electoral vote was more decisive, 301 to 191. Wallace won 10 million votes, 13.5 percent of the total, the best showing by a third-party candidate since Robert La Follette in 1924. All but one of Wallace's 46 electoral votes were from the Deep South. Nixon swept all but four of the states west of the Mississippi, while Humphrey's support came almost exclusively from the Northeast.

So at the end of a turbulent year, near the end of a traumatic decade, power passed peacefully to a president who was associated with the superficial stability of the 1950s. A nation that had seemed on the verge of consuming itself in spasms of violence looked to Richard Nixon to provide what he had promised in the campaign: "peace with honor" in Vietnam and a middle ground on which a majority of Americans, silent or otherwise, could come together.

MAKING CONNECTIONS

- The reform movements of the 1960s galvanized the baby-boom generation into a new youth movement, described in the next chapter, that continued through the early 1970s.

- The conflict in Vietnam, America's longest war, would come to a bitter end for American forces, but the divisions it spawned would echo through the rest of the century.

- The Immigration Act of 1965 would have profound and unexpected consequences on American society: see Chapter 36.

- The success of the civil rights movement in the 1960s led to similar movements for women, gays, Native Americans, and Hispanics, as we see in the next chapter.

FURTHER READING

Herbert Parmet traces the influence of John F. Kennedy in two volumes, *Jack: The Struggle of John Fitzgerald Kennedy* (1980) and *JFK: The Presidency of John Fitzgerald Kennedy* (1983). Critical assessments can be found in Thomas C. Reeves's *A Question of Character: The Life of John F. Kennedy* (rev. ed., 1998) and Bruce Miroff's *Pragmatic Illusions: The Presidential Politics of John F. Kennedy* (1976). The best study of the Kennedy administration's domestic policies is Irving Bernstein's *Promises Kept: John F. Kennedy's New Frontier* (1991). For details on the assassination, see David W. Belin's *Final Disclosure: The Full Truth about the Assassination of President Kennedy* (1988). A more recent critique of the conspiracy theories is Gerald L. Posner's *Case Closed: Lee Harvey Oswald and the Assassination of John F. Kennedy* (1993).

The most comprehensive biography of LBJ is Robert Dallek's two-volume work, *Lone Star Rising; Lyndon Johnson and His Times, 1908–1960* (1991) and *Flawed Giant: Lyndon B. Johnson, 1960–1973* (1998). An intriguing analysis of the tense relationship between Johnson and Robert Kennedy is Jeff Shesol's *Mutual Contempt: Lyndon Johnson, Robert Kennedy, and the Feud That Defined a Decade* (1997).

Among the works that interpret liberal social policy during the 1960s, John Schwarz's *America's Hidden Success: A Reassessment of Twenty Years of Public Policy* (1983) offers a glowing endorsement of Democratic programs. For a contrasting perspective, see Charles Murray's *Losing Ground: American Social Policy, 1950–1980* (rev. ed., 1995).

On foreign policy, see *Kennedy's Quest for Victory: American Foreign Policy, 1961–1963* (1989), edited by Thomas G. Paterson. To learn more about Kennedy's problems in Cuba, see Mark White's *Missiles in Cuba: Kennedy, Khrushchev, Castro and the 1962 Crisis* (1997). For an understanding of the Alliance for Progress, see Jerome Levinson and Juan de Onis's *The Alliance That Lost Its Way* (1970). On the Peace Corps, see Elizabeth Hoffman's *All You Need Is Love: The Peace Corps and the Spirit of the 1960s* (1998).

American involvement in Vietnam has received voluminous treatment from all political perspectives. For an overview, see Larry Berman's *Planning a Tragedy: The Americanization of the War in Vietnam* (1982) and *Lyndon Johnson's War: The Road to Stalemate in Viet-*

nam (1989), as well as Stanley Karnow's *Vietnam: A History* (rev. ed., 1991). Tensions between the secretary of defense and the military leadership are detailed in H. R. McMaster's *Dereliction of Duty: Johnson, McNamara, the Joint Chiefs of Staff and the Lies That Led to Vietnam* (1997). Works that portray American policy in a favorable light include Norman Podhoretz's *Why We Were in Vietnam* (1982), Guenter Lewy's *America in Vietnam: Illusion, Myth and Reality* (1978), and Leslie Gelb and Richard Bett's *The Irony of Vietnam: The System Worked* (1979). An excellent analysis of policy making concerning the Vietnam War is David M. Barrett's *Uncertain Warriors: Lyndon Johnson and His Vietnam Advisors* (1994). Former secretary of defense Robert McNamara confesses his mistakes in *In Retrospect: The Tragedy and Lessons of Vietnam* (1995).

Many scholars have dealt with various aspects of the civil rights movement and race relations of the 1960s. See especially Carl Brauer's *John F. Kennedy and the Second Reconstruction* (1977), David Garrow's *Bearing the Cross: Martin Luther King, Jr., and the Southern Christian Leadership Conference* (1986), Adam Fairclough's *To Redeem the Soul of America: The Southern Christian Leadership Conference and Martin Luther King, Jr.* (1987), and David Lewis's *King: A Biography* (2nd ed., 1978). For the legal turns the civil rights movement took during the 1960s, see J. Harvey Wilkinson's *From Brown to Bakke: The Supreme Court and School Integration, 1954–1978* (1978). William Chafe's *From Civilities to Civil Rights: Greensboro, North Carolina and the Black Struggle for Freedom* (1980) details the original sit-ins. An award-winning study of racial and economic inequality in a representative American city is Thomas J. Sugrue's *The Origins of the Urban Crisis: Race and Inequality in Postwar Detroit* (1996).

34 ∽ REBELLION AND REACTION IN THE 1960s AND 1970s

CHAPTER ORGANIZER

This chapter focuses on:

- rebellion and struggles for rights in the 1970s.

- ending the war in Vietnam.

- Watergate and Nixon's resignation.

- the Ford and Carter administrations.

s Richard Nixon entered the White House, he faced a nation whose social fabric was in tatters. Everywhere, it seemed, traditional institutions and notions of authority had come under attack. The turbulent events of 1968 revealed how deeply divided American society had become and how difficult a task Nixon faced in carrying out his pledge to restore social harmony. Yet the stability he promised proved to be elusive. His policies and his combative temperament served to heighten rather than reduce the tensions wracking the nation. Those tensions had been long in developing and reflected profound fissures in the postwar consensus promoted by Eisenhower and inherited by Kennedy and Johnson. What had caused such a seismic breakdown in social harmony? Ironically, many of the same forces that had promoted the flush times of the Eisenhower years helped generate the social upheavals of the 1960s and 1970s.

THE ROOTS OF REBELLION

YOUTH REVOLT By the 1960s, the postwar "baby-boomers" were maturing. Now young adults, they differed from their elders in that they had experienced neither economic depression nor a major war. Record numbers of these young people were attending American colleges and universities during the 1960s: college enrollment quadrupled between 1945 and 1970. At the same time, many universities had become sprawling institutions increasingly dependent upon research contracts from giant corporations and the federal government. As these "multiversities" grew more bureaucratic and hierarchical, they unknowingly invited resistance from students wary of involvement in what Eisenhower had called the "military-industrial complex."

The Greensboro student sit-ins in 1960 not only precipitated a decade of civil rights activism; they also signaled an end to the supposed apathy that had enveloped college campuses and social life during the 1950s. Although primarily concerned with the rights and status of black people, the sit-ins, marches, protests, principles, and sacrifices associated with the civil rights movement provided inspiring models and rhetoric for other groups demanding justice, freedom, and equality.

During 1960–1961, a small but significant number of white students joined the sit-in movement. They and many others were also inspired by President Kennedy's direct appeals to their youthful idealism. Thousands enrolled in the Peace Corps and VISTA. But soon it became clear that politics was mixed with principle in the president's position on civil rights. Later, as criticism of escalating American involvement in Vietnam mounted, more and more young people grew disillusioned with the government and other institutional bastions of the status quo. By the mid-1960s, a full-fledged youth revolt erupted on many campuses, and rebellious students began to flow into two distinct, yet frequently overlapping, movements: the New Left and the counterculture.

THE NEW LEFT The explicitly political strain of the youth revolt coalesced when Tom Hayden and Al Haber, two student radicals at the
University of Michigan, formed the Students for a Democratic Society
(SDS) in 1960. An ardent critic of American capitalism, Hayden had
been inspired during his college years by Jack Kerouac's *On the Road*
and Jean-Jacques Rousseau's notion of participatory democracy. Two
years later, Hayden drafted what became known as the Port Huron
Statement: "We are the people of this generation, bred in at least moderate comfort, housed in universities, looking uncomfortably to the
world we inherit."

Hayden's earnest manifesto focused on the absence of individual
freedom in modern American life. The country, he insisted, was dominated by huge organizational structures—governments, corporations,
universities—all of which conspired to oppress and alienate the individual. Inspired by the example of black activism in the South, Hayden declared that students had the power to restore "participatory democracy"
to American life by wresting "control of the educational process from
the administrative bureaucracy" and then forging links with other dissident movements. He and others soon adopted the term "New Left" to
distinguish their efforts at grassroots democracy from the Old Left of
the 1930s, which had espoused an orthodox Marxism.

In the fall of 1964, students at the University of California at Berkeley took Hayden's program to heart. When Clark Kerr, the university
chancellor, announced that sidewalk solicitations for political causes
would no longer be allowed, several hundred students staged a sit-in.
Soon thereafter over 2,000 more joined in, including even the conservative student members of Youth for Goldwater. After a tense standoff the
administration relented. Student groups then formed the Free Speech
Movement (FSM).

Led by Mario Savio, a philosophy major and compelling public
speaker, the FSM initially protested on behalf of student rights. But it
quickly escalated into a more general criticism of the modern university
and what Savio called the "depersonalized, unresponsive bureaucracy"
infecting all of American life. In 1964 Savio led hundreds of students
into the administration building and organized a sit-in. In the early
morning hours, 600 police officers moved in and arrested the protesters.

The program and tactics of the FSM and SDS soon spread to universities throughout the country, but their focus changed as escalating

American involvement in Vietnam brought a dramatic expansion of the military draft, and millions of young men faced the grim prospect of participating in an increasingly unpopular war. In fact, however, Vietnam, like virtually every other American war, was a poor man's fight. In 1965–1966, thanks to deferments and exemptions, college graduates made up only 2 percent of all military inductees. Yet several thousand male collegians would flee to Canada or Sweden to escape the draft, while hundreds of thousands engaged in various protests against a war they considered to be immoral.

In the spring of 1967, 500,000 marchers of all ages converged on New York's Central Park, chanting "Hey, hey, LBJ, how many kids did you kill today?" Dozens of young men ceremoniously burned their draft cards, and the so-called Resistance phase of the antiwar movement was born. Thereafter a coalition of protest groups around the country sponsored draft-card burning rallies and sit-ins that led to numerous arrests.

Meanwhile, some SDS leaders were growing even more militant. Inspired by the rhetoric and revolutionary violence of black power spokesmen such as Stokely Carmichael, Rap Brown, and Huey Newton, Tom Hayden abandoned his earlier commitment to participatory democracy and passive civil disobedience. "If necessary," he now could "shoot to kill." As the SDS embraced violence, it also grew more centralized and authoritarian. Capitalist imperialism replaced university bureaucracy as the primary foe.

During that eventful spring of 1968, spreading campus unrest reached a climax with the disruption of Columbia University. Mark Rudd, leader of the campus SDS chapter, and a small group of radicals protested the university's insensitive decision to disrupt a neighboring black community in order to build a new gymnasium. They occupied some campus buildings, and the protest quickly spread. During the following week, more buildings were occupied, faculty and administrative offices were ransacked, and classes were cancelled. University officials finally called in New York City police. While arresting the protesters, the police injured a number of innocent bystanders. Their excessive force angered many unaligned students, who staged a strike that shut down the university for the remainder of the semester. That same spring, similar clashes between students, administrators, and eventually police occurred at Harvard, Cornell, and San Francisco State.

At the 1968 Democratic convention in Chicago, the polarization of American society reached a tragic and bizarre climax. Inside the tightly guarded convention hall, Democrats were nominating Lyndon Johnson's faithful vice-president, Hubert Humphrey. At the same time, Chicago's streets were filled with the whole spectrum of antiwar dissenters, from the earnest supporters of Eugene McCarthy, through the Resistance and SDS, to the nihilistic Yippies (the Youth International Party). The Yippies were especially determined to provoke anarchy in the streets of Chicago. Abbie Hoffman, one of their leaders, explained that their "conception of revolution is that it's fun."

The outlandish behavior of the Yippies and other anarchic protesters did not justify the unrestrained response of Chicago's arch-conservative Mayor Richard Daley and his army of 12,000 police. As a national television audience watched, many of the police went berserk, clubbing and gassing demonstrators as well as bystanders caught up in the chaotic scene. The spectacle lasted three days and generated a wave of anger among many middle-class Americans, anger that Richard Nixon and the Republicans shrewdly exploited at their convention in Miami. At the same time, the Chicago riots helped to fragment the antiwar movement.

By 1968 the SDS was breaking up into rival factions, the most extreme of which was the Weathermen, a term derived from folksinger

The violence at the 1968 Democratic National Convention in Chicago seared the nation.

Bob Dylan's lyrics: "You don't need a weatherman to know which way the wind blows." These hardened young activists launched a campaign of violence and disruption, firebombing university and government buildings and killing innocent people—as well as several of themselves. Government forces responded in kind, arresting most of the Weathermen and sending the rest underground.

By 1971 the New Left was dead as a political movement. In large measure it had committed suicide by abandoning the democratic and pacifist principles that had originally inspired participants and given the movement its moral legitimacy. The larger antiwar movement also began to fade. There would be a final wave of student protests against the Nixon administration in 1970–1971, but thereafter campus unrest virtually disappeared as American troops returned home from Vietnam and the draft ended.

If the social mood was changing during the Nixon years, a large segment of the public still persisted in the quest for personal fulfillment *and* social justice. The burgeoning environmental and consumer movements attested to the continuity of sixties idealism. A *New York Times* survey of college campuses in 1969 revealed that many students were transferring their attention from the antiwar movement to the environment. This ecological conscience would blossom in the 1970s into one of the most compelling items on the nation's social agenda.

THE COUNTERCULTURE The numbing events of 1968 led other disaffected activists away from radical politics altogether and toward another manifestation of the sixties youth revolt: the "counterculture." Long hair, blue jeans, tie-dyed shirts, sandals, mind-altering drugs, rock music, and group living arrangements were more important than revolutionary ideology or mass protest to the "hippies," the direct descendants of the Beats of the 1950s. These advocates of the counterculture were, like their New Left peers, primarily affluent, well-educated young whites alienated by the Vietnam War, racism, political corruption and parental demands, runaway technology, and a crass corporate mentality that equated the good life with material goods. Disillusioned with organized political action, they eagerly embraced the tantalizing credo announced by the zany Harvard professor Timothy Leary, "Turn on to the scene, tune in to what's happening, and drop out."

For some the counterculture primarily entailed the study and practice of Oriental mysticism. For others it focused on the daily use of hallucinogenic drugs such as LSD. Collective living in urban enclaves such as San Francisco's Haight-Ashbury district or New York's East Village was the rage for a time among the hippies, until conditions grew so crowded and violent that residents migrated elsewhere.

Rural communes also attracted bourgeois rebels. During the 1960s and early 1970s, thousands of young and inexperienced romantics flocked to the countryside, eager to be liberated from parental and institutional restraints, to live in harmony with nature, and to coexist in an atmosphere of love and openness. Only a handful of these utopian homesteads survived more than a few months.

Huge outdoor rock music concerts were also a popular source of community for hippies. The largest of these was the Woodstock Music Festival, held in 1969 on a 600-acre farm near the tiny rural town of Bethel, New York. For three days some 500,000 young people reveled in good music and cheap marijuana. According to one journalist, the country had never "seen a society so free of repression." But the Woodstock karma was short-lived. When promoters tried to repeat the scene four months later, this time at a Rolling Stones concert in Altamont, California, members of the Hell's Angels motorcycle gang beat to death a man wielding a knife in front of the stage.

The Woodstock festival drew nearly half a million people to a New York farm in August 1969. The concert was billed as three days of "peace, music, . . . and love."

Just as the 1968 Democratic convention in Chicago marked the end of the New Left as a vital political force, the violence at Altamont sharply diminished the appeal of the counterculture. Moreover, many of the flower children themselves grew tired of their riches-to-rags existence and returned to school to become lawyers, doctors, politicians, or accountants. The search on the part of alienated youth for a better society and a good life was strewn with both comic and tragic aspects, and it reflected the deep social ills that had been allowed to fester throughout the post–World War II period.

FEMINISM   The logic and lure of liberation that spanned the sixties helped accelerate a powerful women's rights crusade. Like the New Left, the new feminism drew much of its inspiration and initial tactics from the civil rights movement. Its aim was to challenge the cult of domesticity that had been touted as the ideal during the 1950s.

The mainstream of the women's movement was led by Betty Friedan. Her influential book, *The Feminine Mystique* (1963), launched a new phase of female protest on a national level. Friedan, a Smith College graduate, had married in 1947. During the 1950s, she raised three children in a New York suburb. In 1957 she conducted a poll of her fellow Smith alumnae and discovered that, despite the rhetoric about the happy suburban housewife during the fifties, many were in fact miserable. This revelation led to more research, which culminated in the publication of *The Feminine Mystique.*

Women, Friedan wrote, had actually lost ground during the years after World War II, when many left wartime assembly lines and settled down in suburbia to care for the kids. Advertisers and women's magazines promoted the "feminine mystique" of blissful domesticity. In Friedan's view, the American middle-class home had become "a comfortable concentration camp" where women saw their individual potential suffocated in an atmosphere of mindless materialism, daytime TV, and neighborhood gossip.

The Feminine Mystique raised the consciousness of many women who had long suffered from a feeling of being trapped in a rut. In 1966 Friedan and a small group of spirited activists founded the National Organization for Women (NOW), whose membership grew rapidly. NOW spearheaded efforts to end job discrimination on the basis of sex, to legalize abortion, and to obtain federal and state support for child-care centers.

Pressured by NOW, Congress and the Supreme Court in the early 1970s advanced the cause of sexual equality. Under Title IX of the Educational Amendments Act of 1972, colleges were required to institute "affirmative action" programs to ensure equal opportunity for women in such areas as admissions, faculty and staff hiring, and athletics. In the same year, Congress overwhelmingly approved the Equal Rights Amendment (ERA) to the Constitution. In 1973 the Supreme Court, in *Roe* v. *Wade,* struck down state laws forbidding abortions during the first three months of pregnancy on the grounds of a constitutional right of privacy. Meanwhile, many bastions of male education, including Yale and Princeton, led a new movement for coeducation that swept the nation. "If the 1960s belonged to blacks," said one feminist, "the next ten years are ours."

By the end of the 1970s, however, sharp divisions between moderate and radical feminists, as well as the failure of the movement to broaden its appeal much beyond the confines of the white middle class, caused reform efforts to stagnate. In 1982 the Equal Rights Amendment died, several states short of ratification. The very success of NOW's efforts to liberalize state abortion laws helped generate a powerful backlash, especially among Catholics and fundamentalist Protestants, who mounted a potent "right to life" crusade.

In 1967 Syracuse University student Kathy Switzer challenged the Boston Marathon's men-only tradition. Officials tried to pull her from the course but with the aid of fellow runners she completed the race. Women became official entrants in 1971.

Yet the success of the women's movement endured despite setbacks. The growing political power of women and their expanding presence in the workforce combined to become one of the most dramatic developments of the era. By 1976 over half the married women in America and nine of ten women college graduates were employed outside the home, a development that one economist called "the single most outstanding phenomenon of this century." Yet many career women did not regard themselves as "feminists"; some took jobs because they and their families needed the money to survive or to achieve higher levels of material comfort. Whatever their motives, women were changing traditional sex roles and childbearing practices to accommodate the two-career family, which had replaced the established pattern of male breadwinner and female housekeeper as the new American norm.

HISPANIC RIGHTS The activism that animated the student revolt, the civil rights movement, and the crusade for women's rights soon spread to various ethnic minority groups. The labor shortages during World War II had led defense industries to offer Hispanic Americans their first significant access to industrial and skilled-labor jobs in the cities, although at the same time a large number of Hispanics still were farm workers. As was the case with African Americans, service in the military during the war years helped to heighten an American identity among Hispanic Americans and to increase their desire for equal rights and opportunities.

But equality was elusive. After World War II, Hispanic Americans still faced widespread discrimination in hiring, housing, and education. Poverty was widespread. In 1960, for example, the median income of a Mexican-American family was only 62 percent of that of a family in the general population. Hispanic-American activists during the 1950s and 1960s mirrored the efforts of black civil rights leaders such as Martin Luther King, Jr. They too denounced segregation, promoted efforts to improve the quality of public education, and struggled to increase Hispanic-American political influence and economic opportunities. Like their black peers, Hispanic college students during the 1960s seized upon ways to heighten their sense of ethnic pride and distinctiveness and to bolster their solidarity.

One of the most popular initiatives was the use of the term *Chicano* as an inclusive label for all Mexican immigrants, Spanish Americans in

New Mexico, as well as old *Californios* (descendants of the inhabitants of California before it was seized by the United States, most of whom were Indians or of mixed ancestry), and *Tejanos* (descendants of the inhabitants of Texas before it became independent). The word *Chicano* was originally a Mexican slang term for a clumsy person. Over the years, Anglo Americans had fastened upon the term as a pejorative reference. Now *Chicano* took on a positive connotation.

In southern California, students formed Young Chicanos for Community Action, a social service group designed to promote greater self-reliance and local involvement within Chicano neighborhoods. Wearing brown berets, the members protested the disproportionate number of Hispanics being killed in the Vietnam War and demanded improvements in their neighborhood schools. Others promoted Hispanic Studies as a new academic discipline. In 1968 nearly 10,000 Chicano students walked out of five Los Angeles high schools as a protest against inadequate facilities, racist teachers, and a high dropout rate. Their actions prompted students in other states to stage similar demonstrations.

Unlike their black counterparts, however, *Chicano* leaders faced an awkward dilemma: what should they do about the continuing stream of illegal Mexican aliens flowing across the border? Many Mexican Americans argued that their own hopes for economic advancement and social equality were put at risk by the influx of Mexican laborers willing to accept low-paying jobs. Mexican-American leaders thus helped to end the *bracero* program (which trucked in *braceros,* Mexican contract day laborers, at harvest time) in 1964 and to form the United Farm Workers (UFW) in 1962 (originally the National Farm Workers Association) to represent Mexican-American migrant workers.

The founder of the UFW was César Chavez. Born in Yuma, Arizona, in 1927 to Mexican immigrant parents, Chavez moved with his parents and four siblings to California in 1939. There they joined thousands of other migrant farm workers traversing the state, moving from job to job, living in tents, cars, or ramshackle cabins. In 1944, at age seventeen, Chavez joined the navy and served for two years in the Pacific. After the war, he married and found work first as a sharecropper raising strawberries and then as a migrant laborer in apricot orchards. In 1952 Chavez joined the Community Service Organization (CSO), a social service group that sought to educate and organize the migrant poor so that they could become more self-reliant. He founded new CSO chapters and was named general director in 1958.

Chavez left the organization in 1962 when it refused to back his proposal to establish a union for farm workers. Other CSO leaders believed that it was impossible to organize migrant workers into an effective union. They thought the farm workers were too mobile, too poor, too illiterate, too ethnically diverse, and too easily replaced by *braceros.* Moreover, farm workers did not enjoy protected status under the National Labor Relations Act of 1935 (the Wagner Act). Unlike industrial laborers, they were not guaranteed the right to organize or to receive a minimum wage. Nor did federal regulations govern the safety of their workplaces.

Despite such obstacles, Chavez resolved to organize the migrant farm workers. His fledgling Farm Workers Association gained national attention in 1965 when it joined a strike by Filipino farm workers against the corporate grape farmers in California's San Joaquin Valley. Chavez's personal charisma and Catholic piety, his insistence on nonviolent tactics and his reliance upon college student volunteers, his skillful alliance with organized labor and religious groups, all combined to attract media interest and popular support. Soon the UFW began organizing migrant workers in the lettuce fields of the Salinas Valley.

Still, the grape strike itself brought no tangible gains. So Chavez organized a nationwide consumer boycott of grapes. Contrary to Chavez's own principles and orders, some of the striking workers used violence to express their frustration at the recalcitrant growers. In an effort to break the impasse and defuse the tension among his followers, Chavez began a personal fast in 1968. He explained that "the truest act of courage, the strongest act of manliness, is to sacrifice ourselves for others in a totally nonviolent struggle for justice." After fasting for three weeks, he had lost thirty-five pounds, and doctors began to fear for his life. A week later he ended his fast by taking communion and breaking bread with Senator Robert F. Kennedy.

Two years later, in 1970, the grape strike and consumer boycott finally succeeded in bringing twenty-six grape growers to the bargaining table. They signed formal contracts recognizing the UFW, and soon migrant workers throughout the West were benefiting from Chavez's strenuous efforts on their behalf. Wages increased and working conditions improved. In 1975 the California state legislature passed a bill that required growers to bargain collectively with the elected representatives of the farm workers. As Robert Kennedy observed, César Chavez was "one of the heroic figures of our time."

But the chief strength of the Hispanic movement lay less in the duplication of the civil rights strategies than in the sheer growth of the Hispanic population. In 1960 Hispanics had numbered slightly more than 3 million; by 1970 they had increased to 9 million, and by 1990 they numbered over 22 million, making them the largest minority in America after African Americans. The most numerous among the Hispanics were Mexican Americans, or Chicanos, who were concentrated in California and the Southwest. Next came the Puerto Rican population, most of whom lived in New York City and the Connecticut Valley. Third largest were the Cubans, many of them refugees from Fidel Castro's Communist regime, concentrated in southern Florida.

During the 1960s, four Mexican Americans—Senator Joseph Montoya of New Mexico and Representatives Elizio ("Kika") de la Garza and Henry B. Gonzalez of Texas and Edward R. Roybal of California—were elected to Congress. In 1974 two Chicanos were elected governor—Jerry Apodaca in New Mexico and Raul Castro in Arizona. In 1981 Henry Cisneros of San Antonio became the first Mexican-American mayor of a large city. He later served as the Secretary of Housing and Urban Development and then as Secretary of Energy in the Clinton administration.

NATIVE AMERICANS American Indians—many of whom now called themselves Native Americans—also emerged as a new political force in the late 1960s. Two conditions combined to make Indian rights a priority: first, white Americans felt a persistent sense of guilt for the destructive policies of their ancestors toward a people who had, after all, been here first; second, the plight of the Native American minority was more desperate than that of any other group in the country. Indian unemployment was ten times the national rate, their life expectancy was twenty years lower than the national average, and the suicide rate was one hundred times higher than that for whites.

Although President Lyndon Johnson recognized the poverty of the Native Americans and attempted to target federal antipoverty program funds into the reservations, militants within the Indian community became impatient with the slow pace of change and organized protests and demonstrations against local, state, and federal agencies. At first the Indian activists copied the tactics of civil rights and black power activists. In 1968 two Chippewas living in Minneapolis, George Mitchell and Dennis Banks, founded the American Indian Movement (AIM) to promote "red power." The leaders of AIM occupied Alcatraz Island in San Francisco Bay in 1969, claiming the site "by right of discovery." And in 1972, a sit-in at the Department of the Interior's Bureau of Indian Affairs (BIA) in Washington attracted national attention to their cause. The BIA, then and since, has been widely viewed as the worst-managed federal agency. Instead of finding creative ways to promote tribal autonomy and economic self-sufficiency, the BIA was a classic example of government paternalism gone awry.

Indian protesters soon discovered a more effective tactic than direct action and sit-ins, however. They went into federal courts armed with copies of old treaties and demanded that these become the basis for restitution. In Alaska, Maine, and Massachusetts, they won significant settlements that provided legal recognition of their tribal rights and financial compensation at levels that upgraded the standard of living on several reservations.

Foot soldiers of AIM marched on Wounded Knee, South Dakota, to bring attention to dependence on welfare, poor living conditions, and rampant alcoholism that plagued Indians on reservations nationwide.

GAY RIGHTS The liberationist impulses of the 1960s also encouraged homosexuals to organize and assert their own right to equal treatment and basic dignity. On June 17, 1969, New York City police raided the Stonewall Inn, a male gay bar in the heart of Greenwich Village. Efforts to close down homosexual gathering places were then commonplace around the country. This time, however, the patrons fought back and the struggle spilled into the streets. Hundreds of other gays and their supporters joined the fracas against the police. Rioting lasted throughout the weekend. When it ended, gays had forged a new sense of solidarity and a new organization called the Gay Liberation Front. "Gay is good for all of us," proclaimed one member. "The artificial categories 'heterosexual' and 'homosexual' have been laid on us by a sexist society. As gays we demand an end to the gender programming which starts when we are born."

As news of the Stonewall riots spread across the country, the gay rights movement assumed national proportions. One of its main tactics was to encourage people to "come out" and make public their homosexuality. This was by no means an easy decision, for professing gays faced social ostracism, physical assaults, exclusion from the military and civil service, and discrimination in the workplace. Yet despite the risks, thousands of homosexuals did "come out." By 1973 almost 800 gay and lesbian organizations had been formed across the country, and every major city had a visible gay community and cultural life.

Like the civil rights crusade and the women's movement, however, the campaign for gay rights soon suffered from internal divisions and aroused a conservative backlash. Gay activists engaged in fractious disputes over tactics and objectives, and conservative moralists and Christian fundamentalists launched a nationwide counterattack against the "gay agenda." They successfully repealed new local laws banning discrimination against homosexuals. By the end of the 1970s, the gay movement had lost its initial momentum and was struggling to salvage many of its hard-won gains.

NIXON AND VIETNAM

The numerous liberation movements of the 1960s fundamentally changed the tone and texture of American social life. By the early

1970s, however, there were signs that the pendulum of national mood was swinging back toward conservatism. The election of Richard Nixon and Spiro Agnew in 1968 and the rise of George Wallace as a serious political force on the radical right reflected the emergence of the "silent majority"—those white working-class and middle-class citizens who were determined to regain control of a society they felt had run amok in permissiveness. Large as the gap was between the "silent majority" and the varied forces of dissent, they agreed on one thing: that the Vietnam War remained the dominant event of the time. Until the war was ended and all American troops were returned home, the nation would find it difficult to achieve the equilibrium that the new president had promised.

GRADUAL WITHDRAWAL The Nixon administration promised a new course in Vietnam. Nixon and his special assistant for national security affairs, Henry Kissinger, claimed to have a secret plan to achieve "peace with honor." But peace was long in coming and not very honorable when it came. The Nixon administration, even while withdrawing American forces, held to a policy that refused to let the North Vietnamese dominate Indochina. By the time a settlement was finally reached in 1973, another 20,000 Americans had died, the morale of the American army had been shattered, millions of Asians were killed or wounded, and fighting in fact continued in Southeast Asia. In the end, Nixon's policy gained little that he could not have accomplished in 1969.

The administration's new strategy in Vietnam moved along three separate fronts. The first front was at the deadlocked Paris peace talks, where American negotiators demanded the withdrawal of North Vietnamese forces from South Vietnam and the preservation of the American-supported regime of President Nguyen Van Thieu. The North Vietnamese and Viet Cong negotiators, however, insisted on retaining a military presence in the South and reunifying the Vietnamese people under a government dominated by the Communists. There was no common ground on which to come together.

Second, Nixon tried to defuse domestic unrest generated by the war. To this end, he sought to "Vietnamize" the conflict by turning over most of the combat missions to Vietnamese units and sharply reducing the number of American ground forces. To assuage the South Vietnamese, he provided more equipment and training for their troops. From a peak of 540,000 in 1969, American combat units were withdrawn at a gradual and steady pace. By 1973 only 50,000 American troops remained in Vietnam. In late 1969 Nixon had also established a lottery system that clarified the likelihood of being drafted—only those with low lottery numbers would have to go. Nixon was more successful in achieving the goal of reducing antiwar activity than at forcing concessions from the North Vietnamese in Paris.

Third, while reducing the number of American combat troops in Vietnam, Nixon and Kissinger secretly expanded the air war in an effort to persuade the enemy to come to terms. On March 18, 1969, American planes began "Operation Menu," a fourteen-month-long bombing of Communist sanctuaries in Cambodia. Over 100,000 tons of bombs were dropped, four times the tonnage dropped on Japan during World War II. Congress did not learn of these raids until 1970, when Nixon announced what he called an "incursion" by United States troops into supposedly "neutral" Cambodia to "clean out" North Vietnamese staging areas.

DIVISIONS AT HOME   News of the Cambodia "incursion" came on the heels of another incident that rekindled public indignation against the war. Late in 1969 the story of the My Lai massacre broke. During the next two years, the public learned the gruesome tale of Army Lieutenant William Calley, who ordered the murder of over 200 Vietnamese civilians in My Lai village in 1968. Twenty-five officers were charged with complicity in the massacre and subsequent cover-up, but only Calley was convicted of murder. Nixon shortly thereafter granted him parole.

The loudest public outcry against Nixon's Indochina policy occurred in the wake of the Cambodian "incursion." Campuses across the country witnessed a new wave of protests in 1970. These student protests against the war led to the closing of hundreds of colleges and universities in May of that year. At Kent State University, the Ohio National Guard was called in to quell rioting, during which the campus Reserve Officer Training Corps (ROTC) building was burned down by antiwar protesters. Pelted by rocks and verbal taunts, the poorly trained guardsmen panicked and opened fire on the demonstrators, killing four bystanders. Eleven days later, on May 15, Mississippi highway patrolmen riddled a dormitory at Jackson State College with bullets, killing two

National Guardsmen shot and killed four student bystanders during antiwar demonstrations on the campus of Kent State University.

black students. Although an official investigation of the Kent State episode condemned the "casual and indiscriminate shooting," polls indicated that the American public supported the National Guard; students had "got what they were asking for."

The following year, in 1971, the *New York Times* began publishing excerpts from a secret Defense Department study on the Vietnam War. The so-called Pentagon Papers, leaked to the press by a former Pentagon official, Daniel Ellsberg, confirmed what many critics of the war had long suspected: Congress and the public had not received the full story on the Gulf of Tonkin incident of 1964. Contingency plans for American entry into the war were being drawn up even while Johnson was promising the American people that combat troops would never be sent to Vietnam. The Nixon administration attempted to block publication of the Pentagon Papers, arguing that publication would endanger national security and prolong the war. By a vote of six to three, the Supreme Court ruled against the government. Newspapers throughout the country began publication the next day.

WAR WITHOUT END Although Nixon's decision in the spring of 1970 to use American forces to root out Communist bases in Cambodia did bring a tactical victory, it also served to widen a war he had promised to end. Moreover, his hopes that the South Vietnamese units replacing American forces could hold their own against the North Vietnamese were dashed when they suffered repeated defeats in 1971 and 1972. Disorganized, poorly led, and lacking tenacity, the South Vietnamese soldiers had to call upon American air power to fend off North Vietnamese offensives.

The deteriorating ground war along with mounting social divisions at home and the approach of the 1972 presidential elections combined to produce a shift in the American negotiating position in Paris. In the summer of 1972 Henry Kissinger dropped his insistence on the removal of all North Vietnamese troops from the South before the withdrawal of American troops. On October 26, only a week before the American presidential election, he announced: "Peace is at hand." But the Thieu regime in South Vietnam objected to the plan for a cease-fire, understandably fearful that the continued presence of North Vietnamese troops in the South virtually guaranteed an eventual Communist victory. Hanoi then stiffened its position by demanding that Thieu resign.

The talks broke off on December 16, and Nixon told his military advisers that only a massive show of American air power would make the North Vietnamese more cooperative at the negotiating table. Two days later, the United States unleashed furious B-52 raids on Hanoi and Haiphong. The so-called "Christmas bombings" aroused worldwide protest, but Henry Kissinger claimed Nixon's "jugular diplomacy" worked, for the talks in Paris soon resumed.

On January 27, 1973, the United States, North and South Vietnam, and the Viet Cong signed an "agreement on ending the war and restoring peace in Vietnam." The agreement showed that despite the Christmas bombings, the North Vietnamese never altered their basic stance: they kept troops in the South and remained committed to the reunification of Vietnam under one government. What had changed since the previous fall was the willingness of the South Vietnamese to accept these terms, albeit reluctantly, on the basis of Nixon's promise that the United States would respond "with full force" to any violation of the agreement.

On March 29, 1973, the last American combat troops left Vietnam, leaving behind several thousand who were declared "missing in action."

On that same day, the last of several hundred American prisoners of war, most of them downed pilots, were released from Hanoi. Within a period of months, however, the war between North and South resumed, and the military superiority and greater political unity of the Communist forces soon became evident. In Cambodia and Laos, where fighting had been more sporadic, Communist victory also seemed inevitable.

In 1975 the North Vietnamese launched a full-scale armored invasion against the South. President Thieu appealed to Washington for assistance, but the Democratic majority in Congress refused, and on April 30, 1975, Americans watched on television as North Vietnamese tanks rolled into Saigon, soon to be renamed Ho Chi Minh City. The scene at the American Embassy in Saigon, where thousands of terrified Vietnamese fought to board the last departing helicopters, provided a poignant and tragic ending to America's greatest foreign policy disaster.

The longest war in American history was finally over, leaving in its wake a bitter legacy. The war described as a noble crusade on behalf of democratic ideals instead suggested that democracy was not easily transferable to Third World regions, which lacked any historical experience with liberal values and representative government. The war eroded respect for the military so thoroughly that many young Americans came to regard military service as inherently corrupting and ignoble. The war, fought to show the world that the United States was united in its convictions, instead divided Americans more drastically than any event since the Civil War. The Vietnam War cost the nation some 58,000 deaths and $150 billion. Little wonder that the dominant public reaction to the war's end was the urge to "put Vietnam behind us" and revert to a noninterventionist foreign policy.

NIXON AND MIDDLE AMERICA

Richard Nixon had been elected in 1968 as the representative of "Middle America," those citizens fed up with the liberal politics and social radicalism of the 1960s. The Nixon cabinet and White House staff reflected the values of this "silent majority." The chief figures were John Mitchell, the gruff attorney-general who had made his fortune as a lawyer in Nixon's old firm, and H. R. Haldeman and John Ehrlichman, advisers on domestic policy whose major experience before their association with the Nixon campaign had been in advertising. The cabinet was all white, all male, all Republican.

DOMESTIC AFFAIRS Confronting a Congress controlled by Democrats, Richard Nixon focused his energies on foreign policy, where presidential initiatives were less restricted and where he, in tandem with Kissinger, achieved several stunning breakthroughs. He also continued to support the American space program and the efforts to beat the Soviets to the moon. In July 1969 American astronaut Neil Armstrong became the first man to walk on the moon. Back on earth, however, Nixon sought to stop social-welfare programs in their tracks. Yet, like Eisenhower before him, he found it difficult to dismantle liberal programs.

Despite the efforts of the Nixon administration, the civil rights legislation enacted during the Johnson years continued to take effect. Administration officials launched a concerted effort in 1970 to block congressional renewal of the Voting Rights Act of 1965 and to delay implementation of court orders requiring the desegregation of school dis-

In July 1969, a program begun by President Kennedy reached its goal: putting a man on the moon.

tricts in Mississippi. Congress then extended the Voting Rights Act over Nixon's veto. The Supreme Court, in the first decision made under the new Chief Justice Warren Burger—a Nixon appointee—ordered the integration of the Mississippi public schools. During Nixon's first term, and despite his wishes, affirmative action made major inroads and more schools were desegregated than in all the Kennedy-Johnson years combined.

Nixon's attempts to block desegregation efforts in urban areas also failed. The Burger Court ruled unanimously in *Swann v. Charlotte-Mecklenburg Board of Education* (1971) that school systems must bus students out of their neighborhoods if necessary to achieve racial integration. Yet protest over desegregation now began to manifest itself more in the North than in the South, as white families in Boston, Denver, and other cities denounced the destruction of "the neighborhood school." Busing opponents won a limited victory when the Supreme Court ruled in 1974 that requiring the transfer of students from the inner city to the suburbs was unconstitutional. This ruling, along with the *Bakke v. Board of Regents of California* (1978) decision, which restricted the use of quotas to achieve racial balance in university classrooms, marked the transition of desegregation from an issue of simple justice to a more tangled thicket of conflicting group and individual rights.

It also reflected the growing conservatism of the Supreme Court, a trend encouraged by Nixon. The litany of liberal decisions during the 1960s had made the Warren Court a prime target for mostly middle-class Americans who resented what they regarded as the federal government's excessive protection of the "undeserving." Fate and the aging of the justices on the Warren Court gave Nixon the chance to make four new appointments. Only one, William Rehnquist, would consistently support Nixon's conservative interpretation of the Constitution, but overall the tenor of the Court did shift toward a more moderate stance.

Nixon also fervently desired to reverse the welfare state policies of his Democratic predecessors. But the administration never succeeded in developing a comprehensive domestic agenda acceptable to Congress. Frustrated by the Democratic majority on Capitol Hill, Nixon sent Vice-President Spiro Agnew on a national speaking tour in the fall of 1969 to assault the opposition. Agnew described war protesters as "anarchists and ideological eunuchs," the liberal news media as "an effete corps of impudent snobs" and "nattering nabobs of negativism."

Meanwhile, the Democratic Congress moved forward with new legislation: the right of eighteen-year-olds to vote in national elections (1970) and, under the Twenty-sixth Amendment (1971), in state and local elections as well; increases in Social Security benefits tied to the inflation rate; a rise in food-stamp funding; the Occupational Safety and Health Act (1970), and the Federal Election Campaign Act (1972). Moreover, in response to Nixon's proposal to decentralize responsibility for various programs, Congress passed in 1972 a five-year revenue-sharing plan that would distribute $30 billion of federal revenues to the states for use as they saw fit.

During Nixon's first term, Americans in large numbers began to lobby for government action to improve and protect the natural environment. In 1970 hundreds of thousands of activists rallied across the country in support of the first "Earth Day." In response, Congress established new programs to control water pollution and passed the Clean Air Act (1970) over Nixon's veto. Congress also created the Environmental Protection Agency (EPA) to oversee federal guidelines for air pollution, toxic wastes, and water quality. The EPA began requiring developers to perform environmental impact studies before new construction could begin. The agency also set fuel efficiency standards for automobiles and required manufacturers to reduce the level of carbon monoxide emissions from car engines.

ECONOMIC MALAISE The major domestic development during the Nixon years was a floundering economy. Exacerbated by the expense of the Vietnam War, the annual inflation rate began to rise in 1967, when it was at 3 percent. By 1973, it reached 9 percent; a year later, it was at 12 percent, and it remained in double digits for most of the 1970s. Unemployment, at a low of 3.3 percent when Nixon took office, climbed to 6 percent by the end of 1970 and threatened to keep rising. Somehow the American economy was undergoing a recession and inflation at the same time. Economists coined the term "stagflation" to describe the syndrome that defied the orthodox laws of economics.

The economic malaise had at least three deep-rooted causes. First, the Johnson administration had attempted to pay for both the Great Society's social-welfare programs and the war in Vietnam without a major tax increase, thus generating larger federal deficits, a major expansion of the money supply, and rapid price inflation. Second, and more important, by the late 1960s, American goods faced stiff competition in international markets from West Germany, Japan, and other emerging industrial powers. This sharply reduced the export of American goods and generated a growing trade deficit. Third, the American economy had grown heavily dependent on cheap sources of energy.

Just as domestic petroleum reserves began to dwindle and dependence on foreign sources increased, the nations in the Organization of Petroleum Exporting Countries (OPEC), centered in the Middle East, combined to use their oil as a political and economic weapon. In 1973, when the United States sent massive aid to Israel during the Yom Kippur War, OPEC announced that it would not sell oil to nations supporting Israel and that it was raising its prices by 400 percent. American motorists thereafter faced long lines at gas stations, schools and offices closed down, factories cut production, and the inflation rate soared.

Another condition leading to stagflation was the flood of new workers—mainly baby-boomers and women—entering the labor market. From 1965 to 1980, the workforce grew by 40 percent, or almost 30 million workers, a figure greater than the total labor force of France or West Germany. The number of new jobs created could not keep up, leaving many unemployed. At the same time, worker productivity declined, pushing up prices in the face of rising demand.

Stagflation posed a new set of economic problems, but the Nixon administration responded erratically and ineffectively with old remedies. First, it tried to reduce the federal deficit by raising taxes and cutting the budget. When the Democratic Congress refused to cooperate with this approach, the White House encouraged the Federal Reserve Board to reduce the money supply by raising interest rates. But the move backfired as the stock market immediately collapsed, plunging the economy into the "Nixon recession."

A sense of desperation then seized the White House. In 1969, when asked about government restrictions on wages and prices, Nixon had been adamant: "Controls. Oh, my God, no! . . . We'll never go to controls." On August 15, 1971, however, he reversed himself. He froze all wages and prices for ninety days, yet the economy still floundered. By 1973 the wage and price guidelines were made voluntary, and therefore almost entirely ineffective. Stagflation continued, and it would plague the economy for the rest of the decade.

NIXON TRIUMPHANT

CHINA If the economy's ailments proved more than Nixon could remedy, in foreign policy his administration managed to improve American relations with the major powers of the Communist world—China and the Soviet Union—and to shift fundamentally the pattern of the cold war. In 1971 Henry Kissinger, Nixon's national security adviser, secretly visited Beijing (Peking) to explore the possibility of American recognition of China. In 1972, Nixon himself arrived in Beijing and made recognition an official and public fact. The irony of the event was overwhelming. Richard Nixon, the former anti-Communist crusader who had condemned the State Department for "losing" China in 1949, had accomplished a diplomatic feat that his Democratic predecessors could not.

DÉTENTE China sought the breakthrough in relations with the United States because its rivalry with the Soviet Union, with which it shares a long border, had become increasingly bitter. Soviet leaders, troubled by the Sino-American agreements, were also anxious for an easing of tensions with the United States now that they had, as the re-

With President Richard Nixon's visit to China in 1972, the United States formally recognized China's Communist government. In this photo, Nixon and Chinese premier Chou-En-lai drink a toast.

sult of a huge arms buildup following the Cuban missile crisis, achieved virtual parity with the United States in nuclear weapons. Once again the president surprised the world, by announcing that he would visit Moscow in 1972 for discussions with Leonid Brezhnev, the Soviet premier.

What became known as "détente" with the Soviets offered the promise of a more orderly and restrained competition between the two superpowers. Nixon and Brezhnev signed the Strategic Arms Limitation Talks (SALT) agreement, which set ceilings for each nation on the number of intercontinental ballistic missiles (ICBMs) and sharp limits on the construction of antiballistic missile systems (ABMs). In effect, the Soviets were allowed to retain a greater number of missiles with greater destructive power while the United States retained a lead in the total number of warheads. No limitations were placed on new weapons systems, though each side agreed to work toward a permanent freeze on all nuclear weapons.

SHUTTLE DIPLOMACY The Nixon-Kissinger initiatives in the Middle East were less dramatic and less conclusive than the agreements with China and the Soviet Union, but they did show that America recognized Arab power in the region and its own dependence on the oil from Islamic states fundamentally opposed to Israel. After Israel recovered from the initial shock of the Arab attacks that triggered the Yom Kippur War of 1973, it recaptured the Golan Heights and seized additional Syrian territory. Kissinger initiated the negotiations leading to a cease-fire and exerted pressure to prevent Israel from taking more Arab territory. American reliance on Arab oil led to closer ties with Egypt and its president, Anwar el-Sadat, and more restrained support for Israel. Kissinger, whose "shuttle diplomacy" among the capitals of the Middle East won acclaim from all sides, failed to find a comprehensive peace formula for the troubled region, however, and ignored altogether the problem of establishing a homeland for Palestinian refugees. But his efforts did lay groundwork for the subsequent accord between Israel and Egypt in 1977.

THE 1972 ELECTION Nixon's foreign policy achievements allowed him to stage the campaign of 1972 as a triumphal procession. The first threat to his reelection came from Democratic Alabama governor

George Wallace, who had the potential to deprive the Republicans of conservative votes. But on May 15, 1972, Wallace was shot and paralyzed below the waist by a deranged man, and he was forced to withdraw from the campaign.

Meanwhile, the Democrats were further ensuring Nixon's victory by nominating Senator George S. McGovern of South Dakota, a former college history professor and crusading liberal whose antiwar and social-welfare positions were associated with the turbulence of the 1960s. At the Democratic convention, party reforms helped McGovern's nomination by increasing the representation of women, blacks, and minorities, but these reforms alienated the party regulars. Chicago's Mayor Richard Daley was actually ousted from the convention, and the AFL-CIO refused to endorse the liberal Democratic candidate.

Nixon won the greatest victory of any Republican presidential candidate in history, capturing 520 electoral votes to only 17 for McGovern. During the course of the campaign, McGovern complained about the "dirty tricks" of the Nixon administration, most especially the curious incident during the summer of 1972 in which burglars were caught breaking into the Democratic National Committee headquarters in the Watergate apartment complex in Washington, D.C. McGovern's accusations seemed shrill and biased at the time. Nixon and his staff made plans for "four more years" as the investigation of the fateful Watergate break-in unfolded.

WATERGATE

During the trial of the accused Watergate burglars, the relentless prodding of Judge John J. Sirica led one of the accused to tell the full story of the Nixon administration's complicity in the episode. James W. McCord, a former CIA agent and security chief for the Committee to Re-elect the President (CREEP), was the first of many informers and penitents in a melodrama that unfolded over the next two years. It ended in the first resignation of a president in American history, the conviction and imprisonment of twenty-five officials of the Nixon administration, including four cabinet members, and the most serious constitutional crisis since the impeachment trial of President Andrew Johnson.

UNCOVERING THE COVER-UP The trail of evidence pursued by Judge Sirica, a grand jury and several special prosecutors, and a televised Senate investigation headed by Samuel J. Ervin, Jr., of North Carolina, led directly to the White House. No evidence surfaced that Nixon had ordered the break-in or that he had been aware of plans to burglarize the Democratic National Committee. From the start, however, Nixon participated in the cover-up, using his presidential powers to discredit and block the investigation. Perhaps most alarming was that the Watergate burglary proved to be one small part of a larger pattern of corruption and criminality sanctioned by the Nixon White House. Since 1970, Nixon had ordered intelligence agencies to spy on his most outspoken opponents, open their mail, and even burglarize their homes in an effort to uncover compromising information.

The cover-up began to unravel as various people, including John Dean, legal counsel to the president, began to believe that they were being set up as fall guys, and began to cooperate with prosecuters. It unraveled further in 1973 when L. Patrick Gray, acting director of the FBI, resigned after confessing that he had destroyed several incriminating documents. On April 30 Ehrlichman and Haldeman resigned, together with Attorney-General Richard Kleindienst. A few days later Nixon nervously assured the public in a television address, "I'm not a crook." New evidence suggested otherwise. John Dean, whom Nixon had dismissed, testified before the Ervin Committee and a rapt television audience that Nixon had approved the cover-up. In another "bombshell" disclosure, a White House aide told the committee that Nixon had installed a taping system in the White House and that many of the conversations about Watergate had been recorded.

A year-long battle for the "Nixon tapes" then began. Harvard law professor Archibald Cox, whom Nixon had appointed as a special prosecutor to handle the Watergate case, took the president to court in 1973 to obtain the tapes. Nixon, pleading "executive privilege," refused to release them and ordered Cox fired. In what became known as the "Saturday Night Massacre," the new attorney-general, Elliot Richardson, and his deputy resigned rather than execute the order. Cox's replacement as special prosecutor, Leon Jaworski, proved no more pliable than Cox, and he also took the president to court. In March 1974 the

Having resigned his office, Richard Nixon waves farewell outside the White House, August 9, 1974.

Watergate grand jury indicted Ehrlichman, Haldeman, and Mitchell for obstruction of justice, and it named Nixon as an "unindicted co-conspirator."

On July 24, 1974, the Supreme Court ruled unanimously that the president must surrender the tapes. A few days later the House Judiciary Committee dramatically voted to recommend three articles of impeachment: obstruction of justice through the payment of "hush money" to witnesses and the withholding of evidence; abuse of power through using federal agencies to deprive citizens of their constitutional rights; and defiance of Congress by withholding the tapes. Before the House of Representatives could meet to vote on impeachment, however, Nixon handed over the complete set of White House tapes. On August 9, 1974, fully aware that the evidence on the tapes implicated him in the cover-up, Richard Nixon resigned from office.

EFFECTS OF WATERGATE Vice-President Spiro Agnew did not succeed Nixon, because Agnew himself had been forced to resign in 1973 when it became known that he had accepted bribes from contractors before and during his term as vice-president. The vice-president at the time of Nixon's resignation was Gerald Ford, the former minority leader in the House from Michigan, whom Nixon had appointed with congressional approval, under the provisions of the Twenty-fifth Amendment (1967). Ford insisted that he had no intention of pardoning Nixon, who was still liable for criminal prosecution. But a month after Nixon's resignation, the new president issued the pardon, explaining that it was necessary to end the national obsession with the Watergate scandals. Many suspected that Nixon and Ford had made a deal, though there was no evidence to confirm the speculation.

If there was a silver lining in Watergate's dark cloud, it was the vigor and resiliency of the institutions that had brought a president down—the press, Congress, the courts, and an aroused public opinion. The Watergate revelations provoked Congress to pass several pieces of legislation designed to curb executive power in the future. The War Powers Act (1973) required presidents to inform Congress within forty-eight hours if U.S. troops were being deployed in combat abroad and to withdraw troops after sixty days unless Congress specifically approved their stay. In an effort to correct abuses of campaign funds, Congress enacted legislation in 1974 that set new ceilings on political contributions and expenditures. In reaction to the Nixon claim of "executive privilege" as a means of withholding evidence, Congress strengthened the 1966 Freedom of Information Act to require prompt responses to requests for information from government files and to place on government agencies the burden of proof for classifying information as secret.

With Nixon's resignation, the nation had weathered a profound constitutional crisis, but the aftershock of the Watergate episode produced a deep sense of disillusionment with the "imperial presidency." Coming on the heels of the erosion of public confidence generated by the Vietnam War, the Watergate affair renewed public cynicism toward a government that had systematically lied to the people and violated their civil liberties. Said one bumper sticker of the day: "Don't vote. It only encourages them." Restoring credibility and respect became the primary challenge facing Nixon's successors. Unfortunately, an array of new economic and foreign crises would make that task doubly difficult.

AN UNELECTED PRESIDENT

While the Watergate crisis dominated the Washington scene, major domestic and foreign problems received little executive attention. The perplexing combination of inflation and recession worsened, as did the oil crisis. At the same time, Henry Kissinger, who assumed control over the management of foreign policy, watched helplessly as the South Vietnamese forces began to crumble before North Vietnamese attacks, attempted with limited success to establish a framework for peace in the Middle East, and supported a CIA role in overthrowing the popularly elected Marxist president of Chile.

THE FORD YEARS Gerald Ford inherited these simmering problems, as well as the burden of being an unelected president. An amiable, honest man, Ford enjoyed widespread popular support for only a short time. "I am a Ford, not a Lincoln," he candidly recognized upon becoming vice-president. His pardon of Nixon on September 8, 1974, generated a storm of criticism. The *New York Times* called it "an unconscionable act."

As president, Ford adopted the posture he had developed as a conservative minority leader in the House: a nay-saying leader of the opposition who believed that the federal government exercised too much power over domestic affairs. In his fifteen months as president, Ford vetoed thirty-nine bills, thereby outstripping Herbert Hoover's veto record in less than half the time. By resisting congressional pressure to reduce taxes and increase federal spending, he succeeded in plummeting the economy into the deepest recession since the Great Depression. Unemployment jumped to 9 percent in 1975, and the federal deficit hit a record the next year. Ford rejected wage and price controls to curb inflation, preferring voluntary restraints.

In foreign policy, Ford retained Henry Kissinger as secretary of state and attempted to pursue Nixon's goals of stability in the Middle East, rapprochement with China, and détente with the Soviet Union. Late in 1974, Ford met with Soviet leader Leonid Brezhnev and accepted the framework for another arms-control agreement that was to serve as the basis for SALT II. Meanwhile Kissinger's tireless shuttling between Cairo and Tel Aviv produced an agreement: Israel promised to return to Egypt most of the Sinai territory captured in the 1967 war, and the two nations agreed to rely on negotiations rather than force to settle future disagreements.

These limited but significant achievements should have enhanced Ford's image, but they were drowned in the sea of criticism and carping that followed the loss of South Vietnam to North Vietnam in 1975. Not only had a decade of American effort in Vietnam proven futile, but the Khmer Rouge, the Cambodian Communist movement, had also won a resounding victory, plunging that country into a fanatical bloodbath. And the OPEC oil cartel was threatening another worldwide boycott, while other Third World nations denounced the United States as a depraved imperialistic power.

THE 1976 ELECTION In the midst of such turmoil, the Democrats could hardly wait for the 1976 election. At the Republican convention, Ford managed to thwart a powerful challenge for the nomination from the former California governor and Hollywood actor, Ronald Reagan. The Democrats chose an obscure former naval officer and engineer turned peanut farmer who had served one term as governor of Georgia. Jimmy Carter capitalized on the post-Watergate cynicism by promising never to "tell a lie to the American people" and by citing his independence from traditional Washington power politics.

To the surprise of many pundits, the little known Carter revived the New Deal coalition of southern whites, blacks, urban labor, and ethnic groups to win the election, 41 million votes to Ford's 39 million. Polls showed that the Carter victory benefited from a heavy turnout of blacks in the South, where he swept every state but Virginia. Minnesota senator Walter F. Mondale, Carter's liberal running mate and a favorite among blue-collar workers and the urban poor, also gave the ticket a big boost. The real story of the election, however, was the low voter turnout. Almost half of America's eligible voters, apparently alienated by Watergate and the lackluster candidates, chose to sit out the election.

THE CARTER INTERREGNUM

EARLY SUCCESSES During the first two years of his term, Carter enjoyed several successes. His administration appointed more blacks, Hispanics, and women than any before. He also offered amnesty to the thousands of young men who had fled the country rather than serve in

Vietnam, closing one of the remaining open wounds of that traumatic event. He reformed the civil service to provide rewards for meritorious performance, and he created new cabinet-level Departments of Energy and Education. Carter also pushed significant environmental legislation through Congress, including a bill to regulate strip mining, and a "superfund" to clean up chemical waste sites.

His success was short-lived, however. Carter's political predicament emerged during the debate over energy policy. His proposed energy bill called for the creation of a cabinet-level Department of Energy, tax incentives and penalties to encourage conservation and new oil and gas production as well as solar power and synthetic fuels, and the increased development of nuclear power as a "last resort." Yet the energy bill passed in 1978 was a gutted version of Carter's original proposal. It focused primarily on new oil and gas production rather than conservation. Carter and his aides lacked the experience and the flexibility to maneuver his proposals around congressional obstacles.

In the summer of 1979, when renewed violence in the Middle East produced a second fuel shortage, motorists were forced to wait in long lines again for limited supplies of gasoline that they regarded as excessively expensive. Soon they directed their frustration at the White House. Opinion polls showed Carter with an approval rating of only 26 percent, lower than Nixon during the worst moments of the Watergate crisis. Faced with such vanishing support, Carter solicited advice from an array of national leaders during an extraordinary retreat at Camp David, Maryland. He emerged ten days later and proclaimed that the nation required "a rebirth of the American spirit." He also announced a "new and positive energy program." It fell on skeptical ears. A Phoenix newspaper editorialized: "The nation did not tune in Carter to hear a sermon. It wanted answers. It did not get them." Congress only partially funded the major feature of his new program—synthetic energy research.

Several of Carter's early foreign policy initiatives also got caught in political crossfires. Soon after his inauguration, Carter vowed that "the soul of our foreign policy" should be the defense of human rights abroad. But the human rights campaign provoked attack from two sides: those who feared that it sacrificed a detached appraisal of national interest for high-level moralizing, and those who believed that human rights were important but that the administration was applying the standard inconsistently.

Carter's successful negotiation of treaties to turn over control of the Panama Canal to the Panamanian government in twenty years also generated intense criticism. Even though the administration reminded Americans that Theodore Roosevelt himself had admitted "stealing" the Canal Zone for American use, many political conservatives flayed Carter's judicious decision all the same. Republican Ronald Reagan manipulated historical fact by claiming that the Canal Zone was sovereign American soil purchased "fair and square." Carter argued that the limitations on American influence in Latin America and the deep resentment toward American colonialism in Panama left the United States with no choice. The Senate ratified the treaties by a paper-thin margin (68 to 32, one vote more than the required two-thirds). The Canal Zone would revert in stages to Panama by 1999.

THE CAMP DAVID ACCORDS Carter's crowning diplomatic achievement was the arrangement of a peace agreement between Israel and Egypt. In 1978 Carter invited Egypt's President Anwar el-Sadat and Israel's Prime Minister Menachem Begin to Camp David for two weeks of difficult negotiations. The first part of the eventual agreement re-

Egyptian president Anwar el-Sadat (left), Jimmy Carter (center) and Israeli prime minister Menachem Begin (right) at the announcement of the Camp David accords, September 1978.

quired Israel to return all land in the Sinai in exchange for Egyptian recognition of Israel's sovereignty. This agreement was successfully implemented in 1982 when the last Israeli settler vacated the Sinai. But the second part of the agreement, calling for Israel to negotiate with Sadat a resolution to the Palestinian refugee dilemma, began to unravel soon after the Camp David summit. Still, Carter and Secretary of State Cyrus Vance had orchestrated a dramatic display of high-level diplomacy that, whatever its limitations, made an all-out war between Israel and the Arab world less likely. It also represented a significant first step toward a comprehensive settlement of the region's volatile tensions.

MOUNTING TROUBLES Carter's crowning failure was his management of the economy. In effect he inherited a bad situation and left it worse. Carter employed the same economic policies as Nixon and Ford to fight stagflation, but he reversed the order of the federal "cure," preferring to fight unemployment first with a tax cut and increased public spending. Unemployment declined slightly, from 8 to 7 percent in 1977, but inflation soared; at 5 percent when he took office, it reached 10 percent in 1978 and kept rising. During one month in 1980, it measured an annual rate of 18 percent. Like previous presidents, Carter then reversed himself to fight the other side of the economic malaise. By midterm he was delaying tax reductions and vetoing government spending programs that he had proposed in his first year. The result, however, was the worst of all possible worlds—a deepened recession with unemployment at 7.5 percent in 1980, mortgage rates at 15 percent, interest rates at an all-time high of 20 percent, and a runaway inflation averaging between 12 and 13 percent.

The signing of a controversial SALT II treaty with the Soviets in 1979 put Carter's leadership to the test just as the mounting economic problems made him the subject of biting editorial cartoons. To pacify his conservative critics, who charged that SALT II would give the Soviets a decided advantage in the number and destructive power of land-based missiles, Carter announced that the United States would build the new MX missile system.

But the SALT II treaty became moot in 1979 when the Soviet army invaded Afghanistan in order to extend "fraternal assistance" to the faltering Communist government there, which was being challenged by Muslim rebels. While continuing the MX missile program, Carter immediately shelved SALT II, suspended grain shipments to the Soviet

Union, and began a campaign for an international boycott of the 1980 Olympics, which were to be held that summer in Moscow.

IRAN Then the Iranian crisis exploded in a year-long barrage of unwelcome events that epitomized the inability of the United States to control world affairs. The crisis began in 1979 with the overthrow of the shah of Iran, long a staunch American ally and right-wing dictator. The revolutionaries who toppled the shah rallied around Ayatollah Ruhollah Khomeini, a fundamentalist Muslim leader who symbolized the Islamic values the shah had tried to replace with Western ways. Khomeini's hatred of the United States dated back to 1953, when the CIA had sponsored the overthrow of Iran's Prime Minister Mohammed Mossadegh, an ardent nationalist who sought to rid his country of Western influence and interests. The 1953 coup had restored the shah's regime to power.

Late in 1979, Carter allowed the exiled shah to enter the United States in order to undergo treatment for cancer. A few days later, on November 4, a frenzied mob stormed the American Embassy in Teheran and seized the staff. Khomeini applauded the mob action and demanded the shah's return along with all his wealth in exchange for the release of the fifty-three American hostages. In the meantime, the Iranian militants staged daily demonstrations, burning the American flag and effigies of Carter for the benefit of worldwide news and television coverage.

Carter was furious, but his options were limited. He appealed to the United Nations, protesting what was a clear violation of diplomatic immunity and international law. But Khomeini scoffed at U.N. requests for the release of hostages. Carter then froze all Iranian assets in the United States and appealed to American allies for a trade embargo of Iran. The trade restrictions were only partially effective—even America's most loyal European allies did not want to lose access to Iranian oil.

So a frustrated Carter, hounded by a public and press demanding "action," authorized a rescue attempt by American commandos in April 1980. The raid, however, was aborted in the Iranian desert because of helicopter malfunctions, and it ended with eight fatalities when another American helicopter collided with a transport plane. Carter's presidency died with them. Secretary of State Cyrus Vance resigned in protest against the risky venture. Meanwhile, nightly television coverage of the taunting Iranian rebels generated a near obsession with the seeming impotence of the United States and the fate of the hostages. The crisis ended after 444 days of captivity when Carter released several billion dollars of Iranian assets to ransom the kidnapped hostages.

The turbulent and often tragic events of the 1970s—the conquest of South Vietnam, the Watergate scandal and Nixon's resignation, the energy shortage and stagflation, the Iranian hostage episode—provoked among Americans what Carter labeled a "crisis of confidence." By 1980, American power and prestige seemed to be on the decline, the economy remained in a shambles, and the rights revolution launched in the 1960s, with the questions it raised for the family and other basic social and political institutions, had sparked a backlash of resentment among "Middle America." With theatrical timing, Ronald Reagan emerged to tap the growing reservoir of public frustration and transform his political career into a crusade to make "America stand tall again." He told his supporters that there was "a hunger in this land for a spiritual revival, a return to a belief in moral absolutes." The United States, he declared, remained the "greatest country in the world. We have the talent, we have the drive, we have the imagination. Now all we need is the leadership."

MAKING CONNECTIONS

- Foreign affairs in the 1970s show the changing patterns of the cold war. The next chapter details the end of both the cold war and the Soviet Union.

- Presidents Nixon and Ford tried, with limited success, to decrease the power of the federal government over domestic affairs. President Reagan was much more successful at advancing the conservative agenda, a topic covered in the next chapter.

- The rebellion and turbulence of the 1960s and 1970s became less apparent in the following decade; as Chapter 36 shows, however, that turbulence reappeared, in a somewhat different form, in the 1990s.

FURTHER READING

Engaging overviews of the cultural trends of the 1960s include William L. O'Neill's *Coming Apart: An Informal History of America in the 1960s* (1972) and Godfrey Hodgson's *America in Our Time* (1976). The scholarly literature on the New Left includes Irwin Unger's *The Movement: A History of the American New Left, 1959–1972* (1974). On the Students for a Democratic Society, see Kirkpatrick Sale's *SDS* (1973) and Allen J. Matusow's *The Unraveling of America: A History of Liberalism in the 1960s* (1984). Also useful is Todd Gitlin's *The Sixties: Years of Hope, Days of Rage* (rev. ed., 1993).

Two influential asessments of the counterculture by sympathetic commentators are Theodore Roszak's *The Making of a Counterculture: Reflections on the Technocratic Society and Its Youthful Opposition* (1969) and Charles Reich's *The Greening of America* (1970). A good scholarly analysis of the hippies that takes them seriously is Timothy Miller's *The Hippies and American Values* (1991). On the communal movement, see Keith Melville's *Communes in the Counter Culture* (1972).

There is a wealth of good books dealing with the women's liberation movement. Among the most powerful accounts are those by participants. See Shulamith Firestone's *The Dialectic of Sex* (1972), Betty Friedan's *It Changed My Life: Writings on the Women's Movement* (1976), Kate Millett's *Sexual Politics* (1971), and *Sisterhood Is Powerful* (1970), edited by Robin Morgan. Sara Evans explains the ambivalent relationship of feminism with the civil rights movement in *Personal Politics: The Roots of Women's Liberation in the Civil Rights Movement and the New Left* (1980).

The organizing efforts of César Chavez are detailed in Ronald Taylor's *Chavez and the Farm Workers* (1975). The struggles of Native Americans for recognition and power are sympathetically described in Stan Steiner's *The New Indians* (1968). On the shifting cultural mood of the 1970s, see Christopher Lasch's influential critique, *The Culture of Narcissism* (1978). Peter Clecak convincingly questions the stereotypic notion of the seventies as an age of apathy and narcissism in *America's Quest for the Ideal Self* (1983).

On Nixon see Stephen Ambrose's *Nixon: The Triumph of a Politician, 1962–1972* (1989) and *Nixon: Ruin and Recovery, 1973–1990* (1991).

Equally valuable is Herbert S. Parmet's *Richard Nixon and His America* (1990). For a solid overview of the Watergate scandal, see Stanley Kutler's *The Wars of Watergate: The Last Crisis of Richard Nixon* (1990).

For the way the Rupublicans handled affairs abroad, consult Tad Szulc's *The Illusion of Peace: Foreign Policy in the Nixon Years* (1978). Secretary of State Henry Kissinger recounts his role in policy formation in *The White House Years* (1978). A less favorable report of the Kissinger role appears in Seymour M. Hersh's *The Price of Power: Kissinger in the Nixon White House* (1983).

The loss of Vietnam and the end of American involvement are traced in Allan E. Goodman's *The Lost Peace: America's Search for a Negotiated Settlement of the Vietnam War* (1978), Frank Snepp's *Decent Interval: An Insider's Account of Saigon's Indecent End Told by the CIA's Chief Strategy Analyst in Vietnam* (1977), and Gareth Porter's *A Peace Denied: The United States, Vietnam and the Paris Agreement* (1975). William Shawcross's *Sideshow: Kissinger, Nixon, and the Destruction of Cambodia* (1978) deals with the broadening of the war, while Larry Berman's *Planning a Tragedy: The Americanization of the War in Vietnam* (1982) assesses the final impact of American involvement. The most comprehensive treatment of the antiwar movement in the United States is Tom Wells's *The War Within: America's Battle over Vietnam* (1994). A recent effort to reflect upon the lingering impact of the Vietnam War is Arnold R. Isaacs's *Vietnam Shadows: The War, Its Ghosts, and Its Legacy* (1997).

To examine the rise of Jimmy Carter, consult Betty Glad's *Jimmy Carter: In Search of the Great White House* (1980). The best overview of the Carter administration is Burton I. Kaufman's *The Presidency of James Earl Carter, Jr.* (1993). A work more sympathetic to the Carter administration is John Dumbrell's *The Carter Presidency: A Re-Evaluation* (1993). Also useful is Kenneth E. Morris's *Jimmy Carter: American Moralist* (1997). Gaddis Smith's *Morality, Reason, and Power* (1986) provides an overview of American diplomacy in the Carter years. Zbigniew Brzezinski's *Power and Principle: Memories of the National Security Advisor, 1977–1981* (1983) and Cyrus Vance's *Hard Choices: Critical Years in America's Foreign Policy* (1983) lend insight into the Carter approach to foreign policy. Background on how the Middle East came to dominate much of American policy is found in William B. Quandt's *Decade of Decisions: American Policy toward the Arab-Israeli Conflict, 1967–1976* (1977).

35 CONSERVATIVE INSURGENCY

President Jimmy Carter and his embattled Democratic administration hobbled through 1979. The economy remained sluggish, double-digit inflation continued unabated, and failed efforts to free the American hostages in Iran made the administration appear indecisive. Carter's inability to mobilize the nation behind his energy program revealed mortal flaws in his reading of the public mood and his understanding of legislative politics. In July 1979, a much ballyhooed presidential address to the nation aroused more criticism than support. Carter's claim that a "crisis of confidence" was paralyzing the nation and his insistence that the days of dramatic economic growth were over fell on deaf or indignant ears. As a Phoenix newspaper editorial declared, the nation did not want "sermons" from the president; it wanted "action."

While the lackluster Carter administration was foundering, Republican conservatives were forging a plan to win the White House in 1980 and to assault the "New Deal welfare state" mentality in Washington. Those plans centered on the popularity and charisma of Ronald Reagan, the Hollywood actor turned California governor and prominent political commentator. Reagan was not a deep thinker, but he was a superb analyst of the public mood, an unabashed patriot, and a committed advocate of conservative principles. He was also charming and cheerful, a likable politician renowned for his folksy anecdotes. Where the dour Carter denounced the evils of free enterprise capitalism and tried to scold Americans into reviving long-forgotten virtues of frugality, a sunny Reagan promised a "revolution of ideas" designed to unleash the capitalist spirit, restore national pride, and regain international respect.

During the late 1970s, Reagan's simple message promoting a grassroots political revolution and a restoration of American pride and prosperity offered an uplifting alternative to Carter's strident moralism. More specifically, Reagan wanted to increase military spending, dismantle the "bloated" federal bureaucracy, reduce taxes and regulations, and in general, undo the welfare state. He also wanted to affirm old-time morality by ending abortions and reinstituting school prayer. Rea-

President Ronald Reagan, "the Great Communicator."

gan's appeal derived from his remarkable skills as a public speaker and his dogmatic commitment to a few overarching ideas and simple themes. As a true believer and an able compromiser, he combined the fervor of a revolutionary with the pragmatism of a diplomat.

Such attributes won Reagan two presidential terms in 1980 and 1984 and ensured the election of his successor, George Bush, in 1988. Just how revolutionary the Reagan era was remains a subject of intense partisan debate. What cannot be denied, however, is that Reagan's actions and beliefs set the tone for the decade.

THE REAGAN REVOLUTION

THE MAKING OF A PRESIDENT As the 1980 election approached, the Republicans eagerly anticipated the contest with a struggling Jimmy Carter. Their candidate, Ronald Reagan, had initially appeared as an even more improbable presidential possibility than Carter had four years earlier. Born in Illinois in 1911, Reagan graduated from tiny Eureka College and then worked as a cheery radio announcer and sportscaster before heading to Hollywood in 1937.

A disciple of New Deal politics, Reagan adopted Franklin Roosevelt's confident rhetoric and engaging smile, and he employed both during World War II when he made uplifting patriotic movies. But after the war his movie career stagnated, and Reagan abandoned his New Deal liberalism. He grew enamored of the Republican party's premise that too much government stifled free enterprise.

In 1964 Reagan entered the political limelight when he delivered a rousing speech on behalf of Barry Goldwater at the Republican convention. During two terms as governor of California (1967–1975), he displayed a commitment to conservative principles as well as a political realism capable of compromise. Nevertheless, by the middle 1970s Reagan's brand of free enterprise conservatism still appeared too extreme for a national audience.

THE MOVE TO REAGAN By the eve of the 1980 election, however, Reagan had become the beneficiary of three developments that made his conservative vision of America much more than a harmless flirtation with nostalgia. First, the 1980 census revealed that the American population (226,505,000) was aging, and was moving in large numbers from the liberal Northeast to the conservative "Sunbelt" states of the South and West. This dual development meant that demographic forces were carrying the electorate toward Reagan's conservative position.

Second, in the 1970s the country experienced a major revival of evangelical religion comparable to the Great Awakenings of the eighteenth and early nineteenth centuries. No longer simply a local or provincial phenomenon, Christian evangelicals and fundamentalists owned their own television and radio stations and operated their own schools and universities. The Reverend Jerry Falwell's "Moral Majority" expressed the political sentiments of the religious right wing: free enterprise should remain free, big government should be shrunk, abortion should be outlawed, prayer in school should be reinstated, evolution should be replaced in schoolbooks by the biblical story of creation, and Soviet expansion should be opposed as a form of pagan totalitarianism. The moralistic zeal and financial resources of the religious right made them effective opponents of liberal political candidates and programs. As defenders of traditional and local values—families in which women stayed home to care for children, tough criminal laws—the religious right rallied to Reagan.

A third factor contributing to the conservative resurgence was a well-organized and well-financed backlash against the feminist movement. During the 1970s, women who opposed the social goals of feminism formed counter-organizations with names such as "Women Who Want to Be Women" and "Females Opposed to Equality." Spearheading such efforts was Phyllis Schlafly, a right-wing Republican activist from Illinois. She orchestrated the campaign to defeat the Equal Rights Amendment (ERA) and thereafter served as the galvanizing force behind a growing antifeminist movement. She characterized feminists as a "bunch of bitter women seeking a constitutional cure for their personal problems." She instead urged women to embrace their God-given roles as wives and mothers. Feminists, she charged, were "anti-family, anti-children, and pro-abortion."

Many of Schlafly's supporters in the anti-ERA campaign also participated in a mushrooming anti-abortion or "pro-life" movement. By 1980 the National Right to Life committee, created by the National Conference of Catholic Bishops, boasted 11 million members representing all religious denominations. The intensity of their commitment made them a powerful political force in their own right, and the Reagan campaign was quick to highlight its own support for traditional family values, gender roles, and the rights of the unborn. Such cultural issues helped convince many northern Democrats to support Reagan. Whites alienated by the increasingly liberal social agenda of the Democratic party became a crucial element in Reagan's electoral strategy.

By 1980 voters seemed eager to embrace Reagan's cheery promises of a new era of less government, lower taxes, renewed prosperity, waning inflation, and revived military strength and national pride. His "supply-side" economic proposals, soon dubbed "Reaganomics" by supporters and "voodoo economics" by critics, suggested that stagflation resulted from governmental intrusions into the marketplace and from excessive taxes that weakened the incentive to work, save, and reinvest. The solution was to slash tax rates. For a long-suffering nation, it was, in theory, an alluring economic panacea.

Reagan was an adept campaigner who presented a consistent message to the voters: Carter and the Democrats, he insisted, believed that the United States had entered an era of permanent limits on economic growth and personal initiative. On the contrary, he asserted, the Republicans believed that America's greatest economic accomplishments were just around the corner. Reagan pledged that his recovery plans would restore prosperity and public confidence. He used folksy maxims and jokes to punctuate his themes. For instance, at one campaign stop he quipped: "A recession is when your neighbor loses his job. A depression is when you lose yours. A recovery is when Jimmy Carter loses his."

On election day Reagan swept to a decisive victory, with 489 electoral votes to 49 for Carter, who carried only six states. The popular vote proved equally lopsided: 44 million (51 percent) to 35 million (41 percent), with 7 percent going to John Anderson, a moderate Republican who had bolted the party after Reagan's nomination and had run on an independent ticket.

In addition to affirming Reagan's conservative agenda, the election reflected the triumph of what one political scientist called the "largest mass movement of our time"—nonvoting. Almost as striking as Reagan's one-sided victory was the fact that his vote total represented only 28 percent of the potential electorate. Only 53 percent of eligible voters cast ballots in the 1980 election.

Where had all the voters gone? Analysts noted that most of the nonvoters were working-class Democrats in the major urban centers. Voter turnout was lowest in poor inner-city neighborhoods such as New York's Bedford-Stuyvesant district, which had a 19 percent voter participation

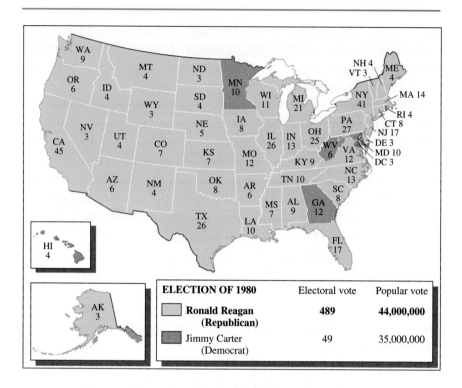

ELECTION OF 1980	Electoral vote	Popular vote
Ronald Reagan (Republican)	489	44,000,000
Jimmy Carter (Democrat)	49	35,000,000

rate. Turnout was highest, by contrast, in the affluent suburbs of large cities, areas where the Republican party was experiencing a dramatic surge in popularity. Such trends meant that American office-holders were being selected during the 1970s by an electorate increasingly dominated by middle- and upper-class white voters.

There were varied explanations for the high levels of voter apathy among working-class Americans. Some stressed the continuing sense of disillusionment with government growing out of the Watergate affair. Others believed that the Democratic party had alienated its traditional blocs of support among common folk. Democratic leaders no longer spoke eloquently on behalf of those at the bottom of America's social scale. By embracing a fiscal conservatism indistinguishable from that of the Republicans, as Carter had done, Democrats had lost their appeal among blue-collar workers and ghetto dwellers. When viewed in this light, Ronald Reagan's victory represented less a resounding victory for conservative Republicans than a self-inflicted defeat by a fractured Democratic party. For the moment, however, such results were masked by the Republicans' euphoric victory celebrations. Flush with a sense of power and destiny, Ronald Reagan headed toward Washington with a blueprint for dismantling the welfare state.

REAGAN'S FIRST TERM

REAGANOMICS Ronald Reagan brought to Washington a simple conservative philosophy. "Government is not the solution to our problem," Reagan insisted; "Government is the problem." Reagan credited Calvin Coolidge and his treasury secretary, Andrew Mellon, with demonstrating that by reducing taxes and easing government regulation of business, free-market capitalism would revive the economy. Like his Republican predecessors of the 1920s, he wanted to unleash entrepreneurial energy as never before. By cutting taxes and domestic federal spending and following a supply-side economic program, he claimed, a surging economy would produce *more* government revenues that would help reduce the budget deficit.

Unlike Carter, Reagan seemed to know exactly what ailed the economy and how to restore America's prestige in the world. Among his first decisions, Reagan abandoned price controls on oil and ended the wheat embargo on the Soviet Union. He then focused on dramatically increasing defense spending, sharply reducing social spending, and passing a sweeping tax reform proposal. Despite loud protests from liberal groups and politicians, Congress passed the entire Reagan economic package by the summer of 1981. Enough Democrats—mostly sympathetic southern conservatives dubbed "boll weevils"—supported the measures to pass them by overwhelming majorities. On August 1, 1981, Reagan signed the Economic Recovery Tax Act, which cut personal income taxes by 25 percent, lowered the maximum rate from 70 to 50 percent for 1982, cut the capital gains tax by a third, and offered a broad array of other tax concessions.

The new legislation embodied an idea that went back to Alexander Hamilton, George Washington's treasury secretary: more money in the hands of the affluent would benefit society at large, since the wealthy would engage in productive investment. A closer parallel was Treasury Secretary Andrew Mellon's tax reduction program of the 1920s. The difference was that the Reagan tax cuts were accompanied by massive increases in defense spending that generated ever-mounting deficits. Reagan's advisers insisted that such unbalanced budgets were only temporary; once the new tax plan began to take effect, the economy would take off and government tax revenues would soar as personal incomes and corporate profits skyrocketed. But it did not work out that way. By the summer of 1983, a major economic recovery was underway, but the federal deficits grew ever larger, so much so that the president, who in 1980 had pledged to have a balanced federal budget by 1983, had in fact run up debts larger than those of all his predecessors combined.

BUDGET CUTS   In trying to slash expenditures, David Stockman, Reagan's budget director, pushed through $35 billion in budget cuts in educational and cultural programs, housing, food stamps, and school lunches in 1981. Reagan assured critics that despite these cuts he was committed to maintaining the "safety net" of government services for the "truly needy." This meant that aid would remain available only to those who could not work because of disability or child care. New Deal welfare programs had had the same purpose, but the Roosevelt administration had also provided federal jobs for those who could work. This was not a part of "Reaganomics." Cuts in programs to the disadvantaged, when added to the sluggish economy, helped raise the percentage of persons living under the poverty level from 11.7 in 1979 to 15.3 in 1983.

While publicly proclaiming a great accomplishment in making such cuts in domestic spending, Reagan and his advisers knew privately that the figures were not adding up to those they had pledged. David Stockman realized that the cuts in domestic spending were far short of what would be needed to balance the budget in four years as Reagan had promised. He pleaded with Reagan to cut back on new defense spending and to slow the proposed tax cuts, but the president refused. The result was a soaring budget deficit and the worst economic recession since the 1930s.

Bankers and investors feared that the rising government debt would send interest rates soaring, a fear expressed in sagging bond and stock markets. A business slump and rising unemployment continued through most of 1982. That same year the federal deficit doubled. Aides finally convinced Reagan that to reassure the public about deficits and the threat of inflation the government needed "revenue enhancements," a euphemism for tax increases. With Reagan's support, Congress passed a new tax bill in 1982 that would raise almost $100 billion.

During the midterm elections of 1982, Reagan rarely mentioned the new tax bill. Instead he focused his campaign speeches on the benefits of supply-side economics and rosy economic forecasts. He urged voters to "stay the course" and appealed for more time to let his economic program take effect. Meanwhile, the economic slump persisted through 1982, with unemployment standing at 10.4 percent, and the Republicans experienced moderate losses in the midterm elections.

CONFLICTS OF INTEREST Like Harding and Coolidge in the 1920s, Reagan named people to government positions who frequently were unsympathetic to the regulatory functions for which they were responsible. The most visible early example was Interior Secretary James Watt, who castigated environmentalists for hindering the commercial use of timber and mineral resources. He was finally forced out of office by the uproar over an offensive joke he made.

The Reagan administration also paralleled the Harding administration by finding itself embroiled in charges of conflict of interest, ethical misconduct, and actual criminal behavior. Public outcry forced the administrator of the Environmental Protection Agency to resign for granting favors to industrial polluters. The president's deputy chief of staff obtained a sweetheart loan from a person who was subsequently given a governmental post. Once he left the White House in 1985, he set up a lucrative consulting business that traded upon his connections with high government officials, as another former presidential aide had done earlier. Both men were later indicted.

Although some 200 other Reagan appointees were also accused of unethical or illegal activities, the president himself remained untouched by any hint of impropriety. His personal charisma and aloof managerial style helped shield him from the political fallout associated with the growing scandals and conflicts of interest among his aides and cronies. Public affection for him as a person remained his most enduring asset. This led one member of Congress to label the Reagan White House the "Teflon Presidency," where the buck never stopped because the blame never stuck.

Organized labor suffered severe setbacks during the Reagan years. Presidential appointments to the National Labor Relations Board tended to favor management, and in 1981 Reagan fired members of the Professional Air Traffic Controllers (PATCO) who had participated in an illegal strike. Even more important, Reagan's smashing electoral victories in 1980 and 1984 broke the political power of the AFL-CIO. His criticism of unions seemed to reflect a general trend in public opinion. Although a record number of new jobs was created during the 1980s, union membership steadily dropped. By 1987 unions represented only 17 percent of the nation's full-time workers, down from 24 percent in 1979.

Reagan also went on the offensive against feminism. He ardently opposed the Equal Rights Amendment, abortion on demand, and the legal guarantee of equal pay for jobs of comparable worth. He did name Sandra Day O'Connor as the first woman justice to the Supreme Court, but critics labeled it a token gesture rather than a reflection of any genuine commitment to gender equality.

Blacks and other minorities shared a similar aggravation at the administration's limited support for affirmative action programs in employment. Reagan cut funds for civil rights enforcement and the Equal Employment Opportunity Commission, and he initially opposed renewal of the Voting Rights Act of 1965, but was overruled by Congress.

THE DEFENSE BUILDUP Reagan's conduct of foreign policy reflected his belief that trouble in the world stemmed mainly from Moscow. At one of his first news conferences he charged that the Soviets were "prepared to commit any crime, to lie, to cheat," and do anything necessary to promote world communism. He and Secretary of Defense Caspar Weinberger embarked on a major buildup of nuclear and conventional weapons to close the gap that they claimed had developed between Soviet and American military forces.

In 1983 Reagan escalated the nuclear arms race by authorizing the Defense Department to develop a Strategic Defense Initiative (SDI). It involved a complex anti-missile defense system using super-secret laser and high-energy particles weapons to destroy enemy missiles in outer space well before they reached their targets. To Reagan its great appeal was the ability to destroy weapons rather than people, thereby freeing defense strategy from the concept of mutually assured destruction that had long governed Soviet and American attitudes toward nuclear war. Journalists quickly dubbed the program "Star Wars" in reference to the popular science fiction film. Despite skepticism among the media and many scientists that such a "foolproof" celestial defense system could be built, it forced the Soviets to launch an expensive research and development program of their own to keep pace. As a West German defense analyst commented, "I have never seen Soviets so emotional as they are over Star Wars."

Reagan borrowed the rhetoric of Harry Truman, John Foster Dulles, and the Kennedy inaugural to express American resolve in the face of "Communist aggression anywhere in the world." Détente deteriorated even further when the Soviets imposed martial law in Poland during the winter of 1981. The crackdown came after Polish workers, united under the banner of an independent union called Solidarity, challenged the Communist monopoly of power. As with Hungary in 1956 and Czechoslovakia in 1968, there was little the United States could do except register protest and impose economic sanctions against Poland's Communist government.

THE AMERICAS Reagan's foremost international concern, however, was in Central America, where he detected the most serious Communist threat. The tiny nation of El Salvador, caught up since 1980 in a brutal struggle between Communist-supported revolutionaries and right-wing extremists, received American commitments of economic and military assistance. Reagan stopped short of sending American troops, but he did increase the number of military advisers and the amount of financial aid to the Salvadoran government. He also abandoned Carter's strident criticism of right-wing Salvadoran militants whose "death squads" engaged in systematic terror and murder. Critics argued that American involvement ensured that the revolutionary forces would emerge as the victorious representatives of Salvadoran nationalism. Supporters countered by warning that American failure to act would allow for a repeat of Communist victories in Nicaragua, and that Honduras, Guatemala, and then all of Central America would eventually enter the Communist camp. By 1984, however, the American-backed government of President José Napoleón Duarte brought a modicum of stability to El Salvador.

Even more troubling was the situation in Nicaragua. The Reagan State Department claimed that the Cuban-sponsored Sandinista government in Nicaragua, which had only recently taken control of the country after ousting a corrupt dictator, was funneling Soviet and

"Shhhh. It's top secret." *A comment on Reagan administration covert operations in Nicaragua.*

Cuban arms to leftist Salvadoran rebels. In response, the administration ordered the CIA to train and supply guerrilla bands of disgruntled Nicaraguans, tagged "Contras," who staged attacks on Sandinista bases and officials from sanctuaries in Honduras. In supporting these "freedom fighters," Reagan sought not only to impede the traffic in arms to Salvadoran rebels but also to overthrow the Communist Sandinistas.

Critics of Reagan's anti-Sandinista policy questioned the motives and ethics of the Contras, accusing them of being mostly right-wing fanatics who indiscriminately killed civilians as well as Sandinista soldiers. They also feared that the United States might eventually commit its own combat forces, thus threatening another Vietnam-like intervention. Reagan warned that if the Communists prevailed in Central America, "our credibility would collapse, our alliances would crumble, and the safety of our homeland would be jeopardized."

THE MIDDLE EAST The Middle East remained a tinderbox of geopolitical conflict throughout the Reagan years. No peaceable end seemed possible to the bloody Iran-Iraq war, which had erupted in 1980, entangled as it was with the passions of Islamic fundamentalism.

In 1984 both sides began to attack tankers in the Persian Gulf, a major source of the world's oil. Although the Reagan administration harbored no affection for either nation, it viewed Iranian fundamentalism as the greater threat and funneled aid to Iraq, a policy that produced unforeseen and grave consequences.

American diplomats continued to see Israel as the strongest ally in the region, all the while seeking to encourage moderate Arab groups. Israel's aim in the area was to secure peaceful borders, America's goal was to prevent Soviet involvement through its ally Syria. But both objectives ran up against the continuing chaos in Lebanon, where ethnic and religious tensions erupted into an anarchy of warring groups. The capital, Beirut, became a battleground for rival Muslim and Christian factions, the Palestine Liberation Organization (PLO) army, Syrian invaders cast as peacekeepers, and Israelis responding to PLO attacks.

In 1982 Israeli forces pushed the PLO out of southern Lebanon all the way north to Beirut, and then the Israelis began bombarding PLO strongholds in Beirut. The United States neither endorsed nor condemned the Israeli invasion, but sent a special ambassador to negotiate a settlement. The PLO agreed to withdraw from Beirut, and Israeli troops moved into the city. While the Israelis looked the other way, Lebanese Christian militiamen took revenge for the murder of their president by slaughtering Muslim women and children left in Palestinian refugee camps.

French, Italian, and American forces thereupon moved into Beirut as "peacekeepers," but in such small numbers as to become targets themselves. On October 23, 1983, an Islamic suicide bomber drove a truck laden with explosives into the U.S. Marine quarters at the Beirut airport. The explosion left 241 Americans dead. Reagan declared that a continued American presence in the city was essential, but he soon began preparations for the withdrawal of the exposed American troops. On February 7, 1984, he announced that the Marines would be redeployed on warships offshore. The Israelis pulled back to southern Lebanon, while the Syrians remained in eastern Lebanon and imposed a tenuous peace upon the faction-ridden country.

GRENADA In a fortunate turn for the Reagan administration, an easy military triumph closer to home eclipsed news of the debacle in Lebanon. On the tiny Caribbean island of Grenada, the smallest independent nation in the Western Hemisphere, a leftist government had admitted Cuban workers to build a new airfield and had signed military agreements with several Communist-bloc countries. In 1983 an even more radical military council seized power.

Appeals from the governments of neighboring islands led Reagan in 1983 to order 1,900 paratroopers and marines to invade the island, depose the radical regime, and evacuate a group of American students at Grenada's medical school. The U.N. General Assembly condemned the action, and many Latin Americans saw it as a revival of gunboat diplomacy. But most Grenadans and their neighbors acclaimed the action, and it was immensely popular in the United States. Although it was a lopsided affair, the attack on the island made Reagan look decisive, and it served notice on Latin American revolutionaries that the president might use force elsewhere in the region.

REAGAN'S SECOND TERM

By 1983 prosperity had returned, and the Reagan economic program seemed to be working as touted. Countervailing policies of fiscal stimulus (tax cuts and heavy defense spending) and monetary restraint (high interest rates) brought at least in the short run an economic recovery with little inflation. Critics argued that the return of prosperity was more the result of the cyclical swings inherent in the economy and the dramatic fall in energy costs following the collapse of the OPEC cartel.

THE ELECTION OF 1984 As the presidential election approached, however, Reagan and the Republicans took credit for the economic recovery. The slogan at the convention was "America Is Back." Reagan had brought new strength and vitality, luster and dignity to the White House and the nation. The Democratic nominee, the former Minnesota senator and vice-president, Walter Mondale, faced an uphill struggle. But he quickly won the endorsement of several major organizations—the AFL-CIO, National Organization for Women, and the NAACP. He also won a lot of media attention by choosing as his running mate a woman, New York representative Geraldine Ferraro. This attention soon focused, however, on her husband's dubious business finances.

Mondale further complicated his campaign by a fit of frankness in his acceptance speech. "Mr. Reagan will raise taxes, and so will I," he told the convention. "He won't tell you. I just did." Reagan in turn vowed never to approve a tax increase, and he chided his opponent's candid stand. Thereafter, Mondale never caught up. Reagan's skill and confidence at campaigning outshone him, and the economic recovery made it difficult for Mondale to attract interest, much less generate enthusiasm.

In the end, Reagan won almost 59 percent of the popular vote and lost only Minnesota and the District of Columbia. His coattails, however, were not as long as in 1980. Republicans had a net gain of only fifteen seats in the House, leaving them still greatly outnumbered by Democrats, 253 to 182. They also lost two Senate seats, leaving their margin only 53 to 47.

DOMESTIC CHALLENGES Although Reagan had won a landslide reelection, domestic problems that he had tried to ignore demanded his attention and shook his complacency. The ethical and criminal violations of his subordinates continued to make headlines, and strains began to appear between the political conservatives in the party and the social conservatives who dominated evangelical religious groups.

Still, for a while, the Reagan luck held out. OPEC continued to lower oil prices, sending inflation down and the stock market up. In his 1985 State of the Union message, the president clarified what had come to be called the Reagan Doctrine in foreign affairs. America, he proclaimed, would support anti-Communist forces around the world seeking to "defy Soviet-supported aggression." In effect, he was challenging the isolationism provoked by the nation's humbling experience in Vietnam. America, he promised, would not hesitate to intervene in world hot spots. Turning to domestic policy, the president dared Congress to raise taxes. His veto pen was ready.

Through much of 1985 Reagan was back again on the campaign trail, this time drumming up support for a tax simplification plan. After a vigorous debate that lasted nearly two years, Congress passed, and in 1986 the president signed, a comprehensive Tax Reform Act. The new measure would by 1988 reduce the number of tax brackets from fourteen to two, and reduce rates from the maximum of 50 percent to

15 and 28 percent—the lowest since Coolidge. Tax shelters were also sharply curtailed.

ARMS CONTROL   Meanwhile Reagan, for all his stern talk about the Soviet Union being "an evil empire," was determined to reach an arms control agreement with the Soviets. In Geneva in 1985 he met with Mikhail Gorbachev, the innovative new leader of the Soviet Union. The two signed several cultural and scientific agreements and issued a statement on arms limitations talks, but no treaty was in the offing. A major stumbling block was Reagan's refusal to consider any restrictions on his pursuit of the Strategic Defense Initiative.

Nearly a year after the Geneva summit, on sudden notice and with limited preparation, Gorbachev and Reagan met in Iceland for two days to discuss arms reduction. Early reports predicted a major break-through, as the two leaders discussed the possibility of a total ban on nuclear weapons, but the talks collapsed over disagreement about SDI. After the Iceland meeting, the two nations reduced the scope of their

Soviet premier Mikhail Gorbachev (left) *and U.S. president Ronald Reagan* (right) *during a light moment at the Geneva summit, November 1985.*

discussions in order to break the impasse. Talks now focused on eliminating short-range nuclear weapons from Europe.

THE IRAN-CONTRA AFFAIR   During the fall of 1986, the Reagan administration suffered a double blow. In the midterm elections the Democrats regained control of the Senate by 55 to 45. For his final two years in office, Reagan would face an opposition Congress. What was worse, on election day, reports surfaced that the United States, with Israeli assistance, had been secretly selling arms to Iran in hope of securing the release of American hostages held in Lebanon by extremist Islamic groups with close ties to Iran. Such action contradicted Reagan's repeated public insistence that his administration would never negotiate with terrorists. It angered America's allies and many Americans who vividly remembered the 1979 Iranian takeover of the American Embassy.

There was more to the story. Over the next several months, a series of revelations reminiscent of the Watergate affair disclosed a more complicated series of covert activities carried out by administration officials. At the center of what came to be dubbed "Irangate" was the much-decorated Marine Lieutenant-Colonel Oliver North. An aide to the National Security Council who specialized in counterterrorism, North had been running secret operations from the basement of the White House involving numerous governmental, private, and foreign individuals. His most far-fetched scheme sought to use the profits gained from the secret sale of arms to Iran to subsidize the Contra rebels fighting in Nicaragua, at a time when Congress had voted to ban such aid.

North's activities, it turned out, had been approved by National Security Adviser Robert McFarlane, his successor Admiral John Poindexter, and CIA Director William Casey. Secretary of State George Shultz and Secretary of Defense Caspar Weinberger both had criticized the sale of arms to Iran, but their objections were ignored. Later, on three occasions, Shultz threatened to resign because no one was trying to stop the "pathetic" scheme. As information about the illegal dealings surfaced in the press, McFarlane attempted suicide, Poindexter resigned, and North was fired. Casey, who denied any connection, left the CIA for health reasons, and died shortly thereafter from a brain tumor.

The White House, meanwhile, assumed a siege mentality as the president's popularity plummeted. Under increasing criticism and amid growing doubts of his own credibility and ability, Reagan appointed both an independent counsel and a three-man commission, led by former Republican senator John Tower, to investigate the spreading scandal.

The Tower Commission issued a devastating report early in 1987 that placed much of the responsibility for the bungled Iran-Contra Affair on Reagan's loose management style. The report portrayed Reagan as uninformed and forgetful, a leader detached from the inner workings of his own administration.

The Iran-Contra Affair left support for the Nicaraguan Contras badly eroded in the Congress, and it undermined much of Reagan's popularity. The investigations of the independent counsel led to six indictments in 1988. A Washington jury found Oliver North guilty of three relatively minor charges but innocent of nine more serious counts, apparently reflecting the jury's reasoning that he had acted as an agent of higher-ups. His conviction was later overturned on appeal. Of those involved in the affair, only John Poindexter got a jail sentence—six months for his conviction on five felony counts of obstructing justice and lying to Congress.

TURMOIL IN CENTRAL AMERICA The Iran-Contra Affair showed the lengths to which members of the Reagan administration would go to support the Nicaraguan Contras. Fearing heightened Soviet and American involvement in Central America, neighboring countries pressed during the mid-1980s for a negotiated settlement to the fighting in Nicaragua. In the spring of 1988 negotiations produced a cease-fire agreement, ending nearly seven years of fighting in Nicaragua. Secretary of State Shultz called the pact an "important step forward," but it surprised and disappointed hardliners within the Reagan administration who saw in it a Contra surrender. The Contra leaders themselves, aware of the eroding support for their cause in the United States Congress, saw the truce as their only chance for tangible concessions such as amnesty for political prisoners, the return of the Contras from exile, and "unrestricted freedom of expression."

Meanwhile, in neighboring El Salvador, the administration's attempt to shore up the centrist government of José Napoleón Duarte through economic and military aid was dealt a body blow when the far-right ARENA party scored an upset victory at the polls during the spring.

AN ECONOMY DRIVEN BY DEBT During the 1980s, all kinds of debt—personal, corporate, and governmental—increased dramatically. Whereas in the 1960s, Americans on average saved 10 percent of their income, in 1987 they saved less than 4 percent. The Reagan budget deficits also reached record levels. Between 1981 and 1987, the federal debt totaled $1.4 trillion, a figure half again larger than the entire debt for the previous two centuries. This statistic led some economists to refer to the nation's "charge card" economic recovery. Caught up in the exhilarating momentum of such prolonged prosperity and what had become a roaring bull market, however, few observers recognized the cost of such carefree spending.

A seeming epidemic of greed and self-absorbed materialism had spread through the country. Wall Street witnessed a rash of arrests and convictions for trading in securities on inside information unavailable to the public. And more government officials, including Attorney-General Edwin Meese, became entangled in the web of corruption. Commentators talked of a compulsive materialism energizing the young, upwardly mobile urban professionals dubbed "Yuppies." Caught up in the race for money, goods, and status, these post–World War II baby-boomers in the fast lane captured the tone and mood of affluent life in the 1980s.

Then, on October 19, 1987, the bill collector suddenly arrived at the nation's doorstep. On that "Black Monday," the stock market, already buffeted by sharp declines the previous week, experienced a tidal wave of selling reminiscent of the 1929 crash. The Dow Jones industrial average plummeted 508 points, or an astounding 22.6 percent. The market plunge nearly doubled the record 12.8 percent fall on October 28, 1929. Almost $560 billion in paper value disappeared, an amount larger than the gross national product of France. With cyclonic suddenness the nation's financial mood went from boom to gloom during the fall of 1987. Several smaller brokerage houses went under amid the speculative whirlpool, thousands of investment bankers and stockbrokers were fired, and consumer confidence took a beating. Wall Street's selling frenzy reverberated throughout the capitalist world, sending stock prices plummeting in Tokyo, London, Paris, and Toronto.

What caused such a goring of the bull market? The reasons were complex and long in developing. Some analysts argued that the runaway market of the 1980s had become artificially high, driven by greed and hope rather than by any relation to the economy's actual performance. Others blamed new computerized trading programs that distorted market activity and misled individual investors. But most agreed that the fundamental problem was the nation's spiraling indebtedness and chronically high trade deficits. Americans were consuming more than they were producing, importing the difference, and paying for it with borrowed money and a dollar sharply declining in value. Foreign investors had lost confidence in Reaganomics and were no longer willing to finance America's spending binge.

In the aftermath of the calamitous selling spree on Black Monday, President Reagan insisted that the "underlying economy remains sound," an unsettling echo of Herbert Hoover's equally sunny assurances in 1929. Few observers actually feared a depression of the magnitude of the 1930s; there were too many safeguards built into the system to allow that. But there was real concern of an impending recession, and within a few weeks, Reagan agreed to work with Congress in developing a deficit reduction package, and for the first time indicated that he was willing to include increased taxes in such a package. Yet the eventual compromise plan was so modest that it did little to restore investor confidence. As one Republican senator lamented, "There is a total lack of courage among those of us in the Congress to do what we all know has to be done."

THE POOR, THE HOMELESS, AND AIDS VICTIMS The 1980s were years of vivid contrasts. Despite unprecedented affluence, there were also uncounted beggars in the streets and homeless people sleeping in doorways, in cardboard boxes, and on heat grates. A variety of causes could be adduced for the shortage of low-cost housing: government had given up on building public housing; with the best of intentions, urban renewal had demolished blighted areas but provided no housing for the displaced; and owners had abandoned unprofitable buildings in poor neighborhoods or converted them into expensive condominiums. The last was called "gentrification."

Other causes of homelessness included family disorganization, and the deinstitutionalization of the mentally ill thanks to new medications for treatment and based on the promise of community mental health services that failed to materialize—a program started under

Despite the nation's prosperity and some efforts to build low-cost housing, the number of homeless people continued to increase during the 1980s.

President Kennedy but never adequately funded. By the summer of 1988, the *New York Times* estimated, more than 45 percent of the city's adult residents were living in poverty, totally outside the labor force for lack of skills, lack of motivation, drug use, and other problems.

Still another group cast aside were those suffering from a strange new malady known as AIDS (acquired immune deficiency syndrome). At the beginning of the decade, public health officials had begun to report that gay men and intravenous drug users were especially at risk for this syndrome. Those infected with AIDS showed signs of fatigue, developed a strange combination of infections, and eventually died. Researchers struggled to discern the origins of the new malady. Eventually they linked it to a virus (HIV) originating in Africa and spread from there to Europe and America. People contracted it by coming into contact with the blood or body fluids of an infected person. One reason the Reagan administration showed little interest in AIDS was that it initially was viewed as a "gay" disease. Patrick Buchanan, the conservative spokesman who served as White House director of communications, said that homosexuals had "declared war on nature, and now nature is extracting an awful retribution."

AN HISTORIC TREATY In the midst of a shaky, unpredictable economic situation, the main prospect for positive achievement before the end of Reagan's second term seemed to lie in arms reduction agreements with the Soviet government. Under Mikhail Gorbachev the Soviets promoted renewed détente in order to free their energies and financial resources to address pressing domestic problems. The logjam impeding the arms negotiations suddenly broke in 1987, when Gorbachev announced that he was willing to deal separately on a medium-range missile treaty. After nine more months of strenuous, highly technical negotiations, Reagan and Gorbachev met amid much fanfare in Washington on December 9, 1987, and signed a treaty to eliminate intermediate-range (300–3,000 miles) nuclear forces (INF).

It was an epochal event, not only because it marked the first time that the two nations had agreed to destroy a whole class of weapons systems but because it represented a key first step toward the eventual end of the arms race altogether. Under the terms of the treaty, the United States would destroy 859 missiles and the Soviets would eliminate 1,752. Provision was also made for on-site inspections by each side to verify compliance. Still, this winnowing of weapons would represent only 4 percent of the total number of nuclear missiles on both sides. Arms-control advocates thus looked toward a second and more comprehensive treaty eliminating long-range strategic missiles.

But virtually all Kremlin watchers were heartened by continuing evidence that Gorbachev was successfully liberalizing Soviet domestic life and aggressively improving East-West foreign relations. The Soviets suddenly began stressing cooperation with the West in dealing with "hot spots" around the world. They urged the Palestine Liberation Organization to recognize Israel's right to exist and advocated a greater role for the U.N. in the volatile Persian Gulf. Perhaps the most dramatic symbol of a thawing cold war was the phased withdrawal of 115,000 Soviet troops from Afghanistan, which began in 1988.

THE REAGAN LEGACY Historians are just beginning to assess the legacy of the nation's fortieth president. Although Reagan had declared in 1981 his intention to "curb the size and influence of the federal establishment," the welfare state remained intact when Reagan left office. Neither the Social Security system nor Medicare nor other major welfare programs had been dismantled or overhauled. And the federal agencies that Reagan had threatened to abolish, such as the Department of Education, not only remained in place in 1989, their budgets grew. The federal budget as a percentage of the gross domestic product (GDP) was actually higher when Reagan left office than when he had entered. Moreover, he did not try to push through Congress the incendiary social issues championed by the religious right such as school prayer and a ban on abortions.

Yet Ronald Reagan nonetheless succeeded in redefining the national political agenda and accelerated the conservative insurgency that had been developing for over twenty years. His greatest successes were in renewing America's soaring sense of possibilities, bringing inflation under control while stimulating the longest sustained period of peacetime prosperity in history, and negotiating the nuclear disarmament treaty and helping to light the fuse of democratic freedom in eastern Europe. By redirecting the thrust of both domestic and foreign policy, he put the Democratic party on the defensive and forced conventional New Deal "liberalism" into a panicked retreat. The fact that Reagan's tax policies widened the gap between the rich and poor and created huge budget deficits for future presidents to confront did not diminish the popularity of the "Great Communicator."

THE 1988 ELECTION As a new presidential election unfolded, eight Democratic presidential candidates entered a wild scramble for their party's nomination. However, as the primary season progressed, it soon became a two-man race between Massachusetts governor Michael Dukakis and Jesse Jackson, the black civil rights activist who had been one of Martin Luther King, Jr.'s chief lieutenants. Dukakis eventually won out, and managed a difficult reconciliation with the Jackson forces that left the Democrats unified and confident as the fall campaign began. As in 1960, they envisioned a popular president and his tired presidency giving way to a cool, poised politician from Massachusetts.

The Republicans nominated Reagan's two-term vice-president, George Bush, who after a bumpy start had easily cast aside his rivals in the primaries. As Reagan's handpicked heir, Bush claimed credit for the administration's successes, but like all dutiful vice-presidents, he also faced the challenge of defining and asserting his own political identity.

Although he was a veteran government official, having served as a Texas congressman, envoy to China, ambassador to the U.N., and head of the CIA, Bush projected none of Reagan's charisma, charm, or rhetorical skills. Cartoonists caricatured the patrician vice-president, the son of a rich Connecticut senator, schooled at Andover and Yale, as a well-heeled "wimp," and one Democrat described him as a man born "with a silver foot in his mouth." Early polls showed Dukakis with a surprisingly wide lead.

Yet at the Republican convention Bush delivered a forceful address that sharply enhanced his stature. Although pledging to continue the Reagan agenda, he also recognized that "things aren't perfect" in America, an admission Reagan rarely acknowledged. Bush promised to use the White House to fight bigotry, illiteracy, and homelessness. The most memorable line was a defiant statement on taxes: "Congress will push me to raise taxes, and I'll say no, and they'll push, and I'll say no, and they'll push again. And all I can say to them is, read my lips: *no new taxes.*"

In a campaign given over to mudslinging, the Bush campaign leaders attacked Dukakis as a camouflaged liberal in the mold of McGovern, Carter, and Mondale, who would increase federal spending, raise taxes, gut the defense program, refuse to intervene against Communist aggression abroad, and oppose the pledge of allegiance to the flag. Dukakis chose not to respond to the Republican attacks. Studiously informed on the issues, he had a Jimmy Carter–like trust in the force of sweet reason. Dukakis was, in Bush's words, "the Iceman," cool, rational, in control of his emotions, blind to the emotional power that trivial issues could exert.

The Republican onslaught took its toll against the less organized, less focused Dukakis campaign. Moreover, the Republicans benefited from the population growth in the Sunbelt states, the shift of population from the Democratic cities to the Republican suburbs, and from the votes of many moderate and conservative Democrats and Independents. Dukakis took ten states plus the District of Columbia, with clusters in the Northeast, Midwest, and Northwest. Bush carried the rest, with a margin of about 54 percent to 46 percent in the popular vote and 426 to 111 in the electoral college—one Democratic elector voted for Lloyd Bentsen, the Texas senator Dukakis had chosen as his running mate.

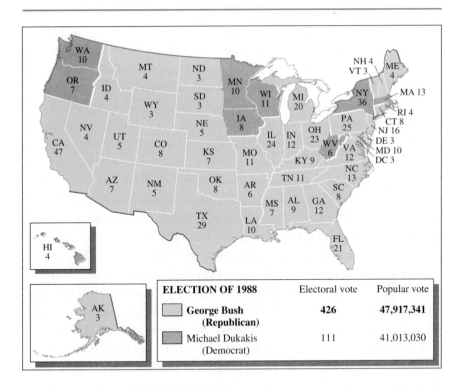

ELECTION OF 1988	Electoral vote	Popular vote
George Bush (Republican)	**426**	**47,917,341**
Michael Dukakis (Democrat)	111	41,013,030

THE BUSH YEARS

George Bush viewed himself as a guardian president rather than an activist. Lacking Reagan's visionary outlook and his skill as a speaker, Bush was a pragmatic caretaker eager to avoid "stupid mistakes" and to find a way to get along with the Democratic majority in Congress. "We don't need to remake society," he announced. As a consequence, Bush sought to consolidate and nurture the programs that Reagan had put in place rather than launch his own array of new programs and policies.

DOMESTIC INITIATIVES The Reagan administration left some issues that demanded immediate attention from the Bush White House. In 1989 Bush tackled the most pressing of these, the savings and loan crisis. One effect of the Reagan administration's efforts to eliminate "unnecessary" federal regulations in the economic sector was a debacle in the savings and loan industry. Savings and loan institutions (also called S & L's or "thrifts") had been set up to help people buy homes. To enable S & L's to compete with commercial banks, Reagan had pushed through Congress a bill that had allowed S & L's to invest depositors' funds in commercial real estate and junk bonds (speculative issues that drew investors into risky investments with the promise of very high returns) as well as in the traditional single-family housing market.

The result was catastrophic. Knowing that the federal government insured deposits up to $100,000, incompetent or corrupt lenders engaged in a frenzy of speculative high-risk investments and freewheeling personal expenditures. By 1989 hundreds of S & L's had failed, and Bush responded with a rescue plan to close or sell ailing S & L's and bail out the depositors. Congress responded the following August by consolidating the insurance fund for savings and loan deposits with the fund covering banks, the Federal Deposit Insurance Corporation (FDIC). A new agency, the Resolution Trust Corporation (RTC), was created to sell off failed S & L's—or at least their assets. At the time, the cost to taxpayers of the bailout was put at $300 billion over thirty years, although in 1990 the General Accounting Office estimated the cost at $500 billion.

The biggest hangover from the 1980s was the national debt, which stood at $2.6 trillion by the time Bush was elected, nearly three times its 1980 level. Bush's taboo on tax increases (meaning mainly income taxes) made it more difficult to reduce the annual federal deficit or trim the long-term national debt.

By early 1990, according to one political writer, the country faced "a horrendous fiscal mess." Bipartisan budget talks between administration and congressional leaders, begun in May, revealed "rancorous partisanship [and] deep divisions within the two parties." Eventually, on June 26, Bush issued a statement: "It seems clear to me that both the size of the deficit problem and the need for a package that can be enacted" required a number of measures, including "tax revenue increases." Congress finally reacted to mounting public anger at the continued indecision and approved a settlement with the Bush administration in October, although most Republicans still opposed it. Through a combination of tax hikes and spending cuts, the measure promised to reduce the budget deficit by $43.1 billion in 1991 and by $331.4 billion in 1991–1995.

THE WAR ON DRUGS There was more symbolism than substance in the Bush administration's plans to deal with the deadly matter of drug abuse. During the 1980s, cocaine addiction had spread through sizable segments of American society. Bush vowed to make drug abuse his number-one domestic priority, and appointed William J. Bennett, former education secretary, as "drug czar," or head of a new Office of National Drug Control Policy, with cabinet status but no department.

Bush's war on drugs was planned along three fronts: more stringent law enforcement, drug testing in the workplace, and heightened efforts to cut off the supply of drugs coming from Colombia and Peru. Although drug-related arrests increased 20 percent from 1988 to 1989, cocaine in its smokable form, known as "crack," remained readily available and immensely popular. In 1989 some 375,000 American babies were born addicted to cocaine or heroin. Equally sobering was the connection between the drug subculture and the street gangs terrorizing inner cities across the country. Like Reagan before him, Bush chose to focus on arrests and interdiction, which failed to address the basic question: why were so many young people attracted by illegal drugs? The answer involved many factors, but the disproportionate incidence of drug and alcohol abuse among poor people pointed to the culture of poverty as a primary culprit.

PERSISTENT POVERTY The United States had clearly lost its thirty-year war on poverty. Among whites, high rates of rural poverty persisted. In addition, the relocation of industries and factories from the Northeast and Midwest to the "Sunbelt" states left behind a "Rust Belt" of abandoned businesses and unemployed workers. Among minority groups, the culture of poverty was especially pervasive. In 1992, 10 percent of whites were classified as "poor," compared to 26 percent of Hispanics and 30 percent of blacks. More than 60 percent of all black children were born to unwed mothers (five times the rate for whites) and 23 percent of Hispanic families were headed by single women. Almost 40 percent of black male high school dropouts were unemployed. Only 4 percent of black males and 6 percent of black females attended college.

Most poverty-stricken Americans subsisted on government welfare checks and lived in rundown, crime-ridden government housing projects and deteriorating ghettos, what one black minister called America's "brand of apartheid." Moreover, by the 1980s it had become difficult to subsist on federal assistance because the value of welfare in real dollars had fallen steadily since the early 1970s. A government official observed that these inner-city dwellers made up a "caste of people almost totally dependent on the state, with little hope of breaking free." Those living amid such squalor and stunted hopes constituted both a tragic refutation of the American dream of upward mobility and a ticking time bomb of anger and frustration waiting to explode.

THE DEMOCRACY MOVEMENT ABROAD Bush entered the White House with more foreign policy experience than most presidents, and he found the spotlight of the world stage more congenial than wrestling with the intractable problems of the inner cities or the deficit. Within two years of his inauguration, George Bush would lead the United States into two wars, a record unequaled by any of his predecessors. Throughout most of 1989, however, he merely had to sit back and observe the dissolution of one totalitarian or authoritarian regime after another. For the first time in years, democracy was suddenly on the march in a sequence of mostly bloodless revolutions that took the world by surprise.

Although in China a suddenly risen democracy movement came to a tragic end in 1989, when government forces mounted a deadly assault on demonstrators in Beijing's (Peking's) Tiananmen Square, eastern Europe had an entirely different experience. Mikhail Gorbachev set events in motion by responding to Soviet economic problems with policies of *perestroika* (restructuring) and *glasnost* (openness), a loosening of central economic planning and censorship. His foreign policy sought rapprochement and trade with the West, to relieve the Soviet economy of burdensome military costs.

Gorbachev backed off from Soviet imperial ambitions. Early in 1989, Soviet troops left Afghanistan, after nine years bogged down in civil war there. Then in July, in Paris, Gorbachev repudiated the "Brezhnev Doctrine," which had asserted the right of the Soviet Union to intervene in the internal affairs of Communist countries. The days when Soviet tanks would roll through Warsaw and Prague were over, and hard-line leaders in the East-bloc countries found themselves beset by demands for democratic reform. With opposition strength building, the old regimes fell in rapid order, and with surprisingly little bloodshed. Communist party rule ended first in Poland and Hungary, then in hard-line Czechoslovakia and in Bulgaria. In Romania, the year of peaceful revolution ended in a bloodbath when the Romanian people were joined by the army in a bloody uprising against the brutal dictator Nicolae Ceausescu. He and his wife were captured, tried, and then executed on Christmas Day. But lacking experienced opposition leaders, as did all the eastern European countries, the new government fell under the control of members of the old Communist establishment.

The most spectacular event in the collapse of the Soviet empire in eastern Europe came on November 9, when the chief symbol of the cold war—the Berlin Wall—was torn down by Germans, and the East German government succumbed to popular pressures for change. With the borders to the West fully open, the Communist government of East Germany collapsed, a freely elected government followed, and on October 3, 1990, the five states of East Germany were united with West Germany. The reunified German nation remained in NATO, and the Warsaw Pact alliance was dissolved.

The democratic movement also reached other parts of the world. During 1990, the Communist party of Mongolia—a country strategically located on the borders of the Soviet Union and China—voted to

West Germans hacking away at the Berlin Wall on November 11, 1989, two days after all crossings between East and West Germany were opened.

give up its monopoly on power, and in Nicaragua, where the ruling Sandinista party avowed Marxism, President Daniel Ortega was defeated in a presidential election in February. Even in isolated Albania, the ruling party yielded to demands for a free election in 1991.

Democratic change overtook authoritarian regimes of a different stripe as well. In Chile, Augusto Pinochet, who had become military dictator in a bloody coup in 1973, yielded to a popular vote against continuing him in office, and was defeated in presidential elections in 1989. In South Africa, to which Congress had applied trade sanctions in protest of its apartheid (racial segregation) policies since 1986, a new prime minister, Frederik W. DeKlerk, came to office in 1989. In early 1990 he freed black nationalist Nelson Mandela, who had served twenty-seven years in prison, and he announced plans to abandon apartheid gradually. By early 1992 DeKlerk had pushed through a constitution ending apartheid and setting up procedures for the full integration of blacks into government and society.

The reform impulse that Gorbachev helped unleash in the East-bloc countries began to career out of control within the Soviet Union itself. Gorbachev proved unusually adept at political restructuring. While yielding to the Communist monopoly of government, he built a new presidential system that gave him, if anything, increased powers. His skills, however, did not extend to an antiquated economy that resisted change. The revival of old ethnic allegiances added to the instability. Although Russia proper included slightly over half the Soviet Union's population, it was only one of fifteen constituent republics, most of which began to seek autonomy, if not independence. Along the fringes of the Russian republic, to the west and south, lay a jigsaw puzzle of about a hundred nationalities and languages.

Gorbachev's popularity in the Soviet Union shrank as it grew abroad. It especially eroded among the Communist hardliners, who saw in his reforms the unraveling of their bureaucratic and political empire. On August 18, 1991, a cabal of political and military leaders suddenly tried to seize the reins of power. They accosted Gorbachev at his vacation retreat in the Crimea and demanded that he sign a decree proclaiming a state of emergency and transferring his powers to them. He replied: "Go to hell," whereupon he was placed under house arrest. Twelve hours later the Soviet news agency reported to the world that Gorbachev was "ill" and had temporarily transferred his powers to his vice-president and an eight-member emergency committee. Political parties were suspended, newspapers were silenced, a curfew was announced, and street demonstrations were banned. Tanks and armored vehicles surrounded strategic installations and government buildings in Moscow. The new leadership promised to end the "chaos and anarchy" they claimed were bedeviling the country.

But the coup was doomed from the start. Poorly planned and clumsily implemented, it lacked effective coordination. The plotters failed to arrest popular leaders such as Boris Yeltsin, the president of the Russian republic, and they neglected to close the airports or cut off telephone and television communications. Most important, the plotters failed to recognize the strength of the democratic idealism unleashed by Gorbachev's reforms. Upon learning of the attempted overthrow, tens of thousands of Muscovites poured into the streets outside Yeltsin's headquarters to act as human shields against efforts to arrest him. Three were killed in the process. Yeltsin himself clambered atop a menacing tank and publicly defied the conspirators, calling them a "gang of bandits."

As the drama unfolded in the Soviet Union, a crescendo of indignation welled up from foreign leaders around the world. On August 20 President Bush, after a day of indecision, responded favorably to Yeltsin's request for support and convinced world leaders to join him in refusing to recognize the legitimacy of the new Soviet government. Siberian coal miners went on strike to oppose the coup. The next day word began to seep out that the plotters had given up and were fleeing. Several committed suicide, and a newly released Gorbachev ordered the others arrested. But his freedom did not bring a restoration of his power. Yeltsin emerged as the most popular political figure in the country. Gorbachev reclaimed the title of president, but he was forced to resign as head of the Communist party and admit that he had made a grave mistake in appointing the men who had turned against him.

What began as a reactionary coup turned into a powerful accelerant for stunning new changes in the Soviet Union. No sooner had the plotters been arrested than most of the fifteen republics proclaimed their independence, with the Baltic republics of Latvia, Lithuania, and Estonia regaining the status of independent nations. The Communist party apparatus was dismantled, prompting celebrating crowds to topple statues of Lenin and other Communist heroes.

By the end of 1991, the Soviet Union had dissolved into a new—and fragile—Commonwealth of Independent States made up of twelve autonomous republics. Held together by little other than historic ties and contiguous borders, the federated republics soon suffered out-breaks of ethnic tensions and separatist movements. For his part, Mikhail Gorbachev found himself out of a job. With the Communist party dissolved, the Soviet Union dismantled, and continuing economic woes raising objections to his leadership, Gorbachev resigned as presi-dent at the end of 1991. Yeltsin, now a national hero, replaced him. The democratic reforms Gorbachev had set in motion to save the Union of Soviet Socialist Republics proved inadequate to the task.

The aborted coup accelerated Soviet and American efforts to reduce the stockpiles of nuclear weapons. In 1991 President Bush stunned the world by announcing that the United States would destroy all its tacti-cal nuclear weapons on land and at sea in Europe and Asia, take its long-range bombers off twenty-four-hour alert status, and initiate dis-cussions with the Soviet Union for the purpose of instituting sharp cuts in ICBMs with multiple warheads. Bush explained that the prospect of a Soviet invasion of Western Europe was "no longer a realistic threat," and this presented an unprecedented opportunity for reducing the threat of nuclear holocaust. The Soviets responded by announcing reci-procal cutbacks. As Joint Chiefs of Staff Chairman Colin Powell re-marked, the cold war "has vaporized before our eyes."

The dilution of the Soviet military threat led the Defense Depart-ment in 1992 to withdraw large numbers of military personnel from bases in Asia and Europe. The Pentagon also announced a plan to shrink the armed forces by 500,000 troops over the next five years. In 1992 Bush and Yeltsin announced their intention to reduce their com-bined arsenals of nuclear weapons from about 22,500 to no more than 7,000 by the year 2003. All land-based multiple-warhead missiles would be destroyed. "The world is becoming a friendlier place," noted one industry analyst.

PANAMA The end of the cold war did not, however, spell the end of international tensions and conflicts. Indeed, in some respects the world was more unstable. Before the end of 1989, American troops were en-gaged in battle in Panama, where General Manuel Noriega, as chief of the Panamanian Defense Forces since 1983, was head of the government in fact if not in title. Years earlier, Noriega had worked secretly with the CIA, providing information about developments in Central America. At the same time, however, he got involved in the lucrative—and illegal—drug trade. In 1988, federal grand juries in Miami and Tampa, Florida, indicted him and fifteen others on charges of international drug smuggling, gun running, and laundering the money through Panamanian banks.

In 1989 Panama's National Assembly named Noriega head of the government and proclaimed that Panama "is declared to be in a state of war" with the United States. The next day, December 16, 1989, four off-duty American servicemen were stopped at a roadblock and one marine was shot and killed. President Bush responded by ordering an invasion of Panama to capture Noriega for trial on the American indictments and installing a government headed by opposition leaders.

The 12,000 American military personnel in Panama were quickly joined by 12,000 more, and in the early morning of December 20, five military task forces struck at strategic targets in the country. They quickly disabled and seized the headquarters of the Panamanian Defense Forces, but Noriega vanished. Resistance collapsed when Noriega took refuge in the Vatican Embassy on Christmas Eve. After intense negotiations, Noriega surrendered to American forces a week later. Twenty-three American servicemen were killed in the action, and estimates of Panamanians killed and wounded ranged up to 4,000, including many civilians caught in the crossfire. Noriega was detained in a U.S. federal jail well over a year after his surrender, before his trial began in late 1991. He was convicted in 1992 on eight counts of racketeering and drug distribution.

THE GULF WAR Months after Panama had moved to the background of public attention, Saddam Hussein, dictator of Iraq, focused attention on the Middle East when his army suddenly fell upon his tiny, wealthy neighbor Kuwait on August 2, 1990. Kuwait had raised its production of oil contrary to agreements with the Organization of Petroleum Exporting Countries (OPEC). The resulting drop in oil prices offended Saddam, deep in debt and heavily dependent on oil revenues. Complaining of "economic aggression" against Iraq, he demanded that Kuwait reduce its oil production and, with Saudi Arabia, cancel Iraqi debts of $30 million.

Saddam did not expect the firestorm of world indignation he ignited. The U.N. Security Council quickly voted 14–0 to condemn the invasion and demand withdrawal. American secretary of state James Baker and Soviet foreign minister Eduard Shevardnadze issued a joint statement of condemnation. The Security Council then endorsed Resolution 661, an embargo on trade with Iraq, by a vote of 13–0, with Cuba and Yemen abstaining. Such unanimity, of course, would have been unlikely during the cold war.

On August 2, President Bush condemned Iraq's "naked aggression" and said he was not ruling out any options. On August 6–7, the United States dispatched planes and troops to Saudi Arabia on a "wholly defensive" mission—to protect Saudi Arabia. British forces soon joined in, as did Arab troops from a half dozen nations. On August 22, Bush ordered the mobilization of American reserve forces for the operation dubbed "Desert Shield."

On November 8, Bush announced that he was doubling American forces in the Middle East from about 200,000 to 400,000, to build up "an adequate offensive military capability." Bush asserted that he already had authority to take such action under the Security Council resolutions. Bush's position was strengthened on November 29 by U.N. Resolution 678, which authorized the use of force to dislodge Iraq from Kuwait, and set a deadline for Iraqi withdrawal of January 15, 1991.

A flurry of peace efforts sent diplomats scurrying all over, but without result. Saddam refused to yield. On January 10, Congress began to debate authorizing the use of U.S. armed forces. The outcome was uncertain to the end, but on January 12 a resolution for the use of force passed the House by 250–183, and the Senate by 52–47.

By January 1991, a twenty-eight-nation allied force was committed to Operation Desert Storm when the first missiles and planes began to hit Iraq at about 2:30 A.M., January 17, Baghdad time. With the allies in control of the air from the beginning, Saddam's only recourse was to fire off lumbering Soviet-made SCUD missiles, which he aimed from the first day into Israel with the hope of provoking Israeli retaliation and undermining the coalition against him. But the damage and casualties were light, and the Israelis showed remarkable restraint in the face of the continuing attacks. The Iraqis responded with desperate moves, which did more damage to the environment than to enemy forces: releasing oil into the Persian Gulf from tankers and loading platforms in Kuwait—and setting fire to hundreds of Kuwaiti oil wells.

U.S. tanks face a burning Kuwaiti oil well, which was set on fire by desperate retreating Iraqi troops.

Saddam concentrated his forces in Kuwait, expecting an allied attack northward into Kuwait. But the Iraqis were outflanked when 200,000 allied troops, largely American, British, and French, vanished with much of their heavy armor and turned up on the undefended border with Saudi Arabia 100–200 miles to the west. The allied ground assault began on February 24, and lasted only four days. Thousands of Iraqi soldiers surrendered, and there was a quick breakthrough into Kuwait.

On February 28, six weeks after the fighting began, President Bush called for a cease-fire, the Iraqis accepted, and the shooting ended. American fatalities were 137. The lowest estimate of Iraqi fatalities, civilian and military, was around 100,000. The coalition forces occupied about one-fifth of Iraq. The Persian Gulf War, the "mother of all battles," in Saddam Hussein's words, had been intense and deadly and had left consequences to be played out far into the future. Yet, despite all the destruction, Saddam Hussein remained in power.

The Middle East, as it had for centuries, resisted any quick fix. The Persian Gulf War was far from a reprise of Vietnam, but it ended with what conceivably could turn into a longer hangover. There was an understanding that the United States would maintain a military presence in the Persian Gulf. It was, ironically, an American missionary who said to one of the British planners carving up the former Ottoman territory after World War I: "You are flying in the face of four millenniums of history." The words retain their haunting quality.

MAKING CONNECTIONS

- As the chapter title indicates, much of what happened in the 1980s, from economic and social policy to presidential leadership style, was reminiscent of the late nineteenth century. The chapter also draws parallels between the 1980s and the 1920s and 1950s.

- Another parallel between the late nineteenth century and the 1980s was a rise in immigration and a change in immigration patterns. This is discussed in the next chapter.

- Chapter 36 shows how the economic and political conservatism of the 1980s became much more ideological in the early 1990s.

FURTHER READING

It is too early for a definitive scholarly analysis of the Reagan administration, but two brief accounts are David Mervin's *Ronald Reagan and the American Presidency* (1990) and Michael Schaller's *Reckoning with Reagan: America and Its President in the 1980s* (1992).

On Reaganomics, see David Stockman's *The Triumph of Politics: How the Reagan Revolution Failed* (1986) and Robert Lekachman's *Greed Is Not Enough: Reaganomics* (1982). On the issue of arms control, see Strobe Talbott's *Deadly Gambits: The Reagan Administration and the Stalemate in Nuclear Arms Control* (1984).

For Reagan's foreign policy in Central America, see James Chace's *Endless War: How We Got Involved in Central America and What Can Be Done* (1984) and Walter LaFeber's *Inevitable Revolutions. The United States in Central America* (2nd ed., 1993). Insider views of Reagan's foreign policy are offered in Alexander M. Haig, Jr.'s *Caveat: Realism, Reagan, and Foreign Policy* (1984) and Caspar W. Weinberger's *Fighting for Peace: Seven Critical Years in the Pentagon* (1990).

On Reagan's second term, see Jane Mayer and Doyle McManus's

Landslide: The Unmaking of the President, 1984–1988 (1988). For a masterful work on the Iran-Contra Affair, see Theodore Draper's *A Very Thin Line: The Iran Contra Affair* (1991). Several collections of essays include varying assessments of the Reagan years. Among these are *The Reagan Revolution* (1988), edited by B. B. Kymlicka and Jean V. Matthews; *The Reagan Presidency: An Incomplete Revolution* (1990), edited by Dilys M. Hill, et al.; and *Looking Back on the Reagan Presidency* (1990), edited by Larry Berman.

On the 1988 campaign see Jack Germond and Jules Witcover's *Whose Broad Stripes and Bright Stars? The Trivial Pursuit of the Presidency, 1988* (1989) and Sidney Blumenthal's *Pledging Allegiance: The Last Campaign of the Cold War* (1990). Major issues in economic and social policy are addressed in Robert Reich's *The Work of Nations: Preparing Ourselves for Twenty-first Century Capitalism* (1991) and William Julius Wilson's *The Truly Disadvantaged: The Inner City, the Underclass, and Public Policy* (1987).

On the banking and other scandals, see L. William Seidman's *Full Faith and Credit: The Great S & L Debacle and Other Washington Sagas* (1993). The onset and growth of the AIDS epidemic are traced in *And the Band Played On: Politics, People, and the AIDS Epidemic* (1987) by Randy Shilts, a journalist who reported much of the story, and in essays edited by historians Elizabeth Fee and Daniel M. Fox, *AIDS: The Burdens of History* (1988) and *AIDS: The Making of a Chronic Disease* (1992).

For further treatment of the end of the cold war, see Michael K. Beschloss's *At the Highest Levels: The Inside Story of the End of the Cold War* (1993), Thomas J. McCormick's *America's Half Century: United States Foreign Policy in the Cold War and After* (2nd ed., 1995), Richard Crockatt's *The Fifty Years War: The United States and the Soviet Union in World Politics, 1941–1991* (1995), and Zbigniew Brzezinski's *Out of Control: Global Turmoil on the Eve of the Twenty-first Century* (1994).

On the Panama and Persian Gulf conflicts, see Edward W. Flanagan's *Battle for Panama: Inside Operation Just Cause* (1993), Bruce W. Jentleson's *With Friends Like These: Reagan, Bush, and Saddam, 1982–1990* (1994), and Lester H. Brune's *America and the Iraqi Crisis, 1990–1992: Origins and Aftermath* (1993).

36 CULTURAL POLITICS

CHAPTER ORGANIZER

This chapter focuses on:

- demographic patterns from the 1990 census and the "new immigrants" of the 1980s and 1990s.

- the Democratic resurgence of the early 1990s; the Republican landslide of 1994; and the Contract with America.

- the remarkable performance of the economy and stock market during the 1990s.

- the revelations of scandal in the Clinton White House that recall earlier sexual escapades during the Harding administration.

D uring the 1980s and 1990s, various cultural and political developments combined to transform American society and institutions. The makeup of the population shifted as the baby-boomers reached middle age. Immigrants to America were now primarily from Asia and Latin America rather than from Europe. In the 1980s and 1990s, the political landscape also began to be transformed, as many conservative politicians won election to local, state, and federal government offices, and many conservative judges were appointed or elected to the courts. In response to the resurgence of conservatism, the Democratic party began to moderate its liberal activism and promote a "moderate" or "centrist" stance. In an effort to become more productive and competitive, American businesses embraced new technology and engaged in "reengineering" efforts that often brought widespread job cuts. As corporations began to downsize, people began to lose faith in company loyalty and job security. At the same time, a backlash against racial preferences created new social tensions. Whites in large numbers began to argue that affirmative action was limiting their access to the nation's colleges and business contracts. They supported a balanced budget, feared for their jobs, and yearned for an end to corruption in government and a revival of "traditional" moral values.

AMERICA'S CHANGING FACE

DEMOGRAPHIC SHIFTS During the 1980s, the nation's population grew by 10 percent, or some 23 million people, boosting the total to almost 250 million. The median age of the quarter-billion Americans rose from thirty to thirty-three, and the much-discussed baby-boom generation—the 43 million people born between 1946 and 1964—entered middle age. Because of its disproportionate size, the baby-boom generation magnifies changes in American society as it moves through the life cycle. As one demographer noted, it resembles a "pig in a python." This generation's maturation and its preoccupation with practical concerns such as raising families, paying for college, and buying houses helped explain the surge of political conservatism during the 1980s. Surveys revealed that baby-boomers wanted stronger family and religious ties and a greater respect for authority. Yet having come to maturity during the turbulent sixties and early seventies, the baby-boomers also displayed more tolerance of social and cultural diversity than their parents.

During the last quarter of the twentieth century, the "Sunbelt" states of the South and West continued to lure residents from the Midwest and Northeast. Fully 90 percent of the nation's total population growth during the 1980s occurred in southern or western states. California gained more people than any other state during the eighties, boosting its total to 30 million, 5 million more than in 1980. Texas and Florida each added more than 3 million new residents, while West Virginia, Iowa, and the District of Columbia experienced a net loss of residents. The Northeast became the least populous region of the country. These population shifts forced a massive redistricting of the House of Representatives, with Florida and California gaining three more seats each and Texas two, while states such as New York lost seats.

Americans in the 1980s tended to settle in large communities. Almost 90 percent of the decade's population growth occurred in large metropolitan areas. In 1990 some 78 percent of the population lived in a metropolitan area, and for the first time, a majority of Americans lived in cities of a million or more people. This move to the cities largely reflected trends in the job market, as the "postindustrial" economy continued to shift from manufacturing to professional service industries, particularly those specializing in telecommunications and information processing. By 1990 fewer than 5 million people out of a total population of 250 million—or 2 percent—lived on farms.

Women continued to enter the workforce in large numbers. Indeed, one of the most significant sociological developments since 1970 was the accelerated entry of women into the world of work outside the home. In 1970, 38 percent of the workforce was female; in 1990 the figure was almost 50 percent. Women workers accounted for 60 percent of labor force growth since 1980, and fully 58 percent of all adult women were gainfully employed. A third of the new medical doctors during the eighties were women (4 percent in 1970); 40 percent of new lawyers were female (8.4 percent in 1970); and 23 percent of new dentists were women (less than 1 percent in 1970).

The decline of the traditional family unit—two parents with children—continued during the 1980s. The proportion of the nation's households in that category dropped from 31 percent in 1980 to 26 percent in 1990. And more people were living alone than ever before, largely as a result of high divorce rates or a growing practice of delaying marriage until well into the twenties. One out of every four households in 1990 was made up of a person living alone, a 26 percent increase over 1980. The number of single mothers increased 35 percent during the decade. The rate was much higher for African Americans: in 1990 less than 38 percent of black children lived with both parents, down from 67 percent in 1960.

Young blacks burdened by the absence of one or both parents faced shrinking economic opportunities in the 1980s. The 1990 census documented a slight rise in the proportion of Americans living in poverty but a substantially heightened inequality in the distribution of income. By 1992, roughly 14.5 percent of the American people were living at or below the official poverty level, pegged at $14,335 in annual income for a family of four. The urban poor were particularly victimized by high rates of crime and violence, with young black males suffering the most. In 1990 the leading cause of death among black males between the ages of fifteen and twenty-four was homicide. Twenty-five percent of black males aged twenty to twenty-nine were in prison, on parole, or on probation, while only 4 percent were enrolled in college. Forty percent of black adult males were functionally illiterate.

THE NEW IMMIGRANTS The racial and ethnic composition of the country also changed rapidly during the 1980s, with nearly one in every four Americans claiming African, Asian, Hispanic, or American Indian

Increased numbers of Chinese risked their money and their lives trying to gain entry into the United States. These illegal immigrants from China are trying to keep warm after being captured when the freighter carrying them to the United States ran aground in Rockaway, New York City.

ancestry. Among an overall population of 250 million, blacks represented 12 percent of the total, Hispanics 9 percent, Asians about 3 percent, and American Indians almost 1 percent. The rate of increase among those four groups was twice as fast as it had been during the 1970s.

The primary cause of this dramatic change in the nation's ethnic mix was a surge of immigration. During the 1980s, legal immigration into the United States totaled over 7 million people, 30 percent higher than the previous decade and more than in any other decade except 1901–1910. These figures do not include the hundreds of thousands of illegal aliens, mostly Mexicans and Haitians. In 1990 the United States welcomed more than twice as many immigrants as all other countries in the world combined.

Even more significant than the overall number of newcomers were their places of origin. For the first time in the nation's history, the majority of immigrants came not from Europe but from other parts of the world. The percentage of European immigrants to the United States declined from 53 percent of the total in the 1950s to 12 percent in the 1980s and 1990s. Asian Americans were the fastest-growing segment of the population in the eighties, with their numbers increasing by 80 percent, a rate seven times as great as the general population. Among the legal immigrants during the decade, Mexicans made up the largest share, averaging about 60,000 a year. The second-highest number came from the Philippines (46,000), while immigrants from mainland China, Taiwan, and Hong Kong totaled 45,000 annually. The next largest groups were Vietnamese and Koreans, followed by Dominicans, Asian Indians, Jamaicans, Iranians, Cubans, Cambodians, and Laotians.

Heightening the social impact of these new immigrants was their tendency to cluster in a handful of states and cities. Most of them gravitated to New York, Illinois, and New Jersey, as well as Florida. Texas, Hawaii, California, and other Sunbelt states. By 1990, California had 64 percent of the Asian Americans in the country and 34 percent of the Hispanics. The population of Miami, Florida, was 64 percent Hispanic, and San Antonio, Texas, boasted 55 percent. Los Angeles contained 2 million Mexican Americans.

The wave of new immigration brought rising conflict between old and new ethnicities. African-American leaders worried that the newcomers were gaining an economic foothold at the expense of poor blacks. And many native whites resented the influx of newcomers into their communities. In 1992 a riot in Los Angeles saw poor blacks and Hispanics loot and destroy stores owned by Asians and whites.

Such reactions recall earlier chapters in American immigrant history, a story marked from the start by ambivalence about the nation's tradition of inclusiveness. With rhetoric reminiscent of the nativist movement a century earlier, critics of the new tide of immigration charged that America was being "overrun" with foreigners; they questioned whether Hispanics and Asians could be "assimilated" into American culture. In 1994 a large majority of California voters approved Proposition 187, a controversial initiative that denied the state's estimated 4 million illegal immigrants access to public schools, nonemergency health care, and other social services. It also required teachers, doctors, and government officials to report anyone suspected of being an undocumented immigrant. Proponents of the new measure claimed it would save taxpayers billions of dollars. Critics labeled Proposition 187 racist in motive and effect. Yet the backlash against the new immigration continued. In 1998 California voters passed a referendum ending bilingual education.

The bitter irony of this new nativism was that it targeted recent immigrants for bringing with them to the United States virtues long prized by Americans—hope, energy, persistence, and an aggressive work ethic.

RESIDENT POPULATION DISTRIBUTION FOR THE UNITED
STATES BY RACE AND ETHNIC ORIGIN: 1980 AND 1990

	1980		1990		
	Number	%	Number	%	Change
Total population	**226,545,805**	**100.0**	**248,709,873**	**100.0**	**9.8**
White	188,371,622	83.1	199,686,070	80.3	6.0
Black	26,495,025	11.7	29,986,060	12.1	13.2
American Indian, Eskimo, or Aleut	1,420,400	0.6	1,959,234	0.8	37.9
Asian or Pacific Islander	3,500,439	1.5	7,273,662	2.9	107.8
Other race	6,758,319	3.0	9,804,847	3.9	45.1
Hispanic origin	14,608,673	6.4	22,354,059	9.0	53.0

Source: U.S. Bureau of the Census, 1991.

IMMIGRANTS ADMITTED BY TOP 15 COUNTRIES OF BIRTH IN FISCAL YEAR 1990

Country of Birth	1990
Total	**656,111**
Mexico	56,549
Philippines	54,907
Vietnam	48,662
Dominican Republic	32,064
Korea	29,548
China (mainland)	28,746
India	28,679
Soviet Union	25,350
Jamaica	18,828
Iran	18,031
Taiwan	13,839
United Kingdom	13,730
Canada	13,717
Poland	13,334
Haiti	11,862
Other	248,265

Source: U.S. Immigration and Naturalization Service, 1991.

Like most of their predecessors who had braved tremendous hardships to make their way to America, the new immigrants toiled long and hard for a share of the American dream, and most economic studies concluded that their presence was beneficial to the nation. They created more wealth than they consumed, and many of them compiled an astonishing record of achievement. The median household income of Asian Americans, for example, exceeded every other group, including native whites, and Asian Americans were disproportionately represented in the nation's most prestigious colleges and universities. Although constituting only 1.6 percent of the total population in 1985, Asian Americans made up over 11 percent of Harvard's freshman class and almost 20 percent at Berkeley and the California Institute of Technology. Yet the very success of the new immigrants contributed to the resentment they encountered from other groups.

THE COMPUTER REVOLUTION Not only were demographic shifts and immigration changing the face of America but technological changes were also transforming the nation. A surge in productivity and prosperity during the 1980s and 1990s resulted from a dramatic revolution in information technology. Cellular phones, laser printers, VCRs, fax machines, and personal computers became commonplace at work and in homes. The computer age had arrived.

The idea of a programmable machine that would rapidly perform mental tasks had been around since the eighteenth century, but it took the crisis atmosphere of World War II to gather the intellectual and financial resources needed to create such a "computer." Funding during the war had enabled a team of engineers at the University of Pennsylvania to create ENIAC (Electronic Numerical Integrator and Computer), the first all-purpose, all-electronic digital computer. Unveiled in 1944, it could perform 5,000 operations per second. ENIAC, however, was so large that it was almost impractical. It took up 3,000 cubic feet of space and included 18,000 vacuum tubes (glass canisters designed to amplify electrical current), 70,000 resistors, 10,000 capacitors, and 6,000 switches. This first new computer was not only bulky; it had too little memory storage, too many tubes, and too lengthy programming.

During the 1950s and 1960s, corporations (such as International Business Machines—IBM) and government agencies transformed

The Electronic Numerical Integrator and Computer (ENIAC), 1946. *Developed for the army, the ENIAC was cumbersome but could perform complex calculations in minutes.*

computers from being mathematical calculators to electronic data-processing machines. The key development in facilitating such a transformation occurred in 1947 when three physicists at Bell Laboratories in central New Jersey invented the transistor (so named because it *trans*fers electric current across a re*sistor,* which is a conductor used to control voltage in an electrical circuit). Transistors took the place of the much larger and more fragile, glass vacuum tubes. Like the vacuum tube, the transistor could amplify an electric signal. Unlike the vacuum tube, however, transistors were cheap, durable, required less power and, as future research would demonstrate, they could be made almost infinitely tiny. The availability of transistors led to the development of hearing aids and portable radios.

They also led to faster and more reliable, smaller and less expensive, mainframe computers. These "second-generation" computers were ten times as fast as the early computers, but programming remained slow, requiring the use of punch cards fed into the machines. The next major breakthrough was the invention in 1971 of the microprocessor—literally a computer on a silicon chip. The functions that had once been performed by computers taking up an entire room could now be performed by a microchip circuit the size of a postage stamp. Microchips were incorporated into television sets, wristwatches, automobiles, kitchen appliances, and the spacecraft being developed by NASA.

The use of such microchips enabled computers not only to be smaller but also cheaper. These "third-generation" computers were so much faster that a new word had to be created to measure their processing speeds: *nanoseconds* (billionths of a second). High-performance computers heightened efficiency throughout the American economy and helped fuel an information revolution that affected virtually every aspect of life.

The invention of the microchip made possible the idea of a personal computer. In 1975, an engineer named Ed Roberts made the first prototype of a "personal computer." The Altair 8800, which cost $397, was imperfect and cumbersome, with no display, no keyboard, and not enough memory to do anything useful. But its potential excited a young Harvard sophomore named Bill Gates. He was a self-described "computer nerd," a student lacking in social skills and addicted to computing, willing to skip his classes in order to work night and day on programming projects. Gates offered his software programming services for the Altair 8800 and formed a new company called Microsoft. By 1977 he and others had helped to transform the personal computer from a hobby machine to a mass consumer product. In 1986 Gates became a billionaire at the age of thirty-one.

The infant personal computer industry soared into the 1980s, offering word processing, games, and perhaps most important, the capacity to calculate financial spreadsheets. This last feature convinced the corporate community that personal computers could indeed become a mass production commodity. By the end of the decade, there were 60 million personal computers in the United States, and people began to talk about an "information superhighway," a worldwide network of linked computers and databases connected by fiber-optic lines that facilitated high-speed transmission. "We're all connected," declared a telephone company commercial.

During the 1990s, the development of the Internet and electronic mail enabled anyone with a personal computer and modem the opportunity to travel on the information superhighway. Such advances had the effect of shrinking the globe and facilitating almost instantaneous

Students at Mansfield University in Pennsylvania work on laptop computers in the school library. Rapid developments in technology have made computers, e-mail, and the Internet readily accessible and affordable.

communication across the continents. Yet those too poor to gain easy access to the information revolution faced a bleak future. To the extent that computers had become essential tools for educational and economic success, they threatened to widen the gap between rich and poor. As always, it seems, technological progress has provided uneven benefits.

CULTURAL CONSERVATISM

Fearing the transformations in the nation's population, technology, and values, dogmatic cultural conservatives helped elect Ronald Reagan and George Bush in the 1980s, but they were disappointed in the results. Once in office, neither president had, in their eyes, adequately addressed their moral agenda, including a complete ban on abortions and the restoration of prayer in public schools. By the 1990s, a new generation of young conservative activists, mostly political independents or Republicans, emerged as a force to be reckoned with in national affairs. They were more ideological, more libertarian, more partisan, and more impatient than their predecessors.

ATTACKS ON LIBERALISM The new breed of conservatives abhorred the excesses of cultural and political liberalism. They lamented the disappearance of basic forms of decency and propriety, and believed that fundamental liberties were at risk. They especially attacked affirmative action programs designed to redress historic injustices against women and minorities. During the 1990s, powerful groups inside and outside the Republican party mobilized to roll back government programs giving preferences to specified social groups. Prominent black conservatives supported such efforts, arguing that racially based preferences were condescending remedies that demeaned their beneficiaries. They argued that preferential government treatment of African Americans raised doubts in the minds of both blacks and whites about the inherent worth of any black achievement.

THE RELIGIOUS RIGHT Although quite diverse, cultural conservatives tended to be evangelical Christians or orthodox Catholics who joined together to exert increasing pressure on the political process. In 1989 the television evangelist Pat Robertson organized the Christian Coalition to replace Jerry Falwell's Moral Majority as the flagship organization of the resurgent religious right. The Christian Coalition encouraged religious conservatives to vote, run for public office, and support only those candidates who shared the organization's views.

With a well-organized grassroots movement in every state, the Christian Coalition chose the Republican party as the best vehicle for transforming its pro-family campaign into new public policies. It encouraged its supporters to withhold political support from any candidate who did not provide an ironclad promise to support the Coalition's school prayer, anti-abortion, anti–gay rights positions. In addition to promoting "traditional family values," it urged politicians to "radically downsize and delimit government."

As a centrist professional politician, George Bush initially tried to keep the cultural conservatives at arm's length, only to find himself the target—and victim—of their in-your-face attacks and take-no-prisoners tenacity. His Democratic successor, Bill Clinton, also underestimated the growing strength of organized groups such as the Christian Coalition. In the 1994 congressional elections, religious conservatives went to the polls in record numbers, and 70 percent of them voted Republican tickets. A third of the voters identified themselves as "white, evangelical, born-again Christians." In many respects, they took control of the political and social agendas in the nineties. As one journalist acknowledged in 1995, "the religious right is moving toward center stage in American secular life."

Bush to Clinton

For months after the Gulf War, President George Bush seemed unbeatable. In the polls his approval rating rose to 91 percent. But the aftermath of Desert Storm was mixed, with Saddam Hussein's grip on Iraq still intact. Despite his image of strength abroad, the president began to look weak even on foreign policy. The Soviet Union meanwhile stumbled on to its surprising end. On December 25, 1991, the Soviet flag over the Kremlin was replaced by the flag of the Russian Federation. The cold war had ended with not just the collapse but the dismemberment of the Soviet Union into its fifteen constituent republics. As a result, the United States was now the world's only superpower.

"Containment" of the Soviet Union, the bedrock of American foreign policy for more than four decades, had lost its reason for being. Bush, the ultimate cold war careerist—ambassador to the U.N., envoy to China, head of the CIA, vice-president under Reagan—struggled to interpret the fluid new international scene. He spoke of a "New World Order" but never defined it. By his own admission he had trouble with the "vision thing." The international situation, in fact, did not lend itself to a simple vision—unless the answer was to drift into isolation, a great temptation, with foreign dangers seemingly lessened.

RECESSION AND DOWNSIZING In 1988, a few days after George Bush was elected president, a journalist observed that the most important issue facing the new administration was the nation's deepening financial debt. "It is the issue that probably will determine the fate of the President. Indeed, it could also be his ultimate undoing."

It was an accurate prediction. For the Bush administration and for the nation, the most devastating development in the early nineties was a prolonged economic recession that began in 1990. The first economic setback in more than eight years, it grew into the longest, if not the deepest, since the Great Depression. By early 1992, over 2 million jobs had dried up. During 1991, 25 million workers—about 20 percent of the labor force—were unemployed at some time.

What made this recession unusual was that its victims included large numbers of white-collar workers. In 1991, for instance, General Motors, Xerox, and IBM cut 100,000 salaried employees from their payrolls. In the corporate world, terms such as "restructuring" and "downsizing" ruled the day. Companies began reducing personnel, switching employees to part-time status to reduce their benefits, and finding other ways to cut labor costs.

Prosperity gave way to firings, growing unemployment, declining sales and profits, the continuing imbalance in foreign trade, and the lack of a plan for the demobilization of the military-industrial complex after the cold war. With soaring expenditures on defense and social entitlement programs, a $150 billion annual deficit had become a $450 billion shortfall during 1991.

Some critics with a historical bent compared Bush to Hoover: both presidents and their aides initially denied that there was a problem with the economy and then assured the nation that the recession would be short and self-correcting. The euphoria over the allied victory in the Gulf War quickly gave way to anxiety and resentment generated by the depressed economy. At the end of 1991, *Time* magazine declared that "no one, not even George Bush" could deny "that the economy was sputtering." With his domestic policies in disarray and his foreign policy abandoned, George Bush tried a clumsy balancing act in addressing the recession, on the one hand acknowledging that "people are hurting" while on the other urging Americans that "this is a good time to buy a car."

THOMAS HEARINGS AND THE WOMEN'S MOVEMENT Other developments affected the president's popularity, among them the retirement in 1991 of the first black Supreme Court justice, Thurgood Marshall, after twenty-four years on the bench. To succeed him Bush named Clarence Thomas, a black federal judge who had been raised in poverty in the segregated South and educated in Catholic schools. After graduating from Yale Law School, Thomas had worked as an aide to a Republican senator before serving as chairman of the Equal Employment Opportunity Commission (EEOC) from 1982 to 1990. Then, after sixteen months on the U.S. Court of Appeals, he was tapped for the Supreme Court.

Thomas's views delighted conservative senators. He questioned the wisdom of the minimum wage, school busing for desegregation, and affirmative action hiring programs, and he preached "black self-help," once declaring that all civil rights leaders ever did was "bitch, bitch, bitch, moan, and whine."

Such opinions promised trouble in the Democratic Senate, but the real explosion occurred when Anita Hill, a soft-spoken law professor at the University of Oklahoma, charged that Thomas had sexually harassed her when she worked for him at the EEOC. Pro-Thomas senators orchestrated an often savage and sometimes absurd cross-examination of Hill. Some accused her of mental instability. An indignant Thomas denied her charges and called the hearings a "high-tech lynching for uppity blacks." He implied that Hill had fabricated the charges at the behest of civil rights groups determined to thwart his confirmation.

The televised hearings revealed that either Hill or Thomas had lied, and the committee's tie vote reflected the doubt: seven to recommend confirmation and seven against. The full Senate then narrowly confirmed Thomas by a 52–48 margin.

The Thomas hearings sparked a new surge in the women's movement. Anita Hill's rough treatment at the hands of male senators revitalized feminism as an organized political movement. As early as 1975, Betty Friedan had broken away from the National Organization for Women (NOW), the organization she had started less than a decade before, claiming that its radical leaders had abandoned the core constituency of working women. By 1992 many claimed that NOW had reached a dead end. Columnist Sally Quinn charged that "many women have come to see the feminist movement as anti-male, anti-child, anti-family, anti-feminine. And therefore it has nothing to do with us."

In the ambiguous aftermath of the Thomas hearings, many women grew incensed at the treatment of Hill, and an unprecedented number of women ran for national and local offices in 1992. The Thomas confirmation struggle thus widened the gender gap for a Republican party already less popular with women than with men. As one political commentator put it: "The war with Anita Hill was not a war Bush needed."

REPUBLICAN TURMOIL The president had already set a political trap for himself when he declared in his 1988 convention address: "Read my lips. No new taxes!" Fourteen months into his term, he decided that the deficit was a greater risk than violating his "no tax" pledge. After intense negotiations with congressional Democrats, Bush announced that reducing the federal deficit required "tax revenue increases." He did not exactly say "new taxes," but as one House Democrat put it, "the charade is over." Bush's backsliding set off a revolt among House Republicans, but a bipartisan majority (most Republicans opposing) finally approved a tax measure raising the top personal rate from 28 to 31 percent, disallowing certain deductions to the upper brackets, and raising various excises. Conservative Republicans would not let George Bush forget his abandoned pledge.

Social issues had been one of the adhesives in the Reagan coalition, keeping the focus away from divisive economic issues, but as hardships crowded in on the attention of blue-collar workers, the economy surged to the fore. Moreover, social issues strengthened the force of the new "Christian Right" and grated on traditional Republicans. Reagan had been adept at exploiting moral issues, especially abortion, while doing little or nothing about them in practice. Bush's efforts to talk up such issues eventually ran out of control when right-wing militants seized the podium and the attention of the TV cameras at the 1992 convention. One television evangelist, for example, insisted that the proposed Equal Rights Amendment represented "a socialist, anti-family, political movement that encourages women to leave their husbands, kill their children, practice witchcraft, destroy capitalism and become lesbians."

DEMOCRATIC RESURGENCE   In contrast to such strident rhetoric, the Democrats presented an image of moderate forces in control. For several years, the Democratic Leadership Council (DLC), in which Arkansas governor William Jefferson Clinton figured prominently, had pushed the party toward a more centrist outlook. A graduate of Georgetown University, Clinton had won a Rhodes scholarship to Oxford, and then earned a law degree from Yale, where he met and married Hillary Rodham. By 1979, at age thirty-two, he was back in his native Arkansas as the youngest governor in the country. He served three more terms as governor and in the process emerged as a dynamic young leader within the national Democratic party, which was committed to winning back the middle-class white voters who had voted Republican during the eighties. Democrats had grown so liberal, he argued, that they had alienated their key constituencies.

A self-described moderate, Clinton promised to cut the defense budget, provide tax relief for the middle class, and create a massive economic aid package for the former republics of the Soviet Union. He was less precise about how such initiatives would be funded. Handsome, witty, intelligent, and a compelling speaker, Clinton reminded many political observers of John F. Kennedy.

Underneath the veneer of Clinton's charisma, however, were several flaws. He often seemed so determined to become president that he was willing to sacrifice consistency and principle. He made extensive use of polls to shape his stance on issues, pandered to special-interest groups, and flip-flopped on controversial issues, leading critics to label him "Slick Willie." Even more enticing to the media and more embarrassing to Clinton were salacious reports that he was a chronic adulterer and that he had manipulated the ROTC program during the Vietnam War to avoid the draft. Clinton's denials of both allegations could not dispel a lingering distrust of his personal character.

After a series of bruising party primaries, Clinton emerged as the front-runner by the time of the Democratic nominating convention in the summer of 1992. The Clinton forces dominated the convention, where Clinton chose Albert Gore, Jr., of Tennessee as his running mate.

Flushed with their convention victory, sporting a ten-point lead in the polls, the Clinton-Gore team stressed economic issues to win over working-class white and black voters. This strategy worked. Exit polls on election day showed that the most important issue had been the economy. Clinton won with 370 electoral votes and about 43 percent of the popular vote; Bush had 168 electoral votes and 39 percent of the popular vote; and off-and-on independent candidate H. Ross Perot of Texas garnered 18 percent of the popular vote but no electoral votes. A feisty billionaire, Perot found a big audience for his simplified explanations of public problems and his offers to just "get under the hood and fix them." Yet during the Democratic convention, Perot withdrew, explaining that the party had "revitalized itself." Later he got back in the race as a third-party candidate and stayed for a surprisingly strong finish, one that suggested a widespread disillusionment with politics-as-usual.

DOMESTIC ISSUES

Once inaugurated and faced with the realities of governing, Clinton alienated many supporters when he reneged on several of his campaign promises. He abandoned his promised middle-class tax cut in order to keep down the federal deficit. When his attempt to allow professed homosexuals in the armed forces provoked strong opposition among military commanders and in Congress, he backed down nine days into office and later announced an ambiguous new policy concerning gays in the military that came to be summed up in the words "Don't ask, don't tell." These inconsistent actions at the start of his administration had a negative effect on public impressions of the president, whom opponents accused on the one hand of putting a leftist agenda first and on the other hand of being too quick to cave in to criticism. In Clinton's first two weeks in office, his approval ratings dropped 20 percent.

Clinton had no traditional honeymoon of bipartisan support as he assumed office, partly because he seemed to live life as a perpetual campaign, partly because his critics permitted no letup. He failed to receive deserved credit for his achievements, such as the Family and Medical Leave Act, which enabled government workers and workers in companies with more than fifty employees to take off twelve weeks (unpaid leave) each year to deal with birth or adoption or an illness in the family. During the campaign, Clinton had promised to submit to Congress within 100 days a comprehensive economic program and a health care reform plan. In both cases, he failed to muster the necessary support of Congress and the public.

THE ECONOMY Clinton entered office determined to reduce the federal deficit without damaging the economy. To this end, on February 17, he laid out a program of tax hikes and spending cuts. He proposed higher taxes for corporations and for individuals in higher tax brackets and called for an economic stimulus package for "investment" in public works (transportation, utilities, and the like) and in "human capital" (education, skills, health, and welfare). Clinton's deficit reduction package of spending cuts and tax hikes on upper incomes provoked opposition from both Republicans and conservative Democrats, but the bill finally passed by 218–216 in the House and 51–50 in the Senate, with Vice-President Gore breaking the tie.

Equally contested was approval of the North American Free Trade Agreement (NAFTA), which the Bush administration had negotiated with Canada and Mexico. The debate revived old arguments on the tariff, pro and con. Clinton stuck with his party's tradition of low tariffs and urged approval of NAFTA, which would make North America the largest free trade area in the world. He and his supporters argued that tariff reductions would open up foreign markets to American industries. Opponents of the bill, such as organized labor, favored barriers against cheaper foreign products and believed that with NAFTA, thousands of American jobs would be lost to Mexico. Nonetheless, NAFTA was approved with solid Republican support but the loss of a sizable minority of Democrats, mostly from the South.

HEALTH CARE REFORM Clinton's major public policy initiative was a new health care plan. Government-subsidized health insurance was not a new idea. Other industrial countries had long since started national health insurance programs, Germany as early as 1883, Britain in 1911. Off and on the idea had been a subject of political discussion in the United States throughout the twentieth century. Medicare, initiated in 1965, provided insurance for people sixty-five and older, and Medicaid supported state medical assistance for the indigent. These programs had grown enormously in the years since, as had business spending on private health insurance.

Sentiment for health care reform spread as annual medical costs approached the trillion-dollar mark, and some 39 million Americans went without insurance either by choice or out of necessity. Universal medical coverage as proposed by Clinton would have entitled every American and legal immigrant to health insurance. But the bill aroused opposition from vested interests, especially the pharmaceutical and insurance industries. Drug companies insisted that they needed large profits to support expensive research. Insurance interests funded TV advertisements that questioned the bill's benefits. Small-business groups attacked the requirements that employers share the cost of medical insurance, already a common practice in old-age, unemployment, and health insurance, even though government would provide subsidies to small business. By midsummer 1994, the health insurance plan was doomed. The Democrats acknowledged defeat and gave up the fight for universal medical coverage.

HANDGUNS AND THE CRIME BILL During Clinton's first year in office, fear of violent crime prompted legislators to limit the availability of unregistered guns. In 1993, Congress passed the Brady Bill, which required a five-day wait to buy a handgun. Clinton called for passage of a crime bill in his State of the Union message. The bill had been passed in both houses in 1993, but when a conference committee reported back a compromise bill, a coalition of unlikely bedfellows—black Democrats who objected to expanding use of the death penalty, pro-gun Democrats who objected to a ban on assault weapons, and Republicans who dismissed crime-prevention programs as "pork" and who sought to embarrass the administration—joined together to oppose the legislation. After Congress voted to postpone consideration of the bill, the Clinton administration pulled out all the stops to win its approval, and the new vote in the House was in favor. When the Senate passed the bill, people characterized it as one of Clinton's greatest victories.

MISTRUST OF GOVERNMENT AND THE MILITIA MOVEMENT
While Clinton sparred with Republicans in Washington, a burgeoning "militia" or "patriot" movement spread across the country in the 1990s. It represented the paranoid and populist strain in cultural politics. Convinced that the federal government was conspiring against individual liberties (especially the right to bear arms), thousands of mostly working-class folk joined well-armed militia organizations. Some militias harkened back to the origins of the Ku Klux Klan and fomented racial and ethnic hatred. Others aligned themselves with right-wing Christian groups, particularly the militant faction of the anti-abortion movement. In the Far West, several of the militias challenged the federal control of public lands, refused to pay taxes, and threatened to arrest and execute local government officials and judges.

Militia groups grew in reaction to dramatic government actions at Ruby Ridge, Idaho, and Waco, Texas. In Idaho in 1992, white supremacist Randy Weaver held off federal agents when they laid siege to his mountain cabin because he had failed to appear in federal court on weapons charges. Crossfire at the cabin killed Weaver's wife and son and convinced many people that the government intended to confiscate all weapons and to start a war against the radical right.

In Waco, Texas, another siege also resulted in catastrophic consequences. Responding to reports and rumors about the stockpiling of weapons, false imprisonment, child abuse, and the violation of immigration laws by the Branch Davidians, an apocalyptic sect headed by David Koresh, agents from the Treasury Department's Bureau of Alcohol, Tobacco, and Firearms (BATF) tried to serve a warrant on the sect on February 28, 1993. When the agents entered the sect's compound, they were met with gunfire. Four agents and two Branch Davidians were killed, and twenty or so people were injured. The next day, the FBI took over the siege of the compound. After fifty days of fruitless psychological warfare against the Branch Davidians, the FBI yielded to frustration and hints of child abuse, and on April 19, the fifty-first day of the siege, agents attacked the compound with armored vehicles and tear gas. Amid the commotion, the compound caught fire and quickly burned to the ground. The fire was so intense that no one could be certain of the number dead, but at least seventy-seven people died in the inferno.

On the second anniversary of the Waco incident, April 19, 1995, a massive truck bomb exploded in front of the federal office building in

Oklahoma City, Oklahoma. The entire front portion of the nine-story building collapsed, killing 168 people, 19 of them children in a day-care center that was in the building. Six hundred others were injured. Within days, the FBI charged Timothy McVeigh and Terry Nichols with the bombing. A third man pleaded guilty to separate charges of conspiring to produce explosives. All three men were militia members who hated the federal government and who had been incensed by the way the BATF and FBI had dealt with the Branch Davidians at Waco.

The Oklahoma City bombing shocked and saddened the nation. It brought to public attention the rise of right-wing militia groups and also revealed the depth of anti-government sentiment among such fringe groups. A year later, in the spring of 1996, the FBI lay siege to a dozen members of the Freemen, a heavily armed militia group that kept federal authorities at bay outside a remote Montana homestead. The Freemen refused to pay taxes or be evicted from the property, which had been foreclosed upon eighteen months earlier. They declared their right to exercise governmental authority, posted bounties for the capture of local police and judges, and threatened to shoot their neighbors' livestock. Unlike the incident at Waco, this time federal officials re-

The Murrah Federal Building in Oklahoma City after it was bombed, April 19, 1995.

solved to wait out the fugitives. "The FBI," said Attorney-General Janet Reno, "has gone to great pains to ensure that there is no armed confrontation, no siege, no armed perimeter, and no use of military-assault-type tactics or equipment. The FBI is trying to negotiate a peaceful solution." The tactics succeeded, and eventually the Freemen were arrested.

REPUBLICAN INSURGENCY

During 1994, Clinton began to see his presidency unravel. After mishandling the volatile militia groups and failing to get either health care reform or welfare reform bills through the Democratic Congress or to carry out his campaign pledge for middle-class tax relief, Clinton and his party found themselves on the defensive. This opened up opportunities for the Republicans to capture control of Congress.

In the midterm elections of 1994, the Democrats suffered a humbling defeat. It was the first election since 1952 in which Republicans captured both houses of Congress at the same time. Not a single Republican incumbent was defeated. Republicans also won a net gain of eleven governorships and fifteen state legislatures. It was a thorough repudiation of the Democratic party, one that had occurred in all regions.

There could be little question that the election signaled a repudiation of Clinton and the Democratic Congress. Squabbling between the president and congressional Democrats did not help matters. Nor did Clinton's response to the Republican takeover of Congress in 1994 endear him to party loyalists. Initially, he and his aides decided to adopt a passive role, letting the Republicans initiate policies and programs and then hoping that they would be decimated by the affected interest groups. He offered no deficit reduction plan, no welfare reform proposal, no new health reform initiative.

Clinton's waffling on major issues began to convince many in his own party that he was a politician rather than a leader, someone who thrived as a campaigner but was bereft of genuine convictions. Said Democratic congressman David Obey: "I think most of us learned some time ago that if you don't like the president's position on a particular issue, you simply need to wait a few weeks." When Clinton joined the chorus of conservatives calling for a scaling back of affirmative action plans designed to remedy historic patterns of racial discrimination in hiring and the awarding of government contracts, liberals felt betrayed.

CONTRACT WITH AMERICA A Georgian named Newton Leroy Gingrich led the Republican insurgency in Congress. In early 1995 he became the first Republican Speaker of the House in forty-two years. Most of the new Republicans in Congress credited "Newt" Gingrich for their election. In the late 1980s he had launched a series of attacks on the ethics of the Democratic leadership in the House, ultimately leading to the resignation of both Democratic Speaker Jim Wright and Democratic Whip Tony Coelho. Gingrich had also helped mobilize religious and social conservatives associated with the Christian Coalition.

In 1995 Gingrich assaulted the "welfare state" and galvanized support for conservative values and principles. He was aided by the freshman Republicans, who promoted what Gingrich called the "Contract with America." The ten-point contract outlined an anti-big-government program with less regulation, less conservation, term limits for members of Congress, a line-item veto for the president, welfare reform, and a balanced-budget amendment. New members hailed their electoral victory as a mandate to enact the Contract.

By April 13, exactly 100 days after taking office, the Republicans had passed twenty-six bills growing out of the Contract with America, and had failed to pass only two: a proposal for an anti-missile ("Star Wars") defense system and term limits for Congress. Nonetheless, twenty-two of these bills did not become law. The four bills that were enacted as laws were: a bill mandating that all laws applicable to ordinary Americans should also apply to members of Congress; a bill by which Congress agreed to stop imposing mandated programs on local and state governments without footing the cost; a large defense spending bill, which Clinton reluctantly accepted, lest Republicans rebel on foreign policy; and a new crime bill providing for stiff penalties for child abuse and pornography. A line-item veto for use by the president would not pass until a year later.

Thereafter, the much ballyhooed GOP revolution and the Contract with America fizzled out. The revolution that Gingrich touted was far too ambitious to enact in so limited a time, with so slim a majority, and with so little sense of crisis. What is more, many of the Republican freshmen in the House disdained compromise, and they limited the

Speaker's room for maneuver. The Senate rejected many of the bills that had been passed in the House, as senators were less under Gingrich's spell and not party to the Contract with America anyway. And beyond them, a presidential veto stood in the path. Finally, President Clinton shrewdly moved to the political center and co-opted much of the Republican agenda. His distinctive strength—at least in the eyes of his supporters—resided in his agile responsiveness to changing public moods. To Clinton, the Republican victory in the 1994 congressional elections and in the passage of the Contract with America initiatives bore a simple message: he must recapture the political center by radically changing his message and agenda.

The Republicans' Contract with America focused public and presidential attention on basic questions of governmental philosophy. But Gingrich and other House Republican insurgents had overestimated the public's interest in dismantling the federal government and many of its social programs. Voters wanted to reduce the size, expense, and intrusiveness of the Washington bureaucracy, but they did not want to return to the laissez-faire approach of Calvin Coolidge. By the end of 1995, Clinton's fortunes were back on the rise as the Gingrich revolution petered out.

LEGISLATIVE BREAKTHROUGH In the late summer of 1996, as lawmakers were preparing to adjourn and participate in the presidential nominating conventions, the 104th Congress broke through its partisan gridlock and passed a flurry of important legislation that President Clinton quickly signed, including a bill increasing the minimum wage and a bill broadening access to health insurance.

Even more significant was the passage of a comprehensive welfare reform measure that ended the federal government's open-ended guarantee of aid to the poor, a guarantee that had been in place since 1935. The Personal Responsibility and Work Opportunity Act of 1996 turned over the major federal welfare programs to the states. In exchange, the states would receive federal grants to fund the programs. The bill also limited the time a person could receive welfare benefits funded by federal money and required that at least half of a state's welfare recipients have jobs or be enrolled in job training programs by the year 2002. Those states failing to meet the deadline would have their federal funds cut.

The Republican-sponsored welfare reform legislation passed the Senate by a vote of 74–24. It had the effect of cutting $56 billion over six years from Aid to Families with Dependent Children, food stamps, and other programs, several of which dated back to Franklin Roosevelt's New Deal. Senator Patrick Moynihan, a New York Democrat, charged that Clinton was abdicating Democratic social principles in order to gain reelection amid the conservative climate of the times. Democratic senator Christopher Dodd of Connecticut called the president's action "unconscionable."

Clinton and his centrist advisers, however, dismissed such criticisms. With his reelection bid at stake, he was determined to live up to his 1992 campaign pledge to "end welfare as we know it." Clinton also knew that most voters in both parties were eager to see major cuts in federal entitlement programs.

THE 1996 CAMPAIGN   After clinching the Republican presidential nomination in 1996, Majority Leader Bob Dole resigned his Senate seat in order to devote his attention to defeating Bill Clinton. "I will seek the presidency," he said, "with nothing to fall back on but the judgment of the people, and nowhere to go but the White House or home."

Born in Kansas in 1923, the product of a hardscrabble existence in a small prairie town, Dole served in Italy during World War II and was severely injured. Despite the permanent paralysis of his right arm and hand as a result of his war injuries, he graduated from college and law school and was elected to the House of Representatives and then to the Senate. In 1976 Dole was Gerald Ford's running mate, but he returned to the Senate after the Carter-Mondale victory. As a senator, Dole was a brilliant legislative tactician and a tough, smart, and honest leader known for his ability to build consensus and forge coalitions.

As the 1996 presidential campaign unfolded, Clinton maintained a large lead in the polls. With a generally healthy economy and with no major foreign policy crises to confront, cultural and personal issues surged into prominence. Concern about Dole's age (seventy-three) and his acerbic manner, as well as rifts in the Republican party between economic and social conservatives over issues such as abortion and gun control, hampered Dole's efforts to generate widespread support.

President Bill Clinton and Vice-President Al Gore at the 1996 Democratic National Convention in Chicago.

Late in the campaign, Dole charged that the Democrats had raised unprecedented sums of money by dubious means. The role of people with foreign connections in the fund-raising even gave rise to suspicions that money from abroad had found its way into Democratic accounts. Yet while Clinton excited extreme animosity in his enemies, he was also like Reagan, the "Teflon president," to whom none of their charges stuck. The polls favored Clinton so heavily that a pall of depression seemed to fall over the Dole campaign.

On November 5 Clinton won again with an electoral vote of 379 to 159 and 49 percent of the popular vote. He lost Georgia, Colorado, and Montana, but he added Arizona and Florida to his column. Dole received 41 percent and Ross Perot got 8 percent of the popular vote. Clinton remained a minority president, and once again the Republicans kept their control of Congress. The resulting deadlock reflected the conservative mood of the times.

ECONOMIC AND SOCIAL TRENDS

After his reelection, Clinton reshuffled his cabinet and other governmental posts. Madeleine Albright, ambassador to the United Nations, became the first woman to head the State Department, and Senator William Cohen, a Republican from Maine, took over at the Defense Department. The overall direction of Clinton's changes was a move to the right.

THE "NEW ECONOMY" As the twentieth century came to a close, the United States benefited from a prolonged period of unprecedented prosperity. Buoyed by low inflation, high employment, declining federal budget deficits, dramatic improvements in productivity, the rapid "globalization" of economic life, and the firm and astute leadership of Federal Reserve Board Chairman Alan Greenspan, American business and industry witnessed record profits.

The stock market soared during the late 1990s. In 1993 the Dow Jones industrial average hit 3,500. By 1996 it had topped 6,000. During 1999, it went past 11,000, defying the predictions of experts that the economy could not sustain such performance. In 1998 unemployment was only 4.3 percent, the lowest since 1970. Inflation was a measly 1.5 percent. "The current economic performance," observed Greenspan, ". . . is as impressive as any I have witnessed." He and others began to talk of a "new economy" that defied the boom-and-bust cycles of the previous hundred years. "It is possible," Greenspan suggested, "that we have moved 'beyond history.'"

By 1999 swelling tax revenues generated a federal budget surplus, the first in over thirty years. Such sustained prosperity seemed to support the "monetarist" philosophy of the Nobel Prize–winning economist Professor Milton Friedman. Keynesian economics, which had emerged against the background of deflation and prolonged depression in the 1930s, had favored fiscal remedies (deficit spending) to stimulate economic growth. Monetarists such as Friedman believed that economic growth would best be promoted by a stable monetary supply (cash plus bank accounts), and they feared inflation more than they feared unemployment. To them, the key to economic stability was the Federal Reserve's power to regulate interest rates.

Before President Clinton took office, he was persuaded to support

Greenspan's monetarist policies and was convinced that a balanced budget was necessary to keep government borrowing from putting inflationary pressure on interest rates. Clinton chose to reduce deficits in part by spending cuts, in part by a tax hike on upper income brackets. At the same time, he abandoned promised tax cuts for middle income brackets.

In the past, invention and innovation had been basic contributors to such economic booms. Much of this had been in electronics, ever since the transistor replaced the vacuum tube in 1947 and created the television revolution at mid-century. Yet, in the 1990s, much of the surging economy resulted from "globalization." The "new" classical economics of Friedman and Greenspan favored free markets on a world scale— markets without tariffs and other barriers. Gigantic corporations such as International Business Machines or General Electric had become international in scope. This encouraged free trade agreements such as NAFTA or most-favored-nation treatment for China and other countries.

Globalization enabled many American companies to "outsource" much of their production to plants in countries with lower labor costs. This led to a decline of the labor union movement in the United States and to corporate moves toward "downsizing," which worked wonders with stock prices, whether or not it served business efficiency. Blue-collar labor lost ground to cheap labor in assembly plants or "sweatshops" elsewhere in the world. Part-time labor became popular because employers could avoid paying for expensive benefits—whether for flipping hamburgers or for teaching.

RACE INITIATIVE Since the triumphs of the civil rights movement in the 1960s, the momentum for minority advancement had run out—except for gains in college admissions and employment under the rubric of "affirmative action." The principle of affirmative action, as stated by President Lyndon Johnson in 1965, involved an effort to overcome the effects of past discrimination. "We seek not just equality as a right and theory," Johnson said, "but equality as a fact and equality as a result." Affirmative action covered a variety of devices, but mainly it involved the inclusion of race among other criteria for jobs and college admissions. Such measures were extended under Richard Nixon.

Despite moves by Reagan and Bush staff members to limit such measures, the outcry from minority leaders caused both administrations to back away from outright opposition to affirmative action. The Supreme Court continued to accept such measures, including voluntary programs of corporations and other institutions, to make up for past discrimination. Race could be a factor among others, but racial quotas were ruled out.

In the 1980s and 1990s, however, the outlook of the federal courts began to shift to the right. One consequence was a challenge to the legality of gerrymandering (redrawing) congressional and legislative districts to create black or Hispanic majorities. Minorities had favored gerrymandering to increase minority officeholding, and Republicans had favored it because such districts would draw minority votes from other districts. But in *Thaw* v. *Reno* (1993), the Court ruled that such districts in North Carolina violated equal protection of the law.

In 1995, a conservative Court again ruled against election districts redrawn to create black or Hispanic majorities, narrowed federal affirmative action programs, and limited the legal remedies for segregated public schools. All were decided by the same vote 5–4 (Chief Justice Rehnquist, and Justices Kennedy, O'Connor, Scalia, and Thomas deciding against Justices Breyer, Ginsburg, Souter, and Stevens).

In one of the cases, *Adarand Constructors* v. *Peña* (1995), the Court assessed a program that gave some advantages to businesses owned by "disadvantaged" minorities. An Hispanic-owned firm had won a highway guard rail contract over a lower bid by a white-owned company. The white-owned company sued on the ground of "reverse discrimination." For the majority, Justice Sandra Day O'Connor said that such programs had to be "narrowly tailored" to serve a "compelling national interest." O'Connor did not define what the Court meant by a "compelling national interest," but the implication of her language was clear: the Court had come to embrace the growing public suspicion of the value and legality of such race-based programs.

In 1996 two major steps were taken against affirmative action in college admissions. In *Hopwood* v. *Texas* (1996), the Fifth Circuit Court ruled that considering race to achieve a diverse student body at the University of Texas was "not a compelling interest under the Fourteenth Amendment." In November, the state of California, while voting for

Clinton, also passed Proposition 209, an initiative that ruled out race, sex, ethnicity, or national origin as criteria for preferring any group.

These rulings eviscerated affirmative action programs and drastically reduced black enrollments, something that caused second thoughts. In Texas, for instance, a new state law guaranteed admission to the state university for the top 10 percent of any high school class—some argued for high school grades as a better predictor of college performance than SAT scores—and in Houston voters rejected a proposition to abandon an affirmative action program adopted by the city.

As the century came to a close, programs of affirmative action remained under siege. And affirmative action still did not address intractable problems that lay beyond civil rights, that is, problems of dependency—illiteracy, poverty, unemployment, urban decay, and slums.

THE SCANDAL MACHINE Just as the administration of Warren G. Harding was rocked by revelations of personal corruption and moral scandal, the Clinton White House also became the focus of investigations and gossip. Since before his first election in 1992, Clinton had faced allegations of both sexual and financial scandals that grew into a relentless inquiry. In the 1970s, the Watergate scandal had provoked the Ethics in Government Act of 1978, which created an office of "special prosecutor" (renamed "independent counsel" in 1988) to investigate allegations against high officials in the government. The law, renewed in 1982 and 1988, was allowed to lapse in 1992, but it was renewed early in 1994.

During his first term, Clinton was dogged by allegations of improper involvement in the Whitewater Development Company. In 1978, as governor of Arkansas, he had invested in a resort project on the White River in northern Arkansas. The project turned out to be a fraud and a failure, and the Clintons took a loss on their investment. Reports surfaced that an Arkansas savings and loan that had put money into the foundering Whitewater project had also misused funds in the Clinton campaign. An independent counsel was named in 1993 to investigate the allegations of improper Clinton involvement in Whitewater. While revealing that Hillary Clinton had handled some legal work for the Whitewater Development Company, evidence was not uncovered that the Clintons were involved in the fraud.

The ongoing Whitewater investigation threatened to supplant more important initiatives as it occupied the attention of the president and Congress.

In 1994, Republican Kenneth Starr was appointed as independent counsel, and he continued to investigate the Whitewater case. Although Starr had a reputation for fairness, many believed that his unwillingness to end the investigation and his former subcabinet position in the Bush administration suggested a taint of partisanship. After nearly four years of expensive investigation, Starr found no criminal involvement by the Clintons, although a number of their close associates had been caught in the web and convicted of various charges, some related to Whitewater and some not.

The office of independent counsel, created to ensure investigations free from conflict of interest, instead contributed to a political culture of scandal. Every president after Nixon saw at least one of his subordinates, if not himself, under criminal investigation. By early 1998, some $50 million had been spent investigating Clinton and his administration. Besides Whitewater, investigators looked into Paula Jones's allegations that Clinton had sexually harassed her while he was governor and she was a state employee in Arkansas.

In the course of the investigation, it surfaced that the president might have had a sexual affair with a former White House intern, Monica Lewinsky, and might have pressed her to lie about it under oath. The public was titillated by the allegations of the alleged affair, yet polls suggested that a majority did not care. This seemed to imply the public's contentment with the way things were going, especially the soaring economy—and perhaps a wish that the scandal would simply go away and not become a constitutional crisis.

But the tawdry scandal would not disappear. In August 1998, in the face of a possible subpoena from the independent counsel, President Clinton agreed to testify before the grand jury investigating the allegations about him. He was the first president in history to do so. During his six hours of testimony, the president recanted his earlier denials and acknowledged having had "inappropriate intimate physical contact" with White House intern Monica Lewinsky, but insisted he had done nothing illegal.

Clinton's admission was a stunning reversal from his insistent public denials over the previous seven months. His dishonesty, he explained, was motivated by a desire to protect his family and "myself from the embarrassment of my own conduct." Had Clinton stopped there, he might have avoided much of the angry criticism that greeted his disclosure. But he went on to attack the "politically inspired" investigation.

Public reaction to Clinton's remarkable about-face was mixed. A majority of Americans expressed sympathy for the president because of his public humiliation and wanted the entire matter dropped. But polls also showed that Clinton's credibility had suffered a serious blow.

Meanwhile, Starr continued his tenacious investigation. On September 9, 1998, he submitted to Congress a 445-page report and eighteen boxes of supporting material. The Starr Report found "substantial and creditable" evidence of presidential wrongdoing. Drawing upon such evidence, the Republican-controlled House Judiciary Committee voted 21–16 to recommend a full impeachment inquiry into perjury and obstruction of justice allegations against Clinton. On October 8, the House of Representatives voted 258–176 to begin a wide-ranging impeachment inquiry of President Clinton. Thirty-one Democrats joined Republicans in supporting the investigation.

During the final two months of 1998, the House Judiciary Committee sifted through evidence and heard testimony from witnesses related to the impeachment inquiry. White House Counsel Charles Ruff, wrapping up Clinton's defense before the committee, declared that the president's behavior was "morally reprehensible," but did not justify impeachment. On December 18, the entire House engaged in a fierce and often venomous debate over whether to impeach the president.

The following day William Jefferson Clinton became the second president to be impeached by the House of Representatives. The House officially approved two articles of impeachment, charging Clinton with lying under oath to a federal grand jury and obstructing justice. Clinton vowed to complete his term and appealed for a bipartisan compromise in the Senate.

With ceremonial flourishes and the world watching, the Senate trial of President Clinton began on January 7, 1999, with the swearing in of Chief Justice William Rehnquist to preside and the senators as jurors. Five weeks later, on February 12, President Clinton was acquitted of the two articles of impeachment. Rejecting the first charge of perjury, 10 Republicans and all 45 Democrats voted "not guilty." On the charge of obstruction of justice, the Senate split 50-50 (which meant acquittal, since 67 votes would have been needed to convict Clinton). In both instances, senators had a hard time interpreting Clinton's sexual adventures as "high crimes and misdemeanors." Responding to the Senate vote, Clinton said he was "profoundly sorry" for the burden he had imposed on the Congress and the American people. His supporters portrayed him as the victim of a puritanical special prosecutor and partisan conspiracy run amok. His critics lambasted him as a lecherous man without honor or integrity.

Both characterizations were accurate, yet incomplete. Politically astute, charismatic, and well-informed, Clinton had as much ability and potential as any president. Yet he was also emotionally fragile and shamelessly self-indulgent. The result was a scandalous presidency punctuated by dramatic achievements in welfare reform, economic growth, and foreign policy.

FOREIGN POLICY CHALLENGES

Like Woodrow Wilson, Lyndon Johnson, and Jimmy Carter before him, Clinton was a Democratic president who came into office determined to focus on the nation's domestic problems, only to find himself mired down in foreign entanglements that had no easy resolution.

Clinton continued the Bush administration's intervention in Somalia, on the northeastern horn of Africa, where collapse of the government early in 1991 had left the country in anarchy, prey to tribal marauders. The televised scenes of starvation horrified American viewers, many of whom demanded action. President Bush in 1992 had gained U.N. sanction for a military force led by American troops to relieve hunger and restore peace. In early 1993, U.S. troop levels peaked and began to shrink with the arrival of international forces. Clinton inherited this situation. The Somalia operation proved successful at its primary mission, but it never solved the political problems that lay at the root of the starvation.

The most successful departure in foreign policy for the Clinton administration during its first term came in Haiti. The end of the cold war had removed any threat of Soviet infiltration in the Caribbean, and brought a new emphasis on Wilsonian themes of democracy. Haiti had emerged suddenly from a cycle of coups with a rebellion in the army rank and file and a democratic election in 1990, which brought to the top a popular priest, Jean-Bertrand Aristide. Old habits returned, however, when a Haitian army general ousted Aristide. The United States immediately announced its intention to bring back Aristide and welcomed the U.N. to the process.

Another new element in the situation was the appearance of thousands of Haitian refugees desperate to reach Florida in leaky wooden boats. Coast Guard vessels began to pick them up and take them back to Haiti or to Guantanamo Bay in Cuba, denying that they were refugees. Public reaction to the flood of new immigrants put the Clinton administration under even greater pressure to resolve the situation.

With drawn-out negotiations leading nowhere, Clinton eventually moved in July 1994 to get a U.N. resolution authorizing force as a last resort. At this juncture, former president Jimmy Carter asked permission to negotiate. He went to Port-au-Prince and convinced the military leaders to quit by October 15. The first American forces were already in the air and landed September 19, without opposition and to a cordial welcome from the people.

Clinton had promised that the bulk of American forces in Haiti would be quickly withdrawn and replaced by an international force of peacekeepers, and in November the American withdrawal began. Aristide returned to Haiti and on March 31, 1995, the occupation was turned over to a U.N. force commanded by an American general. Only about 2,400 American troops remained to retrain Haitian military and police in orderly procedures.

Clinton also continued the Bush policy of sponsoring patient negotiations between Arabs and Israelis. A new development was the inclusion of the Palestine Liberation Organization (PLO) in the negotiations. In 1993 a draft agreement between Israel and the PLO resulted from secret talks between Israeli and Palestinian representatives in Oslo, Norway. It provided for the restoration of Palestinian self-rule in the occupied Gaza Strip and in Jericho on the West Bank, in an exchange of land for peace as provided in U.N. Security Council resolutions. A formal signing occurred at the White House on September 13, 1993. With President Clinton presiding, Israeli prime minister Yitzhak Rabin and PLO leader Yasir Arafat exchanged handshakes, and their foreign ministers signed the agreement.

In the aftermath of this dramatic agreement, talks continued by fits and starts, interrupted by violent incidents provoked by extremist Jewish settlers and Palestinian factions. In October 1994 Israel and the kingdom of Jordan signed an agreement at ceremonies on their border, which were attended by President Clinton. But the Middle East peace process suffered a terrible blow in early November 1995 when Israeli prime minister Yitzhak Rabin was assassinated at a peace rally in Tel Aviv. The gunman was an Israeli Jewish zealot who resented Rabin's efforts to negotiate with the Palestinians.

Some observers feared that the assassin had killed the peace process as well when seven months later conservative hard-liner Benjamin Netanyahu narrowly defeated the U.S.-backed Shimon Peres in the election for a new prime minister. Netanyahu campaigned against the Rabin-Peres peace efforts, arguing that returning land to Arab control endangered Israeli security. In the face of a flurry of suicide bombings conducted by Islamic extremists against Israelis, he promised to slow the peace process, build new Jewish settlements along the West Bank, block the creation of a Palestinian state in the West Bank and Gaza, and retain control of the Golan Heights, captured from Syria in 1967.

Arab leaders responded to Netanyahu's election by threatening to reconsider the concessions they had made over the previous five years. Yet in October 1998, Clinton brought Arafat and Netanyahu together at a conference center in Wye Mills, Maryland, and with the ailing King Hussein of Jordan brokered an agreement whereby Israel would surrender land in return for security guarantees by the Palestinians. As hardliners attempted to derail the tenuous peace process, Netanyahu decided to call elections early. A public weary of war swept into power former general Ehud Barak in May 1999. Barak promised to jump-start the peace process.

Clinton's foreign policy also was affected by the transition in eastern Europe. With the collapse of Communist power, old ethnic and religious enmities quickly resurfaced in eastern Europe and elsewhere, often leading to violent clashes that were difficult to resolve quickly. In response, the Clinton administration operated mostly on an ad hoc basis, often failing to win international backing for its initiatives. As one of Clinton's own ambassadorial appointees admitted, "We're always too ramshackle, we've never been smooth."

The basis of Clinton's foreign policy was to promote free-market democracies throughout the world. One place to expand democratic capitalism was in Russia itself. On this, as on other issues, Clinton continued the Bush administration policy of support for Russian president Boris Yeltsin, a position articulated in Secretary of State Warren Christopher's statement that "helping to consolidate democracy in Russia is not a matter of charity but a security concern of the highest order." American assistance continued to be centered on the exchange of goods, expertise, and training instead of financial assistance.

An especially contentious area of the world in the 1990s proved to be the former Yugoslavia, a volatile, fractious mixture of warring ethnic groups, chiefly Eastern Orthodox Serbs, Catholic Croats, and Bosnian or Albanian Muslims. When Yugoslavia imploded in 1991, fanatics and tyrants provoked ethnic conflict as four of its six republics seceded. Serb minorities, backed by Serbia itself, stirred up civil wars in Croatia and Bosnia. In Bosnia especially, the war involved "ethnic cleansing"—driving Muslims from their homes and towns—and mass rape of Muslim women. The options facing the United States were sobering: to ignore the butchery, to accept the refugees, to use American airpower, or to risk introducing ground troops.

Once in the White House, Clinton backed off from his hawkish campaign statements about using force in Yugoslavia. Western European countries dispatched "peacekeeping" forces and put an embargo on arms shipments—which favored Serbs who had fallen heir to the equipment of the Yugoslav army. Clinton started with the apparent purpose of acting vigorously, but confronted by European reluctance, he settled for dropping food and medical supplies to besieged Bosnians and sending planes to retaliate for attacks on places designated "safe havens" by the United Nations.

Despite a cease-fire agreement at the end of 1994, fighting continued in many parts of the faction-ridden country. In 1995 American negotiators finally convinced the foreign ministers of Croatia, Bosnia, and Yugoslavia to agree to a comprehensive peace plan. Bosnia would remain a single nation but would be divided into two states: a Muslim-Croat federation controlling 51 percent of the territory and a Bosnian Serb republic controlling the remaining 49 percent. Basic human rights would be restored and free elections held to appoint a parliament and joint presidency. To enforce the agreement, 20,000 American troops would be dispatched to Bosnia as part of a 60,000-person NATO peacekeeping operation. A cease-fire went into effect in October 1995 and a final agreement confirming these provisions was signed in Paris in December.

In 1998 the Balkan tinderbox flared up again, this time in the Yugoslav province of Kosovo. A rugged rural region the size of Connecticut, Kosovo has long been considered sacred ground to Christian Serbs. It includes many ancient monasteries and was the site of a fabled fourteenth-century battle against the Ottoman Turks. By 1989, however, over 90 percent of the 2 million Kosovars were ethnic Albanian Muslims. In that year, Yugoslav president Slobodon Milosevic decided to reassert Serbian control over the province. He stripped Kosovo of its autonomy and established de facto martial law. When the Albanian Kosovars resisted and large numbers of Muslim men began to join the Kosovo Liberation Army, Serbian soldiers and state police ruthlessly suppressed them and launched a program of "ethnic cleansing," burning Albanian villages, murdering males, and displacing hundreds of thousands of Muslim Albanian Kosovars.

On March 24, NATO launched air strikes against Yugoslavia. "Ending this tragedy is a moral imperative," explained President Clinton.

Using cruise missiles and an armada of 1,100 planes, NATO forces attacked Yugoslav air defenses, command and control centers, fuel depots, ammunition dumps, and military forces. Operation "Allied Force" relied heavily upon American military resources and leadership. It initially was greeted with skepticism. Critics charged that air power alone would not stop the "ethnic cleansing" in Kosovo. Yet after 72 days of unrelenting bombardment, Slobodon Milosevic sued for peace on NATO's terms. An agreement was reached on June 3, 1999. It was an unprecedented victory for air power and for NATO, which was celebrating its fiftieth birthday. Not a single allied pilot was killed in combat.

As the Albanian Kosovars started to return to Kosovo, however, large numbers of Serbs began to leave the province in fear of Muslim retribution. Some Serbs were killed by angry Albanian Kosovars wishing for revenge. Members of the Kosovo Liberation Army stepped into the vacuum left by the departing Serbs and began to take control of the province.

FIN-DE-SIÈCLE AMERICA

The approach of the year 2000 prompted contradictory reflections upon American life at the end of the millennium and the start of the twenty-first century. As at the close of the last century, referred to as the *fin-de-siècle* (a French term for "end of the century"), many people celebrated the unprecedented prosperity and amazing technological breakthroughs of the times. But, as in 1900, other observers were more gloomy. Skeptical of material notions of perpetual progress and worried about the cohesion of an increasingly diverse population, they expressed an anxious foreboding about societal dissolution and decay.

As the twentieth century drew to a close, the United States seemed to be experiencing the best and worst of times. The economy remained on the crest of a wave of record-setting productivity and profits, inflation was dormant, and the federal government was enjoying balanced budgets for the first time in over a generation. The cold war was over, the nuclear arms race had ended, and the digital revolution was in full swing. Americans were enjoying their personal freedoms, their cornucopia of consumer goods, and their sophisticated technologies. They were also living longer than ever.

Yet a *Times Mirror* survey portrayed a prosperous nation awash in anxiety and self-doubt, with some 73 percent of Americans expressing dissatisfaction with "the way things are going." New technologies were improving productivity and efficiency, but many people were working harder and longer than ever before to keep up with the "wired" workplace and a culture of rising expectations.

The most acute concern today, however, remains the ability of our multicultural society to get along in the midst of our seductive freedoms. Seemingly intractable issues threaten to unravel the social fabric. Religious, racial, and ethnic-related tensions are growing, and the gap between rich and poor is widening. Our obsession with individual rights is eroding our ability to behave socially. In-your-face confrontation, narrow group loyalties, and bipartisan moral arrogance have displaced respectful dialogue and civic virtue. As the perceptive cartoonist Walt Kelly once observed in his Pogo comic strip, "We have met the enemy and he is us."

Some cultural analysts worry that the ferocious, take-no-prisoners nature of public discourse and political campaigns is undermining the consensus needed for democracy to work. Divisive issues such as abortion, gun control, doctor-assisted suicide, affirmative action, prayer in schools, political correctness, and gay rights, to name a few, have fostered a special-interest sectarianism that has disrupted and divided communities, political parties, and churches.

In 1995 Harvard political scientist Robert Putnam addressed such issues in a provocative essay entitled "Bowling Alone: The Decline of Social Capital" in which he declared that the "social fabric is becoming visibly thinner, our connections among each other are becoming visibly thinner. We don't trust one another as much, and we don't know one another as much. And, of course, this is behind the deterioration of the political dialogue, the deterioration of public debate." Putnam highlighted plummeting membership in organizations such as the PTA, Red Cross, Boy Scouts, and the League of Women Voters, as well as civic clubs and labor unions. He blamed such declining civic involvement on many aspects of popular culture—television, VCRs, and personal computers—for distracting people from their social responsibilities. Technological change, Putnam noted, is privatizing leisure time by promoting solitary forms of entertainment.

But Putnam's influential thesis overlooks contrary evidence of civic energy and social interaction. Today Americans engage with each other in many different forms of association. Voluntarism is soaring, as are other group activities. Youth soccer leagues and spectator sports, fitness centers and social clubs, for instance, are examples of popular culture activities that generate a shared discourse and bring people together.

Yet more needs to be done to strengthen the social fabric. "Our greatest responsibility," said President Clinton in his second inaugural address, "is to embrace a new spirit of community for a new century." It is an old ideal. In 1630 Governor John Winthrop told the Puritan colonists settling near Boston that "We must delight in each other, make others' conditions our own, rejoice together, mourn together, labor and suffer together, having always before our eyes our community as members of the same body." *E pluribus unum*—one out of many. At the start of a new century, it remains the best definition of what the unique American experiment in self-government means. It also remains America's greatest hope—and its greatest challenge.

FURTHER READING

On the Bush presidency, see Ryan J. Barilleaux and Mary E. Stuckey's *Leadership and the Bush Presidency: Prudence or Drift in an Era of Change* (1992), Charles Tiefer's *The Semi-Sovereign Presidency: The Bush Administration's Strategy for Governing without Congress* (1994). Among the journalistic accounts of the presidential election of 1992, the best narrative is Jack Germond and Jules Witcover's *Mad as Hell: Revolt at the Ballot Box, 1992* (1993). The best scholarly study is Theodore J. Lowi and Benjamin Ginsberg's *Democrats Return to Power: Politics and Policy in the Clinton Era* (1994).

On Bill Clinton, up to his presidency, the best treatment is David Maraniss's *First in His Class: A Biography of Bill Clinton* (1995). The early months of the Clinton presidency are most thoroughly covered in Elizabeth Drew's *On the Edge: The Clinton Presidency* (1994). Bob Woodward's *The Agenda: Inside the Clinton White House* (1994) focuses on financial policies and the economy. For a psychoanalytic assessment of Clinton, see Stanley A. Renshon's *High Hopes: The Clinton*

Presidency and the Politics of Ambition (1996). Recent analysis of the Clinton years can be found in *The Clinton Presidency: First Appraisals* (1995), edited by Colin Campbell and Bert A. Rockman, and *Back to Gridlock?: Governance in the Clinton Years* (1996), edited by James L. Sundquist. For a Republican perspective, see Haley Barbour's *Agenda for America: A Republican Direction for the Future* (1996).

On social and cultural problems and issues of the times, a good account is Haynes Johnson's *Divided We Fall: Gambling with History in the Nineties* (1994), based on street interviews. Collections of magazine and newspaper articles are in John Leo's *Two Steps Ahead of the Thought Police* (1994), Molly Ivins's *Nothin' But Good Times Ahead* (1993), and George F. Will's *The Leveling Wind: Politics, the Culture, and Other News, 1990–1994* (1994).

Aspects of fundamentalist and apocalyptic movements are the subject of Paul L. Boyer's *When Time Shall Be No More: Prophecy and Belief in Modern American Culture* (1992), George M. Marsden's *Understanding Fundamentalism and Evangelicalism* (1991), and Ralph Reed's *Politically Incorrect: The Emerging Faith Factor in American Politics* (1994).

Aspects of recent cultural debates can be found in *Culture Wars: Documents from the Recent Controversies in the Arts* (1992), edited by Richard Bolton; Gerald Graff's *Beyond the Culture Wars: How Teaching the Conflicts Can Revitalize American Education* (1992); and *The Politics of Liberal Education* (1992), edited by Darryl Gless and Barbara Herrnstein Smith.

Aspects of corporate restructuring and downsizing are the subject of Bennett Harrison's *Lean and Mean: The Changing Landscape of Corporate Power in the Age of Flexibility* (1994). The story of the Whitewater affair is the subject of Martin L. Gross's *The Great Whitewater Fiasco: An American Tale of Money, Power, and Politics* (1994).

APPENDIX

THE DECLARATION
OF INDEPENDENCE

WHEN IN THE COURSE OF HUMAN EVENTS, it becomes necessary for one people to dissolve the political bands which have connected them with another, and to assume the Powers of the earth, the separate and equal station to which the Laws of Nature and of Nature's God entitle them, a decent respect to the opinions of mankind requires that they should declare the causes which impel them to the separation.

We hold these truths to be self-evident, that all men are created equal, that they are endowed by their Creator with certain unalienable rights, that among these are Life, Liberty, and the pursuit of Happiness. That to secure these rights, Governments are instituted among Men, deriving their just powers from the consent of the governed. That whenever any Form of Government becomes destructive of these ends, it is the Right of the People to alter or to abolish it, and to institute new Government, laying its foundation on such principles and organizing its powers in such form, as to them shall seem most likely to effect their Safety and Happiness. Prudence, indeed, will dictate that Governments long established should not be changed for light and transient causes; and accordingly all experience hath shown, that mankind are more disposed to suffer, while evils are sufferable, than to right themselves by abolishing the forms to which they are accustomed. But when a long train of abuses and usurpations, pursuing invariably the same Object evinces a design to reduce them under absolute Despotism, it is their right, it is their duty, to throw off such Government, and to provide new Guards for their future security.— Such has been the patient sufferance of these Colonies; and such is now the necessity which constrains them to alter their former Systems of Government. The history of the present King of Great Britain is a history of repeated injuries and usurpations, all having in direct object the establishment of an absolute Tyranny over these States. To prove this, let Facts be submitted to a candid world.

He has refused his Assent to Laws, the most wholesome and necessary for the public good.

He has forbidden his Governors to pass Laws of immediate and pressing importance, unless suspended in their operation till his Assent should be obtained; and when so suspended, he has utterly neglected to attend to them.

He has refused to pass other Laws for the accommodation of large districts of people, unless those people would relinquish the right of Representation in the Legislature, a right inestimable to them and formidable to tyrants only.

He has called together legislative bodies at places unusual, uncomfortable, and distant from the depository of their public Records, for the sole purpose of fatiguing them into compliance with his measures.

He has dissolved Representative Houses repeatedly, for opposing with manly firmness his invasions on the rights of the people.

He has refused for a long time, after such dissolutions, to cause others to be elected; whereby the Legislative powers, incapable of Annihilation, have returned to the People at large for their exercise; the State remaining in the mean time exposed to all dangers of invasion from without, and convulsions within.

He has endeavoured to prevent the population of these States; for that purpose obstructing the Laws of Naturalization of Foreigners; refusing to pass others to encourage their migrations hither, and raising the conditions of new Appropriations of Lands.

He has obstructed the Administration of Justice, by refusing his Assent to Laws for establishing Judiciary powers.

He has made Judges dependent on his Will alone, for the tenure of their offices, and the amount and payment of their salaries.

He has erected a multitude of New Offices, and sent hither swarms of Officers to harass our People, and eat out their substance.

He has kept among us, in times of peace, Standing Armies without the Consent of our legislature.

He has affected to render the Military independent of and superior to the Civil Power.

He has combined with others to subject us to a jurisdiction foreign to our constitution, and unacknowledged by our laws; giving his Assent to their Acts of pretended Legislation:

For quartering large bodies of armed troops among us:

For protecting them, by a mock Trial, from Punishment for any Murders which they should commit on the Inhabitants of these States:

For cutting off our Trade with all parts of the world:

For imposing taxes on us without our Consent:

For depriving us of many cases, of the benefits of Trial by jury:

For transporting us beyond Seas to be tried for pretended offences:

For abolishing the free System of English Laws in a neighbouring Province, establishing therein an Arbitrary government, and enlarging its Boundaries so as to render it at once an example and fit instrument for introducing the same absolute rule into these Colonies:

For taking away our Charters, abolishing our most valuable Laws, and altering fundamentally the Forms of our Governments:

For suspending our own Legislatures, and declaring themselves in vested with Power to legislate for us in all cases whatsoever.

He has abdicated Government here, by declaring us out of his Protection and waging War against us.

He has plundered our seas, ravaged our Coasts, burnt our towns, and destroyed the lives of our people.

He is at this time transporting large armies of foreign mercenaries to compleat the works of death, desolation, and tyranny, already begun with circumstances of Cruelty & perfidy scarcely paralleled in the most barbarous ages, and totally unworthy the Head of a civilized nation.

He has constrained our fellow Citizens taken Captive on the high Seas to bear Arms against their Country, to become the executioners of their friends and Brethren, or to fall themselves by their Hands.

He has excited domestic insurrections amongst us, and has endeavoured to bring on the inhabitants of our frontiers, the merciless Indian Savages, whose known rule of warfare, is an undistinguished destruction of all ages, sexes, and conditions.

In every stage of these Oppressions We have Petitioned for Redress in the most humble terms: Our repeated Petitions have been answered only by repeated injury. A Prince, whose character is thus marked by every act which may define a Tyrant, is unfit to be the ruler of a free people.

Nor have We been wanting in attention to our British brethren. We have warned them from time to time of attempts by their legislature to extend an unwarrantable jurisdiction over us. We have reminded them of the circumstances of our emigration and settlement here. We have appealed to their native justice and magnanimity, and we have conjured them by the ties of our common kindred to disavow these usurpations, which, would inevitably interrupt our connections and correspondence. They too must have been deaf to the voice of justice and of consanguinity. We must, therefore, acquiesce in the necessity, which denounces our Separation, and hold them, as we hold the rest of mankind, Enemies in War, in Peace Friends.

WE, THEREFORE, the Representatives of the UNITED STATES OF AMERICA, in General Congress, Assembled, appealing to the Supreme Judge of the world for the rectitude of our intentions, do, in the Name, and by Authority of the good People of these Colonies, solemnly publish and declare, That these United Colonies are, and of Right ought to be FREE AND INDEPENDENT STATES; that they are Absolved from all Allegiance to the British

Crown, and that all political connection between them and the State of Great Britain, is and ought to be totally dissolved; and that as Free and Independent States, they have full Power to levy War, conclude Peace, contract Alliances, establish Commerce, and to do all other Acts and Things which Independent States may of right do. And for the support of this Declaration, with a firm reliance on the Protection of Divine Providence, we mutually pledge to each other our Lives, our Fortunes, and our sacred Honor.

The foregoing Declaration was, by order of Congress, engrossed, and signed by the following members:

John Hancock

NEW HAMPSHIRE
Josiah Bartlett
William Whipple
Matthew Thornton

MASSACHUSETTS BAY
Samuel Adams
John Adams
Robert Treat Paine
Elbridge Gerry

RHODE ISLAND
Stephen Hopkins
William Ellery

CONNECTICUT
Roger Sherman
Samuel Huntington
William Williams
Oliver Wolcott

NEW YORK
William Floyd
Philip Livingston
Francis Lewis
Lewis Morris

NEW JERSEY
Richard Stockton
John Witherspoon
Francis Hopkinson
John Hart
Abraham Clark

PENNSYLVANIA
Robert Morris
Benjamin Rush
Benjamin Franklin
John Morton
George Clymer
James Smith
George Taylor
James Wilson
George Ross

DELAWARE
Caesar Rodney
George Read
Thomas M'Kean

MARYLAND
Samuel Chase
William Paca
Thomas Stone
Charles Carroll, of Carrollton

VIRGINIA
George Wythe
Richard Henry Lee
Thomas Jefferson
Benjamin Harrison
Thomas Nelson, Jr.
Francis Lightfoot Lee
Carter Braxton

NORTH CAROLINA
William Hooper
Joseph Hewes
John Penn

SOUTH CAROLINA
Edward Rutledge
Thomas Heyward, Jr.
Thomas Lynch, Jr.
Arthur Middleton

GEORGIA
Button Gwinnett
Lyman Hall
George Walton

Resolved, That copies of the Declaration be sent to the several assemblies, conventions, and committees, or councils of safety, and to the several commanding officers of the continental troops; that it be proclaimed in each of the United States, at the head of the army.

ARTICLES OF
CONFEDERATION

To all to whom these Presents shall come, we the undersigned Delegates of the States affixed to our Names send greeting.

Whereas the Delegates of the United States of America in Congress assembled did on the fifteenth day of November in the Year of our Lord One Thousand Seven Hundred and Seventy-seven, and in the Second Year of the Independence of America agree to certain articles of Confederation and perpetual Union between the States of Newhampshire, Massachusetts-bay, Rhodeisland and Providence Plantations, Connecticut, New York, New Jersey, Pennsylvania, Delaware, Maryland, Virginia, North-Carolina, South-Carolina and Georgia in the Words following, viz.

Articles of Confederation and perpetual Union between the States of Newhampshire, Massachusetts-bay, Rhodeisland and Providence Plantations, Connecticut, New-York, New-Jersey, Pennsylvania, Delaware, Maryland, Virginia, North-Carolina, South-Carolina and Georgia.

Article I. The stile of this confederacy shall be "The United States of America."

Article II. Each State retains its sovereignty, freedom and independence, and every power, jurisdiction and right, which is not by this confederation expressly delegated to the United States, in Congress assembled.

Article III. The said States hereby severally enter into a firm league of friendship with each other, for their common defence, the security of their liberties, and their mutual and general welfare, binding themselves to assist each other, against all force offered to, or attacks made upon them, or any of them, on account of religion, sovereignty, trade or any other pretence whatever.

ARTICLE IV. The better to secure and perpetuate mutual friendship and inter-course among the people of the different States in this Union, the free inhabi-tants of each of these States, paupers, vagabonds and fugitives from justice ex-cepted, shall be entitled to all privileges and immunities of free citizens in the several States; and the people of each State shall have free ingress and regress to and from any other State, and shall enjoy therein all the privileges of trade and commerce, subject to the same duties, impositions and restrictions as the inhabitants thereof respectively, provided that such restrictions shall not ex-tend so far as to prevent the removal of property imported into any State, to any other State of which the owner is an inhabitant; provided also that no im-position, duties or restriction shall be laid by any State, on the property of the United States, or either of them.

If any person guilty of, or charged with treason, felony, or other high misde-meanor in any State, shall flee from justice, and be found in any of the United States, he shall upon demand of the Governor or Executive power, of the State from which he fled, be delivered up and removed to the State having jurisdic-tion of his offence.

Full faith and credit shall be given in each of these States to the records, acts and judicial proceedings of the courts and magistrates of every other State.

ARTICLE V. For the more convenient management of the general interests of the United States, delegates shall be annually appointed in such manner as the legislature of each State shall direct, to meet in Congress on the first Monday in November, in every year, with a power reserved to each State, to recall its delegates, or any of them, at any time within the year, and to send others in their stead, for the remainder of the year.

No State shall be represented in Congress by less than two, nor by more than seven members; and no person shall be capable of being a delegate for more than three years in any term of six years; nor shall any person, being a del-egate, be capable of holding any office under the United States, for which he, or another for his benefit receives any salary, fees or emolument of any kind.

Each State shall maintain its own delegates in a meeting of the States, and while they act as members of the committee of the States.

In determining questions in the United States, in Congress assembled, each State shall have one vote.

Freedom of speech and debate in Congress shall not be impeached or ques-tioned in any court, or place out of Congress, and the members of Congress shall be protected in their persons from arrests and imprisonments, during the time of their going to and from, and attendance on Congress, except for trea-son, felony, or breach of the peace.

ARTICLE VI. No State without the consent of the United States in Congress assembled, shall send any embassy to, or receive any embassy from, or enter into any conference, agreement, alliance or treaty with any king, prince or state; nor shall any person holding any office of profit or trust under the United States, or any of them, accept of any present, emolument, office or title of any kind whatever from any king, prince or foreign state; nor shall the United States in Congress assembled, or any of them, grant any title of nobility.

No two or more States shall enter into any treaty, confederation or alliance whatever between them, without the consent of the United States in Congress assembled, specifying accurately the purposes for which the same is to be entered into, and how long it shall continue.

No State shall lay any imposts or duties, which may interfere with any stipulations in treaties, entered into by the United States in Congress assembled, with any king, prince or state, in pursuance of any treaties already proposed by Congress, to the courts of France and Spain.

No vessels of war shall be kept up in time of peace by any State, except such number only, as shall be deemed necessary by the United States in Congress assembled, for the defence of such State, or its trade; nor shall any body of forces be kept up by any State, in time of peace, except such number only, as in the judgment of the United States, in Congress assembled, shall be deemed requisite to garrison the forts necessary for the defence of such State; but every State shall always keep up a well regulated and disciplined militia, sufficiently armed and accoutred, and shall provide and constantly have ready for use, in public stores, a due number of field pieces and tents, and a proper quantity of arms, ammunition and camp equipage.

No State shall engage in any war without the consent of the United States in Congress assembled, unless such State be actually invaded by enemies, or shall have received certain advice of a resolution being formed by some nation of Indians to invade such State, and the danger is so imminent as not to admit of a delay, till the United States in Congress assembled can be consulted: nor shall any State grant commissions to any ships or vessels of war, nor letters of marque or reprisal, except it be after a declaration of war by the United States in Congress assembled, and then only against the kingdom or state and the subjects thereof, against which war has been so declared, and under such regulations as shall be established by the United States in Congress assembled, unless such State be infested by pirates, in which case vessels of war may be fitted out for that occasion, and kept so long as the danger shall continue, or until the United States in Congress assembled shall determine otherwise.

ARTICLE VII. When land-forces are raised by any State of the common defence, all officers of or under the rank of colonel, shall be appointed by the

Legislature of each State respectively by whom such forces shall be raised, or in such manner as such State shall direct, and all vacancies shall be filled up by the State which first made the appointment.

ARTICLE VIII. All charges of war, and all other expenses that shall be incurred for the common defence or general welfare, and allowed by the United States in Congress assembled, shall be defrayed out of a common treasury, which shall be supplied by the several States, in proportion to the value of all land within each State, granted to or surveyed for any person, as such land and the buildings and improvements thereon shall be estimated according to such mode as the United States in Congress assembled, shall from time to time direct and appoint.

The taxes for paying that proportion shall be laid and levied by the authority and direction of the Legislatures of the several States within the time agreed upon by the United States in Congress assembled.

ARTICLE IX. The United States in Congress assembled, shall have the sole and exclusive right and power of determining on peace and war, except in the cases mentioned in the sixth article—of sending and receiving ambassadors—entering into treaties and alliances, provided that no treaty of commerce shall be made whereby the legislative power of the respective States shall be restrained from imposing such imposts and duties on foreigners, as their own people are subjected to, or from prohibiting the exportation or importation of and species of goods or commodities whatsoever—of establishing rules for deciding in all cases, what captures on land or water shall be legal, and in what manner prizes taken by land or naval forces in the service of the United States shall be divided or appropriated—of granting letters of marque and reprisal in times of peace—appointing courts for the trial of piracies and felonies committed on the high seas and establishing courts for receiving and determining finally appeals in all cases of captures, provided that no member of Congress shall be appointed a judge of any of the said courts.

The United States in Congress assembled shall also be the last resort on appeal in all disputes and differences now subsisting or that hereafter may arise between two or more States concerning boundary, jurisdiction or any other cause whatever; which authority shall always be exercised in the manner following. Whenever the legislative or executive authority or lawful agent of any State in controversy with another shall present a petition to Congress, stating the matter in question and praying for a hearing, notice thereof shall be given by order of Congress to the legislative or executive authority of the other State in controversy, and a day assigned for the appearance of the parties by their lawful agents, who shall then be directed to appoint by joint consent, commissioners or judges to constitute a court for hearing and determining the matter in question: but if they cannot agree, Congress shall name three persons out of each of the United States, and from the list of such persons each party shall alternately strike out one, the petitioners beginning, until the number shall be reduced to thirteen; and from that number not less than seven, nor more than nine names as Congress shall direct, shall in the presence of Congress be drawn out by lot, and the persons whose names shall be so drawn or any five of them, shall be commissioners or judges, to hear and finally determine the controversy, so always as a major part of the judges who shall hear the cause shall agree in the determination: and if either party shall neglect to attend at the day appointed, without reasons, which Congress shall judge sufficient, or being present shall refuse to strike, the Congress shall proceed to nominate three persons out of each State, and the Secretary of Congress shall strike in behalf of such party absent or refusing; and the judgment and sentence of the court to be appointed, in the manner before prescribed, shall be final and conclusive; and if any of the parties shall refuse to submit to the authority of such court, or to appear or defend their claim or cause, the court shall nevertheless proceed to pronounce sentence, or judgment, which shall in like manner be final and decisive, the judgment or sentence and other proceedings being in either case transmitted to Congress, and lodged among the acts of Congress for the security of the parties concerned: provided that every commissioner, before he sits in judgment, shall take an oath to be administered by one of the judges of the supreme or superior court of the State where the case shall be tried, "well and truly to hear and determine the matter in question, according to the best of his judgment, without favour, affection or hope of reward:" provided also that no State shall be deprived of territory for the benefit of the United States.

All controversies concerning the private right of soil claimed under different grants of two or more States, whose jurisdiction as they may respect such lands, and the states which passed such grants are adjusted, the said grants or either of them being at the same time claimed to have originated antecedent to such settlement of jurisdiction, shall on the petition of either party to the Congress of the United States, be finally determined as near as may be in the same manner as is before prescribed for deciding disputes respecting territorial jurisdiction between different States.

The United States in Congress assembled shall also have the sole and exclusive right and power of regulating the alloy and value of coin struck by their own authority, or by that of the respective States—fixing the standard of weights and measures throughout the United States—regulating the trade and managing all affairs with the Indians, not members of any of the States, provided that the legislative right of any State within its own limits be not infringed or violated—establishing and regulating post-offices from one State to another, throughout all of the United States, and exacting such postage on the papers passing thro' the same as may be requisite to defray the expenses of the said office—appointing all officers of the land forces, in the service of the United States, excepting regimental officers—appointing all the officers of the naval forces, and commissioning all officers whatever in the service of the United States—making rules for the government and regulation of the said land and naval forces, and directing their operations.

The United States in Congress assembled shall have authority to appoint a committee, to sit in the recess of Congress, to be denominated "a Committee of the States," and to consist of one delegate from each State; and to appoint such other committees and civil officers as may be necessary for managing the general affairs of the United States under their direction—to appoint one of their number to preside, provided that no person be allowed to serve in the office of president more than one year in any term of three years; to ascertain the necessary sums of money to be raised for the service of the United States, and to appropriate and apply the same for defraying the public expenses—to borrow money, or emit bills on the credit of the United States, transmitting every half year to the respective States an account of the sums of money so borrowed or emitted,—to build and equip a navy—to agree upon the number of land forces, and to make requisitions from each State for its quota, in proportion to the number of white inhabitants in such State; which requisition shall be binding, and thereupon the Legislature of each State shall appoint the regimental officers, raise the men and cloath, arm and equip them in a soldier like manner, at the expense of the United States; and the officers and men so cloathed, armed and equipped shall march to the place appointed, and within the time agreed on by the United States in Congress assembled: but if the United States in Congress assembled shall, on consideration of circumstances judge proper that any State should not raise men, or should raise a smaller number of men than the quota thereof, such extra number shall be raised, officered, cloathed, armed and equipped in the same manner as the quota of such State, unless the legislature of such State shall judge that such extra number cannot be safely spared out of the same, in which case they shall raise officer, cloath, arm and equip as many of such extra number as they judge can be safely spared. And the officers and men so cloathed, armed and equipped, shall march to the place appointed, and within the time agreed on by the United States in Congress assembled.

The United States in Congress assembled shall never engage in a war, nor grant letters of marque and reprisal in time of peace, nor enter into any treaties or alliances, nor coin money, nor regulate the value thereof, nor ascertain the sums and expenses necessary for the defence and welfare of the United States, or any of them, nor emit bills, nor borrow money on the credit of the United

States, nor appropriate money, nor agree upon the number of vessels to be built or purchased, or the number of land or sea forces to be raised, nor appoint a commander in chief of the army or navy, unless nine States assent to the same: nor shall a question on any other point, except for adjourning from day to day be determined, unless by the votes of a majority of the United States in Congress assembled.

The Congress of the United States shall have power to adjourn to any time within the year, and to any place within the United States, so that no period of adjournment be for a longer duration than the space of six months, and shall publish the journal of their proceedings monthly, except such parts thereof relating to treaties, alliances or military operations, as in their judgment require secresy; and the yeas and nays of the delegates of each State on any question shall be entered on the Journal, when it is desired by any delegate; and the delegates of a State, or any of them, at his or their request shall be furnished with a transcript of the said journal, except such parts as are above excepted, to lay before the Legislatures of the several States.

ARTICLE X. The committee of the States, or any nine of them, shall be authorized to execute, in the recess of Congress, such of the powers of Congress as the United States in Congress assembled, by the consent of nine States, shall from time to time think expedient to vest them with; provided that no power be delegated to the said committee, for the exercise of which, by the articles of confederation, the voice of nine States in the Congress of the United States assembled is requisite.

ARTICLE XI. Canada acceding to this confederation, and joining in the measures of the United States, shall be admitted into, and entitled to all the advantages of this Union: but no other colony shall be admitted into the same, unless such admission be agreed to by nine States.

ARTICLE XII. All bills of credit emitted, monies borrowed and debts contracted by, or under the authority of Congress, before the assembling of the United States, in pursuance of the present confederation, shall be deemed and considered as a charge against the United States, for payment and satisfaction whereof the said United States, and the public faith are hereby solemnly pledged.

ARTICLE XIII. Every State shall abide by the determinations of the United States in Congress assembled, on all questions which by this confederation are submitted to them. And the articles of this confederation shall be inviolably observed by every State, and the Union shall be perpetual; nor shall any alteration at any time hereafter be made in any of them; unless such alteration be agreed to in a Congress of the United States, and be afterwards confirmed by the Legislatures of every State.

And whereas it has pleased the Great Governor of the world to incline the hearts of the Legislatures we respectively represent in Congress, to approve of, and to authorize us to ratify the said articles of confederation and perpetual union. Know ye that we the undersigned delegates, by virtue of the power and authority to us given for that purpose, do by these presents, in the name and in behalf of our respective constituents, fully and entirely ratify and confirm each and every of the said articles of confederation and perpetual union, and all and singular the matters and things therein contained: and we do further solemnly plight and engage the faith of our respective constituents, that they shall abide by the determinations of the United States in Congress assembled, on all questions, which by the said confederation are submitted to them. And that the articles thereof shall be inviolably observed by the States we respectively represent, and that the Union shall be perpetual.

In witness thereof we have hereunto set our hands in Congress. Done at Philadelphia in the State of Pennsylvania the ninth day of July in the year of our Lord one thousand seven hundred and seventy-eight, and in the third year of the independence of America.

THE CONSTITUTION OF THE UNITED STATES

WE THE PEOPLE OF THE UNITED STATES, in order to form a more perfect Union, establish Justice, insure domestic Tranquility, provide for the common defence, promote the general Welfare, and secure the Blessings of Liberty to ourselves and our Posterity, do ordain and establish this Constitution for the United States of America.

ARTICLE. I.

Section. 1. All legislative Powers herein granted shall be vested in a Congress of the United States, which shall consist of a Senate and House of Representatives.

Section. 2. The House of Representatives shall be composed of Members chosen every second Year by the People of the several States, and the Electors in each State shall have the Qualifications requisite for Electors of the most numerous Branch of the State Legislature.

No Person shall be a Representative who shall not have attained to the Age of twenty five Years, and been seven Years a Citizen of the United States, and who shall not, when elected, be an Inhabitant of that State in which he shall be chosen.

Representatives and direct Taxes shall be apportioned among the several States which may be included within this Union, according to their respective Numbers, which shall be determined by adding to the whole Number of free Persons, including those bound to Service for a Term of Years, and excluding Indians not taxed, three fifths of all other Persons. The actual Enumeration shall be made within three Years after the first Meeting of the Congress of the United States, and within every subsequent Term of ten Years, in such Manner as they shall by Law direct. The Number of Representatives shall not exceed one for every thirty Thousand, but each State shall have at Least one Representative; and until such enumeration shall be made, the State of New Hampshire shall be entitled to chuse three, Massachusetts eight, Rhode-Island and

Providence Plantations one, Connecticut five, New-York six, New Jersey four, Pennsylvania eight, Delaware one, Maryland six, Virginia ten, North Carolina five, South Carolina five, and Georgia three.

When vacancies happen in the Representation from any state, the Executive Authority thereof shall issue Writs of Election to fill such Vacancies.

The House of Representatives shall chuse their Speaker and other Officers; and shall have the sole Power of Impeachment.

Section. 3. The Senate of the United States shall be composed of two Senators from each State, chosen by the legislature thereof, for six Years; and each Senator shall have one Vote.

Immediately after they shall be assembled in Consequence of the first Election, they shall be divided as equally as may be into three Classes. The Seats of the Senators of the first Class shall be vacated at the Expiration of the second Year, of the second Class at the Expiration of the fourth Year, and of the third Class at the Expiration of the sixth Year, so that one third maybe chosen every second Year; and if Vacancies happen by Resignation, or otherwise, during the Recess of the Legislature of any State, the Executive thereof may make temporary Appointments until the next Meeting of the Legislature, which shall then fill such Vacancies.

No Person shall be a Senator who shall not have attained to the Age of thirty Years, and been nine Years a Citizen of the United States, and who shall not, when elected, be an Inhabitant of that State for which he shall be chosen.

The Vice President of the United States shall be President of the Senate, but shall have no Vote, unless they be equally divided.

The Senate shall chuse their other Officers, and also a President pro tempore, in the Absence of the Vice President, or when he shall exercise the Office of President of the United States.

The Senate shall have the sole Power to try all Impeachments. When sitting for that Purpose, they shall be on Oath or Affirmation. When the President of the United States is tried, the Chief Justice shall preside: And no Person shall be convicted without the Concurrence of two thirds of the Members present.

Judgment in Cases of Impeachment shall not extend further than to removal from Office, and disqualification to hold and enjoy any Office of honor, Trust or Profit under the United States: but the Party convicted shall nevertheless be liable and subject to Indictment, Trial, Judgment and Punishment, according to Law.

Section. 4. The Times, Places and Manner of holding Elections for Senators and Representatives, shall be prescribed in each State by the Legislature thereof; but the Congress may at any time by Law make or alter such Regulations, except as to the Places of chusing Senators.

The Congress shall assemble at least once in every Year, and such Meeting shall be on the first Monday in December, unless they shall by Law appoint a different Day.

Section. 5. Each House shall be the Judge of the Elections, Returns and Qualifications of its own Members, and a Majority of each shall constitute a Quorum to do Business; but a smaller Number may adjourn from day to day, and may be authorized to compel the Attendance of absent Members, in such Manner, and under such Penalties as each House may provide.

Each House may determine the Rules of its Proceedings, punish its Members for disorderly Behaviour, and, with the Concurrence of two thirds, expel a Member.

Each House shall keep a Journal of its Proceedings, and from time to time publish the same, excepting such Parts as may in their Judgment require Secrecy; and the Yeas and Nays of the Members of either House on any question shall, at the Desire of one fifth of those Present, be entered on the Journal.

Neither House, during the Session of Congress, shall, without the Consent of the other, adjourn for more than three days, not to any other Place than that in which the two Houses shall be sitting.

Section. 6. The Senators and Representatives shall receive a Compensation for their Services, to be ascertained by Law, and paid out of the Treasury of the United States. They shall in all Cases, except Treason, Felony and Breach of the Peace, be privileged from Arrest during their Attendance at the Session of their respective Houses, and in going to and returning from the same; and for any Speech or Debate in either House, they shall not be questioned in any other Place.

No Senator or Representative shall, during the Time for which he was elected, be appointed to any civil Office under the Authority of the United States, which shall have been created, or the Emoluments whereof shall have been encreased during such time; and no Person holding any Office under the United States, shall be a Member of either House during his Continuance in Office.

Section. 7. All Bills for raising Revenue shall originate in the House of Representatives; but the Senate may propose or concur with Amendments as on other Bills.

Every Bill which shall have passed the House of Representatives and the Senate shall, before it become a Law, be presented to the President of the United States; If he approve he shall sign it, but if not he shall return it, with his Objections to that House in which it shall have originated, who shall enter the Objections at large on their Journal, and proceed to reconsider it. If after such Reconsideration two thirds of that House shall agree to pass the Bill, it shall be sent, together with the Objections, to the other House, by which it shall likewise be reconsidered, and if approved by two thirds of that House, it shall become a Law. But in all such Cases the Votes of both Houses shall be determined by yeas and Nays, and the Names of the Persons voting for and against the Bill shall be entered on the Journal of each House respectively. If any Bill shall not be returned by the President within ten Days (Sundays excepted) after it shall have been presented to him, the Same shall be a Law, in like Manner as if he had signed it, unless the Congress by their Adjournment prevent its Return, in which Case it shall not be a Law.

Every Order, Resolution, or Vote to which the Concurrence of the Senate and House of Representatives may be necessary (except on a question of Adjournment) shall be presented to the President of the United States; and before the Same shall take Effect, shall be approved by him, or being disapproved by him, shall be repassed by two thirds of the Senate and House of Representatives, according to the Rules and Limitations prescribed in the Case of a Bill.

Section. 8. The Congress shall have Power To lay and collect Taxes, Duties, Imposts and Excises, to pay the Debts and provide for the common Defence and general Welfare of the United States; but all Duties, Imposts and Excises shall be uniform throughout the United States;

To borrow Money on the credit of the United States;

To regulate Commerce with foreign Nations, and among the several States, and with the Indian Tribes;

To establish an uniform Rule of Naturalization, and uniform Laws on the subject of Bankruptcies throughout the United States;

To coin Money, regulate the Value thereof, and of foreign Coin, and fix the Standard of Weights and Measures;

To provide for the Punishment of counterfeiting the Securities and current Coin of the United States;

To establish Post Offices and Post Roads;

To promote the Progress of Science and useful Arts, by securing for limited Times to Authors and Inventors the exclusive Right to their respective Writings and Discoveries;

To constitute Tribunals inferior to the supreme Court;

To define and punish Piracies and Felonies committed on the high Seas, and Offences against the Law of Nations;

To declare War, grant Letters of Marque and Reprisal, and make Rules concerning Captures on land and Water;

To raise and support Armies, but no Appropriation of Money to that Use shall be for a longer Term than two Years;

To provide and maintain a Navy;

To make Rules for the Government and Regulation of the land and naval Forces;

To provide for calling forth the Militia to execute the Laws of the Union, suppress Insurrections and repel Invasions;

To provide for organizing, arming, and disciplining, the Militia, and for governing such Part of them as may be employed in the Service of the United States, reserving to the States respectively, the Appointment of the Officers, and the Authority of training the Militia according to the discipline prescribed by Congress.

To exercise exclusive Legislation in all Cases whatsoever, over such District (not exceeding ten Miles square) as may, by Cession of Particular States, and the Acceptance of Congress, become the Seat of the Government of the United States, and to exercise like Authority over all Places purchased by the Consent of the Legislature of the State in which the Same shall be, for the Erection of Forts, Magazines, Arsenals, dock-Yards, and other needful Buildings;—And

To make all Laws which shall be necessary and proper for carrying into Execution the foregoing Powers, and all other Powers vested by this Constitution in the Government of the United States, or in any Department or Officer thereof.

Section. 9. The Migration or Importation of such Persons as any of the States now existing shall think proper to admit, shall not be prohibited by the Congress prior to the Year one thousand eight hundred and eight, but a Tax or duty may be imposed on such Importation, not exceeding ten dollars for each Person.

The Privilege of the Writ of Habeas Corpus shall not be suspended, unless when in Cases of Rebellion or Invasion the public Safety may require it.

No Bill of Attainder or ex post facto Law shall be passed.

No Capitation, or other direct, Tax shall be laid, unless in Proportion to the Census or Enumeration herein before directed to be taken.

No Tax or Duty shall be laid on Articles exported from any State.

No Preference shall be given by any Regulation of Commerce or Revenue to the Ports of one State over those of another: nor shall Vessels bound to, or from, one State, be obliged to enter, clear, or pay Duties in another.

No Money shall be drawn from the Treasury, but in Consequence of Appropriations made by Law; and a regular Statement and Account of the Receipts and Expenditures of all public Money shall be published from time to time.

No Title of Nobility shall be granted by the United States: And no Person holding any Office of Profit or trust under them, shall, without the Consent of the Congress, accept of any present, Emolument, Office, or Title, of any kind whatever, from any King, Prince, or foreign State.

Section 10. No State shall enter into any Treaty, Alliance, or Confederation; grant Letters of Marque and Reprisal; coin Money; emit Bills of Credit; make any Thing but gold and silver Coin a Tender in Payment of Debts; pass any Bill of Attainder, ex post facto Law, or Law impairing the Obligation of Contracts, or grant any Title of Nobility.

No State shall, without the Consent of the Congress, lay any Imposts or Duties on Imports or Exports, except what may be absolutely necessary for executing its inspection Laws: and the net Produce of all Duties and Imposts, laid by any State on Imports or Exports, shall be for the Use of the Treasury of the United States; and all such Laws shall be subject to the Revision and Controul of the Congress.

No State shall, without the Consent of Congress, lay any Duty of Tonnage, keep Troops, or Ships of War in time of Peace, enter into any Agreement or Compact with another State, or with a foreign Power, or engage in War, unless actually invaded, or in such imminent Danger as will not admit of delay.

Article. II.

Section. 1. The executive Power shall be vested in a President of the United States of America. He shall hold his Office during the term of four Years, and, together with the Vice President, chosen for the same Term, be elected, as follows:

Each State shall appoint, in such Manner as the Legislature thereof may direct, a Number of Electors, equal to the whole Number of Senators and Representatives to which the State may be entitled in the Congress: but no Senator or Representative, or Person holding an Office of Trust or Profit under the United States, shall be appointed an Elector.

The Electors shall meet in their respective States, and vote by Ballot for two Persons, of whom one at least shall not be an Inhabitant of the same State with themselves. And they shall make a List of all the Persons voted for, and of the Number of Votes for each; which List they shall sign and certify, and transmit sealed to the Seat of the Government of the United States, directed to the President of the Senate. The President of the Senate shall, in the Presence of the Senate and House of Representatives, open all the Certificates, and the Votes shall then be counted. The Person having the greatest Number of Votes shall be the President, if such Number be a Majority of the whole Number of Electors appointed; and if there be more than one who have such Majority, and have an equal Number of Votes, then the House of Representatives shall immediately chuse by Ballot one of them for President; and if no Person have a Majority, then from the five highest on the List the said House shall in like Manner chuse the President. But in chusing the President, the Votes shall be taken by States, the Representation from each State having one Vote; A quorum for this Purpose shall consist of a Member or Members from two thirds of the States, and a Majority of all the States shall be necessary to a Choice. In every Case, after the Choice of the President, the Person having the greatest Number of Votes of the Electors shall be the Vice President. But if there should remain two or more who have equal Votes, the Senate shall chuse from them by Ballot the Vice President.

The Congress may determine the Time of chusing the Electors, and the Day on which they shall give their Votes; which Day shall be the same throughout the United States.

No Person except a natural born Citizen, or a Citizen of the United States, at the time of the Adoption of this Constitution, shall be eligible to the Office of President; neither shall any Person be eligible to that Office who shall not have attained to the Age of thirty five Years, and been fourteen Years a Resident within the United States.

In Case of the Removal of the President from Office, or of his Death, Resignation, or Inability to discharge the Powers and Duties of the said Office, the Same shall devolve on the Vice President, and the Congress may by Law provide for the Case of Removal, Death, Resignation or Inability, both of the President and Vice President, declaring what Officer shall then act as President, and such Officer shall act accordingly, until the Disability be removed, or a President shall be elected.

The President shall, at stated Times, receive for his Services, a Compensation, which shall neither be encreased or diminished during the Period for which he shall have been elected, and he shall not receive within that Period any other Emolument from the United States, or any of them.

Before he enters on the Execution of his Office, he shall take the following Oath or Affirmation:—"I do solemnly swear (or affirm) that I will faithfully execute the Office of President of the United States, and will to the best of my Ability, preserve, protect and defend the Constitution of the United States."

Section. 2. The President shall be Commander in Chief of the Army and Navy of the United States, and of the Militia of the several States, when called into the actual Service of the United States; he may require the Opinion, in writing, of the principal Officer in each of the executive Departments, upon any Subject relating to the Duties of their respective Offices, and he shall have Power to grant Reprieves and Pardons for Offences against the United States, except in Cases of Impeachment.

He shall have Power, by and with the Advice and Consent of the Senate, to make Treaties, provided two thirds of the Senators present concur; and he shall nominate, and by and with the Advice and Consent of the Senate, shall appoint Ambassadors, other public Ministers and Consuls, Judges of the supreme Court, and all other Officers of the United States, whose Appointments are not herein otherwise provided for, and which shall be established by Law;

but the Congress may by Law vest the Appointment of such inferior Officers, as they think proper, in the President alone, in the Courts of Law, or in the Heads of Departments.

The President shall have Power to fill up all Vacancies that may happen during the Recess of the Senate, by granting Commissions which shall expire at the End of their next Session.

Section. 3. He shall from time to time give to the Congress Information of the State of the Union, and recommend to their Consideration such Measures as he shall judge necessary and expedient; he may, on extraordinary Occasions, convene both Houses, or either of them, and in Case of Disagreement between them, with Respect to the Time of Adjournment, he may adjourn them to such Time as he shall think proper; he shall receive Ambassadors and other public Ministers; he shall take Care that the Laws be faithfully executed, and shall Commission all the Officers of the United States.

Section. 4. The President, Vice President and all civil Officers of the United States, shall be removed from Office on Impeachment for, and Conviction of, Treason, Bribery, or other high Crimes and Misdemeanors.

ARTICLE. III.

Section. 1. The judicial Power of the United States, shall be vested in one supreme Court, and in such inferior Courts as the Congress may from time to time ordain and establish. The Judges, both of the supreme and inferior Courts, shall hold their Offices during good Behavior, and shall, at stated Times, receive for their Services, a Compensation, which shall not be diminished during their Continuance in Office.

Section. 2. The judicial Power shall extend to all Cases, in Law and Equity, arising under this Constitution, the Laws of the United States, and Treaties made, or which shall be made, under their Authority;—to all Cases affecting Ambassadors, other public Ministers and Consuls;—to all Cases of admiralty and maritime Jurisdiction;—the Controversies to which the United States shall be a Party;—to Controversies between two or more States;—between a State and Citizens of another State;—between Citizens of different States;—between Citizens of the same State claiming Lands under Grants of different States, and between a State, or the Citizens thereof, and foreign States, Citizens or Subjects.

In all cases affecting Ambassadors, other public Ministers and Consuls, and those in which a State shall be Party, the supreme Court shall have original Jurisdiction. In all the other Cases before mentioned, the supreme Court shall have appellate Jurisdiction, both as to Law and Fact, with such Exceptions, and under such Regulations as the Congress shall make.

The Trial of all Crimes, except in Cases of Impeachment, shall be by Jury; and such Trial shall be held in the State where the said Crimes shall have been committed; but when not committed within any State, the Trial shall be at such Place or Places as the Congress may by Law have directed.

Section. 3. Treason against the United States, shall consist only in levying War against them, or in adhering to their Enemies, giving them Aid and Comfort. No Person shall be convicted of Treason unless on the Testimony of two Witnesses to the same overt Act, or on Confession in open Court.

The Congress shall have Power to declare the Punishment of Treason, but no Attainder of Treason shall work Corruption of Blood, or Forfeiture except during the Life of the Person attainted.

ARTICLE. IV.

Section. 1. Full Faith and Credit shall be given in each State to the public Acts, Records, and judicial Proceedings of every other State. And the Congress may by general Laws prescribe the Manner in which such Acts, Records and Proceedings shall be proved, and the Effect thereof.

Section. 2. The Citizens of each State shall be entitled to all Privileges and Immunities of Citizens in the several States.

A Person charged in any State with Treason, Felony, or other Crime, who shall flee from Justice, and be found in another State, shall on Demand of the executive Authority of the State from which he fled, be delivered up, to be removed to the State having Jurisdiction of the Crime.

No Person held to Service or Labour in one State, under the Laws thereof, escaping into another, shall, in Consequence of any Law or Regulation therein, be discharged from such Service or Labour, but shall be delivered up on Claim of the Party to whom such Service or Labour may be due.

Section. 3. New States may be admitted by the Congress into this Union; but no new State shall be formed or erected within the Jurisdiction of any other State; nor any State be formed by the Junction of two or more States, or Parts of States, without the consent of the Legislatures of the States concerned as well as of the Congress.

The Congress shall have Power to dispose of and make all needful Rules and Regulations respecting the Territory or other Property belonging to the United States; and nothing in this Constitution shall be so construed as to Prejudice any Claims of the United States, or of any particular States.

Section. 4. The United States shall guarantee to every State in this Union a Republican Form of Government, and shall protect each of them against Invasion; and on Application of the Legislature, or of the Executive (when the Legislature cannot be convened) against domestic Violence.

ARTICLE. V.

The Congress, whenever two thirds of both Houses shall deem it necessary, shall propose Amendments to this Constitution, or, on the Application of the Legislatures of two thirds of the several States, shall call a Convention for proposing Amendments, which, in either Case, shall be valid to all Intents and Purposes, as Part of this Constitution, when ratified by the Legislatures of three fourths of the several States, or by Conventions in three fourths thereof, as the one or the other Mode of Ratification may be proposed by the Congress; Provided that no Amendment which may be made prior to the Year One thousand eight hundred and eight shall in any Manner affect the first and fourth Clauses in the Ninth Section of the first Article; and that no State, without its Consent, shall be deprived of its equal Suffrage in the Senate.

ARTICLE. VI.

All Debts contracted and Engagements entered into, before the Adoption of this Constitution, shall be as valid against the United States under this Constitution, as under the Confederation.

This Constitution, and the Laws of the United States which shall be made in Pursuance thereof; and all Treaties made, or which shall be made, under the Authority of the United States, shall be the supreme Law of the Land; and the Judges in every State shall be bound thereby, any Thing in the Constitution or Laws of any State to the Contrary notwithstanding.

The Senators and Representatives before mentioned, and the Members of the several State Legislatures, and all executive and judicial Officers, both of the United States and of the several States, shall be bound by Oath or Affirmation, to support this Constitution; but no religious Test shall ever be required as a Qualification to any Office or public Trust under the United States.

ARTICLE. VII.

The Ratification of the Conventions of nine States, shall be sufficient for the Establishment of this Constitution between the States so ratifying the Same.

Done in Convention by the Unanimous Consent of the States present the Seventeenth Day of September in the Year of our Lord one thousand seven hundred and Eighty seven and of the Independence of the United States of America the Twelfth. In witness thereof We have hereunto subscribed our Names,

G°. WASHINGTON—Presd^t.
and deputy from Virginia.

New Hampshire	{ John Langdon Nicholas Gilman		
		Delaware	{ Geo: Read Gunning Bedford jun John Dickinson Richard Bassett Jaco: Broom
Massachusetts	{ Nathaniel Gorham Rufus King		
Connecticut	{ Wm Saml Johnson Roger Sherman	Maryland	{ James McHenry Dan of St Thos Jenifer Danl Carroll
New York: . . .	Alexander Hamilton		
		Virginia	{ John Blair— James Madison Jr.
New Jersey	{ Wil: Livingston David A. Brearley. Wm Paterson. Jona: Dayton		
		North Carolina	{ Wm Blount Richd Dobbs Spaight. Hu Williamson
Pennsylvania	{ B Franklin Thomas Mifflin Robt Morris Geo. Clymer Thos FitzSimons Jared Ingersoll James Wilson Gouv Morris	South Carolina	{ J. Rutledge Charles Cotesworth Pinckney Charles Pinckney Pierce Butler.
		Georgia	{ William Few Abr Baldwin

AMENDMENTS TO THE CONSTITUTION

ARTICLES IN ADDITION TO, and Amendment of the Constitution of the United States of America, proposed by Congress, and ratified by the Legislatures of the several States, pursuant to the fifth Article of the original Constitution.

AMENDMENT I.

Congress shall make no law respecting an establishment of religion, or prohibiting the free exercise thereof; or abridging the freedom of speech, or of the press; or the right of the people peaceably to assemble, and to petition the Government for a redress of grievances.

AMENDMENT II.

A well regulated Militia, being necessary to the security of a free State, the right of the people to keep and bear Arms, shall not be infringed.

AMENDMENT III.

No Soldier shall, in time of peace be quartered in any house, without the consent of the Owner, nor in time of war, but in a manner to be prescribed by law.

AMENDMENT IV.

The right of the people to be secure in their persons, houses, papers, and effects, against unreasonable searches and seizures, shall not be violated, and no Warrants shall issue, but upon probable cause, supported by Oath or affirmation, and particularly describing the place to be searched, and the persons or things to be seized.

AMENDMENT V.

No person shall be held to answer for a capital, or otherwise infamous crime, unless on a presentment or indictment of a Grand Jury, except in cases arising in the land or naval forces, or in the Militia, when in actual service in time of War or public danger; nor shall any person be subject for the same offence to be twice put in jeopardy of life or limb; nor shall be compelled in any criminal case to be a witness against himself, nor be deprived of life, liberty, or property, without due process of law; nor shall private property be taken for public use, without just compensation.

AMENDMENT VI.

In all criminal prosecutions, the accused shall enjoy the right to a speedy and public trial, by an impartial jury of the State and district wherein the crime shall have been committed, which district shall have been previously ascertained by law, and to be informed of the nature and cause of the accusation; to be confronted with the witnesses against him; to have compulsory process for obtaining witnesses in his favor, and to have the Assistance of Counsel for his defence.

AMENDMENT VII.

In Suits at common law, where the value in controversy shall exceed twenty dollars, the right of trial by jury shall be preserved, and no fact tried by a jury, shall be otherwise re-examined in any Court of the United States, than according to the rules of the common law.

AMENDMENT VIII.

Excessive bail shall not be required, nor excessive fines imposed, nor cruel and unusual punishments inflicted.

AMENDMENT IX.

The enumeration in the Constitution, of certain rights, shall not be construed to deny or disparage others retained by the people.

AMENDMENT X.

The powers not delegated to the United States by the Constitution, nor prohibited by it to the States, are reserved to the States respectively, or to the people. [The first ten amendments went into effect December 15, 1791.]

AMENDMENT XI.

The Judicial power of the United States shall not be construed to extend to any suit in law or equity, commenced or prosecuted against one of the United States by Citizens of another State, or by Citizens or Subjects of any Foreign State. [January 8, 1798.]

AMENDMENT XII.

The Electors shall meet in their respective states, and vote by ballot for President and Vice-President, one of whom, at least, shall not be an inhabitant of the same state with themselves; they shall name in their ballots the person voted for as President, and in distinct ballots the person voted for as Vice-President, and they shall make distinct lists of all persons voted for as President, and of all persons voted for as Vice President, and of the number of votes for each, which lists they shall sign and certify, and transmit sealed to the seat of the government of the United States, directed to the President of the Senate;—The President of the Senate shall, in the presence of the Senate and House of Representatives, open all the certificates and the votes shall then be counted;—The person having the greatest number of votes for President, shall be the President, if such number be a majority of the whole number of Electors appointed; and if no person have such majority, then from the persons having the highest numbers not exceeding three on the list of those voted for as President, the House of Representatives shall choose immediately, by ballot, the President. But in choosing the President, the votes shall be taken by states, the representation from each state having one vote; a quorum for this purpose shall consist of a member or members from two-thirds of the states, and a majority of all the states shall be necessary to a choice. And if the House of Representatives shall not choose a President whenever the right of choice shall devolve upon them, before the fourth day of March next following, then the Vice-President shall act as President, as in the case of the death or other constitutional disability of the President.—The person having the greatest number of votes as Vice-President, shall be the Vice-President, if such number be a majority of the whole number of Electors appointed, and if no person have a majority, then from the two highest numbers on the list, the Senate shall choose the Vice-President; a quorum for the purpose shall consist of two-thirds of the whole number of Senators, and a majority of the whole number shall be necessary to a choice. But no person constitutionally ineligible to the office of President shall be eligible to that of Vice-President of the United States. [September 25, 1804.]

AMENDMENT XIII.

Section 1. Neither slavery nor involuntary servitude, except as a punishment for crime whereof the party shall have been duly convicted, shall exist within the United States, or any place subject to their jurisdiction.

Section 2. Congress shall have power to enforce this article by appropriate legislation. [December 18, 1865.]

AMENDMENT XIV.

Section 1. All persons born or naturalized in the United States, and subject to the jurisdiction thereof, are citizens of the United States and of the State wherein they reside. No State shall make or enforce any law which shall abridge the privileges or immunities of citizens of the United States; nor shall any State deprive any person of life, liberty, or property, without due process of law; nor deny to any person within its jurisdiction the equal protection of the laws.

Section 2. Representatives shall be apportioned among the several States according to their respective numbers, counting the whole number of persons in each State, excluding Indians not taxed. But when the right to vote at any election for the choice of electors for President and Vice President of the United States, Representatives in Congress, the Executive and Judicial officers of a State, or the members of the Legislature thereof, is denied to any of the male inhabitants of such State, being twenty-one years of age, and citizens of the United States, or in any way abridged, except for participation in rebellion, or other crime, the basis of representation therein shall be reduced in the proportion which the number of such male citizens shall bear to the whole number of male citizens twenty-one years of age in such State.

Section 3. No person shall be a Senator or Representative in Congress, or elector of President and Vice President, or hold any office, civil or military, under the United States, or under any State, who, having previously taken an oath, as a member of Congress, or as an officer of the United States, or as a member of any State legislature, or as an executive or judicial officer of any State, to support the Constitution of the United States, shall have engaged in insurrection or rebellion against the same, or given aid or comfort to the enemies thereof. But Congress may by a vote of two-thirds of each House, remove such disability.

Section 4. The validity of the public debt of the United States, authorized by law, including debts incurred for payment of pensions and bounties for services in suppressing insurrection or rebellion, shall not be questioned. But neither the United States nor any State shall assume or pay any debt or obligation incurred in aid of insurrection or rebellion against the United States, or any claim for the loss or emancipation of any slave; but all such debts, obligations and claims shall be held illegal and void.

Section 5. The Congress shall have power to enforce, by appropriate legislation, the provisions of this article. [July 28, 1868.]

AMENDMENT XV.

Section 1. The right of citizens of the United States to vote shall not be denied or abridged by the United States or by any State on account of race, color, or previous condition of servitude—

Section 2. The Congress shall have power to enforce this article by appropriate legislation.—[March 30, 1870.]

Amendment XVI.

The Congress shall have power to lay and collect taxes on incomes, from whatever source derived, without apportionment among the several States, and without regard to any census or enumeration. [February 25, 1913.]

Amendment XVII.

The Senate of the United States shall be composed of two senators from each State, elected by the people thereof, for six years; and each Senator shall have one vote. The electors in each State shall have the qualifications requisite for electors of the most numerous branch of the State legislature.

When vacancies happen in the representation of any State in the Senate, the executive authority of such State shall issue writs of election to fill such vacancies: *Provided,* That the legislature of any State may empower the executive thereof to make temporary appointments until the people fill the vacancies by election as the legislature may direct.

This amendment shall not be so construed as to affect the election or term of any senator chosen before it becomes valid as part of the Constitution. [May 31, 1913.]

Amendment XVIII.

After one year from the ratification of this article, the manufacture, sale, or transportation of intoxicating liquors within, the importation thereof into, or the exportation thereof from the United States and all territory subject to the jurisdiction thereof for beverage purposes is hereby prohibited.

The Congress and the several States shall have concurrent power to enforce this article by appropriate legislation.

This article shall be inoperative unless it shall have been ratified as an amendment to the Constitution by the legislatures of the several States, as provided in the Constitution, within seven years from the date of the submission thereof to the States by Congress. [January 29, 1919.]

AMENDMENT XIX.

The right of citizens of the United States to vote shall not be denied or abridged by the United States or by any State on account of sex.

The Congress shall have power by appropriate legislation to enforce the provisions of this article. [August 26, 1920.]

AMENDMENT XX.

Section 1. The terms of the President and Vice-President shall end at noon on the twentieth day of January, and the terms of Senators and Representatives at noon on the third day of January, of the years in which such terms would have ended if this article had not been ratified; and the terms of their successors shall then begin.

Section 2. The Congress shall assemble at least once in every year, and such meeting shall begin at noon on the third day of January, unless they shall by law appoint a different day.

Section 3. If, at the time fixed for the beginning of the term of the President, the President-elect shall have died, the Vice-President-elect shall become President. If a President shall not have been chosen before the time fixed for the beginning of his term, or if the President-elect shall have failed to qualify, then the Vice-President-elect shall act as President until a President shall have qualified; and the Congress may by law provide for the case wherein neither a President-elect nor a Vice-President-elect shall have qualified, declaring who shall then act as President, or the manner in which one who is to act shall be selected, and such person shall act accordingly until a President or Vice-President shall have qualified.

Section 4. The Congress may by law provide for the case of the death of any of the persons from whom the House of Representatives may choose a President whenever the right of choice shall have devolved upon them, and for the case of the death of any of the persons from whom the Senate may choose a Vice-President whenever the right of choice shall have devolved upon them.

Section 5. Sections 1 and 2 shall take effect on the 15th day of October following the ratification of this article.

Section 6. This article shall be inoperative unless it shall have been ratified as an amendment to the Constitution by the legislatures of three-fourths of the several States within seven years from the date of its submission. [February 6, 1933.]

Amendment XXI.

Section 1. The eighteenth article of amendment to the Constitution of the United States is hereby repealed.

Section 2. The transportation or importation into any State, Territory or possession of the United States for delivery or use therein of intoxicating liquors, in violation of the laws thereof, is hereby prohibited.

Section 3. This article shall be inoperative unless it shall have been ratified as an amendment to the Constitution by convention in the several States, as provided in the Constitution, within seven years from the date of the submission thereof to the States by the Congress. [December 5, 1933.]

Amendment XXII.

Section 1. No person shall be elected to the office of the President more than twice, and no person who has held the office of President, or acted as President, for more than two years of a term to which some other person was elected President shall be elected to the office of the President more than once. But this Article shall not apply to any person holding the office of President when this Article was proposed by the Congress, and shall not prevent any person who may be holding the office of President, or acting as President, during the term within which this Article becomes operative from holding the office of President or acting as President during the remainder of such term.

Section 2. This article shall be inoperative unless it shall have been ratified as an amendment to the Constitution by the legislatures of three-fourths of the several states within seven years from the date of its submission to the States by the Congress. [February 27, 1951.]

Amendment XXIII.

Section 1. The District constituting the seat of government of the United States shall appoint in such manner as the Congress may direct:

A number of electors of President and Vice-President equal to the whole number of Senators and Representatives in Congress to which the District would be entitled if it were a State, but in no event more than the least populous State; they shall be in addition to those appointed by the States, but they shall be considered, for the purposes of the election of President and Vice-President, to be electors appointed by a State; and they shall meet in the District and perform such duties as provided by the twelfth article of amendment.

Section 2. The Congress shall have the power to enforce this article by appropriate legislation. [March 29, 1961.]

AMENDMENT XXIV.

Section 1. The right of citizens of the United States to vote in any primary or other election for President or Vice President, for electors for President or Vice President, or for Senator or Representative in Congress, shall not be denied or abridged by the United States or any State by reason of failure to pay any poll tax or other tax.

Section 2. The Congress shall have power to enforce this article by appropriate legislation. [January 23, 1964.]

AMENDMENT XXV.

Section 1. In case of the removal of the President from office or of his death or resignation, the Vice President shall become President.

Section 2. Whenever there is a vacancy in the office of Vice President, the President shall nominate a Vice President who shall take office upon confirmation by a majority vote of both Houses of Congress.

Section 3. Whenever the President transmits to the President pro tempore of the Senate and the Speaker of the House of Representatives his written declaration that he is unable to discharge the powers and duties of his office, and until he transmits to them a written declaration to the contrary, such powers and duties shall be discharged by the Vice President as Acting President.

Section 4. Whenever the Vice President and a majority of either the principal officers of the executive departments or of such other body as Congress may by law provide, transmit to the President pro tempore of the Senate and the Speaker of the House of Representatives their written declaration that the President is unable to discharge the powers and duties of his office, the Vice President shall immediately assume the powers and duties of the office as Acting President.

Thereafter, when the President transmits to the President pro tempore of the Senate and the Speaker of the House of Representatives his written declaration that no inability exists, he shall resume the powers and duties of his office unless the Vice President and a majority of either the principal officers of the executive departments or of such other body as Congress may by law provide, transmit within four days to the President pro tempore of the Senate and the Speaker of the House of Representatives their written declaration that the President is unable to discharge the powers and duties of his office. Thereupon Congress shall decide the issue, assembling within forty-eight hours for that purpose if not in session. If the Congress, within twenty-one days after receipt of the latter written declaration, or, if Congress is not in session, within twenty-one days after Congress is required to assemble, determines by two-thirds vote of both Houses that the President is unable to discharge the powers and duties of his office, the Vice President shall continue to discharge the same as Acting President; otherwise, the President shall resume the powers and duties of his office. [February 10, 1967.]

Amendment XXVI.

Section 1. The right of citizens of the United States, who are eighteen years of age or older, to vote shall not be denied or abridged by the United States or by any State on account of age.

Section 2. The Congress shall have power to enforce this article by appropriate legislation [June 30, 1971.]

Amendment XXVII.

No law, varying the compensation for the services of the Senators and Representatives shall take effect, until an election of Representatives shall have intervened. [May 8, 1992.]

PRESIDENTIAL ELECTIONS

Year	Number of States	Candidates	Parties	Popular Vote	% of Popular Vote	Electoral Vote	% Voter Participation
1789	11	**GEORGE WASHINGTON**	No party designations			69	
		John Adams				34	
		Other candidates				35	
1792	15	**GEORGE WASHINGTON**	No party designations			132	
		John Adams				77	
		George Clinton				50	
		Other candidates				5	
1796	16	**JOHN ADAMS**	Federalist			71	
		Thomas Jefferson	Democratic-Republican			68	
		Thomas Pinckney	Federalist			59	
		Aaron Burr	Democratic-Republican			30	
		Other candidates				48	
1800	16	**THOMAS JEFFERSON**	Democratic-Republican			73	
		Aaron Burr	Democratic-Republican			73	
		John Adams	Federalist			65	
		Charles C. Pinckney	Federalist			64	
		John Jay	Federalist			1	
1804	17	**THOMAS JEFFERSON**	Democratic-Republican			162	
		Charles C. Pinckney	Federalist			14	

Year	Number of States	Candidates	Parties	Popular Vote	% of Popular Vote	Electoral Vote	% Voter Participation
1808	17	**JAMES MADISON**	Democratic-Republican			122	
		Charles C. Pinckney	Federalist			47	
		George Clinton	Democratic-Republican			6	
1812	18	**JAMES MADISON**	Democratic-Republican			128	
		DeWitt Clinton	Federalist			89	
1816	19	**JAMES MONROE**	Democratic-Republican			183	
		Rufus King	Federalist			34	
1820	24	**JAMES MONROE**	Democratic-Republican			231	
		John Quincy Adams	Independent			1	
1824	24	**JOHN QUINCY ADAMS**	Democratic-Republican	108,740	30.5	84	26.9
		Andrew Jackson	Democratic-Republican	153,544	43.1	99	
		Henry Clay	Democratic-Republican	47,136	13.2	37	
		William H. Crawford	Democratic-Republican	46,618	13.1	41	
1828	24	**ANDREW JACKSON**	Democratic	647,286	56.0	178	57.6
		John Quincy Adams	National-Republican	508,064	44.0	83	

Year	Number of States	Candidates	Parties	Popular Vote	% of Popular Vote	Electoral Vote	% Voter Participation
1832	24	**ANDREW JACKSON**	Democratic	688,242	54.5	219	55.4
		Henry Clay	National-Republican	473,462	37.5	49	
		William Wirt	Anti-Masonic	101,051	8.0	7	
		John Floyd	Democratic			11	
1836	26	**MARTIN VAN BUREN**	Democratic	765,483	50.9	170	57.8
		William H. Harrison	Whig	739,795	49.1	73	
		Hugh L. White	Whig			26	
		Daniel Webster	Whig			14	
		W. P. Mangum	Whig			11	
1840	26	**WILLIAM H. HARRISON**	Whig	1,274,624	53.1	234	80.2
		Martin Van Buren	Democratic	1,127,781	46.9	60	
1844	26	**JAMES K. POLK**	Democratic	1,338,464	49.6	170	78.9
		Henry Clay	Whig	1,300,097	48.1	105	
		James G. Birney	Liberty	62,300	2.3		
1848	30	**ZACHARY TAYLOR**	Whig	1,360,967	47.4	163	72.7
		Lewis Cass	Democratic	1,222,342	42.5	127	
		Martin Van Buren	Free Soil	291,263	10.1		
1852	31	**FRANKLIN PIERCE**	Democratic	1,601,117	50.9	254	69.6
		Winfield Scott	Whig	1,385,453	44.1	42	
		John P. Hale	Free Soil	155,825	5.0		
1856	31	**JAMES BUCHANAN**	Democratic	1,832,955	45.3	174	78.9
		John C. Frémont	Republican	1,339,932	33.1	114	
		Millard Fillmore	American	871,731	21.6	8	

Year	Number of States	Candidates	Parties	Popular Vote	% of Popular Vote	Electoral Vote	% Voter Participation
1860	33	**ABRAHAM LINCOLN**	Republican	1,865,593	39.8	180	81.2
		Stephen A. Douglas	Democratic	1,382,713	29.5	12	
		John C. Breckinridge	Democratic	848,356	18.1	72	
		John Bell	Constitutional Union	592,906	12.6	39	
1864	36	**ABRAHAM LINCOLN**	Republican	2,206,938	55.0	212	73.8
		George B. McClellan	Democratic	1,803,787	45.0	21	
1868	37	**ULYSSES S. GRANT**	Republican	3,013,421	52.7	214	78.1
		Horatio Seymour	Democratic	2,706,829	47.3	80	
1872	37	**ULYSSES S. GRANT**	Republican	3,596,745	55.6	286	71.3
		Horace Greeley	Democratic	2,843,446	43.9	66	
1876	38	**RUTHERFORD B. HAYES**	Republican	4,036,572	48.0	185	81.8
		Samuel J. Tilden	Democratic	4,284,020	51.0	184	
1880	38	**JAMES A. GARFIELD**	Republican	4,453,295	48.5	214	79.4
		Winfield S. Hancock	Democratic	4,414,082	48.1	155	
		James B. Weaver	Greenback-Labor	308,578	3.4		
1884	38	**GROVER CLEVELAND**	Democratic	4,879,507	48.5	219	77.5
		James G. Blaine	Republican	4,850,293	48.2	182	
		Benjamin F. Butler	Greenback-Labor	175,370	1.8		
		John P. St. John	Prohibition	150,369	1.5		
1888	38	**BENJAMIN HARRISON**	Republican	5,477,129	47.9	233	79.3
		Grover Cleveland	Democratic	5,537,857	48.6	168	
		Clinton B. Fisk	Prohibition	249,506	2.2		
		Anson J. Streeter	Union Labor	146,935	1.3		

Year	Number of States	Candidates	Parties	Popular Vote	% of Popular Vote	Electoral Vote	% Voter Participation
1892	44	**GROVER CLEVELAND**	Democratic	5,555,426	46.1	277	74.7
		Benjamin Harrison	Republican	5,182,690	43.0	145	
		James B. Weaver	People's	1,029,846	8.5	22	
		John Bidwell	Prohibition	264,133	2.2		
1896	45	**WILLIAM McKINLEY**	Republican	7,102,246	51.1	271	79.3
		William J. Bryan	Democratic	6,492,559	47.7	176	
1900	45	**WILLIAM McKINLEY**	Republican	7,218,491	51.7	292	73.2
		William J. Bryan	Democratic; Populist	6,356,734	45.5	155	
		John C. Wooley	Prohibition	208,914	1.5		
1904	45	**THEODORE ROOSEVELT**	Republican	7,628,461	57.4	336	65.2
		Alton B. Parker	Democratic	5,084,223	37.6	140	
		Eugene V. Debs	Socialist	402,283	3.0		
		Silas C. Swallow	Prohibition	258,536	1.9		
1908	46	**WILLIAM H. TAFT**	Republican	7,675,320	51.6	321	65.4
		William J. Bryan	Democratic	6,412,294	43.1	162	
		Eugene V. Debs	Socialist	420,793	2.8		
		Eugene W. Chafin	Prohibition	253,840	1.7		
1912	48	**WOODROW WILSON**	Democratic	6,296,547	41.9	435	58.8
		Theodore Roosevelt	Progressive	4,118,571	27.4	88	
		William H. Taft	Republican	3,486,720	23.2	8	
		Eugene V. Debs	Socialist	900,672	6.0		
		Eugene W. Chafin	Prohibition	206,275	1.4		

Year	Number of States	Candidates	Parties	Popular Vote	% of Popular Vote	Electoral Vote	% Voter Participation
1916	48	**WOODROW WILSON**	Democratic	9,127,695	49.4	277	61.6
		Charles E. Hughes	Republican	8,533,507	46.2	254	
		A. L. Benson	Socialist	585,113	3.2		
		J. Frank Hanly	Prohibition	220,506	1.2		
1920	48	**WARREN G. HARDING**	Republican	16,143,407	60.4	404	49.2
		James M. Cox	Democratic	9,130,328	34.2	127	
		Eugene V. Debs	Socialist	919,799	3.4		
		P. P. Christensen	Farmer-Labor	265,411	1.0		
1924	48	**CALVIN COOLIDGE**	Republican	15,718,211	54.0	382	48.9
		John W. Davis	Democratic	8,385,283	28.8	136	
		Robert M. La Follette	Progressive	4,831,289	16.6	13	
1928	48	**HERBERT C. HOOVER**	Republican	21,391,993	58.2	444	56.9
		Alfred E. Smith	Democratic	15,016,169	40.9	87	
1932	48	**FRANKLIN D. ROOSEVELT**	Democratic	22,809,638	57.4	472	56.9
		Herbert C. Hoover	Republican	15,758,901	39.7	59	
		Norman Thomas	Socialist	881,951	2.2		
1936	48	**FRANKLIN D. ROOSEVELT**	Democratic	27,752,869	60.8	523	61.0
		Alfred M. Landon	Republican	16,674,665	36.5	8	
		William Lemke	Union	882,479	1.9		
1940	48	**FRANKLIN D. ROOSEVELT**	Democratic	27,307,819	54.8	449	62.5
		Wendell L. Willkie	Republican	22,321,018	44.8	82	
1944	48	**FRANKLIN D. ROOSEVELT**	Democratic	25,606,585	53.5	432	55.9
		Thomas E. Dewey	Republican	22,014,745	46.0	99	

Year	Number of States	Candidates	Parties	Popular Vote	% of Popular Vote	Electoral Vote	% Voter Participation
1948	48	**HARRY S. TRUMAN**	Democratic	24,179,345	49.6	303	53.0
		Thomas E. Dewey	Republican	21,991,291	45.1	189	
		J. Strom Thurmond	States' Rights	1,176,125	2.4	39	
		Henry A. Wallace	Progressive	1,157,326	2.4		
1952	48	**DWIGHT D. EISENHOWER**	Republican	33,936,234	55.1	442	63.3
		Adlai E. Stevenson	Democratic	27,314,992	44.4	89	
1956	48	**DWIGHT D. EISENHOWER**	Republican	35,590,472	57.6	457	60.6
		Adlai E. Stevenson	Democratic	26,022,752	42.1	73	
1960	50	**JOHN F. KENNEDY**	Democratic	34,226,731	49.7	303	62.8
		Richard M. Nixon	Republican	34,108,157	49.5	219	
1964	50	**LYNDON B. JOHNSON**	Democratic	43,129,566	61.1	486	61.9
		Barry M. Goldwater	Republican	27,178,188	38.5	52	
1968	50	**RICHARD M. NIXON**	Republican	31,785,480	43.4	301	60.9
		Hubert H. Humphrey	Democratic	31,275,166	42.7	191	
		George C. Wallace	American Independent	9,906,473	13.5	46	
1972	50	**RICHARD M. NIXON**	Republican	47,169,911	60.7	520	55.2
		George S. McGovern	Democratic	29,170,383	37.5	17	
		John G. Schmitz	American	1,099,482	1.4		

Year	Number of States	Candidates	Parties	Popular Vote	% of Popular Vote	Electoral Vote	% Voter Participation
1976	50	**JIMMY CARTER**	Democratic	40,830,763	50.1	297	53.5
		Gerald R. Ford	Republican	39,147,793	48.0	240	
1980	50	**RONALD REAGAN**	Republican	43,901,812	50.7	489	52.6
		Jimmy Carter	Democratic	35,483,820	41.0	49	
		John B. Anderson	Independent	5,719,437	6.6		
		Ed Clark	Libertarian	921,188	1.1		
1984	50	**RONALD REAGAN**	Republican	54,451,521	58.8	525	53.1
		Walter F. Mondale	Democratic	37,565,334	40.6	13	
1988	50	**GEORGE H. BUSH**	Republican	47,917,341	53.4	426	50.1
		Michael Dukakis	Democratic	41,013,030	45.6	111	
1992	50	**BILL CLINTON**	Democratic	44,908,254	43.0	370	55.0
		George H. Bush	Republican	39,102,343	37.4	168	
		H. Ross Perot	Independent	19,741,065	18.9	0	
1996	50	**BILL CLINTON**	Democratic	47,401,185	49.0	379	49.0
		Bob Dole	Republican	39,197,469	41.0	159	
		H. Ross Perot	Independent	8,085,295	8.0	0	

Candidates receiving less than 1 percent of the popular vote have been omitted. Thus the percentage of popular vote given for any election year may not total 100 percent.

Before the passage of the Twelfth Amendment in 1804, the Electoral College voted for two presidential candidates; the runner-up became vice-president.

ADMISSION OF STATES

Order of Admission	State	Date of Admission	Order of Admission	State	Date of Admission
1	Delaware	December 7, 1787	26	Michigan	January 26, 1837
2	Pennsylvania	December 12, 1787	27	Florida	March 3, 1845
3	New Jersey	December 18, 1787	28	Texas	December 29, 1845
4	Georgia	January 2, 1788	29	Iowa	December 28, 1846
5	Connecticut	January 9, 1788	30	Wisconsin	May 29, 1848
6	Massachusetts	February 7, 1788	31	California	September 9, 1850
7	Maryland	April 28, 1788	32	Minnesota	May 11, 1858
8	South Carolina	May 23, 1788	33	Oregon	February 14, 1859
9	New Hampshire	June 21, 1788	34	Kansas	January 29, 1861
10	Virginia	June 25, 1788	35	West Virginia	June 30, 1863
11	New York	July 26, 1788	36	Nevada	October 31, 1864
12	North Carolina	November 21, 1789	37	Nebraska	March 1, 1867
13	Rhode Island	May 29, 1790	38	Colorado	August 1, 1876
14	Vermont	March 4, 1791	39	North Dakota	November 2, 1889
15	Kentucky	June 1, 1792	40	South Dakota	November 2, 1889
16	Tennessee	June 1, 1796	41	Montana	November 8, 1889
17	Ohio	March 1, 1803	42	Washington	November 11, 1889
18	Louisiana	April 30, 1812	43	Idaho	July 3, 1890
19	Indiana	December 11, 1816	44	Wyoming	July 10, 1890
20	Mississippi	December 10, 1817	45	Utah	January 4, 1896
21	Illinois	December 3, 1818	46	Oklahoma	November 16, 1907
22	Alabama	December 14, 1819	47	New Mexico	January 6, 1912
23	Maine	March 15, 1820	48	Arizona	February 14, 1912
24	Missouri	August 10, 1821	49	Alaska	January 3, 1959
25	Arkansas	June 15, 1836	50	Hawaii	August 21, 1959

POPULATION OF THE UNITED STATES

Year	Number of States	Population	% Increase	Population per Square Mile
1790	13	3,929,214		4.5
1800	16	5,308,483	35.1	6.1
1810	17	7,239,881	36.4	4.3
1820	23	9,638,453	33.1	5.5
1830	24	12,866,020	33.5	7.4
1840	26	17,069,453	32.7	9.8
1850	31	23,191,876	35.9	7.9
1860	33	31,443,321	35.6	10.6
1870	37	39,818,449	26.6	13.4
1880	38	50,155,783	26.0	16.9
1890	44	62,947,714	25.5	21.1
1900	45	75,994,575	20.7	25.6
1910	46	91,972,266	21.0	31.0
1920	48	105,710,620	14.9	35.6
1930	48	122,775,046	16.1	41.2
1940	48	131,669,275	7.2	44.2
1950	48	150,697,361	14.5	50.7
1960	50	179,323,175	19.0	50.6
1970	50	203,235,298	13.3	57.5
1980	50	226,504,825	11.4	64.0
1985	50	237,839,000	5.0	67.2
1990	50	250,122,000	5.2	70.6
1995	50	263,411,707	5.3	74.4

IMMIGRATION TO THE UNITED STATES, FISCAL YEARS 1820–1990

Year	Number	Year	Number	Year	Number	Year	Number
1820–1989	**55,457,531**	**1871–80**	**2,812,191**	**1921–30**	**4,107,209**	**1971–80**	**4,493,314**
1820	8,385	1871	321,350	1921	805,228	1971	370,478
1821–30	**143,439**	1872	404,806	1922	309,556	1972	384,685
1821	9,127	1873	459,803	1923	522,919	1973	400,063
1822	6,911	1874	313,339	1924	706,896	1974	394,861
1823	6,354	1875	227,498	1925	294,314	1975	386,914
1824	7,912	1876	169,986	1926	304,488	1976	398,613
1825	10,199	1877	141,857	1927	335,175	1976	103,676
1826	10,837	1878	138,469	1928	307,255	1977	462,315
1827	18,875	1879	177,826	1929	279,678	1978	601,442
1828	27,382	1880	457,257	1930	241,700	1979	460,348
1829	22,520	**1881–90**	**5,246,613**	**1931–40**	**528,431**	1980	530,639
1830	23,322	1881	669,431	1931	97,139	**1981–90**	**7,338,062**
1831–40	**599,125**	1882	788,992	1932	35,576	1981	596,600
1831	22,633	1883	603,322	1933	23,068	1982	594,131
1832	60,482	1884	518,592	1934	29,470	1983	559,763
1833	58,640	1885	395,346	1935	34,956	1984	543,903
1834	65,365	1886	334,203	1936	36,329	1985	570,009
1835	45,374	1887	490,109	1937	50,244	1986	601,708
1836	76,242	1888	546,889	1938	67,895	1987	601,516
1837	79,340	1889	444,427	1939	82,998	1988	643,025
1838	38,914	1890	455,302	1940	70,756	1989	1,090,924
1839	68,069	**1891–1900**	**3,687,564**	**1941–50**	**1,035,039**	1990	1,536,483
1840	84,066	1891	560,319	1941	51,776		
1841–50	**1,713,251**	1892	579,663	1942	28,781		
1841	80,289	1893	439,730	1943	23,725		
1842	104,565	1894	285,631	1944	28,551		
		1895	258,536	1945	38,119		
		1896	343,267	1946	108,721		

Year	Number	Year	Number	Year	Number
1843	52,496	1897	230,832	1947	147,292
1844	78,615	1898	229,299	1948	170,570
1845	114,371	1899	311,715	1949	188,317
1846	154,416	1900	448,572	1950	249,187
1847	234,968	**1901–10**	**8,795,386**	**1951–60**	**2,515,479**
1848	226,527	1901	487,918	1951	205,717
1849	297,024	1902	648,743	1952	265,520
1850	369,980	1903	857,046	1953	170,434
1851–60	**2,598,214**	1904	812,870	1954	208,177
1851	379,466	1905	1,026,499	1955	237,790
1852	371,603	1906	1,100,735	1956	321,625
1853	368,645	1907	1,285,349	1957	326,867
1854	427,833	1908	782,870	1958	253,265
1855	200,877	1909	751,786	1959	260,686
1856	200,436	1910	1,041,570	1960	265,398
1857	251,306	**1911–20**	**5,735,811**	**1961–70**	**3,321,677**
1858	123,126	1911	878,587	1961	271,344
1859	121,282	1912	838,172	1962	283,763
1860	153,640	1913	1,197,892	1963	306,260
1861–70	**2,314,824**	1914	1,218,480	1964	292,248
1861	91,918	1915	326,700	1965	296,697
1862	91,985	1916	298,826	1966	323,040
1863	176,282	1917	295,403	1967	361,972
1864	193,418	1918	110,618	1968	454,448
1865	248,120	1919	141,132	1969	358,579
1866	318,568	1920	430,001	1970	373,326
1867	315,722				
1868	138,840				
1869	352,768				
1870	387,203				

Source: U.S. Immigration and Naturalization Service, 1991.

IMMIGRATION BY REGION AND SELECTED COUNTRY OF LAST RESIDENCE, FISCAL YEARS 1820–1989

Region and Country of Last Residence[1]	1820	1821–30	1831–40	1841–50	1851–60	1861–70	1871–80	1881–90
All countries	8,385	143,439	599,125	1,713,251	2,598,214	2,314,824	2,812,191	5,246,613
Europe	7,690	98,797	495,681	1,597,442	2,452,577	2,065,141	2,271,925	4,735,484
Austria-Hungary	—[2]	—[2]	—[2]	—[2]	—[2]	7,800	72,969	353,719
Austria	—[2]	—[2]	—[2]	—[2]	—[2]	484[3]	63,009	226,038
Hungary	—[2]	—[2]	—[2]	—[2]	—[2]	7,124[3]	9,960	127,681
Belgium	1	27	22	5,074	4,738	6,734	7,221	20,177
Czechoslovakia	—[4]	—[4]	—[4]	—[4]	—[4]	—[4]	—[4]	—[4]
Denmark	20	169	1,063	539	3,749	17,094	31,771	88,132
France	371	8,497	45,575	77,262	76,358	35,986	72,206	50,464
Germany	968	6,761	152,454	434,626	951,667	787,468	718,182	1,452,970
Greece	—	20	49	16	31	72	210	2,308
Ireland[5]	3,614	50,724	207,381	780,719	914,119	435,778	436,871	655,482
Italy	30	409	2,253	1,870	9,231	11,725	55,759	307,309
Netherlands	49	1,078	1,412	8,251	10,789	9,102	16,541	53,701
Norway-Sweden	3	91	1,201	13,903	20,931	109,298	211,245	568,362
Norway	—[6]	—[6]	—[6]	—[6]	—[6]	—[6]	95,323	176,586
Sweden	—[6]	—[6]	—[6]	—[6]	—[6]	—[6]	115,922	391,776
Poland	5	16	369	105	1,164	2,027	12,970	51,806
Portugal	35	145	829	550	1,055	2,658	14,082	16,978
Romania	—[7]	—[7]	—[7]	—[7]	—[7]	—	11	6,348
Soviet Union	14	75	277	551	457	2,512	39,284	213,282
Spain	139	2,477	2,125	2,209	9,298	6,697	5,266	4,419
Switzerland	31	3,226	4,821	4,644	25,011	23,286	28,293	81,988
United Kingdom[5,8]	2,410	25,079	75,810	267,044	423,974	606,896	548,043	807,357
Yugoslavia	—[9]	—[9]	—[9]	—[9]	5	—[9]	—[9]	—[9]
Other Europe	—	3	40	79	5	8	1,001	682

Asia	6	30	55	141	41,538	64,759	124,160	69,942
China[10]	1	2	8	35	41,397	64,301	123,201	61,711
Hong Kong	—[11]	—[11]	—[11]	—[11]	—[11]	—[11]	—[11]	—[11]
India	1	8	39	36	43	69	163	269
Iran	—[12]	—[12]	—[12]	—[12]	—[12]	—[12]	—[12]	—[12]
Israel	—[13]	—[13]	—[13]	—[13]	—[13]	—[13]	—[13]	—[13]
Japan	—[14]	—[14]	—[14]	—[14]	—[14]	186	149	2,270
Korea	—[15]	—[15]	—[15]	—[15]	—[15]	—[15]	—[15]	—[15]
Philippines	—[16]	—[16]	—[16]	—[16]	—[16]	—[16]	—[16]	—[16]
Turkey	1	20	7	59	83	131	404	3,782
Vietnam	—[11]	—[11]	—[11]	—[11]	—[11]	—[11]	—[11]	—[11]
Other Asia	3	1	1	11	15	72	243	1,910
America	387	11,564	33,424	62,469	74,720	166,607	404,044	426,967
Canada & Newfoundland[17,18]	209	2,277	13,624	41,723	59,309	153,878	383,640	393,304
Mexico[18]	1	1	6,599	3,271	3,078	2,191	5,162	191,319
Caribbean	164	3,834	12,301	13,528	10,660	9,046	13,957	29,042
Cuba	—[12]	—[12]	—[12]	—[12]	—[12]	—[12]	—[12]	—[12]
Dominican Republic	—[20]	—[20]	—[20]	—[20]	—[20]	—[20]	—[20]	—[20]
Haiti	—[20]	—[20]	—[20]	—[20]	—[20]	—[20]	—[20]	—[20]
Jamaica	—[21]	—[21]	—[21]	—[21]	—[21]	—[21]	—[21]	—[21]
Other Caribbean	164	3,834	12,301	13,528	10,660	9,046	13,957	29,042
Central America	2	105	44	368	449	95	157	404
El Salvador	—[20]	—[20]	—[20]	—[20]	—[20]	—[20]	—[20]	—[20]
Other Central America	2	105	44	368	449	95	157	404
South America	11	531	856	3,579	1,224	1,397	1,128	2,304
Argentina	—[20]	—[20]	—[20]	—[20]	—[20]	—[20]	—[20]	—[20]
Colombia	—[20]	—[20]	—[20]	—[20]	—[20]	—[20]	—[20]	—[20]
Ecuador	—[20]	—[20]	—[20]	—[20]	—[20]	—[20]	—[20]	—[20]
Other South America	11	531	856	3,579	1,224	1,397	1,128	2,304
Other America	—[22]	—[22]	—[22]	—[22]	—[22]	—[22]	—[22]	—[22]
Africa	1	16	54	55	210	312	358	857
Oceania	9	2	9	29	158	214	10,914	12,574
Not specified[22]	300	33,030	69,902	53,115	29,011	17,791	790	789

Region and Country of Last Residence[1]	1891–1900	1901–10	1911–20	1921–30	1931–40	1941–50	1951–60	1961–70
All countries	3,687,564	8,795,386	5,735,811	4,107,209	528,431	1,035,039	2,515,479	3,321,677
Europe	3,555,352	8,056,040	4,321,887	2,463,194	347,566	621,147	1,325,727	1,123,492
Austria-Hungary	592,707[23]	2,145,266[23]	896,342[23]	63,548	11,424	28,329	103,743	26,022
Austria	234,081[3]	668,209[3]	453,649	32,868	3,563[24]	24,860[24]	67,106	20,621
Hungary	181,288[3]	808,511[3]	442,693	30,680	7,861	3,469	36,637	5,401
Belgium	18,167	41,635	33,746	15,846	4,817	12,189	18,575	9,192
Czechoslovakia	—[4]	—[4]	3,426[4]	102,194	14,393	8,347	918	3,273
Denmark	50,231	65,285	41,983	32,430	2,559	5,393	10,984	9,201
France	30,770	73,379	61,897	49,610	12,623	38,809	51,121	45,237
Germany	505,152[23]	341,498[23]	143,945[23]	412,202	114,058[24]	226,578[24]	477,765	190,796
Greece	15,979	167,519	184,201	51,084	9,119	8,973	47,608	85,969
Ireland[5]	388,416	339,065	146,181	211,234	10,973	19,789	48,362	32,966
Italy	651,893	2,045,877	1,109,524	455,315	68,028	57,661	185,491	214,111
Netherlands	26,758	48,262	43,718	26,948	7,150	14,860	52,277	30,606
Norway-Sweden	321,281	440,039	161,469	165,780	8,700	20,765	44,632	32,600
Norway	95,015	190,505	66,395	68,531	4,740	10,100	22,935	15,484
Sweden	226,266	249,534	95,074	97,249	3,960	10,665	21,697	17,116
Poland	96,720[23]	—[23]	4,813[23]	227,734	17,026	7,571	9,985	53,539
Portugal	27,508	69,149	89,732	29,994	3,329	7,423	19,588	76,065
Romania	12,750	53,008	13,311	67,646	3,871	1,076	1,039	2,531
Soviet Union	505,290[23]	1,597,306[23]	921,201[23]	61,742	1,370	571	671	2,465
Spain	8,731	27,935	68,611	28,958	3,258	2,898	7,894	44,659
Switzerland	31,179	34,922	23,091	29,676	5,512	10,547	17,675	18,453
United Kingdom[5,8]	271,538	525,950	341,408	339,570	31,572	139,306	202,824	213,822
Yugoslavia	—[9]	—[9]	1,888[9]	49,064	5,835	1,576	8,225	20,381
Other Europe	282	39,945	31,400	42,619	11,949	8,486	16,350	11,604

Asia	74,862	323,543	247,236	112,059	16,595	37,028	153,249	427,642
China[10]	14,799	20,605	21,278	29,907	4,928	16,709	9,657	34,764
Hong Kong	—[11]	—[11]	—[11]	—[11]	—[11]	—[11]	15,541[11]	75,007
India	68	4,713	2,082	1,886	496	1,761	1,973	27,189
Iran	—[12]	—[12]	—[12]	241[12]	195	1,380	3,388	10,339
Israel	—[13]	—[13]	—[13]	—[13]	—[13]	476[13]	25,476	29,602
Japan	25,942	129,797	83,837	33,462	1,948	1,555	46,250	39,988
Korea	—[15]	—[15]	—[15]	—[15]	—[15]	107[15]	6,231	34,526
Philippines	—[16]	—[16]	—[16]	—[16]	528[16]	4,691	19,307	98,376
Turkey	30,425	157,369	134,066	33,824	1,065	798	3,519	10,142
Vietnam	—[11]	—[11]	—[11]	—[11]	—[11]	—[11]	335[11]	4,340
Other Asia	3,628	11,059	5,973	12,739	7,435	9,551	21,572	63,369
America	38,972	361,888	1,143,671	1,516,716	160,037	354,804	996,944	1,716,374
Canada & Newfoundland[17,18]	3,311	179,226	742,185	924,515	108,527	171,718	377,952	413,310
Mexico[18]	971[19]	49,642	219,004	459,287	22,319	60,589	299,811	453,937
Caribbean	33,066	107,548	123,424	74,899	15,502	49,725	123,091	470,213
Cuba	—[12]	—[12]	—[12]	15,901[12]	9,571	26,313	78,948	208,536
Dominican Republic	—[20]	—[20]	—[20]	—[20]	1,150[20]	5,627	9,897	93,292
Haiti	—[20]	—[20]	—[20]	—[20]	191[20]	911	4,442	34,499
Jamaica	—[21]	—[21]	—[21]	—[21]	—[21]	—[21]	8,869[21]	74,906
Other Caribbean	33,066	107,548	123,424	58,998	4,590	16,874	20,935[21]	58,980
Central America	549	8,192	17,159	15,769	5,861	21,665	44,751	101,330
El Salvador	—[20]	—[20]	—[20]	—[20]	673[20]	5,132	5,895	14,992
Other Central America	549	8,192	17,159	15,769	5,188	16,533	38,856	86,338
South America	1,075	17,280	41,899	42,215	7,803	21,831	91,628	257,954
Argentina	—[20]	—[20]	—[20]	—[20]	1,349[20]	3,338	19,486	49,721
Colombia	—[20]	—[20]	—[20]	—[20]	1,223[20]	3,858	18,048	72,028
Ecuador	—[20]	—[20]	—[20]	—[20]	337[20]	2,417	9,841	36,780
Other South America	1,075	17,280	41,899	42,215	4,894	12,218	44,253	99,425
Other America	—[22]	—[22]	—[22]	31[22]	25	29,276	59,711	19,630
Africa	350	7,368	8,443	6,286	1,750	7,367	14,092	28,954
Oceania	3,965	13,024	13,427	8,726	2,483	14,551	12,976	25,122
Not specified[22]	14,063	33,523[25]	1,147	228	—	142	12,491	93

Region and Country of Last Residence[1]	1971–80	1981–89	1984	1985	1986	1987	1988	1989	Total 170 Years 1820–1989
All countries	4,493,314	5,801,579	543,903	570,009	601,708	601,516	643,025	1,090,924	55,457,531
Europe	800,368	637,524	69,879	69,526	69,224	67,967	71,854	94,338	36,977,034
Austria-Hungary	16,028	20,152	2,846	2,521	2,604	2,401	3,200	3,586	4,338,049
Austria	9,478	14,566	2,351	1,930	2,039	1,769	2,493	2,845	1,825,172[3]
Hungary	6,550	5,586	495	591	565	632	707	741	1,666,801[3]
Belgium	5,329	6,329	787	775	843	859	706	705	209,729
Czechoslovakia	6,023	6,649	693	684	588	715	744	526	145,223
Denmark	4,439	4,696	512	465	544	515	561	617	369,738
France	25,069	28,088	3,335	3,530	3,876	3,809	3,637	4,101	783,322
Germany	74,414	79,375	9,375	10,028	9,853	9,923	9,748	10,419	7,071,313
Greece	92,369	34,490	3,311	3,487	3,497	4,087	4,690	4,588	700,017
Ireland[5]	11,490	22,229	1,096	1,288	1,757	3,032	5,121	6,983	4,715,393
Italy	129,368	51,008	6,328	6,351	5,711	4,666	5,332	11,089	5,356,862
Netherlands	10,492	10,723	1,313	1,235	1,263	1,303	1,152	1,253	372,717
Norway-Sweden	10,472	13,252	1,455	1,557	1,564	1,540	1,669	1,809	2,144,024
Norway	3,941	3,612	403	386	367	372	446	556	800,672[6]
Sweden	6,531	9,640	1,052	1,171	1,197	1,168	1,223	1,253	1,283,097[6]
Poland	37,234	64,888	7,229	7,409	6,540	5,818	7,298	13,279	587,972
Portugal	101,710	36,365	3,800	3,811	3,804	4,009	3,290	3,861	497,195
Romania	12,393	27,361	2,956	3,764	3,809	2,741	2,915	3,535	201,345
Soviet Union	38,961	42,898	3,349	1,532	1,001	1,139	1,408	4,570	3,428,927
Spain	39,141	17,689	2,168	2,278	2,232	2,056	1,972	2,179	282,404
Switzerland	8,235	7,561	795	980	923	964	920	1,072	358,151
United Kingdom[5,8]	137,374	140,119	16,516	15,591	16,129	15,889	14,667	16,961	5,100,096
Yugoslavia	30,540	15,984	1,404	1,521	1,915	1,793	2,039	2,464	133,493
Other Europe	9,287	7,324	611	719	771	708	785	741	181,064

Asia	1,588,178	2,416,278	247,775	255,164	258,546	248,293	254,745	296,420	5,697,301
China[10]	124,326	306,108	29,109	33,095	32,389	32,669	34,300	39,284	873,737
Hong Kong	113,467	83,848	12,290	10,795	9,930	8,785	11,817	15,257	287,863[11]
India	164,134	221,977	23,617	24,536	24,808	26,394	25,312	28,599	426,907
Iran	45,136	101,267	11,131	12,327	12,031	10,323	9,846	13,027	161,946[12]
Israel	37,713	38,367	4,517	4,279	5,124	4,711	4,444	5,494	131,634[13]
Japan	49,775	40,654	4,136	4,552	4,444	4,444	5,085	5,454	455,813[14]
Korea	267,638	302,782	32,537	34,791	35,164	35,397	34,151	33,016	611,284[15]
Philippines	354,987	477,485	46,985	53,137	61,492	58,315	61,017	66,119	955,374[16]
Turkey	13,399	20,028	1,652	1,690	1,975	2,080	2,200	2,538	409,122
Vietnam	172,820	266,027	25,803	20,367	15,010	13,073	12,856	13,174	443,522[11]
Other Asia	244,783	557,735	55,998	55,595	56,179	51,793	53,717	74,458	940,099
America	1,982,735	2,564,698	208,111	225,519	254,078	265,026	294,906	672,639	12,017,021
Canada & Newfoundland[17,18]	169,939	132,296	15,659	16,354	16,060	16,741	15,821	18,294	4,270,943
Mexico[18]	640,294	975,657	57,820	61,290	66,753	72,511	95,170	405,660	3,208,543
Caribbean	741,126	759,416	68,368	79,374	98,527	100,615	110,949	87,597	2,590,542
Cuba	264,863	135,142	5,699	17,115	30,787	27,363	16,610	9,523	739,274[12]
Dominican Republic	148,135	209,899	23,207	23,861	26,216	24,947	27,195	26,744	468,000[20]
Haiti	56,335	118,510	9,554	9,872	12,356	14,643	34,858	13,341	214,888[20]
Jamaica	137,577	184,481	18,997	18,277	18,916	22,430	20,474	23,572	405,833[21]
Other Caribbean	134,216	111,384	10,911	10,249	10,252	11,232	11,812	14,417	762,547
Central America	134,640	321,845	27,626	28,447	30,086	30,366	31,311	101,273	673,385
El Salvador	34,436	133,938	8,753	9,093	10,881	10,627	12,043	57,628	195,066[20]
Other Central America	100,204	187,907	18,873	18,354	19,205	19,739	19,268	43,645	478,319
South America	295,741	375,026	38,636	40,052	42,650	44,782	41,646	59,812	1,163,482
Argentina	29,897	21,374	2,287	1,925	2,318	2,192	2,556	3,766	125,165[20]
Colombia	77,347	99,066	10,897	11,802	11,213	11,482	10,153	14,918	271,570[20]
Ecuador	50,077	43,841	4,244	4,601	4,518	4,656	4,736	7,587	143,293[20]
Other South America	138,420	210,745	21,208	21,724	24,601	26,452	24,201	33,541	623,454
Other America	995	458	2	2	2	11	9	3	110,126
Africa	80,779	144,096	13,594	15,236	15,500	15,730	17,124	22,485	301,348
Oceania	41,242	38,401	4,249	4,552	4,352	4,437	4,324	4,956	197,818
Not specified[22]	12	582	295	12	8	63	72	86	267,009

Source: U.S. Immigration and Naturalization Service, 1991.

[1]Data for years prior to 1906 relate to country whence alien came; data from 1906–79 and 1984–89 are for country of last permanent residence; and data for 1980–83 refer to country of birth. Because of changes in boundaries, changes in lists of countries, and lack of data for specified countries for various periods, data for certain countries, especially for the total period 1820–1989, are not comparable throughout. Data for specified countries are included with countries to which they belonged prior to World War I.

[2]Data for Austria and Hungary not reported until 1861.

[3]Data for Austria and Hungary not reported separately for all years during the period.

[4]No data available for Czechoslovakia until 1920.

[5]Prior to 1926, data for Northern Ireland included in Ireland.

[6]Data for Norway and Sweden not reported separately until 1871.

[7]No data available for Romania until 1880.

[8]Since 1925, data for United Kingdom refer to England, Scotland, Wales, and Northern Ireland.

[9]In 1920, a separate enumeration was made for the Kingdom of Serbs, Croats, and Slovenes. Since 1922, the Serb, Croat, and Slovene Kingdom recorded as Yugoslavia.

[10]Beginning in 1957, China includes Taiwan.

[11]Data not reported separately until 1952.

[12]Data not reported separately until 1925.

[13]Data not reported separately until 1949.

[14]No data available for Japan until 1861.

[15]Data not reported separately until 1948.

[16]Prior to 1934, Philippines recorded as insular travel.

[17]Prior to 1920, Canada and Newfoundland recorded as British North America. From 1820 to 1898, figures include all British North America possessions.

[18]Land arrivals not completely enumerated until 1908.

[19]No data available for Mexico from 1886 to 1893.

[20]Data not reported separately until 1932.

[21]Data for Jamaica not collected until 1953. In prior years, consolidated under British West Indies, which is included in "Other Caribbean."

[22]Included in countries "Not specified" until 1925.

[23]From 1899 to 1919, data for Poland included in Austria-Hungary, Germany, and the Soviet Union.

[24]From 1938 to 1945, data for Austria included in Germany.

[25]Includes 32,897 persons returning in 1906 to their homes in the United States.

—represents zero.

NOTE: From 1820 to 1867, figures represent alien passengers arrived at seaports; from 1868 to 1891 and 1895 to 1897, immigrant aliens arrived; from 1892 to 1894 and 1898 to 1989, immigrant aliens admitted for permanent residence. From 1892 to 1903, aliens entering by cabin class were not counted as immigrants. Land arrivals were not completely enumerated until 1908. For this table, fiscal year 1843 covers 9 months ending September 1843; fiscal years 1832 and 1850 cover 15 months ending December 31 of the respective years; and fiscal year 1868 covers 6 months ending June 30, 1868.

PRESIDENTS, VICE-PRESIDENTS, AND SECRETARIES OF STATE

	President	Vice-President	Secretary of State
1.	George Washington, Federalist 1789	John Adams, Federalist 1789	Thomas Jefferson 1789 Edmund Randolph 1794 Timothy Pickering 1795
2.	John Adams, Federalist 1797	Thomas Jefferson, Dem.-Rep. 1797	Timothy Pickering 1797 John Marshall 1800
3.	Thomas Jefferson, Dem.-Rep. 1801	Aaron Burr, Dem.-Rep. 1801 George Clinton, Dem.-Rep. 1805	James Madison 1801
4.	James Madison, Dem.-Rep. 1809	George Clinton, Dem.-Rep. 1809 Elbridge Gerry, Dem.-Rep. 1813	Robert Smith 1809 James Monroe 1811
5.	James Monroe, Dem.-Rep. 1817	Daniel D. Tompkins, Dem.-Rep. 1817	John Q. Adams 1817
6.	John Quincy Adams, Dem.-Rep. 1825	John C. Calhoun, Dem.-Rep. 1825	Henry Clay 1825
7.	Andrew Jackson, Democratic 1829	John C. Calhoun, Democratic 1829 Martin Van Buren, Democratic 1833	Martin Van Buren 1829 Edward Livingston 1831 Louis McLane 1833 John Forsyth 1834
8.	Martin Van Buren, Democratic 1837	Richard M. Johnson, Democratic 1837	John Forsyth 1837
9.	William H. Harrison, Whig 1841	John Tyler, Whig 1841	Daniel Webster 1841

President	Vice-President	Secretary of State
10. John Tyler, Whig and Democratic 1841	None	Daniel Webster 1841 Hugh S. Legaré 1843 Abel P. Upshur 1843 John C. Calhoun 1844
11. James K. Polk, Democratic 1845	George M. Dallas, Democratic 1845	James Buchanan 1845
12. Zachary Taylor, Whig 1849	Millard Fillmore, Whig 1849	John M. Clayton 1849
13. Millard Fillmore, Whig 1850	None	Daniel Webster 1850 Edward Everett 1852
14. Franklin Pierce, Democratic 1853	William R. King, Democratic 1853	William L. Marcy 1853
15. James Buchanan, Democratic 1857	John C. Breckinridge, Democratic 1857	Lewis Cass 1857 Jeremiah S. Black 1860
16. Abraham Lincoln, Republican 1861	Hannibal Hamlin, Republican 1861 Andrew Johnson, Unionist 1865	William H. Seward 1861
17. Andrew Johnson, Unionist 1865	None	William H. Seward 1865
18. Ulysses S. Grant, Republican 1869	Schuyler Colfax, Republican 1869 Henry Wilson, Republican 1873	Elihu B. Washburne 1869 Hamilton Fish 1869
19. Rutherford B. Hayes, Republican 1877	William A. Wheeler, Republican 1877	William M. Evarts 1877

	President	Vice-President	Secretary of State
20.	James A. Garfield, Republican 1881	Chester A. Arthur, Republican 1881	James G. Blaine 1881
21.	Chester A. Arthur, Republican 1881	None	Frederick T. Frelinghuysen 1881
22.	Grover Cleveland, Democratic 1885	Thomas A. Hendricks, Democratic 1885	Thomas F. Bayard 1885
23.	Benjamin Harrison, Republican 1889	Levi P. Morton, Republican 1889	James G. Blaine 1889 John W. Foster 1892
24.	Grover Cleveland, Democratic 1893	Adlai E. Stevenson, Democratic 1893	Walter Q. Gresham 1893 Richard Olney 1895
25.	William McKinley, Republican 1897	Garret A. Hobart, Republican 1897 Theodore Roosevelt, Republican 1901	John Sherman 1897 William R. Day 1898 John Hay 1898
26.	Theodore Roosevelt, Republican 1901	Charles Fairbanks, Republican 1905	John Hay 1901 Elihu Root 1905 Robert Bacon 1909
27.	William H. Taft, Republican 1909	James S. Sherman, Republican 1909	Philander C. Knox 1909
28.	Woodrow Wilson, Democratic 1913	Thomas R. Marshall, Democratic 1913	William J. Bryan 1913 Robert Lansing 1915 Bainbridge Colby 1920
29.	Warren G. Harding, Republican 1921	Calvin Coolidge, Republican 1921	Charles E. Hughes 1921
30.	Calvin Coolidge, Republican 1923	Charles G. Dawes, Republican 1925	Charles E. Hughes 1923 Frank B. Kellogg 1925

President	Vice-President	Secretary of State
31. Herbert Hoover, Republican 1929	Charles Curtis, Republican 1929	Henry L. Stimson 1929
32. Franklin D. Roosevelt, Democratic 1933	John Nance Garner, Democratic 1933 Henry A. Wallace, Democratic 1941 Harry S. Truman, Democratic 1945	Cordell Hull 1933 Edward R. Stettinius, Jr. 1944
33. Harry S. Truman, Democratic 1945	Alben W. Barkley, Democratic 1949	Edward R. Stettinius, Jr. 1945 James F. Byrnes 1945 George C. Marshall 1947 Dean G. Acheson 1949
34. Dwight D. Eisenhower, Republican 1953	Richard M. Nixon, Republican 1953	John F. Dulles 1953 Christian A. Herter 1959
35. John F. Kennedy, Democratic 1961	Lyndon B. Johnson, Democratic 1961	Dean Rusk 1961
36. Lyndon B. Johnson, Democratic 1963	Hubert H. Humphrey, Democratic 1965	Dean Rusk 1963
37. Richard M. Nixon, Republican 1969	Spiro T. Agnew, Republican 1969 Gerald R. Ford, Republican 1973	William P. Rogers 1969 Henry Kissinger 1973
38. Gerald R. Ford, Republican 1974	Nelson Rockefeller, Republican 1974	Henry Kissinger 1974
39. Jimmy Carter, Democratic 1977	Walter Mondale, Democratic 1977	Cyrus Vance 1977 Edmund Muskie 1980

	President	Vice-President	Secretary of State
40.	Ronald Reagan, Republican 1981	George Bush, Republican 1981	Alexander Haig 1981 George Schultz 1982
41.	George Bush, Republican 1989	J. Danforth Quayle, Republican 1989	James A. Baker 1989 Lawrence Eagleburger 1992
42.	William J. Clinton, Democrat 1993	Albert Gore, Jr., Democrat 1993	Warren Christopher 1993 Madeleine Albright 1997

CREDITS

CHAPTER 17: p. 594, Courtesy, Massachusetts Historical Society, Boston; **p. 597,** Library of Congress; **p. 601,** Library of Congress; **p. 608,** National Portrait Gallery, Smithsonian Institution/Art Resource, NY; **p. 616,** Corbis-Bettman; **p. 620,** Library of Congress; **p. 625,** Library of Congress.

CHAPTER 18: p. 647, The Granger Collection, New York; **p. 652,** Library of Congress; **p. 653,** The Warder Collection; **p. 656,** The Denver Public Library, Western History Collection; **p. 661,** Princeton University Press; **p. 662,** National Archives (111-SC-82522); **p. 668,** Western History Collections, University of Oklahoma Library.

CHAPTER 19: p. 676, Amon Carter Museum, Fort Worth, Texas; **p. 679,** Union Pacific Museum Collection; **p. 684,** The Warder Collection; **p. 687,** Carnegie Library, Pittsburgh; **p. 689,** Reprinted with permission of Joanna T. Steichen; **p. 691,** Courtesy of Sears, Roebuck and Co.; **p. 701,** Archives of Labor and Urban Affairs, Wayne State University; **p. 705,** Brown Brothers.

CHAPTER 20: p. 710, Library of Congress; **p. 714,** New York Transit Museum Archives, Brooklyn; **p. 717,** Museum of the City of New York; **p. 719,** Museum of the City of New York; **p. 724,** Library of Congress; **p. 728,** Brown Brothers; **p. 732,** Library of Congress; **p. 745,** The Salvation Army; **p. 747,** Jane Addams Memorial Collection, Special Collections, University Library, University of Illinois at Chicago.

CHAPTER 21: p. 758, Library of Congress; **p. 763,** The Warder Collection; **p. 767,** Corbis-Bettman; **p. 773,** Corbis-Bettman; **p. 777,** Kansas State Historical Society; **p. 778,** University of North Carolina, Chapel Hill; **p. 782,** Library of Congress.

CHAPTER 22: p. 800, State Archives of Hawaii; **p. 803,** Library of Congress; **p. 806,** National Archives (War and Conflict # 299); **p. 808,** Library of Congress; **p. 810,** National Archives (War and Conflict # 319); **p. 818,** Library of Congress.

CHAPTER 23: p. 828, Library of Congress; **p. 830,** Library of Congress; **p. 831,** Underwood & Underwood/Corbis-Bettman; **p. 833,** (*top*) © Collection of the New-York Historical Society, and (*bottom*) Library of Congress; **p. 839,** Library of Congress; **p. 842,** Library of Congress; **p. 844,** Library of Congress; **p. 849,** Stock Montage.

CHAPTER 24: p. 859, Corbis-Bettman; **p. 863,** National Archives (War and Conflict # 620); **p. 867,** *The New York Times;* **p. 869,** Corbis-Bettman; **p. 874,** National Archives; **p. 880,** National Archives (War and Conflict # 613); **p. 882,** National Archives (111-SC-63502); **p. 887,** Library of Congress.

CHAPTER 25: p. 897, Corbis-Bettman; **p. 899,** Corbis-Bettman; **p. 901,** *Chicago Daily News,* DN-097010, Chicago Historical Society; **p. 903,** Ramsey Archive; **p. 905,** Life Picture Service; **p. 906,** Brown Brothers; **p. 908,** AP/Wide World Photos.

CHAPTER 26: p. 920, Brown Brothers; **p. 923,** Library of Congress; **p. 928,** © Globe Photos, Inc.; **p. 930,** From the Collections of the Henry Ford Museum & Greenfield Village; **p. 934,** The Warder Collection; **p. 936,** Herbert Hoover Presidential Library; **p. 941,** Museum of the City of New York; **p. 944,** *New York Daily News* Photo.

CHAPTER 27: p. 949, AP/Wide World Photos; **p. 953,** National Archives; **p. 958,** National Archives; **p. 969,** Corbis-Bettman; **p. 970,** Corbis-Bettman; **p. 972,** Corbis-Bettman; **p. 975,** Library of Congress, Prints & Photographs Division [LC-USZ62-34309].

CHAPTER 28: p. 991, AP/Wide World Photos; **p. 995,** National Archives (War and Conflict # 746); **p. 999,** Library of Congress; **p. 1002,** National Archives; **p. 1010,** National Archives (War and Conflict # 1134).

CHAPTER 29: p. 1014, The Warder Collection; **p. 1021,** Culver Pictures; **p. 1022,** AP/Wide World Photos; **p. 1033,** Army Photographic Agency; **p. 1034,** Corbis-Bettman; **p. 1043,** National Archives (War and Conflict # 750); **p. 1046,** Globe Photos, Inc.; **p. 1050,** UN/DPI Photo by Yuichiro Sasaki, 149443.

CHAPTER 30: p. 1066, University of Louisville, Photographic Archives; **p. 1076,** U.S. Information Agency; **p. 1079,** Corbis-Bettman; **p. 1081,** C. K. Berryman, *The Washington Star,* 1948; **p. 1082,** Harry S. Truman Library; **p. 1085,** Eastfoto; **p. 1089,** AP/Wide World Photos; **p. 1093,** Yale Joel/LIFE Magazine © TIME, Inc.

CHAPTER 31: p. 1101, AP/Wide World Photos; **p. 1104,** Life Picture Service; **p. 1108,** Joe Steinmetz Studio; **p. 1110,** © Archive Photos/PNI; **p. 1114,** UPI/Corbis-Bettman; **p. 1116,** AP/Wide World Photos; **p. 1119,** Rudolph Burckhardt.

CHAPTER 32: p. 1131, Corbis-Bettman; **p. 1135,** "Don't Be Afraid—I Can Always Pull You Back"—from the *Herblock's Here and Now* (Simon & Schuster, 1955); **p. 1137,** Photoworld; **p. 1146,** AP/Wide World Photos; **p. 1148,** University of Louisville, Standard Oil Collection; **p. 1150,** Black Star.

CHAPTER 33: p. 1159, Paul Schutzer/LIFE Magazine © TIME Inc.; **p. 1162,** National Archives; **p. 1164,** National Archives, American Image # 190; **p. 1171,** Yoichi R. Okamoto, Lyndon B. Johnson Library, Austin, TX; **p. 1178,** Los Angeles Times Syndicate; **p. 1180,** National Archives; **p. 1184,** Bill Canfield, © 1963, *The Star-Ledger,* all rights reserved, reprinted with permission.

CHAPTER 34: p. 1196, Magnum Photos, Inc.; **p. 1198,** John Dominis/LIFE Magazine © TIME Inc.; **p. 1200,** Corbis-Bettman; **p. 1205,** Black Star; **p. 1209,** *Valley News Dispatch,* John Filo; **p. 1212,** NASA; **p. 1216,** John Dominis/LIFE Magazine © TIME Inc.; **p. 1220,** AP/Wide World Photos; **p. 1225,** AP/Wide World Photos.

CHAPTER 35: p. 1232, Corbis-Bettman; **p. 1242,** Los Angeles Times Syndicate; **p. 1246,** AP/Wide World Photos; **p. 1251,** Los Angeles Times Syndicate; **p. 1259,** © Alexandra Avakian/Woodfin Camp; **p. 1265,** Corbis.

CHAPTER 36: p. 1271, AP/Wide World Photos; **p. 1275,** Library of Congress; **p. 1277,** AP/Wide World Photos; **p. 1288,** AP/Wide World Photos; **p. 1293,** AP/Wide World Photos; **p. 1298,** Bob Englehart, Courtesy *Hartford Courant.*

INDEX

elections and, 926, 951, 1126, 1133–34, 1254
in French Indochina, 1136–39
Great Depression and, 965–66, 973–74, 977
internal security precautions against, 1091, 1094, 1132–33
in Korean War, 1087, 1089, 1093
McCarthy's crusade against, 1092–93, 1130–32, 1152, 1156
New Look military posture toward, 1135
Nixon's crusade against, 1125–26, 1156, 1216
in post–World War II eastern Europe, 1044–45
in Truman years, 1068, 1082
in Vietnam War, 1181–82, 1185, 1207–8, 1210–11
in youth culture, 1115–16
see also China, People's Republic of; Red Scares; Soviet Union
Community Action Program, 1173
Community Service Organization (CSO), 1202–3
company unions, 933–34
Compromise of 1877, 629
computer revolution, 1274–78, 1305
Comstock Lode, 658
Confederate States of America (Confederacy), 602–3, 605, 643, 706, 836, 866, 896
in Civil War, 595–96, 599, 602
Confiscation Act (1862), 597–98
conformity, 1106–13, 1118, 1121
big business and, 1107, 1109
community in, 1109–10
critics of, 1110–13
women and, 1107–9, 1112–13
Congress, U.S., 780–81, 785, 818, 858, 900, 907, 918, 929, 1011, 1090, 1093, 1099, 1105, 1110, 1116, 1129, 1142, 1144, 1149, 1200, 1204, 1264, 1296
agricultural crisis and, 771, 775–78
in annexation of Philippines, 808–9, 811
big business and, 680–81
in Bush administration, 1255–56, 1260
in Carter administration, 1224–25, 1231
Civil War and, 594–95, 598
in Clinton administration, 1284–86, 1289–91, 1298–99
cold war and, 1073–74, 1087
in Cuban missile crisis, 1165
elections and, 628–29, 781, 813, 847, 883, 940, 951, 969, 979, 1019, 1067–68, 1080–82, 1127, 1140, 1152, 1156, 1159, 1170, 1254, 1279, 1289–90, 1293
in Gilded Age, 755–56, 758–59, 761–63, 765, 767–70
in Grant administration, 623–24, 627
Great Depression and, 940–43, 952–54, 956–58, 965, 974–77
in Harding administration, 921, 924
in Hoover administration, 936, 940–43
immigration and, 695, 718, 721–22, 896

and internment of Japanese Americans, 1025–26
isolationism of, 998–99
A. Johnson and, 605–6, 610–12
in L.B. Johnson administration, 1169–70, 1172, 1174–75, 1177, 1181
Joint Committee on Reconstruction of, 604, 606
lend-lease program and, 1004–5
in New Era, 927, 932–33
New West and, 657–60
in Nixon administration, 1212–15
in Progressive Era, 827, 832–38, 840, 848
in Reagan administration, 1237, 1239–40, 1245, 1247–48, 1250, 1253
in Reconstruction, 599–600, 603–13, 623
in F.D. Roosevelt administration, 979, 982–83
Spanish-American War and, 803–4
in Truman administration, 1065, 1067–69, 1083–84
unions and, 695–96, 699
Vietnam War and, 1181–82, 1209, 1211
war-debt tangle and, 989–90
Watergate scandal and, 1220–21
Wilson's relations with, 847–49
World War I and, 868, 870–73, 877, 881, 883, 886–88
World War II and, 998–1006, 1016–20, 1052
see also House of Representatives, U.S.; Senate, U.S.
Congress of Industrial Organizations (CIO), 981
Congress of Racial Equality (CORE), 1161
Conkling, Roscoe, 759–62
Connor, Eugene (Bull), 1162
conscription:
in Vietnam War, 1194–95, 1208, 1223–24
in World War I, 873
in World War II, 1003, 1016
conservation, *see* environment, environmental movement
conservatives, conservatism, 1115, 1194, 1213, 1281–82
Carter administration and, 1225–26
Clinton administration and, 1285, 1289–90, 1292–93
cultural, 1278–79
dynamic, 1128–30
elections and, 1041, 1125, 1173, 1207, 1218, 1232–36, 1268–69, 1278–79, 1292–93
of Ford, 1222
Kennedy administration and, 1159–60, 1164
Reagan administration and, 1237, 1245, 1251, 1253
in Reconstruction, 621–22
Truman administration and, 1065, 1079, 1083
World War II and, 1018–19
Constitution, U.S., 628, 650, 811, 813, 933, 979, 1160, 1200, 1213, 1299
and A. Johnson's impeachment and trial, 611–12

90° N (North Pole)

180° 165° W 150° W 135° W 120° W 105° W 90° W 75° W 60° W 45° W 30°

80° N

70° N

ALASKA
(U.S.)   Arctic Circle

GREENLAND
(Denmark)

60° N

ICELA

50° N

CANADA

N O R T H

A M E R I C A

UN

40° N

Chicago

NORTH PACIFIC OCEAN

30° N

Los Angeles

UNITED STATES

New York

NORTH ATLANTIC OCEAN

PO

MIDWAY ISLAND
(U.S.)

Tropic of Cancer

Gulf of
Mexico

BAHAMAS

HAITI
DOMINICAN REPUBLIC

WESTE
SAH
(Moro

20° N

HAWAII
(U.S.)

MEXICO

CUBA

PUERTO RICO (U.S.)
VIRGIN ISLANDS (U.S./U.K.)
ST. KITTS & NEVIS
ANTIGUA & BARBUDA

MAU

Mexico City

BELIZE
JAMAICA

DOMINICA
ST. LUCIA

CAPE
VERDE

SEN

GUATEMALA
EL SALVADOR

HONDURAS

GRENADA

ST. VINCENT & THE GRENADINES
BARBADOS

THE GAMBIA
GUINEA-BISSAU

10° N

NICARAGUA

Caribbean Sea

TRINIDAD & TOBAGO

COSTA RICA

VENEZUELA

GUYANA

SIERRA L

0°

Equator

PANAMA
COLOMBIA

SURINAME
FRENCH GUIANA

ECUADOR

WESTERN
SAMOA

PERU

S O U T H

10° S

AMERICAN SAMOA
(U.S.)

SOUTH PACIFIC OCEAN

A M E R I C A

BRAZIL

SOUTH AT

OCE

20° S

Tropic of Capricorn

BOLIVIA

PARAGUAY

Rio de Janeiro

São Paulo

30° S

SOUTH PACIFIC OCEAN

CHILE

URUGUAY

Buenos Aires

40° S

ARGENTINA

50° S

FALKLAND
ISLANDS
(U.K.)

60° S

Antarctic Circle

70° S

80° S

90° S (South Pole)

180° 165° W 150° W 135° W 120° W 105° W 90° W 75° W 60° W 45° W 30°

Bergen

Oslo

Stockholm

FINLAND

Helsinki

L. Ladoga

St. Petersburg

NORWAY

SWEDEN

North
Sea

Ålborg

Göteborg

Tallinn

Gulf of
Finland

Nizhni
Novgorod

ESTONIA

DENMARK

Copenhagen

Baltic
Sea

Riga

LATVIA

Moscow

Hamburg

LITHUANIA

Gdansk

Vilnius

RUSSIA

NETH.

Amsterdam

Berlin

Minsk

BEL.

GERMANY

POLAND

Warsaw

BELARUS

Brussels

LUXEMBOURG

Prague

Kiev

Kharkov

FRANCE

CZECH
REPUBLIC

SLOVAKIA

Dnepropetrovsk

LIECHT.

Munich

Bratislava

UKRAINE

SWITZ.

Bern

Vienna

AUSTRIA

HUNGARY

Budapest

MOLDOVA

Milan

SLOVENIA

Ljubljana

Zagreb

Kishinov

Odessa

Venice

Sea of
Azov

MONACO

CROATIA

ROMANIA

Trieste

BOSNIA
HERZ.

Belgrade

Bucharest

Constanta

SAN
MARINO

Rome

VATICAN
CITY

Sarajevo

YUGOSLAVIA

Black Sea

Corsica

Adriatic Sea

Varna

ITALY

Naples

Skopje

BULGARIA

Sofia

MACEDONIA

Istanbul

Tirane

Thessaloniki

Ankara

Sardinia

Tyrrhenian
Sea

ALBANIA

Aegean
Sea

Bursa

TURKEY

Palermo

Ionian
Sea

GREECE

Izmir

Adana

Sicily

MALTA

Patras

Athens

Nicosia

TUNISIA

Valletta

Mediterranean Sea

Crete

CYPRUS

THE
WORLD